PERSONNEL/
HUMAN RESOURCE
MANAGEMENT TODAY

PERSONNEL/ HUMAN RESOURCE MANAGEMENT TODAY
Readings and Commentary

Second Edition

Craig Eric Schneier
College of Business and Management
University of Maryland

Richard W. Beatty
Institute of Management and Labor Relations
Rutgers University

Glenn M. McEvoy
College of Business
Utah State University

ADDISON-WESLEY PUBLISHING COMPANY

Reading, Massachusetts □ Menlo Park, California
Don Mills, Ontario, □ Wokingham, England □ Amsterdam □ Sydney □ Singapore
Tokyo □ Mexico City □ Bogotá □ Santiago □ San Juan

Sponsoring Editor: Connie Spatz
Packaging Service: Spencer Graphics
Text Designer: Catherine Johnson Dorin
Cover Designer: Marshall Henrichs
Manufacturing Supervisor: Hugh Crawford

Library of Congress Cataloging-in-Publication Data
Main entry under title:

Personnel/human resource management today.

  Rev. ed. of: Personnel administration today. c1978.
  1. Personnel management—Addresses, essays, lectures.
I. Schneier, Craig Eric.   II. Beatty, Richard W.
III. McEvoy, Glenn M.   IV. Personnel administration today.
HF5549.P45146   1986   658.3   85–15013
ISBN 0-201-05794-8

To Helen and Leon Schneier,
Russell and Thelma Beatty,
Bob and Mona Harlan,
Glenna, Raymond, Raedeen, and Jim

PREFACE TO THE SECOND EDITION

In the first edition to this book we noted the complexity and volatility of the field of personnel administration and the pressure on professionals to use techniques and skills that produce programs with impact. Those observations regarding change are even more relevant today, as the original title for the book no longer describes the field's breadth and importance. The appropriate title is now Personnel/Human Resource Management (P/HRM), indicating the inclusion of responsibilities well beyond such traditional employment functions as recruiting and benefit administration. Today, P/HRM reflects an ever-increasing influence on the organization's competitive edge, effectiveness, and perhaps survival itself. We have again set out to capture the present thrust of P/HRM in this contemporary and diverse set of readings.

As did the first edition, this book follows the same structure to P/HRM as does our text, *Personnel Administration: An Experiential/Skill-Building Approach* (Addison-Wesley). Together, the two books provide a thorough, realistic view of the field. The model of P/HRM provided in the Introduction to this edition is again consistent with that in our experiential text. *Personnel/Human Resource Management Today* was also designed to be used with any one of the numerous textbooks available, and a table indicating how the parts of this book fit with the chapters of the texts follows this Preface.

Personnel/Human Resource Management Today, second edition, is a thorough revision. We have retained the unique and successful features of the first edition — the integrative P/HRM model, the realistic and contemporary focus, the variety of sources tapped for readings, the emphasis on P/HRM programs and skills, the interviews with P/HRM professionals, the questions for discussion and review — but *ninety percent* of the selections are new. These readings reflect the diversity and activity in the P/HRM field. New topics covered in this edition include strategic HRM, human resource information systems, competency-based appraisal systems, genetic screening, behavior modeling, comparable worth, benefits, safety and health, pregnancy discrimination, sexual harassment, physical fitness, stress, employment-at-will, and P/HRM research. This breadth is not meant to exhaust all relevant P/HRM topics. We sought again to reflect today's critical issues, with contributions which were well-written, accurate, and timely. In addition, we assessed the relevance of readings to all types of organizations, both large and small, public and private. These selection criteria help assure that our book is useful to the student, the manager, and the P/HRM professional.

The response to our interviews — a unique feature of the first edition — has been very positive. We have interviewed a group of new professionals for this edition, including two recent graduates of P/HRM programs who are now working in the field. Their comments are enlightening and stimulating and offer a rare opportunity for readers to put the contents of such a book into perspective.

In addition to our select group of gracious P/HRM professionals, we would like to acknowledge those authors and publications who gave permission to reprint their work, our colleagues who offered their valuable opinions on the manuscript (Jim McFillen, Bowling Green State University; Wayne Cascio, University of Colorado/ Denver; Lloyd Baird, Boston University; Alan Thayer, Boston College; and George Cole, Pennsylvania State University), our assistants (Ginny Manz, Cris Giannantonio, and Christine Lemyze) who provided expert help in all phases of preparing the book, and the staff at Addison-Wesley for their support and assistance. We remain responsible, however, for any deficiencies in this work.

Washington, D.C.   CES
Princeton, New Jersey   RWB
Logan, Utah   GMM

FULL CITATIONS FOR ENTRIES IN TABLE OF TEXTS (pp. xi to xiii)

1. Anthony, W. P., and Nicholson, E. A. *Management of Human Resources.* Columbus, Ohio: Grid, 1977.

2. Beach, D. S. *Personnel: The Management of People at Work.* New York: Macmillan, 1985.

3. Beatty, R. W., and Schneier, C. E. *Personnel Administration: An Experiential/Skill-Building Approach,* 2nd ed. Reading, Mass.: Addison-Wesley, 1981.

4. Brock, J. *Managing People in Public Agencies: Personnel and Labor Relations.* Boston: Little, Brown, 1984.

5. Burack, E. H., and Smith, R. D. *Personnel Management: A Human Resource System Approach.* New York: John Wiley & Sons, 1982.

6. Byors, L. L., and Rue, L. W. *Personnel Management: Concepts and Applications.* Philadelphia: W. B. Saunders, 1979.

7. Carrell, M. R., and Kuzmits, F. E. *Personnel Management of Human Resources.* Columbus, Ohio: Merrill, 1982.

8. Cascio, W. F. *Applied Psychology in Personnel Management,* 2nd ed. Reston, Va.: Reston, 1982.

9. Cascio, W. F., and Awad, E. M. *Human Resources Management: An Information Systems Approach.* Reston, Va.: Reston, 1981.

10. Cherrington, D. J. *Personnel Management: The Management of Human Resources.* Dubuque, Iowa: W. C. Brown, 1983.

11. Chruden, H. J., and Sherman, A. W. *Managing Human Resources,* 7th ed. Cincinnati: South-Western, 1984.

12. Crane, D. P. *Personnel: The Management of Human Resources,* 3rd ed. Boston: Kent, 1982.

13. Dessler, G. *Personnel Management: Modern Concepts and Techniques,* 3rd ed. Reston, Va.: Reston, 1984.

14. Douglas, J., Klein, S., and Hunt, D. *The Strategic Managing of Human Resources.* New York: John Wiley & Sons, 1985.

15. Dresong, D. L. *Public Personnel Management and Public Policy.* Boston: Little, Brown, 1984.

16. DuBrin, Andrew J. *Personnel and Human Resource Management.* New York: D. Van Nostrand, 1981.

17. Flippo, E. B. *Personnel Management,* 6th ed. New York: McGraw-Hill, 1984.

18. French, W. L. *The Personnel Management Process: Human Resources Administration and Development,* 5th ed. Boston: Houghton-Mifflin, 1982.

19. Heneman, H. G., Schwab, D. P., Fossum, J. A., and Dyer, L. D. *Personnel/Human Resource Management.* Homewood, Ill.: Irwin, 1983.

20. Holley, W. H., and Jennings, K. M. *Personnel Management: Functions and Issues.* Hinsdale, Ill.: Dryden, 1983.

21. Ivancevich, J. M., and Glueck, W. F. *Foundations of Personnel/Human Resource Management.* Plano, Tex.: Business Publications, Inc., 1983.

22. Jucius, M. J. *Personnel Management,* 8th ed. Homewood, Ill.: Irwin, 1975.

23. Klatt, L. A., Murdick, R. G., and Schuster, F. E. *Human Resource Management.* Columbus, Ohio: Merrill, 1985.

24. Mathis, R. L., and Jackson, J. H. *Personnel: Contemporary Perspectives and Applicatons*, 4th ed. St. Paul: West, 1985.

25. Middlemist, R. D., Hitt, M. A., and Greer, C. R. *Personnel Management: Jobs, People, and Logic.* Englewood Cliffs, N.J.: Prentice-Hall, 1983.

26. Milkovich, G. T., and Glueck, W. F. *Personnel/Human Resource Management: A Diagnostic Approach*, 4th ed. Plano, Tex.: Business Publications, Inc., 1985.

27. Miner, J. B., and Miner, M. G. *Personnel and Industrial Relations: A Managerial Approach*, 4th ed. New York: Macmillan, 1985.

28. Mondy, R. W., and Noe, R. M. *Personnel: The Management of Human Resources.* Boston: Allyn & Bacon, 1981.

29. Pigors, P., and Myers, C. A. *Personnel Administration: A Point of View and a Method*, 9th ed. New York: McGraw-Hill, 1981.

30. Robbins, S. P. *Personnel: The Management of Human Resources*, 2nd ed. Englewood Cliffs, N.J.: Prentice-Hall, 1982.

31. Rowland, K. M., and Ferris, G. R. *Personnel Management.* Boston: Allyn & Bacon, 1982.

32. Sayles, L. R., and Strauss, G. *Managing Human Resources*, 2nd ed. Englewood Cliffs, N.J.: Prentice-Hall, 1981.

33. Schuler, R. S. *Effective Personnel Management.* St. Paul: West, 1983.

34. Schuler, R. S. *Personnel and Human Resource Management*, 2nd ed. St. Paul: West, 1984.

35. Sloane, A. A. *Personnel: Managing Human Resources.* Englewood Cliffs, N.J.: Prentice-Hall, 1983.

36. Stahl, O. G. *Public Personnel Administration*, 8th ed. New York: Harper & Row, 1983.

37. Stone, T. H. *Understanding Personnel Management.* Hinsdale, Ill.: Dryden, 1982.

38. Strauss, G., and Sayles, L. R. *Personnel: The Human Problems of Management*, 4th ed. Englewood Cliffs, N.J.: Prentice-Hall, 1980.

39. Wallace, M. J., Crandell, N. F., and Fay, C. H. *Administering Human Resources: An Introduction to the Profession.* New York: Random House Business Division, 1983.

40. Werther, W. B., and Davis, K. *Personnel Management and Human Resources*, 2nd ed. New York: McGraw-Hill, 1985.

41. Yoder, D., and Staudohar, P. D. *Personnel Management and Industrial Relations*, 7th ed. Englewood Cliffs, N.J.: Prentice-Hall, 1982.

Table for Coordinating Contents of *Personnel/Human Resource Management Today*, 2nd Ed., with Chapters of Current Texts

AUTHOR(S) OF TEXT (Numbers in table refer to chapters of these texts)	1. Personnel/Human Resource Management: The Organizational Function and the Profession	2. Strategic Planning and Analysis of P/HRM Systems	3. Appraising Performance in Organizations	4. Human Resource Selection and Staffing	5. Training and Development of Human Resources	6. Maintaining and Improving Satisfaction, Commitment, and Performance	7. Personnel/Human Resource Management in the Contemporary Environment
1. Anthony and Nicholson	1,2	3,4,5		6	7,8	9,11	10
2. Beach	1,2,3	4,5,6	10	7,8	11,12,13	14,22,23,24,25	9,15,16,17,18, 19,20,21,26,27
3. Beatty and Schneier	1	2,3	4,5	6,7,8,9,	10,11,12	13,14,15,16	17,18,19,20
4. Brock	1,2,3	5	9	4	10	6,7,8,9, 11,12,13,14	16
5. Burack and Smith	1	2,3,4,6	13	5	15,16,17,18	7,8,9,11,12	10,14,18
6. Byors and Rue	1	3	17	7,8	9,10,20	11,12,13,14, 15,16,19	2,4,5,6,18
7. Carrell and Kuzmits	1,2	3,4	8	6,7,12	9,10,11,12	4,13,14,15,19	5,16,17,18
8. Cascio	1,3	4,5	16	6,7,8,10, 11,12,13	14,15	17	2,9,18
9. Cascio and Awad	1,2	3,4,6,7,8	16	9,10	11,12,17	13,14,15,18,21	5,19,20,22
10. Cherrington	1	4	8	5,6	3,12,13,17	7,9,10,11, 16,17	2,14,15,17
11. Chruden and Sherman	1,22	3,4,5	10	5,6,7	8,9	11,12,13,16, 17,18,19,20	2,14,15,21
12. Crane	1	3	16	5,6	13,14,17	4,9,18,19,20,21	2,8,10,11, 12,15,22

(Continued)

Table for Coordinating Contents of *Personnel/Human Resource Management Today*, 2nd Ed., with Chapters of Current Texts *(Cont.)*

AUTHOR(S) OF TEXT (Numbers in Table refer to chapters of these texts)	1. Personnel/Human Resource Management: The Organizational Function and the Profession	2. Strategic Planning and Analysis of P/HRM Systems	3. Appraising Performance in Organizations	4. Human Resource Selection and Staffing	5. Training and Development of Human Resources	6. Maintaining and Improving Satisfaction, Commitment, and Performance	7. Personnel/Human Resource Management in the Contemporary Environment
13. Dessler	1	3,4	14	4,5,6	7,8,15	9,10,11,12,18	2,13,16,17,19
14. Douglas et al.	1,3,5	4,7	13	8,9	10,11,12	14,15	2,16,17,18,19,20
15. Dresong	1	6,7,15,16	8	9	10	12,13,14	2,3,4,5
16. DuBrin	1	2	5	3,4	6,7,8,19	9,10,11,12,18	13,14,15,16,17,20
17. Flippo	1,2,3	5,6	10	7,8	9,11	12,13,14,15,16,21,22,23	4,17,18,19,20,24
18. French	1,2,3,4	5,9,10,11	15	11,12	16,17,18,27	6,7,13,14,19,20,21,26	8,22,23,24,25,28
19. Heneman et al.	1,2	3,7,18	5	8,9,10,11	12	4,6,13,14,15,18,19,20	16,17
20. Holley and Jennings	1,2,3	4	8	5,6,7	9	10,11,12,13	14,15,16,17,18,19,20
21. Ivancevich and Glueck	1,2	4,5	8	6,7	9,10,11	12,13,14,15,16,19,20	3,17,18,21
22. Jucius	1,2,3,4,5,28	6,7	12,23	6,7,8,9,10	13,14,15	11,16,17,18,19,20,21,22,24,27	19,22,23,24,25,26,27,28
23. Klatt et al.	1,3	4,5	13	6,7	9,11,12	8,10,14,15,18	2,16,17,19,20
24. Mathis and Jackson	1,2,3	6,7,8	12	7,8,9	8,10,11	13,14,15,16	4,5,17,18,19,20,21

25. Middlemist *et al.*	1	2,3,4,6	15	5,6,7,8	9,10,11	12,13,14,16, 19,20,21,22	17,18,23
26. Milkovich and Glueck	1,3,4,5	2	11	8,9	10	14,15,16	2,7,12,13,17
27. Miner and Miner	1,2,3	6,7	8,9	10,11,12,13	14,15	16,17,18,20,21	4,5,19,22
28. Mondy and Noe	1	2,3,4	9	5,6	7,8,18	10,11,12,15	2,13,14,16, 17,19
29. Pigors and Myers	1,2,3,4	14,19	15,16,17	10	15	5,6,7,12,13, 18,19,20,21,22	8,9,11,23
30. Robbins	1	4	14	5,6,7	8,9,10,11	12,13,15,16, 17,18	2,3,19,20,21
31. Rowland and Ferris	1	3,4	8	5,6,7	11,12,13	9,10,16	2,7,14,15,17
32. Sayles and Strauss	1,2,3	8	15	9	10,14,16	5,6,7,13, 17,18,19,20,21	4,11,12,22
33. Schuler	1	2,3	9	4,5,6	14,15	7,10,11,12,13, 16,17	8,16,18,19,20
34. Schuler	1	2,3	7,8	4,5,6	12	9,10,11,13,14	15,16,17,18
35. Sloane	1	3	9	5,6	7,8	2,10,11,12,13, 14,15	4,16,17,18,19
36. Stahl	1,3,10	4,9	2	5,6	8,14	7,11,12,13, 15,16,17,18,19	20,21,22,23,24, 25,26,27,28
37. Stone	1,2	4,5	10	6,7	8,9,11	12,13,14	3,15,16
38. Strauss and Sayles	15	3,14,16	23	17	18,22,24	1,2,3,4,5,6,8,9, 10,11,12,13,21, 25,26,27,28	7,19,20,29
39. Wallace *et al.*	1,2,15	5,6	13	7	8,9	10,11,14	3,4,12
40. Werther and Davis	1	2,4,5	11	6,7	8,9,10,18	12,13,14,15, 17,19	3,16,20,21,22
41. Yoder and Staudohar	1,2,3	4	7	5,6	8,9	10,11,12	13,14,15,16

CONTENTS

PART IV

HUMAN RESOURCE SELECTION AND STAFFING

MAINTAINING AND IMPROVING SATISFACTION,
COMMITMENT, AND PERFORMANCE

PART VII

PERSONNEL/HUMAN RESOURCE MANAGEMENT
IN THE CONTEMPORARY ENVIRONMENT

PERSONNEL/ HUMAN RESOURCE MANAGEMENT TODAY

INTRODUCTION

This book presents a realistic and timely view of all major aspects of personnel/human resource management (P/HRM). P/HRM refers to the entire spectrum of an organization's interaction with its human resources, from its initial recruiting activities to the exit interview or retirement planning process. It involves human resource planning and forecasting, appraising performance, selection and staffing, training and development, and maintenance and improvement of performance and productivity through such programs as compensation administration, benefits, and incentives (both financial and nonfinancial). In addition, P/HRM exists in an environment of ever-increasing change, diversity, competitiveness, and regulation. Employee rights regarding termination, discrimination, quality of work life, and labor unions are but a few of the more visible examples of such influences. P/HRM is obviously a large and complex field, one that is closely tied to an organization's overall effectiveness.

Human resource managers in today's organizations face an immense task. The diversity and technical nature of the programs they administer and the external constraints they face make their job extremely difficult. Administrators or P/HR managers not only must manage their subordinates in the P/HRM department, but also must design, implement, and evaluate the basic human resource programs that attract, develop, maintain and utilize an organization's most vital asset — its people. In addition, today's professional must interact with line managers and others in the organization, often in an advisory or staff position. Therefore, a delicate interface between those in P/HRM departments and employees, managers, unions, and government must be maintained. Further, the operation of today's P/HRM department is influenced by social, economic, and technological trends, including the demand for high productivity, foreign competition, expectations for a quality work life, Equal Employment Opportunity (EEO) and other types of legislation, the changing composition of the work force toward more women and professionals, and the impact of unionization.

Thus P/HRM professionals have begun to assume the power, status, and authority commensurate with the importance of their function. P/HRM is very much an emerging and dynamic academic field and profession. More and more information pertinent to the field is being generated continually by behavioral science research, and P/HRM managers and administrators must keep abreast of the flow if they are to maintain their effectiveness. The articles in this volume are a representative sampling of the current literature in this field.

Personnel/Human Resource Management Today also includes, at the end of each section, one or two interviews with key figures in the field, including two recent

P/HRM students. These conversations enable readers to obtain a sense of what those currently engaged in P/HRM work think of the field, its challenges, and its potential. As noted in the preface, these interviews *are* P/HRM today.

AN INTEGRATIVE MODEL OF P/HRM PROGRAMS

The seven parts in this book reflect the basic programs in P/HRM. The ultimate objective of these programs — the primary criterion for judging their worth — is organizational effectiveness. Each program, policy, or activity of the P/HRM function must contribute in terms of product or service (sales volume, cost reduction, persons "educated," programs completed, elections won, and so on) to the results an organization seeks. This contribution to organizational effectiveness is, in the case of P/HRM, accomplished through the procurement, development, and utilization of human resources.

Figure 1 is a model of the P/HRM process. The five major functions of the process leading to organizational effectiveness appear in the solid boxes. These, along with the dashed-line box at the top of the figure, represent Parts II through VII of the text. Part I, a discussion of the nature of the P/HRM professional's job, is not included in the figure. So that you may have a better idea of what to expect from the text, let's take a brief look at each of the seven parts.

Part I, "Personnel/Human Resource Management: The Organizational Function and the Profession," provides an overview of the academic field of P/HRM, the profession, and its role and power in an organization. Personal characteristics that can help personnel managers work effectively with the various groups they encounter, trends that have influenced and enhanced P/HRM status and visibility, and practical suggestions for the administration of P/HRM programs are discussed. This part sets the stage for what is to follow.

Part II, "Strategic Planning and Analysis of P/HRM Systems," is the first major category of personnel programs represented by a box in Figure 1. The placement of this box reflects the fact that these activities occur first in the sequence of major P/HRM tasks. Planning and forecasting human resource needs is a prerequisite to decisions on selection, training, and all other personnel decisions. Job analysis and preparation of job descriptions — what people will do in the organization — are also required before individuals can be obtained to fill these positions.

Part III discusses the next task in the P/HRM system. "Appraising Performance in Organizations" examines the establishment of standards or criteria against which to evaluate performance, the development of various methods to appraise performance, and the utilization of effective performance feedback. Before a manager or supervisor can select the right person for the job, he or she needs to know what the person will be required to do (that is, a job description) and how to determine when the person has done it correctly (a set of standards and a method for appraising performance).

After the tasks of planning and definition of desired performance are completed, the P/HRM staff is adequately prepared to assist in the procurement process. Part IV, "Human Resource Selection and Staffing," deals with the various techniques used to make selection decisions, the problems typically encountered, the technical knowledge required, and the legal implications.

Once the procurement phase of human resource management is accomplished, the next task is to develop those human resources selected to their fullest potential. Part V, "Training and Development of Human Resources," focuses on providing people with skills, abilities, and knowledge to perform effectively. The design, implementation, and evaluation of programs to meet this objective are discussed.

FIGURE 1
An Integrative Model of the P/HRM Process

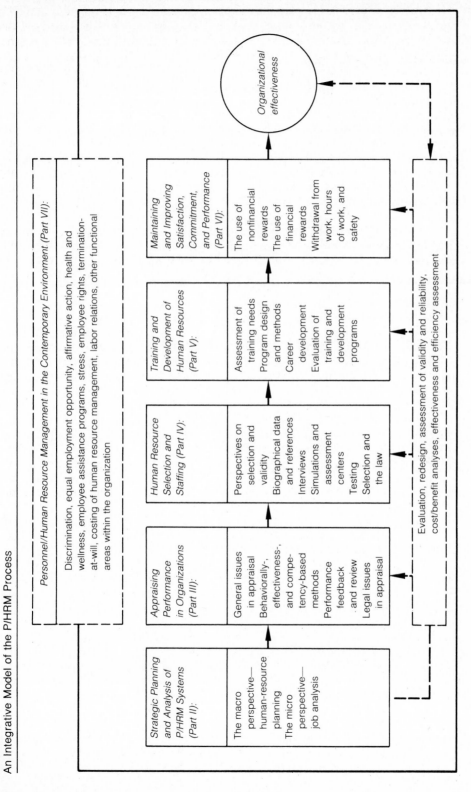

Part VI, "Maintaining and Improving Satisfaction, Commitment, and Performance," examines the utilization of human resources — the issue of performance maintenance and improvement. Many different techniques, certainly not limited to financial rewards, are used to achieve these ends. Part VI reviews these techniques and provides a basis for understanding their foundations and evaluating their effectiveness.

We noted earlier that the environment in which the P/HRM professional operates has changed drastically in recent years. Part VII, "Personnel/Human Resource Management in the Contemporary Environment," deals with several aspects of the external environment that have had a major impact on the P/HRM function. Examples are programs related to equal employment opportunity, affirmative action, employee assistance programs, stress, termination-at-will, and activities of unions. In addition, such P/HRM tools as costing techniques and research methods are included in this section in order to provide a realistic view of how professionals today can deal with environmental influences.

As Figure 1 depicts, these areas influence *all* of the P/HRM programs, as do such factors as an organization's size, structure, product or service, and cultural norms and general economic conditions. Hence, each program, if it is to be successful, must be designed with these factors in mind. In addition, because the entire personnel process is dynamic, it requires constant monitoring, redesign, and assessment of effectiveness, as the feedback lines in Figure 1 indicate.

Figure 1 is a general integrative model. It can be applied to all types of organizations, because they all must procure, develop, and utilize human resources, no matter what their location, size, product, or service. The model is sequential and thus reflects the order in which we believe P/HRM activities should take place. As you read each part, try to keep this framework in view as a constant reminder that P/HRM today is an ongoing, dynamic field whose objective is to contribute to organizational effectiveness.

PART I

PERSONNEL/HUMAN RESOURCE MANAGEMENT: THE ORGANIZATIONAL FUNCTION AND THE PROFESSION

A.

PERSONNEL/HUMAN RESOURCE MANAGEMENT (P/HRM)
IN CONTEMPORARY ORGANIZATIONS

Historical Overview: The Genesis of Personnel in the United States
Arthur A. Sloane

☐ Gives a historical overview of the inception of and developments in P/HRM.

Trends and Issues in Personnel Management
Margaret Magnus

☐ Identifies current social trends and evaluates their impact on P/HRM.

B.

THE HUMAN RESOURCE MANAGEMENT PROFESSIONAL TODAY

Personnel Directors Are the New Corporate Heroes
Herbert E. Meyer

☐ Describes the new, visible role and enhanced status of the P/HR manager.

Big Hat, No Cattle: Managing Human Resources
Wickham Skinner

☐ Critiques P/HRM's limited accomplishments and gives suggestions
for improvement.

C.

P/HRM OVERVIEW

Interview with Joe Zaccaro

D.

RECENT GRADUATES

Interview with Virginia L. Manz

Interview with Daniel J. Montgomery

A.

PERSONNEL/HUMAN RESOURCE MANAGEMENT (P/HRM) IN CONTEMPORARY ORGANIZATIONS

Historical Overview: The Genesis of Personnel in the United States

Arthur A. Sloane

Personnel is, as a formal functional area of administration, hardly an ancient one. The first professional personnel group, the Boston Employment Managers' Association, was founded in 1912. The pioneering college personnel course, a training program for employment managers, dates only from 1915 when the Amos Tuck School of Dartmouth College offered such a selection. The first textbook in the field, *Personnel Administration* by Ordway Tead and Henry C. Metcalf, did not appear until 1920. And personnel was not officially recognized as a profession — if the granting of professional degrees is a valid criterion — until 1946, when Cornell University's newly opened School of Industrial and Labor Relations awarded the initial personnel diploma.

Yet the roots of the profession do go back some distance. They can — although a bit tenuously — even be traced as far back as the Babylonian Hammurabi Code of approximately 1800 B.C., with its minimum wage rate and incentive pay plans. They certainly reach back to the fifteenth century's late medieval period: as Ling has pointed out in his classic history of the field, the first notion of modern industrial training and education can be found in the apprenticeship programs of this era and employee benefit programs, too, derive from this period.[1] And personnel is directly indebted for its existence to at least two nineteenth-century United States developments: the advent of "scientific management" and the coming into being of what was then called, unabashedly, the "welfare secretary."

Scientific management, fathered by Frederick W. Taylor in 1885 and refined by him over the next four decades, represented one man's crusade against worker inefficiency. Taylor's overriding goal was to eradicate excessive fatigue, wasted time and lost motion from the workplace by discovering and then implementing what he called the "one best way" of performing a given operation. In pursuit of this maximum possible efficiency, Taylor advocated four cardinal principles. First, standards for all jobs should be established and incentive wages paid for all output above this standard. Taylor, always the perfectionist, insisted that the subjective judgment methods in use at the time for determining wage payments could be substantially improved upon by such

---

Arthur A. Sloane, *Personnel: Managing Human Resources,* © 1983, pp. 8–18. Reprinted by permission of Prentice-Hall, Inc., Englewood Cliffs, N.J.

avenues as time studies. Second, the best person for the job should be selected — again, not by chance, but by "exact scientific investigation" — and then trained in the best method ("the one best way") of doing the work. Third, employees should be persuaded that changes in their methods could result in greater earnings for themselves. Finally, there should be the maximum possible cooperation between managerial efforts and those of the work force.

No direct interest in establishing a personnel department was ever shown by Taylor or his followers, and "scientific management" to the end was above all an industrial engineering concept. But as its influence grew enormously in these turn-of-the-century years, it did have a large impact on what would someday emerge as personnel. By focusing on the relationship of human resources to organizational profitability and by stressing the importance of employee selection and training, wage administration, and labor-management cooperation to company economic health, it provided incentive for these employee-related areas to be more thoroughly explored in the future. Managers would never again overlook the human dimension.

The *welfare secretary*, sometimes called instead a "social secretary," was also an innovation of the last years of the nineteenth century. Inspired in part by the labor unrest of this period, in part by a burning desire to remain non-union in the time of growing union successes, and to some extent also by a recognition that the increasing size of businesses at this time were weakening employee loyalties and personal relationships with management, companies created such offices in an attempt at augmenting worker morale and thus — it was hoped — productivity.

The exact duties of welfare secretaries varied widely from firm to firm. Tolman reports that one such job-holder had among his responsibilities

> the supervision and initiative of the traveling library of selected books, . . . literature class during winter; question box; . . . the free and careful use of the medicine chest; . . . ice water during summer months; trips to various points of interest on Saturday afternoons; . . . [and] bringing odds and ends to give others less fortunate.[2]

Others supervised cadres of visiting nurses, administered bulletin boards that were designed (often) to inform the work force about events and developments well beyond the narrow place of work, and introduced safety devices. Still others went to the homes of employees and — if the latter were found to be deserving — gave them financial aid. And other secretaries were available to provide, above all, personal advice.

Perhaps not surprisingly, all of these welfare secretary activities were vigorously attacked by the rising union movement. As one source has commented:

> The visiting nurse was looked upon as an instrument of management to spy on workers in their homes; bulletin boards were interpreted as devices of soporific propaganda; first-aid stations were often ridiculed as places where no "he-man" would permit any fussing over a minor injury; even the costs of safety devices were sometimes objected to on the grounds of lowering wages.[3]

And in the face of this opposition, as well as the continuing refusal of many employers to hire welfare secretaries for philosophical and/or financial reasons, the job itself never proved to be much of a growth area. As late as 1916 only 141 firms out of 431 engaged in welfare work employed such secretaries[4] and a few years later the position as such was all but extinct. But, as in the case of "scientific management," the rise and fall of this first industrial personnel specialist had definite consequences for the field. The emerging office of employment manager was to incorporate these social welfare traditions as part of its responsibilities and personnel was thenceforth always to have a major interest in the broad and varying territory once covered by the welfare secretary.

The first formalized personnel department appears to have been that of the B. F. Goodrich Company. Formed in 1900 as a narrowly defined "employment department," it took its title literally, confined its efforts strictly to hiring, and thus allowed the National Cash Register Company, when its much more ambitious personnel unit was created two years later, also to claim credit for innovation in the field.

National Cash Register's operation, called a "labor department," showed a merging of both Taylorism and welfarism. It encompassed such concerns as wage administration, selection and training, what was termed the "improvement" of workers and foremen, employee grievances, counseling, communications, working conditions, record keeping, discharges and — of course — the hiring function. Already known as a welfare pioneer for its origination in 1892 of the first known company employee newspaper, its 1897 implementation of modern industry's first employee suggestion plan and its 1899 initiating of a company-sponsored social club, National Cash Register quickly attracted favorable attention for its "labor department" as well and spawned over the next few years a host of imitators. Fifty such companies, indeed, combined to form the already-mentioned Boston Employment Managers' Association in 1912. Five years later there were at least ten such associations, with over one thousand member companies.

World War I, 1917–1919, gave personnel both new impetus and another basic ingredient. The war's overnight creation of labor shortages on the home front provided the impetus: the reduction of labor turnover became an absolute necessity and the recruiting and training of new workers to replace those who had gone to war was of at least equal importance. The new ingredient was a relatively deep penetration of *psychology* into personnel.

Earlier years of the twentieth century had seen some influence on the nascent personnel field on the part of psychologists. In particular, James Cattell of Columbia, Walter Dill Scott of Northwestern, and Hugo Munsterberg of Harvard had developed the discipline of psychology as applied to practical industrial problems and all three had introduced psychological testing to business executives. The war, however, allowed psychology to make a far more important contribution to personnel: the Army, flooded now with recruits of all mental sizes and shapes, requested leaders in the discipline to design intelligence tests for use in placement and training, and the Army Alpha and Army Beta tests, the first group intelligence tests, were the result. Administered to almost two million men during the war, they survived to be widely used in industry and, in particular, by civilian governmental agencies. Psychologists also, in response to governmental invitation, developed rating scales through which military subjects were evaluated against relevant criteria. These contributions similarly outlived the Armistice, to become incorporated into the personnel function.

Personnel's growth, so visible before the war and clearly not hurt a bit by the success of the military personnel efforts, resumed and to some extent even accelerated during the prosperous 1920s. Even as the title "welfare secretary" was dying, *welfare capitalism* was born in a widespread managerial effort to demonstrate to employees that unions (again viewed as a menace) were unnecessary: a host of employee benefit programs, running a gamut from lavish cafeterias to company-sponsored sports teams arose, as did "employee representation" plans whereby workers could make known their views on employment conditions in a strictly advisory manner. Both types of activities tended to be administered by the personnel unit, which in the latter years of the decade was given further luster by pioneering sociological studies (by Elton Mayo and his Harvard research associates, in particular) that served to show definitively that worker morale and need satisfaction did have an effect on company profits.

Even in these halcyon days, however, the function remained without much real status in the management hierarchy. Personnel's overall realm was unclear, its influence on top management policy-making was generally negligible, and the claim of its practitioners to professional standing remained quite unsubstantiated in view of the total absence of commonly recognized professional standards. Worse yet, personnel was often viewed with animosity by managers in other fields for seemingly having provided a haven from which naive do-gooders could infiltrate the organization. Quantitatively, the field had of course grown considerably in the first three decades of the century, and its undertakings now clearly went well beyond simple "employment." But at the executive ball it was still very much of a wallflower.

THE DEPRESSION AND WORLD WAR II YEARS

In the course of the most pronounced economic disaster in American history — the Great Depression of the 1930s, with its stunning 24.9 percent unemployment rate of 1933 and its chronically bleak economic statistics throughout the decade — even the quantitative progress achieved by personnel was reversed. To employers, "welfare capitalism" was an idea whose time had gone. It could no longer be afforded and, given the unemployment data, it was no longer needed in any event. Within months, most such programs were abruptly ended — and with their demises, quite often, went the entire personnel unit (Elton Mayo, psychological testing and the other growth factors notwithstanding).

Yet even in such a situation the wheels were being set in motion for a new version of the field. Organized labor, which — despite its previously mentioned successes — had never before enlisted in its ranks more than a relative handful of mass production workers almost overnight unionized large numbers of them . . . Mass job insecurities combined with a favorable governmental climate and inspired labor leadership to all but sweep employees in the automobile, steel, rubber, petroleum, electrical, glassmaking and meatpacking industries (among many others) into unions. There were less than 3 million union members in 1932; nine years later the total stood at 10.2 million and was growing fast.

The need for specialists to deal with the labor movement was, obviously, large. And since the avowed and consistent focus of union attention was the personnel arena — matters of wages and other conditions of employment — this was seen as the repository for such specialists. If personnel *per se* was now anything but a hot commodity, "labor relations" — in many ways, personnel as applied to union interests — was. And if only a short while earlier a personnel unit that had any kind of meaningful backing from top management was about as common as an impoverished geneticist or a struggling ophthalmologist is in the 1980s, with the advent of rampant unionism personnel was back in business in a hurry.

In addition, while many managers who were entrusted with the new responsibility possessed no relevant experience — understandably, given the recency of major industry labor relations — help here, too, was on the way. In short order, industrial and labor relations centers were established at a host of universities — Michigan, Stanford, M.I.T., and the California Institute of Technology conspicuously among them — to build upon the existing courses in the labor area that were being developed by a handful of pioneers at Wisconsin, Chicago, Princeton, and Carnegie Tech (now Carnegie-Mellon). Generally offering instruction not only to their own students but also to the outside community through adult education courses, and conducting major research projects as well, they lent status to the new field and, of course, added to its body of knowledge.

World War II, beginning for the United States in late 1941 and lasting until mid-1945, redirected attention to the personnel function well beyond the labor-management relations ingredient. As in the case of the first World War, its rapid creation of tight labor markets made optimal manpower utilization a necessity and interest in both psychological testing and performance appraisal, more or less quiescent since the earlier war, once again burgeoned. More sophisticated versions of both activities now encompassed such refinements as the Army General Classification Test (to select Officer Candidate School admittees) and the Link Trainer in testing and the critical incident and forced choice techniques in performance rating. All four of these and many other wartime-originated testing and rating developments continue, as modified to meet industrial needs, within the personnel function to this day.

But the war's contribution to a renaissance of personnel did not end here. A mammoth Training Within Industry (TWI) program, geared to accommodate the urgent needs of wartime production in the face of millions of inexperienced newcomers to the civilian labor force was developed by the War Manpower Commission. Emphasizing the four steps of "preparation, presentation, performance, and follow-up," it focused on the "key" or "critical" points in the job and helped supervisors to train approximately one-third of the nation's non-military labor force. TWI's basic concepts were hardly new: indeed, they were not decades but centuries old. But, as Ling has observed, "For using these methods, testing them, and popularizing them, TWI is owed a debt by the personnel area."[5]

Other notable wartime training projects that stimulated renewed interest in personnel endeavors were the Federal Security Agency's Engineering, Science, and Management War Training Program and Harvard's Advanced Management Program (which not only survived the end of hostilities but continues to be an esteemed training ground for top managers four decades later). Both did for executive development what TWI did for worker training.

The far-reaching governmental War Labor Board, charged with both general control over wages and hours and the settlement of labor-management disputes during the emergency, further enlarged the size of the personnel department. The Board's often frustrating mandate of wage constraint led it to develop such now-common tools of wage and salary administration as wage surveys and cost of living adjustments and to thenceforth make this personnel sub-field a more important one. The Board's inability to grant wage increases in the face of the legal controls over them fostered the first major growth in the fringe benefit area — particularly at the time, through such substitute employee inducements as paid meals, vacations, and holidays, and health and life insurance.

The Board's influence was felt in labor relations, too. Its efficient settlement of some 20,000 dispute cases gave enormous impetus to the now almost universal institution of voluntary labor-management arbitration, both by showing an appropriate framework and by serving as an invaluable training ground for literally hundreds of young arbitrators. The latter would form not only the center of the profession but essentially *all* of it for the next few decades. The ingredients for all of personnel's labor relations function were now firmly in place.

Finally, the war generated an unprecedented amount of government-sponsored research, both psychological and sociological, into such personnel-related areas as formal and informal groups, motivation, morale, leadership, communications, technological change and productivity. Interest in all of these fields, first kindled years earlier by the pioneering industrial psychologists and sociologists, was stimulated to the point where it was now both widespread and, seemingly, permanent.

Personnel was, in short, definitely a war profiteer. But its new allure was destined only to be temporary.

In 1962, seventeen years after the war had ended, a major personnel consultant wrote, presumably with some sadness,

> Since [personnel] . . . is not so obviously linked to profits or survival as are sales or production, its standing in industry has often been uncertain and its course unclear. Sometimes the value of personnel administration is "discovered" only when the very survival of the business is threatened. During the war years, for example . . . a competent "personnel man" was jewel of great value, and his prestige and organizational status were greatly enhanced. But he was recognized as important only as long as the crisis existed; when conditions returned to normal, the personnel function in many companies returned to its second-class status in the organization.[6]

And "second-class status" was accurate. The great expectations for the field that had been nurtured by the many wartime developments outlined above had simply dissipated. With the sole and conspicuous exception of personnel's labor relations function — where it could be argued (although normally with considerable hyperbole) that "the very survival of the business" was "threatened" — personnel finished the 1940s and remained for perhaps two decades more to some considerable extent the province of the "good old-Joe," clerically-oriented routine-surrounded functionaries alluded to at the beginning of this chapter. There were, of course, exceptions: Sears Roebuck, IBM, General Telephone and Electronics, General Motors and Allegheny Ludlum — among many others — had consistently given their personnel operations considerable authority and significance. But many more organizations seemed content to let their units in this field fulfil what McFarland could deem, in the early 1960s, a "trash can" function, performing a potpourri of unrelated, rather minor activities.[7]

There is no scientific body of knowledge to explain why this should have happened to personnel, but neither is there any shortage of theories. One of them, vocalized by Wilking writing in this period, has it that "Because everyone deals with people more or less successfully every day, there is a natural tendency to fail to see the need for specialized staff assistance in that area. . . . The chief executive often feels no need for high-powered, intelligent, aggressive, high-salaried people in . . . personnel. . . . As a result, he pays relatively low salaries, obtains relatively mediocre people, and, not surprisingly, finds that they can handle only relatively routine assignments."[8] In this scheme of things, personnel's relative stagnation in peacetime, until recent years, constituted the natural state for the profession; its wartime experiences by the same process formed the exception.

Another explanation, advanced by Miner and Miner, focuses on "conceptual" difficulties. Many approaches, procedures and techniques employed by personnel simply had not proven very effective: "Research increasingly indicated that the long-accepted assumption of a constant, positive relationship between job satisfaction and work output was basically incorrect. . . . The selection interview . . . was sorely deficient in a number of respects. . . . [And] the stresses and strains associated with manpower shortages and technological change were increasing, and few companies had been able to find adequate solutions to the problems thus created."[9]

Still other theories are credible. One of them contends that personnel outwore its welcome because its practitioners tended, in the earlier period, to specialize in narrow areas that were of limited concern to general management; the latter could, for example, muster only so much interest in secretarial skill testing or in the design of new evaluation forms. As another explanation, the profession was, again, said to be perceived as a spawner of "soft," as opposed to "hard-hitting" executives ("the best personnel man," declared a joke of mid-1960s' vintage, "is the one who gives away the company's money the least rapidly").

Personnel management also, it was argued, had become mechanics-bound, concerned primarily with procedures as opposed to organizational goals, techniques as opposed to policy, and methodology as opposed to genuine problem-solving. It had become, in short, a victim of its own routinized files, standard operating procedures and forms, and thus fully deserved its low-echelon standing.

Finally, the field, to many, had been increasingly marked by shallowness and oversimplification, with its practitioners all too willing to talk with pride about their programs but quite oblivious to the possibility that *other* programs might be better, and ill-equipped to generate these alternative programs anyhow: "[Even] though it has been abundantly shown that money is an effective incentive when used in combination with other motivating principles," wrote Dunnette and Bass, for example, in 1963, "most personnel managers lack the spirit of innovation and research mindedness necessary to work out effective combinations of money and other types of motivation."[10]

Each of the above indictments must, of course, be taken as a generalization. Exceptions to each, if they did not exactly abound in the community of personnel managers, surely could at least always be located. But even considering this factor, the prognosis for the field as the 1960s neared their termination was hardly an optimistic one. There was very little evidence to indicate that personnel would shortly start to undergo its major transformation.

PERSONNEL TODAY

"The '70s was the decade when personnel administration became professionalized," Odiorne has written.[11] And if a "profession" above all requires the possession of specialized knowledge by its members, there can be no dispute with this long-time student of the field. Symbolically, the American Society for Personnel Administration (the largest organized group of personnel people) had implemented a variety of certification programs, complete with examinations and the designation of different levels of professional standing, over these years. But such programs were no more mandatory for most personnel administrators than was membership in the Society itself, and the professionalism extended well beyond the ASPA boundaries.

The factors that have been especially responsible for personnel's recent upgrading have, of course, dictated to a large extent the types of specialized knowledge needed. Personnel units lacking either detailed or current information as to the ever expanding realm of employment legislation nowadays proceed only at their (and their organization's) peril. Employee benefits, seemingly undergoing a process of continuous liberalization, are today commonly viewed as being both too technical and too complex in their administration to be left to the amateur. Similarly, organizations have increasingly turned to personnel specialists who are steeped in the behavioral sciences (particularly psychology) for help in countering the many problems being presented by the new breed of worker referred to earlier in this chapter.

Far more expertise, too, is demanded from the labor relations staff within the personnel function. At times, in fact, even considerable in-house (as well as outside) legal talent may well be required since it has become ever more risky to state definitively what is legal in bargaining relationships and what is not, and for this reason alone the law school graduate is no longer a tourist attraction in the personnel office. But lawyers or no lawyers, the handling of contract negotiations and contract administration by an expert is, from the organization's viewpoint, vital.

And specialized knowledge is no longer a luxury, either, in: the design, implementation and administration of wage and salary programs; manpower planning; recruitment; training and development; employee counseling; employee communications (including such invaluable and thus fast-growing activities as attitude surveys); job design; and organization planning. In any of these fields, each of whose linkage to profits is nowadays far more visible than it once was, it has become increasingly apparent that a little knowledge is a dangerous thing. Smaller organizations can hardly justify individual specialists in each, but even they as a rule are quite aware of the risks in assigning these duties to personnel executives ungrounded in the subject matter.

Nor is it any longer *just* a knowledge of the subject matter that is needed. The personnel specialist is increasingly expected to possess a working familiarity with relevant mathematical and statistical techniques, a thorough foundation in at least the basic principles of economics, psychology and sociology, and an acquaintanceship with the computer. Membership in the new profession now thus commands — if implicitly rather than by any universal licensing criteria — a considerable amount of tool and methodological knowledge. And if even today personnel contains the entire gamut of practitioner abilities (ranging, as one observer could write a few years ago, "from the highly skilled performances of real pros to that of people who performed like an orangutan with a violin"),[12] ever higher expectations have been placed in the field and employing organizations demand far greater sophistication in their personnel executives than they did.

On the basis, at least primarily, of the needed specialized expertise, personnel administrators have fared very well financially in recent years. By the early 1980s, it was not at all unusual for senior executives in the field to be making $80,000 and even more and some personnel vice-presidents at the largest corporations were earning as much as $250,000 annually (including bonuses).[13] Moreover, a survey of 2,000 chief executives of major business and financial institutions by Information Science, Inc., had revealed that pay for the top personnel administrators under these chief executives had recently risen significantly, to the point where a majority of the respondents said it was equal to or more than the pay for their top legal, administrative and manufacturing officers. And 41 percent of these respondents also said that their top personnel executives made at least as much as their top marketing people.[14] All in all, it was not a bad performance for a field about which it had been said only a decade earlier, by the former Chairman of the Board of the American Management Associations no less, that "if some radical changes are not made in the attitudes and practices of most of the members of the personnel profession, it may disappear as such. . . . Their common denominator is paper shuffling; their criterion is how many times and to how many different documents a person can sign his name."[15]

Yet if there is general agreement nowadays that personnel's new trappings of success are (within limits) deserved, there remains some controversy as to *how* it should contribute its talents to the organization. There is, certainly, agreement that in a sense all managers are personnel managers, concerned with their human resources if for no other reason than that managerial success above all stems from the cooperative endeavors of everyone within the group. It is recognized beyond this that however helpful the personnel office may be, the ultimate responsibility for achieving effective results through people cannot be abdicated by any manager: that, in Lawrence A. Appley's famous dictum of many years ago, "Management *is* personnel administration." And it is no more in question that, on the other hand, since what is everyone's concern in time may well become the concern of no one, the need for the specialist to service line management in the personnel endeavor arises. But here the unanimity ends.

Should this service, for example, be confined to the giving of guidance, which would be reasonably consistent with Appley's view that "it is the job of the personnel executive officer to see that [personnel management by line managers] is done well, rather than do it himself"?[16] Or should the personnel executive be less of an advisor and more of a decision-maker in such a liaison with the line? Trice and Ritzer some time ago argued that the shift to decision-maker had already occurred ("As the occupation has become more important, there has been a shift from doing trivial work and advising to making decisions with others in the organization. For example, the labor relations expert may be the best qualified to decide whether a new union contract is good for the company or not."[17]) They tended to favor this development, which they thought was not as visible as it could have been because personnel managers themselves had carefully concealed it in order to maintain their "precarious organizational relationships" and thus to keep their power.

On the other hand, many personnel practitioners continue to see themselves strictly as advisors and are very happy with the situation: they prefer, as Yoder has put it, to

> minimize their managerial responsibility and authority. They propose to get most of their satisfactions out of planning and directing programs. To a degree, they view themselves as semi-independent consultants, on retainer to line managers as clients.[18]

And should the personnel representative providing the service to the line management give the help even if the line management limits this help to that making use of very little special expertise, or even none at all? Foulkes and Morgan, in words reminiscent of an earlier day, could state even in this relative golden age of personnel that

> dealing with people is a critical part of any manager's job, and most managers believe that they are competent at the practical level. They may seek help when they are overextended, but they do not want the personnel department to do things for them that they feel competent to do.[19]

Calling the providing of such service the "bread and butter" of the personnel job, they suggest that personnel accommodate the request for service in any event. They thus see a need for the personnel generalist, offering a broad portfolio to line management, although they in no way argue against the simultaneous need for the personnel specialist (above all, to establish standards and procedures to ensure that organizational policies are maintained and to research and develop new programs).[20]

But Foulkes and Morgan are not dogmatic about it. They freely admit that "what is effective for Texas Instruments may not be for Polaroid, or vice versa."[21] And they, as all other thoughtful students of the personnel field, would presumably agree (whatever their own preferences) that the test is in how efficiently the desired organizational goals are effected, and not in the superficialities of exact personnel office form and operating style. The field's impressive growth figures eloquently testify that personnel is, on the whole, perceived to be doing well in this test.

NOTES

1. Cyril C. Ling, *The Management of Personnel Relations* (Homewood, Illinois: Richard D. Irwin, Inc., 1965).

2. William H. Tolman, *Social Engineering* (New York: McGraw-Hill Book Co., Inc., 1909), as quoted in Ling, *The Management of Personnel Relations*, p. 79.

3. Walter Dill Scott, Robert C. Clothier, Stanley B. Mathewson, and William R. Spriegel, *Personnel Management*, 3rd ed. (New York: McGraw-Hill Book Co., Inc., 1941), p. 4.

4. *Welfare Work for Employees in Industrial Establishments in the United States* (U.S. Bureau of Labor Statistics Bulletin No. 250) (Washington, D.C.: U.S. Government Printing Office, 1919), p. 119.

5. Ling, *The Management of Personnel Relations*, p. 469.

6. S. Vincent Wilking, "The Status of Today's Personnel Man," in *The Personnel Man and His Job* (New York: American Management Association, Inc., 1962), p. 25.

7. Dalton McFarland, *Conflict and Cooperation in Personnel Administration* (New York: American Foundation for Management Research, 1962), p. 48.

8. Wilking, "The Status of Today's Personnel Man," p. 27.

9. John B. Miner and Mary Green Miner, *Personnel and Industrial Relations: A Managerial Approach*, 2nd ed. (New York: The Macmillan Company, 1973), p. 31.

10. Marvin D. Dunnette and Bernard M. Bass, "Behavioral Scientists and Personnel Management," *Industrial Review*, May 1963, p. 119.

11. George S. Odiorne, "Personnel Management for the '80's," in Lloyd L. Byars et al., eds., *Readings and Cases in Personnel Management* (Philadelphia: W. B. Saunders Company, 1979), p. 21.

12. Wiley Beavers, "Accreditation: What Do We Need That For?" in Mary Green Miner and John B. Miner, eds., *Policy Issues in Contemporary Personnel and Industrial Relations* (New York: Macmillan Publishing Co., Inc., 1977), p. 54.

13. *Wall Street Journal*, December 30, 1980, p. 1.

14. *Wall Street Journal*, October 16, 1979, p. 1.

15. Lawrence A. Appley, "Management *Is* Personnel Administration," *Personnel*, March-April 1969, p. 8.

16. *Ibid.*, p. 12.

17. Harrison Trice and George Ritzer, "The Personnel Manager and His Self-Image," *Personnel Administration*, 35:1 (1972), p. 49.

18. Dale Yoder, "Personnel Administration," in *The Next Twenty-Five Years of Industrial Relations* (Madison, Wisc.: Industrial Relations Research Association, 1973), p. 148.

19. Fred K. Foulkes and Henry M. Morgan, "Organizing and Staffing the Personnel Function," *Harvard Business Review*, May-June 1977, p. 147.

20. *Ibid.*

21. *Ibid.*, p. 153.

Trends and Issues in Personnel Management
Margaret Magnus

The rapidly changing demands on personnel professionals often make us wish for a crystal ball that we could use to foresee the future and be ready to meet the problems and issues head on.

While predictions are often hazardous, they also can be helpful. In reviewing *Personnel Journal* surveys, along with the writings of management sages, we found that some issues of concern to personnel managers continually emerge: training, compensation and benefits, communications, and employee relations.

However, the components and forms of these particular issues change over time, depending upon internal and external forces influencing the organization.

DEMOGRAPHIC CHANGES

Dr. Peter Morrison at Rand Corporation in Santa Monica, California, speaking recently before the Town Hall in Los Angeles, identified several major demographic changes that are affecting personnel practices.

Changes in Household and Family Makeup

The "average American household" no longer exists. In addition, household size is shrinking. In 1995, projections indicate 2.3 persons per household, compared with 3.7 persons per household in 1940.

These smaller households are not shrunken versions of larger ones — the makeup of households is also changing. Only 31% of the population is married with children. Another third are married without children, and almost a fifth are living alone. The remaining households are single-parent families and people living with other non-family members.

Changes in the Age Profile and Participation of the Work Force

Morrison says we are now faced with the "baby boom" and the "baby bust" generations, both leaving a legacy of uneven population growth.

The decline in the birthrate represents a decline in the entry-level work force of the future. On the other hand, the increase in the 65+ population represents an increase in older workers, especially as older people are now opting for later retirement.

The baby boom generation will continue to impact the organization as it moves through the age span. The influx of the baby boom in the 1970s created congestion and high unemployment in entry-level positions and is now moving through the corporation and causing congestion at middle management levels.

Changes in Geographical Preferences

The trend from North to South is well documented, but other changes will also include the move from big cities to smaller communities and the increase in immigration to the U.S. from Asia and South and Central America.

TECHNOLOGICAL DEVELOPMENTS

The number one societal trend, according to John Naisbitt in his book *Megatrends,* is the shift from an industrial to an information society.

In an information society, says Naisbitt, the strategic resource is information. Thus, we move from a capital-intensive to a brain-intensive society.

If the strategic resource is information, what will the economy look like? According to Peter F. Drucker in his book *The Changing World of the Executive,* we will enter "production sharing" on a world-wide basis.

In production sharing, says Drucker, the underdeveloped or developing countries of the world take over the labor-intensive stages of production that cannot be automated. This shift is due, in part, to the availability of an enormous and growing surplus of low-skilled, entry-level workers in developing countries and the decline of entry-level workers in developed countries.

Thus, the developed countries, with their highly educated labor force, will be responsible for the skill-intensive stages of production, such as design, engineering, quality control, and marketing.

What are the implications of the above technological and demographic trends? These changes, at a minimum, influence training, compensation and benefits, organizational structure, employee communications, employee rights, and personnel accountability.

TRAINING

Naisbitt says the formidable challenge of the next several years will be to train people to work in the information society. "Jobs will become available, but who will possess the high technology skills to fill them?" he asks.

Drucker calls this training "redundancy planning," or anticipating the structural and technological changes in the economy and retraining or finding new jobs for workers who will have to be laid off.

Responsibility for this training will, most likely, fall to the personnel/human resources department and may take several forms.

The training itself will include entry-level personnel who need basic training, management training to understand technology and how to apply it for organizational growth and innovation, technical training to maintain state-of-the-art proficiency for experienced technicians, and re-training for new skills.

In-house Training Programs

The larger companies will continue to develop in-house training programs modifying the content to meet technological developments, while utilizing the technology for more sophisticated, more individualized training sessions.

Cooperatives with Universities and Colleges

Many organizations have already begun to work with nearby universities and colleges to develop extension, in-service, and other educational training programs.

These cooperatives are particularly beneficial for organizations without the resources to develop in-house programs, but who can work with other companies requiring employees with similar skills. Also, as Naisbitt points out, these cooperatives are helpful to colleges and universities, which see a declining enrollment due to the drop in birthrate.

Business and Government Partnerships

In some communities, the Private Industry Councils (PICs) formed under CETA have been successful in training and skill development. They can serve as models of cooperative funding and management for training programs that reach the often hard-to-employ, such as youths, minorities, older workers, and re-entry women.

Business Community Training Programs

Other organizations have made manpower forecasts five and 10 years ahead to determine the types of skills needed in the workplace. In response, many companies are now developing training programs, available to the community, which develop the skills required in the workplace of the future. From this population, they will recruit new employees.

Also required of the personnel department will be counseling and placement help along with the corporate resources necessary for the relocation of retrained employees.

COMPENSATION AND BENEFITS

Demographics and technology are also working to change compensation and benefits practices, most notably to tailor them to individual needs and individual performance.

Flexible Benefits

Obviously, the changing makeup of the work force necessitates a modification in compensation and benefits packages. Without a "typical American worker" there is no typical, satisfactory benefits package that applies to all employees.

The result is flexible benefits, or "cafeteria compensation," whereby each employee picks the combination of benefits most suited to his or her needs. The computer makes this personalization possible, by allowing for the storage, retrieval, and use of the information required to develop tailor-made benefits packages.

Decline in Entitlements

The trend has been to bigger and better benefits packages, often without a clearly measurable return on the corporate investment.

Employers are now more closely examining the addition of new benefits and re-evaluating the level of existing benefits, particularly in the area of health care. Here, as elsewhere, employers are beginning to look for a return on their investment and to make decisions based on this analysis.

Pay for Performance

As with benefits, employers are also examining the return on compensation. If human resources are becoming the organization's most important resource, then it becomes imperative to be able to quantify that resources' contribution to production, to the organization, and to profit.

Employees, on the other hand, are demanding rewards for their skills, their creativity, and for their inventions. They, too, want to see a direct relationship between compensation and results produced.

Thus, organizations will develop ways to tie compensation to performance. Traditionally, this has always been true in areas such as sales because it has been easy to measure performance. In areas such as management or research and development, it is more difficult to measure output or productivity. The challenge to personnel management will be to develop ways to tie pay to performance.

Pension Plans

Already under scrutiny by Tax Equity and Fiscal Responsibility Act (TEFRA), pension plans will be reexamined to determine if they can support a retired baby boom generation, if they need to include incentives for staying in the work force longer, and if they need further modifications due to Social Security and other changes.

ORGANIZATIONAL STRUCTURE

Another of Naisbitt's megatrends is the move from organizational hierarchies to networking. "Simply stated," he says, "networks are people talking to each other, sharing ideas, information, and resources."

The important part, he continues, is not the finished product but the process of getting there — the communication that creates the linkages between people and clusters of people.

Networks are important, he says, because they create another type of communication and flow of information that is stifled in the traditional hierarchical pyramid. The information society now requires greater speed and more flexibility, and that can only be accomplished by changing the ways we now communicate and work with each other.

The other reason Naisbitt and Drucker see a change in organizational structure is the highly educated baby boom generation with nowhere to go up the organizational ladder.

Drucker says the concept of natural and consistent upward mobility in organizations has to be de-emphasized. "In the last 15 years, emphasis in many organizations has not been on the job at all, but on promotions. This was short-sighted, even when promotions were plentiful. Even then most employees weren't moving up. Promotions have always been the exception, and now the emphasis will be back where it belongs: on the job."

Naisbitt sees networks and restructuring as the solution. "What will we do with all those well-educated Indians with chief-like tendencies?" he asks. His answer is to restructure our organizations into smaller and smaller working units that interact with each other.

Smaller groups of talented people will then govern their own work environments and participate in their own management decisions.

If organizations restructure, and indeed, become more lateral, personnel managers will be faced not only with new personnel issues around "management," but also will be required to develop new communications systems and networks, redesign training programs, change job descriptions, evaluate performance appraisal systems and compensation plans geared to promotions, and reexamine the entire organization.

EMPLOYEE RIGHTS

Peter Drucker also sees a fundamental change in the way jobs are viewed. He says that jobs have traditionally been considered a contractual agreement, but they are beginning to be treated as a species of property.

As such, employees will be accorded all the rights of property owners. In employment terms, that can include due process in dismissal actions, free speech on and off the job, protection when blowing the whistle on illegal corporate practices, participatory management, equal pay for equal work, flexible work "contracts," privacy issues, and more.

While most of the issues are not new to personnel professionals, many of them will receive greater attention and focus in the next few years. Models of employee privacy or equal pay will become the standard for all organizations. Employee rights is one more area in which the personnel manager has to develop his or her expertise in order to protect the organization and to help employees.

PERSONNEL ACCOUNTABILITY

While personnel managers will be reexamining their responsibilities for training, compensation and benefits, organizational development, and employee rights, they also will be called upon to quantify and justify their own activities.

Based on *Personnel Journal* readers' questions and comments, personnel accountability has become a widespread issue throughout many organizations.

Specifically, questions are asked about how to measure the personnel department's contribution to profits, how to set measurable objectives and quantify results, and how the personnel department can influence organizational productivity.

The return on investment concern applied to employees will also apply to the personnel department. The challenge will be to quantify and measure the corporate return on dollars invested in the personnel function in a way that maximizes human resources management.

CONCLUSION

While the legislation of the '60s and '70s created a new and expanded role for the personnel manager, the demographic and technological changes of the '80s will test the adaptability, ingenuity, and far-sightedness of the personnel manager.

The personnel department will continue to have its traditional set of problems — sometimes in new forms — but it will also have an opportunity to initiate and develop new programs and policies that will increase the importance, visibility, and worth of the personnel department to the organization.

The forward-looking human resources manager will need to think about:

▫ training and retraining existing and future staff to meet the technological changes within existing and new industries

▫ changing compensation practices that reward performance both for employee satisfaction and for corporate investment

▫ reexamining organizational structures and lines of communications to develop new networks for problem solving, while deemphasizing promotions and upward mobility

▫ reexamining corporate policies on employee rights and developing policies and procedures that protect both employees and employers

▫ incorporating accountability into the human resources management function in order to justify, evaluate, and measure the role of personnel management in the organization

While many personnel managers have already tackled these problems, others are just facing the complexities and intricacies of these issues. Regardless of the developmental stage, the changes are rapid and will alter the way we view the work force and the workplace, and the manager of both: the human resources director.

REFERENCES

Drucker, Peter F. *The Changing World of the Executive* (New York: Truman Talley Books, 1982).

Naisbitt, John. *Megatrends: Ten New Directions Transforming Our Lives* (New York: Warner Books, Inc., 1982).

B.

THE HUMAN RESOURCE MANAGEMENT PROFESSIONAL TODAY

Personnel Directors Are the New Corporate Heroes

Herbert E. Meyer

The personnel department has been represented on many a corporate organization chart as an orphaned box — one that came from nowhere and didn't seem to fit anywhere. To many businessmen, including many chief executives, the people who worked in "personnel" appeared to be a bunch of drones whose apparent missions in life were to create paperwork, recruit secretaries who couldn't type, and send around memos whose impertinence was exceeded only by their irrelevance. As a result of this perception, personnel directors, whatever their individual competence, suffered the *sui generis* image of being good-old-Joe types — harmless chaps who spent their careers worshiping files, arranging company picnics, and generally accomplishing nothing whatsoever of any fundamental importance.

In some cases, this depressing image was accurate. Companies *have* been known to use their personnel departments as a sort of dumping ground for executive misfits, or for burned-out vice presidents who needed just a little while longer on the payroll to be eligible for their pensions. But there have always been some personnel directors who found the job a springboard to higher corporate office, and in some companies the executive in charge of personnel management has traditionally been regarded not as an outcast but as an heir apparent.

The current chairman and chief executive of Delta Airlines, W. T. Beebe, was once Delta's senior vice president for personnel. Both Richard D. Wood, the chairman of Eli Lilly & Co., and one of his predecessors as chief executive served as corporate personnel directors on their way to the top — and a former president had followed the same route. Right now, the top Lilly executive responsible for personnel, Harold M. Wisely, holds the rank of executive vice president and has a seat on the company's board of directors.

A STEP TOWARD THE TOP

In the last few years, many companies have joined Delta and Lilly in putting their personnel departments in the hands of powerful senior executives. That old chestnut

---

From *Fortune* 93 (February 1976): pp. 84–88, 140. Reprinted by permission.

21

about a transfer to personnel being a one-way ticket to oblivion is no longer true. Absolutely no one at First National City Bank viewed it as a setback for Lawrence M. Small when he was transferred from the commercial-banking division to head the personnel division in August, 1974. Indeed, it was universally regarded as one very impressive step up the ladder: the job carries the title of senior vice president, and Small was only thirty-two years old at the time. And at I.B.M., to cite just one other example, the former director of personnel resources, David E. McKinney, is now president of the Information Records Division, an important marketing and manufacturing unit.

Those good-old-Joes of yesteryear would be stunned by the amount of power and prestige today's personnel directors can claim within their companies. At Dow Chemical Co., for example, the man in charge of personnel, Herbert Lyon, reports directly to President Ben Branch, the chief executive. Lyon is a member of Dow's board of directors, and is responsible for, among other things, global product planning and corporate administration. At Warnaco Inc., most of the executives promoted to jobs in top management during the last three years were singled out for advancement by John Limpitlaw, the company's vice president for personnel.

The executives who are being put in charge of personnel departments today are hard-driving business managers who speak what they call "bottom-line language"; they are as interested in profits as any other executives. George A. Rieder, senior vice president for personnel at Indiana National Bank in Indianapolis, provides an almost textbook example of how today's personnel executives perceive their role. "I'm not a personnel manager," Rieder says, in a tone of voice conveying scorn for that traditional title. "I'm a business manager with responsibilities for personnel."

Rieder quickly adds that this difference is much more than merely semantic. "It's a difference of style, scope, and approach. I view myself as a businessman first, whose job has as much of an impact on the bottom line around here as anybody else's. To be effective I have got to understand every aspect of my company's business, and I have got to participate actively in major management decisions before they're made." As a senior vice president, Rieder reports to John R. Benbow, the bank's president, and participates actively in day-to-day management of the business.

"GOOD ONES ARE WORTH A LOT"

Salary scales provide a measure of the growing importance of personnel. When the average salaries of executives in different specialties are compared — manufacturing, finance, and so on — personnel directors come out as the lowest paid. But they've begun catching up, because they are getting bigger raises than other executives. According to the American Management Association, the average compensation for personnel directors of industrial companies with sales of $500 million to $1 billion was $61,400 in 1975. Executives in charge of manufacturing for those companies got an average of $83,400, chief financial officers got $103,400, and chief executives $225,700. But since 1970, the average compensation of personnel directors has increased by 20 percent, compared with just 13.5 percent for chief financial officers, 15 percent for manufacturing executives, and 18 percent for chief executives.

It's likely that personnel directors will continue to receive larger raises than other kinds of executives, according to Pearl Meyer, a compensation expert who is executive vice president of Handy Associates. "These poor guys in personnel won't be at the bottom of the scale for too much longer," Mrs. Meyer predicts. "Companies are recognizing that good ones are worth a lot." Last year, when Chase Manhattan Bank went looking for an executive to head its human-resources division (modern corporations don't have personnel departments anymore), the bank put out word that for the right man, it would pay up to $120,000. Chase was obviously not in the market for a mere picnic planner. (The right man turned out to be Alan Lafley, from General Electric.)

Clearly, things are not at all what they used to be in the once dull world of personnel or, if you please, human-resource management. And just as clearly, much of the pressure for change came from the economic environment in which corporations have been operating. As Warnaco's John Limpitlaw points out, "The business climate out there today is a whole lot different from what it was ten years ago." In the economy of the 1970's, just about everybody has found the going tough and profits hard to come by. The cost of labor — union contracts, executive salaries, pension plans, and so on — keeps moving up.

Furthermore, many companies that had expanded geometrically during the 1960's discovered that their acquisition programs had left them with a tangle of incompatible compensation plans, and with scores of highly paid executives who now seemed to be in the wrong jobs or, worse, were superfluous. And with the stock market remaining in the doldrums, stock-option plans that had looked like money machines during the 1960's suddenly seemed most unsatisfactory; new compensation plans had to be devised to keep key executives contented. The job of personnel director took on new dimensions — especially as chief executives began scrambling to minimize the adverse effects of the recession.

Companies eager to increase their workers' productivity — and which were not? — discovered that an alert personnel director was in a unique position to contribute to the company's welfare. For example, George Sherman, the vice president of industrial relations at Cleveland's Midland-Ross Corp., got to wondering just why productivity rates in Japanese factories were so high. He flew to Japan, visited some factories, and concluded that part of the answer lay in the use of committees, made up of both workers and supervisors, that met regularly to hear suggestions for meeting production goals. On his return to the U.S., Sherman got clearance to form Japanese-style committees of workers and supervisors at the company's electrical-equipment plant in Athens, Tennessee. One modification of the Japanese plan involved the offer of a cash bonus to both workers and managers if productivity really did increase beyond the goal set by Midland-Ross. One year and 400 suggestions later, productivity at the Athens plant was up by 15 percent. The company was able to cancel plans to invest $250,000 in added manufacturing capacity, because output increased without it. Now Sherman expects to set up similar committees at other plants.

TIME OFF WHEN IT COUNTS

An idea developed by I.B.M.'s vice president for personnel, Walton Burdick, further illustrates how a personnel executive can help his company, and its workers, through a difficult economic period. Burdick developed a policy allowing I.B.M.'s employees to defer vacation time for as long as they wanted. Postponement was actively urged during years of booming business activity, thus keeping a lid on the number of employees. The payoff for both I.B.M. and its employees came during the past year, when the recession took a bite out of I.B.M.'s production. Workers who had saved up weeks or even months of vacation time were encouraged (rather firmly, one gathers) to use it.

I.B.M. Chairman Frank Cary credits the policy of deferred time off for helping the company get through a rough period without any layoffs. "You can't put a dollar sign on this sort of thing," Cary says. "The real benefit is in terms of morale. Our people know our policies are designed to keep them on the payroll. It makes them a lot more willing to go along with organizational changes we propose from time to time."

Pressure on American corporations from their not-so-silent partner, Uncle Sam, has done a great deal to add luster to the job of personnel director. In the last twenty years, there have been more than a hundred individual pieces of federal legislation directly affecting the relationship between corporations and their employees — e.g., the Work Hours Act of 1962, the Occupational Safety and Health Act of 1970, and the Employees Retirement Income Security Act of 1974. There has been a whole basket of laws and regulations to outlaw discrimination, including the Civil Rights Act of 1964, the Equal Pay Act of 1963, and the Age Discrimination in Employment Act of 1967.

SUITS THAT CONCENTRATE THE MIND

Personnel directors complain that the federal rules and regulations are poorly conceived, sloppily written, and almost impossible to comply with because they change so rapidly. But many of those same personnel directors concede that the federal government's antidiscrimination activities have done wonders for their own prestige and power. To paraphrase Samuel Johnson, there is something about being sued for a lot of money that concentrates a chief executive's mind wonderfully. While some antidiscrimination suits involve just one aggrieved person and not much money, there have also been some class-action suits whose costs to corporations have been considerable. American Telephone & Telegraph Co. has settled two antidiscrimination suits — one for $38 million and another for $25 million — and nine steel companies settled one for a total of $31 million. The threat of class-action suits by aggrieved employees or disgruntled job applicants has made chief executives very much interested in having their personnel directors come up with ways to avoid even the appearance of discrimination. "Boy, do they listen to us now," says one personnel expert rather cheerfully.

In addition to setting affirmative-action goals, such as for the number of women and blacks to be hired during the coming year, and the number to be promoted into various levels of management, personnel directors develop procedures to make sure the goals are reached. That may involve new hiring systems or special training programs for those already hired and marked for fast promotion. Personnel directors must spend a lot of time these days with supervisors at all levels, helping them to meet their targets.

At Chemetron Corp., Melvin Shulman, corporate director of human resources, works directly with Chief Executive John P. Gallagher to set the affirmative-action goals and develop the procedures for reaching them. Then he works with Chemetron's line executives to make sure they understand what those goals are, and also that they understand how serious could be the consequences of failing to reach them. Says Shulman: "I tell them of the possible damage to the company, but in a sense I'm making sure they realize that their own careers here are involved. When they understand how directly the chief executive is involved, and that in effect I'm representing him, they're more than willing to get cracking."

Personnel directors probably would have come in from the cold even without the help of a topsy-turvy economy or a flood of legislation. It would have happened because attitudes within the American corporation itself have been changing steadily for at least a generation — the attitude of chief executives toward their subordinates as well as the attitude of employees at all levels toward the companies for which they work.

It is so commonplace now for chief executives to deliver speeches extolling "people" as their companies' most important resource that one tends to dismiss the phrase as cant. For some chief executives, of course, it may be. But a growing number of them really do realize that the quality and morale of their employees can make the difference between success and failure for their companies. One chief executive who is especially articulate on the importance of a company's human resources is Delta Airlines' Tom Beebe. "The name of the game in business today is personnel," he says emphatically. "You can't hope to show a good financial or operating report unless your personnel relations are in order, and I don't care what kind of a company you're running. A chief executive is nothing without his people. You've got to have the right ones in the right jobs for them, and you've got to be sure employees at every level are being paid fairly and being given opportunities for promotion. You can't fool them, and any chief executive who tries is going to hurt himself and his company."

Since Beebe is a former personnel man, there is some temptation to pooh-pooh his views as those of a man loyal to his old specialty. But one cannot argue with success. Delta hasn't had a strike in twenty years, and as airlines go, it is uncommonly profitable.

COURSES FOR THE COMERS

Every chief executive has to be especially concerned about bringing along capable successors. One company that is justifiably famous for the breadth and quality of its management-training programs is I.B.M. Frank Cary works closely with Walton Burdick, the vice president for personnel, to develop those programs and to assign the executive "graduates" to appropriate jobs within I.B.M. "It's the chief executive's responsibility to make sure the company has personnel policies and practices that can select the best people, then train them for management positions," says Cary.

Dresser Industries' senior vice president for industrial relations, Thomas Raleigh, spends a lot of time with President John V. James developing and administering the company's executive-training programs. At the recently established Dresser Leadership Center, a campus-like training center near the company's Dallas headquarters, executives enroll for courses lasting one to four weeks. They take courses in business management, and also study aspects of Dresser's energy-related business that may be unconnected to their immediate assignments. And Raleigh gets a chance to size up Dresser officials who work far from Dallas.

Few personnel managers work only with executives, of course, and the changed attitudes of employees toward their companies present a constant flow of new challenges. Today's blue- and white-collar workers want more from their jobs than just a paycheck; they want satisfaction, and they want to be treated fairly. Specifically, they want a salary that's fair in relation to their co-workers' salaries, and they want a fair chance for promotion that's based on an objective evaluation of their performances rather than the subjective whims of their immediate supervisors, or on their sex or skin color.

When Harold Johnson joined Philadelphia's INA Corp. as vice president for personnel a few months ago — he was formerly with American Medicorp Inc. — the insurance company did not have a fully developed system for setting the salaries of new employees. Nor were there clear ground rules for awarding raises, or for evaluating employee performance. "Things worked pretty much according to the whims of individual supervisors," says Johnson. "There were no company-wide standards at all. The employees were unhappy because they felt their salaries were sometimes unfair, and because they felt top management wasn't aware of the quality work they were doing. And top management needed a tool to help identify the high performers so they could be promoted, or selected for advanced training."

INA Chairman Ralph Saul has ordered Johnson to develop a system to identify the company's most promising executives, and to establish corporate salary scales so that employees in similar jobs will be paid within an established range. Johnson is also devising an evaluation system to assure that raises will be awarded in a consistent way, based on individual performance. Once the system is in effect, Johnson will be responsible for getting supervisors to use it. Saul has told Johnson that the latter's own job performance will be measured in part by how quickly he can get the new pay and evaluation system working.

26

*PART I
P/HRM: THE
ORGANIZATIONAL
FUNCTION AND
THE PROFESSION*

POWER FOR THE TEAM

In many companies, the personnel director's responsibilities have become so complex that they can only be shouldered by topflight business managers who have the backing of the chief executive. The people who do the job like to say that in the years to come, a tour of duty in the personnel department (more likely the division of human resources) will be mandatory for any executive who aims to be chairman. Though that may prove to be an exaggeration, it is true that more companies are transferring up-and-coming executives into personnel for a while, en route to greater things. Dow Chemical's Herbert Lyon says it's a good thing for personnel departments to have a mix of professional experts, who have worked exclusively in personnel, and generalists who are brought in for a tour of duty from other parts of the company. I.B.M.'s Walton Burdick agrees, and adds that in his view the professional personnel types — of whom he is one — benefit even more than the generalists from having a mix. "It gives the specialists a better sense of what's really going on out there," he explains.

Citibank's Larry Small reflects a perspective common to executives who have moved into personnel but who do not expect to remain in it forever. "I'm not a personnel guy," he says carefully, displaying the annoyance of a man who has explained this to others before and who knows he'll have to explain it again to somebody else. "I'm a businessman — a manager. I just happen to be handling personnel at the moment, because it's a very important part of managing a business today."

As more and more personnel departments become populated with managers like Small, what were once enclaves will increasingly be seen as key corporate divisions. And the executives who run them, whether they are called personnel directors or executive vice presidents for human resources, will finally be recognized for what they now are and what in retrospect they always should have been — power-wielding members of their companies' management teams.

Big Hat, No Cattle:
Managing Human Resources
Wickham Skinner

In the Dallas airport the other day I saw many tall, well-dressed, and impressive-looking men wearing large, immaculate Stetson cowboy hats. As I walked by one such hat-wearer, I noticed two middleaged, sunburned men in faded blue jeans standing nearby. They eyed the same fellow, looked him up and down, and then one said quietly to the other, "Big hat, no cattle."

The same can be said of the massive efforts to improve the management of people in U.S. industry. Since World War II, calling it "human relations," "personnel management," "labor relations," and now "management of human resources," business has spent millions to make employees productive, loyal, and motivated.

First, academics, with minds opened by the Hawthorne experiments, led the movement to effectively manage people. Now, eager consultants and zealous staff experts nurture it. *Fortune* writes of personnel directors as the "new corporate heroes." Library shelves overflow with people management books, and a hundred new ones appear every year. Two hundred documented attempts are going on to improve the quality of work life (QWL), and three nationally known institutions have charters to improve productivity and QWL.

Since Hawthorne, successive waves of people-problem solutions and programs have washed and tumbled industry. In some desperation, managers have steadily invested in supervisory training, organizational behavior, interpersonal behavior, T-groups, sensitivity training, employee attitude surveys, job enrichment, flexible benefits, and expanded fringe benefits — bigger pensions, subsidized insurance, more holidays, shorter work days, four-day weeks, and canned communications packages — and now companies are attempting to revive the "work ethic" with human resources departments. Big programs, but where are the payoffs?

Not in productivity. Recent figures show a decline in employee productivity for the United States.

Not in absence of strikes.

Not in widespread amicable labor relations.

Not in the strategic position of many U.S. industries in international competition.

Not in the absence of government intervention, such as OSHA and EEO regulations.

Not in public confidence, support, and credibility in our business system or big corporations.

Not in the image of managers as a benign, trusted group in our society.

Not in the absence of hostility or class warfare.

Not in enthusiastic employee acceptance of new technology, machinery, or equipment in factories, of stripped-down offices, or of efficiency gains in the ever-expanding industries.

Big hat, no cattle!

Human resources management seems to be mostly good intentions and whistling in the dark or averting unionization. And the results of the 1970s suggest that we may not even be holding our own. The poor management of the work force in this country is damaging the nation and our standard of living. It is making us uncompetitive with the Japanese and some other Asians, the West Germans, the Swiss, and many others.

I do not wish to exaggerate the gloomy aspects of this picture. A handful of large (and certainly many medium-sized and smaller) companies appear to have made their work forces into competitive assets. And surely modest progress has occurred nearly everywhere. For the most part, sweatshops are a thing of the past. Workplaces are better lit and ventilated and are generally safer than in the past. The atmosphere at work is less coldly formal, and decision making more participative. Managers are more aware of feelings and relationships and make fewer overt demands of employees. Fewer "bulls of the woods" charge about offices and factories. Personnel people are more professional, more companies have clearly stated grievance procedures, and house publications regularly explain how and why companies are managing themselves for their employees' benefit.

Some will argue that we've been doing many of the right things and that it is societal factors such as the "declining work ethic," the "new breed," and the "new sociology" that are eroding management's efforts. Regardless, in most companies the results of enlightened people management are simply more comfort, more relaxation, more freedom from pressure, more security, more benefits, and higher pay, not more productivity and loyalty.

What's gone wrong? Why do so few companies actually make use of the greatest competitive weapon of all — the powerful resources of motivated, energized, cooperative, trusting people?

Few managers need much convincing about the importance of people. All the managers I've talked to say, "People are our greatest asset." But they also report, "We don't know how to motivate them." "People are getting harder to manage." "Personnel departments don't give us the leadership we need." "We're just hanging in there trying to cope."

WHAT'S BEEN WRONG?

Managers have had difficulty managing human resources for four reasons:

1. Achieving wholehearted cooperation, energy, and commitment from large numbers of employees is difficult, so managers are often unrealistic in their hopes.*

2. Concepts concerning the management of large numbers of people often convey contradictory messages to managers.

3. Critical problems in the corporate management of personnel, such as the place of human resources management (HRM) in corporate decision making, the role of personnel staff, and a lack of sufficient human resources management knowhow at top management levels, remain largely unresolved.

4. Some management assumptions concerning HRM undermine the efforts of many managers, no matter how well intentioned they may be.

Achieving Employee Commitment

Capturing the loyalty of hundreds or thousands of individuals in one business enterprise so that they direct their energies toward the goals of the company is enormously difficult. The goals of the corporation are long-range and general in nature — profit and growth. But employees usually focus on short time horizons to meet their needs in wages, salaries, working conditions, fair treatment, and promotion. Drawing a connection between these sets of goals is not easy.

Effective relationships between individuals and companies rest on employees' trust that the goals are connected. But developing trust often requires overcoming years of bad experience and many employees' belief that companies exploit people. Of every 100 employees, 5 or 10 will have been disappointed or burned by some job-related experience, which may have been beyond the company's control. Their subsequent alienation can subvert the efforts of managers and personnel officers to build morale.

Given that working in a social, industrial operation requires people to give up many freedoms and that groups acting collectively play on that loss of freedom to

---

*The term *large numbers* is used in this article to distinguish between the management issues concerning interpersonal and small group relationships and those relating to large groups, departments, divisions, or entire companies and institutions. My focus is on the latter, not on the former.

better their own short-term interests, that the work force is uncommitted should be no surprise.

Seen this way, the fight for a motivated work force is an uphill battle. It's rosy idealism to think that every employee is going to turn on and perform with 100% devotion to a company and its objectives. Short-term economic interests are in clear conflict. Employees see their share of the pie as being cut smaller to serve up larger profits to owners. Further, political factors such as Nader's Raiders and the anti-big-business wing of the Democratic party exploit employees' distrust of business, the corporation, and managers, whom employees often see as being out for themselves and siding with their corporate bosses against the employee.

People instinctively resent forces that manage and control them — big business, directors, the industrial establishment, the boss, the boss's boss. The antiestablishment seeds sown in the late 1960s and early 1970s are bearing fruit, and more employees than ever are unwilling to subject themselves wholly to an organization or the discipline of a trade, profession, or team.

Given these obstacles to collaboration, that cooperation occurs within the corporate world at all is miraculous.

Conflicts in Theory

Managers use many different organizational techniques to achieve collaboration and productivity. Researchers can take large credit for the multitude of concepts and tools on hand. They must also, however, accept responsibility for the fact that their different disciplines often conflict and work at cross-purposes.

For example, in most companies managers employ four different disciplines to improve employee performance and relations — human relations, labor relations, personnel administration, and industrial engineering. Since human relations itself includes at least three major schools, six fairly distinct sets of ideas and concepts can be at work in the same organization at the same time:

1. *Human relations.* Theories of *group behavior* deal with social interaction and interpersonal relationships through such tools as theories X and Y and sensitivity training. The school's precept is that because group behavior is critical to collaboration and success, groups must bestow authority and control upward.

   The *individual behavior* school of human relations focuses on individual psychology, leadership, power, authority, responsibility, and the subconscious. Its main concern is the individual's feelings and drives and how they affect the workplace.

   Organizational development goes further and focuses on the need for people to reason together about their common difficulties. Its central belief is that employees can often manage themselves better than managers can.

2. *Labor relations.* Labor laws, public policy, and economics of wages and costs, demographics and manpower management, collective bargaining, contract administration, and grievances are under the purview of labor relations. It sees politics at the plant, corporation, union, state, and national levels together with labor laws as keys to any situation. Its stance is usually adversarial and tough — sticking to contract terms, denying exceptions, avoiding precedents, and building a powerful position for bargaining.

3. *Personnel management.* Activities involved in managing large numbers of people in the aggregate — namely, recruiting, selecting, training, compensating, and developing them — are the province of personnel. This discipline holds that if companies perform those tasks well, they will acquire a set of employees with

appropriate motives, habits, and behavior. Personnel holds that if managers are consistent and apply policies that induce desired behavior, a good climate will result.

4. *Industrial engineering.* This school concentrates on designing jobs to fit technology and human capabilities and controlling performance with standards based on industrial engineering studies. It holds that efficiency and productivity are products of economic rewards and hard-nosed, disciplined supervision.

Each of these four schools focuses on acquiring an effective, loyal, and committed group of employees but in very different ways. My concern is not that disagreement arises among these experts or that they have different approaches to the same problem. I do not think that one school is right and the others wrong, that one is better than another, or that any should be ignored. On the contrary, they all offer ideas and tools that are often very effective, though perhaps not when used at the same time.

The problem is a little like having a car that has good wheels, a shiny body, an efficient engine, excellent brakes, and a terrific hydraulic system but that won't go or that no one in the family wants to drive. Big hat, no cattle.

Each school of thought makes a contribution, a vital contribution, like the wheels and the engine, but the whole system sputters and founders and doesn't produce enough involved, energetic, and loyal workers. Usually companies do not know how to put these ingredients together in one effective corporate system, for the four schools each offer managers contradictory advice.

Two things appear to be missing from the systems. One is a comprehensive unifying concept. Another is a general manager who can effectively mix and match these necessary ingredients. Unfortunately, such a person is a rare breed.

Corporate Management of Personnel

The third set of problems holding back progress toward better people management has to do with the structure of corporations, their size, diversity, and allocation of authority.

As corporations grow in size and diversity, the difficulty of managing employee relations increases. With size come organizational layers that effectively remove top managers from the large numbers of employees at the base of the pyramid. By necessity, communication processes, which are handled via mass media broadcasts, house organs, speeches, and employee letters, become more political and less personal.

When a company grows, the connection between the corporate well-being and the needs of separate divisions and locations can break. In principle, headquarters may be willing to let the divisions deal with their local labor forces on their own, but in letting the divisions take different courses, the corporation may endanger its bargaining position with the union. And even if the company is not unionized, the personnel office might fear that one division's low-cost demands could bring in a union, be short-sighted, or give the company a bad reputation as a place to work.

Also, the Equal Employment Opportunity Act has vastly increased the need for headquarters to be in control, union or not. Yet each division has different tasks and needs, different skills and attitudes in its work force. Division A may need a labor force that is especially cost effective, while Division B, where the strategy may call for rapid product turnover, requires employees to be adaptive.

Given these potential conflicts, experimenting with new approaches becomes riskier in large organizations than in small. Decisions become more sensitive, have longer shadows, and, understandably, executives may become more cautious and may procrastinate or pass the buck when they can.

These problems of size and diversity plague many large corporations these days. Their effects are perplexity and conflict at headquarters, frustration and irritation at divisional and plant locations, and a mishmash of personnel policies and practices that have no clear focus. Policies that swing from the corporate to the divisional point of view, with the responsibility resting in neither location, are often ineffective.

Time Is an Enemy.   Human resources management faces a further fundamental problem that few companies have resolved. Acquiring and developing the right talents for the business as it changes strategy, technology, and products requires more shrewd, wise, long-range planning than any other corporate endeavor. Companies can usually replace or rebuild technology, physical facilities, products, markets, or business systems in 3 to 5 years. But how long does it take to change the attitudes of 1,000 employees with an average age, let's assume, of 40 and with 10 years of seniority?

Clearly, management cannot dismiss the work force and start over again. But it often takes years to effect much genuine change, and one bad decision or unfortunate sequence of events can undo those years of slow progress.

In contrast to the nature of the HRM task, which is a function that requires long-term thinking, consistency, and staying power, short-range pressures such as budgets and annual plans force short-term reactions. Successful managers seldom stay put long enough to see their HRM investments pay off. Also, executive compensation systems seldom reward a manager for five years' investment in HRM policies and activities.

The scarcity of general managers who are as capable, confident, and experienced in the management of large numbers of people as they are in production, marketing, finance, and control is a further problem in many companies. Nonetheless, despite their inexperience, executives who reach the top must select and integrate the six different concepts and disciplines of human relations, personnel administration, and industrial engineering. They must also manage the conflicts among the interests of the corporation as a whole, the different divisions, and the separate plants and facilities.

Why do so many general managers usually lack these skills? Several factors contribute to the difficulty.

The first is that personnel work has seldom been attractive to fast-moving, younger general managers, who see the field as out of the mainstream of the business. Also, they see personnel as a staff function that is strictly advisory, that lacks authority and power, and that deals with small-scale, troublesome problems. A personnel job is seldom an attractive position for a manager who wants to run something independently. Because of personnel's conflict-ridden, pressured, contradictory nature, the decisions personnel managers make are touchy and cumbersome. Because they involve many other managers, they are not only time-consuming but also often frustrating.

For these reasons, few outstanding managers move into personnel, and those in it often have problems getting out. The detail, the time required to gain expertise, the low status in the organization, and the lack of clear-cut authority can swallow up and overwhelm all but the very best in the field.

Questionable Management Premises

Finally, a few commonly held assumptions, the validity of which is increasingly doubtful, are at the root of the HRM problem.

With Good Managers HRM Takes Care of Itself.   If one believes that well-intentioned managers naturally do well at HRM, the following will also seem valid:

> Responsible, generous, enlightened top management will develop an effective employee group because its considerate and humane practices will inevitably trickle down and permeate the organization.

Management may share its prerogative to manage if it wishes, but philosophically employees have no right to manage.

People are fortunate to have jobs for which someone else has invested the capital.

People are adaptable to a wide variety of tasks and conditions.

Someone will turn up able and willing to do any job if the pay is right.

These premises are no longer valid. Widespread dissatisfaction with jobs despite adequate pay has been documented. More workers now see good jobs as rights. Employees demand more autonomy at work and question management's right to administrate, and indeed its competence and wisdom to manage, without participation.

Personnel Is Not Very Important.   If the personnel department is a housekeeping function, it follows that:

It makes available services and advice that line managers can accept or reject since they have the responsibility for line operations.

Personnel's job is to get good people and keep everybody reasonably happy.

Managers responsible for line operations can accept or reject personnel's advice as a "staff" department. Relegating to housekeeping or staff advice activities that directly impinge on a corporation's most vital competitive resource no longer makes sense.

Decisions affecting human resource quality should not be dealt with in a secondary, catch-up, tidy-up, reactive way. Doing so gives a lower priority to personnel activities than to production, sales, or finance; results in personnel management assignments being a sentence to oblivion; fosters second-rate, sloppy personnel activities; and removes accountability from personnel officers for setting up reactive, short-term HRM policies.

Control Is All.   If control systems are really what make an organization run well, it follows that:

By establishing careful and detailed annual forecasts and budgets and monitoring results by month, quarter, and year to meet the plans adopted, managers can effectively control and operate companies.

This premise drives out long-range thinking as well as the long lead times required to build effective human resources. The quantifiables remain, but the "soft quality" items such as training and development, appropriate compensation stuctures, and communication activities are expendable.

Every Problem Has a Solution.   The eternally optimistic macho belief is that if reason is applied:

When managers put good minds to work on a problem, it will yield quickly.

When good managers who will be held accountable are armed with good solutions, substantial improvements will result.

This premise accounts for many "big hats"; managers have adopted programs "to fix" poor morale or low productivity instead of getting at basic underlying causes. Short-term fixes or "programs" do not work in human resources development any better than they do in government.

Managers wishing superior human resources must get at fundamental rather than superficial symptoms; they need to accept disappointments and unexpected outcomes of solutions to complex problems, and they need the staying power to work persistently at improving the quality of human resources. These problems are massive and stubborn. When disillusionment and frustration hit, many managers react judgmentally, blaming the union or the government, the "vanishing work ethic" or "the new breed," instead of their own piecemeal, reactive approach to the management of people.

Since changing habits, skills, values, beliefs, and attitudes in a work force takes years, the lack of long-range planning in human resources is frequently disastrous. So the ultimate irony is that the personnel function — which deals with the most fundamental and central corporate competitive resource and that has the longest time horizon of any function — is left with no long-range strategy and allowed to react merely to transient pressures and events.

TOWARD IMPROVING HUMAN RESOURCE PERFORMANCE

To develop human resources, corporate management will have to make some fundamental changes in its conventional wisdom.

Let me suggest five processes to include in a new approach:

1. Managers need to tackle the mistaken premises head on and cast them out in favor of a new set like the following —

   □ If managers continually fail to listen, communicate, explain, anticipate, and in every way nurture commitment and mutual understanding, employees will inevitably become alienated. In the nature of people and organizations there is a relentless gravitational slide toward alienation.

   □ Managers can develop and tailor a work force to meet the particular performance needs of an organization.

   □ Because superior human resources create the most central, basic, and powerful strategic competitive advantage possible, human resources management should receive top priority.

   □ Employees are stakeholders in the enterprise. Their interest in the conditions of employment and work are as real as those of stockholders and managers. The problem is not whether to keep them involved in the management of the enterprise, but how.

   □ As a function, personnel has as much a right and an obligation to monitor the quality and prescribe the processes of personnel activity (selection, compensation, communication development, et cetera) as accountants do to prescribe and monitor accounting policies and procedures. The top echelon of leading companies in this respect, such as Hewlett-Packard and Dana Corporation, gives the personnel function broad license in any and all HRM activities.

2. Any company can begin to improve the management of human resources simply by doing the basics better. The most practical way to start is by performing all the routine ongoing personnel activities with extraordinary care. Research suggests that for the many reasons cited earlier, recruiting, selection, compensation, job design, training, and communications procedures are in many companies hastily and inadequately carried out.

   Worst of all is supervision — the oldest and most written about of management skills. The business schools neglect it, and economics, schedules, costs, and time pressures allow careless and inhumane practices to characterize it.

   Poor supervision is absolutely unnecessary — yet millions of workers have to put up with it. It hurts American manufacturing and service industries beyond belief. The importance of good supervision is so obvious that its rarity is astounding.

The enormous improvements in HRM at General Motors began when managers went back to the basics of good supervision and communication. For instance, although QWL programs were behind the turnaround at Tarrytown, the fundamental changes were achieved by supervisors simply treating people with care and respect.

3. Managers need to set a seven-year time horizon for their human resources planning and operation. I pick seven years simply to make the point that it's not one, two, three, or even five. Planning in personnel needs at least that amount of time to survive several generations of top executives' strategy shifts, economic recessions, division and companywide crises, government policy changes, legislative revolutions, and technological advances. It takes at least seven years for managers to install, live with, improve, and reap the benefits of major change in personnel activities; to weed out unproductive skills or attitudes; and to hire a new generation. And it takes that long for employees to live through a period of history in a company that forms a new foundation of trust.

Seen as a seven-year ongoing problem, the task of human resources management takes on a whole new cast demanding staying power as well as clear philosophy and strategy. For example, IBM's philosophy that people are valuable to the company has permeated the organization from the beginning. Similarly, at Hewlett-Packard the founders enunciated a set of standards that placed people first. To this day, these values persist with great benefit to these companies.

4. Having a seven-year horizon requires that managers develop a philosophy, some objectives, and a strategy. Since human resources strategic planning is as yet a largely unknown art and since it may take researchers years to develop competence, managers would do better to begin on their own rather than wait for the perfect approach.

But how to begin? The combined experiences of four major U.S. corporations that have been working at HRM for a long time (Honeywell, American Hospital Supply, Dana Corporation, and Westinghouse) offer several lessons —

□ A first step is to identify the *implicit* tendencies of present personnel policies and practices in terms of the skills, attitudes, and behavior they develop. Each corporate unit and division has implicit objectives in its personnel activities — to develop a work force that achieves low costs, to be flexible, or to acquire the skills for special projects, for instance. In most companies, such analysis will show that the implicit goals of the various personnel policies and activities are contradictory. Further, the uniformities in policy and practices across divisions, departments, and functions are also frequently dysfunctional in meeting the strategic needs of those separate groups.

□ A second useful step in human resources strategy planning is to identify by function, department, and division the desired behavioral characteristics of each employee group. These will depend on the company's or division's objectives and plans for gaining competitive advantage. That plan requires certain product, marketing, manufacturing, and financial strategies. These in turn will each have specific human resources implications. Managers need to uncover these implications and clearly specify them.

□ When managers juxtapose the human resources implications of their plans with those implicit in their personnel policies and activities, the need for change will emerge. From this process they can develop a human resources strategy that details by division, department, or function the human resources and specific policies and practices needed in the basic areas of human resources management. Then they can make long-term plans.

▢ Pioneers in human resources strategy make such planning a central part of their annual plans, budgets, and long-range strategy. In other companies, however, managers commonly let HRM become a residual or an outcome of the plans rather than a key input. At best, most divisional or company managers merely project from extrapolations the number of various personnel categories they will need in the future.

Experience in HRM strategic planning shows that the process nearly always raises a fundamental problem: the divisions or departments of the company have different competitive strategies and often need different performance from their people. Similarly, within a division or a location, groups may need different personnel policies and activities. But can a company, for example, pay people differently in engineering than it can in purchasing or accounting? The answer is yes, but only when management discards the old uniformity rules and designs personnel policies to achieve strategically essential objectives.

5. Companies wishing to improve their HRM need to establish a long-term program to develop general managers with human resources management skills and experience. Considering the personnel department as a functional operation with strong authority and responsibility for effective human resources management practices has helped several companies to attract and keep good personnel managers.

By regarding the development of superior human resources as an essential competitive requirement that needs long-range, functional strategic plans, top managers can attract many of the best managers in the company to the HRM function. Some companies that have moved outstanding managers into personnel functions for two- to four-year periods have, after five to seven years, developed a top management group, a high proportion of which has had in-depth experience in the formulation and implementation of human resources strategy.

A group of loyal, productive employees is an organization's most effective competitive weapon. But during the last decade variations among persons available for employment appear to have greatly increased. Subtle differences in job and personal skills and in attitudes toward work and employers have made selecting an outstanding set of employees even more difficult. Mass education, which makes schooling level as a selection criterion less meaningful, has compounded the problem. Leading companies in HRM have learned that the old adage that "people are people" is wrong: there are enormous differences between a good employee and a superb one. A small fraction of companies have learned to insist stubbornly on hiring only the very best.

These increased problems in achieving a "quality level" set of employees have made this HRM strategy, when successfully carried out, a uniquely dynamic competitive weapon. But it is more important than ever to recruit and develop a high-quality group of employees, for companies with a head start are hard to catch. Their good people attract others like them, while conventional organizations have to accept what is left.

Human resources planning can act as a catalyst and an operating mechanism to accelerate the building of an effective work force. Where this is accomplished, people are energized and committed and become the most powerful, fundamental corporate competitive resource of all.

C.

P/HRM OVERVIEW

Interview with Joe Zaccaro

Joe Zaccaro is presently principal of the Human Resource Consulting Group, Inc. His consulting efforts are broad-based and include organization design, performance management and appraisal, management training, human resource strategic planning, compensation, executive search, and outplacement. Prior to his present position, Mr. Zaccaro was vice-president for human resources at Mattel Toys. He is a member of the American Society for Personnel Administration (ASPA) and a past participant on ASPA's Employment Practices Committee. His articles have appeared in the *Rocky Mountain News* and the *National Business Employment Weekly*. Mr. Zaccaro holds a Master's degree in Psychology/Industrial Relations from the University of Minnesota.

1. *How has the role of the personnel/human resources management (P/HRM) professional changed over the past twenty years? To what do you attribute these changes?*

   I see three primary ways the role has changed. It has become more legal and technical especially in areas such as EEO, OSHA, and, most recently, employment-at-will. Secondly, the P/HRM professional has become more of a businessperson and a strategic thinker — part of the top management team in many cases. And third, the P/HRM professional has changed from an administrator to a "people and organization developer."

   In terms of attributing those changes, I'd say the first change is a specific and direct result of a great deal of new protective legislation over the last ten or fifteen years. Regarding the change to a businessperson, changes in society have made it clear that businesses have to respond and synchronize their P/HRM practices and programs with their business plans and strategies. No longer do we have the clear direction and simple economic structure that existed in the forties and fifties. Instead, we have a much more complex worldwide economic structure with rapid changes in society. And finally, in terms of changing from an administrator to a people developer, there is a great deal of free movement of people from company to company. Promises of security — which companies have not been able to live up to anyway — no longer are adequate. We cannot any longer assume that people will stay with a single company for an entire career. We must give them good career reasons to stay in the same organization — such as growth assignments and personal development opportunities on a continuing basis.

2. *Do P/HRM professionals today differ from those of twenty years ago in terms of the background and experience they bring to their jobs? If so, how?*

Yes, definitely. There is more employee and organization development schooling and experience in their backgrounds. I see them much more balanced in their concern for both the company and the employee rather than being just an administrator of management practices, or on the other end of the spectrum, an ombudsman. The P/HRM professional has to take a much more balanced view of the business situation in order to be optimally effective.

3. *In your previous position as vice-president for human resources at Mattel, what were your greatest challenges? What activities consumed the majority of your time?*

There were two primary concerns. The first was the development of management succession planning fast enough and well enough to handle the growth of the business. The second was responding to the needs of different work forces with the proper reward systems. In terms of the activities which consumed the majority of my time, I would say there were three or four primary ones. First, planning — both strategic business planning and strategic human resources planning. Second, executive selection — both internal and external in terms of the actual recruiting and setting up of systems to allow it to happen in an effective manner. Third, employee and labor relations. And fourth, compensation and merit issues.

4. *How should the performance of a personnel professional be evaluated? How should his or her department's performance be evaluated?*

I think the primary measurement has to be the ability to set, and successfully accomplish, objectives based on the needs of the line organization. Too many times P/HRM functions have operated based on what they thought was right or needed without the input of the line organization. Secondly, I think P/HRM professionals need to be measured on their technical human resources know-how when that's applicable to their current position. There is a good deal of technical knowledge necessary, and I think we should not ignore that while we're worried about broader issues. And third, I think they need to be evaluated based on specific objectives with the solicited input of their internal clients. Do the internal clients, meaning the line organization, perceive them as meeting their needs successfully?

5. *As a staff activity, P/HRM functions differently from line activities. What differences have you observed? How might P/HRM departments structure themselves for maximum effectiveness?*

The P/HRM function is much less predictable than line functions. The needs change more rapidly and in a more volatile way. Secondly, I think the activities are often less concrete than those of the line functions. Often the P/HRM function is charting new ground with little or no guidance as to what will work — they find out as they go along. Therefore, there is a greater risk of becoming only reactive, not proactive. I think P/HRM people must take that risk of looking for the things that need to be done in the business (by understanding the business) and then doing them. The P/HRM professional must understand that his/her role is to become part of the organization and help it to change as necessary.

As for P/HRM department structure, you need to look first at the line organization structure. How does the business run? How is it organized? Then organize the P/HRM function to fit. Is the organization primarily a product organization? A geographic one? A functional one? Then build a P/HRM organization with the expertise to best help that actual company structure. Again, as I mentioned earlier, there has been a tendency in the past to organize P/HRM for the convenience of P/HRM or for the functional logic which might exist within the P/HRM area. This is a classic mistake, and I see more and more P/HRM functions beginning to realize it by trying to respond to the line organization.

6. *We have heard and read much recently about the increasing status and influence of personnel departments. They no longer simply keep the records and schedule company picnics. Do you personally sense an increase in the influence and status that P/HRM professionals have in organizations? If so, to what do you attribute this increase?*

Yes. But I don't think as much yet as is necessary. The changes have occurred because of the increasing complexity of our society, changes in the work force, and the demands of employees to grow within the organization. However, top management is still in the process of recognizing the proper role and status of human resources. Human resource executives themselves are still on a learning curve, and therefore they don't display all the characteristics that will eventually earn them the status that P/HRM needs to have. The better run organizations in the country are recognizing the essential role that P/HRM can play in the organization — that it can be part of top management; and that's where we see the greatest change taking place. There are many, many organizations, however, that still lag behind in that realization. My only suggestion for speeding up this process is for P/HRM executives to take the initiative by convincing their company presidents that P/HRM needs to be represented on top company committees (executive committee, strategic planning committee), and how such involvement will benefit the organization.

7. *What strikes you about the young people entering the field today? Do they possess adequate backgrounds? What courses of study would you recommend they pursue to prepare themselves while in college? What types of initial employment would seem to be most beneficial as they prepare for a professional personnel position?*

Let me say that I see P/HRM people having a better understanding of the business world and society. They're less naive. They take less for granted. In terms of what they might study, they need more knowledge of business and broad humanities in addition to human resources. In other words, become a whole person while you're in college. We should avoid the tendency of trying to study too specifically when we're in college and not coming out with a broad education that will allow us to guide people in more general ways. Also, upon entering the business arena, they might consider line positions in operations, marketing and finance. Maybe line positions should be interspersed with other P/HRM jobs before individuals settle into the human resources field. This will give them a better understanding of how those line organizations run and what their needs are. In the process, they will enhance their credibility with the line organizations when they are actually working in the P/HRM area.

8. *What personal characteristics are important for the modern personnel professional to possess? In other words, what type of person do you think would have the best chance of success, given the demands of the job?*

First, business savvy. P/HRM professionals can no longer afford a narrow professional orientation focused only on technical P/HRM affairs. I also like to see high, focused energy — well-organized people who are truly interested in organizational dynamics and how to deal with them. So, when I am looking for people in the P/HRM field, I look for those who are able to perform effectively while under pressure, who are well organized in getting their functions performed, but who never lose sight of the fact that they're working within organizational dynamics. They need the ability to push back from the organization periodically and look at it to see what's really happening.

Most importantly, human resources people need to become excellent managers. I'd like to see P/HRM professionals become excellent managers themselves so they become role models for the line people with whom they're interfacing. That way they can better advise line management from experience rather than from "the book."

9. *Are you familiar with the ASPA accreditation program (through the Personnel Accreditation Institute)? If so, what is your sense of how important accreditation is, and will become, for the personnel profession?*

Yes, I am; any program that will maintain high standards in the profession is desirable. Equally important, however, is the pursuit of a continuing broad education and on-the-job training. As I mentioned earlier, in order for P/HRM professionals to succeed in the future, they will need to be well balanced — in their knowledge and skills in human resources, business and the broader world picture.

10. *What changes do you envision in the human resources profession in the next twenty years? How will the duties of the P/HRM specialist change? On what premises do you base these predictions?*

I see a diet composed more of strategic planning, creation of reward systems for a continually changing work force, more interface with the line organization, keeping up to date with societal directions, and helping the organization respond to the way people are motivated. My premise is that in the next twenty years change will be even faster and more profound than in the past twenty.

D.

RECENT GRADUATES

Interview with Virginia L. Manz

Virginia L. Manz is currently employed at Staffing Consultants in Vienna, Virginia. At the time of this interview, she was working at Contel Information Systems, a job she had held since graduation from college. At Contel, Ms. Manz was a personnel generalist whose primary responsibility was in the area of high-technology employee recruiting. She graduated from the University of Maryland in December 1983 with a Bachelor's degree in business management. Her area of concentration was personnel/ human resource management.

1. *Let's begin by having you tell us why you decided on a position in personnel/ human resource management (P/HRM) as your first job after college. Do you presently plan to make P/HRM a career?*

The decision to work in P/HRM after college was directly a result of my having selected Personnel as my major area of concentration within the business school. I transferred to the University of Maryland from Syracuse University, where I had been enrolled as a general business student. I had taken the basic marketing, accounting, and finance courses, and had done well in them. But, I felt like I didn't want to do just one thing in my career — such as work with numbers like accountants do. In the P/HRM field I found a middle ground where one can engage in a variety of activities. The compensation area, for example, primarily involves the numerical skills of an accounting major, while recruiting requires the selling skills of a marketing major. Thus, P/HRM demands a variety of skills, making it a more interesting field in which to work for me. Also, P/HRM is a career that can be undertaken in a wide variety of organizations.

Do I intend to make P/HRM my career? Yes, I think so — at least presently. Unfortunately, I feel that personnel people at many organizations are undervalued and therefore underpaid. At Contel Information Systems, as at many service firms, the "product" essentially is the mental (rather than physical) effort of many people. The role of the P/HRM function is to find, develop, and keep these people. It is hard to imagine a more critical role within an organization. As firms begin to realize the importance of the personnel function to business success, P/HRM people will gain the status already accorded to marketing and finance positions. Personnel will evolve into a department that does less paper pushing and more responsible decision making. So,

I feel as though P/HRM is a good place to be in terms of a career because the impending changes will bring more recognition and responsibility to the field.

2. *Can you tell us exactly what your present job consists of, and the skills and abilities you believe are necessary for successful accomplishment of this job?*

My present job involves several responsibilities. Most of my efforts are devoted to recruiting. Contel is a rapidly growing high-tech firm that has a more or less continuous need for hard to find engineering and technical talent. In 1984, for example, I interviewed about 200 people, and brought in about 75 new employees. That's a substantial number for a firm that had only 110 employees at the beginning of the year!

As the personnel department at Contel is small, I also engage in a variety of other P/HRM activities. The most important of these would be the scheduling and administration of performance appraisal reviews and the administration of employee benefit programs.

Each of these responsibilities requires a different mix of skills. Recruiting and interviewing require strong social skills. You have to learn to like everybody, to be a good salesperson for your organization, and to ask about sensitive issues (salary demands, for example). Verbal skills and self-confidence are very important.

Another side of the recruiting function is producing advertising. At Contel, we probably spend $50,000 a year on help wanted advertising in the *Washington Post* and other local newspapers. Strong writing skills are important here. You must be creative to elicit response, and yet concise to contain your advertising costs. As for overseeing performance reviews, this part of my job requires good organizational skills along with the ability to be persuasive. Many technical managers resist doing performance reviews because they can be unpleasant. In addition, many don't understand the importance of feedback to employees — especially newer employees. Therefore, my job is to make sure that these reviews happen, and happen in a timely manner. In benefit administration, writing skills again become very important, along with just plain patience.

3. *In your job as a recruiter, you must see a lot of people engaging in "job jumping" in an effort to improve their positions. Do you have any advice for these people?*

Yes, job jump very carefully! I see a lot of engineers and computer professionals job jumping because the market is very good. Changing jobs purely for salary reasons is a poor decision. These workers need to look at themselves and their careers with a longer term perspective. Internal advancement is available for those who give an organization two to three years of good work. With these promotions come increased responsibilities and improved salaries. These types of opportunities may never be available to those workers who are constantly changing jobs.

4. *What parts of your present job have been hardest to get used to?*

Two aspects of my job come to mind. The first has to do with interviewing. As I mentioned earlier, I interviewed about 200 candidates for jobs in 1984. Many of these candidates are considerably older than I am, and are earning salaries two and three times greater than mine. Initially, it was very easy to be intimidated in this type of situation. Yet, as the interviewer, I had to learn to control the situation and control the flow of conversation to satisfy my objectives.

I have also found that in the "real world" — as opposed to college — you have to learn when it is worth pushing for your own point of view and when it is better to back off and maintain harmony in working relations. You can't win every argument, so you must learn to prioritize those things you think need to be changed in the work setting and push for only those changes of top priority.

5. *You mentioned a difference between the "real world" and college. In what ways did your formal education fail to prepare you for your present job? Do you have any suggestions for current college students as to choices of coursework that would prove helpful in P/HRM positions?*

Well, for the most part my formal education did a good job preparing me for my present position. The courses I had that stressed writing skills were particularly helpful, because, as I mentioned earlier, writing is such an important part of my job — or almost any job for that matter.

I guess my major disappointment regarding formal education is that it raised my expectations of the P/HRM profession to an unrealistic level. I was not prepared for the poor image of P/HRM that unfortunately still exists in some organizations. My readings and studies in the personnel area in college had not presented this side of the picture. Too much was said of corporate-level P/HRM programs, and not enough time was devoted to how local-level P/HRM personnel operate. Had the coverage been more balanced, maybe my initial expectations would have been a little more realistic upon entry into the work world.

As for recommendations for present personnel students, I would make two. First, consider taking a job as a recruiter right out of school. Recruiting is considered by many to be the heart of the personnel management process, it has more visibility than other functions, and it often is more lucrative in terms of salary. My second recommendation flows directly from the first. In recruiting for a high-tech organization, you need to know at least a little about the technical side of business. Therefore, some coursework in science and computers is highly advisable. You don't have to be a technological expert by any means, but you do need to be conversant with engineers and computer scientists. Besides, the P/HRM field is becoming increasingly tied in with computers, so a solid foundation in this area will pay off well in the future.

6. *Let's follow-up on your last response. Which areas of personnel do you see as growth areas in terms of future jobs and opportunities?*

Many P/HRM functions are going to become highly automated over the next twenty years. The whole area of human resource information systems will become increasingly important. I would expect there to be quite a few job opportunities in both the design of these types of information systems, and in teaching noncomputer people how to use them. Many organizations will need in-house specialists in these areas.

I also expect that more job opportunities are going to be available in the benefits administration area. Organizations are spending an incredible amount of money on benefits, and they are beginning to wonder if that money is well spent. There will be more emphasis in the future on communicating the value of benefit packages to employees and on the design and implementation of flexible (or so-called cafeteria-style) benefit programs. This will require more sophisticated benefit administrators in the future than most organizations have at present.

Interview with Daniel J. Montgomery

Dan Montgomery received an M.B.A. from the University of Colorado at Boulder in December 1982. Since then, he has been employed as a human resource information analyst at Bergan Mercy Hospital in Omaha, Nebraska. In this capacity he has been involved in the development of a computerized human resource information system, a behaviorally-based performance appraisal system, and a timesharing payroll and personnel system. The emphasis in his M.B.A. program was information science.

1. *Please start by telling us a little about yourself and why you decided on a position in personnel/human resource management (P/HRM) as your first job after college. Do you intend to make P/HRM a career?*

I have an undergraduate degree in psychology, and following receipt of that degree I gravitated toward the personnel field because it seemed like an opportunity to apply psychology to a business situation. Later on, I also worked as a counselor in a mental health center and as a personnel administrator in that context. As I got more interested in business issues in the mental health field, I decided I'd go back to business school. My initial intention was to focus on organization management. As I went through the business school program, however, I was introduced to computers. I quickly became very interested in working with them, and switched my emphasis to information science. So naturally I gravitated toward combining computers with personnel information.

It had always intrigued me that the major portion of what makes an organization tick is the people that work there. In spite of the fact that "people" are a major expense in running an organization — and they can make or break an organization — it always struck me how very little most organizations really know about what they have going for them in terms of people. Computers seemed to me to be a way of getting a picture — a snapshot if you will — of what the organization looks like. I saw computers as a very practical approach to management. So, I was very attracted to a situation where I could combine my interest in computers and personnel management.

At this point in my career I want to continue to focus on working with human resource information systems and develop more expertise in how to set them up. I anticipate continuing to work in a human resource context, but as something of a hybrid between a systems analyst or a systems manager and a human resource manager.

2. *What have been your greatest challenges on your present job? What has been most difficult adjusting to in this position compared to the life of a college student?*

I think the greatest challenges I've had in my present job have been political. Business school does a good job of teaching you a set of intellectual techniques, but deals little with the practicalities of how organizations work. I think you get a picture — a very rational model — of an organization to start with, which is a good thing. But you have to have a bit of a sense of humor because in practical terms you are not always able to carry out activities rationally. You may come in with a set of intellectual tools that people are not really interested in — in terms of how they actually make decisions in that organization.

As a college student you are generally given a pretty specific set of guidelines at the beginning of the semester. Usually the first meeting of the class the professor will outline exactly what he or she expects of you to get a certain kind of grade. I have found in my present job — and in other jobs I've had before — that this is not the way things operate in the real world. The critical thing in a real business situation seems to be knowing how to work with people and how to identify what people's motivations are. There's a time to bring out the tools and techniques and a time to let them go, depending on the kind of people you're working with. "Technique" is really a first step in business. It's the science of business, and beyond that there's an awful lot of art which people simply have to develop on their own.

In studying personnel management, my tendency was to look at the field in terms of implementing programs that made the best use of people — get people into the situation that is the best for them and develop programs that improve their health and welfare. You find once you actually get into personnel management practice that you come up against a lot of tough situations where you're really not able to be a nice guy. Situations may come up where layoffs are necessary or you're involved in a labor-management conflict. The guidelines are never as clear as they were when you were in school. It's really up to you on your own to get a sense of where the organization seems to be headed, what the relationships are among people in the organization, and what sort of approach you ought to take. Even though there may be a set of formal goals and objectives for the organization, in reality the things that are happening are always so complex that you have to adjust those guidelines day to day and learn to be very sensitive to the direction things are going. If you're lucky, you might work in an organization that is very explicit about what the corporate culture is; where people make a strong effort to mentor you and give you a good idea of the current situation. However, I don't really believe that's the case in most organizations; it's certainly not been the case in the organizations for which I've worked. So there's a real difference between being in a work environment and being in school!

3. *Can you tell us exactly what your present job consists of, and the skills and abilities you believe are necessary for successful accomplishment of this job? What do you foresee as your next career move, and how will the requisite skills and abilities change upon making this move?*

My present position involves finding ways to use computers to carry out the on-going work of my department (the human resource department) more efficiently, and also to find ways to support new projects and programs that come up — all the while trying to keep the data bases and the programs integrated in such a way that there's a basic blueprint we can build on for the future. At the present time I'm heavily involved in implementing a time-share payroll system. I'm working in conjunction with the accounting department, my own department, and several outside companies in trying to pull everything together. What we're generally doing is moving away from having a centralized computer system into managing a distributed data base within the human resource department. This calls for developing a lot of new skills in terms of getting people in the habit of interacting directly with the computer and teaching them how to use that resource on their own rather than relying on more of a "canned" approach where forms go out the door and reports mysteriously come back.

The job I have requires a fairly broad range of skills — from technical skills to the ability to identify organizational strategies to abilities to work with people. Based on where the organization and the human resource function is headed, I have to be able to identify what we ought to be doing and then determine what the information needs are in order to support those directions. Therefore, I have to be able to put technical details in a larger perspective. I have to be able to simplify technical problems to present them to the managers I work for. Finally, I need to be able to take organizational strategies and try to turn them into specific programs that fit in with the way work goes through the HR department.

As far as the immediate future is concerned, I see myself doing something similar — continuing in this job and possibly in the next job in terms of learning the basics of identifying information needs and having the ability to set up an information system that works with the needs of the human resource department. Beyond that, having developed HR information systems, I'd like to develop more skill in using the HR information systems to support more effective decision making on the part of managers. As this develops, I see more and more of a need to develop my skills in working with, training, and motivating other people.

4. *In what ways did your formal education prepare you, and fail to prepare you, for your present job? Can you make suggestions for those presently studying in Business Schools regarding choices of coursework appropriate for positions in P/HRM?*

As I wasn't a personnel major at the University of Colorado, I'll have to confine my comments to talking about the quality of the M.B.A. program as a whole and, specifically, to my major which was information systems. I felt that intellectually in the information systems emphasis I received a very good set of basic tools for analyzing information flow, for looking at the elements that go into computer systems, and for determining trends in the data processing field. As I move ahead in my career, I'm realizing more and more that I need to take the time occasionally to pay attention to those trends because even in the short space of two years they keep changing. I see a real need to stay on top of those.

As far as the basic ways that the M.B.A. program at the University of Colorado was organized, one of the things that I look back on as being the most helpful was the fact that in many of my classes — particularly in the second year — the professors had us take a team approach to doing projects. This was very frustrating at the time in a lot of respects because you'd end up with a group of people with very diverse interests and abilities. But having to work with a group of people that way and get something done was very helpful. Otherwise, it's really much too easy to focus on just doing your own work your own way and trying to get a good grade. I think taking the individual approach might get you through business school, but it's not really relevant to what you find when you get out. In the work world you often have to deal with people who are different from you in terms of backgrounds and motivations.

I do have one suggestion to business students who are contemplating a career in the personnel management field. Don't kid yourself into thinking that personnel management is a field in which you don't have to pay attention to numbers. I've encountered this attitude among a number of people who are personnel majors. It's true that you can get into a lot of entry-level positions in the personnel field without a real good head for numbers. Further, if you want to confine yourself to working in an area that's more specifically people oriented, like recruitment in particular, that's fine. But if you're interested in taking more of a global approach to personnel management, the most important thing becomes selling your ideas to top management. You have to be able to pay a lot of attention to corporate strategies which are very often, if not all of the time, interpreted in terms of bottom-line results over the long haul. Similarly, accounting is a very important thing to pay attention to because accounting is the language that defines whether a business is doing well or not. Furthermore, computers are playing a larger and larger role in all kinds of management activities, and personnel management is no exception.

5. *What is your sense of how important continuing education is for yourself and for others in the personnel profession?*

I think, in general, these kinds of programs are a very good thing because there is a tendency to pick up a lot of new ideas while you're in school and go out working with that set of ideas. But if you don't watch it, within a surprisingly short period of time you can find that you're presenting ideas based on things that you learned a number of years ago and meanwhile the whole society and business climate has shifted. You really have to take responsibility for keeping up with those changes in order to make a contribution to your organization and your own career.

6. *Which areas of P/HRM do you see as growth areas in terms of future jobs and opportunities? Why?*

I think there are a lot of well-documented changes happening in American industry that have obvious effects on the personnel management function. The key to identifying the growth area is to look at the changes that are happening in industry as a whole, and how P/HRM can contribute to those things. The biggest thing that we see is an increasingly rapid rate of organizational change. You may have whole functions getting phased out while other ones are being phased in. And yet, you always work with a particular pool in terms of the labor market from which you recruit. Therefore, I would say that training and management development are extremely important areas in P/HRM today because there's such a dynamic atmosphere with job roles changing all the time. Things are not static. In management and administrative staff jobs, people have to learn to negotiate their job role in the organization rather than moving into a predetermined slot.

Similarly, I see an increasing need for more sophistication in employee recruitment, selection and career management. On the recruitment end, it's a matter of being able to go out and identify the kinds of people you need and get them into the jobs that need to be filled. On the other end, outplacement and transfer services are very much a growing area. This involves the ability to look at a given person's set of skills and envision other situations which would provide a growth opportunity for them. I think we have to take a much more creative attitude about those things.

And finally, I think the increasing rate of change demands that human resource managers be able to get a good picture of the characteristics of the workforce. This is where I see a tremendous growth area in human resource information systems because a good snapshot of the organization can really help executives minimize the disruption involved in moving from point A to point B in a time when corporate strategy and tactics may be changing rapidly. With better information you can minimize the disruption to the whole organizational system, to the bottom line of the business, and also to the people who are involved.

PART I: FOR DISCUSSION AND REVIEW

A.

Sloane

- ☐ Describe the influence of scientific management on the development of P/HRM.
- ☐ How did personnel as a field benefit from World Wars I and II?
- ☐ Have the basic goals of P/HRM changed over the years? Explain.

Magnus

- ☐ Describe the impact of demographic and technological changes on the P/HRM function.

□ Explain specifically how the training function and organizational structure will be affected by recent changes in society and technology.

B.

Meyer

□ Describe how the typical personnel specialist was generally regarded by others in the organization some years ago. Why? How has that image changed?

□ Why do today's P/HRM people have more status and influence than in the past?

Skinner

□ Overall, has P/HRM as a function in organizations been successful? Why or why not?

□ Explain why P/HR managers have not benefited significantly from the results of the research conducted by scholars in the field.

□ Discuss the widespread notion that "with good managers, P/HRM takes care of itself."

□ What are the changes advocated by the author and how do they address current problems in P/HRM?

PART II
STRATEGIC PLANNING AND ANALYSIS OF P/HRM SYSTEMS

A.

THE MACRO PERSPECTIVE: HUMAN RESOURCE PLANNING AND FORECASTING

Personnel Widens Its Franchise
Business Week

- □ Presents current samples of the increased role of P/HRM in corporate planning.
- □ Provides an analysis of P/HRM planning activities.

Strategic Planning and Human Resource Management
Mary Anne Devanna, Charles Fombrun, Noel Tichy, and Lynn Warren

- □ Presents the results of the authors' recent survey of planning activities of senior P/HRM executives.
- □ Develops a framework and a set of guidelines for helping P/HRM become more strategically focused and hence effective.

B.

THE MICRO PERSPECTIVE: JOB ANALYSIS

How Do the Experts Do It?
Edward L. Levine

- □ Describes and compares several courses of job analysis information and the most popular methods used to conduct a job analysis.

C.

HUMAN RESOURCE INFORMATION SYSTEMS

The Newest Job in Personnel: Human Resources Data Administrator
Alfred J. Walker

- □ Outlines the responsibilities of human resource data administrators.
- □ Concludes that the HRDA requires multi-disciplinary skills in data processing and personnel.

D.

HUMAN RESOURCE PLANNING

Interview with Les Woller

E.

JOB ANALYSIS

Interview with Walter W. Tornow

A.

THE MACRO PERSPECTIVE: HUMAN RESOURCE PLANNING AND FORECASTING

Personnel Widens Its Franchise
Business Week

Until three years ago, the personnel department at Standard Brands Inc. was virtually indistinguishable from those that have existed since the dawn of the corporate era. Composed of a director of labor relations and a director of benefits — each with a salary in the $30,000 range — and a staff of about 20, the department routinely administered hiring and firing procedures, handled labor negotiations, maintained employee records, administered benefits, and saw to it that paychecks went out on time. Its decisions could vitally affect individual employees, but they had little impact on the direction of the corporation, and the department was buried well below finance, marketing, and planning in the corporate bureaucracy.

The old personnel staff is still performing many of the same functions at Standard Brands today, but now it is part of a new human resources department, four times the size of the original personnel department and headed up by a corporate vice-president, Madelyn P. Jennings, whose salary and responsibilities are easily double those of the two directors combined. Part of that growth is the result of a flood of new government regulations that have increased the importance and the complexity of traditional personnel administration tasks. Since joining the company in 1976, Jennings has instituted a national compensation program, overhauled benefits, and developed an employee appraisal system.

But much of the stunning growth of Jennings' department is the result of a brand-new role that has been assigned to personnel administration at Standard Brands: the development and implementation of the company's first manpower planning system, one that is directly tied to carrying out corporate strategies. This new personnel function at Standard Brands is typical of similar changes taking place in most other large corporations that promise to lift top personnel administrators, who increasingly are adopting the human resources designation, into prominence as powerful officers in the corporate hierarchy. Already, experts estimate, such human resources executives — whether they carry the title or not — now hold key manpower planning responsibilities in almost all of the nation's 500 largest industrial companies, compared with only a handful of companies five years ago.

Reprinted from the February 26, 1979, issue of *Business Week* by special permission, © 1979 by McGraw-Hill, Inc., pp. 116–121.

HIRED BY CEOS

While their staffs still handle such mundane chores as allocating spaces in the company parking lot, they are also expected to work closely with senior operating managers to create staffing plans that are designed to meet corporate goals and to satisfy the growing demands by employees for clear career paths they can follow. "Management realizes that its important assets are not simply financial resources but having the people on hand at the right time and in the right place to make a thing go," observes Thomas C. Stevens, who in 1974 filled a new post as corporate director of human resources at J. I. Case Co., the construction and farm equipment subsidiary of Tenneco Inc.

Not surprisingly, personnel executives able to tackle such herculean tasks are commanding top dollar. A recent study by Heidrick & Struggles Inc., a Chicago-based executive-search firm, shows that the average salary of senior human resources executives is $79,000, compared with $52,000 for personnel executives who normally do not perform manpower planning. Even senior personnel executives who may handle human resources responsibilities but do not have the title average $61,000. And one human resources officer recently told *Business Week* that, counting performance incentives, his annual compensation can top $250,000. "Today corporations recognize that the right executive in human resources can add to profits," comments Lester B. Korn, president of Korn/Ferry International, an executive-search firm that conducted 28 searches for human resources vice-presidents in the last two years, a 30% increase from the prior two years.

PIPELINE TO THE TOP

Chief executive officers are increasingly taking an active role in such searches, a clear indication that the human resources position is gaining importance. Standard Brands' Jennings recalls one prehiring interview with F. Ross Johnson, the company's chairman, that lasted seven hours. William M. Buck Jr., who holds the new post of senior vice-president of human resources at Peabody Coal Co., was hired by President and Chief Executive Officer Robert H. Quenon. And at American Express Co., Chairman James D. Robinson III and President Roger H. Morley insisted on interviewing all potential candidates for the job themselves before hiring Philip H. Prince last August as AmEx's senior vice-president for personnel and management development.

The pipeline to the top rarely stops after hiring. Many human resources executives such as Buck report directly to the CEO. Others — Jennings is one — sit on corporate policy committees. "More and more, key human resources people are sitting at the CEO's right elbow," notes Gerard R. Roche, president of Heidrick & Struggles.

Tenneco is typical of the trend to relate manpower planning to corporate goals and strategies. The company recently started requiring vice-presidents to submit a five-year "executive resources" projection along with their five-year business plans. Both are closely reviewed by Kenneth L. Otto, senior vice-president of employee relations, who determines if they are compatible. If a division, for example, is planning to shift from a marketing to a production orientation, Otto must make certain that it is planning not only to develop a large enough production staff to meet the new demands in that area but also to make a suitable reduction of marketing specialists. "We're looking at how people figure into the equation as a long-range problem," says Otto.

DEVELOPMENT GOALS

Such planning is essential for companies with ambitious growth goals. AmEx, for example, has plans to expand into new business areas that will double its employee population to 70,000 over the next ten years. Even without this growth, the company's annual turnover rate produces a need for more than 500 new people a year. As a result, a manager's performance will be judged on how well he has been able to grow people in his own organization, and up to 10% of an executive's bonus could be negatively affected for failure to meet management development goals. That, in turn, is already placing a heavy demand on Personnel Senior Vice-President Prince to develop new programs to teach AmEx executives necessary skills in employee recruitment, training, and career counseling.

The new stress on human resources planning has resulted in a major expansion in the entire area of personnel, and experts estimate that the number of specialists in the field has doubled in the last five years. At Hibernia Bank, in San Francisco, Max H. Forster, the new vice-president and director of personnel, more than doubled the size of his unit from 6 to 14 people in only six months. At Levi Strauss & Co., Harold M. Goldstein, director of employee selection and development, recently was authorized to hire human resources staffers "at a time when we were trying as a company to hold the line."

Unlike its predecessors in personnel, who thought mostly in terms of answering or silencing employee complaints, the new breed of human resources executives focuses much more sharply on profits. That often means reorienting personnel staffs toward a bottom-line view that once seemed alien to them. Laurence E. Mullen recalls that when he became vice-president of personnel and organization at Allegheny Ludlum Industries Inc., in 1974, his staff "not only lacked awareness of how they could impact the profitability of a business, but they weren't aware that people wanted them to." Mullen's solution: A series of intensive training seminars in corporate finance were given to the company's entire personnel staff.

WAY STATION

Luckily, corporations are starting to get an influx of people with both an interest in human resources and a thorough grounding in business. In many companies, personnel was once considered a dumping ground for executives who could not succeed in running operating divisions. More common now are executives such as James W. Kennedy, manager of human resources planning and employment for General Foods Corp., who switched careers after 12 years as a successful marketing executive. Also typical are a growing number of line managers who believe that two- to three-year stints as human resources executives can be a major way station in their route to the top. And they can point to a lengthening list of examples to support that belief, including W. Thomas Beebe, chairman of Delta Airlines Inc., and J. Stanford Smith, chairman of International Paper Co., both of whom spent time as personnel executives.

Business schools are accommodating this trend by turning out more MBAs who believe that human resources is where the action is. "Since 1975, we've had a 50% increase in the number of graduates who are interested in this position," comments J. Frederic Way, associate dean of placement and career services at Columbia University's Graduate School of Business. Similarly, Frank H. Cassell, professor of industrial relations at Northwestern University's Graduate School of Management, watched attendance at his seminar for human resources soar from only six students eight years ago to 275 students this year — roughly 80% of the entire graduating class. And at the University of Pennsylvania's Wharton School of Business, three to five students each semester are taking independent majors in human resources, majors that were not even provided five years ago.

While a variety of factors explain the growing role of corporate human resources departments, the one most commonly cited is government. Dozens of new federal laws — from the Employee Retirement Income Security Act to the Equal Employment Opportunity Act — spell out how companies must treat existing and prospective employees, and compliance often involves expensive new programs. Peabody Coal's human resources department, for example, began supervising a program costing more than $500,000 in 1973 that simulates various mining conditions in order to train some 15,000 miners a year — all to ensure compliance with the Mining Safety & Health Act. And Standard Brands' Jennings notes that the number of statutes enforced by the Labor Dept. has increased from 40 in 1960 to 130 now.

A less obvious but equally important reason for the closer attention large companies are giving to human resources is the skyrocketing cost of employee benefits, which has risen from just above 20% of an average employee's salary five years ago to 35% today. With so much invested in an employee, reducing turnover rates is crucial. At Tenneco's J. I. Case subsidiary, the human resources department is credited with helping the company reduce its monthly turnover rate to 1.1%, compared with an industry average of 1.5% a month, by developing clearer job performance criteria and better training programs and by emphasizing promotion from within. Thanks to a new system for spotting and tracking internal managerial talent, Case fills 80% of its salaried slots with insiders, up from 50% five years ago.

THE PAYOFF

Yet human resources executives are by no means over all of the hurdles in establishing their new role in the corporation. The problem of putting manpower training programs in place and "getting management to buy them" still remains, observes Ruben Krigsman, manager of personnel research at Union Carbide Corp. But he notes that a "new breed" of operating managers is coming along who show far more respect for personnel executives. Five years ago, Krigsman figures, he initiated 90% of all of his contacts with top management. Now they come to him about 60% of the time.

One major reason for that, says Krigsman, is that top management increasingly appreciates the profit potential of human resources executives. To illustrate, he recalls how in 1976 he was dispatched to Carbide's Pleasantville (N. Y.) plant to try to boost employee productivity and morale. After running various surveys, Krigsman instituted new training programs and reorganized the workplace to give blue-collar workers more responsible jobs. In just three months, productivity soared by 25%; the amount of finished goods passing inspection jumped from 60% to 80%; and absenteeism dropped from 5% to 3%. As a result of such triumphs in human resources management, says Krigsman, "managers recognize that there's a payoff for both the business and the employees."

Strategic Planning and Human Resource Management

Mary Anne Devanna, Charles Fombrun, Noel Tichy, and Lynn Warren

Every period has its dominant concern. The recent wave of interest in productivity, quality circles, quality of work life, or Japanese management is a rekindling of old fires that stressed the importance of the human element in organizational performance. We have gone through other dominant concerns. It wasn't long ago that strategic planning had its moment of glory. Or that marketing sat at the right hand of the Chief Executive, himself a representative of sophisticated finance.

It is impossible to deny the fad-like nature of the current interest in management skills. The automobile industry is blamed for poor management. Government is said to be poorly managed. In fact, every sector of our economy is said to be lacking in one or the other of the people skills required to be effectively managed. Human resources management is therefore the keyword of the day, encouraged by foreign competition, a slow growth economy, and a cumbersome political system.

In fact, the recent popularity of human resources management is causing major problems for traditional personnel departments. For years they have been explaining their mediocre status by bewailing their lack of support and attention from the CEO. Now they are getting it, but find themselves quite unprepared to respond.

Whether the human resources component survives as a valuable and essential contribution to effective management will largely depend on the degree to which it is integrated as a vital part of the planning system in organizations. In large part, the management of human resources must become an indispensable consideration in both strategy formulation and strategy implementation.

In the survey reported in this article, both senior planning and senior personnel executives were asked to rate the degree to which human resource activities are and should be used in formulating strategies and in implementing strategies. Only twenty percent responded that human resource considerations have a great impact on either strategy formulation or implementation. However, fifty-one percent indicated that human resources should be instrumental in shaping strategic decisions and sixty-four percent that human resources should be used as strategy implementation tools.

Such results suggest two conclusions. First, we need to build a consensus among planners and human resource specialists about their role in the organization. Second, human resource issues must be brought in both before strategic decisions are taken and integrated into the strategy implementation process.

The purpose of this article is to: 1) present the results of a recent survey of senior planning and human resource executives, and 2) develop a framework and set of guidelines for helping human resource management become more strategic.

OVERVIEW OF STUDY

A questionnaire was sent to the chief human resource executives and strategic planners in 224 *Fortune* companies. Responses were received from 252 executives representing 168 companies. The survey was conducted to ascertain how the heads of strategic planning and human resource management viewed the role of human resource management in strategy formulation and implementation in their firms.

An interesting result of the study was that there was no statistically significant difference between the responses of the strategic planners and the human resource managers. This indicates that both groups' perceptions with regard to these issues are congruent. Therefore, in reporting the results, the responses of both groups have been combined.

The sample consisted not only of a large number of top firms, but also covered a cross section of industries. The survey was sent to aerospace, chemical, automotive, banking, life insurance, food and beverage, and leisure time industries, to name a few. Table 1 details the respondents in the survey.

PREVALENCE OF STRATEGY PLANNING ACTIVITIES AND THEIR OVERALL EFFECTIVENESS

Fifty-three percent of the respondents reported that formal strategic planning activities were used to a great extent in their company. Thirty-nine percent saw a moderate amount of strategic planning in use at their company. Clearly, the majority of the companies responding have a good deal of formal strategic planning going on. Although strategic planning processes seem very much a part of corporate activities today, results showed that fifty-two percent of the executives had seen these used at their companies for less than six years. Strategic planning can then be viewed as a somewhat recent addition to corporate life.

Human resource managers and strategy planners varied in their judgment as to the contribution of the strategic planning process to the overall performance of their companies. Thirty-one percent of the respondents reported that they found the strategic planning activities of their company moderately effective. Forty-eight percent found strategic planning more than moderately effective and twenty-one percent found the process less than moderately effective. In essence, executives found that formal strategic planning processes are at least moderately, if not more than moderately, useful in contributing to the overall effectiveness of the company.

THE ROLE OF HUMAN RESOURCE MANAGEMENT IN STRATEGY FORMULATION

Respondents were asked two questions concerning the utility of human resource data in strategy formulation: 1) Is human resource data systematically available? 2) To what extent does it influence strategy formulation?

As seen in Figure 1, the executives were asked to apply these two questions to six categories of human resource data. They are listed on the left vertical axis of the chart. The results show where the majority of the respondents fell on the scale. Four of the six types of information were quite available to strategy planners: 1) an inventory of managerial talent; 2) forecasts of an inventory of future talent; 3) an inventory of technical talent and 4) succession plans for top management.

The least available and least utilized information is a human resource audit of considered acquisitions. When a company sets out to expand by getting into new ventures or by acquiring a company in a different line of business, it usually obtains detailed analyses from the financial and marketing staff. Only recently have companies begun to seek information about the human resources of the target company. Such information would be extremely useful in the strategic planning of considered acquisitions. A company may offer an array of assets, making it a desirable purchase; however, if that company's human resources are, for any number of reasons, incongruent with the type of human resources existing in the purchasing company, assimilation will

TABLE 1
Respondents to Survey

Industry Type	Respondents		Companies Receiving and Responding to Questionnaires	
	Strategic Planning Exec's.	*Human Resource Exec's.*	*Rec'd.*	*Resp.*
Aerospace	4	2	5	5
Appliances	1	1	3	2
Automotive	2	1	5	2
Auto parts & equip.	2	2	5	3
Building materials	3	3	5	4
Chemical	7	6	8	7
Conglomerates	1	1	3	1
Containers	1	2	3	3
Commercial banking	21	17	27	24
Diversified financial	2	1	5	2
Drugs	3	4	7	5
Electronics	1	1	5	1
Electrical	2	2	4	3
Food & beverage	7	11	14	12
Fuel	8	15	18	17
Information processing	9	7	10	9
Instruments	0	0	2	0
Machinery	4	5	6	5
Metals & mining	3	2	4	3
Miscellaneous mfg.	3	1	4	9
Leisure time	2	3	4	3
Life insurance	12	9	17	13
Personnel & home care	1	2	6	2
Retailers	2	4	10	5
Paper	4	4	5	5
Steel	3	2	3	3
Semiconductors	3	3	5	4
Tire & rubber	1	3	3	3
Transportation	4	7	11	9
Utilities	6	8	12	9
Total	122	130	168	224

be difficult and problems may be exacerbated because they are neglected. *Business Week,* in the November 16, 1981 issue, pointed to the problems Sears can expect as they venture into the area of financial services.

Companies are beginning to pay more attention to their human resources for many reasons. Today's employee has expectations, needs, and personal desires which

FIGURE 1

Availability and Use of Human Resource Data

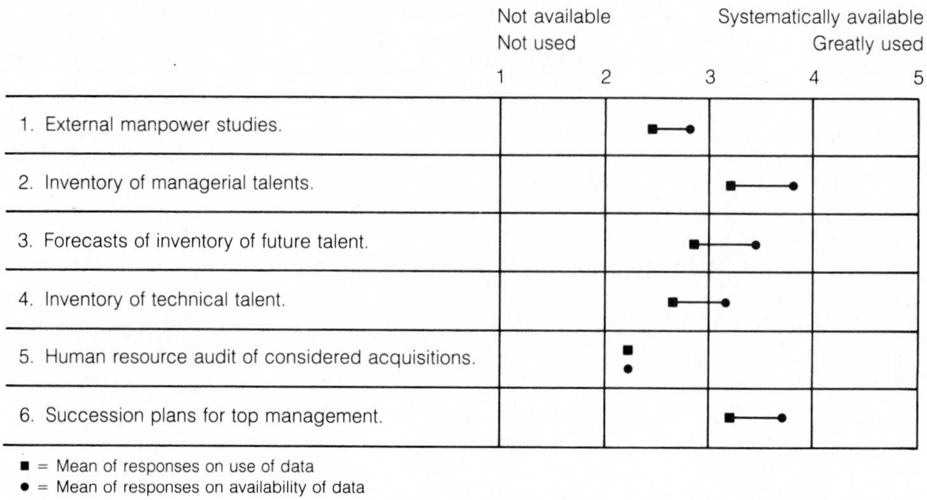

	Not available Not used		Systematically available Greatly used		
	1	2	3	4	5
1. External manpower studies.		■—●			
2. Inventory of managerial talents.			■—●		
3. Forecasts of inventory of future talent.			■—●		
4. Inventory of technical talent.			■—●		
5. Human resource audit of considered acquisitions.		■ ●			
6. Succession plans for top management.			■—●		

■ = Mean of responses on use of data
● = Mean of responses on availability of data

make the work options for employees and employers more varied and complex. It follows then that human resource considerations become an integral part of strategic decision making. Unfortunately, companies are only beginning to recognize the value of having accurate and comprehensive human resource data for planning activities. With this trend of companies and individuals having a more interactive relationship in establishing satisfying work-life styles, for their mutual benefit, human resource management departments are likely to find themselves assuming an increasing responsibility for developing useful manpower inventories.

Respondents reported that there are consistently more human resource data available than are actually utilized in the various decision making processes. The one exception, as noted above, is a human resource audit of considered acquisitions since this information tends to be collected only for immediate use in considering an acquisition.

Executives wish to see more human resource information utilized in the strategic planning process. Fifty-three percent of the respondents felt that human resource considerations had less than a moderate effect on strategy formulation. Forty-seven percent felt that this information had a moderate or greater impact on the formulation process. More important was the response to the question concerning the desired impact. Eighty percent of the executives said that they would like to see human resource considerations have more than a moderate impact on strategy formulation. Only twenty percent felt that human resource information should play a minor role in formulating corporate strategy. In general, it seems that both human resource executives and strategic planners see a need to utilize more human resource data in strategy formulation. (See Figure 2.)

THE ROLE OF HUMAN RESOURCE MANAGEMENT IN STRATEGY IMPLEMENTATION

Strategy planning is a two-step process; formulation and implementation. The third phase of the survey focuses on strategy implementation issues. The questions asked were: 1) to what extent are human resource activities used in strategy implementation?

FIGURE 2
Impact of Human Resource Considerations on Strategy Formulation

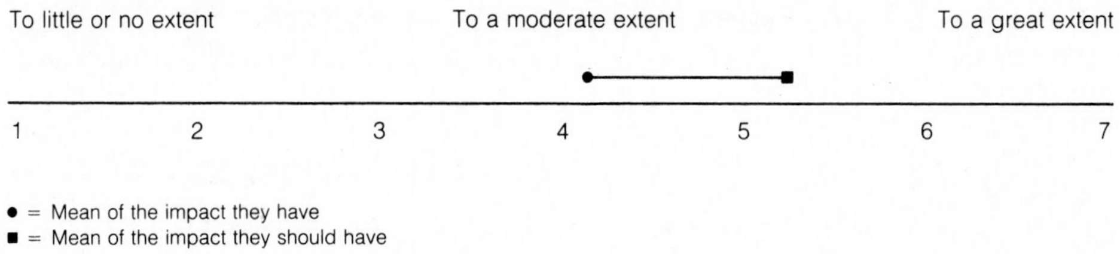

To little or no extent   To a moderate extent   To a great extent

| 1 | 2 | 3 | 4 | 5 | 6 | 7 |

● = Mean of the impact they have
■ = Mean of the impact they should have

and 2) to what extent should human resource activities be used in strategy implementation?

There were seven types of human resource activities considered as potentially useful for the strategy implementation phase of planning. These seven tools are enumerated on the left hand axis of Figure 3.

For the first five out of seven activities, the majority of respondents reported moderate utilization of human resource tools in strategy implementation. The last two activities (conducting development programs designed to support strategic changes, and conducting career planning to help develop key personnel for strategic plans) were regarded as less than moderately utilized in the implementation process at this time.

It seems, from these results, that formal training and development programs have not been nearly as prevalent in corporations as assessment activities. Until recently, corporations have relied primarily on job rotation and teaching executives the skills

FIGURE 3
The Extent to Which Human Resource Activities Are Used in Strategy Implementation and the Extent to Which They Should Be Used

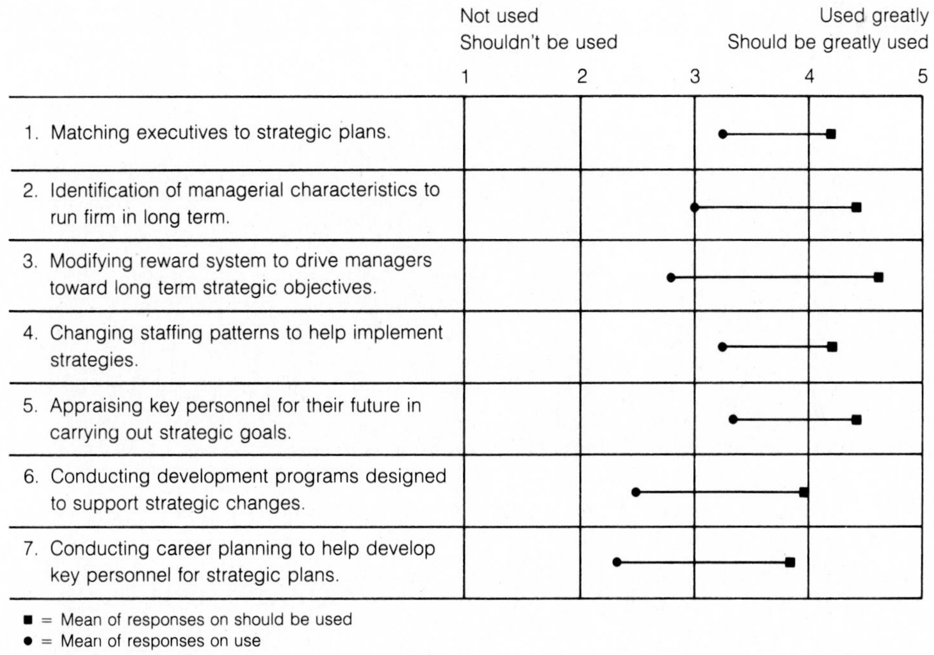

	Not used Shouldn't be used			Used greatly Should be greatly used	
	1	2	3	4	5
1. Matching executives to strategic plans.			●—■		
2. Identification of managerial characteristics to run firm in long term.			●———————■		
3. Modifying reward system to drive managers toward long term strategic objectives.			●—————————■		
4. Changing staffing patterns to help implement strategies.			●——■		
5. Appraising key personnel for their future in carrying out strategic goals.			●————■		
6. Conducting development programs designed to support strategic changes.		●————■			
7. Conducting career planning to help develop key personnel for strategic plans.		●————■			

■ = Mean of responses on should be used
● = Mean of responses on use

they need to aid in strategy implementation. With today's constrained economy and with the increased immobility of today's employees, job rotation is a less feasible human resource tool.

Figure 3 shows a consistently large difference between the use of human resource activities and how much the executives feel they should be used in implementing strategies. With regard to every activity, the respondents indicate a desire to see higher utilization of human resource activities in strategy implementation. The greatest difference between the actual and desired amount of utilization of personnel tools can be seen in the last two activities. It's interesting that even though these two activities are the least used in implementation now, they are equally as desirable as the other five for future use. This seems to verify the fact that formal training programs are becoming a necessity in today's corporate world.

In the final analysis, the respondents reported that they wish to see a much larger use of human resource activities in the strategy implementation process. Eighty-three percent of the respondents felt that human resource tools were currently being moderately or less than moderately utilized in the implementation phase of the strategic planning process. When asked about the extent to which they would like to see human resource activities utilized, ninety-six percent of the respondents reported that they would like to see a moderate or greater than moderate use of human resource tools for implementing strategies.

Historically, personnel has played a mostly reactive role in the company, supplying the necessary human resources post-strategy formulation. It would seem that this role would lead to more involvement on the part of human resource departments at the implementation stage. Strategic planners have formulated corporate strategies and they wish to have help in implementing these plans from the personnel department. The data seems to support this notion. Fifty-seven percent of the respondents reported a moderate or greater use of human resource tools in the implementation state of strategic planning, and only forty-seven percent reported a moderate or greater use of these tools in the formulation stage.

With regard to the respondents' desire to see human resource tools used in the strategic planning process, the results were similarly skewed toward a greater desire to see information utilized in the implementation phase than in the formulation phase. Eight-six percent of the respondents wished to see a moderate or greater use of human resource information in the formulation of strategies, and ninety-six percent wished to see these tools used in the implementation phase. It seems that from the responses of the executives, there is still a very important role for human resource departments at the implementation stage of the planning process. And, while all tools offered to aid in implementation are important, there is an increasingly apparent need for formal training programs and career planning programs.

Given the importance of human resource activities in the implementation stages of strategy planning, it would seem that companies would benefit from recognizing what human resource managers can offer in the formulation stage. Too often, the human resource issues of the strategy planning process are the implicit part of the plan; the unknown factor. It makes it very difficult to implement a new strategy when personnel has to find ways after the fact to deal with human resource needs that are incongruent with existing policies. Fombrun *et al*, state that:

> The trends suggest that competing in the 80's will require a sophisticated set of tools for dealing with the problems of a highly educated work force in a slack labor market, competing for fewer jobs in an increasingly service economy. Organizations will have to carefully consider the implications of alternative recruitment and training strategies to ensure effective implementation of their

plans. Indeed, the viability of these plans may largely depend on how well human resource needs and implications are understood and built-in to the planning process in the early stages of formulation.

HOW HUMAN RESOURCE STAFF ARE GENERALLY REGARDED BY SENIOR LINE MANAGERS

In the final questions, researchers asked the executives: 1) to what extent senior line managers used their human resource staff for operational and strategic services, and 2) what role do they believe personnel departments should play in the corporation. Managers were asked to rate the role of the human resource staff on a scale of 1 to 5. The numbers were representative of the degree of operational versus strategic services personnel people were asked to supply. The exact descriptions were:

1. only looked to for operational (day-to-day) personnel services.
2. mostly looked to for operational services but once in a while for strategic services.
3. looked to for operational and strategic services.
4. looked to somewhat for operational but more for strategic.
5. totally looked to for strategic services.

Fifty-seven percent of the respondents saw human resources staff as providing mostly operational services. That is to say, that fifty-seven percent of the respondents fell between numbers 1 and 2 on the scale. Only five percent were looked to for mostly strategic services with the remaining percent looked to for both services. Fifty percent of the total response to this question was on number 2.

There was a vast difference between these results and the results of the question about how they would wish to see the human resources staff viewed. On that question, ninety-eight percent of the response rate fell between numbers 3 and 5 on the scale, clearly indicating that the respondents should wish to see human resource staff providing more strategic services. Sixty-five percent of the total respondents wished to see personnel as an operational and strategic function, but the majority of respondents felt that it was mostly looked to for operational services.

WHAT NOW? HUMAN RESOURCE MANAGEMENT'S NEW ROLE

Regardless of the role that personnel assumes in the coming years, there are two kinds of data critical to the effective performance of this function: 1) internal human resource stock, and 2) external labor market data.

Both kinds of data have fairly obvious uses for the corporation. Human resource managers must be able to have an up-to-date index of the people in the company and the existing human resource market outside the company in order to perform its role in guiding the human resources of a company.

While both sets of data are important, neither is sufficient for strategic purposes. These kinds of inventories only describe present conditions; but what is needed is scenario forecasting: projecting the future trends and needs of human resources. Equipped with these two types of data and projections about future trends, human resource departments have two linkages with strategists: formulation and implementation linkages. The critical task for personnel at this point is to:

1. Design a strong link from the human resource function to the strategic planning function at the formulation stage in order to ensure their consistency.

2. Build a sufficient information base for human resource projection to support the business and corporate plans.

Human resource departments all have some responsibility for four basic **generic** activities:

1. Selection: recruiting qualified personnel.
2. Evaluation: managing the performance appraisal process.
3. Rewards: maintaining adequate compensation and fringe benefits packages.
4. Development: creating systems to enhance skills, promotional opportunities, and career paths.

On an operational level, these functions can be performed to satisfy immediate company needs and desires. On a strategic level, however, these activities should be performed to reflect the long-term goals and strategies of the company. This would involve projecting the internal and external labor market conditions, and designing processes for performing these activities that would fulfill the thrust of the human resources plans of the company.

There are three basic things that human resource functions must be willing to do in order to improve their capacity to operate on a strategic level. They must:

1. Improve data collection and retrieval systems. Attitudinal appraisal and skills data must be readily available in flexible form.
2. Encourage strategic thinking within the different activity units of human resource management. Officers must be educated to the realities of corporate planning and constantly monitor trends in terms of their consequences for the company's human resources.
3. Link the activities of the human resource functions to the strategic plans of the company. Interact with executive line officers around strategy formulation.

DESIGNING THE CORPORATE HUMAN RESOURCE STRATEGY

The task corporations now face is designing human resource strategies that complement their range of business and business strategies. In companies with several businesses at various stages of growth and decline, it becomes essential to differentiate particular human resource strategies to suit the shape of the business. With this in mind, the company's human resource staff has to be designed to fulfill the requirements of its function. So, a personnel department in a start-up business will have to emphasize recruitment activities, while a more established business will require more training and development expertise.

The corporation must also be ready to integrate the different human resource functions of their various businesses. The corporate position should be to differentiate the different personnel departments when necessary and to look for ways of integrating them whenever possible, so they can maintain some feeling of corporate affiliation.

CONCLUSION

The reseachers believe that if personnel is to move into the realm of strategic planning, both formulation and implementation, several things must happen. First, the corporation has to design a philosophy that encompasses its attitudes and values, and relates them to its strategic plans. Next, companies must design systems that reflect their philosophy and maintain their strategy.

The objective of injecting human resource management into the strategic arena is not to enhance the status of traditional personnel resource staff, but rather it is to alter the way managers set priorities and make decisions. And the final caveat is that the whole process must happen *over time,* lest the radical change aggravate rather than help potential problems.

B.

THE MICRO PERSPECTIVE: JOB ANALYSIS

How Do the Experts Do It?

Edward L. Levine

Out of the variety of building blocks available, the job analysis experts (both professionally acclaimed and self-styled) have chosen particular ones and constructed their particular approaches. Their choices of which building blocks to use in developing a job analysis method are usually based on the human resource activity they are interested in, be it training, performance appraisal or any of [several] . . . others. . . . But they also make choices based on their experiences and those of others about the advantages of one building block compared to another. A choice may be made strictly for practical considerations, like the extent to which workers can be gathered together in a group. To a lesser extent the choices of building blocks flow from scientific studies concerned with what building blocks work best in particular situations. Unfortunately, the science of job analysis is not far enough advanced to govern the choices to any great extent.

Nevertheless, if you want to become knowledgeable about job analysis you do need to be exposed to some of the methods that have been devised by the best known of the job analysis experts. (I'll leave it to you to search on the seamy side of town for the methods proffered by the self-styled experts.) I have selected the following seven methods to acquaint you with:

1. Threshold Traits Analysis
2. Critical Incident Technique
3. Job Element Method
4. Position Analysis Questionnaire (PAQ)
5. Functional Job Analysis
6. Ability Requirements Scales
7. the Task Inventory Approach paired with a particular set of computer programs called CODAP.

Edward L. Levine. "How Do the Experts Do It?" *Everything You Always Wanted to Know About Job Analysis*, Chapter 4, pp. 41–58. Tampa, Florida: Mariner Publishing, 1983. Reprinted by permission.

Each method will be described in the form of a brief capsule summary to whet your appetite. Then for those of you who want more details, some suggested readings are offered. The descriptions are condensed from published material, manuals, and in some cases, interviews with the developers of the methods.

THRESHOLD TRAITS ANALYSIS

In this method, which was developed by Felix M. Lopez, three types of information about jobs are focused on. They are:

1. tasks (what gets done on the job)
2. demands (conditions under which tasks are performed)
3. traits (human abilities, skills and personality factors needed to perform the tasks)

The tasks and demands required for job performance are collected in a two-step procedure. The first step involves a series of interviews with job holders, who are asked about the tasks they perform and the demands of the job.

In the second step, the information obtained in the interviews is used to develop a questionnaire. The questionnaire lists all the tasks and demands drawn from the interviews and requests that job holders rate the importance of the tasks and demands. The ratings are then computer analyzed, and the computer provides a printout listing all the significant tasks and demands for the job being analyzed, with their ratings. The computer also provides a 40–60 page report which organizes the tasks and demands into a pre-existing list of 21 job functions. The 21 job functions have been carefully devised and include the following examples: Physical Exertion, Information Processing, Quantitative Computation, Stressful Working Conditions, and Interpersonal Contact.

The traits required to perform the job also come from a standard, pre-existing list. There are 33 "threshold traits," and each one is linked to a corresponding job function. For example, the job function Physical Exertion has two traits linked to it, Strength and Stamina. A few other examples of traits are: Personal Appearance, Oral Expression, Memory, and Adaptability to Change. This standard list of traits is intended, as are the job functions, to apply to all kinds of jobs.

The traits analysis begins with a meeting of the job analyst and a group of supervisors. The supervisors are trained to understand the 33 traits and the rating scales they will use to evaluate each trait in relation to the job being analyzed. Supervisors then proceed to identify those traits that are considered relevant to the job. The relevant traits are rated on the level required for acceptable performance on the job and on how practical it is to expect applicants for the job to possess the level of the trait required.

Let's consider an example — the trait Problem Solving, which is linked to the job function Information Processing. Problem Solving is defined as the ability of the job holder to analyze information and to reason in order to arrive at a specific solution to a problem. There are four levels of Problem Solving:

1. Solving very minor, simple problems, such as giving someone directions. A bus driver's job would require this level.
2. Solving somewhat more difficult problems but problems with only a few variables, such as solving a customer complaint. A customer representative's job would require this level.
3. Solving problems with many variables that are known to the job holder but are complex, such as computer programming. A systems analyst's job would require this level.

4. Solving very difficult problems with many variables, some of which are unknown to the job holder, such as conducting research on a cure for cancer. A Supreme Court Judge's job would require this level.

Only traits requiring a level above the first are considered relevant for a job.

After a two-hour meeting of the supervisors, their ratings of the traits are entered into a computer. The computer then analyzes the ratings to produce a list of relevant traits that are practical to expect among applicants, the levels of the traits and the weights they have in the overall job performance picture.

As a final step the reports on tasks, demands and traits are compared to see if they relate well to each other. Disagreements are rarely found in practice, but the reports are subject to change if disagreements arise.

There it is! One method already covered and you are not even breathing hard. Let's go on to the next one, the Critical Incident Technique.

CRITICAL INCIDENT TECHNIQUE

The inventor of this method, J. C. Flanagan, defines an incident as a job activity complete enough to allow an observer to make inferences about an employee's capabilities. To be *critical*, an incident must occur where:

1. the purpose of the act is clear,
2. the consequences of the act are definite, and
3. the act is crucial to either *outstanding* or *poor* job performance.

When you put all the incidents for a job together, the job may be defined in terms of specific job behavior that are necessary for successful job performance.

How does one go about an analysis of a job using this method? First, the analyst must formulate the general objectives of the job to be analyzed. Second, persons are picked who are knowledgeable about the job in question. They are provided with the list of general objectives and given instructions on how to describe critical incidents. Third, they proceed to write or describe as many critical incidents as they can, and the job analyst collects them. Fourth, the job analyst edits the incidents, deletes redundant ones and organizes them into a set of categories such as Job Dimensions. Fifth, a report is written which includes the critical incidents and such other items as the education and experience of those persons who supplied the incidents.

Critical incidents must be written in a special format. Each incident must describe:

1. what led up to the incident and the setting in which it occurred,
2. exactly what the employee did that was so effective or ineffective,
3. the consequences of the employee's actions, and
4. whether the consequences were actually within the control of the employee (if this is not obvious).

Here are a couple of critical incidents for the job of Accountant that was analyzed by a team of analysts under my supervision some years ago:

1. When the employee received telephone inquiries regarding retirement withholding, the employee bluffed his way through the inquiries rather than seeking assistance to learn the correct answers to the questions.
2. When a misunderstanding developed between the data processing and accounting divisions, the employee met with the data processing manager, explained the problem and developed compromise solutions.

Here are a couple of critical incidents for the job of Mental Health Technician that the same team analyzed. These incidents were written to specify what an employee is expected to do if performing well or poorly.

1. At the time of discharging a patient, the employee may be expected to talk with the patient's parents to explain his present condition, what to expect and what to look for in the patient's future behavior.

2. After physically holding a combative patient in order to administer medication, this staff member can be expected to feel guilty and to alleviate the guilt feelings by giving the patient food and cigarettes.

The critical incidents can be collected by means of interviews, questionnaires or notes kept in a diary. At least two points of view, such as job holders and supervisors, need to be included. According to the developer of this method, between 2,000 and 4,000 critical incidents are required to establish a comprehensive statement of job requirements for a managerial job. Between 1,000 and 2,000 incidents are adequate to cover the critical behaviors for semiskilled and skilled jobs. However, others, myself included, have found that several hundred incidents may be adequate. Even with this smaller number, a critical incident job analysis may take several weeks to complete.

THE JOB ELEMENT METHOD

The developer of the Job Element Method, E. S. Primoff, focused his method strictly on worker traits and completely ignored tasks or actual job behaviors. The worker traits are referred to as Knowledges, Skills, Abilities and Other Personal Characteristics (KSAO's). These in fact are the *job elements* from which the method gets its name. Examples to illustrate what KSAO's are like include:

1. knowledge of accounting principles,
2. skill with woodworking tools,
3. ability to manage a program, and
4. willingness to do simple, repetitive tasks.

The method relies on a panel session and begins with the identification of 6 to 12 experienced supervisors and experienced workers or others knowledgeable about the job, who will serve as panel members. The panel session consists of two phases, job element *generation* and job element *rating*. These two phases may be expected to take one to five days time. In the first phase, the job analyst explains the purpose of the job analysis, defines the terms Knowledge, Skill, Ability and Other Personal Characteristics, and asks the panelists to describe all the KSAO's needed for job performance. As the panelists provide the KSAO's, they are carefully written down. A good session might yield 100 or more elements for a fairly complex job.

When the panelists have completed the generation phase, they, or a new group of panelists, are asked to rate each element on four scales:

1. *Barely Acceptable* (B). What proportion of even barely acceptable workers possess the KSAO. Ratings range from "all are good" to "almost none are good."

2. *Superior* (S). How important is an element for separating the truly superior workers from the average workers. Ratings range from "very important" to "does not differentiate."

3. *Trouble Likely* (T). How much trouble is likely if the element is ignored when selecting applicants. Ratings range from "much trouble" to "safe to ignore."

4. *Practical* (P). How practical is it to expect workers to possess the element. Ratings range from "all openings can be filled" to "almost no openings can be filled if this element is demanded."

Now the panelists are dismissed and the analysis of the BST & P ratings is begun. First, the ratings are combined by special formulas to determine which 8 to 12 elements are the most important or critical. Then the remaining elements are grouped with each of these 8 to 12 critical elements on the basis of their similarity to each of the critical elements. The next step involves the use of additional computational formulas and the total pattern of ratings to determine the role to be played by the elements in personnel selection and training programs.

Some elements, based on their pattern of ratings, are specially earmarked to serve as the guideposts for training programs. As you might expect, these elements are ones which are rated high on Superior, but low on the Practical scales. The remainder are earmarked for personnel selection. Again, based on the pattern of their ratings, the particular role of the elements or KSAO's earmarked for selection is decided. Some elements may be designated for use in developing tests to rank applicants for jobs. An example of an element that might be used for ranking applicants for the job of Water and Fuels Analyst in an Electric Generating Power Plant might be, Ability to Read and Follow Complex Directions.

Other elements may be used on a pass-fail basis as minimum qualification requirements. An example of such an element for the job of Water and Fuels Analyst might be, Willingness to Work Unusual Schedules.

The final product of the job analysis is a report which contains a listing of critical elements and all the other KSAO's grouped with them. The report will also contain the actual ratings for each element, and will identify which elements are to be used for training, for selection on a pass-fail basis, or for selection on a ranking basis.

Still with me? Great! (Give yourself 10 points for staying awake.) Let's get on to the next method.

POSITION ANALYSIS QUESTIONNAIRE (PAQ)

The foundation of this method is a long questionnaire developed by E. J. McCormick and his associates at Purdue University. The questionnaire, which can be used to describe any job, contains 194 items. The first 187 items relate to job activities or the work situation, while the last 7 deal with compensation. Items cover the various mental processes the worker engages in, interpersonal relationships, actions taken by the worker, the work environment and various other aspects of work.

An example of an item from the PAQ is drawn from a section on the use of hand-held tools or equipment. The item refers specifically to long-handle tools such as brooms, mops or rakes. The person who completes the questionnaire rates the importance of such tools to the job on a six point scale ranging from N ("does not apply") to 5 ("extremely important").

The procedure for completing a job analysis depends on who is to complete it. If job holders and supervisors are to complete it, they should have college level reading skills because the PAQ and its instructions are rather difficult to read. When job holders and supervisors are used, the procedure is as follows:

1. An expert in job analysis serves as discussion leader to interpret the PAQ items in terms directly related to the job being analyzed.

2. Each worker and supervisor completes the PAQ independently. Only about one supervisor and three workers are needed.

3. The completed questionnaires are sent to the PAQ developers for computer analysis.
4. The computer reports are interpreted and used as the situation requires.

When a job analyst completes the PAQ, the procedure is as follows:

1. The job analyst becomes familiar with the PAQ items.
2. The analyst interviews job holders and supervisors, and may also observe job holders while they work.
3. The analyst completes the PAQ.
4. The completed questionnaire is sent to the PAQ developers for computer analysis.
5. The computer reports are interpreted and used as the situation requires.

In either case the computer analysis takes one or two weeks.

Because they have done a great deal of research with the PAQ, McCormick and his associates are able to provide a wealth of information with their computer analysis. However, anyone who wishes to use the computer reports should be well versed in statistics.

Among the kinds of information an analyst will get from the PAQ are the following:

1. Job dimension scores on many different dimensions in the form of a profile. These dimension scores are based on comparisons between a job's scores and the average scores of thousands of jobs in the U. S. economy. One such dimension is Making Decisions. This dimension is composed of (PAQ) items dealing with reasoning, planning and scheduling, decision making (obviously!), using mathematics, etc. Jobs with high scores on this dimension include Corporate Lawyers and Physicians. Jobs with average scores include Auto Mechanics and Librarians. Jobs with low scores include Kettle Cooks and Bus Drivers.
2. Scores on selected human attributes needed to perform the work, such as arithmetic reasoning or capacity to deal with time pressures.
3. The average scores to be achieved by workers on the job, if they were to take the General Aptitude Test Battery. This is a group of tests that measures verbal ability, math ability, and several other mental abilities.
4. Scores on special indexes, such as amount of education required by a job, the type of supervision received, and the job's prestige.

FUNCTIONAL JOB ANALYSIS

The Functional Job Analysis method, devised by S. A. Fine, focuses on tasks and ratings of the tasks on a number of different scales. Tasks describe what a worker does and what gets done on a job. A more formal definition of the term task in Functional Job Analysis is as follows:

A task is an action sequence grouped through time designed to contribute a specified end result to the accomplishment of a work objective.

A task statement must follow a standard format. The format includes an action verb to describe the worker's action as well as the tools, methods or equipment used.

In addition a task statement should contain a statement describing the purpose of the worker's action. Here is an example of a task statement for the job of Social Worker:

> Suggests/explains to client reasons for making a good appearance and particular areas where he can make improvements to conform to local standards in order that client makes applications for jobs appropriately dressed and groomed.

However, the statement alone is not a task. It does not qualify as a task in Functional Job Analysis until *worker function levels* and a *worker function orientation* are provided. There are three worker *functions*, which are the basis for the name of this job analysis method. They are:

1. *Data,* which describes the way the worker relates to information, ideas, facts and numbers. There are six levels of the Data Function, ranging from the simple ("Comparing") to the complex ("Synthesizing").

2. *People,* which describes the way the worker interacts and communicates with others. There are seven levels of the People Function, ranging from the simple (Taking Instructions, Helping) to the complex (Mentoring, e.g., guiding a scientist in his or her research).

3. *Things,* which describes the way the worker interacts with machines, tools and equipment. There are only three levels of the Things scale, ranging from the simple (Handling) to the complex (Setting Up).

The worker function levels for the Social Worker task statement are 3 for Data (moderate complexity), 3 for People and only 1 for Things.

The worker function *orientation* is the percentage of the worker's involvement in the performance of the task that deals with Data, People and Things. The sum of the three percentages must equal 100%. For the Social Work Task Statement, the worker function orientation is 35% in Data, 60% in People and only 5% in Things.

The procedure for gathering task information and rating the tasks on worker functions and a number of other scales is fairly simple. One or more job analysts first review available background information about a job under analysis. Then they interview a number of people who are knowledgeable about the job, usually job holders and supervisors. The number interviewed may vary from job to job, but the idea is to interview enough people to get full coverage of all the tasks performed. Sometimes they may observe workers as they perform their jobs. After the interviews and observations task statements are written. The task statements are reviewed by a group of job experts, who verify that the tasks are indeed part of the job, and who add any tasks that are missing from the list.

When the list of task statements is complete, the job analysts who are specially trained to do so, rate each of them on the worker functions and on other scales. The last step is the preparation of a task bank. The task bank contains index cards, one for each task statement. The index cards also contain the worker function *levels* and *orientation,* ratings on several other scales, standards for performance of the task and the content to be used for training a worker on the task. The Social Worker task on explaining to clients the need for good grooming would have the performance standard that clear, complete, accurate information must be given to clients. The training content would include a segment devoted to teaching a Social Worker how to explain grooming standards to clients applying for jobs. The typical task bank might contain 50 to 60 index cards, each covering one task.

How about those other rating scales I have mentioned? What are they? They include the following:

1. A scale related to the amount of discretion the worker has in his or her job,
2. A scale dealing with the level and kind of reasoning required in the job,
3. A scale dealing with the level and kind of mathematical ability required in the job, and
4. A scale dealing with the level and kind of verbal ability required in the job.

Why not get yourself a cup of strong coffee, and we'll get on to the last two methods.

ABILITY REQUIREMENTS SCALES

Like the Job Elements Method, the Ability Requirements Scales approach does not concern itself with tasks or what gets done on the job. Rather it focuses on the human abilities needed to perform the work. But unlike the Job Elements Method, where the KSAO's are generated anew for each job, the Ability Requirements Scales rely on a standard, pre-existing list of 37 human abilities. First, let's explore the nature of these abilities, and then I will describe the procedure.

The list of abilities in this method was prepared by E. A. Fleishman and his associates with two ideas in mind:

1. the abilities should provide a way of specifying the individual differences in worker performance and learning ability, and
2. the abilities should be applicable to all tasks.

An ability is defined as a general human trait that makes some people better performers than others on groups of related tasks. After careful study, 37 abilities were selected to represent the full range of human performance. The abilities are grouped into four categories:

1. mental abilities, such as Verbal Comprehension,
2. physical abilities, such as Stamina,
3. psychomotor abilities which require some action to be taken when specific sensory cues are present, such as Choice Reaction Time (how quickly a person can respond when presented with one particular cue, e.g., a red light, rather than another, e.g., a green light), and
4. abilities having to do with the way incoming sensory material is perceived, such as Spatial Orientation (how well people can figure out the way objects are laid out in space).

The scales used in the job analysis, the Ability Requirements Scales themselves, are 5 to 7 point rating scales. One example of the way the scales are laid out is as follows for the Verbal Comprehension scale:

Requires the understanding of complicated detailed information which contains novel words and phrases and requires fine distinctions among words.	7
	6
	□ Understand a mortgage contract for a new home
	5

(continued)

4

3

☐ Understand a newspaper article

Requires only a basic knowl-   2
edge of language to understand   ☐ Understand a comic book
simple communications   1

The rater is also given a definition of each ability and a brief description of how the ability in question differs from other, related abilities. For example Verbal Comprehension is distinguished from Ideational Fluency (understanding of words vs. production of ideas), and Verbal Expression (understanding by the receiver of information vs. ability to express or communicate information).

The procedure requires that incumbents and supervisors rate a total job or, if tasks are available, each task on the level of ability required for performing the job or the task. The larger the number of raters, the better. One estimate offered by the developer of the number required was between 25 and 30 supervisors and between 25 and 30 job holders. The ratings may be made easier by following a step by step checklist procedure designed by the developers of the method. The final product of this analysis is a report which contains information on the procedure followed, the raters used, and a listing of the 37 abilities along with the average ratings on the level of each ability required for performing the job.

TASK INVENTORY PAIRED WITH THE COMPREHENSIVE OCCUPATIONAL DATA ANALYSIS PROGRAM (TI/CODAP)

TI/CODAP is a computer based method devised by R. E. Christal and his colleagues at the U. S. Air Force Human Resource Laboratory. The method relies on task inventories, which accounts for the TI part of the name, and a well developed package of computer programs (the CODAP part) to analyze information provided by job holders who complete the task inventories.

Task inventories in this method are actually questionnaires which ask for a variety of information from job holders in the jobs being analyzed. The core of the task inventory is really a list of *activities*. . . . The activities . . . are defined as meaningful units of work recognizable to the worker. Each activity is rated by job holders on a Relative Time Spent scale. This scale refers to the relative time spent performing a particular activity relative to all the other activities. Levels on the scale (usually 7 or 9 levels are used) may range from "Very Much Below Average" to "Very Much Above Average." Job holders may also be asked to rate the tasks on other kinds of scales, and to provide additional information. The additional information might cover their work experience, race, sex, use of equipment and job satisfaction.

After a particular job or job family is chosen for analysis, the process of developing the task inventory begins. This is a fairly complicated procedure which may take as long as four months' time and which involves the following steps:

1. Research background information such as previous job analyses and already available task inventories. Interviews with job experts may also be done.

2. Develop a list of broad duties for the job or job family being analyzed.

3. Write the activity statements and assign them to their respective duties.

4. Verify and refine the task listing by having job experts review it.

The outcome of this phase is a questionnaire that may contain from 200 to 1,400 task statements depending on the purpose of the analysis and the complexity of the job. The average task inventory in the Air Force contains about 450 items.

Now the inventories are distributed to job holders. When a job family has 3,000 or fewer job holders, the Air Force attempts to have all job holders complete the inventories. When there are more than this, the Air Force uses a large, randomly selected sample of job holders. The job holders usually use a computer scorable answer form to record their answers. The collection of all this information, and putting it into the computer may take as long as four weeks.

At this point, CODAP comes into the picture, and the data are subjected to a variety of analyses. Some of the results of these analyses include the following:

1. a listing of all data in the form of a master file,
2. a set of clusters or categories into which similar jobs or positions are placed, and
3. a set of job descriptions.

The analysis of all these task inventory data may take up to two months' time.

Finally, management reports and other types of products such as written tests for use in selection are prepared. It's almost too obvious to say that someone who uses this method must be capable of developing survey questionnaires, knowledgeable about computers and well versed in statistics.

NOW FOR A TEST

You have done it! You have gotten through the seven methods in one piece.
Here is a quick test for you:

1. How many traits are there in the Threshold Traits Analysis method?
2. What do B, S, T, and P stand for in the Job Element method?
3. Which job analysis method contains information on aptitudes from the General Aptitude Test Battery?
4. What does CODAP stand for?
5. How do you define a task when you are doing a Functional Job Analysis?

Give yourself 100 points if you can answer these questions without checking back. Give yourself 50 points if you need to go back but can quickly spot the answers. Give yourself 0 points if you don't know where to start looking. You readers with 0 points, please pinch yourself, get a cup of coffee and reread the chapter.

These methods I described are only a few among many. The availability of so many methods is a blessing or a curse, depending on your point of view. On the one hand, there should presumably be a method just right for a particular situation. On the other hand, the large number of methods makes it hard to settle on one. . . .

Now I will deliver what I promised at the beginning of this chapter. If your appetite for a particular method has been whetted by my brief descriptions, here is a list of references where you can read more about each one.

1. Threshold Traits Analysis — Lopez, F. M., Kesselman, G. A., and Lopez, F. E. An empirical test of a trait oriented job analysis technique. *Personnel Psychology*, 1981, v. 34, pp. 479–502.

2. The Critical Incident Technique — Flanagan, J. C. The critical incident technique. *Psychological Bulletin*, 1954, v. 51, 327–358.

3. The Job Element Method — Primoff, E. S. *How to prepare and conduct job element examinations.* Washington, D.C.: U.S. Government Printing Office, 1975.

4. The Position Analysis Questionnaire — McCormick, E. J., Jeanneret, P. R. & Mecham, R. C. A study of job characteristics and job dimensions as based on the Position Analysis Questionnaire (PAQ). *Journal of Applied Psychology*, 1972, v. 56, pp. 347–368.

5. Functional Job Analysis — Fine, S. A. & Wiley, W. *An introduction to functional job analysis: Methods for Manpower Analysis.* Kalamazoo, Mich.: Upjohn Institute for Employment Research, 1971 (Methods for Manpower Analysis #4). A closely related method is described in the U.S. Department of Labor's *Handbook for Analyzing Jobs.* Washington, D.C.: U.S. Government Printing Office, 1972.

6. Ability Requirements Scales — Fleishman, E. A. Toward a taxonomy of human performance. *American Psychologist*, 1975, v. 30, pp. 327–358.

7. TI/CODAP — Christal, R. E. The United States Air Force occupational research project. *JSAS Catalog of Selected Documents in Psychology*, 1974, v. 4, 61 (Manuscript Number 651).

C.

HUMAN RESOURCE INFORMATION SYSTEMS

The Newest Job in Personnel: Human Resources Data Administrator

Alfred J. Walker

THE PERSONNEL DATABASE IS BEST MANAGED BY A PERSONNEL PROFESSIONAL WITH COMPUTER SKILLS

The position of human resource data administrator (HRDA), a position that virtually did not exist in the top echelons of personnel management five years ago, is taking on increased significance in the evolution of the modern personnel office. This trend reflects a growing need for personnel-oriented database administration, to protect and make the most of corporate investment in human resource information systems (HRIS).

The reasons for this are clear to anyone who has participated in the development of an HRIS: personnel data needs are different both qualitatively and quantitatively from the needs of accounting, inventory control, engineering, or production. Human resources — being human — are infinitely more complex and variable than most other corporate resources.

Not the least of the differences between the personnel database and other databases is the need to protect the privacy rights of individuals, while assuring that data are available to those with a genuine need to know.

The Technical Administrator

In the past, database administration has usually fallen to the data systems function or department, where technically skilled people with no particular understanding of personnel needs and problems have provided access to the database.

As long as personnel users of the HRIS were relatively few and they limited their requests to fixed reports — such as EEO headcounts, recurring reports on benefits, or standard salary information requests — technically oriented database administrators have served most personnel users adequately. In these situations, however, the role of the database administrator was primarily that of guardian of the database and protector of the integrity of data, its currency, and technical procedures — such as standardization of input, error correction, edits, table maintenance, report formats, and specifications for system changes.

These and other administrative tasks are crucially important in the efficient maintenance of any database, but personnel users require more. For example:

1. Who decides whether and how to interface the personnel system with the payroll system?
2. How do you create the most cost-effective and retrievable hierarchies for personnel functions?
3. Which editing criteria are appropriate for different kinds of human resources data?
4. What equipment or software will more efficiently provide the methodology for a new application?
5. Which new applications should have priority?
6. Are user requests for data or reports redundant to their needs? Or insufficient?
7. Does the database administrator understand personnel functions well enough to negotiate with users and participate in cost/benefit analysis of proposed usage?

The Perfect Database?

In a sense, it would be ideal if each of the personnel functions — benefits, pensions, staffing, etc. — could have its own database. Personnel users who are responsible for different functions — from the employment process to pension planning — have different, function-specific objectives in terms of what reports should look like, timing of reports, who should see which data, and other function-specific needs.

Because so much human resource information can be used in any number of systems, however, such an arrangement would clearly defeat the purpose of an HRIS. Data such as names, salaries, job codes, department number and the like can be used in as many as 15 or 20 different internal subsystems. Efficiency dictates that such data be collected only once, uniformly coded, appropriately related to other data or programs, and, when changes occur, revised once-and-for-all.

In the design of the HRIS, the database is normally structured in such a way — through modular design, tables, and interfaces — as to permit separate functional entities such as benefits administration to have their own databases and retrieval methodologies. Nonetheless, much of the efficiency of the overall HRIS comes from the universality of much personnel data, standardization of codes, and data upkeep that automatically maintains the accuracy of all fields and files.

HRDA Tasks

In large companies, the HRDA manages a large service organization. In smaller firms he or she may operate alone. In either case, the role played by the HRDA often makes the difference between an accurate, up-to-date, secure, and usable database, and one that falls short of its full potential as a management-support system. The organization of the many functions that are part of effective human resource data administration will depend on the size of database, its main components, and the kinds of applications needed.

In whatever organizational structure, the HRDA function, in most cases, will bear ultimate responsibility for these tasks:

- □ *Data management,* including inputs, scheduling, updates, and error correction.
- □ *Standardization of codes and procedures,* including data interpretation and accuracy programs.
- □ *Enhancements,* including new edits as well as new data and processes, and the setting of priorities for changes that are inevitable.
- □ *Retrieval procedures,* including the maintenance of hierarchies and development of various kinds of canned and ad hoc report formats.
- □ *Security and privacy maintenance,* protecting both the corporate investment and employees' privacy rights.
- □ *Interface with other systems,* such as payroll, that must be managed and monitored to minimize redundant data collection and assure compatibility.
- □ *Consultation* with users on problems, improvements, and new subsystems (e.g., a management selection system).
- □ *Continuing research* into new technologies, such as the use of microcomputers in distributed networks, electronic mail, and other developments that may be applicable.
- □ *Budget and billing control,* including the preparation of cost estimates for alternative procedures and reports.

There are other duties as well, some more important to different organizations at different stages of HRIS development. Vendor evaluation, for example, is a key responsibility of the HRDA in organizations planning to purchase prepackaged software.

Multidisciplinary Skills Are Needed

The skills required for effective human resource data administration include a range of technical, personnel, and managerial qualifications and abilities that together define a new kind of human resources technocrat. In practice, HRDA practitioners usually have gained some of these skills in formal education. They have been able to acquire the other needed skills on-the-job, supplemented by company or outside training.

The data processing skills required should accentuate computer usage and applications, and thus requires the broad perspective of systems analysis rather than mere computer programming. The job of HRDA calls for some understanding of systems interfaces, database issues, vendor evaluations, and retrieval problems.

Human resources qualifications are essential to understanding the effects of computerization in each area mechanized by the HRIS, and how to achieve maximum productivity of the system through functionally feasible edits, inputs, and outputs.

Traditional management skills will of course mean the difference between an HRDA function that is merely capable, and one that gets the job done in a manner that most efficiently achieves corporate objectives. The role of the database administrator should include both supervision and responsibility for day-to-day HRIS administration — from updates and changes to accuracy standards and training.

The HRDA function also requires planning and decision-making about the future applications of using the human resources database as a corporate resource. This means that the HRDA must fully understand top management's views on personnel priorities, and must be able to help shape the uses and outputs of the personnel information system to meet the most essential objectives — in a way that does not discourage promising new applications. In many cases, the HRDA's skill at juggling the different kinds of demands made on the database will be the administrator's most important management skill.

A Top Manager

The position of human resources data administrator has emerged as one of the top personnel spots in large to medium-sized personnel departments — equal in importance to the jobs of salary administrator, benefits administrator, etc. In the growing number of companies that have invested in an HRIS, top management has come to two realizations:

1. These systems do not run themselves.
2. As personnel data uses proliferate — take full advantage of the efficiencies of computerized information systems — administration of human resources data systems will require personnel expertise and management skills in addition to technical database management abilities.

D.

HUMAN RESOURCE PLANNING

Interview with Les Woller

At the time of this interview, Les Woller was director of human resources at Petro-Lewis Corporation. Prior to joining Petro-Lewis in 1981, he held several personnel management positions at General Electric, Envirotech, and Cobe Laboratories. Woller was production manager at N N Dataforms, a Wisconsin manufacturer of business forms and data processing papers. He is presently managing partner of Wargo and Company's Denver office.

Woller is founder and chairman of the Rocky Mountain Human Resource Planners Group. He also chairs the Professional Development Committee of the Human Resource Planning Society, and is a member of the society's board of directors.

1. *What is human resource planning (HRP) and how does it benefit the organization in general and the personnel department in particular?*

Human resource planning is the process of identifying and responding to human resource issues and charting new policies, systems and programs that assure effective human resource management under changing conditions. The human resource planning process is comprised of two major elements: needs forecasting and program planning. Needs forecasting involves the analysis of internal conditions and external conditions. It requires an understanding of future human resource requirements netted against your future human resource availability, and results in a forecast of human resource needs. Program planning primarily consists of performance management, career management, succession planning, and compensation management.

The essential benefit of a human resource planning process is the help it gives management in maintaining an effective and successful organization. There are a number of traditional measures that have been used to determine the benefits of a human resource planning process. Some of these are: number of qualified back-ups for managerial positions, job offer acceptance rates for professionals, cost per hire, turnover rates, participation rates in training programs, cost per participant in programs, length of time before positions are filled, occurrence and cost of internal movement, achievement of affirmative action goals, organization's compliance with performance appraisal policies, indicators of pay adjustments, and employee attitude measures. However, the ultimate measures to determine the benefit of human resource planning processes are the subjective judgments that can be made only by managers. The better managers feel about the human resource planning process, the more involved the personnel department will be in future operations that impact the organization. Therefore, it becomes a circular kind of thing that feeds on itself. The better the managers feel about the process, the better the process will be ultimately.

2. *How important is it that the human resource planning system be formalized in today's larger organizations? How does the HRP process work at Petro-Lewis?*

In my opinion, some parts of the human resource planning process need to be formalized in any organization. In the area of program planning, the performance appraisal system and the reward systems need to be formalized. These are the cornerstones of any sound human resource planning process. They affect employees' attitudes about the corporation and set the tone for the corporate culture. Therefore, they have tremendous impact on the measures that determine how beneficial a planning process is. In addition, the effect on productivity is enormous. I feel these two areas are key.

In terms of the human resource planning process at Petro-Lewis, we do an annual forecast of our future needs, play that against availability, and come up with our annual manpower plan. We have a formalized performance appraisal system, compensation system, and internal and external employment process. Our career management area is one that we have begun to do some additional work on and is not formalized. However, senior human resource management is an active participant in career decisions relating to individuals — particularly management succession issues.

3. *What background and skills should a human resource planner possess? Do you envision any changes in these qualifications over the next twenty years? If so, how and why?*

It is much better for a human resource planner to have been in an operating or line position. In fact, more than one operating role would be ideal. The in-depth knowledge of the business that comes from being a hands-on contributor or manager in another part of the business either before an assignment in human resource (HR) planning or between assignments in HR gives an individual the perspective to really contribute in these roles. Other qualifications the individual needs are: a good communicator — particularly verbally; persuasive; good process skills; and, as I previously mentioned, a thorough understanding of the business. Also, being very analytical while still being action oriented is helpful.

In general I don't see these qualifications changing dramatically over the next twenty years. However, I do feel that the day of the generalist or the bionic HR planner is definitely at hand. The specialist — the individual who is strictly interested in either one segment of human resources or has not had experience with the business — is going to have difficulty over the next few years because of the focus on cost and productivity. I believe many human resource departments will not have the luxury to carry on their staff a cadre of specialists. These generalists who can do one assignment this week and another the next week, are going to be the wave of the future. There are a number of experienced specialists available from the consulting area to shore up a human resource department in many specialist areas. Plus the tremendous development of computer applications makes decision-making data related to human resources more accessible to line managers and HR generalists.

4. *Many recent articles have argued, in theory, for more integration of HRP activities with overall organizational planning and strategy formulation. Has it been your experience, in practice, that personnel concerns are as important as financial, marketing, or operations concerns in the formulation and implementation of*

business strategy? If not, why do you think this is so and do you perceive any changes in this area?

I think that it has always been important to integrate human resources into the business plan. I see no change. In fact, I feel it will become more and more important as many changes take place in the business environment. These changes include a focus on decentralized, autonomous divisions or work units; a focus on marketing; increasing international competition; a continuation of merger and acquisition activity making for larger, more diverse kinds of corporations. As these changes occur, the emphasis on planning and allocating your human resources is going to become more and more critical. In fact, it is my view that you will not implement your strategic business plan or your financial, marketing, or operation strategies without people. People energize your plans. Without a "people" segment of the plan, you have no plan.

5. *Forecasting an organization's future need for human resources is an important part of the HRP process. This would seem to be a particularly difficult task in a business as volatile as the oil business. How does Petro-Lewis approach this problem?*

We do an annual manpower forecast as part of our budgeting process. Because, as you point out, our business is very volatile, doing more than an annual plan is really not feasible. And many times we have to change directions and revise the plan during the plan year. And I think that this points out that any good plan has a mechanism in it for change and a management team that is willing to make changes as appropriate.

6. *Another important part of the HRP process is planning for executive and managerial succession. To what degree is the personnel department involved in this process and how is it done at Petro-Lewis? Does succession planning differ from HRP? If so, how?*

Different organizational levels in the personnel department are involved in the succession planning process. I would describe our succession planning process as somewhat ad hoc. By that I mean we do not have a formal review process where layer by layer managers are reviewed and a determination is made for what positions they will be successors. However, there are discussions periodically throughout the year with key members of senior management to determine where we are thin, what we were doing about backups, who might be a backup for what and what it is that needs to be done. These are not done necessarily when a crisis occurs. They are done as part of a normal interaction that we have with senior management and it takes the appearance of an ad hoc or informal system.

Succession planning is part of the human resource planning process. It is not different from — it is a subset of — HRP. Management succession includes things like individual assessment, position requirements, replacement charting, an overall succession plan, and tracking of progress. This is part of a career management element of the program planning section of the HRP process.

7. *To what degree are computers utilized in the HRP process in your organization or others with which you are familiar?*

We utilize computers at Petro-Lewis to a great degree. We have our monthly manpower tracking report computerized. We have computerized productivity-type measures and ratios that we utilize to validate our manpower forecast and to determine what kinds of people are needed to do certain tasks based on past productivity and forecasted ratios. Plus we have mechanized compensation and training data. Additionally, we have access through our system to many other data bases in the company. I feel that we have as much capability as most organizations, if not more. And it has worked well for us, considering the volatility of our business. Organizations are becoming more and more interested in computer applications in HRP, and I think that you will see more creative applications and different variations of software offered in this field that will be extremely useful to many companies.

8. *Which organizations that you know of seem to be doing the best job in HRP? What do they do differently than other organizations?*

The book *In Search of Excellence* detailed this as well as has ever been done. I think the sales of that book certainly verifies this. However, there are a number of companies that do an excellent job, and rather than categorize them, which I think Peters and Waterman did a thorough job of, let me just take an example that comes to mind. General Electric Corporation, I think, does an absolutely outstanding job in the area of human resource planning. And they don't do this with a huge organization of planners. Under the leadership of Jack Welch, who I had the pleasure of working for in the 1970s, GE has clearly taken the position that planning is a managerial responsibility. I think there are some keys that General Electric and Jack Welch are a perfect example of. One, they have a leader who is committed to constantly improving his human resources through the development of his managers. By that I mean not necessarily formal training, but on-the-job development. The company is also able to move managers around because of the diversity of GE's various businesses. Most good HRP planning processes involve moving managers around so that they can get in-depth knowledge of different positions and different jobs. Additionally, performance appraisals are directly linked to the reward system. That is the cornerstone, in my mind, of a good human resource planning process. And lastly, GE is not afraid to try new things. They operate on a decentralized, divisional kind of basis, and these business units try things on their own — they are not part of a large bureaucratic process that is forced upon them.

9. *Much of the recent academic literature on HRP has involved the application of sophisticated mathematical techniques (e.g., Markov Analysis) to HRP problems. In your experience, have these mathematical treatments begun to have an impact on HRP in practice? If not, do you believe that they will in the future?*

I believe that in practice the mathematical approach has really not had an impact on HRP and I believe it will not in the future. The subjective, if you will, and qualitative forecasting techniques and other planning processes in HRP are much more appropriate for the changing environment we're trying to manage in. In my opinion the future will see more acceptance of the entrepreneur's "feel" for problem solving, business planning and HRP issues.

10. *What do you think are some of the key behaviors required for an individual to be successful in human resources?*

I think there are seven key kinds of behaviors that make an individual successful in human resources. One, view yourself as an internal consultant and view the employees as clients. Remember, they are the customers and you need to keep them involved. Two, link what you're doing with the direction the corporation is going. Pick your targets carefully because you only have a limited number of "silver bullets." You need to use them judiciously and link up with operational and strategic issues around the corporation. Three, do your homework. Know more about what you're doing than anyone else. Four, use the power of data. By that I mean make sure you've done your homework and have got your facts and when it's appropriate to use them. Make sure others know that you know what's going on. Five, form follows function. Determine what you're trying to do, and then let the approach follow. Six, keep it simple and be practical. Deal with the simple issues first, and don't use a lot of jargon or come up with solutions that are so complicated that it is hopeless to implement them. And lastly, show progress. Don't try to eat the "whole elephant." The theory of small wins always applies — particularly in human resource issues. Try to take it a little at a time, but also keep reminding people where you're going.

E.

JOB ANALYSIS

Interview with Walter W. Tornow

Walter Tornow is presently vice-president and executive consultant at Control Data Business Advisors, where he is in charge of organization research services — including employee surveys, performance appraisal, program evaluation and personnel research. He is also involved in advanced product design, job analysis systems integration and micro-technology applications. Dr. Tornow is a licensed consulting psychologist, an Accredited Personnel Diplomate, and a frequent contributor to both scholarly and practitioner journals in the personnel field. He received his Ph.D. in industrial organizational psychology in 1970 from the University of Minnesota.

Three colleagues at Control Data Business Advisors collaborated with Dr. Tornow in this interview. They were Dennis T. Caskey, Louis J. Huether, and Ronald C. Page.

1. *What is job analysis and why is it an important process for personnel administration?*

    Job analysis is the systematic collection of information on job content, including job behaviors, competencies, and level (or value) information. It is an important process for personnel administration because it is a base technology that provides information to such key personnel functions as compensation, staffing, and training and development. Most personnel/human resources management (P/HRM) decisions are based on some information about job content. It is of fundamental importance to the company in that it is the foundation of many P/HRM decisions. For example, through job analysis, we can identify important job components — a first step in defining job groups or units in the work force. Once defined, these common groups can be compared internally as well as to the external market to define equitable pay practices. With increased government regulations, companies must know why jobs are different from each other, and be able to monitor their characteristics.

2. *How does the process generally work at Control Data Corporation? Is there one method that is commonly used, or are a variety of methods utilized?*

    There are various job analysis approaches used at Control Data (CDC), depending on the purpose. However, a quantitative, questionnaire-based approach has grown predominant and has several applications. This method is called FOCAS (Flexible Occupational Analysis System) and is based on job-oriented questionnaires that are computer analyzed. This system has primary application for compensation, but also has application for performance appraisal, career pathing, and selection. More specifically, in the past CDC has used the typical benching procedure with jobs (e.g., Engineering, Administrative) and point plans (e.g., production, office). CDC now has made the transition to the more behavior-based FOCAS system. This method captures the time-spent data, along with compensable factor data which then can be used for multiple human resource functions (e.g., pay programs, training, hiring requirements). Employees and their managers are heavily involved in this method as they provide actual task data in work sessions.

3. *What background, education, and skills should a competent job analyst possess? Is this a good area for recent college graduates to start a career in personnel management? Why or why not?*

Job analysts should have a background in personnel and quantitative methods, and a proficiency in running computer applications. In addition, the analyst should have sound communication skills: interviewing skills for data gathering, and writing skills to document the findings. Since job analysis requires information be gathered on all company jobs, it is an excellent way to become familiar with the organization. This knowledge can serve well for growth in P/HRM or other areas.

I prefer analysts that have at least a master's degree in fields such as industrial/organizational psychology or industrial relations. If traditional observation/interview techniques are used, then a B.A. degree is adequate. If a questionnaire approach is used, I prefer the strong quantitative training of an advanced degree.

4. *In theory, a job analysis forms the basis for most all other personnel activities (e.g., performance appraisal, selection, training). Despite this importance, many suspect that job analysis in practice is not done as carefully and as thoroughly as it could be. What has been your experience, both at Control Data and with other organizations, in this regard?*

Small organizations usually ignore job analysis because everyone knows what everyone else is doing. If they experience growth, the company usually loses touch with employees' duties rather quickly. Large companies have a large number of diverse positions, and it is difficult to keep current with changes in positions. If managers and employees sense that job descriptions are not current, they gradually lose credibility. To be effective, job descriptions have to be accurate and easy to revise since it is the basic structure for other P/HRM programs.

At CDC, we are implementing FOCAS, which is computer based for data analysis. Thus, we are beginning to use a single job analysis strategy for multiple applications. This is in contrast to the past, when job analysis was usually performed, but it was done independently by different departments to meet their specific needs. The FOCAS approach is systematic and allows us to access a common data base to address multiple applications.

5. *Unlike most other P/HRM professionals, you do a lot of research and writing for scholarly journals. Why do you believe that this is important? What is your sense of the present relationship between scholars in the personnel field and P/HRM practitioners? Is there a gap? Should it be narrowed? If so, how?*

It is important to describe to others what is currently occurring in industry. Industry practices have significant impact because they show which practices are accepted by industry management and provide considerable data for research studies. The present relationship between scholars in the personnel field and P/HRM practitioners is not as active as it could be. There is indeed a gap. Scholars in academic positions tend to publish more articles, but may not be as interested in bottom-line issues of implementation and maintenance. Although difficult from a time perspective, the P/HRM field would benefit by industrial practitioners increasing their contributions to scholarly journals. Practitioners need better guidance from scholars on the best methods for addressing their needs. Ideally, increased interaction between representatives from academe and industry could be enhanced by such activities as six-month job swapping, special assignments to academe or industry, etc.

6. *What do you see as one of the areas in job analysis that should be given more emphasis?*

With the explosion of micro-computers, new and experienced compensation analysts must prepare themselves to use this valuable tool. As more and more job data are manipulated, the analyst must have not only a systems understanding, but a hands-on operating ability at the terminal. The analyst must be able to structure job information systems to satisfy management needs, or be specifically knowledgeable of a vendor's system such as CDC's FOCAS system. I predict that within 10 years it will be virtually impossible to function in the P/HRM areas without a working knowledge of micro-computers and their applications packages.

7. *Has the importance of job analysis changed over the last twenty years? If so, to what do you attribute this change? Do you think job analysis will be more or less important in the future? Why?*

Yes — the importance of job analysis has increased over the last twenty years, as improved methods of doing job analysis have emerged. Government guidelines, constant changes in job content, addition of new jobs, and productivity concerns as profits are squeezed — all have caused management to show increased interest in what employees are really doing, and what is the best job match for their skills. The importance of job analysis will continue and probably accelerate because it is the foundation of making appropriate and informed P/HRM decisions. For example, EEOC and comparable worth issues will force organizations to better document the job relatedness of their P/HRM decisions. Management will be looking at more complex positions with higher paid people in them since automation will likely replace current production jobs.

PART II: FOR DISCUSSION AND REVIEW

A.

Business Week

- ☐ Explain the concept of manpower planning as used in the article. How does it relate to or differ from that of strategic planning?
- ☐ What is the recent emphasis on P/HRM attributable to?

Devanna et al.

- ☐ Briefly describe the purpose and the results of the survey conducted by the authors.

□ Discuss the following statement: "Historically, personnel has played a mostly reactive role in the company." What is the alternative proposal provided?

B.

Levine

□ Define the concept of critical incident. How is it used in the Critical Incident Technique of job analysis?

□ Which of the methods described in the reading focus primarily on (1) tasks, (2) worker traits, and (3) job behavior?

C.

Walker

□ What types of questions are Human Resource Information Systems designed to answer?

□ Why does an HRDA need multidisciplinary skills?

PART III
APPRAISING PERFORMANCE IN ORGANIZATIONS

A.

GENERAL ISSUES IN APPRAISAL

Performance Appraisal Formats
Wayne F. Cascio

☐ Describes and reviews the most widely used appraisal techniques and discusses their advantages and disadvantages.

The Rater as Information Processor
Stephen J. Carroll and Craig E. Schneier

☐ Focuses on the perspective of appraisal as essentially an information-processing activity and builds a model of the rater as an imperfect observer, recaller, and processor of information about the behavior of ratees.

Another Perspective of Managers' Performance — From Subordinates
Management Review

☐ Argues for assessing subordinates' perceptions of their bosses' performance and discusses how this information can be used.

B.

BEHAVIORALLY-BASED, EFFECTIVENESS-BASED, AND COMPETENCY-BASED
PERFORMANCE APPRAISAL METHODS

Developing Behaviorally-Anchored Rating Scales (BARS)
Craig Eric Schneier and Richard W. Beatty

☐ Details a step-by-step procedure for designing a behaviorally-based appraisal system and argues for its utility.

Implementation of MBO
Stephen J. Carroll, Jr., and Henry L. Tosi, Jr.

☐ Reviews the basics of MBO, a commonly used appraisal system for managers.

Competency-Based Management
Alice Sargent

▫ Describes a recently developed approach to determine those personal characteristics that lead to successful performance in an organization.

C.

PERFORMANCE FEEDBACK AND REVIEW

The Performance Appraisal Interview: A Review, Implications, and Suggestions
Douglas Cederblom

▫ Reviews the findings of recent research on the appraisal interview.

▫ Provides practical suggestions for improving the effectiveness of this activity.

D.

LEGAL ISSUES IN PERFORMANCE APPRAISAL

Implications of Performance Appraisal Litigation for Personnel Decisions
Wayne F. Cascio and H. John Bernardin

▫ Cites and explains the impact of relevant court decisions on personnel systems, such as job analysis.

▫ Discusses the practical influence these decisions would have on those designing appraisal systems.

E.

PERFORMANCE APPRAISAL

Interview with Charlene Bradley

A.

GENERAL ISSUES IN APPRAISAL

Performance Appraisal Formats

Wayne F. Cascio

TYPES OF PERFORMANCE MEASURES

Objective Measures

Performance measures may be classified into two general types: objective and subjective. *Objective performance* measures include production data (dollar volume of sales, units produced, number of errors, amount of scrap) as well as personnel data (accidents, turnover, absences, tardiness). These variables directly define the goals of the organization, but they often suffer from several glaring weaknesses, the most serious of which are performance unreliability and modification of performance by situational characteristics. For example, dollar volume of sales is influenced by numerous factors beyond a particular salesperson's control — territory location, number of accounts in the territory, nature of the competition, distances between accounts, price and quality of the product, and so forth. Our objective in performance appraisal, however, is to judge an individual's *performance*, not factors beyond his or her control. Moreover, objective measures focus not on behavior, but rather on the outcomes or results of behavior. Admittedly, there will be some degree of overlap between behavior and results, but the two are qualitatively different (Levinson, 1976). Finally, in many jobs (e.g., those of middle managers), there simply are no good objective indices of performance, and in the case of personnel data, variables in this category are usually present in less than 5% of the cases examined (Landy & Trumbo, 1980). Hence, they are often useless as performance criteria. In short, although objective measures of performance are intuitively attractive, theoretical and practical limitations often make them unsuitable. Although they can be useful when used as supplements to supervisory judgments, correlations between objective and subjective measures are often low (Cascio & Valenzi, 1978) and when used as bases for personnel decisions, the combination of such measures may be weighed differently for different ethnic groups (Bass & Turner, 1973).

Subjective Measures

The disadvantages of objective measures have led researchers and managers to place major emphasis on *subjective measures* of job performance. However, since subjective

Wayne F. Cascio, *Applied Psychology in Personnel Management*, 2nd ed., 1982. Reprinted by permission of Reston Publishing Company, a Prentice-Hall Company, Englewood Cliffs, NJ 07632.

measures are dependent upon human judgment, they are prone to certain kinds of errors associated with the rating process. To be useful, they must be based on a careful analysis of the behaviors viewed as necessary and important for effective job performance.

We will have more to say about developmental procedures for rating formats in a later section, but for the present, it is important to point out that there is enormous variation in the types of subjective performance measures used by organizations. Some use a long list of elaborate rating scales; others use only a few simple scales; still others require managers to write a paragraph or two concerning the performance of each of their subordinates.

In addition, subjective measures of performance may be *relative* (in which comparisons are made among a group of ratees) or *absolute* (in which a ratee is described without reference to others). Regardless of their form, subjective performance appraisals frequently suffer from various behavioral barriers that limit their effectiveness. . . .

SYSTEMATIC APPROACHES TO SUBJECTIVE APPRAISAL

Performance appraisal systems were classified earlier either as relative or absolute. Within this taxonomy, the following methods may be distinguished:

Relative	*Absolute*
Rank order	Essays
Paired comparisons	Behavior checklists
Forced distribution	Critical incidents
	Graphic rating scales

Relative Rating Systems (Employee Comparisons)

Simple ranking requires only that a rater order all ratees from highest to lowest, from "best" employee to "worst" employee. *Alternation ranking* requires that the rater initially list all ratees on a sheet of paper. From this list the rater first chooses the best ratee (#1), then the worst ratee (#n), then the second best (#2), then the second worst (#n − 1), and so forth, alternating from the top to the bottom of the list until all ratees have been ranked.

Both simple and alternation ranking implicitly require a rater to compare each ratee with every other ratee, but systematic ratee-to-ratee comparison is not a built-in feature of these methods. For this we need *paired comparisons*. The number of pairs of ratees to be compared may be calculated from the formula $[n(n-1)]/2$. Hence if 10 individuals were being compared, $[10(9)]/2$ or 45 comparisons would be required. The rater's task is simply to choose the better of each pair, and each individual's rank is determined by counting the number of times he or she was rated superior.

Employee comparison methods are easy to explain and are helpful in making personnel decisions. They also provide useful criterion data in validation studies, for they effectively control leniency, severity, and central tendency errors. Like other systems, however, they suffer from several weaknesses that should be recognized.

Employees are usually compared only in terms of a single overall suitability category. The rankings, therefore, lack behavioral specificity, and may be subject to legal challenge (Cascio & Bernardin, 1981). Halo is merely obscured, not eliminated (Guion, 1965), and in addition, employee comparisons yield only ordinal data — data that give no indication of the relative distance between individuals. Moreover, it is often impossible to compare rankings across work groups, departments, or locations. The last two problems can be alleviated, however, by converting the ranks to normalized standard scores that form an approximately normal distribution. . . .

A further problem stems from the tendency of employee comparison methods to reward members of an inferior group and penalize members of a superior group. Reliability also may suffer, for when asked to re-rank all individuals at a later date, the extreme high or low rankings will probably remain stable, but the rankings in the middle of the scale may shift around considerably.

A final employee comparison method, the *forced distribution*, has been discussed previously. Its primary advantage is that it controls leniency, severity, and central tendency errors rather effectively, but it assumes that ratees conform to a normal distribution. This may introduce a great deal of error if a group of ratees, *as a group*, is either superior or substandard. In short, rather than eliminating error, forced distributions may simply introduce a different kind of error!

Absolute Rating Systems

Absolute rating systems enable a rater to describe a ratee without making direct reference to other ratees. Perhaps the simplest absolute rating system is the *narrative essay*, in which the rater is asked to describe, in writing, an individual's strengths, weaknesses, and potential, together with suggestions for improvement. The assumption underlying this approach is that a candid statement from a rater who is knowledgeable of a ratee's performance is just as valid as more formal and more complicated appraisal methods.

The major advantage of narrative essays (when they are done well) is that they can provide detailed feedback to ratees regarding their performance. On the other hand, essays are almost totally unstructured and they vary widely in length and content. Comparisons across individuals, groups, or departments are virtually impossible since different essays touch on different aspects of ratee performance or personal qualifications. Finally, essays provide only *qualitative* information; yet in order for the appraisals to serve as criteria or to be compared objectively and ranked for the purpose of a personnel decision, some form of rating that can be *quantified* is essential. Behavioral checklists provide one such scheme.

Behavioral Checklists

When using a behavioral checklist, the rater is provided with a series of descriptive statements of job-related behavior. His task is simply to indicate ("check") which of the statements are descriptive of the ratee in question. In this approach raters are not so much evaluators as they are reporters of job behavior. Moreover, ratings that are descriptive are likely to be higher in reliability than ratings that are evaluative (Stockford & Bissell, 1949).

To be sure, some job behaviors are more desirable than others; checklist items can, therefore, be scaled by using attitude scale construction methods (cf. Edwards, 1957). In one such method, the Likert method of *summated ratings*, a declarative statement (e.g., "she follows through on her sales") is followed by several response categories, such as "always," "very often," "fairly often," "occasionally," and "never." The rater simply checks the response category he feels best describes the ratee. Each response category is weighted — for example, from 5 ("always") to 1 ("never") if the statement describes desirable behavior, or vice versa if the statement describes undesirable behavior. An overall numerical rating for each individual can then be derived by summing the weights of the responses that were checked for each item, and scores for each performance dimension can be obtained by using item analysis procedures (cf. Anastasi, 1976).

The selection of response categories for summated rating scales is often made arbitrarily, with equal intervals between scale points simply assumed. Scaled lists of adverbial modifiers of frequency and amount are available, however, together with statistically optimal 4 to 9 point scales (Bass, Cascio, & O'Connor, 1974). Scaled values are also available for categories of agreement, evaluation, and frequency (Spector, 1976). A final issue concerns the optimal number of scale points for summated rating scales. Lissitz and Green (1975), using a Monte Carlo approach, have shown that for relatively homogeneous items, reliability increases up to five scale points, and levels off thereafter.

Checklists may also be constructed using Thurstone's method of *equal-appearing intervals*. First, a large number of statements that describe both desirable and undesirable job behaviors are generated, and judges sort the statements into piles representing steps along 7-, 9-, or 11-point scales of desirability. Means and standard deviations are then computed for each statement. Mean judgments represent scale values, while the standard deviations of judgments represent measures of statement ambiguity. Statements with large standard deviations are discarded, for they apparently mean different things to different people. Unambiguous statements representing the full range of scale values are then assembled into a checklist for rating. Fortunately, this rather laborious preliminary effort is not really necessary since Uhrbrock (1950, 1961) has published lists of 724 and 2,000 scaled items, each with mean and standard deviation. An independent check on the stability of these scale values, using a different sample of judges and a different technique, correlated .97 with those reported by Uhrbrock (Prien & Campbell, 1957).

An example of an equal-appearing intervals scale is presented in Table 1; in practice, raters would not be shown statement means and standard deviations. They simply check as many statements as apply to describe a particular ratee, and an individual's overall rating is equal to the sum of the scale values of the items checked.

The item "has surly attitude" would ordinarily be dropped from the scale because it is ambiguous (S.D. = 12.1). This ability to evaluate statement ambiguity is clearly the main advantage of the equal appearing intervals approach.

Halo has not been a serious problem with checklists since they yield only an overall

TABLE 1
Sample Equal-Appearing Intervals Scale

Item	*Mean*	*S.D.*
Is a dynamic leader who stimulates enthusiasm	109.4	2.4
Is very well informed on all phases of work	99.4	7.5
Conveys ideas well to others	89.4	5.6
Learns quickly	78.8	5.9
Doesn't waste much time	68.1	6.3
Makes occasional errors and mistakes	58.1	3.9
Wanders from subject in conversation	48.8	4.8
Is slow	37.5	5.6
Too often needs to be shown what to do next	28.1	6.3
Has surly attitude	18.8	12.1
Cannot be trusted	10.6	2.4

Adapted from Uhrbrock, R. S. 2000 scaled items. *Personnel Psychology*, 1961, *14*, 375–420.

summary rating. However, there is no control for leniency, although special scoring procedures can be developed for this purpose (Bass, 1956). Despite these advantages, it is sometimes difficult for a rater to give diagnostic feedback based on checklist ratings, for he does not see the scale values of the items he chooses. On balance, the many advantages of checklists (developed either by Likert or Thurstone scaling procedures) probably account for their widespread popularity in organizations today.

Forced-Choice Systems

A special type of behavioral checklist is known as the forced-choice system — a technique developed specifically to reduce leniency errors and to establish objective standards of comparison between individuals (Sisson, 1948). In order to accomplish this, checklist statements are arranged in groups, from which the rater chooses statements that are most or least descriptive of the ratee. An overall rating (score) for each individual is then derived by applying a special scoring key to the rater's descriptions.

Forced-choice scales are constructed according to two statistical properties of the checklist items: (1) *discriminability*, a measure of the degree to which an item differentiates effective from ineffective workers, and (2) *preference*, an index of the degree to which the quality expressed in an item is valued (i.e., is socially desirable) by people. The rationale of the forced-choice system requires that items be paired so that they appear equally attractive (socially desirable) to the rater. Theoretically, then, the selection of any single item in a pair should be based solely upon the item's discriminating power, not its social desirability.

Although many different item arrangements have been used, Berkshire and Highland (1953) found optimal a form that included four statements, all favorable (and equally socially desirable), from which the rater selects the two statements most like the ratee. It was most resistant to deliberately induced bias, it demonstrated adequate reliability and validity, and it was one of the two forms most preferred by the raters. For example, in rating Air Force instructors, the following tetrad was used by Berkshire and Highland (1953):

a. Patient with slow learners.

b. Lectures with confidence.

c. Keeps the interest and attention of class.

d. Acquaints classes with the objective for each lesson in advance.

All four statements are approximately equal in preference value, but only *a* and *c* were found to be characteristic of effective instructors. Modifications of this basic forced-choice system have been tried (Kay, 1959; Obradovic, 1970), with mixed success.

The main advantage claimed for forced-choice scales is that a rater cannot distort a person's ratings higher or lower than is warranted since he or she has no way of knowing which statements to check in order to do so. If the rater deliberately attempts to be lenient in assigning ratings, he or she is most likely to choose statements that are socially desirable, but can also be said of almost everyone, and therefore do not discriminate effective from ineffective performers. Hence, leniency should theoretically be reduced. However, when forced-choice scales have been administered first under guidance conditions and later under employment selection conditions, marked distortion in a positive direction has been observed (Hedberg, 1962; Maher, 1959), although this is not always the case (Gordon & Stapleton, 1956).

Forced-choice scales can always be beaten by using an "ideal employee" strategy. When a rater wants to give average employee Linda Middle a high rating, the rater simply describes the very best employee he knows on Linda Middle's forced-choice form. Forced-choice systems do not, in general, control for halo (King et al., 1980). They usually give only a single, global indication of merit, rather than ratings of specific dimensions of performance. Sets of items are usually not developed for specific dimensions because a great deal of time and effort is required to write and scale items and then to develop tetrads that: (a) are matched on social desirability, and (b) discriminate adequately among individuals. For example, King et al. (1980) evaluated 1,200 one-page essays of effective state trooper performance in order to develop a 4-dimension forced-choice instrument.

There are two further problems with forced-choice scales. The most serious is rater resistance. Since control is removed from the rater, he or she cannot be sure just how she rated a subordinate. Raters often become irritated with forced-choice scales; they want to say openly how they rate someone and not be second-guessed or tricked into making "honest" appraisals (Oberg, 1972). Finally, forced-choice forms are of little use (and may even have a negative effect) in performance appraisal interviews, for the rater is unaware of the scale values of the items he chooses. In order to overcome these difficulties, some form of critical incident scale may be used.

Critical Incidents

This method of performance appraisal has generated a great deal of interest in recent years, and several variations of the basic idea are currently in use. As described by Flanagan (1954), the critical requirements of a job are those behaviors that make a crucial difference between doing a job effectively and doing it ineffectively. *Critical incidents* are simply reports by knowledgeable observers of things employees did that were especially effective or ineffective in accomplishing parts of their jobs. Critical incidents are recorded for each employee by supervisors, as they occur. Thus, they provide a behaviorally based starting point for appraising performance. For example, in observing a police officer chasing an armed robbery suspect down a busy street, a supervisor recorded the following:

> June 22, officer Mitchell withheld fire in a situation calling for the use of weapons where gunfire would endanger innocent bystanders.

Critical incidents typically provide information on both the static and dynamic aspects of a job. These little anecdotes force attention on the situational determinants of job behavior and also on ways of doing the job successfully that may be unique to the person described (individual dimensionality). The critical incidents method looks like a natural for performance appraisal interviews because supervisors can focus on actual job behavior rather than on vaguely defined traits. Performance, not personality, is being judged. Ratees receive meaningful feedback and they can see what changes in their job behavior will be necessary in order for them to improve. While the ratee may not agree with his supervisor's standards, at least he knows what those standards are (Oberg, 1972). In addition, when a large number of critical incidents are collected, abstracted, and categorized, they can provide a rich storehouse of information about job and organizational problems in general and are particularly well-suited for establishing objectives for training programs (Flanagan & Burns, 1955).

As with other approaches to performance appraisal, the critical incidents method also has its drawbacks. First of all, it is time-consuming and burdensome for supervisors to record incidents for all of their subordinates on a daily or even weekly basis. Feedback may, therefore, be delayed. Moreover, the rater sets the standards by which subordinates are judged; yet subordinates are likely to be more motivated if they have some say in setting their own behavioral standards. Finally, in their narrative form, incidents do not readily lend themselves to quantification, which, as we noted earlier, poses problems in between-individual and between-group comparisons as well as in statistical analyses.

For these reasons two variations of the original idea have been suggested. Kirchner and Dunnette (1957), for example, used the method to develop a behavioral checklist (using the method of summated ratings) for rating sales performance. After incidents were abstracted and classified, selected items were assembled into a checklist. For example,

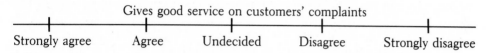

Gives good service on customers' complaints

| Strongly agree | Agree | Undecided | Disagree | Strongly disagree |

A second modification has been the development of behaviorally anchored rating scales, an approach we will treat more fully in the next section.

Graphic Rating Scales

Probably the most widely used method of performance appraisal is the *graphic rating scale*. Landy and Trumbo (1980), for example, reported that 72% of the validation studies published in the *Journal of Applied Psychology* between 1955 and 1975 relied on some form of rating scale, examples of which are presented in Figure 1.

In terms of the amount of structure provided, the scales differ in three ways: (1) the degree to which the meaning of the response categories is defined, (2) the degree to which the individual who is interpreting the ratings (e.g., a personnel manager or researcher) can tell clearly what response was intended, and (3) the degree to which the performance dimension being rated is defined for the rater.

On a graphic rating scale each point is defined on a continuum. Hence, in order to make meaningful distinctions in performance within dimensions, scale points must be defined unambiguously for the rater. This process is called *anchoring*. Scale *a* uses qualitative end anchors only. Scale *b* includes numerical and verbal anchors, while scales *c*, *d*, and *f* use verbal anchors only. These anchors are almost worthless, however, since what constitutes high and low quality or "outstanding" and "unsatisfactory" is left completely up to the rater. A "commendable" for one rater may only be a "competent" for another. Scale *e* is better, for the numerical anchors are described in terms of what "quality" means in that context.

The scales also differ in the relative ease with which a person interpreting the ratings can tell exactly what response was intended by the rater. In scale *a*, for example, the particular value that the rater had in mind is a mystery. Scale *e* is less ambiguous in this respect.

Finally, the scales differ in terms of the clarity of the definition of the performance dimension in question. In terms of Figure 1, what does quality mean? Is quality for a nurse the same as quality for a cashier? Scales *a* and *c* offer almost no help in defining quality, scale *b* combines quantity and quality together into a single dimension (although they are typically independent), and scales *d* and *e* define quality in different terms altogether (thoroughness, dependability, and neatness versus accuracy, effectiveness, and freedom from error). Scale *f* is an improvement in the sense that, while quality is taken to represent accuracy, effectiveness, initiative, and neatness (a combination of scale *d* and *e* definitions), at least separate ratings are required for each *aspect* of quality.

An improvement over all the examples in Figure 1 is shown next. It is part of a graphic rating scale using to rate nurses. The response categories are defined clearly, an individual interpreting the rating can tell what response the rater intended, and the performance dimension is defined in terms that both rater and ratee understand and can agree on.

Graphic rating scales may not yield the depth of narrative essays or critical incidents, but they: (a) are less time-consuming to develop and administer, (b) permit quantitative results to be determined, (c) promote consideration of more than one performance dimension, and (d) are standardized and therefore comparable across individuals. On the other hand, graphic rating scales give maximum control to the rater,

FIGURE 1
Examples of Graphic Rating Scales

(a) Quality   High └___┴__✓__┴_____┴___•_┘ Low

JOB PERFORMANCE—	LEVEL	Employee's and Supervisor's Comments and Suggestions for Making Improvement
(b) QUALITY AND QUANTITY OF WORK PERFORMED: Consider neatness and accuracy as well as volume and consistency in carrying out work assignments.		

KEY TO LEVELS OF PERFORMANCE
3. COMMENDABLE
2. COMPETENT
1. NEEDS IMPROVING

Factor	OUT-STANDING	ABOVE AVERAGE	AVERAGE	BELOW AVERAGE	MARGINAL
(c) QUALITY OF WORK Caliber of work produced or accomplished compared with accepted quality standards.	◯	◯	◯	◯	◯
	Comments:				

(d)

QUALITY OF WORK
(Consider employee's thoroughness, dependability and neatness in regard to the work.)

Unsatisfactory		Satisfactory		Excellent		Outstanding	

Comments _____

(e)

QUALITY OF WORK
Accuracy and effectiveness of work. Freedom from error.

Consistently good quality. Errors rare.	4	Usually good quality, few errors.	3	Passable work if closely supervised.	2	Frequent errors. Cannot be depended upon to be accurate.	1

COMMENTS:

(f)

QUALITY OF WORK

☐ Accuracy
☐ The achievement of objectives; effectiveness
☐ Initiative and resourcefulness
☐ Neatness of work product
☐ Other _____

CHECK ITEMS
☐ +	Excels	☐ −	Unsatisfactory
☑	Satisfactory	☐ NA	Not Applicable
☐ 0	Needs Improvement		

EMERGENCY PROCEDURE AWARENESS is the knowledge an individual has of his or her DR.
HEART, STAT, CODE 13, CODE D and CODE RED responsibilities

1 2 3	4 5 6	7 8 9	10 11 12	13 14 15
Unaware or not interested	Needs additional training	Knows responsibilities and has participated in drills	Superior knowledge of responsibilities and performance during drills	Very thorough knowledge of responsibilities; able to assist in training of others.

Comments: _____

_____

_____

thereby exercising no control over leniency, severity, central tendency, or halo errors. For this reason, they have been widely criticized. Nevertheless, when simple graphic rating scales have been compared against more sophisticated forced-choice ratings, the graphic scale consistently proved just as reliable and valid (King et al., 1980) and was more acceptable to raters (Berkshire & Highland, 1953). Now let us consider two interesting variations of graphic rating scales — mixed standard scales and behaviorally anchored rating scales.

Mixed Standard Scales. These are designed specifically to minimize halo and leniency errors and to permit evaluations of the reliability with which each individual is rated, each scale rates, and each rater rates (Blanz & Ghiselli, 1972). The procedure is as follows. Items that discriminate effective from ineffective performance are first obtained from knowledgeable persons (usually supervisors). For each performance dimension to be rated, three items are chosen that represent good, average, and poor performance, respectively. These are "standards" or degrees of performance, and the rater must respond to each standard, indicating whether he considers the ratee to be better than the description (+), to fit the description (0), or to be worse than the description (−).

The performance dimensions and the standards describing them are then randomly mixed so that no clear order-of-merit descriptions exist for each dimension. A mixed standard scale using only three (of the 18) dimensions used by Blanz and Ghiselli (1972) is presented in Figure 2.

If all ratings are assigned accurately, then whenever the rater checks one statement as "fits the ratee" (0), all statements in that scale that describe superior behavior should be checked as "the ratee is poorer than this statement" (−), and all those that describe inferior behavior should be checked as "the ratee is better than this statement" (+). If all three standards in a scale are checked (+), then in the rater's opinion, the ratee is truly exceptional on this dimension since he or she exceeds even the best of the three standards. On the other hand, if all three standards are checked (−), then according to the rater the ratee is very poor since his or her performance is worse than even the poorest of the three standards. According to the scoring scheme in Figure 3, the individual in Figure 2 received a score of 6 on dimension I (efficiency), a 4 on dimension II (self-confidence), and a 7 on dimension III (report-making).

Obviously, not all raters will respond accurately and logically. For example, a rater might say that an individual was worse than the "poor" statement but better than the "average" statement. In this case, the scoring scheme in Figure 3 would not apply. Saal (1979) has developed a scoring scheme that will handle such logically inconsistent errors, but results to date do not indicate that the new scoring scheme is qualitatively superior to the old one.

FIGURE 2

Mixed Standard Rating Scale Where I, II, and III Represent the Dimensions of Efficiency, Self-confidence, and Report-Making, Respectively, and "G," "A," and "P" Represent Good, Average, and Poor Performance (Adapted from Blanz, F., & Ghiselli, E. E. The mixed standard scale: A new rating system. *Personnel Psychology,* 1972, *25,* 185–199.)

		Rating
II.	1. Has normal self-confidence, with only occasional uncertainty. He usually is open and assured. (A)	0
I.	2. There is some lack of efficiency on his part. He may take too much time to complete his assignments, and sometimes he does not really finish them. (P)	+
III.	3. Both his written and oral reports are well formulated, thorough, and well thought out. They rarely need additional explanation. (G)	+
II.	4. He is a little shy and uncertain. Occasionally avoids situations which require him to take a position. (P)	+
I.	5. He is efficient enough, usually getting through his assignments and work in a reasonable time. (A)	+
III.	6. Sometimes his reports are so incomplete and poorly organized that they are of little value, or must be done over. (P)	+
I.	7. He is quick and efficient, able to keep his work on schedule. He really gets going on a new task. (G)	0
II.	8. Behaves confidently. Reacts in all situations without hesitation and with assurance. (G)	−
III.	9. His reports are useful and meaningful, but they usually require some additional explanations. (A)	+

The rationale for mixing standards stems directly from the logic of forced-choice formats — namely, that halo and leniency are likely to be reduced if ratings are not made on a scale with statements arranged in an obvious order-of-merit hierarchy. Empirical findings lend support to these hypotheses (Dickinson & Zellinger, 1980; Saal & Landy, 1977). In addition, raters tend to use all seven scale points. A final advantage of mixed

FIGURE 3

Scoring Scheme for a Mixed Standard Scale
(Adapted from Blanz & Ghiselli, 1972.)

Statements			Points
G	A	P	
+	+	+	7
0	+	+	6
−	+	+	5
−	0	+	4
−	−	+	3
−	−	0	2
−	−	−	1

+ = the ratee is better than the statement
0 = the statement fits the ratee
− = the ratee is worse than the statement

standard scales, and one that is not to be taken lightly, is that they are capable of providing indices of the extent of error for different raters and ratees and for different scales.

Mixed standard scales are not without their disadvantages, however. Completion of each statement for each ratee is a painstaking task. When a large number of statements must be responded to individually, negative rater reaction may be anticipated, and interrater reliabilities may be low. Scoring may also be time-consuming (although computer scoring is possible). Finally, since items and dimensions are both scrambled, mixed standard scales may not be very useful in performance appraisal interviews. Nevertheless, the mixed standard format is well suited for other uses of performance appraisals; hopefully, its advantages will stimulate further development and more widespread use in the future.

Behaviorally Anchored Rating Scales. So far, it seems that the performance appraisal systems that are most acceptable to raters (e.g., narrative essays, employee comparisons, graphic scales) are often least acceptable in terms of their psychometric characteristics. Conversely, those that are psychometrically acceptable (e.g., forced-choice scales) are often resisted by raters. Where is the happy medium? According to Smith and Kendall (1963):

> Better ratings can be obtained, in our opinion, not by trying to trick the rater (as in forced-choice scales) but by helping him to rate. We should ask him questions which he can honestly answer about behaviors which he can observe. We should reassure him that his answers will not be misinterpreted, and we should provide a basis by which he and others can check his answers. (p. 151)

Their procedure is as follows. At an initial conference, groups of workers and/or supervisors attempt to identify and define all of the important dimensions of effective performance for a particular job. Graphically:

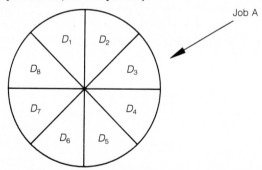

A second group then generates, for each dimension, critical incidents illustrating effective, average, and ineffective performance. A third group is then given a list of dimensions and their definitions, along with a randomized list of the critical incidents generated by the second group. Their task is to sort or allocate incidents into the dimensions they best represent. Graphically:

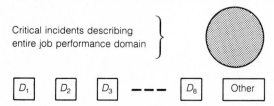

This procedure is known as *retranslation* since it resembles the quality control check that is used to insure the adequacy of translations from one language into another. Material is translated into a foreign language and then retranslated back into the original by an independent translator. In the context of performance appraisal, this procedure insures that the meaning of both the job dimensions and the behavioral incidents chosen to illustrate them is specific and clear. Incidents are eliminated if there is not clear agreement among judges (usually 60–80%) regarding the dimension to which each incident belongs. Dimensions are eliminated if incidents are not allocated to them. Conversely, dimensions may be added if many incidents are allocated to the "other" category.

Each of the items within dimensions that survived the retranslation procedure is then presented to a fourth group of judges, whose task is to place a scale value on each incident (e.g., in terms of a 7- or 9-point scale from "highly effective behavior" to "grossly ineffective behavior"). Graphically:

D_1	D_2	...	D_8
7 C.I.	7 C.I.		7 C.I.
6 C.I.	6 C.I.		6 C.I.
5 C.I.	5 C.I.		5 C.I.
4 C.I.	4 C.I.		4 C.I.
3 C.I.	3 C.I.		3 C.I.
2 C.I.	2 C.I.		2 C.I.
1 C.I.	1 C.I.		1 C.I.

Means and standard deviations for each incident are then computed. Items in the final scale for each dimension must have mean scale values covering the entire range of performance and low standard deviations. The end product looks like that in Figure 4.

Finally, the behaviorally anchored rating scales (BARS) are pilot-tested with a sample of supervisors who are asked to rate their subordinates on each of the dimensions. Each subordinate is rated independently by at least two raters, and the ratings are correlated to provide an estimate of interrater reliability. Scale scores are also intercorrelated as a check on dimension independence. Periodically thereafter (e.g., annually), the behavioral anchors are checked for their continued relevance, clarity, and scale values.

BARS development is a long, painstaking process that may require many individuals. Moreover, separate BARS must be developed for dissimilar jobs. Consequently, this approach may not be practical for many organizations. As BARS grow in popularity and use, however, it is likely that scales that have generality across organizations (e.g., BARS for computer programmers, purchasing agents) will be developed.

The retranslation approach to developing job behavior rating scales holds considerable promise and many advantages are claimed for it. BARS are rooted in, and referable to, actual job behavior, not vaguely defined personality traits. A second advantage may be attributed to an aspect of the developmental procedure that is unrelated to the measurement of performance *per se* — namely, intense rater-ratee involvement throughout all phases of BARS development. High participation serves a dual purpose: (1) it insures acceptability of the resulting scales and a commitment to make them work, and (2) it guarantees that the scales are relevant to the jobs in question. Performance dimensions and behavioral anchors are rigorously defined and can be distinguished from one another easily and accurately. Moreover, the scales are phrased in the jargon of the users, not the jargon of the psychologist or scale developer. Finally, even though specific behaviors may be observed in different situations, they are referred to a common set of expectations that serves as a mutual frame of reference (Smith & Kendall, 1963).

FIGURE 4

103

*A. GENERAL ISSUES
IN APPRAISAL*

Scaled Expectations Rating Scale for the Effectiveness with Which the Department Manager
Supervises His Sales Personnel

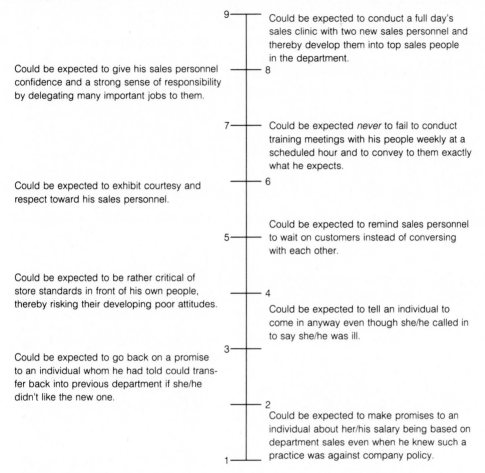

9 — Could be expected to conduct a full day's sales clinic with two new sales personnel and thereby develop them into top sales people in the department.

Could be expected to give his sales personnel confidence and a strong sense of responsibility by delegating many important jobs to them. — 8

7 — Could be expected *never* to fail to conduct training meetings with his people weekly at a scheduled hour and to convey to them exactly what he expects.

Could be expected to exhibit courtesy and respect toward his sales personnel. — 6

5 — Could be expected to remind sales personnel to wait on customers instead of conversing with each other.

Could be expected to be rather critical of store standards in front of his own people, thereby risking their developing poor attitudes. — 4

Could be expected to tell an individual to come in anyway even though she/he called in to say she/he was ill.

3 —

Could be expected to go back on a promise to an individual whom he had told could transfer back into previous department if she/he didn't like the new one.

2 —

Could be expected to make promises to an individual about her/his salary being based on department sales even when he knew such a practice was against company policy.

1 —

Source: From Campbell, J. P., Dunnette, M. D., Arvey, R. D., & Hellervik, L. V. The development and evaluation of behaviorally based rating scales. *Journal of Applied Psychology,* 1973, 57, 15–22. (Copyright © 1973 by the American Psychological Association. Reprinted by permission.)

    How have BARS worked in practice? An enormous amount of research on BARS has accumulated over the past decade, and much of it has been summarized by Dunnette and Borman (1979), Jacobs et al. (1980), and Schwab, Heneman, and DeCotiis (1975). At the risk of oversimplification, major known effects of BARS with respect to *quantitative* criteria are summarized in Table 2.

    In short, there is little empirical evidence to support the superiority of BARS over other performance appraisal systems. Moreover, several *qualitative* criteria for appraisal systems have been relatively ignored by empirical studies of BARS (as well as by other appraisal systems). For example (Jacobs et al., 1980):

Relevance — any rating scale construction method should incorporate a job analysis. BARS can serve as a job analysis procedure (Blood, 1974), but to do so,

TABLE 2
Known Effects of BARS

Participation	Participation does seem to enhance the validity of ratings, but no more so for BARS than for simple graphic rating scales.
Leniency, Central tendency, Halo	BARS not superior to other methods.
Reliability	BARS not superior to other methods (reliabilities across dimensions in published studies range from about .52 to .76)
External validity	Moderate (R_s^2 of .21 to .47 — Shapira & Shirom, 1980) relative to the upper limits of validity in performance ratings (Borman, 1978).
Comparisons with other formats	BARS no better or worse than other methods.
Variance in dependent variables associated with differences in rating systems	Less than 5%
Convergent/discriminant validity	Low convergent validity, extremely low discriminant validity

information regarding importance, frequency, level of difficulty, and consequence of error for the examples/dimensions must be included.

Data Availability — three questions are subsumed under this topic: (1) Is direct observation of performance possible or must inferences be made in the absence of direct ratee contact? (2) Who should do appraisal — supervisors, peers, self, subordinates, or clients served? (3) What additional performance data (e.g., production records) are available to augment the appraisal? Little research has been done using BARS to answer questions 1 or 2.

Practicality — consideration of time and cost for both development and implementation of an appraisal system are essential. The organization should be able to offset these costs by more effective utilization of performance appraisal data. The use of BARS is problematic when viewed in this light. The job specificity of BARS limits its application to many jobs which are occupied by only a small number of incumbents, and an extensive investment in time (and money) may be required to develop and implement the scales. On the other hand, a longitudinal study of BARS with engineers reported more favorable attitudes toward the system and improved job performance (Ivancevich, 1980).

Equivalence — the situation under which all ratees are evaluated and the ways in which different raters actually evaluate ratees should be comparable. For BARS systems, the question is whether one set of BARS can be used across several job positions.

Interpretability — the extent to which all raters (and ratees) interpret observed behaviors in a similar manner. While research indicates that BARS examples are perceived similarly by a group (Zedeck et al., 1976), this is probably not the case for other methods. For example, using a graphic rating scale, does "above average" mean the same thing to all raters?

In summary, if BARS are to be used *solely* for performance ratings, simpler systems might well be used. This is a narrow view of the problem though, as Jacobs et al. (1980) pointed out:

What is desperately needed is a more far reaching approach to performance evaluation, one which includes scale construction and utilization as a starting point, incorporates performance feedback, and culminates in organizational efforts toward training, selection, placement, and promotion. In this light BARS has a future. To continue the current research applications is to uncover nothing new and to do a disservice to the methodology specifically and the area of performance evaluation in general. (p. 635)

In weighing the costs/benefits of BARS as opposed to other types of appraisal systems, these additional benefits should not be overlooked. Formal performance appraisal systems are neither worthless (as some critics contend) nor panaceas (as some of us might wish). They are, at the very least, a commendable attempt to make visible, and hence improvable, a set of essential organization activities (Oberg, 1972). BARS can be of considerable value here because of the wealth of additional information they provide.

REFERENCES

Anastasi, A. *Psychological Testing* (4th edition). New York: Macmillan, 1976.

Bass, A. R. and Turner, J. N. Ethnic group differences in relationships among criteria of job performance. *Journal of Applied Psychology*, 1973, 57, 101–109.

Bass, B. M. Reducing leniency in merit ratings. *Personnel Psychology*, 1956, 9, 359–369.

Bass, B. M., Cascio, W. F. and O'Connor, F. J. Magnitude estimations of expressions of frequency and amount. *Journal of Applied Psychology*, 1974, 59, 313–320.

Berkshire, J. R. and Highland, R. W. Forced-choice performance rating: A methodological study. *Personnel Psychology*, 1953, 6, 355–378.

Blanz, F. and Ghiselli, E. E. The mixed standard scale: A new rating system. *Personnel Psychology*, 1972, 25, 185–199.

Blood, M. R. Spin-offs from behavior expectation scale procedures. *Journal of Applied Psychology*, 1974, 59, 513–515.

Borman, W. C. Exploring upper limits of reliability and validity in job performance ratings. *Journal of Applied Psychology*, 1978, 63, 135–144.

Cascio, W. F., and Bernardin, H. J. Implications of performance appraisal litigation for personnel decisions. *Personnel Psychology*, 1981, 34, 211–226.

Cascio, W. F. and Valenzi, E. R. Relations among criteria of police performance. *Journal of Applied Psychology*, 1978, 63, 22–28.

Dickinson, T. L., and Zellinger, P. M. A comparison of the behaviorally anchored rating and mixed standard scale formats. *Journal of Applied Psychology*, 1980, 65, 147–154.

Dunnette, M. D. and Borman, W. S. Personnel selection and classification systems. *Annual Review of Psychology*, 1979, 30, 477–525.

Edwards, A. L. *Techniques of attitude scale construction*. New York: Appleton-Century-Crofts, 1957.

Flanagan, J. C. The critical incident technique. *Psychological Bulletin*, 1954, 51, 327–358.

Flanagan, J. C. and Burns, R. K. The employee performance record: A new appraisal and development tool. *Harvard Business Review*, 1955, 33, 95–102.

Gordon, L. V. and Stapleton, E. S. Fakability of a forced-choice personality test under realistic high school employment conditions. *Journal of Applied Psychology,* 1956, *40,* 258–262.

Guion, R. M. *Personnel testing.* New York: McGraw-Hill, 1965.

Hedberg, R. More on forced-choice test fakability. *Journal of Applied Psychology,* 1962, *46,* 125–127.

Ivancevich, J. M. A longitudinal study of behavioral expectation scales: Attitudes and performance. *Journal of Applied Psychology,* 1980, *65,* 139–146.

Jacobs, R., Kafry, D., and Zedeck, S. Expectations of behaviorally anchored rating scales. *Personnel Psychology,* 1980, *33,* 595–640.

Kay, B. R. The use of critical incidents in a forced-choice scale. *Journal of Applied Psychology,* 1959, *43,* 269–270.

King, L. M., Hunter, J. E. and Schmidt, F. L. Halo in a multi-dimensional forced-choice performance evaluation scale. *Journal of Applied Psychology,* 1980, *65,* 507–516.

Kirchner, W. K. and Dunnette, M. D. Identifying the critical factors in successful salesmanship. *Personnel,* 1957, *34,* 54–59.

Landy, F. J. and Trumbo, D. A. *Psychology of work behavior* (rev. ed.). Homewood, IL: Dorsey, 1980.

Levinson, H. Appraisal of *what* performance? *Harvard Business Review,* 1976, *54,* 30–32, 34, 36, 40, 44, 46, 160.

Lissitz, R. W. and Green, S. R. Effect of the number of scale points on reliability: A Monte Carlo approach. *Journal of Applied Psychology,* 1975, *60,* 10–13.

Maher, H. Studies of transparency in forced-choice scales: I. Evidence of transparency. *Journal of Applied Psychology,* 1959, *43,* 275–278.

Oberg, W. Make performance appraisal relevant. *Harvard Business Review,* 1972, *50,* 61–67.

Obradovic, J. Modification of the forced-choice method as a criterion of job proficiency. *Journal of Applied Psychology,* 1970, *54,* 228–233.

Prien, E. P. and Campbell, J. T. Stability of rating scale statements. *Personnel Psychology,* 1957, *10,* 305–309.

Saal, F. E. Mixed standard rating scale: A consistent system for numerically coding inconsistent response combinations. *Journal of Applied Psychology,* 1979, *64,* 422–428.

Saal, F. E. and Landy, F. L. The mixed standard rating scale: An evaluation. *Organizational Behavior and Human Performance,* 1977, *18,* 19–35.

Schwab, D. P., Heneman, H. G. III, and DeCotiis, T. A. Behaviorally anchored rating scales: A review of the literature. *Personnel Psychology,* 1975, *28,* 549–562.

Shapira, Z. and Shirom, A. New issues in the use of behaviorally anchored rating scales: Level of analysis, the effects of incident frequency, and external validation. *Journal of Applied Psychology,* 1980, *65,* 517–523.

Sisson, D. E. Forced choice, the new Army rating. *Personnel Psychology,* 1948, *1,* 365–381.

Smith, P. C. and Kendall, L. M. Retranslation of expectations: An approach to the construction of unambiguous anchors for rating scales. *Journal of Applied Psychology,* 1963, *47,* 149–155.

Spector, P. E. Choosing response categories for simulating rating scales. *Journal of Applied Psychology,* 1976, *61,* 374–375.

Stockford, L. and Bissel, H. W. Factors involved in establishing a merit rating scale. *Personnel*, 1949, 26, 94–116.

Uhrbrock, R. S. Standardization of 724 rating scale statements. *Personnel Psychology*, 1950, 3, 285–316.

Uhrbrock, R. S. 2000 scaled items. *Personnel Psychology*, 1961, 14, 375–420.

Zedeck, S., Jacobs, R. and Kafry, D. Behavioral expectations: Development of parallel forms and analysis of scale assumptions. *Journal of Applied Psychology*, 1976, 61, 112–115.

The Rater as Information Processor

Stephen J. Carroll and Craig E. Schneier

Most people who have either provided or received an appraisal of performance in an organization would agree that there are some very difficult problems associated with this task. While there are potential advantages and disadvantages to each of a number of appraisal formats, experience and research (see, e.g., Landy and Farr, 1980) have shown that rating format or instrument differences do relatively little to improve the performance appraisal *process*.

The difficult problems for raters and ratees arise in the judgmental or evaluative aspects of appraisal: two raters observe and rate the same ratee, but judge performance differently; or a rater and ratee disagree about an evaluation. This [article] explores the nature of such differences, analyzing rater and ratee characteristics that account for them. The judgmental nature of appraisal is emphasized. A view of judgment in PAR [Performance Appraisal and Review] systems includes how information about performance is *processed* — observed, stored, categorized, selected, constructed, organized, recalled — in order to form an evaluation.*

This process occurs before the measurement or rating process (i.e., the use of rating scales or other types of formats) because it occurs before the rating is made. Insights into the rater's information-processing activities and other characteristics of raters and ratees can do much to augment our understanding and prediction of what will be said or written about a ratee in a PAR system.

---

*Recently, an emphasis in performance appraisal research and theory has been on the information-processing approach, a view that much can be gained by assessing the process used by raters to make their evaluations of ratee performance (see, e.g., Landy and Farr, 1980; Feldman, 1981; Banks, 1979; Borman, 1978, 1979; Lewin and Layman, 1979; Schneier, 1977; Stone and Shlusher, 1974).

FIGURE 1

Classes of Rater (and Ratee) Characteristics That Influence the Appraisal Process

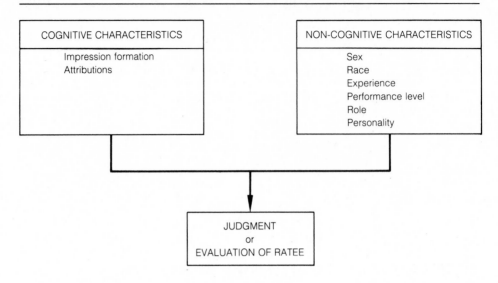

Two Classes of Characteristics That Explain Judgments

As we begin to dismantle the complex process of evaluating performance in organizations, two broad classes of rater (and ratee) characteristics can be distinguished (see Figure 1). The first class refers to the information-processing activity of the rater as he or she makes judgments. Included in this class of characteristics are impression-formation processes and attribution processes. As noted above, these activities help explain how a judgment is formed in a rater's mind. Hence they can be loosely called "cognitive" processes (the subject of this chapter).

The second class of characteristics that affect the judgments made in an appraisal situation are external to a rater's (or ratee's) cognitive processes and are more or less fixed or static aspects. Such variables as sex, experience, race, and role of the rater are examples, along with various personality characteristics. . . .

IMPLICIT PERSONALITY THEORIES: THE FORMATION OF IMPRESSIONS OF RATEES

When someone encounters another person in almost any setting, he or she is interested in finding out what the other person is like. As a result of interactions, even fleeting ones, we form impressions of others. We see people as friendly or unfriendly, intelligent or dull, ambitious or apathetic, trustworthy or devious. But how are our impressions formed? We typically do not have access to others' innermost thoughts and feelings and are therefore uncertain whether a specific comment was, for example, actually intended to be unfriendly or was harmless. We must therefore *infer* various things about people based upon the behavior we observe.

Using the sample of behavior we observe and our own feelings, thoughts, motives, and the manner in which we select and process this behavioral information, we *construct* our own version of reality (see Figure 2). This version is often quite different from that which others construct, so we may find ourselves constructing a picture of someone in very positive terms while a friend informs us that he or she has decided

FIGURE 2
A Simple Model of the Formation of Impressions

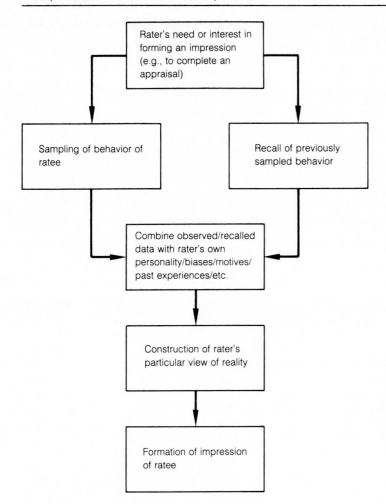

that the same person is not to be trusted. In addition, our initial impressions of, for example, intelligence, often are not confirmed by subsequent data.

In a PAR situation, raters are called upon to go through the same inferential process in order to make judgments about others. They observe samples of ratees' behavior, construct their version of reality, and form impressions. The inferences they make, however, are quite often based upon their individual theories of the manner in which various aspects of behavior are related, as well as the way in which they infer personal characteristics from observed behavior. Further, raters make inferences about traits *not* observed from those they have observed.

In short, raters possess their own theories of personality which guide their inferences about others. These theories are often called *implicit personality theories,* since they are not articulated overtly by the persons making the inferences. Researchers have been able to identify and describe the implicit personality theories held by groups of people and have even been able to demonstrate that an entire set of characteristics, forming a clear impression, can be attributed to people on the basis of a very small sample of behavior (see DiNisi and Pritchard, 1978; Norman and Goldberg, 1966; Schneider, 1973).

Authors in this area have stated that the inferences made about others have much more to do with the characteristics of the person making the inference than they do with the characteristics of the ratee (Hakel, 1974). The implication of this statement is enormous for the PAR situation. Could it be that ratings are as much, or more, a result of the *rater's* judgment characteristics and processes than of a *ratee's* actual performance?

The Development of Implicit Personality Theories. The work on implicit personality theories is fairly recent, falling within the broad framework of human information-processing, specifically, the processing of information about others typically referred to as *person perception* (Schneider, Hastorf, and Ellsworth, 1979). Initially, implicit personality theorists were concerned with the assumed relationship of traits which led to the formation of impressions. The work has since broadened, however, to include a search for the causes of behavior or attribution of motives (see Kelley and Michela, 1980; Schneider, 1973). (This work is discussed later in this chapter.)

Four distinct processes that lead to impression formation have been identified (see Figure 3). First, a portion of information is selected from all that which is available. Next, additional information is generated, based upon that which has already been selected. Information then must be organized and finally combined in order to complete the impression-formation process. Each of these four phases is discussed below as they occur in the formation of judgments in a PAR situation, as well as in other judgment settings.

Selecting Information

When we encounter someone, we select and attend to various aspects of, for example, their appearance, to note and later use in constructing our judgment of the person. One observer may note a person's height or eye color, but not whether clothes are stylish. Another observer may note height and style of clothes, but not eye color. We attend to and select only a portion of the total information available to us. We then make our impressions and/or attribute characteristics to people based upon this sample of information (Feldman, 1981).

See what aspects of a ratee's performance you notice, by reading the vignettes in Figure 4.

One rater in a PAR situation may note that a vice president of finance (VPF) . . . analyzes data very carefully before making decisions. An impression of thoroughness is hence formed. Another rater may choose to ignore this piece of information and note instead that the VPF has fired several people in the recent past. An impression of impatience is hence formed. As noted above, the information we select to use from all that is presented to us depends as much or more upon our own cognitive structure, perspective, and expectations as upon the actual characteristics of the person being perceived (Passini and Norman, 1966).

Research has confirmed that people not only selectively attend to and recall different cues when processing information (see Wegner and Vallacher, 1977), but also attend to less information than the total available (Slovic, 1969). In actual PAR situations, raters are often unable to obtain all of the information that would be relevant. This could be due to lack of opportunity to observe behavior, or to lack of knowledge that certain behaviors are relevant to the appraisal criteria being employed.

FIGURE 3

111
The Formation of an Implicit Personality Theory

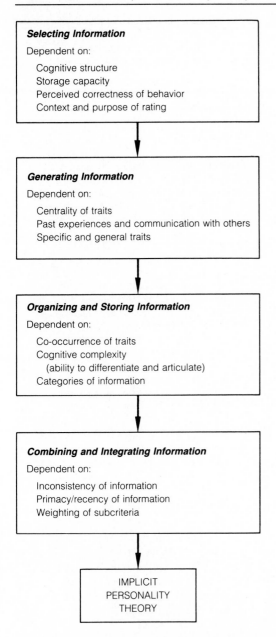

Cognitive Complexity. The particular aspects of a ratee's behavior a rater attends to and recalls are dependent upon several variables. One is cognitive complexity, that is, the number of dimensions or characteristics used to evaluate persons and whether or not fine distinctions can be made within each dimension (see Schneier, 1979; Bieri, 1971). Some persons attend only to a few cues when viewing others, some attend to many. Some research has shown that cognitively complex raters, those who attend to

FIGURE 4

What Specific Aspects of These Two Ratees' Performance Do You Selectively Attend To?

Instructions

Read the vignettes quickly, then jot down your perceptions of the two auditors' performance, indicating what information you recall to defend your judgment. After you have done this, follow the directions given below.

Vignette A	*Vignette B*
Rosena Marley, an auditor assigned to review budget expenditures on a defense department project, recognized immediately that the audit segment she was assigned was off track. She redirected the project by submitting audit guidelines that accurately determined the amount, extent, and location of the work to be performed. She obtained the information requested by the team leader without consultation with other team members in a timely manner and referenceable form. The accuracy of the data collected was verified by sourcing all information gathered to the audit program. Her discovery that portions of the agency's comments were not germane to the project enabled the draft report to be succinctly edited. Her section of the written report clearly identified the major findings and provided supporting evidence. She continually requested input and feedback from other team members. During the course of the audit, she passed relevant information up and down the chain of command as soon as it was learned.	Edward Allan Marks, a newly promoted auditor, drafted audit guidelines, based on the agency manual, which were used in the final guidelines without substantial review. His team was studying the impact and effectiveness of Environmental Protection Agency standards. He was specifically assigned to gather information on auto emission controls. As the team began to assemble the information, several gaps became evident in the data he had gathered. He had to return to the agency twice to provide complete information. His rush to make up for lost time resulted in poorly organized summaries which omitted basic format requirements. His written report failed to fill in the reader on necessary background information. Over the course of the audit, he disrupted several meetings by arguing irrelevant points. He went to great lengths to single out errors made by other members of the team. One woman scientist who served as technical advisor to the project insisted on working with another auditor.

After judgments have been made and data supporting judgments are noted, see what patterns there might be to the information you selected (e.g., all personal characteristics, all work output). Ask someone else to perform the same task. Are your judgments similar? Did either of you use a different rationale for your judgments due to the sex of the ratee?

multiple dimensions of others' behavior and are able to make distinctions as to degree within dimensions, may be more accurate raters, particularly when using a complex rating system (Schneier, 1977). While contradictory results have also been found (Bernardin and Cardy, in press), additional data are required to confirm this notion. Work is being done to help describe the process of attending to cues. Which behavioral characteristics are used and which are ignored can be identified. Patterns that emerge, coupled with other cognitive characteristics such as cognitive complexity, will eventually assist in understanding and predicting the information-selection process raters use (Banks, 1979).

Storage Capacity. Related to the type of information and number of categories a person's cognitive structure permits to be assessed is the capacity to store information. It has been known for some time that human information storage capacity and ability to discriminate among types of information is limited (Kafry, Jacobs, and Zedeck, 1979; Miller, 1956). The total amount of information that can be stored may be determined by several factors, including how discrepant the information is, the length of time between observations, the number of categories or dimensions observed, and the perceived importance of the task.

This final characteristic, perceived importance, seems to be crucial. We can hardly expect a rater to store and recall information about, for example, how our VPF solves a particular problem, if we have already told the rater that the result of such problem-solving, not the process, is important. The rater in this case may not even be observing and hence storing any information related to the problem-solving process.

Considering all the information available is an awesome task for any rater. The data is not only voluminous, but only a subset of rater behavior at the workplace is appropriate for use in formation of an impression regarding performance level (Bazerman and Atkin, 1979). Coupled with raters' typical interest in minimizing their time expenditure, they select a relatively small amount of behavior and make decisions without exhaustive searches (Newell and Simon, 1972). When asked to recall the behavior, raters probably recall what has been stored. Their storage "bins" contain evaluations and judgments of behavior they have observed, as opposed to information about the behaviors themselves. When searching their "bins" of recalled information to make a rating, what they find is that the ratee is not dependable, a *judgment* based on behavior, rather than a behavior itself. Difficulty in defending their evaluations with observable behavior is thus common for raters as they perhaps never even stored the behavioral information.

Correctness of Behavior. Another determinant of what cues raters may differentially respond to as they observe performance is the accuracy and correctness of the behavior. Raters have been shown to rate correct behavior more accurately than incorrect behavior (Gordon, 1970). Others have found that unfavorable information is given more weight than favorable information when evaluating others (London and Poplawski, 1976).

Context and Purpose of Rating. Selective attention to cues can be determined by the situational context in which they are perceived. Ratings have been found to be influenced by the degree to which the environment contained ratees who were perceived by raters to be noncompliant (i.e., the degree of support ratees show for their supervisors' orders), with evaluations of compliant raters higher the more noncompliant their peers were (Grey and Kipnis, 1976; see also DeNisi and Stevens, 1981). Raters may thus base their ratings on their perceptions of the degree to which a ratee is contrasted with those who make up the overall rating environment.

Furthermore, raters may not even be aware of information about ratee performance unless it causes problems for them as they interact with ratees or unless it deviates from their expectations. In this view, a "management by exception" principle becomes operative. Raters assume things are moving along well until a problem arises. They then focus their attention on this problem — an exception to normal events. Since we would expect negative performance to be atypical and to lead to problems requiring a supervisor's attention, the heightened weighting and interest in negative performance noted above is predictable.

The type of information selected to form impressions of ratees may also depend upon the type of decision to be made from the appraisal results. A rater making a promotion decision might focus on whether or not ratee performance has been stable. Would he or she continue to perform well in the new job? A bonus allocation decision might lead a rater to select for analysis information about a ratee's ability and motivation (see Bazerman and Atkin, 1979). Was the ratee sufficiently motivated to warrant more money?

Generating Information

Our implicit personality theories and the impressions formed as a result of them depend upon the particular information we select from all that is available. The final judgments also depend, however, upon information generated by us — information not actually available from our observations but, in a sense, "manufactured." Inferences, as noted above, are made on surprisingly little information. On the basis of one piece of information, such as whether or not a person is wearing a suit and tie, we may generate an entire set of inferences about his or her knowledge, motives, or intelligence.

Central Traits. In a series of well-known experiments, Asch (1946) found that, given only a list of traits about a person, subjects were able to generate an entire impression of the person. The central traits of warm and cold significantly changed overall impression when only one was substituted for the other, with other traits remaining the same. More extreme judgments are made on the basis of these central traits than on peripheral traits, and central traits are used more in evaluating others (Schneider, 1973).

This can account for the halo effect. *Halo* is defined as the coloring of an entire judgment based upon knowledge of one or a few key characteristics. Perhaps a central trait for VPFs would be intelligence. Like the subjects in Asch's original experiments, raters of VPFs would color their judgment of other traits based upon their knowledge of the VPF's intelligence. Those known to be intelligent would be given a high rating on other traits, perhaps those not even observed directly, such as attention to detail or conscientiousness. Information would thus be generated by raters.

Central traits are also those traits perceived to be most stable. If we can identify the set of central (i.e., important, evaluative, stable) traits in a particular organizational setting and see them influencing ratings unduly, weights can be given to such traits, or very specific definitions can be used so as to counterbalance their unequal effect on an overall rating.

Specific and General Traits. Certain attributes are applied specifically to only a few people, while others are more general, applied in various degrees to almost everyone we encounter. An example of the former would be knowledge of the stock market, an attribute that would be important in evaluating VPFs but not people in general. An example of the latter would be consideration, an attribute that could be applied to all groups of people in varying degrees, including VPFs. An important distinction between general and specific attributes is that specific attributes are often applied in a categorical or bipolar manner. A VPF is considered either knowledgeable in the stock market or not. Fine distinctions of degree of knowledge are not made. General attributes, on the other hand, are applied with many fine degrees because they are used to describe and compare larger numbers of people.

The Origin of Inferences. Our previous experiences are interpreted and inferences are made of future situations on the basis of such interpretations of past events. A type of social learning takes place. Based on past experiences with VPFs, for example, we may have developed a stereotype of them as impersonal, cold people. On the basis of this interpretation, if he or she is observed punishing a subordinate, we may evaluate a specific VPF as not being concerned with others' feelings. Even though the punishing behavior may have been justified, this may be ignored as we generate information to form our evaluation. The observations have confirmed our inferences from previous experience.

Generation of information concerning unobserved ratee characteristics from observed characteristics, and use of such information in the making of evaluations, can obviously lead to biased and/or inaccurate ratings. How can such rater behavior be explained? People come to judgment settings with expectations regarding the relationship of characteristics possessed by others. Some traits are seen as related and others are not. After a rater has selected a sample of information from that which is available about a ratee, he or she can construct an entire impression and hence an evaluation.

Organizing and Storing Information

Cognitive Maps. The relationships we perceive among traits originate from two sources: communication with others and our own experiences. Both sources lead us to organize and store information in certain ways that form our own "cognitive map." After information is selected and perhaps generated, the third impression-formation process is the organization and storage of information. Confirmation of our preconceived inferences is an important aspect of the judgment process. Information is organized on the basis of which attributes are perceived to go together and which are not. Compatible attributes form an inference which seems to make sense to us. If we could look at a "cognitive map" of a person's inferential process, we would see those traits or attributes perceived as being related to each other are closer together spatially. Cognitive maps have been built, with the aid of computer programs, to depict the manner in which information about others is organized (see Rosenberg and Jones, 1972; Goodman, 1968).

We can ask a rater to describe various ratees and note when and how attributes co-occur. For example, does the rater describe ratees as young and energetic, or honest and modest? If so, we can see that the rater tends to place these traits together in his or her cognitive map. When using the trait *young,* the rater would also have a tendency to attribute to a ratee the trait *energetic.* The rater who observes a young ratee might thus describe this ratee as energetic even though there was no observation of "energetic" behavior. The organization, or co-occurrence, of a set of attributes here determines the rating, regardless of observed performance.

Cognitive Structure. Not only are the relationships among various attributes important in evaluating others, but the number of attributes used and the number of degrees with which each is distinguished can help determine attributions. The relationships that persons assume to hold between traits allow them to develop an inferred personality profile of a person. But the number of attributes they use when making inferences and the degree to which they distinguish among traits or personality dimensions allow them to make discriminations *across* people.

How does cognitive complexity influence one's implicit personality theory and hence one's ratings in a performance appraisal situation? Cognitively complex raters, as opposed to simple raters, have been found to be better able to deal with discrepant or inconsistent information about ratees and to have more confidence in their ratings (Schneier, 1975). Cognitive complexity of raters interacts with the cognitive requirements of rating formats to influence judgments (Schneier, 1976; 1977), leading to a *cognitive compatibility* theory in performance appraisal. While additional data is required to confirm this notion (see Bernardin and Cardy, in press), cognitively complex raters have been shown to be more accurate raters when using a rating format, such as Behaviorally-Anchored Rating Scales (BARS), which require many complex judgments. Simple raters were found to be more accurate in their ratings when they used a rating format which required them to make few distinctions and judgments (i.e., a format that made cognitive demands of them which were compatible with their own cognitive structure).

FIGURE 5
Sample Prototypes for Various Categories of Ratees

Category: Workers
Prototype: Clean-cut, deferent to authority, middle-aged, hard-working, responsible, honest

Category: Finance Vice Presidents
Prototype: Professional-looking, usually white male, conservative values, loyal to company, egotistical, intelligent, smooth

Category: Engineers
Prototype: Slightly rumpled in appearance, not too articulate, very bright, interest in gadgets, somewhat introverted

Categories of Information. Recent work on human information-processing, particularly storage and retrieval (Feldman, 1981), indicates that we place information into categories after it is gathered. Such placement influences subsequent evaluations. "Prototypes" are developed in each category on the basis of previous experience. Raters might have a prototype VPF, for example, who exhibits certain characteristics (see Figure 5). The categories do not have well-defined boundaries, however, and people are placed in them without possessing every characteristic of a prototype.

When encountering a VPF to be rated, his or her behavior and characteristics will be compared to those of the prototype the rater has formed. If they match, the ratee is assimilated into the category. Recall about the person being rated may include information that is part of the rater's prototype but in fact was never presented by the ratee. The categories are hence stereotypes, based upon raters' experiences. To the extent that they do not accurately describe all members in the category, judgments about certain members will be biased.

When people do not fall into one of our categories — they do not fit our prototype — we begin an active process which can be called *attribution* (Feldman, 1981).* After a person is placed in a category, the prototype of that category is evoked as a representation of that person, and characteristics of the prototype could be recalled if a rating were required. Once a VPF is placed into the category of VPs with, for example, a prototype containing the trait "egotistical," the rater will be able to recall egotism when evaluating the VPF. Furthermore, the rater may be inclined not only to seek information about the VPF's egotism to confirm his or her stereotype but also to elicit egotistical behavior from the VPF.

Perhaps our beleaguered VPF will be heard to say to his or her superior, "I can't do anything right around here!" But all hope is not lost for an objective or rational process. Additional information gathered about ratees can help to overcome rater stereotypes (DiNisi and Pritchard, 1978). If raters can be provided with enough information about ratee performance, either through their own efforts at recall, observation, and/or record-keeping, or through use of a rating form that requires them to recall and report critical incidents before they make their judgment, performance-related factors may outweigh those characteristics (e.g., sex, age, experience level) which often lead to stereotypical judgments (Schneier and Beusse, 1980).

Combining and Integrating Information to Form a Judgment

The fourth aspect of implicit personality theories and the formation of impressions is the combining and integrating of information. We will consider here the combining of

---

*For more detailed discussion of attribution theories and processes, see Kelley and Michela (1980); Green and Mitchell (1979); Calder (1977); Jones and Davis (1965).

inconsistent information, the relative importance of information gathered immediately preceding a judgment to that gathered earlier, and the weighting of various aspects of performance into a whole or summary judgment.

Inconsistent Information.   When we are given inconsistent information about a person — for example, one who in one instance is seen to be very personable and at another time to treat subordinates cruelly — we are able to reconcile the discrepancies by discounting certain information. A generally positive or negative view thus emerges. We may be able to combine and integrate the seemingly inconsistent information by assuming, for example, that the person described above is personable but has a bad temper.

When we receive a large amount of information, however, it becomes very difficult to combine or assimilate it in a meaningful way, particularly if there is inconsistent information. We do not know whether to average the good and bad traits and come up with a moderate evaluation or to discount either one or the other type of information in order to come up with a consistent positive or negative evaluation. Judgments become much more subjective, and the frustration often leads to further subjectivity as the amount of information increases (Wegner and Vallacher, 1977). Common strategies for raters are either to develop a univalent (all good or all bad) judgment, an aggregated (some good and some bad, but separate) judgment, or an integrated judgment. In the integrated judgment good and bad are tied together by reasoning (e.g., variable behavior is justified by differing situations) (see Figure 6). Each judgment may be both inaccurate and more a result of the rater's judgmental behavior than of the ratee's performance.

Primacy and Recency Effects.   Another aspect of combining information is the relative importance of recent versus more primary information in our evaluations. Early research suggested that judgments were based heavily on first impressions. This information was said to be primary, and the primacy effect was used to explain how impressions were formed. Later research found that the most recent information a rater receives has the most influence on his judgment (recency effect).* A supportable conclusion is that a primacy effect occurs when there is inconsistent information given to a rater over a relatively brief period of time, but that the recency effect seems to be operating to influence judgments when inconsistent information is received over a longer period of time.

FIGURE 6
Raters' Strategies for Dealing with Inconsistent Information about Ratees

Strategy 1: Univalent	*Strategy 2: Aggregated*	*Strategy 3: Integrated*
Rating: The ratee is only a marginally competent manager due to weak interpersonal skills.	Rating: The ratee is an excellent writer and technician, but is weak in interpersonal skills and tact. Has potential if interpersonal skills can be strengthened.	Rating: The ratee is a very competent technician and manager. Problems in past were due to difficulty in managing particularly diverse and troublesome work group.
Summary judgment: Weak	Summary judgment: Competent	Summary judgment: Strong

*Personality characteristics of the raters themselves can also influence the choice of internal or external motives.

Policy Capturing.   Raters have described their judgment strategies — the manner in which they combine information — in overly complex and often inaccurate ways. Research into an area called *policy capturing* attempts to identify raters' actual judgment policies as they integrate information in order to evaluate people. These actual policies are then compared to the stated policies of the raters. Statistical models can be used to describe a decision-maker's actual decision strategy mathematically (see, e.g., Adler and Kafry, 1980; Sackett and Hakel, 1979; Slovic, Fischoff, and Lichtenstein, 1977; Zedeck and Kafry, 1977). Policy-capturing techniques can ascertain, for example, whether a stated policy to weight each specific criterion equally when making evaluations is actually followed by raters.

MOTIVATION THEORY: THE ATTRIBUTION OF CAUSES OF RATEE BEHAVIOR

The Relationship between Impressions and Attributions

The implicit personality theories people develop help to describe behavior of those they encounter. In most cases, however, we are not only interested in developing a personality profile or an evaluation of those with whom we interact, but also in discovering the causes or motives for their actions. In a PAR situation, raters are similarly interested in ascertaining the causes of ratees' behavior. Just as each rater develops implicit personality theories and resultant impressions, he or she develops what can be termed implicit *motivation* theories which attribute motives or causes to ratees' behavior.

Attributions might begin when the more or less automatic impression-formation process is unable to explain, describe, or categorize observed behavior. When observed behavior contradicts the normal categories and their prototypical performers (e.g., a humble, as opposed to egotistical, VPF), a different information-processing activity may take place. In the absence of an appropriate category in which to place observed behavior, the ratee begins an active, rational attribution process to uncover causes for observed behavior (Feldman, 1981; Weiner et al., 1971; Jones and Davis, 1965). The person and the situation are scanned. Once a suitable cause or motive is found, a trait is attributed to the person by the observer and a new category (e.g., humble VPFs) may be established in which to funnel and store future information (see Figure 7).

Internal versus External Motives

One of the most important and pervasive distinctions between motives or causes of behavior is that between internal and external causes (Heider, 1958; Jones and Davis, 1965; Kelley, 1971). Behavior is perceived to be caused either by the situation and environment in which the actors find themselves (external causes) or by characteristics attributed to the actors themselves (internal causes). If external causes are hypothesized, an observer might feel that others in the same situation would behave in a similar manner — the environment would affect most others similarly. If internal causes are assumed, an observer might expect other people to behave differently in the same situation — each person's individual make-up would cause a different reaction. Whether attributions of motives are due to internal or external causes has been shown to depend upon (a) the sources of information available to the observer, (b) the ways in which this information is selected and processed, and (c) the level of expectations of the observer. Each is discussed below.

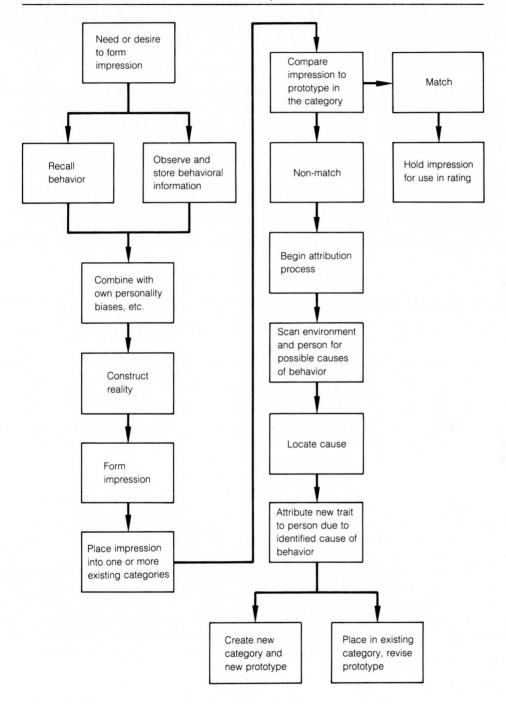

Attribution Theory

Distinctiveness. When people use information available to them in order to make attributions about causes of behavior, they assess several aspects of the information, one of which is called distinctiveness (Kelley, 1971).* *Distinctiveness* refers to the specificity of the behavior toward a person or object. Suppose we observe a manager struggling over several rewrites of a report. The question we ask is, "Does this manager struggle this way over all reports?" The more the struggling is specific or distinctive to the particular report, the less likely this source of information is to tell us something unique about the person. High distinctiveness leads us to external attributions. If we see that the struggling is distinct to the particular report, we may assume that the report is exceedingly difficult, an attribution to a cause external to the person (i.e., the report itself), rather than to any incompetence on the part of the manager.

Attribution of Motives as a Function of Type of Decision. Another characteristic of the situation, particularly a PAR situation, which may determine whether internal or external causes are chosen, is the type of decision to be made. As noted earlier, raters might allocate bonuses only if they feel recent performance was due to the ratee's own ability or effort, not to any easy job assignment. Feedback about performance might be more mild than called for if raters attribute poor performance to lack of ability (Ilgen and Knowlton, 1980). Telling people they are not competent may be more devastating than telling them they didn't put forth enough effort.

Attribution of Success and Failure

In a PAR situation, it is important to identify when raters attribute performance, either success or failure, to the ratee's abilities or personal characteristics as opposed to such external causes as luck or level of task difficulty. The attribution of causes here can have a bearing on the way the results of a PAR system are used, regardless of the score attained by a ratee. For example, a superior may decide not to promote a highly evaluated ratee if he or she felt the cause of recent job success was external (i.e., an easy assignment).

Four Common Attributions: Ability, Effort, Task Difficulty, and Luck. Let's return to our example of a manager struggling with a report. We can advance any of the following four hypotheses to explain his or her observed behavior.

1. The manager is having trouble because he or she is not, and never has been, competent (a stable, internal cause — ability).
2. The manager is having trouble because the report is especially difficult to write and any manager would no doubt have trouble with it (a stable, external cause — task difficulty).
3. The manager is having trouble because he or she is not trying very hard on this particular assignment and did not take the time required to prepare the report (an unstable, internal cause — effort).
4. The manager is having trouble because he or she was unlucky in getting an assignment outside his or her area of expertise (an unstable, external cause — luck).

Figure 8 illustrates the four types of attributions for success or failure of the manager's report-writing.

---

*Personality characteristics of the raters themselves can also influence the choice of internal or external motives.

FIGURE 8
Classification Scheme for Perceived Determinants of Success and Failure

	Locus of Control	
Stability	*Internal*	*External*
Stable	Ability	Task difficulty
Unstable	Effort	Luck

Source: From Weiner et al. (1972).

Research Evidence.   Research has found that internal versus external attributions do have a bearing on appraisal results and subsequent behavior of raters and/or ratees. Workers showing improvement over time and/or who are consistent in their performance over time are judged to have higher motivation (an internal cause) than those whose performance falls and/or who are inconsistent performers (Scott and Hamner, 1975). More extreme ratings may be given based on effort attributions (Knowlton and Mitchell, 1980) and internal attributions were found to lead to more punitive consequences than external ones (Mitchell and Wood, 1980). The utility of attribution notions in explaining ratings in an organizational setting is considerable.

The Influence of Sex on Attributions of Success and Failure

One important issue which has obvious implications in organizational settings is whether female managers are evaluated higher or lower than males in the same task setting. Research has generally found women to be rated less desirable than men for managerial positions, but contrary evidence is also available.* Where women are traditionally expected to perform less well than men in an organizational setting, their high performance is inconsistent or unstable and hence might be attributed to extra effort. They may thus be seen as more worthy of reward and receive higher ratings than their male counterparts. Above-average performance of a female on a "masculine" task might reasonably be attributed to luck rather than skill. The attitude of a supervisor, whether male or female, toward women might influence his or her attributions of causes of behavior.

The important and timely issue of women's ratings relative to men's seems to be traceable, at least in part, to the implicit motivation theories that influence the attributions of raters of both sexes. Attribution theory points out that the sources of information which generate these theories and their resultant attributions of causes of behavior must be attacked if various sex-role stereotypes are to be shattered. Simply providing evidence that women can perform as well as men may be ineffective in loosening negative stereotypes if the need to interpret the new information in a consistent manner with present biases simply causes people to attribute success to luck.

Expectations of Performance and the Consequences of Attributions

Earlier it was noted that attributions of causes of behavior are not only determined by the source of information available and selected by an observer but also by the ob-

---

*This research is reviewed by White, Crino, and DeSanctis (1981), Terborg (1977), and Nieva and Gutek (1980). In research where data in addition to sex are presented to raters, ratings are less influenced by sex (see Stevens and DeNisi, 1980).

server's expectations and biases. This was seen to be operating in the evaluation of women. Those who hold low expectations of women's abilities attribute success to extra effort. Those who hold biases against women as managers attribute success to luck. Expectations are related to ratings of a person's chances for promotion, and again sex is a determinant (Mai-Dalton, Feldman-Summers, and Mitchell, 1979). When females behave as expected of males in managerial work roles (e.g., calm and unemotional), they are rated as being as promotable as males.

Consequences of Attributions for Future Performance

The attribution process is not only an explanation for the identification of *causes* of behavior but also its *consequences*. Those who succeed may attribute future performance to their ability as opposed to luck, while those who fail may attribute future performance to effort as opposed to ability (Kovenklioglu and Greenhaus, 1978). Optimism after failure is more reasonable if one attributes performance to factors within his or her own control (e.g., effort) which he or she can change in the future.

Attributions, Labeling, and Self-Fulfilling Behavior. The actual subsequent behavior of raters or ratees, not merely their satisfaction levels (discussed above), can be determined by attributions (see Chacko, Stone, and Brief, 1979; Stone and Slusher, 1974). Perhaps early attributions of high ability explain why there are few "late bloomers" in the work force. That is, persons labeled as less than competent to reach top management may revise their self-image downward. There has also been discussion in the literature and research on assessment centers of the "crown prince" or "princess" effect (see Figure 9). Certain candidates who go through an assessment center early in their careers are evaluated favorably and labeled as having potential. Their future performance appraisals are thus in part based upon these previous attributions of high potential for advancement. They are seen by both superiors and themselves as being

FIGURE 9
Labeling and Self-Fulfilling Behavior

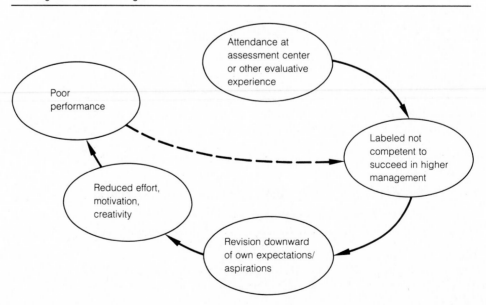

very competent. They therefore rise quickly in the organization. (It is difficult to rate someone low who has just been highly evaluated by professional assessors in an intensive, expensive assessment center.) To the extent that such early attributions are valid, achievement would be expected. Where the attributions are not accurate or are biased, the future successful behavior of the candidates may be, at least in part, due to the labeling. The "crown prince" or "princess" label is a self-fulfilling prophecy of advancement.

Attribution of Traits as a Consequence, Not Cause, of Performance. Attributions made about performance can also serve as cues through which characteristics are subsequently ascribed to a work group. People can develop different profiles of a successful and an unsuccessful work group. In one study, high-performing groups were attributed higher amounts of openness to change, cohesiveness, and communication than were low-performing groups, based upon self-ratings (Staw, 1975). These attributions were argued to represent the *consequences,* not the *causes,* of performance (see Figure 10). The implication for the PAR situation is that performance data may be used by raters as a basis for their views on attribution of personal characteristics to ratees.

In those cases in which PAR criteria contain both performance-based and personal criteria, ratings on personal criteria or traits can be highly suspect. Are these ratings simply attributed to ratees based upon their perceived performance levels, or do they accurately reflect ratees' personal characteristics? There may be a logical and stable relationship between performance level and personal characteristics (e.g., poorer performers really are less dependable) such that attributions about the personal characteristics from knowledge of performance are valid. More research on this issue is needed.

Errors in the Attribution Process

Errors made as persons attribute motives to others are typical. Such errors are common in interpersonal judgment settings, including PAR. It is important not only to understand the attributional process of human judgment but also to be cognizant of its potential inaccuracies. A brief listing of the more common errors in the attribution process is presented in Figure 11.

FIGURE 10
Causal Sequences of Attributions and Performance

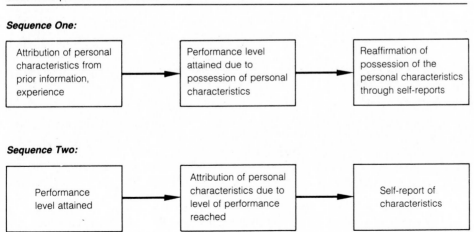

Sequence One:

Attribution of personal characteristics from prior information, experience → Performance level attained due to possession of personal characteristics → Reaffirmation of possession of the personal characteristics through self-reports

Sequence Two:

Performance level attained → Attribution of personal characteristics due to level of performance reached → Self-report of characteristics

Source: After Staw, 1975.

FIGURE 11
Possible Errors in the Attribution Process

1. Understating situational (external) causes and over-estimating personal (internal) causes of behavior.
2. Emphasis on situational (external) causes by the actors themselves and emphasis on personal (internal) causes by observers.
3. Causal aspects of the environment are seen as those persons or situations which are novel.
4. Tendency to attribute internal causes when the observer is emotionally involved in the situation.
5. Internal attributions overstated when behavior has led to reward.

Source: See Feldman (1981).

SUMMARY

PAR is an interpersonal judgment process carried out in an organization setting. As such, much of what we know about interpersonal perception in general and impression formation and attribution in particular goes a long way toward explaining how raters transform their observations of ratee behavior into evaluative judgments.

The manner in which information about others is selected, generated, organized, and combined can explain to a large degree why and how persons form their impressions and implicit personality theories of others. Of course, additional influences such as individual personality characteristics of the rater also affect judgments of others. Raters also employ a number of implicit personality theories about ratees. These lead them to judgments which may be more a function of the manner in which they feel traits are related than the actual behavior of the ratee.

Further, raters tend to attribute causes of behavior to ratees, not on the basis of specific data about such causes but, rather, on the basis of inferences they make concerning why people behave in specified ways in each setting in which they are observed. The implicit theories about people's motives that raters bring to the PAR setting also account in part for the resultant ratings. The important conclusion to be noted from this discussion is that a rating made by a rater in a PAR situation may be due more to the cognitive characteristics — implicit personality and attribution theories — that *raters* develop than to the actual behavior of *ratees*. These areas are perhaps the most important for exploration in order to understand and improve the PAR process.

IMPLICATIONS FOR THE DESIGN AND IMPLEMENTATION OF PAR SYSTEMS IN APPLIED SETTINGS

Even the preliminary empirical and conceptual investigations into cognitive characteristics of raters reviewed [here] have enormous consequences for the PAR situation. The body of work is as yet too unsettled to make firm conclusions or recommendations. Many ideas have received little empirical support. However, the following implications of this emphasis on rater cognitive characteristics for PAR system design and implementation seem obvious.

1. *Do not assume raters are aware of their judgment characteristics.* Raters are not cognitive psychologists. They are unaware of the impact of their judgment process on their ratings and so this must be pointed out to them, perhaps by feedback about judgment in rater training sessions.

2. *Encourage raters to gather performance-related information over time.* Ratings depend upon information selection. All information available to raters on ratee performance is typically not used and ratings are obviously influenced by that sample information which is obtained. Raters should be reminded to sample often and note their judgments. This will result in better recall and less of a recency effect.

3. *Encourage raters to identify their own stereotypes and expectations.* Ratee behavior is typically compared to expectations for desired performance held by raters. To the extent that such expectations are unrealistic, ratings may be inaccurate. Raters should be asked to make their expectations explicit to themselves and to their ratees.

4. *Unusually high or low performance may be given too much weight.* As raters "manage by exception," they concentrate on unusual behavior, both positive and negative. In fact, they may be aware of ratee performance only when it is unusual. Fair ratings, however, must take into account typical and atypical behavior. A ratee should not receive a low rating for one glaring error in several dozen successive assignments.

5. *Trait ratings may be redundant, or an artifact of performance, and vice versa.* If people attribute specific personal characteristics to certain performance levels, asking only for trait ratings may result in invalid ratings. Those who perform well might be the only ones perceived as possessing, for example, leadership qualities. On the other hand, once someone has been labeled a good leader, his or her performance might be automatically assumed to be high — a self-fulfilling prophecy. The issue is accuracy. Some relationship between personal traits and performance surely exists, but raters should be encouraged to deal separately with each type of criterion where performance is impacted.

6. *Performance-related data helps raters overcome their stereotypes.* If raters hold stereotypes against certain groups, such as younger or female workers, their ratings can be made more accurate as they receive actual data on the workers' performances, and this may help to override their concentration on non-performance-related data.

7. *Policies which specify criteria weights may be thwarted by raters.* As raters combine information on several criteria to form a judgment, they may unintentionally weigh certain factors more heavily than others, despite organizational policy indicating equal weights. Sensitizing raters to this by having them rate on each characteristic separately can help mitigate this problem.

8. *Attributions for failure tend to be external causes.* There is a tendency for persons to attribute their failures to their environment or others and their successes to themselves. Before the appraisal period begins, raters should delineate which aspects of the situation are within the control of ratees and for which aspects they will be held accountable. Environments may be legitimate but only partial explanations of performance.

9. *The sex of the ratee may affect attributions.* Raters (male and female) often attribute a woman's success to luck rather than ability, perhaps due to unrealistically low expectations of women's ability and/or prejudice which precludes raters from admitting their competence. Providing performance-relevant data and clearly defined standards might help to reduce this problem, as might providing feedback to raters on their differential expectations for males and females.

REFERENCES

Adler, I., & Kafry, D. Capturing and clustering judges' policies. *Organizational Behavior and Human Performance*, 1980, 25, 384–394.

Asch, S. E. Forming impressions of personality. *Journal of Abnormal and Social Psychology*, 1946, 41, 258–290.

Banks, C. G. An experimental study of rating process: Correlates of rating behavior. Paper presented at the annual meeting of the Western Psychological Association, 1979.

Bazerman, N. H., & Atkin, R. S. Performance appraisal: An information-processing and attributional perspective. Graduate School of Industrial Administration. Carnegie-Mellon University, Working Paper 25-78-79, 1979.

Bernardin, H. J., & Cardy, R. L. Cognitive complexity and appraisal effectiveness: Back to the drawing board? *Journal of Applied Psychology* (in press).

Bieri, J. Cognitive structures in personality. In H. M. Schroder and P. Suedfeld (eds.), *Personality theory and information processing*. New York: Ronald, 1971.

Borman, W. C. Exploring upper limits of reliability and validity in job performance ratings. *Journal of Applied Psychology*, 1978, 63, 135–144.

Borman, W. C. Individual differences correlates of accuracy in evaluating others' performance effectiveness. *Applied Psychological Measurement*, 1979, 3, 103–115.

Calder, B. J. An attributional theory of leadership. In B. Staw and G. Salanick (eds.), *New directions in organizational behavior*. Chicago: St. Clair, 1977.

Chacko, T. I., Stone, T. H., & Brief, A. P. Participation in goal-setting programs: An attributional analysis. *Academy of Management Review*, 1979, 4, 433–438.

DeNisi, A., & Pritchard, R. Implicit theories of performance as artifacts in survey research: A replication and extension. *Organizational Behavior and Human Performance*, 1978, 21, 358–366.

DeNisi, A. S., & Stevens, G. E. Profiles of performance, performance evaluations, and personnel decisions. *Academy of Management Journal*, 1981, 24, 592–602.

Feldman, J. M. Beyond attribution theory: Cognitive processes in performance appraisal. *Journal of Applied Psychology*, 1981, 66, 127–148.

Goodman, B. S. The measurement of an individual's organization map. *Administrative Science Quarterly*, 1968, 13, 246–265.

Gordon, M. E. The effect of the correctness of the behavior observed on the accuracy of ratings. *Organizational Behavior and Human Performance*, 1970, 5, 336–377.

Green, S., & Mitchell, T. R. Attributional processes of leaders in leader-member interactions. *Organizational Behavior and Human Performance*, 1979, 23, 429–458.

Grey, R. J., & Kipnis, D. Untangling the performance appraisal dilemma: The influence of perceived organizational context on evaluative processes. *Journal of Applied Psychology*, 1976, 61, 329–335.

Hakel, M. D. Normative personality factors recovered from ratings of personality descriptors: The beholder's eye. *Personnel Psychology*, 1974, 27, 409–421.

Heider, F. *The psychology of interpersonal relations*. New York: Wiley, 1958.

Ilgen, D. R., & Knowlton, W. A. Performance attributional effects on feedback from superiors. *Organizational behavior and human performance*, 1980, 25, 441–456.

Jones, E. E., & Davis, K. E. From acts to dispositions: The attribution process in person perception. In L. Berkowitz (ed.), *Advances in experimental social psychology* (Vol. 2). New York: Academic Press, 1965.

Kafry, D., Jacobs, R., & Zedeck, S. Discriminability in multidimensional performance evaluations. *Applied Psychologist Measurement*, 1979, 3, 187–192.

Kelley, H. H. Attribution in social interaction. In E. E. Jones, D. E. Kanouse, H. H. Kelley, R. E. Nisbett, S. Valines, & B. Weiner (eds.), *Attribution: Perceiving the causes of behavior*. Morristown, N.J.: General Learning Press, 1972.

Kelley, H. H., & Michela, J. L. Attribution theory and research. *Annual Review of Psychology*, 1980, 31, 457–501.

Knowlton, W. A., & Mitchell, T. R. Effects of causal attributions on a supervisor's evaluation of subordinate performance. *Journal of Applied Psychology*, 1980, 65, 459–466.

Kovenklioglu, G., & Greenhaus, J. H. Causal attributions, expectations, and task performance. *Journal of Applied Psychology*, 1978, 63, 698–705.

Landy, F. J., & Farr, J. L. Performance rating. *Psychological Bulletin*, 1980, 87, 72–107.

Lewin, A. Y., & Layman, S. S. Information processing models of peer nominations. *Personnel Psychology*, 1979, 32, 63–81.

London, M., & Poplawski, J. R. Effects of information on stereotype development in performance appraisal and interview contexts. *Journal of Applied Psychology*, 1976, 61, 199–205.

Mai-Dalton, R. R., Feldman-Summers, S., & Mitchell, T. R. Effect of employee gender and behavioral style on the evaluations of male and female banking executives. *Journal of Applied Psychology*, 1979, 64, 221–226.

Miller, G. A. The magical number 7, plus or minus two: Some limits on our capacity to process information. *Psychological Review*, 1956, 63, 81–97.

Mitchell, T. R., & Wood, R. E. Supervisor's responses to subordinate poor performance: A test of an attributional model. *Organizational Behavior and Human Performance*, 1980, 25, 123–138.

Newell, A., & Simon, H. A. *Human problem solving*. Englewood Cliffs, N.J.: Prentice-Hall, 1972.

Nieva, V. F., & Gutek, B. A. Sex effects on evaluation. *Academy of Management Journal*, 1980, 5, 267–276.

Norman, W. T., & Goldberg, L. R. Raters, ratees, and randomness in personality structure. *Journal of Personality and Social Psychology*, 1966, 4, 681–691.

Passini, F. T. , & Norman, W. T. A universal conception of personality structure? *Journal of Personality and Social Psychology*, 1966, 4, 44–49.

Rosenberg, S., & Jones, R. A. A method for investigating a person's implicit theory of personality: Theodore Dresier's view of people. *Journal of Personality and Social Psychology*, 1972, 22, 372–386.

Sackett, P. R., & Hakel, M. D. Temporal stability and individual differences in using assessment information to form overall ratings. *Organizational Behavior and Human Performance*, 1979, 23, 120–137.

Schneider, D. J. Implicit personality theory: A review. *Psychological Bulletin*, 1973, 79, 294–309.

Schneider, D. J., Hastorf, A. H., & Ellsworth, P. C. *Person perception* (2nd ed.). Reading, Mass.: Addison-Wesley, 1979.

Schneier, C. E. Performance appraisal in organizations: An empirical field investigation of the influence of rater cognitive complexity on rater behavior and of behaviorally-anchored rating scales as a performance appraisal format. Unpublished doctoral dissertation, University of Colorado, 1975.

Schneier, C. E. Toward a cognitive theory of the performance appraisal process. Paper presented at the National Meeting of the Academy of Management, Kansas City, 1976.

Schneier, C. E. The operational utility and psychometric characteristics of behavioral expectation scales: A cognitive reinterpretation. *Journal of Applied Psychology,* 1977, 62, 541–548.

Schneier, C. E. Measuring cognitive complexity: Developing reliability, validity, and norm tables for a personality instrument. *Educational and Psychological Measurement,* 1979, 39, 599–611.

Schneier, C. E., & Beusse, W. E. The impact of sex and time in grade on management ratings in the public sector: Prospects for the Civil Service Reform Act. *Proceedings, Academy of Management National Meetings,* Detroit, 1980.

Scott, W. E., & Hamner, W. C. The influence of variations in performance profiles on the performance evaluation process: An examination of the validity of the criterion. *Organizational Behavior and Human Performance,* 1975, 14, 360–370.

Slovic, P. Analyzing the expert judge: A descriptive study of a stockbroker's decision processes. *Journal of Applied Psychology,* 1969, 53, 255–263.

Slovic, P., Fischhoff, B., & Lichtenstein, S. Behavioral decision theory. *Annual Review of Psychology,* 1977, 28, 1–39.

Staw, B. M. Attribution of the "causes" of performance: A general alternative interpretation of cross-sectional research on organizations. *Organizational Behavior and Human Performance,* 1975, 13, 414–432.

Stevens, G. E., & DeNisi, A. S. Women as managers: Attitudes and attributions for performance by men and women. *Academy of Management Journal,* 1980, 23, 355–361.

Stone, T. M., & Slusher, E. A. *Attributional insights into performance appraisal* (Working Paper Series no. 74-15). Iowa City: Bureau of Business and Economic Research, University of Iowa, 1974.

Terborg, J. R. Women in management: A research review. *Journal of Applied Psychology,* 1977, 62, 647–664.

Wegner, D. M., & Vallacher, R. R. *Implicit psychology.* New York: Oxford University Press, 1977.

Weiner, B., et al. Perceiving the causes of success and failure. In E. E. Jones, D. E. Kanouse, H. H. Kelley, R. E. Nisbett, S. Valines, & B. Weiner (eds.), *Attribution: Perceiving the causes of behavior.* Morristown, N.J.: General Learning Press, 1972.

White, M. C., Crino, M. D., & DeSanctis, G. L. A critical review of female performance, performance training and organizational initiatives designed to aid women in the work-role environment. *Personnel Psychology,* 1981, 34, 227–248.

Zedeck, S., & Kafry, D. Capturing rater policies for processing evaluation data. *Organizational Behavior and Human Performance,* 1977, 18, 269–294.

Another Perspective of Managers' Performance — From Subordinates

Management Review

"It just blew my mind," recalls John Endee, when one of his subordinates told him that he frightened people and was too aggressive. But Endee, president of Photocircuits, a division of Kollmorgen Corporation, was grateful for the feedback. He is among nearly 300 managers and supervisors at Photocircuits who are having their performances assessed by their subordinates at the company's two plants, in Glen Cove and Riverhead, New York.

So far, participation has been voluntary; but starting this month, every manager and supervisor will be assessed by his or her subordinate as a matter of company policy. This will be done by a formal review process which is almost identical to traditional performance appraisals, except that the roles of reviewer and reviewee are reversed. Therefore the procedure has been labeled as a "reverse review."

"The basic thing we are trying to do," explains Endee, "is to build up the relationship between managers and subordinates so that they talk to each other as equals. We are convinced that this relationship makes all the difference as far as productivity is concerned."

However, there is still the question of whether subordinates will be honest in their assessments. "I expect that some people will be afraid and I don't expect all will be 100 percent honest," Endee admits. "But if they are only 10 percent honest, it will be a beginning. When they see that 10 percent has positive results, they'll go for another 10 percent."

"I was skeptical when the reverse review was proposed," says Frank Fuggini, vice-president, human resources. "But it's been a real eye opener. I learned more about myself . . . I found people in general were very candid and in most cases welcomed the opportunity. That really surprised me."

"I think employees will speak frankly if their attitude is right and the personal relationships between them and their managers are good," says Hugo Barucco, a principal of Barucco Associates, a New York management consulting firm. The reverse review is in fact a product of the training seminars and personal consultations with management personnel he has been conducting at Photocircuits during the past year.

Initially, Photocircuits, which manufactures printed circuit boards, was concerned with changing the behavior and attitudes of its managers and getting them to communicate more effectively with the people they work with. "The important difference in American and Japanese management is not technical competence but attitude," says Endee. "And in order to get improvements, managers must have continuous feedback on their performance."

The company first set up a "buddy system" for managers. Every manager was supposed to team up with a colleague with whom he would meet weekly. Their objective was to criticize each other on how well they had handled a particular problem or a specific incident and suggest how it could have been done better.

The buddy system didn't succeed. "There were too few buddies who were prepared to be really candid," explains Endee.

During Barucco's in-company training seminar, the realization emerged that, if a manager really wanted to find out how he was doing, he should talk to the people he manages. Thus the idea for the reverse review began.

The managers agreed to proceed voluntarily. A form was designed to ensure that vital areas concerning performance, attitudes, and relationships were covered, and to guide those "who might find it difficult to articulate what bugs them," as Barucco puts it. With some minor deviations, the items on the form were keyed in directly to the principles and concepts discussed in Barucco's seminars.

The box below lists the questions on the form. On a separate sheet, subordinates summarize their manager's outstanding qualities and areas he could improve upon. The summary sheet also contains two additional questions: How would you like to see your supervisor change in order to improve your relationship? and Do you feel that he was positive in his reaction to this review?

After the form is completed, the subordinate and his manager discuss the appraisal. The report is then signed by the subordinate and the individual being reviewed, who may add his own comments if he wishes. Copies may be made of the form, but

---

Reverse Review Form

All questions are answered "Often," "Sometimes," or "Rarely,"— except for Question Four (which is answered "Definitely," "Satisfactory," or "Inadequate") and Question 15 ("Always," "Sometimes," or "Rarely").

1. Does he [your manager or supervisor] show interest in you as an individual?
2. Is he a good listener who tries to understand your point of view?
3. Does he show you understanding and support when required?
4. Does he assure that you receive the training that you need?
5. Is he fair and explicit in his assignment of work?
6. Does he provide challenge in your job?
7. Does he keep you informed on developments in your group and the company?
8. Does he attempt to "set an example" (through personal appearance, attendance, punctuality, commitment to the job)?
9. Does he encourage you to come out with questions, problems, or complaints without being afraid?
10. Does he react to change positively?
11. Does he accept suggestions easily?
12. Does he give credit when credit is due and show appreciation when appropriate?
13. Does he give criticism in a fair and considerate manner?
14. Does he accept criticism in a positive way and when wrong, does he admit to it?
15. Does he discuss your performance and how it will be measured before your review is given?
16. Is your review regularly given as scheduled?

the original moves to the next managerial level for signature and then to the vice-president of human resources.

Virtually all managers assessed by their subordinates thus far have found out some surprising things about themselves. Fuggini, for instance, was criticized by one of his subordinates for being too quick to praise. "I always thought I was a good manager, patting people on the back when I felt it was appropriate," he says. "But, as I praised him for small things as well as important ones, he never knew when he deserved it."

Photocircuits has not decided whether reverse reviews should be held at the same time as traditional performance appraisals. The company is experimenting with a different approach at each plant. But it seems likely the two appraisals will be carried out separately in the future. "The main reason is that salary increases are tied in with regular performance appraisals," explains Endee. "I also don't think it would be fair to expect managers to deal with assessments at the same time."

The main problem is getting subordinates to overcome their fear. "It's difficult enough for supervisors assessing their subordinates to tell them about their weaknesses," observes Endee. "Imagine the pressure on a subordinate who has to tell his boss that he is not up to par."

The first time around, many appraisals were glowing. Almost everything about the managers was rated highly. But for the sake of credibility, subordinates did not generally give a top score for every question; some areas were merely rated satisfactory. "There's the crack in the door!" exclaims Endee. "Why am I rated lower in that area? That's where a manager really interested in finding out about his weak points must start to question the subordinate."

In his case, Endee discovered one reason that people were frightened of him was his tendency to speak quickly, particularly when he gets excited about something. His initial reaction was that a senior executive must be aggressive and enthusiastic about what he is doing.

"That's my nature," Endee told Barucco. "I'm not willing to change it." Barucco persuaded him that it is not necessary to change his basic nature, but simply the way he projects it.

Endee welcomes the feedback; but will other managers be afraid of being assessed by their subordinates? "Only managers who lack self-confidence in their abilities are afraid of criticism," maintains Endee. "However, a company can't just suddenly spring a form on a subordinate and tell him to assess his boss's performance. The whole system needs to be introduced and explained properly. It's a matter of education and experience.

"The company environment must also be right," he adds. "This sort of program doesn't work in a climate of fear. It requires a lot of sensitivity on the part of a manager to encourage a subordinate's honesty."

Will reverse reviews be a deterrent in recruiting managers externally? "I hope so," Endee says with a smile. "The reverse review is another filter screen. We want people who accept our open-communication policy. Anyone unwilling to be evaluated, by anyone, would not work out well here."

The reverse review is also expected to help identify specific training needs. By analyzing all review forms, the company will pick up trends, zero in on common problems, and develop training courses. "We have already discerned a need for a course on how to listen properly, for instance," says Fuggini.

The reverse review will also give the company a better perspective of a manager, because while he has only one supervisor, he may have seven or more subordinates, Barucco points out. "So the amount of feedback on a manager is substantially increased. I'm sure we'll get more than one image of the same person, since a manager will generally behave differently with his boss than he does with his subordinates."

Says Endee: "I have already noticed that people who defer to me because of my title expect their subordinates to be deferential toward them for the same reason. Our reverse review bears that out. We don't like to place that kind of value on titles here. I believe in managers earning the respect of others, not expecting it simply because of the position they hold."

And, of course, the whole exercise has already opened a new channel of communication between supervisors and their subordinates. Endee believes this will lead to more effective communication throughout the organization. "I think that managers and supervisors will become much more open and start to speak more frankly to each other as a result," he explains.

"After all," he concludes, "criticism of management exists in any organization. Employees constantly criticize their boss — behind his back. Hopefully, the manager who has a problem — who needs to improve his behavior or attitude — will be made aware of this by the very people who can help him most."

B.

BEHAVIORALLY-BASED, EFFECTIVENESS-BASED, AND COMPETENCY-BASED PERFORMANCE APPRAISAL METHODS

Developing Behaviorally-Anchored Rating Scales (BARS)

Craig Eric Schneier and Richard W. Beatty

For several years organizations have been moving toward goal-setting, results-oriented performance appraisal systems, such as Management by Objectives (MBO). While certainly useful, goal-setting performance programs can easily fall into the trap of concentrating too heavily on final *results* or objectives and ignoring the *methods* required to achieve objectives. First, a "results at any price" philosophy often rewards behaviors which can be harmful to an organization in the long run, but which may facilitate short-run goal attainment. Second, guidelines in terms of specific behaviors are seldom given employees in the goal-setting sessions, thus the opportunity to improve effectiveness through engaging in alternative (i.e., more desirable) behaviors is often not provided. In short, a question coming up with increasing frequency among professionals in appraisal is "How do we use MBO to set goals *and* develop specific information on how to attain them?"

Identifying those desired behaviors necessary to attain both long- and short-run objectives is the function of the action planning phase of goal-setting or MBO programs. The action planning process is difficult, but can be aided by using Behaviorally-Anchored Rating Scales (BARS), a recently developed technique which offers a systematic procedure for identifying desired behavior. With BARS, MBO programs are not only able to specify desired ends, but also provide the parameters of the means used to reach those ends.

The purpose of this . . . article . . . on performance appraisal is to describe the procedure for integrating effectiveness-based and behavior-based appraisal systems. Based on the objectives and problem sources of appraisal systems . . . behaviorally-based and effectiveness-based systems . . . each [have been] found to have noteworthy advantages, as well as a few disadvantages. Through the use of BARS, these systems can be integrated. . . .

Management by Objectives (MBO) is a firmly established and well-supported technique for improving performance, reducing role ambiguity and redirecting effort to important organizational goals. MBO has been used successfully in organizations of all types and sizes as a general planning process, a control technique and a form of individual performance appraisal.[1]

Most MBO programs have three basic phases. First, goals or objectives are jointly set by superiors and subordinates. Second, action plans are developed (often by the employee alone) to meet objectives, giving people considerable freedom to perform their tasks. Third, performance is reviewed in order to ascertain the degree to which objectives were attained. While there are innumerable variations of MBO programs in actual practice, all incorporate these three essential activities in some form. The first and third phases of the typical MBO process have received a great deal of attention. Many guidelines are available for setting specific, quantifiable and/or challenging goals and discussions note the importance of mutual (i.e., supervisor and subordinate) goal setting.[2] The various types of goals which can be used in MBO, including personal growth goals, performance goals and staff development goals have been frequently stressed.

Further, there are available in the MBO literature several useful discussions regarding the problems and pitfalls of MBO review sessions. Allowing for authentic subordinate input, using a problem-solving orientation, ending with an action plan and using non-threatening language to reduce defensiveness have all been suggested and used successfully. Making salary and promotion actions contingent upon performance would also facilitate the motivational impact of the review session.

However, little has been written and few guidelines have been offered to those implementing MBO programs concerning the second phase of MBO noted above, action planning. In fact, contributors to the field generally feel that the method of goal accomplishment should largely be left to the subordinate. But action planning can be of obvious importance when it refers to the identification and definition of specific activities necessary to accomplish goals. In short, action planning is the "how do we get there" phase of MBO. Not everyone possesses the skills required to determine which are the most appropriate and efficient methods for accomplishing objectives. Further, newer or inexperienced workers typically welcome assistance in planning how to attain their goals effectively. Because it is often difficult to translate objectives into specific actions in an MBO program, guidelines for the action planning phase of MBO are offered in this discussion.

Several authors[3] have recognized the importance of the action planning phase of MBO and have noted the necessity of specifying those activities which lead to objective attainment. But few suggestions are offered. Actually specifying activities when MBO is implemented is a difficult and time-consuming process if attempted without a detailed procedure. When we see what the action planning phase entails, the problems become obvious reasons why it is often the most neglected aspect of the MBO system. For example, defining the duties and responsibilities of one's job in order to specify action plans makes conflicts between subordinates and supervisors explicit. Such potential conflicts are not often confronted and MBO systems become ineffective.

DIVERGENCE IN ROLE PRESCRIPTIONS

Supervisors and subordinates operate from different perspectives, in large part due to their divergent role prescriptions. Supervisors may evaluate technical aspects of the job as these seem to reflect outputs directly, outputs against which they themselves may be evaluated. On the other hand, subordinates may perceive cooperation and interpersonal aspects of the job as primary since, as they deal with their peers, these factors influence their ability to perform.[4] Such differences are identified as goals and

135

*B. BEHAVIORALLY-BASED,
EFFECTIVENESS-BASED,
AND COMPETENCY-
BASED PERFORMANCE
APPRAISAL METHODS*

are mutually set in MBO. Further, the process of planning how objectives will be met may point out ambiguous and inconsistent organizational policy regarding performance or can pinpoint the failure of superiors to communicate that policy across levels of the organizations. These potential problems can thwart an MBO effort by amplifying conflict and lessening commitment before the program is even under way.

CRITIQUE OF MBO

The action planning phase of MBO has often been the focus of criticism of MBO programs. . . . [5] Most MBO objectives are measures of *effectiveness*. That is, they are designed to measure a person's contribution to the attainment of organization goals or overall effectiveness. When objectives are stated in overtime units, in terms of cost reductions, in deadlines met, or in profit margins, they refer to indices of effectiveness. *Behavior,* on the other hand, refers simply to work activity on the job — what people *do* at work (hopefully in pursuit of objectives). Behaviors are *how* objectives are accomplished while the objectives are *what* is accomplished. When this behavior is evaluated or measured in an organization, it is called *performance*. For example, if a salesperson meets with a client (a behavior) and their behavior in the meeting facilitates a sales quota being met (a measure of effectiveness), the behavior would be termed excellent performance. If the customer is lost as a result of certain behaviors exhibited in the meeting (e.g., abrasiveness, incorrectly citing product characteristics), performance would be poor.

The Cost of "Results at Any Price"

The relationship between behavior, performance and effectiveness and their meaning in an MBO program help explain the criticism of MBO noted above. MBO concentrates heavily on effectiveness or results. While this concentration on results is of obvious use since it redirects efforts toward key performance areas, an overemphasis on results can lead to undesirable outcomes. For when performance objectives are stated only as effectiveness indices (e.g., profit margins) and behaviors or the *means* to attain these objectives are ignored, people could be damaging the organization in the long run in order to meet short-run effectiveness objectives.

To illustrate, consider the example of a manager who has attained an objective of reduced delivery times (an effectiveness index) but has done so only by using extremely punitive supervision of his subordinates (a behavior). If the behavior which led to the goal attainment was ignored, long-run problems such as employee dissatisfaction may manifest themselves in increasing organizational costs through absenteeism, turnover, poor quality work and perhaps sabotage.

Thus, the "results at any price" philosophy often comes at an extremely *high* price. That is, possible undesired behaviors (e.g., a punitive supervisory style in the example above) are reinforced by the organization. This occurs when the undesired or potentially harmful behaviors lead to short-run objective attainment. But consider the possible long-run consequences. Since close supervision, a behavior, led to rewards, that behavior will be used again and again by the manager because it worked. By simply looking at results (ends) and not behavior (means to reach ends), the possible undesired means used to reach a desired end are not uncovered in MBO and thus will persist.

Ignoring Desired Behavior

If an MBO program is too heavily oriented toward results, it might also fail to recognize behaviors which we desired, but which did *not* lead to goal attainment. For example, a manager may have used desirable behaviors which characterize discretion and judgment in handling a delicate customer complaint or may have been innovative in devising a problem solution, but if the customer still returned the merchandise or the innovative solution was not implemented due to budget cuts, overall effectiveness — or results — may still look poor. Thus, the effectiveness index used in MBO may not be totally within the worker's control, as in the cases when general economic conditions, prevailing interest rates, or product demand affect a worker's or a department's goal attainment. Again, desired behaviors may go unnoticed if only results are evaluated in MBO.

A Systematic Procedure for the Action-Planning Phase of MBO

Outlined below is a systematic procedure for identifying desired behavior which can also facilitate the attainment of objectives in MBO. It is a performance appraisal technique called Behaviorally-Anchored Rating Scales (BARS) developed to specify desired behavior in an organization and to judge the level of performance certain behaviors indicate. BARS can supply managers attempting to implement MBO with a procedure whereby action plans can be developed in specific terms and MBO programs can be developed with an emphasis on desired behavior, as well as results or effectiveness. BARS can thus help fill a gap in the guidelines available for the important action-planning phase of MBO.

BARS is a technique used to specify the behaviors required to attain objectives — they supply the means necessary to attain ends. The BARS process can be used after major objectives are set and desired behavior or activities needed to meet objectives are required.

What Are BARS?

BARS were designed as a behaviorally-based performance appraisal tool.[6] They are a set of scales — one scale for each major job dimension, or broad class of duties, responsibilities, or activities of a job. Placed on the scales are a set of anchors, or statements illustrative of worker behavior on the particular job dimension. There are usually several such anchors attached to each scale. The anchors illustrate specific degrees of performance, ranging, for example, from *Excellent Performance,* noted at the top of the scale, to *Unacceptable Performance,* noted at the bottom of the scale.

Figure 1 is an example of one such scale. The scale was written for a job dimension found in many managerial jobs which can be called "planning, organizing and scheduling project assignments and due dates." On the left of the scale are the scale values illustrated by the anchors. The values on this scale run from seven (Excellent) to one (Unacceptable). The behavioral anchors appear on the right side of the scale. These are the brief statements of actual worker *behavior* which, when exhibited on the job, indicate the degree of performance on the scale opposite that particular anchor. Figure 2 is an example of a scale written for a computer programmer/systems analyst position, whereas Figure 3 is an example of a scale developed for a chemical plant worker. Each is different, but possesses the saliant features of the behaviorally-anchored format. BARS can be designed for any position — clerical, technical, staff, executive, or operating level.

To rate someone's performance with BARS, raters read through the list of anchors on each scale until they find the group of anchors most typical of the ratee's job behavior during the performance period. The performance level opposite those anchors is then checked. This procedure is followed for each job dimension identified for the job and a total numerical score can be obtained by summing the scale values checked across all dimensions.

137

*B. BEHAVIORALLY-BASED,
EFFECTIVENESS-BASED,
AND COMPETENCY-
BASED PERFORMANCE
APPRAISAL METHODS*

FIGURE 1
Example of a Behaviorally-Anchored Rating Scale

Job Dimension: Planning, Organizing and Scheduling Project Assignments and Due Dates

---

7 [ ] EXCELLENT | Develops a comprehensive project plan, documents it well, obtains required approval and distributes the plan to all concerned.

6 [ ] VERY GOOD | Plans, communicates and observes milestones; states week-by-week where the project stands relative to plans. Maintains up-to-date charts of project accomplishments and backlogs and uses these to optimize any schedule modifications required.

Experiences occasional minor operational problems, but communicates effectively.

5 [ ] GOOD | Lays out all the parts of a job and schedules each part; seeks to beat schedule and will allow for slack.

Satisfies customers' time constraints; time and cost overruns occur infrequently.

4 [ ] AVERAGE | Makes a list of due dates and revises them as the project progresses, usually adding unforeseen events; instigates frequent customer complaints.

May have a sound plan, but does not keep track of milestones; does not report slippages in schedule or other problems as they occur.

3 [ ] BELOW AVERAGE | Plans are poorly defined; unrealistic time schedules are common.

Cannot plan more than a day or two ahead; has no concept of a realistic project due date.

2 [ ] VERY POOR | Has no plan or schedule of work segments to be performed.

Does little or no planning for project assignments.

1 [ ] UNACCEPTABLE | Seldom, if ever, completes project because of lack of planning and does not seem to care.

Fails consistently due to lack of planning and does not inquire about how to improve.

Some Terminology

There are a few key terms which must be clearly understood in order to use BARS effectively. Job *dimensions* are those broad categories of duties or responsibilities which comprise a job. If a job is comprised of six separate dimensions, there will be six separate scales with anchors used to describe total performance on that job. *Anchors* are those very specific statements generated to illustrate various degrees of performance along each scale. They are behaviors, or worker activity. As they appear beside each level or degree of performance, they are said to "anchor" each of the scale values along a scale. The BARS rate worker *behavior,* not contribution to department or organization goals (i.e., effectiveness). Measures of effectiveness are best typified in the objectives themselves in an MBO program, not in the action plan.

How Are BARS Developed?

BARS are typically developed through a series of small group discussions which include both superiors and subordinates.[7] Figure 4 contains an outline of the major steps in

FIGURE 2
Example of a Behaviorally-Anchored Rating Scale

Job Dimension: Knowledge and Use of Job Control Language (JCL)

EXCELLENT
- ☐ Has used or has knowledge of the majority of important JCL statements, systems function better since is able to take advantage of the computer's ability through JCL, new situations are little or no problem due to abundant knowledge.
- ☐ Can solve the most complicated JCL problem and writes simple JCL so others can follow it.
- ☐ Knows JCL and SSG, and creates smooth running streams for every run, always willing to try out new phases of JCL and SSG.

VERY GOOD
- ☐ Uses JCL effectively and efficiently, may review job streams to upgrade systems, pays particular attention to newer methods of using JCL.
- ☐ Utilizes JCL very effectively both from machine and operator viewpoint.
- ☐ Is aware of good JCL technique, makes JCL efficient and easily followed by others who might use it. Tries to keep up to date with knowledge of JCL.

GOOD
- ☐ Has few problems with JCL and causes few operations problems.
- ☐ Creates good JCL job streams and will upgrade them when and if necessary, needs little help.

SLIGHTLY BETTER THAN AVERAGE
- ☐ JCL works and follows standards.
- ☐ Able to write JCL that works correctly.

AVERAGE
- ☐ Can make a JCL job stream for usual type jobs, can maintain existing JCL jobs with some help.
- ☐ Knows how to set up standard, or relatively simple job stream.

SLIGHTLY LESS THAN AVERAGE
- ☐ Does not make maximum use of JCL, has limited knowledge of JCL.
- ☐ Does not assign files correctly and leaves some files on desk at end of job.

POOR
- ☐ Possesses little knowledge of JCL, quite often runs have to be killed due to impossible situations, such as requesting the same tape on different drives at the same time.
- ☐ Needs constant supervision to write JCL.

VERY POOR
- ☐ This programmer's knowledge of JCL is virtually nonexistent, runs consistently error off or else have to be killed by the operator.
- ☐ Avoids use of JCL if at all possible.

UNACCEPTABLE
- ☐ Unwilling to learn the most basic JCL commands.

developing BARS, along with approximate time frames for each. The following discussion details these steps.

Step one in the procedure is usually a brief orientation in which the terminology and purposes of BARS are discussed. In step two, several of the job incumbents and their supervisors (the eventual reviewers of performance in an MBO program) meet to discuss the job in question. Their task is to identify all of the relevant job dimensions

FIGURE 3
Example of a Behaviorally-Anchored Rating Scale

139

B. BEHAVIORALLY-BASED,
EFFECTIVENESS-BASED,
AND COMPETENCY-
BASED PERFORMANCE
APPRAISAL METHODS

Job Dimension: Centrifuge Operation

7 — This operator could be expected to:
vary the centrifuge speed in order to obtain the best speed for unfamiliar material, constantly monitor evenness of cake.

6 — This operator could be expected to:
contact superiors immediately when material does not spin, install bags correctly and quickly, washes cake evenly and completely.

5 — This operator could be expected to:
determine correct rate of spin by material appearance, not wash product over basket, always check effluent for solids when starting to spin.

4 — This operator could be expected to:
dig out cakes too slowly, load properly but incorrectly judge the amount in centrifuge versus the amount in pot to obtain correct number of spins, never try to spin without turning on pump, occasionally let cakes run down too long, cause centrifuge to wobble resulting in uneven wet cake.

3 — This operator could be expected to:
wash cake at such a speed that only part of the cake gets washed, forget to blow down hose from bottom of pot after loading each spin.

2 — This operator could be expected to:
select wrong washing material, forget to place honey cart under centrifuge when digging it out, run effluent over top of bag, overrun centrifuge, or overrun surge tank.

1 — This operator could be expected to:
forget to turn on centrifuge pump or open proper outlet valves, frequently tear bags or not report holes in them until end of shift.

FIGURE 4
Steps Required to Develop BARS and Approximate Time Required

1. Orientation to BARS purpose and terminology: Meetings of about two hours for each group used. Groups of 20 to 30 are most effective.

2. Identification of all relevant job dimensions: Meetings of about two hours for each group of 20 to 30 used.

3. Writing behavioral anchors for each job dimension illustrative of various degrees of performance: About one hour for each participant for each job dimension.

4. Attach randomized group of anchors back to job dimensions: About two hours for each participant.

5. Deciding on scale values for remaining anchors: About two hours for each participant. (Can be combined with step 4 above.)

6. Computing percentage of participants who agree on placement of anchors to job dimensions and mean scale value given each anchor by participants: Time required varies depending on number of anchors and participants. (Electronic calculators simplify the process greatly.)

7. Arranging anchors surviving step 6 above on scales according to appropriate scale value and job dimension: Time required depends on number of anchors and job dimensions.

8. Reading over final scales to assure proper terminology, adding any necessary anchors, final editing, etc.: Time required varies according to number of job dimensions used and number of people involved in this stage.

for the job. It is best either to compare such a list with that generated by another group of subordinates and superiors or to ask the initial group to review their list after a few days in order to make sure all of the relevant job dimensions were identified. Step three is to write the behavioral anchors for each of the job dimensions. A work sheet with good, fair and poor performance written along the left margin can be used for each dimension and should be given to several superiors and subordinates (see Figure 5). As many anchors as possible should be written for each level of performance on each dimension.

Writing anchors is not an easy task for some people as they typically think of job performance in terms of *results* rather than *behavior*. Using as many job incumbents as possible as suppliers of anchors not only helps assure a large and representative pool of behaviors, but also facilitates the participation of a wide number of people in the development of *their* appraisal system. Such participation fosters commitment.

Anchors should not contain such words as feel, think, know, expect, or other psychodynamic concepts which cannot be explicitly ascertained. For example, to assess whether someone knows a work procedure, we must observe it being done, ask to have it explained, etc. Anchors are behavioral statements and thus should contain action verbs. Figure 6 contains some characteristics of useful anchors and offers suggestions for their development.

In step four of the BARS process, the users must reach consensus as to which job dimension each anchor most clearly illustrates. If there is disagreement . . . as to which job dimensions an anchor best illustrates, even though the anchor's original author intended it for a specific dimension, the anchor is probably too ambiguous to be meaningful. Consensus as to the dimension which an anchor best illustrates is accomplished by randomly ordering all anchors written by participants in step three above, after any

FIGURE 5
BARS Anchor Worksheet

Instructions: After you have inserted the appropriate job title and job dimension in the spaces below, write at least three specific behavioral statements for good performance, three for fair performance, and three for poor performance on this sheet. These are examples of what people in the job actually *do* which you feel can be judged as good, fair, or poor performance. Please be very precise.

Job title: _____

Job dimension: _____

Anchors for GOOD Performance

　　1.

　　2.

　　3.

Anchors for FAIR Performance

　　1.

　　2.

　　3.

Anchors for POOR Performance

　　1.

　　2.

　　3.

FIGURE 6

141

Suggestions for Developing Useful Behavioral Anchors for BARS

1. Use specific examples of behavior, not conclusions about the "goodness" or "badness" of behavior.

   Use this: This supervisor could be expected to tell a secretary when the work was to be completed, the degree of perfection required, the amount of space it must be typed within and the kind of paper necessary.

   Not this: This supervisor could be expected to give very good instructions to a secretary. Instructions would be clear and concise.

2. Avoid using quantitative values (numbers) within anchors.

   Use this: This accountant could be expected to submit reports on time which contain no misinformation or mistakes. If discrepancies occur on reports from the last period this accountant knows the cause.

   Not this: This accountant could be expected to meet 90 percent of deadlines with 95 percent accuracy.

3. Avoid using *adjective qualifiers* in the anchor statements, use descriptions of actual behavior.

   Use this: This supervisor can be expected to understand employees such that the supervisor can repeat both the employee's communication and the intent of the message. They also make certain they talk in private when necessary and do not repeat the conversation to others.

   Not this: When supervising associates this supervisor does a good job of understanding their problems. This supervisor is kind and friendly.

4. Avoid using anchors which make assumptions about employee *knowledge* about the job, use descriptions of behavior.

   Use this: This employee can perform the disassembly procedure for rebuilding a carburetor by first removing the cap and then proceeding with the internal components, gaskets, etc. If in doubt about the procedure the mechanic will refer to the appropriate manual.

   Not this: This mechanic knows how to disassemble a carburetor and will do so in an efficient and effective manner.

redundancies have been removed and any minor editing required has been performed. The entire group of randomly ordered anchors is given to several participants who are asked to indicate which job dimension each anchor illustrates. A sample worksheet used for this process appears as Figure 7. As a general rule, any anchor which 75 percent or more of the participants have not agreed to as a job dimension should be discarded due to ambiguity. In addition, dimensions which have very few or no anchors attached to them should be eliminated, reworded and/or combined into others.

Step five in the BARS process consists of deciding exactly what scale value (one through seven when a seven-point scale is used, one through five when a five-point scale is used, etc.) each of the anchors remaining after step four best illustrates (see Figure 5). Here the anchors are attached to their job dimensions and participants are asked to indicate the scale value each should be given. The mean scale value given by the group is used as the final scale value. This would be an "average" of the group's opinion.[8]

The anchors are then placed on the appropriate scales according to their exact mean group scale values or the values can be rounded to the nearest whole number and attached to the scale opposite the scale value (see Figures 1 to 3). Finally, the scales are read carefully by the members of the groups and top management to be sure that the job incumbent's terminology was used in the anchors, that any additional anchors required to illustrate certain performance levels are added and that all anchors reflect the organization's policy regarding performance.

USING BARS IN AN MBO PROGRAM

As noted earlier, a major use of BARS in MBO programs would be to specify those desired behaviors which can be used by workers to reach objectives, or the means to reach their ends. For example, if a performance objective for a manager was to reach a certain level of competence in "planning, organizing and scheduling project assignments and due dates" (see Figure 1), the BARS would help specify *how* the goal is to be reached, or what specific behaviors are required, expected and necessary in order to reach the goal. These behaviors appear as the anchors in BARS.

Many MBO authorities have pointed out that one key motivational aspect of MBO is that workers are typically given the freedom, within certain limits, to perform in those ways which facilitate objective attainment. The many behavioral anchors listed on BARS, as well as the process of writing anchors itself, can facilitate the identification of several possible behavioral strategies or action plans which can attain objectives.

Because BARS may precisely specify how objectives are to be reached, they enable barriers to goal attainment to be uncovered, such as impractical time frames or inadequate staffs. BARS aid in specifying the degree to which goal attainment might in-

FIGURE 7
BARS Anchor Reassignment and Scale Value Worksheet

Instructions: Randomly order all anchors below in the right hand column. Then put all of the job dimensions in the middle column. Ask participants to decide which job dimension each anchor most clearly illustrates by placing an "x" in one and only one job dimension column. Then participants note the degree of performance they feel is illustrated by each anchor by placing an "x" in one of the columns numbered 1–7. (Five, nine, or four point scales can also be used.)

Behavioral Anchors	Job Dimensions							Scale Values						
	No. 1	No. 2	No. 3	No. 4	No. 5	No. 6	etc.	Excellent 7	Very Good 6	Good 5	Average 4	Below Average 3	Very Poor 2	Un-acceptable 1
1.														
2.														
3.														
4.														
5.														
6.														
7.														
8.														
9.														
10.														
11.														
12.														
13.														
14.														
15.														
etc.														

143

B. BEHAVIORALLY-BASED,
EFFECTIVENESS-BASED,
AND COMPETENCY-
BASED PERFORMANCE
APPRAISAL METHODS

volve help from other persons, they offer a way to estimate resource and time requirements in quantitative terms and they may identify areas in which superiors' help is required in order to reach goals. The behaviors specified by BARS reduce role ambiguity for workers in that they help pinpoint their responsibilities and authority.

An Aid in the Performance Review Phase of MBO

Any MBO program requires a review of performance and a method by which goal attainment can be measured. BARS help in this process by providing performance standards in the form of behavioral anchors against which performance can be judged. The scales also serve as cues to reviewers as to what behaviors to observe as they evaluate a ratee. Typical ratee behaviors can be noted and anecdotal records can be kept by raters in MBO to facilitate fair and comprehensive evaluation at the end of review periods.

Further, BARS serve as a focal point for discussion in the MBO performance review session. They provide job-related, specific behavioral statements which can be used to discuss actual performance in a problem-solving manner. BARS offer a way to provide specific feedback to ratees in MBO. Rather than evaluating goal attainment as merely good, fair, or poor, BARS enable raters to pinpoint ratee strengths and weaknesses and to show ratees exactly where they excelled or were deficient. The scales enable the parties to end the review session with a plan indicating what behaviors are necessary to reach goals and to gain commitment both to the plan and to performance improvement itself by stressing specifically which behaviors on the form need to be improved.

Employees usually know when their performance was deficient and may fear the performance review session because they feel their deficiencies are over-emphasized. With BARS the supervisor can offer suggestions in terms of how workers may improve as he or she notes specific behaviors on the form which would lead to improvement. Further, if an innovative procedure or unusual effort has led to accomplishment beyond set goals, the BARS system is flexible enough to build in these new behaviors. New behaviors can be added as BARS anchors any time they are identified and it is often wise to leave space on the BARS to insert them. BARS, like MBO itself, must be a dynamic, not a static, system and must recognize changes in worker behavior, jobs and job environments over time.

An Aid in the Goal-Setting Phase of MBO

BARS can improve the goal setting process of MBO by bringing differences of opinion between parties into the open as job dimensions and anchors are developed. Superiors and their subordinates often have differing expectations regarding desired performance, responsibility and authority boundaries, as noted above. Such ambiguities and conflict can be resolved as the BARS process forces a thorough job analysis which makes duties, responsibilities, and authority explicit. Further, BARS can pinpoint ambiguities in job objectives themselves. For if parties in MBO are unable to list and agree upon the desired way to reach an objective (i.e., if they cannot write behavioral anchors for BARS), the objective itself may be at fault and thus needs to be reworked as it is perceived differently by different people.

General Performance Improvement Technique

Any performance appraisal technique, including MBO, would seem to have two objectives. It must be able to accurately measure present performance and must be able to help develop or improve future performance. There is empirical evidence that BARS can lead to improved performance.[9] Its motivational base is essentially that of MBO and hence its compatibility to MBO is enhanced.

Essentially, BARS can improve performance at two different time periods. After job dimensions are identified and anchors are written and scaled, ambiguity regarding performance is reduced. Employees now have a clear statement of what aspects of job performance are required. The anchors are essentially behavioral goals which, when set explicitly, can improve performance by redirecting effort to important job duties. As BARS are used in the MBO review session, the feedback generated by comparing performance to targets, and hence identifying specific behavioral deficiencies, has a motivating effect. This goal-setting and feedback on performance model has been well documented as a facilitator of performance improvement.[10]

An Aid to Personnel Programs in Addition to MBO

BARS can facilitate effective training programs as the behavioral deficiencies which are noted in performance review sessions can serve as objectives around which training program content is built. BARS aid selection programs as jobs are analyzed carefully and major duties and responsibilities are identified which can be translated into realistic selection criteria. In addition, the behavioral anchors specified by BARS themselves can be used as selection criteria which are job-related. Hence validity studies are more feasible. Wage and salary administration can be improved as the job dimensions derived in BARS for each job can be compared to those in other jobs so as to rank the jobs in importance, complexity, or skill requirements. Relative wage and salary levels can then be calculated for different jobs and a rational, data-based wage structure can be developed in an organization. Motivation programs can also be designed which tie rewards to those specific desired behaviors identified in the BARS procedure.

POTENTIAL PROBLEMS

Like other appraisal techniques, BARS are not problem-free, either when used in conjunction with MBO or alone. The information derived in BARS can be biased if too few participants are used or if participants come from only one level in the hierarchy. In addition, BARS can be difficult to develop. Because they are so detailed and thorough, because they are tailor-made for one type of job and because they require much subordinate and superior participation, they may be time consuming and thus costly. For jobs which have only one or a few incumbents, developing the BARS can place a large burden on these people. Identifying job dimensions and numerous specific behavioral anchors requires concentration and serious commitment. Some persons may find it difficult to generate anchors and to make the many, fine discriminations required as raters.[11] This commitment to the development and use of BARS must begin at the top of the organization and be carried downward in order for the data to be effectively used. But for MBO programs, as well as for other personnel activities, BARS seem to be worth the effort. Many organizations are finding that the job-related, behaviorally-based information generated by BARS outweighs their initial cost.

Behaviorally-based appraisal systems have advantages regarding relevance and job relatedness. If developed according to the procedure outlined here for Behaviorally-Anchored Rating Scales (BARS), commitment of raters is built through their participation in the system's development.

BARS facilitate the action planning phase of Management by Objectives (MBO) by specifying what behavior is desired by the organization in order to attain objectives.

It thus details *how* to become effective once the goals in MBO have specified *what* outcomes are expected.

BARS can also facilitate performance review sessions as specific feedback is available to ratees regarding what behaviors deterred or facilitated the attainment of their objectives. Ratee strengths and weaknesses can be identified, developmental or remedial task assignments can be made and behaviorally-based job-related data on the form assist raters in presenting a rationale for their ratings. Such a rationale helps alleviate halo and leniency in judgments.

A behaviorally-based appraisal system such as BARS augments other human resource programs. It can identify training needs, provide a content-valid criterion for validation of selection systems and form a basis for wage, salary, benefit, and promotion decisions. While more time-consuming to develop than other types of scales, BARS have several operational advantages as an appraisal system and as a technique for the management of performance.

REFERENCES

1. See e.g., S. J. Carroll and H. Tosi, *Management by Objectives*, NY: Macmillan, 1973.

2. For example see Exercise 6 in R. W. Beatty and C. E. Schneier, *Personnel Administration: An Experiential/Skillbuilding Approach*, Reading, MA: Addison-Wesley, 1977.

3. Among these are Carroll and Tosi, *op. cit.*, and A. P. Raia, *Managing by Objectives*, Glenview, IL: Scott Foresman, 1974.

4. See C. E. Schneier and R. W. Beatty, "The Influence of Role Prescriptions on the Performance Appraisal Process," *Academy of Management Journal*, 1978, 21, 129–134; C. E. Schneier, "Performance Appraisal: Does the Use of Multiple Raters Groups Help or Hinder the Process?", *Public Personnel Management*, 1977, 6 (1), 13–20.

5. See R. W. Beatty and C. E. Schneier, "A Case for Positive Reinforcement," *Business Horizons*, Vol. 18, No. 2 (April, 1975), 57–66.

6. See W. J. Kearney, "The Value of Behaviorally Based Performance Appraisals," *Business Horizons*, Vol. 19, No. 6 (June, 1976), 75–83; Beatty and Schneier, Personnel Administration, *op. cit.*; C. E. Schneier and R. W. Beatty, *Personnel Administration Today*, Reading, MA.: Addison-Wesley, 1978.

7. For a more detailed explanation, see Exercise 5 in Beatty and Schneier, *Personnel Administration . . . ; op. cit.*

8. Anchors with standard deviations of 1.5 or greater (on a seven-point scale) should be discarded as the large standard deviation indicates the group varied considerably in their opinions of what degree of performance a behavior illustrated.

9. See R. W. Beatty, C. E. Schneier and J. R. Beatty, "An Empirical Investigation of Ratee Behavior Frequency and Ratee Behavior Change Using Behavioral Expectation Scales (BES)," *Personnel Psychology*, 1977, 30, 647–658.

10. See eg., E. A. Locke, N. Cartledge and C. S. Knerr, "Studies in the Relationship Between Satisfaction, Goal-setting and Performance," *Psychological Bulletin*, 1968, 70, 474–485; Carroll and Tosi, *op. cit.*

11. See C. E. Schneier, "The Operational Utility and Psychometric Soundness of Behavioral Expectation Scales (BES): A Cognitive Reinterpretation," *Journal of Applied Psychology*, 1977, 62, 541–548.

Implementation of MBO

Stephen J. Carroll, Jr., and Henry L. Tosi, Jr.

SOME ORGANIZATIONAL CONSIDERATIONS

Some broad-policy problems must be resolved before MBO can effectively be implemented. For example, MBO must be integrated with the other components of the formal structure, such as the subsystems of budgeting, man-power planning, appraisal, and development. If such compatibility does not exist, several problems may arise in the future, as in [a] case study of an English firm cited [by Wickens (1968)], in which there was no integration of the subsystems with the MBO program.[1]

There must be some consideration given to the manner in which goal setting will take place. Some advocates of MBO would argue for a fairly formalized and scheduled series of meetings between superiors and subordinates to ensure that the conditions for effective goal setting are present. Others argue that goal setting should be the responsibility of the superior and the subordinate and that how it is done should be left to them.

Such mechanistic questions as the following: What kind of appraisal forms are to be used? How are they to be used? Should the interview between the boss and the subordinate be the primary vehicle for the evaluation, or should the evaluation be recorded on some form? must be resolved. More important, however, is the answer to the question: What should be the content of the interview? Meyer, Kay, and French suggested the separation of discussions about performance from salary considerations.[2] Also in an English case study, the separation of performance review from the establishment of merit pay increases seemed to result in fewer problems.[3] However, when performance and compensation are discussed separately, it becomes very difficult for the individual to link performance with salary and promotion, thus potentially reducing the effectiveness of salary as an incentive. Previous research has shown that managers who perceive a relationship between performance and the reward system perform at a higher level.[4] Thus, if management prefers to link incentives and performance, goal accomplishment and salary can be considered at the same time.

Frequency of performance appraisal is an important issue. There should be at least one required annual performance review. This should be supplemented with intermittent reviews. Our research suggests that the frequency of performance review is related to many positive managerial attitudes and to higher performance.

Once an individual's performance has been evaluated and discussed extensively with him, how much of the information gleaned from this process needs to be submitted to higher levels of management, recorded in his personnel file, and made generally available to others in the organization? What information should be provided to the subordinate? Such information may have substantial impact on an individual's future in the organization and must be handled with care.

In the event that a manager lacks the necessary skills to set goals or appraise performance, will some sort of training effort be available? Or should the development of these skills be the responsibility of one's immediate superior? If there are deficiencies, especially in goal setting, the whole MBO process breaks down. Because this skill is so critical to the success of MBO, its development should be provided for either by training or intensive coaching.

Once major goal areas have been set at the top-management level, the freedom of action that lower and middle managers have in choosing their own goals should be interfered with only when necessary. However, if the original goals have been formally recorded, a change in them should be made formally. Otherwise, at the end of the appraisal period, goals that are no longer relevant will still be listed on a form, and a manager may well become uneasy. In later periods when the form on which the original goals were recorded is examined by others, a manager might be evaluated as a failure because he did not achieve those particular goals.

The answers to all these questions will serve as a guide in the implementation of MBO and are problems that top management must contend with before attempting to implement any type of formal MBO system.

MANAGERIAL RESISTANCE TO MBO

Individuals may not be fully receptive to a formal MBO program. Although most managers no doubt feel that the philosophy of MBO is an important one — one that they believe that they use — a formal program will cause some problems and encounter some managerial resistance to change. . . .

Time Expenditures

"I've always managed this way. Why do I have to spend time in training? Why do I need to write these goals? My people know what is expected." Comments such as these indicate that some managers feel that the determination of objectives takes an unreasonable amount of time. There is little question that the development and statement of objectives and subsequent programs of action will take a great deal of a manager's effort and time. When a formal MBO program is used, the manager must communicate the goals and objectives of the organization. These must be developed and prepared in such a way that they can be clearly stated to his subordinates, as well as to his superiors. This means that a manager will be forced to spend time, which may be in very short supply for him, to prepare his objectives and to assist his subordinates in preparing their objectives in such a way as to facilitate communication.

Subordinate Deficiencies

Another problem is that some managers may not believe their subordinates capable of using MBO because they lack the adequate decision discretion necessary to participate effectively in MBO or are not competent enough to make the proper decisions. However, what is more likely to be the case is that managers who resist MBO are either underestimating the competence of their subordinates or rationalizing their own unwillingness to allow additional subordinate involvement and participation.

Erosion of Authority

Because of subordinate participation in setting objectives, a superior may feel that he is losing some control, that his authority is being eroded. This concern probably arises from a lack of understanding of the relationship among participation, discretion, and decision parameters. To participate means that an individual has influence on the decision. If subordinates do, in fact, participate in decision making, their input should be valued and used when appropriate. Essentially, the subordinate must have some discretion to act in the area in which he is participating. (Discretion can come either from a general policy or from the delegation of responsibility and authority by a superior.) However, in some cases, it may not be appropriate for the subordinate to influence the decision; for instance, parameters such as budget limitations imposed by top management may make certain decisions nonnegotiable. What is of utmost importance in this case is that the subordinate know what these nonnegotiable areas are. In this way, there is better understanding between the superior and the subordinate as to which areas the subordinate may participate in, and which areas he cannot participate in.

Lack of Planning Ability

MBO forces managers, especially at the top levels, to look ahead to the future. In two organizations studied, the authors found a great deal of reluctance on the part of certain high-level but very disorganized managers to look ahead and establish specific objectives for their organizational units. As MBO forces an analysis of the future, managers who are reluctant to do this may resist MBO.

Status of the Group Proposing the Program

In the University of Kentucky studies cited [by Ivancevich, Donnelly, and Lyon (1970)], a new MBO program was more successful when it was initiated by the top-management group than when it was initiated by the personnel department.[5] Certainly perceptions of the initiator will influence acceptance. Initiators of any new program who are perceived by others to be of low status, low competence, untrustworthy, or who are disliked because of past behavior will have difficulty in gaining acceptance for their suggested programs.

MBO as a "Club"

Some managers feel that MBO is a club used by the organization or superiors to compel them to perform at higher levels than they are able to. In an unpublished study, Stein, who interviewed several hundred managers participating in an MBO program[6] found that a manager may feel that he is forced to commit himself to unrealistic or undesirable goals simply because he is unable to argue effectively against such goals.

The MBO Cycle and Work Cycle

Other planning and work cycles may not be compatible with the formal MBO cycle. For example, sometimes there will be scheduled evaluations whose dates may not coincide with the planning and control cycles of the various units in the organization. The end of the fiscal year may be the time specified for the annual performance evaluation under MBO, but some units may be operating on a calendar-year basis. This means that different goal-setting and evaluation cycles would be appropriate for them. Different cycles must be taken into account.

Dislike of the Performance Review Requirements

When MBO is implemented, the intended review and feedback may not take place as needed or required. Many managers make the mistaken assumption that when they interact with their subordinates, the subordinates receive feedback about their performance. Such is not the case. When goals are set in MBO, they represent a statement of the superior's expectation of the subordinate's work and provide the subordinate with guidelines delineating his responsibilities and activities. Having these stated in "objective form" leads the individual to expect some feedback. When performance feedback is not forthcoming, particularly with respect to goals set, he may be somewhat upset, frustrated, and concerned with how he is being evaluated. Therefore, if MBO does create an expectancy for feedback, we must ensure that it occurs *and that the subordinate perceives it as feedback.* Some managers dislike the face-to-face discussion of performance with their subordinates. One manager interviewed by one of the authors indicated that he hated to review performance with his subordinates. This activity caused him considerable discomfort and was decidedly unpleasant to him. He did not like the MBO program, preferring instead the old performance review program, which involved using groups of superiors from several levels to review the performance of engineering personnel. Obviously he liked the group evaluations because he could share responsibility for his judgments and suggestions.

Paper-work Problems

In our research we have found paper work to be an irritant for a certain number of managers. There is no doubt that more work is involved for the MBO manager. Goals and evaluations should be documented, which means additional forms. Becoming bogged down in paper work does reduce time for other managerial activities. However, it is possible that the paper-work syndrome is simply the easiest rationalization for failing to use MBO. Furthermore, it has been our experience that this is only an initial response. Later, managers are more willing to use the MBO system and prepare a goal statement, if the program is implemented with the true support and assistance of top management.

IMPLEMENTATION OF MBO

To implement MBO, an integrated, well-designed program should be developed that will enhance the chances of MBO's acceptance by managers and will contribute to its effectiveness. Like any new program, MBO must be fully understood; managers must know why and how it works. In addition, they must both be motivated to use it and have the ability to implement it. The implementation effort should take place in at least three stages: learning, implementation, and follow-up.

The Learning Phase

There are some important skills that managers must develop before they can use MBO effectively. In addition, there are various types of information that will facilitate its use. The following areas are of utmost importance and must be covered in the "learning phase."

What MBO Is.   Managers must know as much as possible about MBO and its value. Emphasis must be placed on the planning aspect as well as on the goal-setting and appraisal dimensions of MBO. In the learning phase, theory and practice should be tied together. Managers should examine the value of participation, feedback, and goal-setting and learn how these relate to performance and satisfaction on the job. The details of goal setting in the organization must be discussed, in addition to the sequencing of goal-setting and evaluation activities. These can be tied in with other organizational activities, such as budgeting, performance evaluation, salary, and promotional review.

The Management Philosophy and MBO.   Managers must know how MBO fits into the general philosophical framework of management in the organization. This is especially important because MBO and top-management philosophy must be consistent. Simply verbalizing support for MBO is not enough to ensure its implementation. However, the process of thinking through the relationship between MBO and management philosophy, especially by top management, forces the kind of commitment and decisions that must be made prior to implementing MBO. Managers, especially those at the higher levels, are also forced to become aware of the problems that will be encountered in the future and, more importantly, to think of specific ways to resolve these problems.

Goal Setting. Managers should know in what ways the general objectives of the organization can be broken down into meaningful objectives for lower-level units. Translation of general objectives into operational terms for lower levels must be part of the training effort. For example, objectives can be viewed as means–end chains to show that the goals and objectives of one unit are the means used by a higher-level unit to achieve its objectives. An understanding of means–end chains is thus helpful in the determination of lower-unit objectives.

Certain training techniques, such as the problem-solving methods of Kepner and Tregoe, and Maier, may be very helpful in goal setting.[7] After all, goals may be viewed as a type of problem to be solved, and the ability to define well the problems to be solved can facilitate the development of various solution strategies.

Managers must know the difference between objectively and subjectively measured goals. This becomes especially acute in the appraisal process and in the development of performance measures, as the nature of the performance standards will have an impact on managerial performance. Because grave misunderstanding can result from using poorly developed and understood performance standards as a basis for evaluation, managers must know the difficulties in the development of effective evaluation criteria.

Appraisal. Part of the training should focus on appraisal. Role playing can make managers more aware of the difficulty of conducting appraisal interviews. For example, defensiveness resulting from criticism can be brought out more directly when experienced in role playing. Using the appropriate training methods, managers can learn techniques to reduce defensiveness in the appraisal process.

Summary. Once these subject areas have been covered in detail, managers are in a better position to know the relationship between MBO and their job. This understanding, developed through active participation and involvement in the learning phase, will facilitate the use of MBO on the job.

An external consultant might be extremely helpful in this phase of the introduction. The practicing manager probably has neither the time nor the inclination to develop an understanding and explanation of the underlying theory of MBO; he is more concerned with practice. The consultant can bring to bear experiences and skills in training managers to use MBO, and can make certain that the manager is exposed to both the positive and negative aspects of MBO.

Training for MBO, however, may cause some of the resistance to it. As many managers may believe that they use it already or that another approach is more effective for them, training is directed at changing a managerial style. This means that the training process must allow the participants the opportunity to practice the skills, assess them, and ultimately arrive at their own judgment regarding the advantages of MBO. Thus, extensive time during the program should be devoted not only to the discussion of how MBO works but to the opportunity to understand the benefits derived from it as well as the typical problems encountered with it.

Essentially, the learning process described so far will increase knowledge of MBO and develop basic skills, but it cannot guarantee that MBO will be used effectively on the job. Thus, the learning phase represents only the first step. Because implementation occurs on the job, the organization's environment must be supportive of the MBO process. That is, the ideas developed in the learning phase must be consistent with existing norms that underlie the superior–subordinate relationship and the managerial philosophy that generally permeates the organization. These, and the decisions and policies resulting from them, will have the most substantial effect on whether managers use MBO effectively and their attitudes toward it. If managers find that the reward system pays off for behavior other than that recommended in the objectives process, MBO will achieve only secondary status. If it is not part of the ongoing system of the organization, it will be shoved aside and viewed as a useless appendage to the manager's job. He will view it as excessive paper work, to be completed only because the personnel department requires it. If this is his perception, MBO will be relatively valueless to him.

151

*B. BEHAVIORALLY-BASED,
EFFECTIVENESS-BASED,
AND COMPETENCY-
BASED PERFORMANCE
APPRAISAL METHODS*

The Implementation of MBO

As stated above, the developmental experiences described in the learning phase will probably expose the manager adequately to the theory of MBO and provide some basic practice in its requisite skills, but the key to successful implementation is the use of MBO by top management. Verbal support is not enough to get managers at lower levels to use the system. Because they are unlikely to use it unless their superiors use it, it may be necessary to implement MBO in a relatively structured fashion.

The Statement of Goals.   The most fundamental problem to be resolved is the definition of the organization's objectives. These must be defined as clearly as possible and then stated both as desired results and as the general plans and programs to achieve them. If not, individuals at lower levels will be unable to determine how they can contribute to the goals. The determination of organizational objectives will be one of the most valuable contributions of MBO, as it forces top management to review and assess the objectives of the firm and state them in an operational fashion.

Goals cannot be stated in simple, general terms. For instance, it is not enough to state that we want to be the "leader in the field." An operational definition of what leadership in the field means must be developed. Is it measured by increased market penetration? If so, how much? Is it the rate of new product introduction for the following year? Broad philosophical statements of abstract ends may be relatively meaningless to lower-level managers — one reason it is important that the organizational goals be the subject of intense concern at the top level.

The Cascading Process.   The responsibility, of course, for developing these goals is top management's — probably the chief executive's. He may do it in conjunction with the board of directors or a group of vice-presidents at the level below him. Once the goals and general plans have been developed, they must be clearly communicated to the next-lower levels. This can be done by a series of cascading meetings. The cascading process is nothing more than a set of meetings between the superior and his work group to deal with the objectives of the boss.

First, the corporate executive officer determines his objectives and general program. Then he meets with all his immediate subordinates, including staff and operating executives in charge of major divisions. At this meeting he defines his objectives and plans for the group. Essentially, this is a statement of what he believes to be the major activities and goal areas for the following year. The purpose of this meeting, especially for the subordinate, is informational.

At the meeting, subordinates should be given the opportunity to increase their understanding of how the chief executive sees the direction, goals, and plans of the company through a free flow of information about objectives. Negotiable and non-negotiable areas and plans should also be discussed, as these will become operating constraints for lower-level managers. At this meeting, there is only slight emphasis on the specific goals and objectives of the subordinates.

From the information received at this group meeting, each manager should develop a plan of action, goals, and appropriate performance measures for each relevant organizational objective in his own unit or division. Then, in a private meeting with the chief executive officer, each manager undertakes to make an assessment of his own goals and what he will do to achieve them. When these goals and specific plans of action are agreed upon, precise goals and ways of achieving them will exist for two levels of management.

Once an executive at the second level knows what his objectives are, he schedules a meeting with his operating and staff personnel. At this meeting, he makes known to that group the goals and action plans that he has agreed to with his boss. This group meeting is essentially an informational one, at which subordinates should be encouraged to ask questions and engage in discussion that will help them understand the kinds of commitments that have been made to the higher level. The subordinate can then make a more accurate assessment of his discretion areas. He will know those areas in which he can make decisions, in addition to those that are nonnegotiable, non-decision-making areas for him.

After this group meeting, each third-level executive individually prepares a set of action plans and objectives for himself and his unit, and then meets individually with his superior. At this time the superior and the subordinate agree upon the goals, activities, and criteria for assessment of success.

When some consensus has been reached and the executive has his set of goals, he should then schedule a meeting with his subordinates and the process described above continues. This cascading process should proceed to the lowest level of the organization feasible. At each succeedingly lower level, the range of individual discretion will, of course, become less and less, as an individual at the lower level will have more of his activities specified for him. This may mean that for the lowest operating managerial level, the meetings are essentially communicational in nature. The subordinate may be given a fairly well-developed set of operating measures and action plans that he must implement. The nature of the organizational beast is such that these managers must operate within tighter organizational constraints than managers at higher levels.

Some difficult problems must be resolved in this cascading process, or else there will be a breakdown in MBO. The first one is timing. For the cascading process to occur effectively, the meetings between superiors and subordinates should be fairly tightly scheduled; otherwise, the goal setting process may extend over a long period of time. Weeks or months could be spent in refining the general organizational goals to meaningful operational components for managers of lower levels. We therefore suggest that a specific period be devoted toward goal setting — perhaps the two-week period immediately following the final budget determination for the following fiscal year. If managers know that a particular time is scheduled for goal setting, they can schedule other commitments appropriately so as to be available to engage in that activity.

Another problem is the amount of individual time involved in the determination of objectives and action plans. We have already noted that one general complaint voiced by managers is that MBO takes what they regard as an inordinate amount of time. Perhaps they are already burdened with too many activities. It is our contention, however, that MBO is a way to be an effective manager. Therefore, managers must either find the time or make it.

Another important problem is the possibility of a break in the goal-setting chain. If, at any level, a manager fails to set goals, those at lower levels cannot effectively use MBO. This is perhaps the primary reason that goal setting should be done during a specific time. Managers can then be held accountable for setting goals. As a matter of fact, one goal that might be set for all managers by their superiors is to have goals set for subordinate groups. Their success in this area can be verified later in the evaluation of performance. Managers can be asked to bring with them to the evaluation discussion the goal statements developed earlier with their subordinates.

The Evaluation of Performance. Our research suggests that managers feel that they do not receive adequate performance review and feedback.[8] On the other hand, most managers would argue that they supply subordinates with adequate information on performance. They say, for example: "I hold a group meeting every Monday morning to discuss the past week's results," or "I sit with my subordinates at least once a week and talk with them about their progress." This is not the kind of review and feedback activity necessary to make MBO effective because subordinates generally do not regard these activities as feedback. Group meetings are usually situations in which there is limited specific information given to any one individual about his performance. (If such specific information were given in a group meeting, it would probably arouse intense defensiveness of those in attendance.) General meetings are usually viewed by subordinates as situations in which the manager, seeking solutions, presents his own problems to his work group. The review and feedback process should be more personalized — one in which the managers and subordinates operate on a one-to-one basis.

In most organizations at least one annual performance review is required. The reason, normally, is to provide data on promotability and appraisal for personnel records, in addition to the desire to convey performance review information to individuals. Our data suggest that one meeting a year is not frequent enough; more frequent feedback is necessary for positive results of MBO.[9] Therefore, intermediate review meetings should be scheduled.

More meetings will undoubtedly take more of the manager's time. But we would argue that this is his job, his responsibility. These intermediate review sessions might be held on a quarterly basis, or perhaps more frequently or randomly through the period. They would no doubt be more effective if they took place at the end of some major activity. For instance, if one of the major components of a subordinate's objectives is to complete a subtask at the end of a specified time, say three months, the intermediate review session should be held at the end of the three-month period. It should be clearly stated that the intermediate review session is a review session, at which progress can be reviewed, problems solved, and some assistance given to the subordinate in working toward his goals. These intermediate sessions will provide an opportunity for both positive feedback, such as praise and recognition, and negative feedback.

It is our contention that there must be some formal mechanism to ensure that appraisal occurs. For example, the personnel department can develop some sort of monitoring system, through which the department operates as a support unit for facilitating the appraisal process rather than requiring it to meet formal requirements. Otherwise, managers may feel that reviews are conducted primarily for providing information to the personnel department rather than for the appraisal of subordinates.

The Follow-Up

After the MBO program has been formally implemented and is in operation, some assessment should be made of how it is used by managers. Undoubtedly, problems will occur that need to be discovered and resolved.

There should be constant ongoing discussion with managers about difficulties with forms, format, and other specific problems of goal setting or appraisal. There is also the need for a well-conceived, formal follow-up evaluation. This formal evaluation — in which there is an examination of the goal-setting process, generally recurring problems with MBO, suggested changes, and the manager's reaction to the program — should probably occur about eighteen months after the program has been formally instituted.

A follow-up may be helpful in uncovering some important problems. For instance, it may help to pinpoint whether the goal-setting and evaluation processes have broken down in any of the departments. If so, action can be taken to reinforce goal setting, and pressure can be brought to bear on those managers who are not using the MBO process. If this is not desirable, a fairly extensive general educational effort can be undertaken to make these managers aware of the value of MBO.

The follow-up will uncover cases in which MBO is incompatible with other systems. For instance, where there are discrepancies between the compensation program and MBO, they will be highlighted in the follow-up study. Constant monitoring of MBO is important because of the benefits to be derived from altering the program to fit the needs of the managers.

It is our feeling that it will take approximately three to five years to build an MBO process into an organization such that it becomes part of the managerial style and philosophy. Follow-up evaluation of the process is necessary to facilitate this integration, as it is only then that the process can be tailored to the needs of the company and the philosophy of the management.

The Use of Consultants.   The external consultant will be of importance in performing this auditing function. In this capacity, he may investigate areas in which the program, once implemented, needs to be changed and improved. . . .

SUMMARY

In this chapter we have described the mechanics for implementing MBO and presented research results about MBO in action. Specifically, attention has been directed to those problems of getting managers to understand this approach and to use it. We have not dealt at length with the nature of forms or the specific types of reporting mechanisms to be used in MBO. These should be developed individually to meet the needs of each organization.

Some will argue that our strategy for implementation is an intensively formalized, rigid one. There is no doubt that such is the case. However, it is our experience that unless it is implemented in this manner, MBO is unlikely to be broadly used throughout the organization in its first stages. If formal requirements are not imposed on managers, they will continue to operate in a style and fashion they believe to be appropriate.

Without an implementation process, such as we described above, we do not believe that MBO will be effectively implemented. This is not to say that it cannot work any other way. It is certainly more desirable that MBO become an integrated part of the managerial style and philosophy in the company than not. But we think that this is most likely to happen if there is a fairly well disciplined, formal MBO effort. Perhaps the implementation process that we have described will allow those managers who use it to see its benefits and facilitate their adoption of the process.

The most important key to the implementation of MBO is its use by top management. This is not a system to be used solely by subordinates. To us, there is little question that the participation by top management in MBO is the fundamental factor that governs the effective implementation of such a system, as participation is the best indicator of top-management support. The earlier discussion of our research suggests that satisfaction with MBO is positively related to the manner in which the subordinate feels that MBO is supported, that is, used, by the boss. We believe our research to be strong evidence of the link between managerial support and the degree of acceptance of MBO by an individual. Only when each level of management reinforces the use of MBO for lower levels by using it itself are there any real benefits.

NOTES

1. Wickens, J. D. "Management by Objectives: An Appraisal," *Journal of Management Studies*, **5** (1968), 365–379.

2. Meyer, H. H., E. Kay, and J. R. P. French, Jr. "Split Roles in Performance Appraisal," *Harvard Business Review*, **43** (1965), 123–129.

3. Preston, S. J. "J. Stone's Management by Objectives," *Personnel* (London) **1** (1968), 22–25.

4. Porter, L., and E. Lawler III. *Managerial Attitudes and Performance*. Homewood, Ill.: Irwin, 1968.

5. Ivancevich, J. M., J. H. Donnelly, and L. Lyon. "A Study of the Impact of Management by Objectives on Perceived Need Satisfaction," *Personnel Psychology*, **23** (1970), 139–151.

6. Stein, C. I. Personal communication, Carroll I. Stein and Associates, Minneapolis, Minn., July, 1970.

7. Kepner, C. H., and B. B. Tregoe. *The Rational Manager: A Systematic Approach to Problem Solving and Decision Making*. New York: McGraw Hill, 1965. Maier, N. R., *Problem Solving Discussions and Conferences: Leadership Methods and Skills*. New York: McGraw Hill, 1963.

8. Tosi, H. L., Jr., and S. J. Carroll, Jr. "Managerial Reaction to Management by Objectives," *Academy of Management Journal*, **11** (1968), 415–425.

9. Carroll, S. J., Jr., and H. L. Tosi, Jr. "The Relationship of Characteristics of the Review Process as Moderated by Personality and Situational Factors to the Success of the 'Management by Objectives' Approach," *Proceedings, Academy of Management*, 1969.

Competency-Based Management

Alice Sargent

INTRODUCTION

To develop effective human resource management systems, organizations need to develop models of managerial effectiveness for use in recruitment and assessment, training and development, and performance appraisal. The development of these models requires both an assessment of the status quo as well as a look at problems to be faced by managers of the 80's and 90's, so competency models can be built that reflect both present and future needs. Reward systems in organizations then need to be brought in line to support these models.

Business and the nation face vast problems in the 80's. These include the transition from an industrial age to an age of communication, the transition from hierarchical organizations to more horizontal models. The transition in values also includes, according to Daniel Yankelovich (professor of psychology at New York University and head of a research firm bearing his name) moving from an ethic of self-centeredness to one of commitment. Those of us who grew up in the 50's were taught guilt and responsibility. The next generation became the "me generation." Now, the 80's call for commitment that is a blend of concern for ourselves, our community and others.

Surprisingly few organizations attempt to develop managers systematically for entry, mid-level, and executive management positions. Many rely on an apprenticeship model or a random learn-as-you-go process, neither of which are systematic or cost-effective. Among the better-known firms that do have programs are IBM at Armonk, General Electric at Croton, Xerox at Leesburg, INA in Philadelphia, the Federal Executive Institute (FET) in Charlottesville, and Texas Instruments in Houston. There are not many executive development programs except for FET, and now several major oil companies are looking at the problems of how to develop their managers to manage the companies' vast resources. The major training firms in the management education field are the American Management Association, particularly their new competency-based Masters in Management Program; the National Training Laboratories; and some of the major universities who operate education centers and certificate programs. These include Harvard Business School, Sloan School at MIT, University of Michigan, Wharton, University of Southern California, and UCLA.

The education of managers is a critical issue. In an article in *The Washington Post*, Walter Mondale was quoted as saying that managers don't know how to manage because business schools have not figured out what skills managers need. The American Association of Collegiate Schools of Business arrived at the same conclusion — MBA programs lack an effective model for developing practitioner managers, partly because they have relied too heavily on the case study method. A number of firms are seeking to grant degrees — major businesses such as Arthur D. Little, Wang, and Massachusetts General Hospital have moved or are moving toward degree granting. While business currently spends $30 billion a year for training, it would seem that business believes schools and colleges have not done, nor are ready to do, the job of "growing" managers effectively.

William Ouchi, in *Theory Z*, concludes that the key issues facing American business today are not technology, investment, regulation or inflation, but that the Japanese

---

Alice Sargent on "Competency-Based Management" in *Human Resource Development*, F. L. Ulschak, Editor, 1983. Reprinted by permission of Reston Publishing Company, a Prentice-Hall Company, Englewood Cliffs, NJ 07632.

157

*B. BEHAVIORALLY-BASED,
EFFECTIVENESS-BASED,
AND COMPETENCY-
BASED PERFORMANCE
APPRAISAL METHODS*

know how to manage better than we do. The Japanese emphasis on intimacy, trust, subtlety in the workplace is more effective and enlightened than our own heavy focus on task and technology. Whether or not we put it as boldly as Ouchi, the task confronting us is to define a curriculum for practitioners in management.

This chapter focuses on competency-based management training as an assessment tool. Competency-based programs identify the key training and development targets for present and future managers.

THE NEED FOR A COMPETENCY MODEL

We have grown up without much education in psychology. What we learned in that area, we tended to learn at home or from our peer group, without the opportunity to select from options. Hence, our society is basically emotionally illiterate. Many people do not express feelings easily, are uncomfortable with conflict, and/or don't work effectively in teams. Instead they try to "problem-solve" feelings rather than be empathetic. Many of these same people become managers without a lot of training in people management skills. They have been promoted on the basis of technical competence. Yet, we know that other competencies — interpersonal, entrepreneurial, self-awareness, analytical — are critical to effective management. What we need are competency models which encompass all those elements which make for effective management.

Engineers, particularly those who have moved into project manager positions, have understood the need for management education. Now politicians and doctors recognize that they never have had applied behavioral science courses, either. In fact, lawyers have been taught exactly the opposite of interpersonal competence; they have learned adversarial skills and mistrust. As lawyers and accountants are being organized in teams of organizations, they are found to lack the skills to work effectively in that mode.

The prevailing theory of management today is situational management or contingency management, which means selecting the appropriate behavior to get the desired results in any given situation. Therefore, the critical skills managers need are to be effective participant observers to diagnose the impact of their behavior.

Buried inside managers is a management curriculum which enables them to be valuable resources in building a model for managerial effectiveness and in developing a common language for organizational management. In developing the new competency-based model of management, it is critical to capture the language of each organizational culture, rather than impose language from outside.

DEVELOPING A COMPETENCY-BASED MODEL

There are a number of approaches to competency-based management. One approach is the "generic" approach. In this approach, general management competencies are overlaid on an organization. It is assumed that the general competencies will be applicable.

A second approach is based on a research model. Using a research approach, external or internal consultants identify the management competencies within the organization and then present them to the organization.

A third approach is based on organizational development. This chapter is built on this approach. The starting point with the organizational development approach is using the language of the organization.

If the language of the particular organizational culture is not used to build the competency model, there may not be validation and ownership. The model may be treated as another instance of social science jargon. It is essential to develop different competency models for executives, for middle managers and for supervisors, and to involve those managers in the development of the model.

Many line managers feel apprehensive about embarking upon the task of building competencies. They may not recognize that they are capable of defining the needs of managers, particularly if they come from a technical specialty such as engineering or law. A half-day to a day should be set aside to work in small groups to build the first iteration of the model. It may be necessary to invite the response to the question, "What words would you use to describe effectiveness?" The intent of this discussion is to begin the process of defining what effectiveness means in the organization.

Subsequently, a refinement of terms can be attempted. The goal is to generate behavioral descriptors that are objectively verifiable but not necessarily quantifiable. Neither are we trying to return to the old-style traits, nor are we trying to come up with only characteristics that can be counted. We are trying to capture the language people use to describe effectiveness.

It is necessary to identify competencies for at least three levels of management: the first-line supervisors, mid-level managers, and executives. Robert Katz (in "Skills of an Effective Administrator") described the degree of competence required at each of these three levels for three competencies he labeled conceptual, human and technical. As we can see from the chart, technical competence diminishes in importance as one moves up the corporate ladder. The executive has really left behind his/her technical specialty, utilizing at best technical judgment, whereas the human or interpersonal competencies remain stable at each level of management.

	Executive	*Mid-level*	*First-line supervisor*
Conceptual	47%	31%	18%
Human	35%	42%	35%
Technical	18%	27%	47%

The Department of the Army has conducted one of the only studies available that differentiates competencies at different levels: those between the colonel (middle manager) and the brigadier general (executive) (see Figure 1). The colonel influences others with a personal style that is charismatic and highly visible. The brigadier general influences others with an interpersonal style that is confidently assertive, but not so dramatic and spectacular. With that much power at the top, one need only say, "I want it this way."

For the colonel as middle manager, however, the concern with subordinates focuses on their supervision and performance evaluations. The executive is more concerned with support and development of employees. The mid-level manager looks after short-term issues, while the view from the top is longer range.

Richard Boyatzis, author of *The Competent Manager* and president of McBer & Company, has compiled an excellent competency list through research on critical incidents involving high performing managers (see Figure 2). The McBer model is useful to hold up to other models compiled in the language of the organization to see what might have been omitted.

The high-performing manager's number one characteristic is holding high standards for self and others. This manager produces compliance by being a role model, not via threats or punishment. Coaches often are held up as models of effective managers. People say, "He/she wouldn't ask the team to do anything that he/she wouldn't do." In the same way, the high performer gets compliance by doing a good job, which others imitate. Old-style management used to be, "Don't do as I do, do as I say." Now we demand congruence in our role models, so they need to know that we will "do as they do, not as they say." Without alliances, cohesiveness and a focus on morale, employees are likely to burn out, to lose motivation.

The major part of the process of developing a competency-based model, then, is spending time building the competencies in the language of the organization. This happens in sessions where various levels of managers talk about what effective management means and what it may mean in the future.

THE ANDROGYNOUS MANAGER

From the beginning, management has been concerned with people and tasks, productivity and morale. The link between the two is becoming obvious. Morale and people are no longer simply frosting for task and productivity. We almost encourage alienation and isolation at work by thinking that business and personal lives should be kept separate. Yet, the critical interface at work is the manager/subordinate relationship and then the work team. These relationships must be characterized by trust if effective

FIGURE 1

U.S. Department of the Army Leadership Profiles

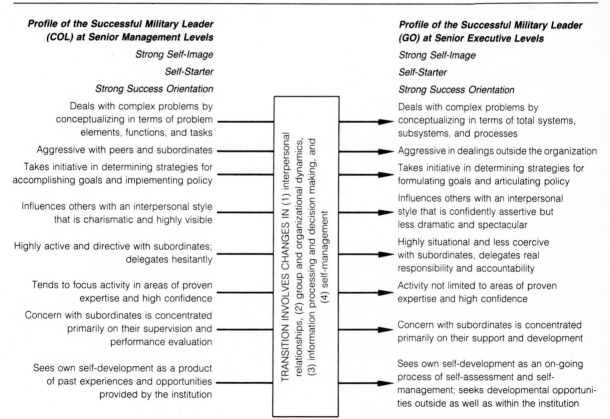

Source: From Bradford F. Spencer and Jerald R. Gregg, "Successful Behaviors Which Breed Failure," *University of Michigan Business Review* (1979). Developed by John Hallen, consultant, Washington, D.C., and Lt. Col. Frank L. Burns, U.S. Army.

FIGURE 2

Managerial Competencies

COMPETENCY: *Some characteristic of a person which underlies or results in effective performance.*

  I. Knowledge competencies
    specific knowledge base

 II. Emotional maturity
    self control
    spontaneity
    perceptual objectivity
    accurate self-perception
    stamina and physical energy
    adaptability

III. Entrepreneurial abilities
    efficiency orientation
    productivity — goal setting and planning
    proactivity — problem-solving and information-seeking skills
    concern for unique achievement
    task efficiency

IV. Intellectual abilities
    logical thought — perceive cause/effect relationships — inductive thinking
    diagnostic use of concepts — deductive thinking
    memory
    conceptual ability
    political judgment

 V. Interpersonal abilities
    social sensitivity
    self-presentation
    counseling skills
    expressed concern with impact
    compliance producing skills
    alliance building skills
    language skills
    non-verbal sensitivity
    respect for others
    effective as team member

VI. Leadership skills
    presence
    persuasive speaking
    positive bias
    negotiating skills
    takes initiative
    management of groups — team building skills

Source: Richard Boyatzis, President, McBer & Co., Boston.

performance management, career development, team effectiveness, even strategic planning — which requires risk and creativity — are to result.

Amid rapid technological changes, people almost have been overlooked as the critical resource. We cannot be effective unless we pay attention to the management of people. If we rely on our current management model, we will end up with the status quo. What is wrong with that model? It does not respond to people's affiliation needs nor does it build the necessary teamwork to get the job done, particularly in a com-

161

*B. BEHAVIORALLY-BASED,
EFFECTIVENESS-BASED,
AND COMPETENCY-
BASED PERFORMANCE
APPRAISAL METHODS*

munication society. It may have worked at times to support a hierarchical, competitive model, but with shifts in forms of management, it is insufficient. We need to focus on self-awareness, competence, interpersonal competence, effectiveness as a team leader and member, and ability as a participant observer.

One model that offers some possibilities in the 80's is the androgynous manager, a blend of masculine and feminine skills and behaviors, of toughness and tenderness, of instrumental and expressive behaviors, of concern for both people and task, of caring for both productivity and morale, of analytical and intuitive thinking (see Figure 3).

The competencies labeled as masculine describe the way organizations have done business and managers have been rewarded. To date, the dominant style has been that of a rational, analytical problem-solver, an instrumental, direct, visible, results-oriented style. It emphasizes having a direct visible impact on people and producing compliance. Such a manager is effective through negotiation, competition, assertiveness, proactivity and thinking in a logical, linear fashion.

To date, however, the behaviors labeled feminine have not been as highly valued and rewarded in organizations. Nonetheless, a number of managerial functions require the full range of androgynous behavior — long-range planning, creative problem-solving, career development, performance management, and team-member effectiveness. These and other management functions require expressive behavior, self-disclosure, a vicarious achievement style in order to enjoy the development of others, mentoring, and skills in producing alliances.

Peter Block and Neil Clapp, consultants at Block Petrella Associates, presented good definitions for instrumental and expressive behavior (see Figure 4). Instrumental behavior is data based, rational and problem solving. It is planned, predictable, and certain. Instrumental behavior avoids surprises, where expressive behavior encourages spontaneity, strives to avoid boredom and welcomes self-disclosure.

Expressive behavior is critical to an intimate relationship at home. "Did you get the car fixed? Did you pay the insurance? Where should we go Saturday night?" all focus on instrumental behavior. It is the same when the parent/child relationship involves only, "Is your room cleaned up? Is your homework done? Did you brush your teeth?" But "How do you feel?" or "What is new?" is expressive behavior that is accepted as important at home. So, too, expressive behavior is needed at work to communicate between boss and subordinate, within work groups, and among work groups.

FIGURE 3
Androgynous Management Competencies

Masculine	*Neutral*	*Feminine*
Instrumental behavior	Command of basic facts	Expressive behavior
Direct achievement style	Balanced learning habits	Vicarious achievement style
Compliance producing skills	Continuing sensitivity to political events	Alliance-producing skills
Negotiating/competing	Quick thinking	Accommodating/mediating
Proactive style	Creativity	Reactive style
Analytical/problem-solving, and decision-making skills	Social skills	Self knowledge
Visible impact on others		Non-verbal sensitivity

FIGURE 4
Managerial Behavior

Description	Instrumental Behavior	Expressive Behavior
Purpose	Problem solving to avoid failure, to achieve success	Self-expression to get acknowledged, to get connected
Exchange	Services, information	Empathy
Basis	Data	Feelings
Needs served	Control, power	Spontaneity
Time orientation	Future-oriented, planned	Spontaneous
Structure	Predictable, certain, clear, agreed-upon, negotiated, contracted	Flexible, ambiguous
Avoid at all costs	Surprise	Boredom

Neale Clapp & Peter Block, Block Petrella Associates. *Source:* see Fig. 3.

Boss/subordinate communication needs to be characterized by conversations that involve "How are things?" "Where do you want to be two years from now?" "What new skills would you like to learn?"

The androgynous blend offers effective behaviors to both sexes to improve communications between male/male, female/female, and male/female, plus cross-cultural relationships: old/young, black/white, Hispanic/white, north/south, east coast/west coast.

NEXT STEPS

We are in the early stages of building competency-based mangement models. It may take several years to go through various iterations of building the competency model. The model needs to be tested by putting it on the performance appraisal form, to see if the organization will put its rewards behind it as well as to institutionalize the model as part of the management system. It also needs to be institutionalized in the assessment process and in training and development modules.

THE COMPETENCY MODEL: ITS USE IN TRAINING

While the ultimate use of competency models relates to performance appraisals and effectiveness, it is very useful in training and development. The outcome of the competency process is a profile of an effective manager. This provides an excellent basis for assessment of managers for training and development needs.

The first step is to ask managers at different levels to do a self-assessment based on the competencies in order to select training modules that develop their flat sides. A number of already developed instruments can be used to assess a baseline competence level in interpersonal competence: Kilman Thomas, the Lead Self, the New FIRO, the Strength Deployment Inventory, Myers Briggs, the Androgyny Scale — all offer data in interpersonal competence.

Once competencies have been identified, the assessment process is readily completed by simply assessing the managers in light of those competencies. Then the individual manager's specific training needs can be targeted.

163

*B. BEHAVIORALLY-BASED,
EFFECTIVENESS-BASED,
AND COMPETENCY-
BASED PERFORMANCE
APPRAISAL METHODS*

CONCLUSION

Competency-based management programs provide unique assessment possibilities. Since competencies have been identified, the process of assessment is readily done. By using a competency-based approach, training can be readily directed to the needs most vital to individual managers.

It is time for the human resource development professionals to involve line managers in building a competency model. In order for this model to be effective it must be institutionalized in the other HRD management systems (assessment, career development training and development, and performance appraisal); and it must be responsive to management issues of the future, not just the status quo.

One such model for the future is the androgynous manager. In effect, androgyny synthesizes the best of the feminine and masculine styles to develop a more complete manager and individual who can handle both technical and interpersonal issues. The androgynous manager is able to express emotions as well as to handle intellectual, analytical tasks. These are the values and behaviors necessary to carry us in the age of communication which requires interaction and understanding.

REFERENCES

Boyatzis, Richard. *The Competent Manager.* New York: John Wiley and Sons, 1982.

Katz, Robert. "Skills of an Effective Administrator." *Harvard Business Review,* Vol. 52 (September 1974).

Ouchi, William. *Theory Z.* Reading, Mass.: Addison-Wesley, 1981.

C.

PERFORMANCE FEEDBACK AND REVIEW

The Performance Appraisal Interview: A Review, Implications, and Suggestions
Douglas Cederblom

The performance appraisal interview is a potentially important part of any organization's performance appraisal system. Clearly, the appraisal interview might function in several important ways: providing feedback to employees, counseling and developing employees, and conveying and discussing compensation, job status, or disciplinary decisions. Although the potential benefits of the performance appraisal interview seem evident, its infrequent and ineffective use in organizations also is widely recognized (Landy & Trumbo, 1980; McGregor, 1957; Meyer, Kay, & French, 1965). Despite the apparent importance of appraisal interviews, superiors often receive no training in conducting these sessions (Burke & Kimball, 1971). Available performance information often is not fed back to employees (Cascio, 1978), or it is given in a perfunctory manner (Porter, Lawler, & Hackman, 1975).

This paper organizes and examines accumulated findings of research concerning appraisal interviews. Several contingency models of performance appraisal systems then are applied to the appraisal interview, providing a broader view of these interviews and suggesting a situational approach for conducting them.

In recent years contingency models of performance appraisal systems have been proposed by Cummings and Schwab (1978), Kane and Lawler (1979), and Keeley (1978). Basically, Cummings and Schwab's model states that the appropriate function of the appraisal, as well as the type and frequency of its feedback, are contingent on the nature of the employee's job and the characteristics of the employee. Keeley maintains that a suitable appraisal technique depends on the degree of structure it provides, the employee, and the employee's job. Kane and Lawler outline a comprehensive model, in which the effectiveness of an appraisal system is contingent on a large number of factors, including the appraisal technique and content, characteristics of the appraiser and appraisee, the purpose and timing of the appraisal, and the appraisee's job.

Building on these models, a review is made of several aspects of the appraisal

From the *Academy of Management Review*, April 1982, 219–227. Copyright, *Academy of Management Review*, 1982. Used with permission of the *Academy of Management Review* and the author.

interview as they are affected by the employee and the employee's job. Unless otherwise specified, it may be assumed that the studies reviewed have been field studies with actual employees. All findings noted below obtained at least the $p < .05$ level of statistical significance.

STRUCTURING THE INTERVIEW

Function

Certainly the function of the appraisal interview must affect the interview process and outcomes. Two main purposes of the interview are counseling and development and the evaluation and discussion of administrative decisions. Many writers have commented on problems involved in using the interview for both of these purposes. Two studies have investigated the specific question of whether the functions of employee counseling/development and salary discussion are served better in separate or in joint sessions. Meyer et al. (1965) concluded from their study at General Electric that interviews attempting to serve both purposes of (1) informing and justifying salary decisions and (2) providing feedback and counseling for improvement are less effective than "split role" interviews dealing with these two purposes. They argued that interviews attempting to accomplish both objectives force the superior into conflicting roles of counselor and judge, cause subordinate defensiveness, and usually become salary discussions with little influence on subordinates' future performance. They reported that employees' performance and attitudes toward their superiors improved when they changed from the joint purpose interview to separate development and salary interviews. The separate development interviews differed from the joint purpose interviews in several ways other than function: they were more frequent, had no summary ratings, and emphasized mutual goal planning. Thus, no conclusions can be derived from this study as to the extent to which the more positive results of separate interviews were due solely to their separate purposes.

Cummings (1973) pointed out that expectancy theory would suggest that development and salary functions should be combined in appraisal interviews. He compared reactions of employees to old and new appraisal systems in a field experiment. Results showed more positive attitudes by employees to the new joint function (salary and development) system, but several other confounding factors again prevent conclusions about any specific effects of combining interview functions.

One study has investigated subordinates' perceptions of the importance of their appraisals for future rewards, and the interview process and outcomes. Burke, Weitzel, and Weir (1978) obtained data from employees in a civil service institution in which no rewards were officially attached to the performance review. Nevertheless, employees who viewed their reviews as more instrumental for pay, promotion, or work rewards reported more goal setting, motivation to improve, and satisfaction in the interview. These results suggest that the review process may be more effective if some rewards are perceived as linked to appraisal reviews.

Considering the potential of appraisal interviews for functioning in several important ways, present empirical understanding of how to structure several interview functions in one or more interviews is quite limited. The particular question of whether separate or joint development and administrative reward sessions function more effectively seems unresolved, and further studies investigating this particular issue would be useful.

A different, comprehensive approach to dealing with the development and evaluation functions has been proposed by Cummings and Schwab (1978). They suggest that appraisals have development potential if meaningful and challenging goals can be established. Both Keeley (1978) and Cummings and Schwab (1978) caution that goal setting is less feasible for some jobs and employees than for others. In many routine jobs employees lack the control or discretion for goal setting to be meaningful. Cummings and Schwab suggest that appraisals have realistic development potential for a limited number of employees. They propose three types of appraisals, whose functions are contingent on the individual performer and job. Developmental appraisals would be used for high performing, high potential employees in fairly discretionary jobs. Most employees would be evaluated by a "maintenance" appraisal system. These employees have performed at a steady, satisfactory level for some time and are not likely to improve due to constraints of ability, motivation, or the nature of their jobs. Their appraisals would focus on maintaining performance at the currently acceptable levels, and on exceptions to established performance patterns. Serious exceptions then would be handled either by developmental appraisals or by the third system — remedial appraisals. These appraisals would be used for low performing or marginal subordinates to attempt to raise performance to acceptable levels. Cummings and Schwab suggest that this approach would separate developmental and evaluative functions insofar as the first type is primarily developmental and the second (maintenance) mainly evaluative. Conflict does seem likely for remedial appraisals, which combine these two functions for performers who are likely to be quite defensive.

Cummings and Schwab's separation of function by type of appraisal seems generally sensible. However, it still would seem important to provide both functions for many employees in all three appraisal situations. Although developmental sessions would be used mainly for high potential employees, evaluations and administrative decisions about such employees still need to be made and discussed. For employees in maintenance situations, development may be appropriate for certain discretionary aspects of their jobs. Both functions clearly are necessary for remedial employees. Sequentially, one way of handling both functions of development and discussion of administrative decisions might be to conduct one or more development sessions, eventually followed by a session focusing on administrative decisions. When possible, goals and incentives could be set during the development sessions. This approach at least would seem to minimize employee surprise and possible resentment about eventual decisions and would provide some opportunity for development.

Cummings and Schwab's model may seem callous toward possibilities of employee development. They recognize that their premises run counter to the "humanistic ideal of universal potential for growth and development." Nevertheless, they suggest that employees do reach growth limits or are placed in jobs constraining further development and that attempts to develop such employees may well prove frustrating to the employee and wasteful for the organization. They may overstate the extent of the limitations for development, but their model nevertheless points out important contingencies and provides a useful framework for focusing the functions of the interview.

Frequency

Officially, the annual employee performance review seems to be a norm in American work organizations. A 1974 Bureau of National Affairs survey of personnel executives from 150 industrial and government organizations indicated that office employees, managers, and production workers were formally evaluated at least annually in approximately 90 percent of these organizations (Miner, 1974, 1975). In the large majority of these cases, the frequency of evaluation was once a year, and in at least 90 percent of the companies the evaluation was accompanied by an appraisal interview with the employee.

However, there are several indications that performance reviews may occur less frequently, at least in the view of subordinates. Both McCall and DeVries (1976) and Meyer et al. (1965) found that in many companies interviews are not actually conducted unless strong control procedures insuring their occurrence have been established. Landy and Trumbo (1980) reported experience with numerous companies in which available performance ratings were not presented to employees, partly because of logistic difficulties for one supervisor interviewing all subordinates, and partly out of superiors' feeling that the ratings served no real use. A study by Hall and Lawler (1969) suggests that superiors and subordinates may have different conceptions of the appraisal interview. They found that when interviewed separately, subordinates reported having no performance review sessions regularly. The interviews indicated that superiors regarded brief, general discussions with subordinates about their performance as review sessions, but that subordinates did not.

How frequently a superior might most effectively conduct appraisal interviews with a subordinate depends on a number of factors, including the function of the interview, the nature of the subordinate's job, and characteristics of the subordinate. Appraisal interviews whose function is primarily developmental, particularly for employees in discretionary, nonroutine jobs in which goal setting or MBO are involved, should be conducted relatively frequently (Cummings & Schwab, 1978; McConkie, 1979; Meyer et al., 1965). It is recommended that such sessions be scheduled on an individual basis, depending on the job and its natural feedback concerning goal progress. Intervals would be more flexible than set, although generally more than annual sessions are recommended. Cummings and Schwab suggest that maintenance appraisals, appropriate for satisfactory employees in more routine jobs, be conducted less frequently — annually or as warranted by exceptions.

Several sources suggest highly frequent reviews with low performers. Cummings and Schwab believe intensive (weekly and possibly daily) sessions are required to raise performance to acceptable levels. A finding by Kay, Meyer, and French (1965) also would argue for more frequent sessions with lower performers. They reported an "overload phenomenon" of subordinate defensiveness in evaluation sessions: as the number of critical statements by the manager increases, subordinate defensiveness increases at an accelerating rate. With more frequent sessions the number of criticisms in each session could be decreased, which might reduce a tendency for subordinates to become overwhelmed by criticism in a given session. From a different perspective, in a review on punishment in organizations Arvey and Ivancevich (1980) propose that punishment will be most effective if delivered immediately after every undesirable response. Considering that feedback sessions for many low performers often will seem somewhat punitive, improved performance may more likely result from very frequent sessions. However, this approach may be emotionally straining for both superior and subordinate. It would be important in this approach to avoid a tendency to focus solely on specific immediate mistakes to the exclusion of a broader picture of performance expectations.

In addition to performance level, another characteristic of individual employees relevant to the frequency of review sessions is tenure. New employees tend to need more frequent appraisals than do long term employees (Kane & Lawler, 1979). It seems to be standard practice in some organizations to conduct appraisals more frequently for new employees (Miner, 1974).

Although it generally is recommended that feedback to employees be given more frequently, present empirical knowledge of the desirability of more frequent appraisal interviews is sparse. Landy, Barnes, and Murphy (1978) reported that subordinates evaluated at least once a year viewed their evaluations as fairer and more accurate than did subordinates evaluated less frequently. However, their results would not necessarily indicate that evaluations made more than once a year would be regarded as fairer or more accurate than annual evaluations.

Further research concerning frequency of interviews is needed. Questionnaire data from superiors and subordinates, separately indicating their preferences for frequency of appraisal interviews, would be useful. Also useful would be field experiments in which the frequency of interviews is manipulated and any attitudinal or behavior effects are obtained. Such research should consider the function of the interview, the nature of the employees' jobs, and the characteristics of employees.

Format

Appraisal Technique. Several writers have suggested that appraisal interviews be based more on mutual goal setting or management by objectives than on the traditional "traits-rated" format (Kelly, 1958; McGregor, 1957; Meyer et al., 1965; Odiorne, 1965). For example, McGregor suggested that a goal oriented evaluation would shift the interview process from appraisal to analysis, thereby reducing the discomfort of the superior in playing "judge" and also reducing subordinate defensiveness. There is some indication of employees' preference for goal based appraisals. In a review of the goal setting and appraisal process of MBO, McConkie (1979) cites four studies showing more positive attitudes by personnel toward MBO appraisals than toward their preceding trait centered appraisals.

Nevertheless, practical limits of goal setting and goal based appraisals need to be considered. As discussed earlier, Keeley (1978) and Cummings and Schwab (1978) point out that goal setting seems inappropriate for highly routine jobs in which employees lack discretion and control. They also cite dangers of goal setting in very uncertain, nonroutine jobs involving vague and conflicting expectations. Goal based appraisals used for these jobs may neglect less quantifiable but important aspects of performance.

Keeley suggests that the appropriate appraisal technique is determined by its fit with a contingency model of organizational structure, the employee's need for independence, and the nature of the job. He cites evidence indicating optimal fits among high organizational structure, employees with low need for independence, and highly routine tasks; and among low organizational structure, employees with high need for independence, and very nonroutine tasks. Accordingly, Keeley recommends the following: (1) behavior based procedures, defining specific procedural and performance expectations, for employees low in need for independence and employed in highly routine jobs; (2) goal based appraisals, defining performance less narrowly, for employees with a moderate desire for autonomy in moderately routine jobs; and (3) multiple subjective judgments, defining performance least specifically, for highly independent employees in very nonroutine tasks.

Appraisers' Knowledge of Employee's Job. Normally, an employee's appraisal interview is conducted one-on-one by the immediate superior, based on a written appraisal previously prepared by the superior (Miner, 1974). Appraisal from multiple raters has been recommended as a more thorough method of appraisal than the traditional "immediate supervisor" approach and particularly appropriate for appraising employees in nonroutine jobs (Kane & Lawler, 1979; Keeley, 1978). In such jobs, the employee is often answerable to a variety of individuals and groups, who hold differing and often incompatible expectations of the employee and who view different aspects of the employee's performance. This useful suggestion poses an issue of who should then participate in the appraisal interview. One approach would be to have all raters participate, which could help clarify conflicting expectations (McConkie, 1979). Another approach would be to have only the superior and subordinate present, with the superior identifying and clarifying prepared feedback from the various sources. This second strategy might reduce subordinate defensiveness often found in the traditional interview by slanting the superior's role more towards interpreter than judge.

Whoever participates in appraising and interviewing, the superior must have adequate knowledge of the subordinate's job duties and behavior. Such knowledge is clearly required for appraisal of the subordinate's performance. This knowledge also is important for superiors to present appraisal feedback credibly and effectively to subordinates. Ilgen, Fisher, and Taylor (1979) concluded from their thorough review of feedback in organizations that providers of feedback must be knowledgeable of the recipients' tasks and performance for their feedback to be accurately perceived and accepted. Landy et al. (1978) found that subordinates, who regard their superiors as highly knowledgeable about the subordinates' jobs and performance, view their own performance as more fairly and accurately evaluated than do subordinates who regard their supervisors as less knowledgeable about their jobs and performance.

Findings from two studies by Greller question subordinates' regard for feedback from superiors. First, employees rating different sources of feedback on the extent to which each provided feedback on performance indicated that their own feelings and ideas and natural feedback from their tasks were more informative about performance than was feedback from their supervisors (Greller & Herold, 1975). Second, employees rating six different sources of feedback on their usefulness as feedback on performance showed supervisor feedback ranked fifth out of six, behind their own comparisons against co-workers, their tasks, the level of their information assignments, and co-worker comments. Also, supervisors' ratings of the same sources overestimated (relative to subordinates' ratings) the importance of their feedback to subordinates (Greller, 1980). These results were discussed in terms of subordinates valuing most highly those sources of feedback psychologically "close" to the subordinate.

These findings suggest that appraisal interviews conducted by superiors who have limited contact and familiarity with subordinates and subordinates' jobs may not have positive outcomes, at least from the viewpoint of subordinates. Superiors "distant" from their subordinates may need to devote extra effort to observe and evaluate their employees. Otherwise, subordinates may regard their appraisal interviews as simply going through the motions or, worse, as tending to be unfair and inaccurate.

PROCESS FACTORS

Goal Setting

Goal setting by or for the subordinate during the interview has consistently related to positive appraisal interview outcomes. In correlational studies, goal setting was positively related to subordinate satisfaction with the interview (Burke & Wilcox, 1969; Burke et al., 1978; Greller, 1975, 1978), perceived fairness and accuracy of the evaluation (Landy et al., 1978), and perceived utility of the appraisal (Greller, 1978). Goal setting also has been related to greater mutual understanding and perceived fairness (Burke et al., 1978), subordinates' desire to improve, and subsequent improvement (Burke & Wilcox, 1969; Burke et al., 1978). In addition, a main finding of the appraisal interview studies conducted at General Electric was that criticism revised into goals is twice as likely to result in improved performance as is simple criticism (French, Kay, & Meyer, 1966). Goal setting generally seems to function positively in appraisal interviews. However, as discussed previously, useful goal setting may be limited by the degree of control employees have in very routine jobs, and by conflicting or less quantifiable aspects of performance in very nonroutine jobs. For highly nonroutine, uncertain tasks, relatively open-ended "directional" goals may function more effectively than fixed, specific goals.

Subordinate Participation

Encouraging Participation. The one aspect of subordinate participation that consistently has related to positive outcomes has been a factor of the superior's "welcoming participation." Burke and Wilcox (1969), Burke et al. (1978), Greller (1975), and Nemeroff and Wexley (1977) all found items such as "opportunity to present ideas or feelings" and "boss asked my opinion" to correlate positively with a variety of outcomes. Nemeroff and Wexley's results also suggest that superiors may underestimate the importance of this factor to subordinates, and they may overestimate the extent to which they effectively welcome subordinates' participation.

Several correlational studies have examined the relation between interview outcomes and actual subordinate participation, defined by proportion of time the subordinate talked (Burke et al., 1978; Greller, 1975; Nemeroff & Wexley, 1977), perceptions of subordinate influence (Burke et al., 1978; Greller, 1978), or participation in goal setting (Greller, 1975; Nemeroff & Wexley, 1977). Results of these studies have been mixed at best.

Two studies have involved manipulations of subordinate participation. French et al. (1966) manipulated subordinate participation by asking each of one group of managers at the close of their appraisal interviews to prepare goals and methods for improvement prior to individual follow-up planning sessions with their superiors. A second group of managers was simply scheduled at the end of their appraisal interviews for individual sessions with their superiors. Effects of this manipulation on performance were conditioned largely by two background factors: usual level of subordinate participation and level of threat to the subordinate during the appraisal interviews. Usual level of subordinate participation was measured by subordinates' reports of their day-to-day influence in their superiors' work components. Threat was measured by observers' reports of the number of critical remarks made to subordinates during interviews. Under conditions of high usual level of participation and low threat during the interview, the manipulation had positive effects on subsequent performance; but under low level of usual participation and high threat during the interview, the manipulation had negative effects on performance.

Bassett and Meyer (1968) manipulated subordinate participation by comparing appraisal interviews based on subordinate-prepared appraisals versus those based on manager-prepared appraisals. They were interested in self-appraisals by subordinates as a vehicle for reducing defensiveness and threat resulting from the judge-defendant roles cast for superiors and subordinates by the traditional manager-prepared appraisal. In the self-appraisal group, subordinates rated themselves on the standard appraisal form prior to the appraisal session. Managers were instructed not to fill out appraisal forms for these subordinates, but they could modify the ratings to their satisfaction during the interview. Self-reviews were preferred over the traditional approach by a majority of managers and generally resulted in less defensive behavior by subordinates. Also, subsequent performance was rated higher for the self-review group of subordinates.

Limitations of Participation and Implications. Several factors seem to moderate the effectiveness of subordinate participation in the interview. Two of these factors are the degree of threat to the subordinate and the previous relationship of supervisor and subordinate. Both the French et al. (1966) and the Bassett and Meyer (1968) studies indicate that participation likely will result in more positive outcomes when threat is low. The evidence from French et al. indicates that increased participation under high threat may actually damage outcomes. These same two studies also demonstrate that the appraisal relationship of superior and subordinate must be considered in the context of their prior relationship. Results from French et al. suggest that a high level of subordinate participation may be ineffective if the subordinate is unaccustomed to such participation. Bassett and Meyer found that when prior contact between the two was frequent and the relationship informal, the shift to a formal interaction represented by the traditional manager-prepared form tended to result in unfavorable attitudes by the subordinate. They also found that newer employees (without a previous appraisal interview with their current supervisor) preferred the manager-prepared format.

Two other factors influencing the effectiveness of subordinate participation in the interview are the subordinate's knowledge concerning interview issues and the subordinate's need for independence. Locke and Schweiger's (1979) review of participation and Vroom and Yetton's (1973) contingency model of leadership indicate that subordinate participation is naturally more effective to the extent that the subordinate has information that the superior lacks. Bassett and Meyer (1968), Keeley (1978), and Locke and Schweiger (1979) cite evidence indicating that participation is less effective for subordinates with low need for independence.

Practical Implications. The above review of subordinate participation in the appraisal interview has practical implications for superiors. First, it seems generally effective for the superior to invite and welcome subordinate participation. For example, the superior might ask several nondirective questions and avoid interrupting the subordinate. Second, the extent to which the superior further structures the interview for subordinate participation should depend on the degree of threatening interview content for the subordinate, the superior's previous relationship with the subordinate, their relative knowledge concerning interview issues, and the subordinate's need for independence. This structuring for greater subordinate participation might take the form of requesting subordinates to appraise themselves or set and discuss goals. Conditions favoring greater participation would be low anticipated threat to the subordinate, a longer tenured subordinate (who had previously received an appraisal interview from the superior), a subordinate accustomed to participating with the superior, and a relatively independent subordinate who is knowledgeable about issues to be discussed in the interview.

Superior's Support and Criticism

The superior's support is a factor dealing with the extent to which the superior is positive, constructive, and accepting of the employee during the interview. Typical measures of this variable have been the items "supervisor was helpful and constructive" and "manager gave recognition for good performance." Although superior's support may seem loosely defined, it has consistently related to positive interview outcomes (Burke & Wilcox, 1969; Burke et al., 1978; Nemeroff and Wexley, 1977; Solem, 1960).

One particular aspect of superior's support is praise. Evidence suggests that praise by the superior may improve interview outcomes, but only if presented effectively. Nemeroff and Wexley (1977) found that praise by the manager correlated positively with subordinate satisfaction with the interview and motivation to improve. However, Kay et al. (1965) concluded that amount of praise by managers had no effect on the interview process or outcomes. Two problems with the managers' administering praise in this situation were, first, subordinates tended not to perceive the praise as being offered sincerely and, second, the superiors seemed to "sandwich" praise in a praise-criticism-praise pattern, so that praise simply conditioned subordinates for the following criticism.

Criticism from superior to subordinate tends to function ineffectively or negatively. Criticism did not relate with any interview outcome in the study by Nemeroff and Wexley (1977). Greller (1978) obtained a positive relationship between criticism and utility of the interview, but a negative relationship between criticism and subordinate satisfaction. Kay et al. (1965) reported that larger numbers of critical statements by superiors resulted in greater defensiveness, more negative attitudes toward appraisals, and less improvement in performance by subordinates.

Although criticism is generally ineffective, criticism in the form of explicit "fair warning" about misbehavior or very poor performance seems appropriate and just. Superiors may be required to present such criticism to the subordinate in writing, with the poor performance specified and possible punitive action explained. An advantage of this formal procedure is that it minimizes misunderstanding (Miner, 1975).

IMPLICATIONS

This review suggests that three factors contribute consistently to effective appraisal interviews. Two of the factors — superior's support and welcoming participation — have related consistently to positive interview outcomes. The third factor — superior's knowledge of the subordinate's job and performance — has been shown by a variety of sources to be important for conducting credible, useful interviews. These behaviors and knowledge may be controlled to some extent by the superior. Thus, one implication of the review is a general guideline that superiors should be knowledgeable about the subordinate's job and performance and should conduct interviews in a manner that provides support and welcomes the subordinate's participation.

Beyond this general guideline, effective management of the appraisal interview is contingent on factors of the employee and the employee's job. Specifically, the employee's performance level, tenure, and need for independence, and the extent of discretion and control available to the employee in the job determine the appropriate function, frequency, and format (appraisal technique and participants) of appraisal interviews for individual employees. These same variables of the employee and job, plus the employee's relationship with the supervisor, set limits on two aspects of the interview process: extent of goal setting and actual subordinate participation. Accordingly, a second implication of the review is that a situational approach be used for conducting appraisal interviews.

An outline of this approach follows. Interviews with high performers in nonroutine jobs should be focused toward development and conducted at flexible intervals. For longer tenure satisfactory employees in routine jobs, interviews should be slanted more toward evaluation of deviations from prior acceptable performance. These interviews should be held relatively infrequently, at set intervals or as warranted by exceptions. Frequent developmental and evaluative interviews should be conducted with newer or lower performing employees. Appropriate appraisal formats would be specific behavioral measures made by the superior for personally dependent employees in routine jobs, goal based appraisals for moderately independent employees in fairly nonroutine jobs, and multiple subjective judgments for highly independent employees in very nonroutine jobs. Appraisal interviews should be structured for high participation by the subordinate when (1) interview content is likely to be relatively nonthreatening to the subordinate, and (2) the subordinate is knowledgeable and personally independent or is a longer term employee accustomed to participation with the superior. When these conditions are not present, interviews should be structured for lower participation. Some goal setting is recommended for most situations, but it would be limited to those aspects of jobs under the subordinate's control.

Training is needed to enable superiors to plan appraisal interviews for different situations and to conduct the interviews. Research in this area of training is limited; nevertheless, several training techniques and suggested contents seem appropriate. Different mock employee situations could be posed to help superiors plan interviews. To increase their knowledge of subordinates' performance, superiors could be trained in methods of observing and recording subordinates' job behavior. One promising approach to developing superiors' interview behavior is indicated by Nemeroff and Cosentino (1979). They found an effective technique that combined (1) questionnaire feedback from subordinates to managers on specific previous interview behaviors of each manager with (2) managers' subsequent goal setting for improvement on their choice of these specific behaviors. Modeling and role playing also are potentially helpful for developing superiors' interview behavior.

CONCLUSION: A SITUATIONAL PERSPECTIVE

Several difficulties with performance appraisal interviews were cited at the beginning of this paper. Organizations have been faulted for allowing appraisal interviews to be conducted infrequently and ineffectively. Superiors have been criticized for conducting perfunctory interviews and failing to see much value in appraisal interviews. Such criticism may stem partly from unrealistic expectations about what appraisal interviews might accomplish. Just as a situational approach seems useful for conducting these interviews, situational expectations for appraisal sessions also seem appropriate. For example, high expectations may be unrealistic for annual interviews with satisfactory employees in routine jobs.

Nevertheless, in many situations the appraisal interview can be much more than routine. To a large extent, effective sessions need to be tailored to individual employees and their jobs. Training superiors to plan and conduct these interviews seems essential, and methods of this training need to be developed further.

REFERENCES

Arvey, R. D., & Ivancevich, J. M. Punishment in organizations: A review, propositions, and research suggestions. *Academy of Management Review,* 1980, 5, 123–132.

Bassett, G. A., & Meyer, H. H. Performance appraisal based on self review. *Personnel Psychology,* 1968, 21, 421–430.

Burke, R. J., & Kimball, L. Performance appraisal: Some issues in the process. *Canadian Journal of Personnel and Industrial Relations,* 1971, 18, 25–34.

Burke, R. J., & Wilcox, D. S. Characteristics of effective employee performance review and development interviews. *Personnel Psychology,* 1969, 22, 291–305.

Burke, R. J., Weitzel, W., & Weir, T. Characteristics of effective employee performance review and development interviews: Replication and extension. *Personnel Psychology,* 1978, 31, 903–919.

Cascio, W. F. *Applied psychology in personnel management.* Reston, Va.: Reston Publishing Company, Inc., 1978.

Cummings, L. L. A field experimental study of the effects of two performance appraisal systems. *Personnel Psychology,* 1973, 26, 489–502.

Cummings, L. L., & Schwab, D. P. Designing appraisal systems for information yield. *California Management Review,* 1978, 20, 18–25.

French, J. R. P., Kay, E., & Meyer, H. Participation and the appraisal system. *Human Relations*, 1966, 19, 3–20.

Greller, M. M. Subordinate participation and reaction to the appraisal interview. *Journal of Applied Psychology*, 1975, 60, 544–549.

Greller, M. M. The nature of subordinate participation in the appraisal interview. *Academy of Management Journal*, 1978, 21, 646–658.

Greller, M. M. Evaluation of feedback sources as a function of role and organizational level. *Journal of Applied Psychology*, 1980, 65, 24–27.

Greller, M. M., & Herold, D. M. Sources of feedback: A preliminary investigation. *Organizational Behavior and Human Performance*, 1975, 13, 244–256.

Hall, D. T., & Lawler, E. E. Unused potential in research and development organizations. *Research Management*, 1969, 12, 339–354.

Ilgen, D. R., Fisher, C. D., & Taylor, M. S. Consequences of individual feedback on behavior in organizations. *Journal of Applied Psychology*, 1979, 64, 349–371.

Kane, J. S., & Lawler, E. E. Performance appraisal effectiveness: Its assessment and determinants. In B. M. Staw (Ed.), *Research in organizational behavior*, 1979, 1, 425–478.

Kay, E., Meyer, H. H., & French, J. R. P. Effects of threat in a performance appraisal interview. *Journal of Applied Psychology*, 1965, 49, 311–317.

Keeley, M. A contingency framework for performance evaluation. *Academy of Management Review*, 1978, 3, 428–438.

Kelly, P. Reappraisals of appraisals. *Harvard Business Review*, 1958, 36 (3), 59–68.

Landy, F. J., & Trumbo, D. A. *Psychology of work behavior.* Homewood, Ill.: The Dorsey Press, 1980.

Landy, F. J., Barnes, J. L., & Murphy, K. R. Correlates of perceived fairness and accuracy of performance evaluation. *Journal of Applied Psychology*, 1978, 63, 751–754.

Locke, E. A., & Schweiger, D. M. Participation in decision-making: One more look. In B. M. Staw (Ed.), *Research in organizational behavior*, 1979, 1, 425–478.

McCall, M. W., & DeVries, D. L. *When nuts and bolts are not enough: An examination of the contextual factors surrounding performance appraisal.* Paper presented at the American Psychological Association, Washington, D. C., 1976.

McConkie, M. L. A clarification of the goal setting and appraisal process in MBO. *Academy of Management Review*, 1979, 4, 29–40.

McGregor, D. An uneasy look at performance appraisal. *Harvard Business Review*, 1957, 35 (3), 89–94.

Meyer, H. H., Kay, E., & French, J. R. P. Split roles in performance appraisal. *Harvard Business Review*, 1965, 43 (1), 123–129.

Miner, M. G. *Management performance appraisal programs* (PPF Survey No. 104). Washington, D. C.: Bureau of National Affairs, Inc., 1974.

Miner, M. G. *Employee performance: Evaluation and control* (PPF Survey No. 108). Washington, D. C.: Bureau of National Affairs, Inc., 1975.

Nemeroff, W. F., & Cosentino, J. Utilizing feedback and goal setting to increase performance appraisal interview skills of managers. *Academy of Management Journal*, 1979, 22, 566–576.

Nemeroff, W. F., & Wexley, K. N. Relationships between performance appraisal characteristics and interview outcomes as perceived by supervisors and subordinates. *Proceedings of the Academy of Management*, 1977, 30–34.

Odiorne, G. S. *Management by objectives.* New York: Pitman, 1965.

Porter, L. W., Lawler, E. E., & Hackman, J. R. *Behavior in organizations.* New York: McGraw-Hill, 1975.

Solem, A. R. Some supervisory problems in appraisal interviewing. *Personnel Administration,* 1960, 23, 27–40.

Vroom, V., & Yetton, P. *Leadership and decision making.* Pittsburgh: University of Pittsburgh Press, 1973.

D.

LEGAL ISSUES
IN PERFORMANCE APPRAISAL

Implications of Performance Appraisal Litigation for Personnel Decisions

Wayne F. Cascio and H. John Bernardin

Over the last 50 years or so, industrial/organizational psychologists have learned a great deal about performance appraisal systems and about the performance appraisal process. At the risk of greatly oversimplifying, one portion of this knowledge is summarized into eight prescriptive categories. We then examine how these prescriptions have been violated in court cases that reached the Federal Appeals or Supreme Court level, recognizing, of course, that the actual number and severity of violations is probably far higher. In a concluding section we consider the implications of this body of case law for I/O scientists and practitioners.

PRESCRIPTIONS FOR PERFORMANCE APPRAISAL SYSTEMS

1. Appraisal of job performance must be based upon an analysis of job requirements as reflected in performance standards. Graphically:

$$\text{Job Analysis} \qquad \text{Performance Appraisal}$$
$$\searrow \qquad\qquad \nearrow$$
$$\text{Performance Standards}$$

2. Appraisal of job performance only becomes reasonable when performance standards have been communicated and understood by employees.
3. Clearly defined individual components or dimensions of job performance should be rated, rather than undefined, global measures of job performance.
4. Performance dimensions should be behaviorally based, so that all ratings can be supported by objective, observable evidence.
5. When using graphic rating scales, avoid abstract trait names (e.g., loyalty, honesty) unless they can be defined in terms of observable behaviors.
6. Keep graphic rating scale anchors brief and logically consistent.

Reprinted with permission from *Personnel Psychology*, Summer 1981, pp. 211–226.

7. As with anything else used as a basis for employment decisions, appraisal systems must be validated, and be psychometrically sound, as well as the ratings given by *individual* raters.

8. Provide a mechanism for appeal if an employee disagrees with a supervisor's appraisal.

Adverse Impact and Appraisal

Unfair discrimination occurs in a variety of ways and there are a number of methods for seeking redress through the courts. Cascio (1978) presents a listing of possible sources for suits involving allegations of employment discrimination. The vast majority of suits involving performance appraisal that reached the U.S. Court of Appeals are filed under Title VII of the 1964 Civil Rights Act.

Although it is sound personnel practice to validate all decision-making methods, validation is legally required only if there is evidence of adverse impact on individuals or groups covered by Title VII of the 1964 Civil Rights Act. Several methods have been used to operationalize the term "adverse impact." One of the most common methods is to compare the selection rates of minority and nonminority groups for the position in question. The 80% rule is suggested by the *Uniform Guidelines* as a "rule of thumb" for assessing adverse impact despite the obvious problem with such a criterion when dealing with small numbers of people. The *Guidelines* do make it clear that the 80% rule is *not* meant to be the sine qua non in determining adverse impact.

In *McDonnell Douglas Corp. v. Green (1973)*, the court specified four criteria for establishing a prima facie case of unfair discrimination. These criteria have been cited often in subsequent cases, and include the following elements: (1) complainant belongs to a racial minority; (2) she/he applies for and is qualified for a job for which the employer is seeking applicants; (3) she/he is rejected despite the qualifications; and (4) after the rejection, the position remained open and the employer continued to seek applicants from persons of the complainant's qualifications. The courts might also look at population statistics for the relevant geographical area (e.g., Standard Metropolitan Statistical Area data) in order to compare percentages of occupants in given positions. Finally, adverse impact could also be defined simply in terms of evidence that the employer *deliberately* denied equal opportunity for individuals or groups covered under Title VII. Horstman (1978) reviewed court cases with respect to the definitions of adverse impact that are imposed. She found that there was little consistency in the definitions applied and that the extraneous factors apparently play a major role in the proceedings of the cases.

RELEVANT CASE LAW

For the sake of parsimony, only pertinent sections of legal rulings will be cited in order to illustrate their impact on the prescriptions presented above.

1. Job Analysis and Performance Standards

In *Patterson v. American Tobacco Co.* (1976, 1978), the Court affirmed a finding of discrimination in the selection of supervisors and ordered the company to develop written job descriptions and objective criteria for appointments. Prior to 1968 each department in the company maintained its own seniority roster, and departments were rigidly segregated by race. The company had no formal, objective, written standards for promotions to supervisory positions. Instead, a system of "unwritten qualifications" was used to deny black employees access to higher paying jobs. A similar pattern of personnel practices was also struck down in *Sledge v. J. P. Stevens & Co.* (1978).

In *Robinson v. Union Carbide Corp.* (1976), the statistical evidence showed substantial adverse impact against blacks in supervisory positions. The Company said it relied on nondiscriminatory data for promotion — foremen were asked to recommend qualified persons for vacant positions. The Court ruled that while the "foreman's recommendation is the indispensable single most important factor in the promotion process, [he is] given no written instructions pertaining to the qualifications necessary for promotion . . . Standards determined to be controlling are vague and subjective. . . . There are no safeguards in the procedure designed to avert discriminatory practices." Similar issues were considered in *Rowe v. General Motors Corp.* (1972), *EEOC v. Radiator Specialty Co.* (1979), and in *Meyer v. Missouri State Highway Commission* (1977), where a female toll bridge collector was never promoted to shift captain. The manager of the bridge hired, fired, and promoted individuals to the position of shift captain. However, since the job of shift captain was "unclassified," there was no written description of job duties or minimum qualifications for the job. "Informal procedures" were used in making promotions (the manager summoned chosen individuals to his office and asked if they wanted the position of shift captain). Personnel practices such as these never have, and probably never will, stand the test of judicial scrutiny.

2. Communication of Performance Standards

In *Donaldson v. Pillsbury Co.* (1977), a female sought relief for wrongful discharge based on race and sex and asked for class action certification. Among other things, she claimed that since she had never been given a job description and never told of policies regarding personal phone calls or other work standards, her subsequent discharge was unlawful. The Eighth Circuit Court of Appeals ruled that similar grievances by others *were* sufficient to constitute a class action, and remanded the case back to the District Court, which it found had excluded certain evidence which might have affected the findings.

Similarly, in *Weahkee v. Perry* (1978), an American Indian sued the chairperson of E.E.O.C. alleging discharge based on racial discrimination. Weahkee claimed he was not given specific instructions as to where to put work priorities when investigating complaints in his job as a complaint investigator for E.E.O.C. Moreover, when given an unsatisfactory evaluation, he was not told how he could improve, and then he was discharged. The District Court ordered judgment for Weahkee, but the Appeals Court reversed, and sent the case back to the District Court for further evidence and findings on issues of fact. In both *Donaldson* and *Weahkee*, clear communication of job requirements and performance standards may well have made formal legal action unnecessary.

3. Define and Rate Individual Performance Dimensions

There are two landmark cases on this point, both dealing with the use of global, undifferentiated paired comparisons — *Albemarle Paper Co. v. Moody* (1975) and *Watkins v. Scott Paper Co.* (1976). In *Albemarle*, the company conducted a concurrent validity study without benefit of any job analyses, among other deficiencies. In gathering criterion data, supervisors were instructed to judge which employee was the better of the two when names were presented in a paired comparison format. Employees in different jobs were compared, and supervisors were given no bases on which to determine the "better" employee of each pair. The Supreme Court found that supervisory ratings based on such "vague and inadequate standards" are subject to a plethora of interpretations of doubtful job relatedness.

In *Watkins*, as in *Albemarle*, the paired comparison system in use did not require supervisors to judge specific skills or work functions. "Nowhere in the record is there any suggestion that the supervisors were asked to determine something other than which of the two employees was 'better.'" As in *Albemarle*, the use of a global paired comparison technique which used no focused or stable body of criteria was rejected. Several of the suggestions the Court made for the company relate to the appraisal process:

(1) "Formulating guidelines that explain the manner in which job-related, objective criteria such as absenteeism and number of reprimands are evaluated, (2) formulating guidelines that explain the relative importance of subjective criteria found to be job-related, and (3) devising a procedure by which Scott can recognize situations where first line supervisors' recommendations might be subject to racial bias."

Other types of appraisal systems that are factorially heterogeneous are also subject to challenge, e.g., when "quantity" and "quality" of work are combined into a single rating dimension as in *James v. Stockholm Valves & Fittings Co.* (1977).

4, 5, and 6. Performance Dimensions Should be Behaviorally Based. Avoid Abstract Trait Names in Graphic Rating Scales. Keep Graphic Rating Scale Anchors Brief and Logically Consistent.

At *Stockholm Valves* employees were evaluated by supervisors using a form composed of seven undefined dimensions: quantity and quality of work, job or trade knowledge, ability to learn, cooperation, dependability, industry, and attendance. In examining these dimensions we are reminded of the study done in the early 1960's in which 47 executives were asked to define the word "dependability" (Bass & Barrett, 1981). The 47 executives produced 75 *different* definitions of "dependability"! Yet today, many appraisal systems still present the dimension "dependability," and leave its definition to the rater. While several of the *Stockholm Valves* dimensions are potentially behaviorally based, abstract traits such as cooperation, dependability, and industry are less defensible, unless they can be defined in terms of observable behaviors. However, when we examine the anchors for each of these dimensions, they are not behaviorally based and they are open to diverse interpretation. On each factor, employees were rated "unsatisfactory," "poor," "average," "superior," or "exceptional." Among other problems that caused a violation of Title VII, the Court noted the following: (1) incumbent foremen (predominantly white) play a critical role in the selection of new foremen or supervisors, (2) recommendations are largely discretionary and there are no adequate safeguards against racial bias, (3) no written guidelines specify necessary qualifications, and (4) criteria for promotion are subjective. On these last two points in awkward, *Gilmore v. Kansas City Terminal Railway Co.* (1975), supervisors were asked to evaluate their subordinates' promotability and to consider "aptitude, ability, and work habits" in doing so. However, the supervisors were given no criteria for effective "aptitude, abilities or work habits." Again, the court ruled in the plaintiff's favor.

As in *Stockholm Valves*, given evidence of adverse impact resulting from the use of ratings, unless each appraisal dimension can be supported by objective, observable evidence, its continued use may well be prohibited. However, there is another issue here, and that is, even if an otherwise legitimate performance appraisal system is *used* improperly it may be struck down. Thus in *U.S.A. v. City of Chicago* (1978), a racial discrimination case involving fire department promotions, appraisal ratings made in a lower level job were used as criteria in a concurrent validation study where the tests were intended for use in a higher level job. The court noted,

> "The only way a correlation between prepromotion efficiency ratings and test scores could comply with the E.E.O.C. Guidelines would be if the employer could establish that requirements of the lower level job and the job for which the test is being administered are identical. No such showing was made in this case."

In *Marquez v. Omaha District Sales Office, Ford Division of the Ford Motor Company* (1971), performance appraisals had been designated formally as an important factor in employee promotions. Mr. Marquez had excellent appraisals for 15 years, together with consistent ratings from his supervisors as promotable to the next higher level job. Nevertheless he was kept at his same position, and for no reason which appears on the record or in his employment files, his name was removed from the list of promotable employees. No reason was given for the removal of his name and the company was found guilty of racial discrimination.

Similarly, in *Cleverly v. Western Electric Co.* (1979), an age discrimination case, a personnel decision to discharge an employee was contradicted by the weight of evidence in 14 years' worth of performance appraisal data. Cleverly had received satisfactory performance ratings and steadily increasing salary during his 14 years of service to the company. When discharged, he was told that one reason for the discharge was to make way for younger engineers in the department, and his discharge occurred just six months prior to the vesting of his pension. The company was found guilty of age discrimination and Cleverly was awarded back pay. As in Chicago and Marquez, an otherwise lawful appraisal system was used improperly.

7. Validate Appraisal Systems and Raters

For those cases involving performance appraisal that reached a U.S. Court of Appeals, rarely are any empirical data presented to justify either the system itself or the ratings given by individual raters. The importance of such data surfaced early in *Rowe v. General Motors Corp.* (1972), *Brito v. Zia Co.* (1973), *Bolton v. Murray Envelope Corp.* (1974), and *Wade v. Mississippi Cooperative Extension Service* (1976). In *Zia*, for example, unsatisfactory performance appraisal ratings were used as the basis for layoffs of 12 Hispanic and three native American workers. When challenged, the company was unable to introduce any evidence of the validity of its appraisal system. No records of performance were maintained, and thus no specific performances were documented to justify the ratings. Employees were not evaluated according to their "average daily amount of acceptable performance," and were not even observed on a daily basis. The appraisal system was struck down because Zia could provide "no empirical data demonstrating that the appraisal system was significantly correlated with important elements of work behavior relevant to the jobs for which the appellants were being evaluated."

It should be pointed out that the type of validity evidence required for performance ratings is linked to the *purposes* for which the ratings are made. For example, if appraisal of past performance is to be used as a predictor of future performance (i.e., promotions), validation evidence must be presented to show first that the ratings of past performances are in fact valid, and second, that the ratings of past performances are related to *future* performance in another job (*U.S.A. v. City of Chicago*, 1978). At the very least, this latter step should entail a job analysis indicating the extent to which the two jobs in question overlap. Given evidence of adverse impact, if appraisal of past performance is to be used for the purpose of making personnel decisions such as merit pay, layoffs, or demotions, defendants must show that the appraisals are valid measures of past performance. This need to validate apparently also applies to appraisal when the data are only used for the empirical validation of some predictor as, for example, in the Supreme Court case of *Albemarle v. Moody* (1975).

Validity data of any kind are rare indeed for appraisal systems since one of the principal reasons for using "soft" criteria is the nonexistence of "hard" criteria such as error rates, production rates, etc. Moreover, it appears that the relationships between ratings and "hard" criteria are weak (e.g., Cascio and Valenzi, 1978; Hausmann and Strupp, 1955).

To put this issue in perspective, Cascio and Valenzi (1978) hypothesized that overall variance in supervisory ratings is composed of four elements: (a) systematic, job-relevant variance that is contained in objective performance indices; (b) systematic, job-relevant variance that is not reflected in strictly objective indices of performance; (c) systematic, but job-irrelevant variance that may or may not be contained in strictly objective measures of performance; and (d) error variance. Consistent with previous research findings, and despite the use of behaviorally anchored rating scales, less than 25% of the variance in supervisors' ratings was accounted for by objective indices. In terms of their model, therefore, it appears that overall variance in supervisory ratings is composed mainly of one or more of the last three elements.

The problem of validating ratings is further illustrated by the following quote from the *Uniform Guidelines*:

> " . . . ratings should be examined for evidence of racial, ethnic or sex bias. All criteria need to be examined for freedom from factors which would unfairly alter scores of members of any group. The relevance of criteria and their freedom from bias are of particular concern when there are significant differences in measures of job performance for different groups" (*Federal Register*, 43, 166, August 25, 1978).

The first two sentences of this quotation imply that there is some way to distinguish true sources of variance from error variance due to biasing factors. In other words, if mean differences are found on some rating scale as a function of race or sex, the *Guidelines* imply there is a method of determining whether the mean differences were due to bias in the system (e.g., prejudiced raters) or actual differences in performance as a function of race or sex. In fact, such a distinction cannot clearly be made in almost any appraisal circumstance. As we have seen in this review, however, the courts continually call for safeguards against such racial, ethnic, or sex bias (e.g., *Robinson v. Union Carbide*; *Watkins v. Scott Paper*; *James v. Stockholm Valves*). We address this issue more fully in a final section of the paper.

The third sentence from the *Uniform Guidelines* quote above (i.e., "relevance of criteria") in fact has been the focus of attention when significant race/sex differences in appraisal ratings exist.

Thus in *U.S.A. v. City of Chicago* (1978), in remanding the case back to the District Court, the Appeals Court noted:

> On remand, the district court should follow this approach in analyzing the legality of the efficiency ratings. This district court should first make specific findings on whether whites received higher efficiency rating scores than minorities. If such a disparity exists, the district court should make additional findings on whether defendants have met their burden of establishing job relatedness. This determination should involve more than face validity; an inquiry into whether the efficiency ratings accurately predict performance in the job being tested for will be required (16EPD 8141, p. 4651).

In order to demonstrate this, Chicago relied on two criterion-related validity studies. In the first study, test results were correlated (inappropriately, as was pointed out earlier) with pre-existing performance appraisals of each candidate's performance in positions held before taking the promotional exam. In the second study, performance ratings were correlated with ratings given in drill tests. The relevance of drill tests as criteria was evaluated by the Appeals Court as follows:

> Indeed, the district court recognized that drill tests "do not clearly distinguish between the individuals' performance and that of the unit under his direction." Moreover, even if the performance of the drill test leader could be effectively isolated, drill test scores would still be an inadequate validation device absent a showing that the drill tests measured the major responsibilities of the promotional positions (126 EPD 8141, FN.9).

And further,

> Defendants contend on appeal that the correlation between efficiency ratings and drill tests demonstrates that the promotional exams are construct valid. A construct valid study is one in which examinations are structured to measure the degree to which job applicants have identifiable characteristics that have been determined to be important in job performance (*Washington v. Davis, supra* at 247, n. 13). This argument does not help defendants, however, because there has been no attempt to determine from a job analysis what traits are necessary for job performance. E.E.O.C. Guidelines, 29 C.F.R. 1607.5(a). Thus the drill tests fail to demonstrate either criterion validity or construct validity because they fail to predict performance in promotional ranks (16 EPD 8141, FN.10).

In short, there is no doubt that performance criteria are subject to the same standards as written tests (as they should be), that the courts in general are quite sophisticated in evaluating their job relatedness, and that the development of criteria must receive the same careful attention to detail as the development of "predictors."

8. Provide a Mechanism for Appeal

One of the few things we do know for certain with respect to appraisal systems is that they must be acceptable to those being rated if they are to work in practice. An appeal procedure does not guarantee that employees will agree with their ratings or even agree with the rating system. But it does help to know that ratings assigned (usually by the immediate supervisor) are reviewable, that the rater is answerable to a higher authority, and that employees have the right to present their side of the story before pursuing more formal, legal means for redress. Personnel practices which permit one person's appraisal to carry complete weight in personnel decisions, as in *Rowe, Robinson, Meyer, Watkins, Stockholm Valves,* and *Wade* are unlikely to be permitted unless they can be supported by documented, objective, reliable evidence for each dimension rated. In most cases, this is difficult, if not impossible, to demonstrate.

IMPLICATIONS OF CASE LAW CITED

Clearly this body of case law has implications for a wide variety of personnel decisions. In this section we consider five such implications.

1. Appraisal Systems Must Meet the Uniform Guidelines Like Other Tests

It is apparent from *Brito v. Zia,* and *U.S.A. v. City of Chicago* that, once adverse impact is shown, performance appraisal systems must be validated in some manner, that they must be psychometrically sound, and that arguments for face or even content validity are unacceptable. *Zia* focused on particular raters and their rating behavior, work habits, and attitudes. In this context, we must thus validate raters as well as appraisal systems. The *Guidelines* state that criteria should represent: "important or critical work behavior(s) or work outcomes . . . " (*Federal Register, 43,* 166, August 25, 1978).

We invoke the term "content domain sampling" here as preferable to "content validity" because we wish to distinguish inferences about the adequacy and representativeness of the content of the rating form vis a vis the content of the job (content domain sampling) from the appropriateness of inferences made about the rating scores (content validity). Both are clearly important. While the use of a behaviorally-based rating form may be *necessary* in order to provide a job-relevant rationale for personnel actions, the use of such a (content domain sampled) form is certainly not *sufficient* for defense of the appropriateness or reasonableness of the actions taken. In short, the validity of the rating scores themselves must also be demonstrated. Arvey (1979) has written that "organizations that have made reasonable efforts to develop criterion measures through carefully developed job analysis, have checked the reliabilities of these measures, and have performed statistical tests to detect differences between ratings of minority and majority groups will likely survive court challenges of these measures" (p. 119). We disagree. While behaviorally anchored rating scales, for example, would certainly be looked upon more favorably than trait-oriented scales, mean differences on the two scales as a function of race or sex would be a more critical issue in any court proceeding (cf., *Brito v. Zia,* 1973; *U.S.A. v. City of Chicago,* 1978). Thus, we prefer to reserve the term "validity" for inferences about scores, rather than contents of appraisal forms.

What then should be done if racial differences are found in appraisal results? To be sure, this is an outcome the individual differences literature would predict more often than not (cf. Humphreys, note 1). Assuming that such differences are found in ratings and the ratings result in adverse impact against a group or individual covered under Title VII, some type of validation evidence must be presented to justify the ratings (parenthetically, if the ratings are used only as criteria in a validation study where adverse impact occurs as a function of the predictor, evidence for the validity of the ratings is also likely to be required).

The most basic issue at this point is the purpose of the appraisal, for as Jacobs, Kafry, and Zedeck (1980) have noted, different purposes require different information to be collected, which in turn requires different methodologies for performance appraisal. Appraisals may be used either as predictors (e.g., in personnel decisions to promote, to train, or to transfer) or as criteria (e.g., in personnel research, in establishing objectives for training programs, as a basis for employee feedback and development, merit pay decisions, disciplinary decisions, layoff decisions). Criterion-related validity strategies seem most appropriate when appraisals are used as predictors, especially when unbiased criteria are or become available (e.g., dollar-valued productivity measures). When appraisals are used as criteria, a construct-oriented strategy seems more appropriate (e.g., Campbell, 1976). The first step is to demonstrate that an adequate content domain sampling procedure has been followed. Thus, a showing of job-relatedness would depend on the adequacy with which the appraisal instrument sampled the content domain(s) of the job, the extent to which critical tasks or work behaviors were assessed, the extent to which any special circumstances were considered in developing the content domains, and the extent to which definitions of psychological constructs were supported by research evidence (American Psychological Association, Division of Industrial-Organizational Psychology, 1980).

Some of the best evidence for the validity of ratings regardless of purpose would be correlations with important, uncontaminated, nonjudgmental criteria (e.g., sales volume). As stated above, however, this type of data is more often than not unavailable.

Thus, we must turn to other methods in order to validate the appraisal system and individual raters.

Bernardin (1979) has proposed two methods for validating raters. One approach is to have raters evaluate any variables that are in fact verifiable along with those which are not verifiable. For example, raters could be asked to rate absenteeism or error rates for ratees and these ratings could be correlated with objective data on these two variables. A high correlation would indicate that the raters are basing their evaluations on observed individual differences. Inferences can then be made regarding ratings on non-verifiable dimensions. With this procedure, individual raters can also be examined for error in ratings (e.g., leniency and severity errors). One obvious criticism of this approach is that the validity of ratings on verifiable dimensions such as absenteeism or error rates may have little or no relationship to the validity of ratings on non-verifiable dimensions. Some research has shown accuracy or validity in ratings may be generalizable across dimensions (Borman, 1977; Mullins and Force, 1962). When one considers the impact of rater motivation on the validity of ratings (e.g., Landy & Farr, 1980), the generalizability of validity within raters and across dimensions is plausible.

The second approach to "validating" raters is to correlate observations of ratee behavior with appraisals. For example, raters could do their evaluations at the regularly scheduled time. However, during the observation period, the raters or, preferably, the ratees would also maintain records of exhibited work behaviors. These incidents of behavior should be as descriptive and nonevaluative as possible. There should be no mention of traits or dimensions, merely behaviors and contexts. Once a fair number of these incidents is recorded for each ratee and, preferably, from more than one observer's perspective, subject matter experts thoroughly familiar with the positions under study would receive randomly ordered lists of these now "anonymous" incidents (behaviors at this point are no longer linked to individual ratees). Ratings of effectiveness and importance could then be derived for each incident and descriptive statistics could be compiled for each incident, for each ratee, and from each rater. A ratee's overall rating for each observation period would be compiled by taking the mean or median effectiveness rating for the group of incidents applicable to him/her, perhaps using importance ratings as multipliers. These ratings could then be correlated with ratings made on the formal evaluation form by each rater. After a test of level differences as a function of rater, a differential accuracy measure (Cronbach, 1955) could then be used to derive an accuracy coefficient for each rater. A high correlation would represent high agreement between a rater's order of evaluations for his/her ratees and subject matter experts' order of evaluations for behaviors exhibited by the same ratees. Thus, with this procedure, a form of construct validity is revealed for each rater's ratings.

While validating raters is indeed a difficult task, such data may be essential if adverse impact has resulted from personnel decisions based on ratings or when significant mean differences are found as a function of race, sex or age when ratings are used as criteria in a test validation study. The presentation of summary statistics on ratings such as convergent or discriminant validity, halo error, or reliability appears to be of limited significance in court cases on appraisal. Rather, the emphasis has been on particular raters and justification for their ratings.

2. Encourage Internal Review of Appraisal Systems

After reading the testimony of company officials in many of these cases, one gets the uneasy feeling that (1) top management was totally unaware of what kind of appraisal system was in effect at lower levels, or (2) the employer was well aware of the (illegal) appraisal system in use but was unaware of what was wrong with it. Like drivers who try unsuccessfully to alibi their way out of a traffic ticket are all too painfully aware (" . . . but officer, I didn't know this was a one-way street"), ignorance is no excuse. One lesson which top managers understand well is that mistakes in the personnel area can be costly. However, improvement in appraisal systems requires a method as well as the motivation to improve. Personnel professionals might well use the eight prescriptions cited earlier as a checklist and encourage organizations to take proactive steps to correct deficiencies rather than reactive steps to cover them up or explain them away. Knowing the issues involved in appraisal litigation helps in diagnosing existing systems, and in convincing line managers of their vulnerability.

3. Fit Practice to Purpose

The lesson from *Chicago, Cleverly* and *Marquez* is clear. Appraisal systems which pass muster in every respect, but which either are disregarded in personnel decisions (such as layoff or promotion), or are used improperly (appraisals made at lower levels used as validation criteria for higher level jobs), will be subject to challenge.

4. Expand Research on Rater Training and Rater Accuracy

As Bernardin and Buckley (1981) and Spool (1978) have shown, we know little about how to train people to observe performance-related behavior. The effects of training to avoid constant errors such as halo and leniency has had mixed results (Bernardin and Pence, 1980; Thornton and Zorich, 1980). There can be little question, however, that some dimensions are more difficult to rate accurately than others, especially when embedded within particular political, social, and emotional contexts. Finally, the characteristics that differentiate easy from difficult dimensions should be investigated. At the outset, however, we must recognize that we don't know what truth is in performance appraisal.

5. Let's Get Back to Basics

One of the important lessons to be learned from this review of litigation in performance appraisal is that appraisal systems are often found wanting because in translating theory into practice we have ignored the fundamental principles that make performance appraisal scientifically sound (i.e., the eight prescriptions noted earlier). Nevertheless, it is clear that factors other than those cited above will, on occasion, influence the ultimate decision of the courts. For example, the scrutiny a decision system receives will depend to a large extent on the overall impact of the system and the affirmative action posture of the employer (Herring, note 2; Horstman, 1978; Kleiman and Faley, 1978; Schneier, 1978). In their review of 66 court cases, most of which were settled at the District Court level, Feild and Holley (Note 3) found that the type of organization of the defendant was the best predictor of case outcome. That is, if a charge was filed against an industrial organization, verdicts were more likely to be found in favor of the plaintiff compared to cases involving a non-industrial employer. Feild and Holley (Note 3) also cited the importance of job analysis, written instructions for raters, a behavioral rating format, and an employee review process as important determinants of the outcomes of cases.

It is clear from case law that high levels of adverse impact in promotion, facilitated by sex or race differences on an appraisal instrument, would be difficult to defend even with a very sophisticated rating format. And, unfortunately, we know all too well that more sophisticated formats are no less subject to rating biases than the simpler types (Landy and Farr, 1980). Prescriptions for scientifically sound, court-proof appraisal systems are not difficult to offer (e.g., job relevance, user acceptability, sensitivity, reliability, practicality). As we have seen, however, the implementation of credible, workable appraisal systems requires diligent attention by organizations to the fundamental principles, plus an enduring commitment to make them work in practice.

REFERENCE NOTES

1. Humphreys, L. G. *Adverse impact on blacks of tests and criterion measures.* Paper presented at the meeting of the American Psychological Association, San Francisco, CA, 1977.
2. Herring, J. W. *Guarding personnel appraisal procedures against charges of unfair bias.* Paper presented at the meeting of the Southeastern Psychological Association, Washington, D.C., 1980.
3. Feild, H. S. and Holley, W. H. *The relationship of performance appraisal system characteristics to verdicts in selected employment discrimination cases.* Unpublished manuscript, Auburn University, 1980.

REFERENCES

Albemarle Paper Co. v. Moody. 422 U.S. 405 (1975).

American Psychological Association, Division of Industrial-Organizational Psychology. *Principles for the validation and use of personnel selection procedures* (Second edition) Berkeley, CA: author, 1980.

Arvey, R. D. *Fairness in selecting employees.* Reading, Mass.: Addison-Wesley, 1979.

Bass, B. M. and Barrett, G. V. *People, work, and organizations (2nd ed.).* Boston: Allyn & Bacon, 1981.

Bernardin, H. J. Implications of the Uniform Selection Guidelines for performance appraisals of police officers. *Proceedings of the national workshop on the selection of law enforcement officers,* 1979, 97–102.

Bernardin, H. J. and Buckley, M. R. A consideration of strategies in rater training. *Academy of Management Review,* 1981, 2, 205–212.

Bernardin, H. J. and Pence, E. C. Effects of rater training: Creating new response sets and decreasing accuracy. *Journal of Applied Psychology,* 1980, 65, 60–66.

Bolton v. Murray Envelope Corp. 493 F.2d 191 (5th Cir., 1974).

Borman, W. C. Consistency of rating accuracy and rating error in the judgment of human performance. *Organizational Behavior and Human Performance,* 1977, 20, 238–252.

Brito v. Zia Co. 478 F.2d 1200 (10th Cir. 1973). Cascio, W. F. *Applied psychology in personnel management.* Reston, Va.: Reston, 1978.

Cascio, W. F. and Valenzi, E. R. Relations among criteria of police performance. *Journal of Applied Psychology,* 1978, 63, 22–28.

Campbell, J. P. Psychometric theory. In Dunnette, M. D. (Ed.), *Handbook of industrial and organizational psychology.* Chicago, Ill.: Rand-McNally, 1976.

Cleverly v. Western Electric Co. 594 F.2d 638 (8th Cir. 1979).

Cronbach, L. J. Processes affecting scores on "understanding of others" and "assumed similarity." *Psychological Bulletin,* 1955, 52, 177–193.

Donaldson v. Pillsbury Co. 554 F.2d 825 (8th Cir. 1977).

E.E.O.C. v. Radiator Specialty Co. 610 F.2d 178 (4th Cir. 1979).

Gilmore v. Kansas City Terminal Railway Co. 509 F2d 48 (8th Cir. 1975).

Hausman, H. J. and Strupp, H. H. Non-technical factors in superiors' ratings of job performance. *Personnel Psychology*, 1955, 8, 201–217.

Horstman, D. A. New judicial standards for adverse impact: Their meaning for personnel practices. *Public Personnel Management*, 1978, 7, 347–353.

Jacobs, R., Kafry, D., and Zedeck, S. Expectations of behaviorally anchored rating scales. *Personnel Psychology*, 1980, 33, 595–640.

James v. Stockholm Valves & Fittings Co. 559 F.2d 310 (5th Cir. 1977).

Kleiman, L. and Faley, R. Assessing content validity: Standards set by the court. *Personnel Psychology*, 1978, 31, 701–713.

Landy, F. J. and Farr, J. L. Performance rating. *Psychological Bulletin*, 1980, 87, 72–107.

Marquez v. Omaha District Sales Office, Ford Division of Ford Motor Co. 440 F2d 1157 (8th Cir. 1971).

McDonnell Douglas Corp. v. Green. 411 US. 792 (1973).

Meyer v. Missouri State Highway Commission. 567 F.2d 804 (8th Cir. 1977).

Mullins, C. J. and Force, R. C. Rater accuracy as a generalized ability. *Journal of Applied Psychology*, 1962, 46, 191–193.

Patterson v. American Tobacco Co. 535 F.2d 275 (4th Cir. 1976). Also 586 f.2d 300 (4th Cir. 1978).

Robinson v. Union Carbide Corp. 538 F.2d 652 (5th Cir. 1976).

Rowe v. General Motors Corp. 457 F.2d 348 (5th Cir. 1972).

Schneier, D. B. The impact of EEO legislation on performance appraisals. *Personnel*, 1978, July-August, 24–34.

Sledge v. J. P. Stevens & Co. 585 F.2d 625 (4th Cir. 1978).

Spool, M. D. Training programs for observers of behavior: A review. *Personnel Psychology*, 1978, 31, 853–888.

Thornton, G. C. and Zorich, S. Training to improve observer accuracy. *Journal of Applied Psychology*, 1980, 65, 351–354.

U.S.A. v. City of Chicago. 573 F.2d 416 (7th Cir. 1978).

Wade v. Mississippi Cooperative Extension Service. 528 F.2d 508 (5th Cir. 1976).

Watkins v. Scott Paper Co. 503 F.2d 159 (5th Cir. 1976).

Weahkee v. Perry, 587 F.2d 1256 (D.C. Div. 1978).

E.

PERFORMANCE APPRAISAL

Interview with Charlene Bradley

Charlene Bradley is currently Manager of the Performance Management Program for civilian employees of the United States Air Force. In this position, she is responsible for the development of appraisal systems, performance-based incentive and awards programs, and productivity and probationary systems. In her eighteen years with the Air Force, Ms. Bradley has also worked in the areas of employee relations, personnel staffing, and computerized personnel systems management. She has been assigned to both overseas and U.S. locations and is a member of the International Personnel Management Association.

1. Can you briefly discuss your professional experience in performance appraisal?

I've had eighteen years' experience in personnel with the Air Force at Base level, at Major Command level, and now with the Air Staff. I am a Personnel Management Specialist in the Directorate of Civilian Personnel. In 1982 I assumed responsibility for the civilian appraisal systems. We have approximately 240,000 civilian employees in the Air Force, and the appraisal systems I am responsible for cover all those employees with the exception of senior executive service members. In 1983, after an extensive evaluation, I decided to revamp our current appraisal systems (we had three at the time) and combine them into one appraisal system utilizing a single form. On July 1, 1984, we established a performance management program for civilian employees in the Air Force. So, I am program manager not only for developing civilian appraisal systems, but incentive awards programs, performance based incentive systems like merit pay, probationary requirements, fitness for duty medical determinations, unemployability, dealing with poor performers, and, more recently, productivity of civilian employees. The latter will include some new ideas to the federal sector such as gain sharing. We will also be looking at quality circles and productivity incentive systems that deal with cash awards. So actually, I am responsible for taking the appraisal system and making it mesh with, and be the basis for, all the other systems that I've just talked about.

2. Why, in your opinion, has performance appraisal received so much visibility in organizations — and in the personnel literature — in the last ten years?

There are several reasons for this increased visibility, and the reasons are different in the public sector compared to the private sector. In the private sector, top management has been concerned for some time about profit and loss. The Japanese are competing effectively with us in just about every business involving high-tech. Consumers have been generally dissatisfied with our products and services, and there have been declines in the productivity of American workers and the quality of American products.

In 1982 I was looking at various performance appraisal systems in use in the private sector. One high-tech company in Colorado that I visited had done very well in the first few years after the company was founded, but then began to see productivity dropping off. In response, they instituted a very sophisticated appraisal system (in fact, a lot like the one we had in the Air Force under the Civil Service Reform Act), and trained their managers and employees extensively in the use of the system. In the short time of about six months that I was corresponding back and forth with these folks and made a visit, they changed their appraisal form four times! In looking for reasons for their declining economic performance, management felt they needed to find a valid appraisal system to determine who the good workers were and be able to weed out the poorer performers.

While the primary impetus for performance appraisal in the private sector has been profits, in the public sector it has been political considerations. The public has had for some time a perception of overpaid and underworked public servants. The mid to late 1970s saw the largest federal government work force that we've ever had, and it was during the Carter administration that the big effort began to make sure that the government provided better service to the public. So, a lot of politics came into play during the Carter administration, and since that time there's been increased emphasis on productivity and performance in the federal sector. The civil rights movement had a great deal to do with it because of the Uniform Guidelines on Employee Selection. Further, the Civil Service Reform Act of 1978 introduced the principles of "merit" in determining which employees you retain, promote, and reward. A valid performance appraisal system is, of course, required for a personnel system based on merit principles. So I think it was a combination of things that were happening — remember, we just came out of the Vietnam War at that time. We were beginning to look inward for things that we wanted to improve, and performance appraisal was one of the places that we looked.

3. *You mentioned the importance of the civil rights movement to the increased visibility of performance appraisal systems. Since performance appraisals are used in promotion decisions, they must meet the legal requirements applicable to selection techniques (i.e., they must be "valid" and nondiscriminatory). What impact has increasing legal scrutiny of performance appraisal systems had on personnel practice related to appraisal systems?*

Well, it's totally changed the way we do business! It used to be that in the federal sector we simply told employees once a year whether they were satisfactory, outstanding, or unsatisfactory. And even though many agencies had a "requirement" to establish standards for employees by which their performance could be measured, I would venture to say that it was rarely done. The Civil Service Reform Act legislated requirements for written performance standards and also for valid performance appraisal systems to be used in promotion. Further, personnel research psychologists have to be concerned about the design of performance appraisal systems to meet validity requirements because of the Uniform Guidelines.

The litigation costs in discrimination cases can be absolutely staggering. One class action discrimination suite at a military base or in a federal agency, for instance, where the agency loses that case based on either performance appraisal systems that haven't been validated or prohibitive personnel practices, could literally cost the agency millions. Yet, the typical first-line supervisor really doesn't have the time or the personnel management expertise to stay up with all the changes and all the requirements. It's very difficult at times to explain to that first-line supervisor, and sometimes to top management, why it's important that we have systems that can bear legal scrutiny. Until they're involved in an actual case, or until they have heard of a case, they are naturally not as concerned. It's just like you don't get really concerned about drunk driving until you're involved in an accident.

4. *While the personnel department is often charged with the responsibility of developing the performance appraisal system, line managers are the ones who must implement the system. What are the major problems P/HRM professionals face in getting a performance appraisal system implemented?*

The biggest problem is that for years it's been "our" system. In other words, performance appraisal systems belong to the personnel people. They were invented by personnel people to be used by personnel people, and in some cases that is still true. Now, with the new legal requirements I mentioned earlier, it seems to managers even more so than before that these systems are being forced on them. They see a significant workload with little return for the time spent.

When personnel people design appraisal systems, we've got to deal with management's needs. That's who we work for; we want to design systems that help them promote and retain their top people with the least amount of paperwork and pain to them. I'd say our biggest problem when we try to do that is really our PR — selling it to managers and convincing them that this is something that is useful and beneficial to them. We had some success with that in our last system when we used managers along with personnel specialists in a team concept to teach the performance management program to other supervisors. Where the managers themselves were sold — where they could see the benefits — they were the best PR people for the system.

Another difficulty in implementing our appraisal systems is that federal employees are becoming more knowledgeable about how personnel systems are affecting them. They are aware — especially since the Civil Service Reform Act of 1978 — exactly how performance appraisal will affect their future. Employees know that their score on an appraisal will be affecting their promotion opportunities, their basic pay, the awards they get, and their longevity with the organization. For that reason, employee unions have become more involved in the development of appraisal systems and in negotiating the impact and implementation of such systems. Unions are very sensitive to changing personnel practices that affect their members. So, we must meet management's needs, while at the same time designing a system that protects employees and the merit systems principles addressed in the Civil Service Reform Act.

5. *Why is performance appraisal so hard for managers to do well? How can difficulties be minimized? Are there particular problems for managers in public sector, as opposed to private sector, organizations?*

Well, in a nutshell, I would say that the number one problem is just plain human nature. No one ever really wants to tell another individual what their weaknesses or strengths are. There's a basic fear of confrontation. It would be a rare individual, I think, that would enjoy sitting down and telling another person that they are not doing well, or they are not doing as well as they could, or that their work habits need improvement. Also there's the possibility of feeling inadequate on one's own part if everything isn't going well with a subordinate. If I have someone working for me who's not really working up to par, there's got to be some feeling of "what haven't I done so that

that employee isn't performing the way he or she should?" "Am I an inadequate leader?" "Am I doing my part as a supervisor?" "What are *my* supervisors going to think of me when they see that I have an employee who's not doing well?" So I think that human nature plays a big part in making it difficult for supervisors to appraise people and give them feedback the way they should.

A second difficulty relates to the many external pressures. Everyone, including Congress, is in the business of telling us how to manage performance. On one hand supervisors are told that "bell curves" are contrary to good performance management; and yet, on the other hand, they're expected to assure that there is an equitable distribution of performance ratings. This is a very hard tightrope for them to walk because if you're going to have a performance-based incentive system (which seems to be the thing these days), then you've got to have good distributions and ratings to make it work. How do you get good distributions and ratings? Of course, the answer is to rate realistically, but even the best supervisors have a hard time with that one, and doing it without forcing bell curves or distributions of ratings is not easy.

Another reason that managers are reluctant to do performance appraisal and care about performance management is that they're just not seeing enough fruits for their labors. In the federal sector since 1978 there's been constant change due to the Civil Service Reform Act. We haven't convinced our supervisors yet, that properly used, performance management is probably the best tool that they have to increase productivity. And when I'm talking performance management, I'm talking performance-based incentive systems, rewards, and dealing with that poor performer who probably is never going to be an adequate performer. To be convinced, supervisors need to see more results.

Compared to their private sector counterparts, public sector managers don't have much flexibility. They have budget constraints, and many more regulations to abide by. They operate in highly structured organizations, and most of the personnel management procedures are dictated to them. Therefore, public sector managers have very little room to maneuver even if they properly appraise employees and are actually good at picking out the top performers. Often there are budget limitations that keep managers from giving top employees adequate monetary rewards for high performance. There is presently no authority, for instance, for gain-sharing programs. So a common complaint I've heard over at least the last three years from management is that there is a lack of flexibility in the use of incentives.

One of the things we can do to minimize the problem is to simplify the appraisal system as much as possible so that it is not such an administrative burden. Then, we need education. By education I mean either training programs or in-house education, and support from top management to show that they believe performance management is a positive thing. And it's not only desirable, but it is a required part of being a supervisor — that it is one of the things managers are being paid for. I think that managers have to be taught — conditioned, I guess, is a better word — that properly used performance appraisals can increase productivity, can make good employees better employees, can bring some poor performers up to an adequate level, and that in those cases where poor performers won't or can't improve, it can be an adequate tool for removing those employees.

6. *Much recent academic research effort has been devoted to exploring the merits of different types of performance rating scales. Are organizations in practice actively involved in searching for better rating instruments? If so, can you describe how an organization would determine what type of appraisal format or form to use?*

People are definitely looking not only for better instruments but better systems. I receive calls on a weekly basis from other federal agencies and from private corporations who've heard that we've done something different in the Air Force, and they just want to know what. Everybody seems to feel that they need to do a better job in performance appraisal and they want to see what our experience is and how it is working for us.

As for how an organization should determine what type of appraisal format or form to use, I would suggest listening to your managers. The best devised, most beautiful performance system will fall flat on its face without their support. As you are designing an appraisal system, you have absolutely got to get input from the people who are going to use that system. Now, that input naturally has got to mix with input from knowledgeable professionals. Our first line supervisors are extremely knowledgeable in what they do, but they don't have time to keep up on what it takes to have content-construct validity in an appraisal system. That's where our job comes in. But we need to listen to them, because without their support the appraisal is not going to work anyway.

7. *What is your sense of the present status of MBO or results-based systems as performance appraisal techniques?*

I think they still have a place (simply for organization and communication if nothing else), but they have got to be supplemented with other appraisal techniques. Measuring results only doesn't identify a problem or tell you what's making something work. MBO has been around for a long time, but it really didn't get to be a big thing in the federal sector until the Civil Service Reform Act. And as I've reviewed work plans over the last few years, I still find that it is very seldom that an employee really has been told what his or her place in the organization is from an MBO standpoint. In a given office or on a given production line, just what part does that employee play in getting the end result done? Because of the Civil Service Reform Act and the emphasis on MBO, the communication lines have just begun to open up to employees as to what is required on their specific job. That is still not being communicated adequately. But even if it were, there would need to be more. Knowing that he or she didn't make an objective doesn't help a manager know *why* it happened. So, yes I think that MBO has a very definite place in the federal sector, as long as there is a supplementary appraisal system to help managers solve performance problems.

8. *How can subjectivity, inconsistency, and/or bias in ratings be alleviated? Is this a practical objective?*

Even the best system will not alleviate bias or prejudice. A good system may temper the effects, but will not eliminate it. The written standards and elements required under the Civil Service Reform Act are helpful if (as I mentioned before), for no other reason than the fact that it has definitely opened up communication between supervisors and employees. But the standards really only give you a checklist or sort of a map to follow. You still have to determine what makes one employee produce ten more widgets than everybody else. What did that employee do? What work behavior or work habit does that employee have that makes him or her perform over and above other employees? And as much as we would like for everything to be quantifiable there still is judgment and subjectivity when it comes to those kinds of decisions.

9. *Do many organizations actually tie their rewards (promotion, salary increases, etc.) to performance-appraisal results? Why or why not? What, from your professional experience actually working with appraisal systems, would be difficulties involved in determining the size of a bonus based on the degree to which people attained*

their objectives or received high appraisal scores? What would be the disadvantages of such a system?

193

E. PERFORMANCE
APPRAISAL

My experience, of course, is with the federal sector, and we are required by law to tie rewards to performance. So performance appraisal is the hub of the wheel for most of our major personnel decisions. There are many advantages of such a system, but I will stick to the question and address some of the disadvantages.

One of the problems I have experienced in our own appraisal system is that no system is "pure." There are varying degrees of performance levels represented by the same appraisal score. The expectations of supervisors are not consistent. You may have ten employees in ten different organizations who receive a rating of "outstanding" but the rating is given by ten different supervisors. If you go back and look at the basic work plans that the ratings were derived from, the plans may vary significantly in degree of difficulty. Further, the substantiations of the ratings may differ. So the system is not really pure enough. It's a little bit scary for pay decisions to be made strictly on appraisal scores!

Also, I think a disadvantage to this type of system is that it tends to focus loyalty inward instead of to the larger unit in which you work. When you get into a performance-based incentive system, even with good motivators built in, sometimes employees will tend to pull inward and it may create unhealthy competition that wasn't there before.

I've heard employees over the years complain bitterly when they see a poor performer who gets consistent rewards simply because he or she happens to work for a supervisor who routinely gives rewards. That is a demotivator. And so, while I think most employees would agree with a system that recognizes good performance, the lack of "purity" in existing appraisal systems sometimes creates employee disenchantment.

10. *Performance appraisal is useful not only for the measurement, but also for the development, of performance. Yet feedback is often so general and subjective (or omitted altogether) as to disallow any improvement. What type of feedback have you found most helpful?*

Feedback needs to be specific and timely. We put out a lot of literature telling our supervisors to have informal, periodic performance discussions with their employees. I think that that's important, too. But I believe that on a day-to-day basis or a weekly basis — actually when the occasion arises — that's the time to give the employee feedback. If you talk to an employee four months after a problem incident, it doesn't have nearly the impact (and it may have an adverse impact) as immediate feedback would have.

The periodic *formal* appraisal discussions then can be a little more general. There's no need to go back over all the little issues that may have come up, but managers can bring those back in a more general way by going down through the performance appraisal and telling the employee how he or she is performing.

11. *Anything else you would like to add?*

There is one other problem I'd like to mention, and that is the reluctance of management (particularly mid-level and top management) to release supervisors for training on performance management. I guess what it gets right down to is interpersonal skills. We spend hundreds of thousands of dollars in organizations to train employees and supervisors in technical skills. We wouldn't think twice about sending someone off full-time to college for engineering or computer training. But we're very reluctant to give those same supervisors time off the job for training in performance management.

There's also a reluctance on the part of the supervisor to take training in personnel-related areas. Maybe it's because it places supervisors in an uncomfortable situation. It's uncomfortable to go to training on social actions or civil rights movements or EEO subjects because they deal with interpersonal sensitivities. It's uncomfortable to go to training when you are being taught how to deal with performance problems.

So, I think that the lack of top management support is a problem that human resource management people face. And I'm not sure what the answer is to that problem except to somehow convince top management that the way to increase productivity is to do a better job of training their supervisors to be good performance managers. I guess the selling job is really on those of us in personnel to *find* some success stories, to *make* some success stories happen, and to thereby convince management of just how much good performance management and performance appraisal can do for them.

PART III: FOR DISCUSSION AND REVIEW

A.

Cascio

- Describe the mixed standard scale and BARS appraisal methods and note how they differ from other approaches.
- What specific problems do forced-choice scales have?
- Discuss the notions of "objective" and "subjective" in regard to appraisal.

Carroll and Schneier

- What is implicit personality theory?
- Why is the information-processing approach to appraisal advocated?
- How should the design of appraisal systems take into account the research on personality theory and information processing?

Management Review

- What are the advantages and disadvantages of allowing subordinates to rate their bosses?
- What conditions and climate would be required in an organization in order for such a system to operate effectively?

B.

Schneier and Beatty

- Why are BARS useful?
- What problems might come with a BARS system?
- What special skills and activities would be required of managers in order to use BARS correctly?
- Does the emphasis on behavior in BARS preclude judgment and reduce bias? Discuss.

- ☐ Why is MBO so popular?
- ☐ What is the relationship of MBO to an organization's planning system?
- ☐ How can the paperwork problems of MBO be overcome?
- ☐ Can MBO and BARS be combined? If so, how?

Sargent

- ☐ What is a competency?
- ☐ Why would competency-based management have appeal to line managers?
- ☐ Do you see any legal problems with using a competency-based approach to performance appraisal?

C.

Cederblom

- ☐ What are the functions of the appraisal interview?
- ☐ What have we learned about appraisal interviews based on research?
- ☐ What are the arguments in favor of goal-oriented interviews with participation by the person being rated?
- ☐ What does the author mean by a "situational approach"?

D.

Cascio and Bernardin

- ☐ What are the laws and legal precedents which are the basis for court cases cited on performance appraisal?
- ☐ What are the keys, based on the outcome of cases on performance appraisal, to avoiding (or at least reducing the probability of) litigation on an organization's appraisal system?

PART IV
HUMAN RESOURCE SELECTION AND STAFFING

A.

PERSPECTIVES ON SELECTION AND VALIDITY

Recruitment, Testing, and Selection
Edgar H. Schein

- □ Provides an overview of the traditional approach to selection instrument validation.
- □ Discusses the premises on which this approach is based, and reviews problems that might be encountered in its use.

Open a New Window: Validities and Values in Psychological Measurement
Robert M. Guion

- □ Details the essence of the concept of validity in industrial and organizational psychology.
- □ Differentiates between the various types of validity notions and specifies their uses.
- □ Relates validation work to the values inherent in validation studies.

Signs, Samples, and Criteria
Paul F. Wernimont and John P. Campbell

- □ Argues for the measurement of actual behavior — samples of job performance — as predictors of future job success.
- □ Develops a consistency model which assumes that past behavior will predict future behavior and hence should be assessed at the time of selection.

B.

BIOGRAPHICAL DATA AND REFERENCES

Development and Use of Weighted Application Blanks
George W. England

- □ Describes a technique to predict job success more effectively by determining which specific responses to application blanks are made by successful job holders.
- □ Addresses validation of weighted application blanks.

Reference Checks: What's Legal
The Effective Manager

☐ Points out potentially illegal questions in reference checking.

☐ Suggests how to conduct legally defensible and useful reference checks.

C.

INTERVIEWS

Confessions of an Interviewer
Robert A. Martin

☐ An inside look at how a professional interviewer sees the process.

The Employment Interview: A Summary and Review of Recent Research
Richard D. Arvey and James E. Campion

☐ Summarizes research, speculates as to why the interview is used so heavily despite dismal research results, and notes implications of the research.

☐ Notes the impact of several characteristics of interviews on the decision process itself.

☐ Offers suggestions for improving interview utility.

D.

SIMULATIONS AND ASSESSMENT CENTERS

Going for Broker: Our Man Takes Part in Stock-Selling Test
Lawrence Rout

☐ Provides a realistic view of what it's like to participate in a business simulation, in this case to help select stockbrokers.

A Critical Look at Some Common Beliefs about Assessment Centers
Paul R. Sackett

☐ Details the research on assessment centers.

☐ Presents a case for more caution in the use of assessment centers and notes some of the hazards to people and organizations.

E.

TESTING

Employment Testing: Old Theories and New Research Findings
Frank L. Schmidt and John E. Hunter

☐ Presents evidence that cognitive ability tests are valid predictors of job performance on a wide variety of job-types

☐ Demonstrates how the use of tests can save millions of dollars in costs associated with selection decisions.

☐ Shows how research can be applied to a large number of studies across jobs and organizations.

The Implications of Genetic Testing
Judy D. Olian and Tom C. Snyder

- □ Defines genetic screening as testing to see whether job applicants carry genes that make them prone to occupational diseases.
- □ Discusses the controversial implications of genetic screening.

F.

SELECTION AND THE LAW

Jobs: The Pursuit of Fairness
Kathy Sawyer

- □ Describes the history of affirmative action, whom it affects, and how it works.
- □ Discusses the lack of evidence available to either support or refute a claim of success for affirmative action.
- □ Presents an update on the Brian Weber reverse discrimination case.
- □ Discusses the impact that affirmative action has had on the power and prestige of personnel departments.

Moving toward Unbiased Selection
Marilyn K. Quaintance

- □ Thoroughly reviews the legal history of our current position as a nation on discrimination at work.
- □ Presents strategies for compliance with the law.
- □ Reviews current status of the *Guidelines*, the basic document outlining legal implications for employers.

G.

SELECTION

Interview with Virginia R. Boehm

A.

PERSPECTIVES ON SELECTION AND VALIDITY

Recruitment, Testing, and Selection
Edgar H. Schein

The process of recruiting candidates and of selecting from among them those likely to be of the greatest use to the organization existed long before the advent of scientific psychology. What psychology has been able to contribute to this process, however, is a higher average rate of success in selection; it has done so by applying scientific criteria to the whole selection process and by developing standard ways of observing candidates which permit systematic comparison and evaluation.

The steps required in order to improve the accuracy of selection are the following:

1. *Develop criteria.* The organizational roles or jobs to be filled must be adequately described to whoever is responsible for selection, and actual performance on the job must be in some way measurable.

2. *Determine predictor variables.* The candidate must be observed on some variables that are presumed to be good predictors of performance on the criteria.

3. *Obtain sufficient candidates to insure adequate variation on the predictor variables.* In order to determine whether the selection procedure is any improvement over pure chance or whatever method has previously been used, it is necessary to obtain candidates who rate both high and low on the predictor. If such variation is not obtained, it is difficult to establish a meaningful correlation between predictor and criterion.

4. *Hire an unselected group of candidates.* They should be hired without consideration of their scores on the predictor variable.

5. *Rate candidates on actual job performance.* These ratings must be obtained in order to correlate them with predictor-variable scores.

6. *Correlate scores or observations on the predictor variable with criterion performance in the unselected group of candidates.* This step is necessary in order to determine whether the predictor does in fact predict; if the correlation

Edgar H. Schein, *Organizational Psychology*, 2nd ed. © 1970, pp. 22–30. Reprinted by permission of Prentice-Hall, Inc., Englewood Cliffs, NJ 07632.

obtained is too low, another predictor has to be tried; if the correlation is acceptable, according to certain standards to be mentioned below, the next step can be implemented.

7. *Select from among further candidates only those who reach a certain score on the predictor variables.* Once a correlation has been established, it is possible to improve the accuracy of selection by using only candidates with scores similar to those of the unselected population who actually did well on the job. The actual cutoff score to be used depends on a number of factors to be mentioned later.

The improvement in selection which results from this type of procedure depends on a number of factors in the situation.

1. *The actual variation in job performance (the criterion) between best and worst workers.* If there is very little variation, a predictor has in fact nothing to predict. Hence, there is little point in going to the expense of developing one.

2. *The reliability of the criterion.* If, for any of a number of reasons, it is difficult to judge whose performance is better and whose performance is worse on a given job, or if the job is so complex that it is difficult to develop criteria in the first place, the criterion scores (ratings of performance) will be unreliable. If they are unreliable, it is difficult to establish a valid correlation between them and the predictor variables. It has been easy to develop tests and other predictors for clerical or manual work because a reliable criterion can be established. On the other hand, selecting managers, for example, has been much more difficult because of the problem of describing the managerial job and reliably judging relative performance.

3. *Success in locating predictor variables.* For many kinds of jobs it is easy to determine a likely predictor variable — for instance, manual dexterity for doing complex manual jobs, good vision for being a pilot, verbal fluency for writing advertising copy, and so on. For many kinds of jobs, however, the predictor may not be obviously relevant; hence, it may require great intuitive skill, much study of cases, and many unsuccessful experiments before a predictor can be located. For example, in the selection of managers, traits such as tolerance for ambiguity and emotional stability may be more important than specific managerial skills, yet they may not have been thought of as relevant when the managerial job was first analyzed.

   Not only must a predictor variable be located, but it must be reliably measurable and it must enable one to discriminate among candidates. If all candidates get the same score, or if the scores vary from one testing to the next, it is impossible to establish a usable correlation between the predictor and the criterion.

4. *Enough candidates to be able to select and to insure variability in the predictor.* The sample of available candidates is largely out of the hands of the recruiter and selection specialist. If the number of candidates is less than or equal to the number of jobs, i.e., if the *selection ratio* is too low, it obviously does not pay to invest in an expensive selection procedure. Only as the number of candidates increases does a selection procedure begin to pay off. The greater the ratio, the greater the payoff, and, because of the sheer difficulty of deciding from among many candidates whom to hire, the greater the necessity for a selection procedure as well. Closely related to the problem of the selection ratio is the problem of the *base rate*. The base rate can be defined as the percentage of

randomly selected candidates who would be successful on the job. A high base rate can result either because all candidates happen to be highly skilled or because the job is one which could be done by virtually anyone. If, for any reason, all the candidates happen to have qualifications such that *any* of them could succeed at the job, it obviously makes little difference who is hired. Only if there is enough variability so that many candidates would be likely to do poorly at the job does it make sense to use a testing procedure.

5. *Enough time to determine the correlation between the predictor and the criterion.* One of the commonest mistakes in developing selection procedures is to skip the step of actually determining the correlation between predictor and criterion before using the scores on the predictor to select candidates. For example, a college desiring to improve the quality of its applicants may decide to emphasize high school grades as a predictor. Before starting to screen applicants on this basis, it is essential that, for an unselected group, the correlation between high school grades and college performance be determined. This step is critical because it may turn out that there is no correlation, that the high school grades in fact do not predict. If this step is skipped and only students with high grades are admitted, it is difficult to obtain a usable correlation because of the reduced variability on the predictor variable. If the correlation in reality is low, the wrong students would be chosen for admission.

If an organization does not have time to test for such correlations with new samples of candidates, or if there is not enough turnover to permit the hiring of an unselected sample, predictor-variable scores can be obtained on present members of the organization and these scores can be correlated with their current and past performance ratings. The problem with the use of such existing samples is that they may already be highly selected in terms of the predictor variable, thus cutting down its variability, or their scores may be influenced by their actual experience on the job. In other words, for many tests, it is essential that the scores be obtained before the person has had specific experiences related to the test. If time is to be invested in developing a selection procedure, it is important to obtain actual correlations with the predictor before using it as a selection aid.

6. *A correlation high enough to improve the selection process.* Obviously the whole procedure hinges on success in predicting the criterion. No matter how much logical sense the predictor variable makes, or how much intuitive confidence the selector has in its use, if it fails to correlate with the criterion, its use will not improve the existing selection process. The correlation obtained is called the *validity* of the predictor: its capacity to predict what it is supposed to predict. How high this validity needs to be depends on the selection ratio, on the base rate, and on whether the organization is more concerned about obtaining successful performers (even if some unsuccessful ones appear also) or eliminating unsuccessful performers (even if some successful ones are also eliminated in this process). Statistical tables have been worked out that permit a selector to determine from his validity, selection ratio, and base rate how much improvement he can expect from the use of his test. These data tell him whether or not to use the test and what cutoff scores to set for acceptance or rejection of a candidate.[1]

Let us now look at two examples where a scientifically designed testing program and selection procedure has significantly improved the efficiency of the selection process. During World War II, the Air Force faced the problem of selecting from many candidates those who would most likely pass flight training and thus become successful pilots. Because it was expensive to bring a candidate into training who might "wash out" after some months, it was desirable to minimize wash-out rates. Psychologists designed a series of tests and developed a procedure for combining the scores into a single aptitude index which came to be known as the "pilot stanine" (stanines range from 1 to 9; each unit is one-ninth of the total distribution). By successive refinement of this index (going repeatedly through the above steps), a useful predictor was eventually worked out.

The success of this predictor index can be judged from the results. Of all pilot trainees with a score of 1, 75 percent were washed out of flight training; of all those with a score of 9, only 5 percent were washed out. For scores in between, the wash-out rates were steadily higher as the stanine score became lower. It was clear that selection could be improved markedly by using the stanine measure in addition to or instead of whatever other procedures were currently in use.

A similar example can be cited from efforts to select life insurance salesmen by an aptitude index, again based on a whole range of tests. Of those men who scored very high on the index, 52 percent survived with the company after one year and 30 percent were considered successful in terms of sales; of those who scored low on the index, only 29 percent remained with the company and only 11 percent were considered successful.

Attempts have been made to predict performance in all kinds of industrial jobs, in schools and colleges, in the military services, and even in private mental clinics where admission may be based on predictors of the patient's "likelihood of responding to treatment." In most instances, some success has been achieved, but the practical problems of developing scientifically sound selection procedures sometimes outweigh the ultimate gains achieved. And, as we will see below, the whole procedure of selection based on testing may have organizational consequences not desired by the organization.

Variables may be observed in the context of an *interview* or a *standardized test situation,* may be elicited in response to questions on an *application blank,* or may be observed in a *job sample* where the applicant is actually asked to perform the work for a limited time. Which procedure is used in the total selection process depends upon a number of considerations. The reliability of the observations is crucial. One of the major reasons why tests are an important part of the selection procedure is that they can produce more standardized and hence more reliable responses than, for example, an interview. But answers elicited on an application blank or in an interview are in principle just as valuable as test scores, provided they can meet the criteria of reliability and precision. The kinds of variables which can be observed and measured in the effort to improve selection can range from obviously relevant ones (for example, the flight trainee's vision) to ones that may seem irrelevant but prove empirically to correlate with the criterion (for instance, the flight trainee's home town). The kinds of variables which can be observed fall into the following general classes. The methods which have proven to be helpful in assessing the variable are indicated in parentheses.

A. Biographical information and work-history (application blank, interview)
B. Intellectual level and aptitude (tests, job samples)
C. Specific areas of knowledge or specific skills (tests, job samples)
D. Attitudes and interests (tests, application blank, interview)
E. Motivation, personality, temperament (tests, interview)

In general, tests have proven to be most valuable in those situations in which the job to be performed can be clearly described and in which a clear-cut criterion of successful job performance exists. Thus, clerks, machine operators, and pilots have been generally easier to select by means of tests than teachers, managers, or salesmen.

The use of tests has not been limited to selection. There are organizational situations where a given group of employees must be assigned to a given group of jobs and the problem is to get the best fit between the people and the jobs. In this case, differential predictions must be made among the candidates rather than individual predictions for each one. Tests have also been used to assess the general potential for advancement of present employees. And tests have aided counseling psychologists in locating possible sources of tension or maladjustment. For example, tests may reveal that a given worker has been asked to do a job which is beyond or too far beneath his intellectual level.

PROBLEMS OF SELECTION AND TESTING

The successful development of a useful test-and-selection procedure depends on a number of circumstances which are in practice difficult to deal with. Since jobs have become more *complex* and *interdependent,* particularly with the advent of automation, it is increasingly difficult to develop adequate job descriptions and adequate criteria of performance. Yet without a knowledge of what he is trying to predict, a psychologist cannot even begin to develop an effective predictor; without clear criteria of who did how well as a function of test scores, the tester cannot determine whether his test, no matter how valid it *seems* to be, is in fact an improvement over previously used selection procedures.

A second, related problem is that the ratio of *management personnel* to hourly paid workers has been steadily rising. This change has made it increasingly important to improve selection devices for managers, yet it is the managerial job which is most difficult to describe and analyze clearly. Many companies are investing great time and effort in developing tests to hire managers at various levels but with relatively little success. Many other companies use complex assessment programs run either by their own staffs or by consulting firms that specialize in such activities, but few data are as yet available on the success of these programs.[2]

A third force which undermines the effectiveness of job description and criterion development is the *fluidity of jobs* themselves in our rapidly changing technology and society. What may serve as a good description today, enabling the tester to select people validly, may in fact be irrelevant tomorrow. For many years, organizations were finding it useful to hire engineers and managers on the basis of *specific* technical courses which they had had in college. Today the rate at which engineers become "obsolete" is so great that companies are beginning to favor college students who have had more *general* educations, who have a solid background in pure mathematics, and who are generally better prepared to cope with a *changing* environment.

Fourth, the kinds of criteria which are applied to job performance tend to be short-run rather than long-run because the tester cannot wait forever before he checks the validity of the test. To the extent that short-run performance is itself highly correlated with long-run performance, this procedure is perfectly acceptable. But on many kinds of jobs and for most kinds of people, the *correlation between short-run and long-run performance tends to be low:* The person who is a good apprentice machinist may not do well when he is in charge of the machine; the good worker may not make a good group member when the job later requires teamwork; the good subordinate may not be effective as a supervisor, and so on.

The reasons for this low correlation are several:

1. A person often redefines a job in subtle ways that make a later measure meaningless because the performance criteria are no longer comparable from

one person to the next. For example, two managers with identical formal responsibilities may develop quite different strategies of doing their job, one working on a refinement of task procedures while the other establishes good working relations with people. Performance measures of these people should take into account the strategies each has adopted if good predictions of future performance are to be made, even if the actual output of the departments is identical.

2. The person starts in one kind of job but later moves to another in which his task is different from what it was in the first job.

3. The longer the person remains in the organization, the more diverse his value is likely to become — he may be a terrible machine operator (for which the test may have been designed) but prove to be an excellent leader and organizer; if the test had eliminated him from one area, the organization might have lost a valuable resource in another area.

4. The person is more likely to be highly motivated to prove himself in the short run thus giving a biased picture of his long-run motivation. If the development of the test is a long-run proposition because the nature of the work is likely to remain static for some period of time, these difficulties can be overcome. They are acute, however, in a rapidly changing technology.[3]

Specialists in personnel selection have attempted to overcome these various problems by developing more sophisticated and refined techniques of establishing criteria, by using multiple criteria in which different factors are given appropriate weights, by taking into account broad measures of performance which include loyalty to company and low absenteeism, by using more refined statistical procedures such as multi-variate analysis and multiple correlation, and so on. But the ultimate problem of finding predictors which will correlate with criteria remains the same.

Another problem with the traditional approach to selection is the questionable assumption that an applicant can be placed into a standard kind of test situation. People are dynamic creatures in constant interaction with their environment. In practice, therefore, standardized performance is difficult to obtain. First, a person may simply refuse the test. Second, he may, for any of a number of reasons, attempt to fake the test. He may fail in presenting an inflated picture of himself, but he may well succeed in rendering the test useless as a measure of his actual potential. Third, the person may resent the whole testing procedure. A classic example occurred some years ago when a well-meaning tester developed a "stress interview" designed to determine how the candidate would handle emotionally difficult situations. The real test consisted of the candidate being told, after many hours of paper-and-pencil tests, that he had failed them all. The purpose was to determine how the candidate would react to failure. The candidate who was most promising handled the failure experience adequately, whereupon he was congratulated and told that he had passed all of the selection criteria. He thanked the tester very much, told him that he was taking a job with another company which did not feel it necessary to put its employees through demeaning and traumatic application procedures, and walked out!

Perhaps the most serious problem with the selection-through-testing approach is that the *individual tends to be viewed as a static entity* to be measured, classified, and fitted into an organizational slot. Lip service is paid to his needs and motives, but the emphasis first and foremost is on the fulfillment of the organization's needs. As the field of selection has developed and become refined, these assumptions have remained essentially unchanged. Several consequences follow from them. First, an organization builds up an image of itself through the manner in which it recruits and selects its members. An applicant may well come to view himself as part of a mechanical, impersonal system which cares little for his needs and dignity. If he develops such an image of the organization, it may well undermine his long-run contribution in creativity and work effectiveness. He may become the good but apathetic worker, carefully keeping his real self-involvement out of the picture.

Second, through its selection policies the organization may reinforce what is already a powerful stereotype among the public at large that it is all-powerful, impersonal, and callous. For example, in a recent rebuttal of an attack by psychologists that personnel men continue to rely too much on the interview even though it has little validity for selection, a member of a personnel department in a large company defended the continued use of it on the grounds that it was *good public relations*. In a way, he was saying that the selection process should use methods which make the applicant feel worthwhile, even if the method is not valid, thus highlighting the company's need to present itself as human.

Finally, many people have begun to raise the ethical question of whether it is legitimate to use tests which probe the personal life of the applicant, sometimes without his knowledge, since good tests often disguise their purpose. This objection raises the whole issue of the ethical limitations of the psychological contract between employee and organization. Does the organization have the right to probe for personal facts in making its decisions about selection? If so, since the organization has available to it certain private facts about him, what implications does this have for an employee's later career development? Some psychologists have argued that the only person who should see the test data is the person himself. He should then be encouraged to share the data with the company, but at his initiative and under his control. This logic would apply especially to the personality assessments which are made of higher-level managers.

None of these points argues that selection and testing should be stopped. However, it is important to recognize the consequences of using this approach because of both the assumptions to which it commits the organization and the image of the organization which it creates. These assumptions and images may well make it impossible for the organization at a later time to demand of its employees behavior based on other assumptions. Or, worse, the organization may bring into itself replication of what it already has, losing the potential innovators and rebels who may become more important to organizational survival in a changing environment.

NOTES

1. L. E. Albright, J. R. Glennon, and W. J. Smith give an excellent summary of this field in *The Use of Psychological Tests in Industry* (Cleveland: Howard Allen, 1963). See also Leona Tyler, *Tests and Measurements* (Englewood Cliffs, N.J.: Prentice-Hall, 1963), and R. M. Guion, *Personnel Testing* (New York: McGraw-Hill, 1965).

2. One of the most extensive efforts is that of the Bell Telephone System. It is described in D. W. Bray and D. L. Grant, "The Assessment Center in the Measurement of Potential for Business Management," *Psychological Monographs* 80 (1966): 1–27.

3. Studies of the salary growth of managers have uncovered some "late bloomers," highly paid senior managers whose success was not predictable from salaries when they were age 35. See L. L. Fergusen, "Social Scientists in the Plant," *Harvard Business Review* 42 (1964): 133–43.

Open a New Window: Validities and Values in Psychological Measurement

Robert M. Guion

In the musical, Mame tells young Patrick that excitement and a full life come not from unimaginative adherence to routine but from change and new perspectives. She advises him to "open a new window," to "travel a new highway that's never been tried before. . . . " She is too shrewd to leave it entirely to him; she herself opens the windows and doors to introduce new challenges.

Maybe it is too fanciful to place Congress in the role of the uninhibited Mame, or the field of industrial and organizational psychology in the role of the naive Patrick; nevertheless, Congress did open a new door for us when it passed the Civil Rights Act of 1964. It was opened wider by the Office of Federal Contract Compliance and the Equal Employment Opportunity Commission when they issued regulations for the validation of tests and other selection procedures. Their documents directed readers to the *Standards for Educational and Psychological Tests and Manuals* (APA, 1966), but readers found the *Standards* wanting in clarity. So, in the form of a joint committee, the American Psychological Association, the American Educational Research Association, and the National Council on Measurement in Education walked through that door to survey a highway that, even if "tried before," seemed strangely obscure.

Presidential addresses come in two forms. Some are research reports; those of us without long-term research programs offer exhortations. This is the latter type. My exhortation is a plea to psychologists to look over new vistas, but to do so with less than Mame's impulsive enthusiasm. I advocate thorough and careful exploration of new terrain lest we, like Mame's Beauregard, "fall off a damned Alp." My comments are based on my work during the last two years as a member of the joint committee. I speak only for myself, not for the committee. I want to share with you my personal conclusions about the meaning and implications of what we have said about validity. My comments necessarily are elementary because elementary concepts seem so often ignored.

DEFINITIONS OF VALIDITY

Validity, in the history of testing, has been a confused concept, although the basic ideas have been present from the beginning. Criterion-related, content, and construct validities were all implicit when Galton said,

> One of the most important objects of measurement . . . is to obtain a general knowledge of the capacities of man by sinking shafts, as it were, at a few critical points. In order to ascertain the best points for the purpose, the sets of measurements should be compared with an independent estimate of the man's powers. We may thus learn which of the measures are most instructive [DuBois, 1970, p. 22].

The criterion problem was acknowledged by Hull (1928): "The most formidable problem encountered by the aptitude psychologist is the location of a trial group of subjects from whom a *valid* and reliable quantitative criterion of *aptitude* may be obtained [p. 374, italics added]."

The construct problem was in Brigham's (1930) complaint:

> Most psychologists working in the test field have been guilty of a *naming fallacy* which easily enables them to slide mysteriously from the score in the test to the hypothetical faculty suggested by the name given to the test. Thus, they speak of . . . perception, memory, intelligence, and the like while the reference is to a certain objective test situation [pp. 159–160].

Brigham was particularly critical of combining independent tests and giving the composite a unitary name. If tests are independent, he argued, they are measuring different things and therefore should not be given a common name. If he were addressing you, his title might come from a different song: "When will they ever learn?"

Constructs, content sampling, and relations with criteria were all intertwined in discussions of validity as the extent to which tests measure what they "purport" to measure (Boynton, 1933; Hunt, 1937; South, 1938). The 1954 *Technical Recommendations* clarified things somewhat, but the "clarification" sparked controversy, such as the opposing positions of Bechtoldt (1959) and Loevinger (1957). Content validity was largely ignored outside of educational circles; industrial psychologists certainly paid little attention to it until the term was thrust upon them in federal regulations. Nearly 20 years after the "clarification," debate still rages over the meanings of these terms. What's more, because of legal issues we have a different term, *job-relatedness*, which must somehow fit into the scheme.

I offer here my understanding of what these terms mean, and I shall illustrate that understanding with examples from a study of packers.*

Workers on this job packed their products — golf balls — a dozen to a carton. Two types of assessment were considered as possible predictors. There was a series of anthropometric measures, of which I shall concentrate only on the simplest, arm length. The other was a home grown dexterity test. The criterion was a brief work sample: the time required to pack a set of eight cartons.

Criterion-Related Validity

Criterion-related validity is the extent to which scores on one variable, usually a predictor, may be used to infer performance on a different and operationally independent variable called a criterion. For convenience we often speak of criterion-related validities in terms of correlation coefficients, but the statistic has nothing to do with the definition.

We can describe two of the measures in the packing study in conventional criterion-related terms. Arm length correlates with speed in packing with a coefficient of −.46; the validity coefficient for the dexterity test is −.41. These seem quite satisfactory.

The names of the predictors are not important. The information about validity is in the correlation coefficients and the regression equations on which they are based. The information I have given would have been as complete had I simply said that variables A and B have validities of −.46 and −.41, respectively. The nature of the measurement is not what is important to this statement. The important fact being reported is that these variables can be used to predict job performance within the limits of accuracy defined by the correlation coefficient.

The criterion in this conventional validation study is quite different from the sort

---

*David P. Jones of Bowling Green State University and I plan to report the study elsewhere; here I refer only to those parts of the study that illustrate certain ideas.

of criterion desired by early testers. In contemporary practice, a criterion usually grows out of a given problem. The problem here is straightforward: How can we select people who will package golf balls more quickly? Pioneers in mental measurement phrased a different question: How can we find a measure in real life that will reflect the attribute our test is measuring? They would have accepted job performance as a criterion for dexterity, but looking for a criterion for a measure of arm length would have seemed awfully silly to them.

The point is that criterion-related validities serve two distinctly different purposes. In some cases, as in the early history of testing, the emphasis is on the test. In other cases, as in selection research, the focus is on the criterion. In the first type, one refers to the validity of the test scores. In the latter case, however, the reference is to the validity of the relationship. In the packing study the validity coefficient tells us nothing at all about one measurement other than that it tends to be related to another measurement. It gives as much information about the validity of the criterion as of the validity of the test. This is an uncommon way to look at these correlations, but it is useful; it may point to some understanding of the performance measure. Understanding criteria is every bit as important as understanding tests.

Construct Validity

When we speak of understanding, we are talking about construct validity, the degree to which scores may be used to infer how well a stated hypothetical construct describes individual differences among the people tested. Construct validity is not expressible in such simple terms as validity coefficients; it is a judgment based on many kinds of information: procedures followed in developing the test, results of experiments testing specific implications of the construct, and patterns of correlations with other measures. The data used to judge the construct validity of a measure may also help to validate the construct; as data accumulate, ideas about the construct may be modified. Describing a construct is more than merely naming it.

Can any of the measures in the packing study be evaluated in terms of construct validity? What construct is being measured by the criterion? If I suggest that the construct we wanted to measure is productivity, as different from production, then I must define what productivity implies. Productivity may imply, for example, endurance at a high rate of performance over an extended period of time in varying conditions of work. Does the timing of a job sample for a few minutes imply endurance? I think not. We cannot defend the criterion in terms of construct validity unless we define the construct simply as short-term speed in packing golf balls — and in such a tautology we are more interested in reliability.

Can we praise the construct validity of the dexterity test? It so happens that we can. The construct of manual dexterity has been established in experimental and factor-analytic literature. This test has been found in factor analysis to have a substantial dexterity loading (Bourassa & Guion, 1959). This is not enough evidence, but it is some; it places this particular test in a well-established network of relationships.

What about the construct validity of the cloth tape measure used to indicate arm length? Here again is a tautology. What sort of a construct, other than physical distance from one end of an arm to the other, could we possibly have in mind? Of course we could say distance is a construct, simply declare the measurement valid, and forget the whole thing. Actually, construct validity is not a very useful idea for physical measurement. There are well-established, well-defined units by which length is measured. A tape measure is not evaluated by experimental or correlational studies placing their results in some nomological net. It is evaluated in terms of its reliability and of the accuracy of its units. These are quite different questions (Guion, 1965).

Let us examine the same three measures from the point of view of content validity. Content validity refers to the fidelity with which a measure samples a domain of tasks or ideas; it is the degree to which scores on the sample may be used to infer performance on the whole.

Consider a test of addition of two single-digit integers. Figure 1 defines the content domain; there are 10 possible digits for the top number and 10 for the lower. The resulting matrix allows 100 possible combinations. If the content domain is defined with every combination weighted equally, then an arithmetic test of less than 100 problems will be a valid sample of the domain if equal numbers of cells are selected for each row and each column of the matrix. With three cells in each column and each row, randomly chosen within this constraint, Figure 1 specifies a 30-item test that will be judged adequate in terms of content validity.

It is up to those concerned about content validity to define a domain appropriately for their situation. If someone defines a domain using the same matrix, but differing in the weights to be given, the 30-item test indicated here would have inadequate content validity. Figure 2 shows the changed definition: Problems using the smaller numbers have only half the weight of those using the larger ones. Relatively more items must be selected from the lower right quadrant to yield adequate content validity according to this definition of the domain.

In real industrial problems, content domains are harder to diagram, but the principles are the same. To speak of content validity, there must be a content domain from which to draw a sample. It must be analyzed in terms of elements; elements must be weighted in some way (perhaps in terms of such characteristics as frequency of occurrence, importance, or complexity); and content validity must be judged in terms of how well the domain as defined has been sampled.

The content validity of our packing criterion depends on the definition of the

FIGURE 1

Sampling of Arithmetic Problems with Equally Weighted Domain

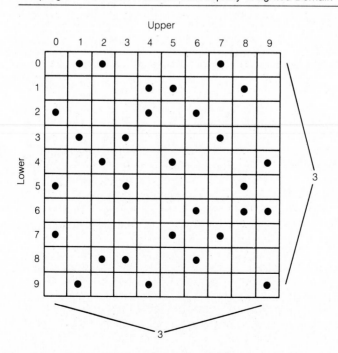

FIGURE 2
Sampling of Arithmetic Problems with Larger Integers More
Heavily Weighted

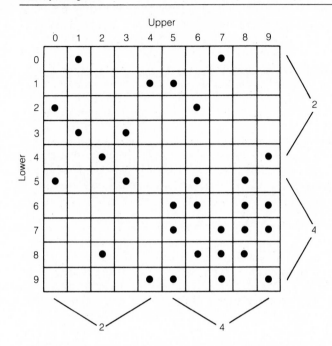

domain of packing tasks. If I define the domain as packing fragile items, this measure lacks content validity, for golf balls are not fragile. If the job of packing golf balls includes crating the cartons, sealing the crates, and stacking them on pallets, and *if I define the content domain as including all of these activities,* then *this* work sample lacks content validity. If, however, I define the content domain simply as the repetitive packing of cartons of golf balls as quickly as possible, then this work sample has substantial content validity.

Can we talk about the content validity of the measure of arm length? Some people will. I will not. Merely recording the number of inches encompassed in the outstretched arm does not, as far as I can tell, sample any defined domain of content. The measure is therefore not reasonably described in terms of content validity.

What about the content validity of the dexterity test? The *construct* of dexterity has been operationally defined with several kinds of related tasks; these tasks could define a content domain. The present test calls on only one of these tasks, so it is not a very good sample. Yet if I am satisfied that I am measuring the construct adequately, I am not likely to worry about content validity. Personally, I tend to think of content validity as a special case of construct validity. Where the task chosen adequately measures the construct, the need for representative sampling of tasks is not apparent to me.

Let us take stock. What has or can be said about validity? First, for any measure there are many validities, not just one. It is and has long been recognized as silly to speak of *the* validity of a test. Second, it is an erroneous shorthand to speak of the validities of the measures themselves; what we really refer to are the validities of *inferences* from the measures (Cronbach, 1971). When we speak of *criterion-related* validity we refer to the use of test scores to infer criterion levels. When we speak of *construct* validity, we refer to the use of test scores to infer degrees to which a particular construct describes the persons, organizations, or objects measured. When we speak of *content* validity, we refer to the use of test scores to infer levels of achievement the persons, organizations, or objects would exhibit in the total domain. These are different facets or "aspects" of validity, and all three kinds of inferences should be valid for most tests. However, the kind of validity statement we seek in any given measurement situation depends on the kinds of inferences we wish to make. This is fundamentally a value judgment. Third, in industrial psychology, the most frequently valued inference is the inference about future performance on a valued criterion. The valued criterion is usually (although not necessarily) either a sample of a performance domain or a performance construct that is identifiably different from the constructs measured by predictors. That is, in employment testing, the validity of major interest is the validity of the *hypothesis* of a predictive relationship between test scores and job performance. Fourth, the validities of criteria need to be investigated. Finally, I suggest that an employment test may provide a basis for inferences that have criterion-related validity, or construct validity, or content validity, or all of these, and still not be job related.

Job-Relatedness

I am not willing to equate "validity" and "job-relatedness." Criterion-related validity is evidence of job-relatedness only if the criterion measure is a valid measure of overall job performance, an element or sample of performance, or a construct related to job behavior.

Construct validity is evidence of job-relatedness only if the construct is related to the job. To defend an employment test on the basis of construct validity, one must first argue from job or need analysis that a particular construct is related to job behavior. Then he must show that the test has acceptable validity for measuring that construct. What he has at this point is the hypothesis that the construct, as operationally defined by the predictor, can be used to infer levels of valued job behavior. This is a hypothesis of criterion-related validity, and it fairly begs to be tested, "where technically feasible."

If it is clearly feasible to do the criterion-related study, it should be done. Where it is clearly *not* feasible to do the study, the defense of the predictor can rest on a combination of its construct validity and the rational justification for the inclusion of the construct in the predictive hypothesis. Where the issue is not clear, we will argue. My position is that I would rather trust the use of valid measures of predictor constructs in a well-developed hypothesis than a typical, done-for-convenience criterion-related study. I think my preference offers better evidence of job-relatedness. There are some highways, Patrick, that are better not traveled; they include those with small *n*s, low variances, or questionable criteria.

So far, these comments implied an assumption that inexperienced people will be hired who will have to learn the job. The employment test is therefore a *predictor* of performance, not a *measure* of it.*

No such assumption is made when content validity is invoked. Either experienced

---

*In the *Griggs* decision, the Supreme Court has said, "What Congress has forbidden is giving these devices and mechanisms controlling force unless they are demonstrably a reasonable measure of job performance." At first glance, in the context of this discussion, the quoted phrase might be interpreted as requiring content validity. This is an unreasonable interpretation. One cannot "measure" job performance among applicants who have not yet performed on the job. One can *predict* job performance, or one can measure performance on tasks that are samples of the job. Either of these is a job-related use of tests and probably satisfies the intent of the phrase.

workers will be hired, or applicants will be expected to have already mastered certain prerequisite components of the job through prior training.

The job-relatedness of content sampling depends on the definition of the content domain. In the most extreme case, one might define job content by listing every non-trivial task performed. A representative sample from this complete catalog of tasks clearly has both content validity and job-relatedness. Despite its virtue, however, it can only be used to select people who already know how to handle the job. If the domain is defined more narrowly as a skill or area of knowledge that can reasonably be expected in applicants and is prerequisite to learning necessary additional skills or information, and if a test is a valid sample of this content, then the test is job related to whatever extent the domain it samples is job related.

How much abstraction is permissible before one questions whether a test is sampling *job* content? Figure 3 may clarify this problem. The large block on the left represents the defined content domain. The smaller blocks represent different ways to sample from that domain. The most direct sample, and therefore the closest, is a probationary period; what could have higher content validity than a well-planned probationary period? Next is the completion of a training program designed to teach a representative sample of job tasks. The third, a simulation exercise, can be a good sample of job content.

As we move to the right, to the use of conventional tests, the sampling is progressively less direct. The farther one goes in assessment from a direct sampling, the greater the inferential leap necessary to relate test content to job content. Where shall we draw the line? How far can we go and still claim to be sampling the content of the job? For the present, I will say only that the greater the inferential leap required, the less relevant content validity is in assessing the job-relatedness of a test; that is, the domain being sampled validly is a less satisfactory definition of the *job* domain.

I have argued that a measure can be described as valid and still not be job related. I will also argue that a requirement may be job related even where the measurement concepts of validity are not applicable. The usual example of a bona fide occupational

FIGURE 3
A Progression of Methods for Sampling Job-Relevant Content for the Assessment of Candidates

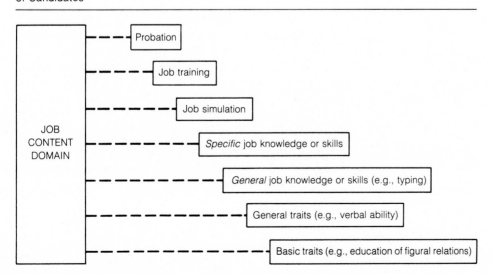

qualification, the requirement that the men's room attendant be male, may soon be archaic, but I think it illustrates the point.

Certain educational requirements may also be job related even where the validity of inferences as described in the *Standards* is not especially relevant. Consider only one example: the requirement of a degree in mechanical engineering for one who is to design heavy equipment. Possession of the degree does not reflect any homogeneous construct. Its content validity for a job-content domain is probably low; it includes performance in nonengineering subjects, many of the engineering subjects studied may be irrelevant to the particular job, and many aspects of the job may not have been reflected in the work toward the degree. In short, the knowledge and skill required to obtain the degree is a sample of a different domain from that of the job. Yet, personally, I would consider a degree in engineering related to the job of designing heavy equipment.*

When I say this, I am implying a hypothesis that people with the degree are more likely to be able to perform the required tasks than are people without the degree. This is a testable hypothesis, but the interests of society are not well served by hiring a lot of nonengineers to design heavy equipment just to do a criterion-related validation study. Moreover, the logic of the hypothesis seems so clear to me that I would accept the requirement as job related without any further evidence of the validity of the hypothesis.

In short, I view job-relatedness as the extent to which the hypothesis of a relationship between the hiring requirement and job behavior can be accepted as logical. If there are gaps in the logical arguments, or if it is based on weak assumptions, then evidence of validity may be useful to support claims of job-relatedness. But validity and job-relatedness are not the same.

VALUES IN VALID HYPOTHESES

Job-relatedness is, of course, a digression from the implications of the *Standards*, so let me return to the main theme.

If we recognize that most criterion-related validation is actually the validation of hypotheses arising from real situations, then we must also recognize the influence and nature of the values implied by the hypotheses we choose to examine. If we examine values carefully and if we take them seriously, we may change the hypotheses to be tested. Look again at the packing study.

If we really value speed in packing cartons, we should consider something other than raw validity coefficients. I am sure it has occurred to you that there *is* something else to consider. Arm length is a valid predictor, but it may also be discriminatory against some women, who, being shorter than men, have shorter arms. Now, discriminating against women may be illegal, but in itself it does not violate our production value unless it also reduces the speed of packing golf balls. Figure 4 shows the scatterplot of arm length against packing time. Solid dots represent data from males; open dots represent data from females. The right-hand part of the chart represents mainly men, the left mainly women, and the composite yields a higher correlation than either because of the increased variance. In a sense, the predictor variable is sex. Arm length, however, is a valid predictor only for women, not for men. Figure 5 presents the regression lines from the same data: Tall women are discriminated against when the composite regression line is used.

---

*This is not a general endorsement of educational requirements, many of which are highly questionable.

FIGURE 4
Scatterplot: Prediction of Speed of Performance from Arm Length

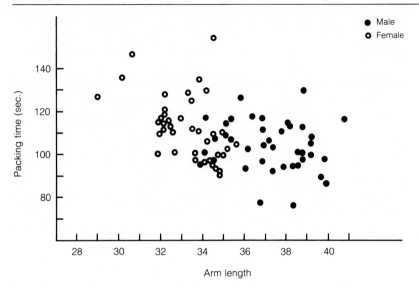

FIGURE 5
Regression Lines in Original Condition

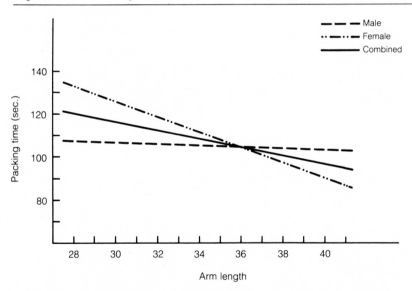

It is time to level with you. The packing study is a laboratory project in which golf balls were fed by gravity into a tray 32 inches from the subject's seat. For most men, reaching the tray presented no problem; for most women it was quite a reach because we planned it that way. The study was repeated with the tray brought closer: 24 inches. Figure 6 shows that the situation was reversed; for men with long arms, the work space was too cramped for fast packing. Arm length became a valid predictor for men. For women, the "test" of arm length had no validity.

FIGURE 6
Regression Lines in Redesigned Task

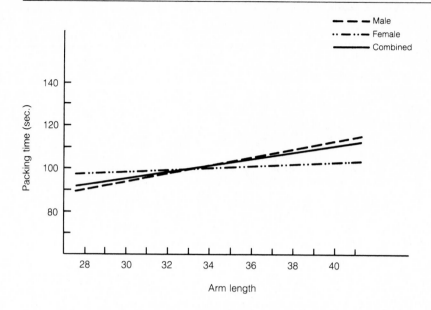

The project was intended mainly to point out two things. First, despite the adverse impact, a silly arbitrary predictor can be valid and its use probably legal. Second, if an employer in such a situation genuinely valued improved performance more than his managerial prerogative to test, he would develop alternate hypotheses and design the validity out of the job. The validity study would be used, not as a basis for selection, but as information about the criterion. If performance is dependent on arm length, then the tray can be set at an optimum distance for each person, male or female. And for the redesigned job, the "predictor" is no longer valid.

VALIDITY AND VALUES IN OTHER AREAS

It would be tempting to stop now if I were not afraid that people would misunderstand. People might think I have been talking about employee selection; I have *not* been. I have been talking about the problem of assessing validity (*a*) in measuring things we value and (*b*) in the hypotheses we pose for explaining them. Consider some rather different measurement areas.

Organized Climate

First, consider that construct, or family of constructs, known as organizational climate. It is generally hypothesized by students of the subject that changes in the climate of an organization will produce changes in such value-laden variables as organizational stability, productivity, satisfaction, and the like. The testing of these hypotheses requires valid measurement on both sides, but let us skip nimbly past the tiresome criterion problem and focus only on the measurement of the climate. In fact, let us narrow the problem a bit more and specify that we shall discuss measurement of perceived organizational climate.

As some of you know, I have argued that perceived organizational climate only pretends to be a new construct when it is really only the rediscovery of the job satisfaction wheel (Guion, 1973). According to Schneider (1973), that is not necessarily so, even if generally true at present. According to his analysis, the perception of organizational climate is the result of concept formation; it is cognitive in nature. In contrast, the perception of job satisfaction is affective — an interpretation of the perceived environment in terms of the individual's own values, needs, or desires. Job satisfaction is a highly personal, subjective construct; different people react to the same organizational stimuli with different kinds and degrees of affect. Organizational climate, however, should be consistently perceived by different people; it is more objective. Climate is an organizational characteristic; satisfaction is an individual characteristic.

Suppose we were to take Schneider's distinctions as a starting point and develop a descriptive measure (or set of measures) of organizational climate. In the light of the concepts of validity, how should we proceed?

First, we should define a *content* domain. Since we plan to differentiate two constructs, content domains should be defined for each. The content of organizational climate must be defined as possible objective, cognitive descriptions of aspects of the work environment, such as what leaders do. The corresponding content domain of job satisfaction must be defined differently as possible affective reactions to various leader behaviors. When the domains have been defined, elements of these domains can be selected for measuring each construct. If the sampling is done well, both instruments, one for measuring climate and the other for satisfaction, should be judged satisfactory in content validity. (Incidentally, although I am thinking largely of questionnaire construction, other types of measurement could be derived from the same beginnings. For example, interviewer or observer checklists could be prepared and evaluated in the same way.)

This content sampling does not, of course, say much about construct validity, but it is a fairly good start. The next step should be an item analysis, based in part on item variances. Items describing organizational characteristics should, according to Schneider's construct, have low variances; items describing individual attitudes should have high variances. Conventional analyses should also be done so that internally consistent subscales can be formed for both climate and satisfaction. The climate scales should yield scores for each organization; the satisfaction scales should yield scores for each person.

The product is an instrument for measuring organizational climate for which preliminary evidence of construct validity is accumulating from the manner of its construction and from its demonstrable independence from a valid measure of a competing construct, if that should be the case. Investigators would then develop a network of experimental and correlational studies, including criterion-related validation, to test hypotheses suggested by the theory of organizational climate. If all goes well, the results may both modify ideas concerning the nature of organizational climate and provide further evidence of construct validity. In the process, the validities of various hypotheses about the correlates or effects of climate variables would either be supported or refuted, and these results would carry much greater weight in theory and in practice than would results based on measures of less well established validity.

Information Content and Related Measures

Let us move to a different measurement problem, one from applied experimental psychology. In 1954, Fitts sought to apply the concepts of information theory to psychomotor performance. A simple task was devised, as diagrammed in Figure 7, where the subject was asked to tap alternately two target areas with a stylus. The width of each target area was always the same, identified as W. The amplitude of the required

FIGURE 7
Schematic Diagram of the Task Used by Fitts (1954)

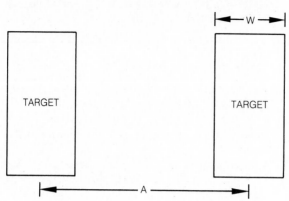

arm movement was identified as A, the distance between the midpoints of the two targets. An index of difficulty was defined by analogy to the information measure using the formula $ID = -\log_2(W/2A)$.

The question of construct validity should be asked about such a measure. Data were reported that support an interpretation of this as a valid measure of difficulty, but as far as I know, the validity of this as a measure of information, as the construct has been defined in information theory, has not been investigated.

Another effort to measure the information content of a job, and more particularly of worker capacity for processing information, is reported by Standing (1971, 1973). Working directly from N-gram analysis (Attneave, 1959), Standing developed a measure of the amount of information in the sequences of operations in an inspection job. No validity information was obtained, but he demonstrated an approach to measuring the information content of work. In the same study he developed a measure of cognitive complexity for individual inspectors, that is, a measure of individual differences in abilities to codify and process the information in the job. The results of his investigation give tentative support for a judgment of construct validity, but there is as yet no network of support.

Uncertainty, or information, as a component of a job or display, and the cognitive complexity of which individual workers or perceivers are capable, are important constructs to people in human engineering, consumer research, job or system design, task simplification, job enlargement, or job enrichment. The motivational hypotheses derivable from information theory seem to have unusual potential for industrial and organizational psychologists and for the states, processes, and outcomes they value highly. Unless we have valid measures of these constructs, however, the best we can offer is idle speculation.

Other Measurement Problems

Let me mention without comment some other constructs of interest to us for which our measures are often valid more by proclamation than by investigation: cognitive strategies, competence, creativity, effort, equity, expectancy, growth, leadership, long-term memory, obsolescence, organizational stability, productivity, utility, valence, work values.

CONCLUSION

I do not mean to imply that the whole of psychology or even the whole of industrial and organizational psychology must work with hypothetical constructs and develop evidence of validity for all measures, experimental conditions, or interventions. Quite the contrary. Just as I believe that an employment requirement can be job related without being also described as valid, I believe the science and practice of psychology can be advanced in some situations by behavioral manipulations, environmental changes, or social interventions for which the concepts of the validities of measurements are as irrelevant as they are for measures of arm length. But I also claim that nearly every branch of psychology entertains problems involving the creation of scientific or technological constructs, that measures are and must be derived for such constructs, and that the ultimate worth of the enterprise does in fact depend on the validity of inferences drawn from such measurement.

It is rather peculiar that it is fashionable from time to time to disparage psychological testing, yet many critics of testing often condone or commend work done with measures never subjected to such rigorous scrutiny as is required in the development or use of a published test. They draw lovely pictures or diagrams and call them models, fill the models with terms they cannot operationalize, and give never a thought to the validities of the operational definitions they *do* use. Much of our field is long on numbers but short on measurement.

It is time for industrial and organizational psychology to rediscover its heritage. The field was built on excellence in measurement. Now, many of us are not particularly excellent. Two important new enterprises — new windows, if you like — are being opened by our brethren in educational psychology. One of these is the content-referenced measurement of mastery, greatly important in personnel applications. The other is the measurement of change or growth in the evaluation of the effectiveness of programs. Few things are more important than program evaluation to those who institute formal programs or speak of their "interventions." If one is going to intervene, his obligation is to find out whether that intervention has helped or hindered the organizational enterprise. We must not only again give measurement its respected place within our specialty, but we must demand that the standards of effective measurement also be respected. We must stop the sophomoric "naming fallacies" that hide the rediscovery of old wheels behind the rhetoric of new labels. In industrial-organizational psychology and in psychology generally, we must identify more clearly than ever before the dependent variables and outcomes we value fundamentally.

We must often open new windows and travel new highways to find these outcomes. But we must not fall victim to the notion that every change, every innovation, every bright idea moves us closer to cherished goals. Every new highway we travel deserves and needs to be explored with the same thoroughness a test developer is expected to use in exploring the validities of his test. The so-called "testing standards" are in fact standards of effective measurement for nearly all of the directions psychological research might take.

REFERENCES

American Psychological Association, American Educational Research Association, & National Council on Measurements Used in Education (Joint Committee). Technical recommendations for psychological tests and diagnostic techniques. *Psychological Bulletin*, 1954, **51**, 201–238.

American Psychological Association, American Educational Research Association, & National Council on Measurement in Education (Joint Committee). *Standards for educational and psychological tests and manuals.* Washington, D.C.: American Psychological Association, 1966.

Attneave, F. *Applications of information theory to psychology.* New York: Holt, 1959.

Bechtoldt, H. P. Construct validity: A critique. *American Psychologist,* 1959, **14,** 619–629.

Bourassa, G. L., & Guion, R. M. A factorial study of dexterity tests. *Journal of Applied Psychology,* 1959, **43,** 199–204.

Boynton, P. L. *Intelligence: Its manifestations and measurement.* New York: Appleton, 1933.

Brigham, C. C. Intelligence tests of immigrant groups. *Psychological Review,* 1930, **37,** 158–165.

Cronbach, L. J. Test validation. In R. L. Thorndike (Ed.), *Educational measurement.* (2nd ed.) Washington, D.C.: American Council on Education, 1971.

DuBois, P. H. *A history of psychological testing.* Boston: Allyn & Bacon, 1970.

Fitts, P. M. The information capacity of the human motor system in controlling the amplitude of movement. *Journal of Experimental Psychology,* 1954, **47,** 381–391.

Guion, R. M. *Personnel testing.* New York: McGraw-Hill, 1965.

Guion, R. M. A note on organizational climate. *Organizational Behavior and Human Performance,* 1973, **9,** 120–125.

Hull, C. L. *Aptitude testing.* Yonkers, N.Y.: World Book, 1928.

Hunt, T. *Measurement in psychology.* New York: Prentice-Hall, 1937.

Loevinger, J. Objective tests as instruments of psychological theory. *Psychological Reports,* 1957, **3,** 635–694.

Schneider, B. *The perceived environment: Organizational climate.* (Tech. Rep. 2) College Park: University of Maryland, Department of Psychology, June 1973.

South, E. B. *A dictionary of terms used in measurements and guidance.* New York: Psychological Corporation, 1938.

Standing, T. E. An application of information theory to individual worker differences in satisfaction with work itself. Unpublished doctoral dissertation, Bowling Green State University, 1971.

Standing, T. E. Satisfaction with the work itself as a function of cognitive complexity. Paper presented at the meeting of the American Psychological Association, Montreal, Canada, August 31, 1973.

Signs, Samples, and Criteria
Paul F. Wernimont and John P. Campbell

Many writers (e.g., Dunnette, 1963; Ghiselli & Haire, 1960; Guion, 1965; Wallace, 1965) have expressed concern about the difficulties encountered in trying to predict job performance, and in establishing the validity of tests for this purpose. In general, their misgivings center around the low validities obtained and misapplications of the so-called "classic validity model." To help ameliorate these difficulties it is proposed here that the concept of validity be altered as it is now applied to predictive and concurrent situations and introduce the notion of "behavioral consistency." By consistency of behavior is meant little more than that familiar bit of conventional wisdom, "The best indicator of future performance is past performance." Surprisingly few data seem to exist to either support or refute this generalization. It deserves considerably more attention.

SOME HISTORY

It is perhaps not too difficult to trace the steps by which applied psychologists arrived at their present situation. During both World War I and World War II general intelligence and aptitude tests were effectively applied to military personnel problems. Largely as the result of these successes, the techniques developed in the armed services were transported to the industrial situation and applied to the personnel problems of the business organization. From a concentration on global measures of mental ability, validation efforts branched out to include measures of specific aptitudes, interests, and personality dimensions. The process is perhaps most clearly illustrated by the efforts of the United States Employment Service to validate the General Aptitude Test Battery across a wide range of jobs and occupations. In general, testing seemed to be a quick, economical, and easy way of obtaining useful information which removed the necessity for putting an individual on the job and observing his performance over a trial period.

It was in the context of the above efforts that an unfortunate marriage occurred, namely, the union of the classic validity model with the use of tests as signs, or indicators, of predispositions to behave in certain ways (Cronbach, 1960, p. 457), rather than as samples of the characteristic behavior of individuals. An all too frequent procedure was to feed as many signs as possible into the classic validity framework in hopes that the model itself would somehow uncover something useful. The argument here is that it will be much more fruitful to focus on meaningful samples of behavior, rather than signs of predispositions, as predictors of later performance.

THE CONSISTENCY MODEL

To further illustrate the point, consider a hypothetical prediction situation in which the following five measures are available:

1. Scores on a mental ability test;
2. School grade-point average (GPA);

3. Job-performance criterion at Time 1;

4. Job-performance criterion at Time 2;

5. Job-performance criterion at Time 3.

Obviously, a number of prediction opportunities are possible. Test scores could be correlated with GPA; school achievement could be correlated with first-year job success; or the test scores and GPA could be combined in some fashion and the composite used to predict first-, second-, or third-year job performance. All of these correlations would be labeled validity coefficients and all would conform to the classic validity model. It is less clear what label should be attached to the correlation between two different measures of job performance. Few would call it validity; many would probably refer to it as reliability. There seems to be a tendency among applied psychologists to withhold the term validity from correlations between measures of essentially the same behavior, even if they were obtained at two different points in time. That is, the subtleties of the concept of reliability and the ingredients of the classic validity model seem to have ingrained the notion that validity is a correlation between a predictor and a criterion and the two should somehow be dissimilar.

However, each of the 10 correlations that one could compute from the above situation represents the degree of common variation between the two variables, given the appropriateness of the linear correlation model. After all, that is what correlation is all about. In this sense there is no logical reason for saying that some of the coefficients represent validity and others reliability, although there certainly may be in other contexts. An implicit or explicit insistence on the predictor being "different" seems self-defeating. Rather one should really be trying to obtain measures that are as similar to the criterion or criteria as possible. This notion appears to be at least implicit in much of the work on prediction with biographical data where many of the items represent an attempt to assess previous achievement on similar types of activities. Behavior sampling is also the basis on which simulation exercises are built for use in managerial assessment programs.

At this point it should be emphasized that for the consistency notion to be consistent, the measures to be predicted must also be measures of behavior. For example, it would be something less than consistent to use a behavior sample to predict such criteria as salary progression, organizational level achieved, or subunit production. The individual does not always have substantial control over such variables, and, even with the more obvious biasing influences accounted for, they place a ceiling on the maximum predictive efficiency to be expected. Furthermore, they are several steps removed from actual job behavior. In this respect, the authors are very much in accord with Dunnette (1966) who argues strongly for the measurement of observable job behavior in terms of its effect on meaningful dimensions of performance effectiveness. A recently developed method for accomplishing this aim is the behavior retranslation technique of Smith and Kendall (1964). The applied psychologist should reaffirm his mandate and return to the measurement of behavior. Only then will one learn by what means, and to what extent, an individual has influenced his rate of promotion, salary increases, or work group's production.

In general terms, what might the selection or prediction procedure look like if one tried to apply a consistency model? First, a comprehensive study of the job would be made. The results of this effort would be in the form of dimensions of job performance well defined by a broad range of specific behavior incidents which in turn have been scaled with respect to their "criticalness" for effective or ineffective performance.

Next, a thorough search of each applicant's previous work experience and educational history would be carried out to determine if any of the relevant behaviors or outcomes have been required of him or have been exhibited in the past. Items and rating methods would be developed to facilitate judging the frequency of such behaviors, the intensity with which they were manifested, the similarity of their context to the job situation, and the likelihood that they will show up again. These judgments can then be related to similar judgments concerning significant and consistent aspects of an individual's job behavior.

Such a procedure places considerable emphasis on background data and is similar in form to the "selection by objectives" concept of Odiorne and Miller (1966). However, the aim is to be considerably more systematic and to focus on job behavior and not summary "objectives."

After the analysis of background data it might be found that the required job behaviors have not been a part of the applicant's past repertoire and it would be necessary to look for the likelihood of that job behavior in a variety of work-sample tests or simulation exercises. A number of such behavior measures are already being used in various management assessment programs.

Finally, individual performance measures of psychological variables would be given wider use where appropriate. For example, the Wechsler Adult Intelligence Scale (Wechsler, 1955) might be used to assess certain cognitive functions. Notice that such a measure is a step closer to actual performance sampling than are the usual kinds of group intelligence tests.

How does the above procedure compare to conventional practice? The authors hope they are not beating at a straw man if the usual selection procedure is described as follows. First, a thorough job analysis is made to discover the types of skills and abilities necessary for effective performance. This is similar to the consistency approach except that the objective seems to be to jump very quickly to a generalized statement of skills and abilities rather than remaining on the behavioral level. The conventional approach next entails a search for possible predictors to try out against possible criteria. Based on knowledge of the personnel selection and individual differences literature, personal experience, and "best guesses," some decisions are made concerning what predictors to include in the initial battery. It is the authors' contention that the classic validity model has forced an undue amount of attention on test and inventory measures at this stage. Witness the large amount of space devoted to a discussion of "test validation" in most books dealing with the selection problem. Again, signs seem to take precedence over samples. Lastly, one or more criterion measures are chosen. Too often the choice seems to be made with little reference to the previous job analysis and is based on a consideration of "objectivity" and relevance to the "ultimate" criterion. Unfortunately, even a slight misuse of these considerations can lead to criteria which are poorly understood. In contrast, working within the framework of a consistency model requires consideration of dimensions of actual job behavior.

It might be added that the above characterization of the conventional approach is meant to be somewhat idealized. Certain departures from the ideal might reinforce the use of signs to an even greater extent. For example, there is always the clear and present danger that the skill requirements will be stated in terms of "traits" (e.g., loyalty, resourcefulness, initiative) and thus lead even more directly to criteria and predictors which are oriented toward underlying predispositions.

RELATIONSHIP TO OTHER ISSUES

The consistency notion has direct relevance for a number of research issues that appear frequently in the selection and prediction literature. One important implication is that selection research should focus on individuals to a much greater extent than it has. That is, there should be more emphasis on intraindividual consistency of behavior. In their insightful discussion of the criterion problem, Ghiselli and Haire (1960) point out that intraindividual criterion performance sometimes varies appreciably over time, that is, is "dynamic." They give two examples of this phenomenon. However, after an exhaustive review of the literature, Ronan and Prien (1966) concluded that a general answer to the question, "Is job performance reliable?" is not really possible with present data. They go on to say that previous research has not adequately considered the relevant dimensions that contribute to job performance and very few studies have actually used the same criterion measure to assess performance at two or more points in time. In the absence of much knowledge concerning the stability of relevant job behaviors it seems a bit dangerous to apply the classic validation model and attempt to generalize from a one-time criterion measure to an appreciable time span of job behavior. Utilizing the consistency notion confronts the problem directly and forces a consideration of what job behaviors are recurring contributors to effective performance (and therefore predictable) and which are not.

In addition, the adoption of signs as predictors in the context of the classic model has undoubtedly been a major factor contributing to the lack of longitudinal research. It makes it far too easy to rely on concurrent studies, and an enormous amount of effort has been expended in that direction. Emphasis on behavior samples and behavior consistency requires that a good deal more attention be devoted to the former, along with very explicit consideration of the crucial parameters of a longitudinal study.

The moderator or subgrouping concept also seems an integral part of the consistency approach. The basic research aim is to find subgroups of people in a particular job family for whom behavior on a particular performance dimension is consistent. Subgrouping may be by individual or situational characteristics but the necessity is clear and inescapable. Only within such subgroups is longitudinal prediction possible.

Lastly, the process the authors are advocating demands a great deal in terms of being able to specify the contextual or situational factors that influence performance. It is extremely important to have some knowledge of the stimulus conditions under which the job behavior is emitted such that a more precise comparison to the predictor behavior sample can be made. Because of present difficulties in specifying the stimulus conditions in an organization (e.g., Sells, 1964), this may be the weakest link in the entire procedure. However, it is also a severe problem for any other prediction scheme, but is usually not made explicit.

It is important to note that the authors' notion of a consistency model does not rest on a simple deterministic philosophy and is not meant to preclude taking account of so-called "emergent" behaviors. Relative to "creativity," for example, the question becomes whether or not the individual has ever exhibited in similar contexts the particular kind of creative behavior under consideration. If a similar context never existed, the research must investigate creative performance and outputs obtained in a test situation which simulates the contextual limitations and requirements in the job situation.

An additional advantage of the consistency approach is that a number of old or persistent problems fortunately appear to dissipate, or at least become significantly diminished. Consider the following:

1. Faking and response sets — Since the emphasis would be on behavior samples and not on self-reports of attitudes, beliefs, and interests, these kinds of response bias would seem to be less of a problem.

2. Discrimination in testing — According to Doppelt and Bennett (1967) two general charges are often leveled at tests as being discriminatory devices:

   a. Lack of relevance — It is charged that test items are often not related to the work required on the job for which the applicant is being considered, and that even where relationships can be shown between test scores and job success there is no need to eliminate low-scoring disadvantaged people since they can be taught the necessary skills and knowledge in a training period after hiring.

   b. Unfairness of content — It is further maintained that most existing tests, especially verbal measures, emphasize middle-class concepts and information and are, therefore, unfair to those who have not been exposed to middle-class cultural and educational influences. Consequently, the low test scores which are earned are not indicative of the "true" abilities of the disadvantaged. Predictions of job success made from such scores are therefore held to be inaccurate.

   The examination of past behaviors similar in nature to desired future behavior, along with their contextual ramifications, plus the added techniques of work samples and simulation devices encompassing desired future behavior, should markedly reduce both the real and imagined severity of problems of unfairness in prediction.

3. Invasion of privacy — The very nature of the consistency approach would seem to almost entirely eliminate this problem. The link between the preemployment or prepromotion behavior and job behavior is direct and obvious for all to see.

CONCLUDING COMMENTS

The preceding discussion is meant to be critical of the concepts of predictive and concurrent validity. Nothing that has been said here should be construed as an attack on construct validity, although Campbell (1960) has pointed out that reliability and validity are also frequently confused within this concept. Neither do the authors mean to give the impression that a full-scale application of the consistency model would be without difficulty. Using available criteria and signs of assumed underlying determinants within the framework of the classic model is certainly easier; however, for long-term gains and the eventual understanding of job performance, focusing on the measurement of *behavior* would almost certainly pay a higher return on investment.

   Some time ago, Goodenough (1949) dichotomized this distinction by referring to signs versus samples as indicators of future behavior. Between Hull's (1928) early statement of test validities and Ghiselli's (1966) more recent review, almost all research and development efforts have been directed at signs. Relatively small benefits seem to have resulted. In contrast, some recent research efforts directed at samples seem to hold out more promise. The AT&T studies, which used ratings of behavior in simulated exercises (Bray & Grant, 1966) and the In-basket studies reported by Lopez (1965) are successful examples of employing behavior samples with management and administrative personnel. Frederiksen (1966) has reported considerable data contributing to the construct validity of the In-basket. In addition, Ghiselli (1966) has demonstrated that an interview rating based on discussion of specific aspects of an individual's previous work and educational history had reasonably high validity, even under very unfavorable circumstances. In a nonbusiness setting, Gordon (1967) found that a work sample yielded relatively high validities for predicting final selection into the Peace Corps and seemed to be largely independent of the tests that were also included as predictors.

   Hopefully, these first few attempts are the beginning of a whole new technology of behavior sampling and measurement, in both real and simulated situations. If this technology can be realized and the consistencies of various relevant behavior dimensions mapped out, the selection literature can cease being apologetic and the prediction of performance will have begun to be understood.

REFERENCES

Bray, D. W., & Grant, D. L. The assessment center in the measurement of potential for business management. *Psychological Monographs,* 1966, 80(17, Whole No. 625).

Campbell, D. T. Recommendations for APA test standards regarding construct, trait, and discriminant validity. *American Psychologist,* 1960, **15,** 546–553.

Cronbach, L. J. *Essentials of psychological testing* (2nd ed.) New York: Harper & Row, 1960.

Doppelt, J. P., & Bennett, G. K. Testing job applicants from disadvantaged groups. *Test Service Bulletin* (No. 57). New York: Psychological Corporation, 1967. Pp. 1–5.

Dunnette, M. D. A modified model for test validation and research. *Journal of Applied Psychology,* 1963, **47,** 317–323.

Dunnette, M. D. *Personnel selection and placement.* Belmont, Calif.: Wadsworth, 1966.

Frederiksen, N. Validation of a simulation technique. *Organizational Behavior and Human Performance,* 1966, **1,** 87–109.

Ghiselli, E. E. *The validity of occupational aptitude tests.* New York: Wiley, 1966.

Ghiselli, E. E., & Haire, M. The validation of selection tests in the light of the dynamic character of criteria. *Personnel Psychology,* 1960, **13,** 225–231.

Goodenough, F. *Mental testing: Its history, principles, and applications.* New York: Holt, Rinehart & Winston, 1949.

Gordon, L. V. Clinical, psychometric, and work sample approaches in the prediction of success in Peace Corps training. *Journal of Applied Psychology,* 1967, **51,** 111–119.

Guion, R. M. Synthetic validity in a small company: A demonstration. *Personnel Psychology,* 1965, **18,** 49–65.

Hull, C. L. *Aptitude testing.* New York: Harcourt, Brace & World, 1928.

Lopez, F. M., Jr. *Evaluating executive decision making: The In-basket technique.* New York: American Management Association, 1965.

Odiorne, G. S., & Miller, E. L. Selection by objectives: A new approach to managerial selection. *Management of Personnel Quarterly,* 1966, **5**(3), 2–10.

Ronan, W. W., & Prien, E. P. *Toward a criterion theory: A review and analysis of research and opinion.* Greensboro, N. C.: Richardson Foundation, 1966.

Sells, S. B. Toward a taxonomy of organizations. In W. W. Cooper, H. J. Leavitt, & W. W. Shelly, II (Eds.), *New perspectives in organization research.* New York: Wiley, 1964.

Smith, P. C., & Kendall, L. M. Retranslation of expectations: An approach to the construction of unambiguous anchors for rating scales. *Journal of Applied Psychology,* 1963, **47,** 149–155.

Wallace, S. R. Criteria for what? *American Psychologist,* 1965, **20,** 411–417.

Wechsler, D. *Manual for the Wechsler Adult Intelligence Scale.* New York: Psychological Corporation, 1955.

B.

BIOGRAPHICAL DATA AND REFERENCES

Development and Use of Weighted Application Blanks
George W. England

PART I: INTRODUCTION

The continuing importance of selection and placement decisions to individuals, employers, and society is highlighted when we are reminded that over thirty million job changes take place each year at an estimated annual cost to industry of more than ten billion dollars. The cost to society and to individuals when selection and placement errors are frequent is incalculable but unquestionably large. It is little wonder that we have been willing to try almost anything to do a better job. In the 1920's, standard methods of selection were based primarily on letters of application in the applicant's own handwriting (graphology, a pseudo-science was in vogue); submission of a photograph (physiognomy, another pseudo-science was also in vogue); the interview in chaotic form; and unstandardized letters of recommendation. Evaluation of these methods showed that they improved predictions of subsequent job success by no more than two or three per cent above chance.[1]

Real progress has been made since then. Selection methods have been improved by developing better measures of job success, standardizing the interview, standardizing blanks for obtaining recommendations, introducing a wide variety of psychological tests into the employment process and by making application blank information more useful through quantification. We have also increased our understanding of the complexities involved in making predictions about how well individuals will perform specific jobs in a given organization. England and Paterson (1960) illustrated the role of selection and placement instruments to be that shown in Figure 1. Such a schema clearly recognizes that it is the complex relationships between person characteristics, job characteristics and organizational setting characteristics that selection and placement efforts must work through. Very straight forward notions such as predictor criterion relations often hide more than they reveal in terms of understanding. Dunnette (1963, 1966) has further specified the complexities of real prediction situations in his model for test validation and selection research as shown in Figure 2.

Adapted, with permission, from *Bulletin 55*, University of Minnesota Industrial Relations Center, Minneapolis, 1971.

FIGURE 1
Selection-Placement Schema

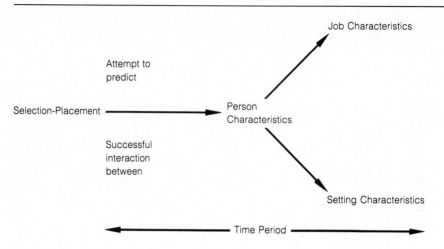

FIGURE 2
A Model for Test Validation and Selection Research as Indicated by Dunnette

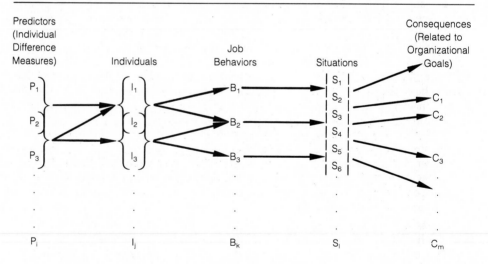

The brackets and arrows serve as reminders of the many possibilities for different prediction strategies that should be considered in any personnel selection or test validation study. The brackets in the diagram signify different groupings of tests for different groups of persons, depending upon the patterns of job behavior to be predicted. The arrows in the diagram show that different avenues based on various groupings of predictors, persons, and behaviors may be utilized. For example, predictors P_2 and P_3 might be tried for individuals I_2 and I_3 or for individuals I_1 and I_2, but they probably would yield differentially accurate predictions for different job behaviors. The diagram also portrays the possibility of different job behaviors leading to various organizational consequences depending upon differing situational contexts. Thus, the prediction model calls attention to the likelihood of complex interactions between predictor groupings, groups or types of individuals, job behavior patterns, and broadly defined organizational consequences. Moreover, the model makes explicit the necessity for predicting actual job behavior and studying it in the context of different job situations rather than simply contrasting groups formed on the basis of overall organizational outcomes.

Selection research, based on this model, becomes a series of investigations designed to discover the optimal groupings or subsets of predictors, persons, job behaviors, and situations within which to study patterns of predictability and to validate and cross-validate prediction strategies. As we have said, most previous selection research has been rather fixedly concerned with predicting organizational consequences directly without first seeking to learn the nature of possible linkages between such consequences and all that goes before in the model — notably the patterns of situational circumstances and the possible differences in job behavior. Our model implies no lessening of interest in predicting organizational outcomes but it does direct research efforts toward a more careful analysis of their behavioral and situational correlates with the hope of understanding these organizational outcomes better, and of predicting them more accurately.

Three major characteristics stand out when we study the improvement in selection over the past forty years. First, it seems that we have done a better job of selecting as our methods have become more standardized. We have, in effect, directed more effort and research toward determining "what we should know about people" and then planned standardized ways of obtaining and using this information. Secondly, our selection methods have become more effective as we have been able to express them in numerical terms (quantification). Finally, we would expect further improvements as understanding directs our approaches and methods toward better approximation of the actual level of complexity found in the real world.

The intelligent development of weighted application blanks (WAB) continues to rely on the three hallmarks of progress in selection: standardization, quantification and understanding.

The rationale behind WAB development can be outlined as follows:

1. Personal history information such as age, years of education, previous occupations, and marital status represent important aspects of a person's total background and should be useful in selection. The major assumption is that how one will behave in the future is best predicted by how one has behaved in the past or by characteristics associated with past behavior.

2. Certain aspects of a person's total background should be related to whether or not he will be successful in a specific position. Numerous studies have shown that information contained in application blanks is predictive in selecting employees for certain types of positions. Personal factors such as age, years of education, previous occupations, and marital status have been found to be correlated with indicators of desirable employee behavior (length of service, supervisory ratings, sales volume, and average salary increase).

3. A way of determining which aspects of a person's total background are important for a given occupation is needed. The WAB technique identifies those items on an application blank which differentiate between groups of desirable and undesirable employees in a given occupation.

4. A way of combining the important aspects of a person's total background is needed so we can predict whether or not he is likely to be successful in a given occupation. By determining the predictive power of each application blank item, it is possible to assign numerical weights or scores to each possible

answer. Weights for these items may then be totaled for each individual and a minimum total score established, which, if used at the time of hiring, will eliminate the maximum number of undesirable candidates with a minimum loss of desirable candidates.

The WAB technique, then, provides one systematic method for determining which personal factors are important in specific occupations and how to use them in selection. Use of the WAB technique in the employment process permits rapid screening of applicants by means of a simple scoring of the application blank. WAB results also can be used in combination with test and interview information to further improve screening and placement.

This technique is applicable in any organization having a relatively large number of employees doing similar kinds of work and for whom fairly adequate records are available. It seems particularly valuable for use with positions requiring long and costly training periods, positions where the turnover rate is abnormally high, or in situations where large numbers of applicants are seeking few positions. Already it has proved useful in the selection of managers, supervisors, production workers, clerical workers, cab drivers, sales personnel, engineers, and military personnel.

Development of weights for the application blank does not need to be a long, expensive, complicated process requiring the services of a specialized consultant. There is no reason why the job cannot be undertaken successfully by any trained member of the company's personnel department staff once he has learned the fundamentals of the technique. No complicated statistic formulas need be involved — just simple arithmetic and a fair amount of clerical aptitude. Ordinarily the process for one type of job can be completed and ready for trial use in as little as 100 working hours, with possibilities of reduction in hiring costs which may repay many times over the original investment in research.

These materials have been prepared to present step-by-step methods which have been found successful in developing weights for an application blank. An attempt is made to present the material in such a way that it may serve as a practical guide to persons who may wish to develop similar weights applicable to their specific local situations. To illustrate the details of the method, an actual study is presented in part. This study concerned department store saleswomen where turnover was the major problem. The intent of the study was to develop a scoring system for the application blank which would indicate whether or not applicants were likely to remain with the company for relatively long time periods. Therefore, length of service was used as the criterion or measure of employee desirability.

Seven major steps will be considered in detail in the following sections. These steps cover the decisions which must be made in developing a WAB and can be listed as follows:

1. Choosing the criterion
2. Identifying criterion groups
3. Selecting application blank items to be analyzed
4. Specifying item response categories to be used in the analysis
5. Determining item weights
6. Applying weights to the holdout groups
7. Setting cutting scores for selection

Developing weights for the application blank is accomplished by a systematic method of determining what application blank item responses were given more frequently by applicants who proved to be desirable employees and, at the same time, were given less frequently by applicants who proved to be undesirable employees. To be useful in the selection process, the personal history responses which are compared are those obtained at time of hiring. This is done by comparing item by item the application blanks of a group of desirable employees with those of a group of undesirable employees. In order to select these two groups for comparison, one must have some index or criterion of desirability. One must decide what employee performance characteristic he wishes most to identify.

Choosing the Criterion

It is often helpful in selecting a criterion of success to consider what characteristics have been most frequently lacking in employees hired by existing techniques. Perhaps the major problem has been in selecting employees who are proficient in their work. If so, the best accessible measure of job proficiency should be the criterion. On the other hand, turnover rather than job performance may be the most pressing problem. In this case, length of service would be the most appropriate criterion. Table 1 lists the types of criteria which are most commonly reported in the literature on weighted application blank studies. . . .

Identifying Criterion Groups

After a criterion has been selected, it is necessary to form two criterion groups (a *high criterion group* — representing desirable employees and a *low criterion group* — representing undesirable employees). It is recommended that these two criterion groups be as large as possible, and that no study be undertaken without, at the minimum, 75 in each of the two groups.

Each criterion group is further separated into a weighting group and a holdout group. The weighting groups are used to identify and weight personal history items which differentiate between desirable and undesirable employees. Each weighting group (high and low) should contain at least 50 individuals. The holdout groups (high and low) are used in evaluating the effectiveness of the WAB and for setting cutting scores to be used in later application of the technique in selection. Each holdout group should contain at least 25 individuals. Figure 3 illustrates the formation of these groups. . . .

TABLE 1
Criteria Used in Weighted Application Blank Studies

1. Length of service
2. Absenteeism
3. School grades
4. Rate of salary increase over a period of time (salary of present job minus salary of first job ever held, divided by the number of years worked).

FIGURE 3
Use of Criterion Groups

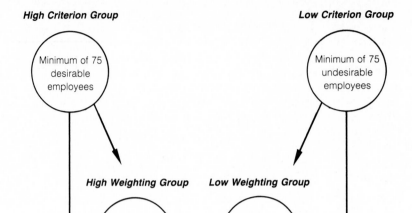

High Criterion Group

Minimum of 75 desirable employees

Low Criterion Group

Minimum of 75 undesirable employees

High Weighting Group

Minimum of 50 individuals

Low Weighting Group

Minimum of 50 individuals

Used to identify and weight personal history items

High Holdout Group

Minimum of 25 individuals

Low Holdout Group

Minimum of 25 individuals

Used to evaluate effectiveness of WAB and to set cutting scores

Selecting Application Blank Items to be Analyzed

The type and number of items which can be analyzed will depend on the content of the application blank used by the organization in which the study is undertaken. Sometimes additional items can be secured from other personnel records filled out at the time of hiring, provided such records are available for all individuals in the criterion groups.

Table 2 lists a wide variety of items which have been found to be predictive of "job success" for different types of jobs.

Specifying Item Response Categories

Names and item responses from the application blanks of all persons in the weighting groups should be recorded on ruled work sheets, using separate sheets for the high and low groups. For the most part, this will be a simple matter of transferring responses from application blank to the appropriate square on the work sheet.

Personal

1. Age
2. Age at hiring
3. Marital status
4. Number of years married
5. Dependents, number of
6. Children, number of
7. Age when first child born
8. Physical health
9. Recent illnesses, operations
10. Time lost from job for certain previous period (last 2 years, etc.)
11. Living conditions, general
12. Domicile, whether alone, rooming house, keep own house, etc.
13. Residence, location of
14. Size of home town
15. Number of times moved in recent period
16. Length of time at last address
17. Nationality*
18. Birth place*
19. Weight and height
20. Sex

Background, General

21. Occupation of father
22. Occupation of mother
23. Occupation of brothers, sisters, other relatives
24. Military service and rank
25. Military discharge record
26. Early family responsibility
27. Parental family adjustment
28. Professionally successful parents
29. Stable or transient home life
30. Wife does not work outside home

Education

31. Education
32. Educational level of wife
33. Educational level of family, relatives
34. Education finances — extent of dependence on parents
35. Type of course studied — grammar school
36. Major field of study — high school
37. Specific courses taken in high school or college
38. Subjects liked, disliked in high school
39. Years since leaving high school
40. Type of school attended, private/state
41. College grades
42. Scholarship level, grammar school and high school
43. Graduated at early age compared with classmates

Employment Experience

44. Educational — vocational consistency
45. Previous occupations (general type of work)
46. Held job in high school (type of job)
47. Number of previous jobs

(Cont.)

TABLE 2 *(Cont.)*

Employment Experience (cont.)

48. Specific work experience (specific jobs)
49. Previous selling experience
50. Previous life insurance sales experience
51. Total length of work experience (total years, months)
52. Being in business for self
53. Previous employee of company now considering application
54. Seniority in present employment
55. Tenure on previous job
56. Employment status at time of application (employed, unemployed)
57. Reason for quitting last job
58. Length of time unemployed
59. Previous salary earned, or salary earned at present employment

Skills

60. Ability to read blueprints
61. Does repair work on own car
62. Amount of previous training for applicant job
63. Amount of previous training for any other job
64. Possesses specific skills required for job
65. Number of machines that a person can operate

Socioeconomic Level — Financial Status

66. Financial responsibility
67. Number of creditors
68. Number of accounts with finance companies
69. Number of accounts with stores
70. Amount loan as a proportion of total income
71. Monthly mortgage payment
72. Highest pay received
73. Debts
74. Net worth
75. Savings
76. Amount of life insurance carried
77. Amount of other insurance carried
78. Kinds of and number of investments
79. Real estate owned (own home, etc.)
80. Owns automobile
81. Make, age of auto owned
82. Owns furniture
83. Has telephone in home
84. Minimum current living expenses
85. Salary requests, limits set for accepting job
86. Earnings expected (in future, 2 yrs., 5 yrs., etc.)

Social

87. Club memberships (social, community, campus, high school)
88. Frequency of attendance at group meetings
89. Offices held in clubs
90. Experience as a group leader
91. Church membership

Interests

92. Prefer outside to inside labor
93. Hobbies

TABLE 2 (Cont.)

235

B. BIOGRAPHICAL DATA
AND REFERENCES

Interests (cont.)

94. Number of hobbies
95. Specific type of hobbies, leisure time activities preferred
96. Sports
97. Number of sports active in
98. Most important source of entertainment

Personal Characteristics, Attitudes Expressed

99. Willingness to relocate or transfer
100. Confidence (as expressed by applicant)
101. Basic personality needs (5 types) as expressed by applicant in reply to question on application blank
102. Drive
103. Stated job preferences

Miscellaneous

104. Time taken for hiring negotiations between applicant and company
105. Former employer's estimate of applicant
106. Interviewer's estimate of applicant's success, based on health, social personality, relationships, etc.
107. Source of reference to company for job application
108. Has relatives or acquaintances presently working for company
109. Number of character references listed
110. Availability for entire season of work stated
111. Availability — can start immediately, can't start immediately
112. Manner of filling out application blank (time taken, method used, way information stated, etc.)
113. Restrictions on hours available for duty

*Some items may violate fair employment practice legislation.

In some cases, however, it may be desirable to translate data into more useable terms. For example, if the application blank shows date of birth, this should be subtracted from date of application and recorded on the work sheet in the form of age at the time of application. Likewise, if the amount of previous experience in the type of work under study is wanted, it may be necessary to draw this information from several places in the applicant's work history and to do a little simple addition in order to arrive at a single figure for the work sheet.

In cases of omitted responses, some standard no-answer entry should be adopted on the work sheets, such as the letters N.A. or a diagonal line through the square.

For some items, suitable response categories to be used in calculation of weights will be obvious. This is particularly true of items which automatically elicit a limited number of possible answers, discrete in nature. Marital status, for example, is an easy item to categorize. Any person can be classified as either single, married, divorced, separated, or widowed.

Continuous variables, on the other hand, such as age and length of residence are somewhat more difficult to classify. With items of this nature, one of three types of classification is most frequently used. These may be described as equal frequency classes, equal interval classes and maximum weight classes. Using the variable of age, each method is illustrated:

1. *The method of equal frequency classes* divides the responses of the combined weighting groups into four or five classes with an approximately equal number

of individuals in each class. The age data shown in columns 2 and 3 of Table 3 would appear as follows:

Age	Group I High Weighting Group	Group II Low Weighting Group	Class Totals
Under 23	9	46	55
24–32	15	39	54
33–48	40	16	56
Over 48	48	11	59
No answer	0	0	0

2. *The method of equal interval classes* classifies age into five or ten year intervals. Five year intervals are used in Table 3 with the exception of the "under 20" group and the "over 40" group.

Age	Group I High Weighting Group	Group II Low Weighting Group
Under 20	30	32
20–40	35	30
Over 40	35	38
Total N	100	100

3. *The method of maximum weight classes* is essentially one of trial and error to determine what response categories or interval limits best bring out differences between the groups. The following *hypothetical* example partially illustrates this method. The first trial sets up age categories of under 20, 20–40, and over 40.

	Age	Group I High Weighting Group	Group II Low Weighting Group
	Under 20	30	32
	20–40	35	30
Over	41–50	5	33
40	Over 50	30	5
	Total N	100	100

Working out the weighting procedure (see next section) would show that age was not a significant variable and should not be used. However, if the "over 40" class actually had the following distribution, the age variable should be weighted for prediction.

Obviously, the distinction between age 41–50 and over 50 is one that is desirable to make. While such sharp reversals as illustrated rarely occur in practice, the trial and error process is a way of detecting such differences. The danger in using strictly a trial and error method is that many chance differences between the two groups may be weighted. These differences will increase the separation of the original groups but may not remain as stable differences which are useful in later application.

TABLE 3
Sample Weighting Work Sheet

Response Category	Number Responding		Percent Responding*		Col. 4 Minus Col. 5	Net Weight	Assigned Weight
	Group I—High Weighting Group	Group II—Low Weighting Group	Group I—High Weighting Group	Group II—Low Weighting Group			
Columns: 1	2	3	4	5	6	7	8
Age							
Under 20	6	28	5%	25%	−20%	−6	0
20–25	7	42	6	38	−32	−9	0
26–30	7	12	6	11	−5	−2	1
31–35	7	6	6	5	1	0	1
36–40	17	8	15	7	8	2	1
Over 40	68	16	61	14	47	12	2
No answer	0	0					
	112	112	99%*	100%			
Marital status							
Single	30	53	27%	47%	−20%	−4	0
Married	45	49	40	44	−4	−1	1
Divorced or separated	9	6	8	5	3	1	1
Widowed	28	4	25	4	21	6	2
No answer	0	0					
	112	112	100%	100%			
Number of dependent children							
None	79	96	70%	86%	−16%	−4	0
One	20	9	18	8	10	2	1
Two or more	13	7	12	6	6	2	1
No answer	0	0					
	112	112	100%	100%			

*Percentages have been rounded to the nearest whole percent. For this reason, they do not always total exactly 100%.

On balance, it seems most useful to categorize continuous variables following the method of equal frequency classes, but to check for reversals within each class. If reversals are found which would change the weighting and are based on the responses of at least ten people in an interval, the classes should be changed. . . .

Determining Item Weights

In order to determine whether or not desirable workers respond to certain items in a way different from that of undesirable workers, information from response work sheets #1 and 2 must be drawn together for comparison on a third work sheet similar to the one shown in Table 3. Appropriate response categories for each item are listed in the first column on Table 3, and the number of persons from the high and low weighting groups whose responses fall into each of these categories is recorded in columns 2 and 3.

After the number of persons from each weighting group whose responses fall into each category have been recorded in Table 3, these numbers are converted to percentages for each group, as shown in columns 4 and 5. The percentages for Group II (Low Weighting Group) are then subtracted from the corresponding percentages for Group I (High Weighting Group) and the differences recorded in column 6, using the appropriate sign, plus or minus. For example, in Table 3 it may be seen that the age category "under 20" includes 5% of Group I and 25% of Group II. Subtracting the percentages for Group II (25%) from the percentage for Group I (5%) gives a minus 20%, and this difference has been recorded in column 6. . . .

Any item which has the same assigned weight for every response category does not differentiate between the high and low weighting groups and should be discarded.

For the three items illustrated in Table 3, adequate responses were available for every person in both criterion groups. There were no omissions. However, in cases where there are persons who have given no answer or inadequate answers on a particular item, the usual procedure is to eliminate these persons from the calculation of weights for that item, and thus to work with a reduced number of subjects. For example, if five individuals in Group I and twelve individuals in Group II had not given their ages, weights for the age item would have been standardized on the remaining 107 subjects in Group I as compared with the remaining 100 in Group II. The percentages in columns 4 and 5 of Table 3 would then have been calculated on the basis of total groups of 107 and 100, rather than 112 and 112. Of course, if the weighting groups are small to begin with and the proportion of "no answer" responses is large for a specific item, it may be necessary to discard the item altogether. . . .

REFERENCES

Dunnette, M. D. A Modified Model for Test Validation and Selection Research. *Journal of Applied Psychology.* Vol. 47, 1963, pp. 317–323.

Dunnette, M. D. *Personnel Selection and Placement.* Belmont, California: Wadsworth Publishing Co., Inc., 1966.

England, G. W. and D. G. Paterson. Selection and Placement — The Past Ten Years. In Industrial Relations Research Association *Employment Relations Research: A Summary and Appraisal.* New York: Harper & Brothers, 1960.

Reference Checks: What's Legal

The Effective Manager

Many managers are under the mistaken impression that it's illegal to make extensive reference checks on prospective employees. While there may be reasons for limiting what you say or ask, there are actually few laws which regulate reference checking. Employers have a legitimate interest in finding out about an applicant's past, and the law respects that right — provided you don't go too far.

QUESTIONS ABOUT APPLICANT

You have a right to collect information about areas such as past employment history, including duration, absences, punctuality, skills and education; military service; dependability and trustworthiness; and reasons for the employee's departure. But you must ask the same questions of all applicants and have good business reasons for seeking the information. Otherwise, you could be open to suits involving privacy or discrimination. There are three principal areas that need to be handled delicately: arrest records, union affiliations, and credit records.

Arrest Records

You should be wary of asking about arrest records. Many courts have held that hiring decisions based on arrest records discriminate because members of minority groups are arrested proportionately more than whites. Questions about arrest records are best avoided unless you have good business reasons for requiring a "clean" applicant (for example, jobs in law enforcement or those giving employees access to valuable and portable commodities).

Conviction records are a different matter. Because they are much more reliable indicators of an individual's past character and conduct, there are fewer restrictions on the use of conviction records. But a word to the wise: Distinguish between minor offenses and major ones; and look at how long it has been since the individual was in trouble. You could be asking for problems if you treat both minor and major offenses the same way.

Union Affiliations and Activities

If you collect any information about an individual's past or present union activities, you are asking for trouble. The right to engage in collective activities is protected by law, and evidence that you sought this kind of information could amount to a "smoking gun."

Credit Records

If you use an outside agency to make a credit or character check on an applicant, you have to follow certain procedures mandated by the Fair Credit Reporting Act. First, applicants must be notified in writing that you plan to make the credit check. Second, if the applicant requests that you do so, you have to make disclosures about the nature and scope of the investigation. Third, if a decision not to hire the person is based in part on the credit report, you have to tell the applicant in writing that the report influenced your decision. You also have to disclose the name and address of the reporting agency.

Unless you can show a business necessity for making credit checks, it's better to avoid this area. The Equal Employment Opportunity Commission found that rejecting applicants on the basis of poor credit ratings has a disparate impact on minority groups.

HOW TO CONDUCT REFERENCE CHECKS

When you make reference checks, you are actually conducting an interview, and you should draw upon your experience as an interviewer. For example, don't appear to be threatening or overly assertive. Ask open-ended questions. Listen carefully for what isn't said, and explore ambiguities. Remember to do the following:

Get the Applicant's Authorization

Make it clear that you have been authorized by the applicant to make the inquiry. (Your application form should include a declaration saying that, by signing it, the applicant authorizes you to contact the references listed.) Then, if someone tries to "stonewall" you, let it be known that he or she is not doing the applicant a favor; that for you, no news is bad news.

Talk to the Right Person

If possible, talk to the applicant's supervisor. Try to avoid dealing with someone who only has a written record of the applicant's performance.

Be Consistent

Set up formal, written policies covering how reference checks will be carried out; when they will be required; and how negative information will be weighed and verified. These policies should be followed consistently to avoid being charged with discriminatory hiring practices.

Establish Whether to Write or Phone

If you use the telephone, it's a good idea to prepare a list of questions to ensure that specific points are covered. Most employers find that telephone checks are more effective than written ones. Telephone checks can save time, and they may produce information that won't appear if a written form is prepared and mailed back. Written checks are more often limited to high-level, sensitive positions.

C.

INTERVIEWS

Confessions of an Interviewer

Robert A. Martin

Most of the corporate recruiters with whom I've had contact are decent, well-intentioned people. But I've yet to meet anyone, including myself, who knows what he (or she) is doing. Many interviewers seem to have an absolute faith in their omniscience, but I suspect that their "perceptiveness" is based more upon preconceived, untested assumptions than upon objectively derived data.

This unscientific approach to the process of selecting employees saddens me. All my life I've accepted, as an unassailable truism, the bromide that "people are our most important asset." Yet I know that many major companies spend more money researching what kind of paint to use for their buildings than they do trying to determine how to recognize and measure talent.

When I bemoan my own inadequacies in such matters to my colleagues, I am, more often than not, rewarded with the bemused sympathy of a master for his servant. I would urge more of my associates to consider the virtue of humility. A humble person is more susceptible to a reexamination of his beliefs and practices. The following quotation, from *The Selection Process* by Milton Mandell, by far the best book on employment practices I have ever encountered, is a classic:

"Many reasons can be advanced for the need of humility among interviewers — just one should be sufficient. The interviewer is trying to obtain in 20 to 60 minutes an accurate understanding of a lifetime of thousands of experiences producing attitudes, motivations, and behavior which, in many cases, are unknown to the applicant himself and which are modified at different times and in different places. Humility motivates the interviewer to avoid hasty judgments, to obtain the evaluations of others in order to check his own conclusions, to improve his skill and knowledge as much as possible, to use other selection devices to contribute to the accuracy of selection, to limit the interview to those factors which can be appraised adequately, and to omit from it those factors which should be measured by other methods." Now that we are all properly humble and open-minded about our beliefs, it might be appropriate to examine those considered to be the most sacrosanct.

It is assumed, first of all, that students who graduate with high grade-point averages are the most intelligent, and therefore the only ones capable of meeting the company's standards. Grades are perhaps the most tenaciously clung to predictor of managerial success. Many major companies use the 3.0 grade-point cutoff as the keystone of their recruiting program.

It is a difficult nut to crack. But let's examine some of the evidence to see if grades are really a reliable predictor of success on the job. Possibly the best-known study on this subject was made by Bell Laboratories in 1962. The company analyzed the records of 17,000 employees who had graduated from college prior to 1950, in order to relate college achievement to progress in management.

The survey found that salary progress was positively correlated with class rank in college, with the college's academic quality, and with extracurricular achievement. At the same time, it found that students who supported themselves in college did not do significantly better in salary, and that undergraduate major made no difference.

The report cautioned: "It would, of course, be a mistake to apply the indices of this study — rank in college, quality of college, and campus achievement — in a blind, mechanical way. Even of the men who stood near the top on all three characteristics, a significant minority have not performed with distinction in business." Conversely, a significant minority of those who did not perform with distinction in college did achieve distinction in business.

In 1957 Purdue University conducted a survey of its engineering graduates since the class of 1911. From 3,799 usable replies the survey concluded that high scholastic achievement is positively correlated with attainment of positions in management, with membership in professional societies, with number of patents, and with salary. The survey also found that doctorates are positively correlated with salary, though M.S. degrees are not. Again, the study cautioned against applying its conclusions too strictly. It emphasized that some of even the lowest decile graduates advanced to the top salary levels (9 percent compared to 25 percent for top decile graduates).

Other recent studies dispute even the mild correlation that these surveys found between job success and various individual achievements. A recently released study done at the University of Utah concluded that "there is almost no relationship between the grades a student gets in medical school and his competence and success in medical practice." No one was more astounded by this finding than the leader of the research team, Dr. Philip B. Price. "It is a shocking finding to a medical educator like myself who has spent his professional life selecting applicants for admission to medical school," he said.

In another study Dr. Eli Ginzberg examined the records of 342 graduate students in various fields who had won fellowships to Columbia University between 1944 and 1950. Ginzberg and his associates set out to learn how successful those graduates had become 15 years after they had completed their fellowships. Their surprising discovery was: "Those who had graduated from college with honors, who had won scholastic medals, who had been on dean's lists, who had been elected to Phi Beta Kappa, were more likely to be in the lower professional performance levels than in the top levels."

In spite of these findings, far too many hiring supervisors continue to proudly insist upon high grades, "good schools," and other questionable criteria for their prospective employees. The corporate effort, in this era of social responsibility, toward understanding "our most important asset" has been almost nonexistent. I would like to see all major corporations establish permanent research departments, staffed by competent people, who would investigate the critical problem of what constitutes valid and reliable predictors of job success. I suspect we would find that those predictors vary among industries, occupations, supervisors, and managerial philosophies.

I am not against high grades. I am appreciative of the hard work and/or intelligence and/or test-taking ability that is required to achieve them. All things being equal, I would choose an A student over a C student. But I don't think an applicant should be recommended for employment simply because of high grades or rejected because of low grades. Success is too dependent upon such other factors as dedication, perseverance, personality, specialized abilities, and so on.

Are there any factors that can be shown to bear a consistent relationship to job success? In an attempt to answer this question, a couple of years ago at the Hughes Aircraft Company we conducted an informal seminar for supervisors who had a reasonable amount of interviewing experience.

We formed two classes, of 24 people each, which met independently for two days. The first assignment was simply to list all possible predictors of job success. A total of 48 were named, ranging from scholastic performance to marital status, hobbies, and motivation.

Next, the two classes were asked to discuss each predictor. The participants were encouraged to champion their favored predictors with as much vehemence as the sensitivities of the others would allow. The results of these discussions were predictable. The hallowed assumptions could not withstand critical analysis and the actual experiences of others. In particular, the sacrosanct grades and "good schools" predictors took a shellacking.

Each group then selected, independently, the ten predictors they considered to be the most important. After comparing and consolidating the resulting two lists, we were able to come up with a list of six general employment predictors. Ranked in order of importance, they are:

1. Specific abilities
2. Ambition
3. Maturely directed energy
4. Ability to communicate
5. General intelligence and knowledge
6. Integrity.

The specific ranking is less important than the recognition that there are a number of factors that should be considered when evaluating an applicant for employment. We agreed that the importance of grades and schools should be downplayed, though certainly not ignored. And we agreed that, although specific abilities are important, they are not the deciding factor with most hires. No longer should I hear such laments as "Martin, Martin, how many times do I have to tell you? I don't need guys experienced in designing the leading edges of turbine blades — I need guys with *trailing* edge experience."

Another workshop I participated in that attempted to determine the most reliable predictors of job success was even less successful. Three years ago at an Employment Managers Association conference, more than 100 employment managers, representing many of the major corporations of the country, attempted to reach some conclusions on this subject in a day-long workshop.

We discussed our experiences with most of the traditional predictors of job success — grades, school quality, extracurricular activities, number of dependents, rate of job change, level of degree, references, interview comments, and so forth.

Every one of us had pet predictors that we proudly offered to the workshop. But every one of them was shot down with humiliating finality. None could stand up under scrutiny.

It was a disillusioning experience. By the end of the day we had reached one unanimous conclusion. We agreed that only one employment predictor does have significant value: the interviewer's gut feeling.

Admittedly, that's a pretty unsatisfactory conclusion to come to in this age of science. Gut feeling takes into account a wide variety of tangible and intangible elements — including the person's appearance, demeanor, ability to express himself, and so on. The resulting overall thumbs-up or thumbs-down feeling is what, according to the recruiters, correlates most often with managerial success.

The implications of this conclusion are important — especially for employers under pressure from the government to provide equal employment opportunity to minorities and women. No longer can they rationalize their possibly discriminatory hiring decisions on the basis of grades or any other single criterion. They must recognize and take into account the entire range of qualifications that a job candidate brings to the interview.

The Employment Interview: A Summary and Review of Recent Research

Richard D. Arvey and James E. Campion

Industrial and organizational psychologists have been studying the employment interview for more than 60 years in an effort to determine the reliability and validity of judgment based on the assessment device and also to discover the various psychological variables which influence these judgements.

Hundreds of research articles have been published and a number of articles have appeared which summarize the current "state of the art" in this particular research domain. The present article falls within this tradition. Not since Schmitt's 1976 review article in [*Personnel Psychology*] has there been a review of the literature in this area. And indeed, there has been much research dealing with this topic since that time.

The objective of the present article is threefold: (1) to summarize the findings of relevant recent research dealing with the employment interview, (2) to provide some interpretation of these findings and offer some noticeable trends in this area, and (3) to spell out our thoughts about how and why the employment interview continues to be used despite its unimpressive research record.

Our plan is to first present a model or "schema" of the variables and processes inherent in the employment interview. Second, we will summarize the research findings as reported by earlier reviewers. Third, we bring these reviews up-to-date by reviewing research published in the past few years. Finally, we will offer some suggestions about possible research avenues and potential methodologies which could be profitably utilized in future exploration of this topic area.

Condensed with permission from *Personnel Psychology*, Summer 1982, pp. 281–322.

Perhaps one way of viewing the variables and processes involved in the employment interview is shown in Figure 1. For elaboration of similar model, the reader is referred to Schmitt (1976). As may be seen in this figure, there are a number of applicant characteristics which may influence the perception of the interviewer and influence the resulting decision. In addition, there are a number of interviewer and situational factors which may also influence the perceptual and judgemental processes. Most of these classes of variables have been the object of research efforts bearing on decision making in the interview. It is expected that some of these variables will interact to influence subsequent decisions. For example, knowing the race and sex of an applicant may differentially shape the expectations, stereotypes, and behaviors of an interviewer which in turn may affect the interview outcome. We have intentionally omitted any hypotheses concerning causality among these variables. We simply do not have sufficient knowledge, even after 60 years or so of research, to accurately pinpoint causal relationship between these variables at the present time.

Prior Research Reviews

Wagner (1949). The first comprehensive review of the research associated with the employment interview was published by Wagner in 1949.

Wagner began his review by noting that one of the earliest investigations of the interview was published in 1911. In that article, Binet reported low reliability for interview-based assessments of intelligence collected from three teachers who had evaluated the same five children. However, the earliest industrial application was in 1915 when Scott reported low reliability for evaluations given by six personnel managers

FIGURE 1

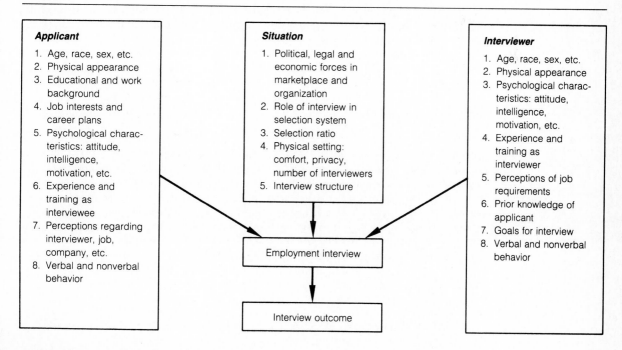

who had interviewed the same 36 sales applicants. These disappointing results have become persistent themes for research on the selection interview.

Wagner located 106 articles dealing with the employment interview. However, only 25 reported any empirical work and the remaining articles were nonempirical and represented a "hodge-podge of conflicting opinions." This early review was organized around several issues. One issue concerned the reliability and validity of interview judgements. Reliability was typically assessed by correlating evaluations of different interviewers who had assessed the same job candidates. Validity was typically assessed by correlating interview judgments with some measure of on-the-job performance. When the measure of performance was collected simultaneously with the interview judgments (e.g., interviews conducted with present employee groups), the design was called a concurrent study. In contrast, predictive designs involved following up at a later date those individuals who had been hired and put on the job. In his review, Wagner noted that reliabilities ranged from .23 to .97 with a median r of .57 for the 174 sets of ratings which were reported. Of the 22 validity coefficients summarized by Wagner, the range was from .09 to .94 with a median r of .27. This value was noted as not being particularly high.

Another issue addressed by Wagner was the capacity of interviewers to integrate information. He suggested that while interviewers may be useful in eliciting from candidates information which may not be obtained through other data gathering mechanisms, the combination of this information may best be done in a statistical rather than clinical fashion.

Wagner was favorably impressed with research results regarding the use of a standardized or patterned interview and recommended its use. He also suggested interviewers consider using several "new" techniques. For example, he suggested that the interviewer might sit on the sidelines and evaluate the candidates as they perform job tasks such as giving a speech or participating in a group discussion — a procedure which today comprises an important component in the assessment center approach. He also recommended using the interviewer to rate the applicant while he (the applicant) carries out some practical job-related task, such as building a simple object. Again, this technique has found wide acceptance today in the work-sample approach to assessing applicant qualifications.

In conclusion, Wagner recommended that the interview may be useful in three situations: (1) where rough screening is needed, (2) where the number of applicants is too small to warrant more expensive procedures, and (3) where certain traits may be most accurately assessed by the interviewer. He also recommends the use of a standardized approach with an emphasis on assessing traits which have been demonstrated to be job related.

Mayfield (1964). Fifteen years later, Mayfield (1964) summarized the interview research literature since the Wagner (1949) review. He noted that the literature still indicated relatively low reliabilities and validities for the employment interview. However, he went on to recommend that research in this area should shift to studying the decisionmaking processes inherent in the interview and to determine what factors were producing or influencing the interview judgments. Moreover, he suggested that research should focus on dividing the interview into smaller chunks and studying one or two variables at a time in a more controlled fashion. Thus, he suggested a re-orientation toward more micro-analytical research. After reviewing the literature, Mayfield felt that the research findings tended to support several general statements. Some of the most important of these statements are as follows:

1. General suitability ratings based on unstructured interviews have low reliability.

2. Material is not covered consistently in unstructured interviews.

3. Interviewers are likely to weight the same information differently.

4. Structured interviews result in higher inter-rater reliability.

5. Interview validity is low.

6. If the interviewer has valid test information available, his predictions based on the interview plus test information are usually no better and frequently less valid than the predictions based on the test alone.

7. Interviewers can reliably and validly assess intelligence but have not been shown to be effective in evaluating other traits.

8. The form of the question affects the answers given.

9. The attitude of the interviewer affects the interpretation of interviewees' responses.

10. In unstructured interviews, interviewers tend to talk most.

11. Interviewers are influenced more by unfavorable than favorable information.

12. Interviewers make their decisions quite early in unstructured interviews.

Ulrich and Trumbo (1965).   Published only six months after Mayfield's (1964) review, Ulrich and Trumbo (1965) reached many of the same conclusions. After agreeing that the interview again seemed deficient in terms of its reliability and validity, Ulrich and Trumbo called attention to the utility of the interview. That is, they suggested that researchers should examine the information gained from the interview separately from information gained from other sources such as employment tests.

These authors also supported Wagner's recommendation for a structured approach to the interview. Further, their interpretation of the evidence suggested that the interview should be used as a selection device with more limited evaluation goals. Specifically, their review indicated that the interview could be useful in assessing interpersonal relations and career motivations. Finally, they reviewed more recent micro-analytic and decision-process research and characterized these studies as interesting and promising for providing insights into interviewing as well as for the field of interpersonal communication in general.

Wright (1969) and Schmitt (1976).   Wright (1969) and later Schmitt (1976) summarized many of the research studies generated in investigating the decision making processes of the employment interview. Both Wright (1969) and Schmitt (1976) relied heavily on the significant research conducted by Webster (1964) and his colleagues at McGill University. The studies summarized by Schmitt and Wright were, indeed, micro-analytical. In fact, Wright (1969) suggested that researchers might profit by returning to the earlier orientation of dealing with the interview more as a totality because the small micro-analytic approach would lead to fragmentation and meaningless results. In a similar vein, Schmitt (1976) indicated that with few exceptions, the studies reviewed suffered from a lack of integration and limited generalizability.

It is worthwhile here to summarize in more depth some of the specific variables and findings reviewed by Schmitt. He organized his review around specific variables and their impact on decision making in the interview.

1. *Information favorability*. A recurring research theme revolved around the relationship between an interviewer's final decision and the kind of information presented in the interview. Schmitt's review of the available data suggested that interviewers reach a final decision quite early in the interview — typically within the first 4 minutes (Springbett, 1958). Also, data revealed that interviewers weigh negative information more heavily than positive information

(Springbett, 1958). Webster (1964) suggests that this phenomenon may be due to the tendency for interviewers to receive feedback only about "bad" employees and, consequently, they may become more sensitive to negative or "knock-out" factors.

2. *Temporal placement of information.* Schmitt reviewed several studies dealing with when during an interview specific positive or negative information is presented. Some of these studies (Farr, 1973) indicated that order has a significant impact and that early impressions are more important than factual information in determining interviewer's judgments. An interpretation was offered by Farr (1973), who suggested that interviewers make up their minds early and then lose attention. Anderson (1960) found that after interviewers form a favorable decision, they spend more time talking than does the interviewee, perhaps to "sell" the candidates on the company. Schmitt suggests that the reason structured interviews are more reliable is because this format may force interviewers to be more attentive which subsequently enhances their agreement with other raters.

3. *Interview stereotypes.* A considerable number of studies reviewed by Schmitt dealt with the stereotypes interviewers have of idealized job candidates. Research by Sydiaha (1961), Bolster and Springbett (1961), and Hakel, Hollman, and Dunnette (1970) tended to confirm the notion that interviewers possess stereotypes of idealized successful applicants against which real applicants are judged. However, London and Hakel (1974) presented data suggesting that these stereotypes diminish or are altered as the evaluation of an applicant progresses.

4. *Job information.* Several studies reviewed by Schmitt indicated that as interviewers receive more information about the job to be filled, inter-rater reliability increases (Langdale and Weitz, 1973), and there is a reduction in the impact of irrelevant attributes on decisions.

5. *Individual differences in the decision process.* Schmitt reviewed several studies investigating whether interviewers use and weight information differently from one another. Hakel, Dobmeyer, and Dunnette (1970) found evidence indicating that actual interviewers gave different weights to academic standing and job experience factors in evaluating applicants than did undergraduate students serving as raters. Valenzi and Andrews (1973) found wide individual differences in cue utilization resulting in considerable inter-rater differences in evaluating applicants.

6. *Visual cues.* Schmitt's review suggested that nonverbal sources of information were more important than verbal cues and that a combination of both kinds of cues were maximally responsible for obtained differences in ratings of job candidates.

7. *Attitudinal, sexual, and racial similarity.* In 1976, Schmitt reviewed a handful of studies which investigated the importance of attitudinal and racial similarities between the interviewer and interviewee. Generally, the findings suggested that attitudinal and racial similarity affected evaluations of candidates (Rand and Wexley, 1975; Wexley and Nemeroff, 1974). In addition, several studies (Dipboye, Fromkin, and Wibach, 1975; Cohen and Bunker, 1975) demonstrated that interviewers tended to give lower evaluations to female applicants. However, both males and females were more likely to be recommended for traditionally role-congruent jobs.

8. *Contrast effects.* A number of studies reviewed by Schmitt had to do with the investigation of the quality of the preceding interviewees on interview ratings.

There appears to be mixed findings in this area. Some studies found a significant, strong, and practical effect (Wexley, Yukl, Kovacs, and Sanders, 1972), while other studies suggest that the effect is either nonsignificant or trivial (Landy and Bates, 1973; Hakel, Dobmeyer, and Dunnette, 1970), especially when professional interviewers are used.

9. *Structured interview guides.* Again, Schmitt found evidence that the use of a structured interview guide increases inter-interviewer agreement.

10. *Miscellaneous.* Carlson, Thayer, Mayfield, and Peterson (1971) conducted a study showing that experienced interviewers were no more reliable than inexperienced interviewers, but that stress for quotas influenced the decisions of experienced interviewers more than the decisions of less experienced interviewers. Also, Carlson (1967) investigated the relative importance of appearance and personal history information.

The review by Schmitt was comprehensive and is illustrative of the kinds of variables and processes investigated in exploring the employment interview during the past 10 years or so.

Arvey (1979).   In 1979, Arvey summarized the research literature concerning evidence of bias in the employment interview with regard to blacks, females, the handicapped, and the elderly. Because of the increased probability that the interview will be subjected to legal scrutiny, Arvey reviewed the legal aspects of the interview. Eight legal cases concerning the employment interview were summarized. It appears litigation has revolved around two basic themes:

1. Do particular kinds of questions convey an impression of an underlying discriminatory attitude or intent? That is, reference to "girls" and inquiries to females into non-job related areas such as marital status, parenthood, child care, etc. when these same questions are not presented to male candidates may be sufficient to convince a court that discriminatory "animus" or intent was operating.

2. Does the inquiry operate in such a way as to demonstrate a differential impact or adverse impact on protected groups? If so, is the particular information valid or job related? Organizations should avoid interview questions which operate in such a way as to differentially affect minority groups, unless such questions are job related.

In his review, Arvey specified the processes inherent in the interview which potentially contribute to differential evaluations according to sex, race, etc.: (1) stereotyping and (2) differential behavior emitted during the interview.

Arvey reviewed a number of studies (17) investigating the effects of applicant's sex in interview evaluations. The studies showed in a reasonably consistent fashion that females were generally given lower evaluations than males when these candidates had similar or identical qualifications.

In addition to reviewing studies dealing with sex as a main effect, Arvey reported that research had also focused on several variables predicted to interact with sex to influence the evaluations given. The variable given the greatest attention was the type of job for which the candidates were being considered. Evidence supported the notion that females are given lower ratings for jobs typically "masculine" in nature, whereas males are also given lower ratings when being considered for typically "feminine" jobs (Shaw, 1972; Cohen and Bunker, 1975; Cash, Gillen, and Burns, 1977).

A second variable commonly investigated in combination with sex was applicant competence or qualifications. Arvey reported that when qualifications were included, sex tended to account for a relatively small percentage of rating variance. A hypothesized interaction between sex and qualifications where competent females would receive lower evaluations than competent males was given only mixed support. Finally, attractiveness was investigated in combination with sex. Arvey's review indicates that attractive candidates are typically preferred regardless of sex.

Somewhat surprisingly, Arvey could locate only three studies dealing with race of the applicant in interview evaluations. Even more surprising was that little evidence was found indicating that unfavorable evaluations were given to black candidates compared to whites (Wexley and Nemeroff, 1974; Haefner, 1977; Rand and Wexley, 1975).

In addition, Arvey reviewed two studies investigating the effects of candidates' age on interviewer evaluations and found a relatively strong pervasive effect due to applicant age (Haefner, 1977; Rosen and Jerdee, 1976).

Finally, Arvey reviewed four studies investigating the effects of applicants' handicap status on interview evaluations. Evidence supported the notion that handicapped applicants received lower evaluations in terms of hiring, but higher evaluations on motivational variables. Arvey suggests that interviewers might attribute higher motivation, effort levels, etc. to handicapped individuals filing applications for jobs because of the interviewer's attribution of greater efforts to overcome disabilities on the part of these applicants.

In his conclusion, Arvey identified a number of areas which need research attention.

1. *Methodological problems.* Arvey called attention to the overreliance on resume and paper-and-pencil methodologies in this area. He suggested that greater efforts should be made to study "real" interview situations and to utilize more full stimulus fields. More use of videotape and face-to-face interview situations are needed. Arvey suggested that researchers need to tap subject pools other than undergraduate and graduate students and that subjects be given the opportunity to view more than *one* particular female, or handicapped individual in studies of this sort. Otherwise, any significant effect observed could be unique to the specific stimulus individuals presented due to other uncontrolled characteristics (hair color, height, etc.).

2. *More research on race, age, and the handicapped.* Arvey specified where more research is needed with each of these minority groups.

3. *Process research.* Arvey indicated that little is known about *why* differential evaluations are made and what goes on in the interview to influence the evaluations. In essence, he called for more research concerning the perceptual processes which might account for the phenomenon observed.

Review of Recent Research

This section of the paper will consist of our summary of the recent literature concerning the employment interview. Basically, process research which has been published since the Schmitt (1976) article will be reviewed. Similarly, research dealing with bias and discrimination in the interview since the Arvey (1979) article will also be reviewed.

This review will be organized by focusing first on the general issues of interviewer reliability, validity, and some methodological concerns. Subsequently, we will review the research on a topic-by-topic basis dealing with many of the topics and variables discussed earlier by Schmitt.

Reliability and Validity

Recent research has not been as pessimistic about the validity and reliability as in prior years. Interviews conducted by a board or panel appear to be promising as a vehicle for enhancing reliability and validity.

For example, reasonably favorable results were reported by Landy (1976) for the validity of board interviews for police officer selection. Data was gathered in a one year period during which 399 white male applicants were interviewed and 150 applicants hired. The ratings made by the interviewing board at the end of each interview comprised the predictor variables. A principal components analysis of the averaged interview trait ratings indicated that there were three major components. A principal component analysis of supervisory ratings of performance identified four oblique performance factors. A validity analysis demonstrated rated performance could be predicted from averaged interview factor scores but not from the averaged overall recommendations of the interviewers. When the validity coefficients were corrected for restriction of range on the predictors, four of the 12 coefficients were significant (.26, .29, .33, and .34). However, given the number of validity coefficients computed and the statistical manipulations involved, these results are not overwhelming. . . .

The themes suggested by research investigating the overall reliability and validity of the interview seem to be twofold:

1. The use of board or panel interviews appears promising as a means of improving the validity and reliability of the interview. Perhaps sharing different perceptions with the different interviewers forces interviewers to become more aware of irrelevant inferences made on non-job related variables.

2. Use of directly related job analysis and other job information as a basis for interview questions is a useful method of improving the accuracy of the interview. This theme has been suggested previously by Schmitt (1976) and others (e.g., Langdale and Weitz, 1973). . . .

Decision-Making Studies

There were several studies reporting evidence for various rating errors in the interview. Kopelman (1975) found evidence of contrast bias in evaluations of videotaped interviews of candidates applying for medical school. Contrast effect counted for 11% of the decision variance and was most influential in the assessment of candidates of intermediate quality. Additional evidence for the contrast effect was provided by Schuh (1978) who had 120 employment interviewers and 180 managers view videotaped interviews of four applicants for a management trainee position.

Farr and York (1975) investigated the influence of amount of information on primacy-recency effects in recruitment decisions. Seventy-two college recruiters evaluated hypothetical candidates described in a written booklet. The analysis indicated that recency effects occurred when interviewers were asked to make repeated judgments during the interview, whereas primacy effects were obtained when only a single judgment was required of each interviewer. The amount of information presented about each applicant had no effect upon judgments.

First impression error was investigated by Tucker and Row (1979). They asked 72 students to read and evaluate interview transcripts after examining a letter of reference. Results suggested that interviewers who first read an unfavorable letter were more likely to give the applicant less credit for past successes and to hold the applicant more personally responsible for past failures. Results also indicated that the decision to hire is closely related to interviewers' causal interpretations of past outcomes.

Keenan (1977) reported evidence suggesting that interviewers' personal feelings about candidates influenced their general evaluations of them. In a study of 551 graduate recruitment interviews conducted by 103 interviewers, Keenan found fairly strong relationships between interviewers liking of the candidate and overall evaluations. The relationship between ratings of candidates' intelligence and general evaluations was only slightly reduced when the effect of liking was held constant. This was interpreted as suggesting that there are both affective and cognitive components in interviewers' evaluations of candidates.

London and Poplowski (1976) found sex differences in rating when they presented 120 male and 120 female undergraduates with information about two groups of hypothetical company employees. Their hypothesis that the distinctiveness in amount and favorability of information would result in differential stereotypes about the two groups was not confirmed. However, they did find that female subjects gave consistently higher ratings.

Finally, Leonard (1976) studied the relationship between cognitive complexity and similarity error in an interview context. Sixty-four undergraduates conducted interviews with confederates who played roles as job applicants. Similarity was manipulated by the confederate roles and by information given to the subjects. Subjects high on cognitive complexity were more likely to evaluate similar applicants more positively, suggesting that cognitive complexity may moderate the impact of similarity error.

A recent study by Osburn, Timmrick, and Bigby (1981) reported that interviewers made accurate discriminations among job candidates on the basis of a videotaped interview when they evaluated the candidates on specific and relevant job dimensions. However, interviewers making evaluations on more generalized job dimensions were not as accurate.

In sum, the recent studies tend to confirm earlier research demonstrating that indeed, interviewers tend to produce ratings or evaluations which are influenced by contrast, primacy-recency, first impressions, personal feelings, and other factors. On the positive side, some research again indicates that when evaluations are in the form of specific predictions of job behavior, less distortion is found.

There have been three studies published which investigated interviewer decision time. Huegli and Tschirgi (1975) examined a sample of 183 recruiting interviews conducted by 16 interviewers at Ohio University. Interviews were recorded and time monitored. The interviewers also completed a questionnaire describing their decisionmaking during the interview. Findings indicated that 77% of the interviewers reported making decisions during the interview itself but only 33% during the first half of the interview. This finding is at variance with those of previously reported studies which indicated that decisions were made very early in the interview. Huegli and Tschirgi also found that hire decisions were made sooner than no-hire decisions; however, interview length was unrelated to the hiring decision. Finally, decisions were unrelated to time of day.

A second study in this area was by Tucker and Row (1977) who conducted an experiment to determine whether consulting the application blank prior to the interview would delay the initial decision. Twenty-eight experienced recruiters interviewed a role-playing job candidate. Half the interviewers were provided with an application blank prior to the interview and half were not. Results indicated that not providing the application blank did not slow down the initial decision nor did it reduce the interviewer's confidence in the decision.

In a third study, Tullar, Mullins, and Caldwell (1979) investigated the effects of interview length (15 minutes versus 30 minutes) and applicant quality (high versus low) on interviewer decision time. Sixty experienced employment counselors observed a videotaped interview and made a decision as soon as they felt they had sufficient information. The interviewers took significantly more time to make the decision for the high quality candidates and for the longer interview. . . .

Interviewee Training

There have been numerous studies exploring how interviewees might be taught to present themselves more effectively in the employment interview. An early example of this was reported by Stevens and Tornatzky (1976) who assigned 26 clients from a drug abuse treatment program to a treatment group and a control group. The treatment was a workshop stressing behavioral interview skills, such as preparing for an interview, application completion, grooming, nonverbal communications, and phrasing of answers to interview questions. A six-month follow up showed no significant attitudinal differences between the two groups but those who participated in the interview workshop obtained higher paying jobs.

Hollandsworth, Dressel, and Stevens (1977) developed a job interviewee skills workshop based on behavioral procedures such as modeling, role playing, and directive feedback, and compared it with a traditional lecture-discussion group approach, as well as with a no-treatment control group. Forty-five college seniors were randomly assigned to one of three groups. Subjects participated in a videotaped, simulated job interview prior to and following each workshop. Analyses of self-report and behavioral measures indicated that the group learning the behavioral procedures made significant gains in percentage of time eye contact was maintained during the interview. The discussion group was found to be superior to the behavioral and control groups in ratings of their ability to explain individual skills, and expression of feelings and personal opinions relevant to the interview. Also, interviewees in the discussion group demonstrated a significant increase in length of speaking time. Thus, both procedures seem to increase interviewee's effectiveness in the interview.

In a follow-up study, Hollandsworth and Sandifer (1979) developed a workshop combining the most effective components of behavioral and discussion group methods, and trained 46 Masters level counselors in the use of the workshop. Subsequently, the counselors conducted over 320 workshops for approximately 4100 secondary and post-secondary students. Data generated by these counselors indicate that the workshop was easily employed as a training procedure. Also, student participants reported high levels of satisfaction with the procedure.

Keith, Engelkes, and Winborn (1977) also investigated training with 66 rehabilitation clients and found experimental support for training effects in improving knowledge of job openings and the number of job leads obtained. Further, eight of the 19 trainees obtained jobs; whereas, only six of 47 control group members were able to find employment. Finally, Speas (1979) assigned 56 prison inmates to one of four treatment conditions or to a waiting list control group. The four instructional techniques were model exposure, role-playing, model exposure plus role-playing, and model exposure and role-playing with videotaped feedback. Judges' ratings of videotaped simulated pre- and post-treatment interviews, and personnel interviewers' ratings of follow-up interviews served as criterion measures. Post-test results indicated that both the model-plus-role-playing and the model-exposure-plus-role-playing-plus-videotaped-feedback treatments were significantly more effective than the control procedure on all dependent variables.

Lastly, two research efforts focused on issues related to what the interviewees can do to impress the interviewers. Harlan, Kerr, and Kerr (1977) administered questionnaires to 274 managers, supervisory personnel, clerical workers, and high school students, and asked them to indicate whether or not they would discuss various types of work-related factors if they were interviewed as applicants for employment. A systematic tendency was found for respondents to prefer to discuss motivator rather than hygiene factors. Responding to a modified version of the questionnaire, 20 professional employment interviewers indicated that it is, in fact, wise to emphasize motivator and de-emphasize hygiene factors if the applicant's intent is to maximize the likelihood of being offered a job.

In a second study, Campion (1978) investigated college recruiter evaluations of 170 job applicants. His findings suggested that undergraduate GPA, membership in fraternity or sorority, and membership in a professional society were significantly related to interviewers' overall general impression, personal liking, and the chances for further consideration in the interview.

This domain of investigation might profit by researchers becoming more acquainted with literature available on impression management. The recent text by Schlenker (1980) provides a review of the theory and research in impression management which may facilitate future research efforts in this area.

Summary and Conclusions

It is clear that research dealing with the employment interview is progressing. A number of themes seems to emerge when reviewing what has been happening in this area over the past five years or so.

1. *There has been an increase in research investigating possible bias in the interview.* One theme which has been fairly consistent is the increased interest in the employment interview as a vehicle for discrimination against women and minority group job candidates. While attention has focused predominantly on group membership variables and how they influence interview decisions, more recent research has investigated the effects of other variables in interaction with protected group status on interviewers decisionmaking. However, as we noted earlier much more research needs to be conducted in this area. With the potential for increased legal challenges to this selection device, there is a pressing need for more research in this area before court decisions are made on the basis of preliminary and perhaps methodologically flawed studies.

2. *More variables associated with the interview have been under investigation.* Our review has revealed a number of studies dealing with variables which previously received little research attention. For example, researchers have begun to probe such topics as nonverbal behavior, interviewees' perceptions of interviewers, interviewees' self-perceptions, and interviewee training. For the most part, these factors are associated with the interviewee rather than with the interviewer. It is somewhat surprising that so little research has been conducted in the past dealing with applicant perceptions. Perhaps researchers felt that it would be somewhat intrusive to ascertain the perceptions, reactions, and so forth of actual candidates.

An important "hole" in the interview research area is the lack of investigations dealing with situational factors as they impact interviewers. For example, what effect does accountability have on interviewer decisions? Are the decisions of interviewers whose evaluations are more "public" more accurate and valid than interviewers who make their decisions with little visibility? Rozelle and Baxter (in press) conducted a study which shows that interviewers who were under conditions of higher accountability and responsibility were more discriminating in their judgments and showed more agreement with other interviewers.

3. *Researchers are becoming more sophisticated in their research methodologies and strategies.* As mentioned earlier, interview research in the past utilized resume designs for the most part. However, recent research efforts are incorporating more realistic stimulus sets into the designs. The use of videotape to capture the employment in-

terview as it progresses is more frequent, due possibly to the lower costs and greater flexibility of these technologies.

Moreover, researchers are realizing the limitations of resume and other pencil-and-paper methodologies and conducting research to demonstrate the differences in results using these methodologies compared to more realistic stimulus and response settings. Some of the ethical issues associated with conducting research unobstrusively without informed consent are being discussed (e.g., Newman and Kryzstofiah, 1979). Yet it is possible that results may have little relevance to employment interviews and associated evaluation processes unless interviewers and interviewees remain unaware of the purpose of the interview.

There has, however, been little attention to more sophisticated decisionmaking models and their incorporation into research on the interview. For example, the Brunswick lens model, policy-capturing methods, and Baysian techniques have seldom been employed. In one interesting, but complex study, Bigby (1977) used a Baysian model to determine the revisions of probabilities made by interviewers evaluating job candidates. His use of a Baysian framework seems particularly fruitful for future research.

Similarly, it appears as if some of the validity generalization models may be applicable. Distribution of validity coefficients based on the interview might be made available and applied to the same kinds of analyses indicated by Schmidt and Hunter (1977) and Callender and Osburn (1980).

4. *Research continues to be microanalytic in nature.* The research reviewed here has most certainly been microanalytic. Researchers have continued to examine a narrow range of variables when conducting their research on the employment interview. In our view, this approach still continues to have some usefulness despite Schmitt's (1976) admonition about conducting research which is too narrow. In our opinion, research efforts should focus on capturing more real or actual behavioral and evaluation processes, but continue to focus on relatively small components of the interview and interview process.

5. *Researchers investigating the employment interview have neglected related research in the person-perception literature.* In reviewing recent research, one is struck by the almost complete lack of attention which has been paid to the person-perception literature by researchers in this area. It is almost as if industrial and organizational psychologists have studied the employment interview in isolation from the rest of psychology, perhaps even ignoring the fact that the phenomenon under investigation is essentially a perceptual process. Thus, one of the recommendations we can offer to researchers in this area is to pay far greater attention to what is going on in other domains regarding person-perception processes. Specifically, researchers could profit from examining the interview from various theoretical models and frameworks which stem from other areas. These include the following:

a. *Attribution models.* The employment interview and the evaluation judgments made by interviewers are surely a function of the attributions they make about interviewees. Hastorf, Schneider, and Polefka (1970) summarized the literature in this area some time ago, which suggests that interviewers form judgments about the success or failure of interviewees and frequently base their judgments on their attributions of cause of the success or failure experience was due to internal factors associated with interviewees or to external factors beyond the control of the interviewee. Moreover, attribution models differentiate between factors which are assumed to be stable (e.g., ability, difficulty of task) or relatively unstable (e.g., effort, luck). The implications which stem from attribution models are clear: Interviewers will form judgments about interviewees according to the attributions they make for the cause of past achievements on the part of job candidates. Yet, attribution theory has been virtually ignored in the investigation of the employment interview process.

b. *Impression formation and management.* A large body of literature has accumulated concerning how individuals form impressions and how impressions may be managed. For example, Schlenker (1980) summarizes a large number of studies dealing with the impact of nonverbal behavior on perceiver impressions and judgments. These studies have been conducted largely by social psychologists. Similarly, Hastorf, Schneider, and Polefka (1970) indicate that an area under investigation is how perceivers combine evaluation data. The same kind of question appears in the employment interview — how do interviewers combine informational cues. Yet, some of the scaling and weighting models developed by psychologists in person-perception research have received little or no attention from industrial psychologists.

c. *Implicit personality theory.* The notion that individuals have their own idiosyncratic models of personality which differ from those of other judges, is seldom recognized by researchers dealing with the employment interview as a broader phenomenon. Few researchers in industrial psychology pay much attention to this perceptual model.

In short, the mainstream of research dealing with the employment interview typically has been without the benefit of the more broadly applicable person-perception models. The price has been somewhat shortsighted and situationally bound research, without the guidance of broader based theories.

WHY THE INTERVIEW IS STILL USED

Perhaps the glaring "black hole" in all previous reviews and in the current literature concerns the issue of why use of the interview persists in view of evidence of its relatively low validity, reliability, and its susceptability to bias and distortion. We know of only one organization that hires a candidate sight unseen, based on resume information only.* One only has to ask researchers in this area the question, "Would you hire somebody without an interview?" to learn that they most likely would also rely on the interview. Why is this so?

The reason for this persistence seems to fall into two major categories: (1) the interview is "really" valid, (2) the interview is not valid but certain practical considerations make it the popular choice, (3) the interview may not be valid but certain psychological processes act to maintain great faith in the selection tool, and (4) the interview is not valid but it does other things well. Let us examine each of these categories in more detail.

1. *The interview is "really" valid.* Under this category fall two quite different explanations. First, some individuals will argue that while the evidence is quite pessimistic overall, the interview still yields valid judgments on several observable interpersonal dimensions of behavior which are manifested in the interview — such as sociability, verbal fluency, etc. In essence, the interview is viewed as a "work sample" of these behaviors and is more likely to allow accurate assessment of these variables than of less observable dimensions. In fact, the evidence tends to support this contention. Validity coefficients are typically higher and more likely to be significant for dimensions of behavior which are more easily observed in the interview. Note, however,

---

*Apparently, Princeton University Philosophy Department hires on the basis of credentials only (personal communication, Dianne Horgan).

that this argument pertains to the accurate and valid assessment of these specific traits or behavioral dimensions and not necessarily to the job behavior.

Similarly, there are some important areas that cannot be assessed well or easily with available psychometric technology. One obvious example is the prediction of work motivation. Attempts to develop motivation measures for predicting work behavior generally have not been successful outside of a counseling context. Consequently, decisionmakers have relied on the interview and discussions of job interest, career plans, likes and dislikes, etc. to make assessments in this important area.

A second argument extended under this category is that while the interview is valid, typical psychometric models are not sufficiently capable of detecting interview validity. The reasoning here is that restriction of range, small samples, homogeneous applicant populations, and so forth, act to attenuate the correlations observed. We may simply expect too much in the way of psychometric evidence. A similar argument is that the linear model is not appropriate for tapping the relationships between interview judgments and on-the-job performance. Possibly more representative would be a multiple-hurdle approach, where candidates need to exhibit a certain "minimum" level of a variable, and subsequent differences beyond this minimum do not translate into differences in job performance.

A related issue concerns whether researchers have been validating the wrong theory. It may be that certain specific interviewers are more valid than others and that researchers perhaps should focus on differences among interviewers rather than the validity of the interview, collapsed across interviewers. In essence, the argument is "some interviewers are more valid than others."

2. *The interview may not be valid but certain practical considerations make it the popular choice.* For example, Wagner (1949) recommended the use of the interview when the number of applicants is too small to warrant more elaborate procedures. Historically, and especially since 1964, the use of other "more sophisticated" selection devices (such as tests) have been limited primarily to those jobs with a large number of incumbents where empirical validation was feasible and clearly cost effective. The vast majority of jobs have too few incumbents to permit traditional validation studies. This may be changing, however. It appears organizations have become increasingly interested in conducting cooperative and industry-wide validation studies. This taken together with recent successes in validity generalization research (Pearlman, Schmidt, and Hunter, 1980) suggest that test usage may become more viable as an alternative or supplement to interviews for selection purposes.

Related to this are arguments regarding the practicality of using job tryouts as a means of assessing applicants' job skills and work experience claims. A practical alternative has been to have the applicant describe and discuss work history in the employment interview, a variation of the oral trade test. Here again, we anticipate change. This is due to the increased interest many organizations have shown for developing content-valid test and work samples as evaluation aids in assessing specific work skills and experience. Finally, some organizations use practicality arguments for removing tests and other scored selection devices in the aftermath of the 1964 Civil Rights Act. It was erroneously thought that total reliance on the unscored selection interview would lessen EEO problems. Of course, the courts have ruled otherwise (Arvey, 1979).

Finally, the interview may be used to forecast to applicants the nature of the job and the responsibilities. Wanous (1980) has called to our attention the importance of exposing job candidates to accurate information about the job which help create realistic job expectations for job candidates. Obviously, the interview can facilitate the communications of accurate job information.

3. *The interview is not valid, but interviewers maintain great faith and confidence in their judgments.* This argument stems predominantly from the work emerging from

the decisionmaking research. While evidence in clinical settings has clearly documented the superiority of statistical prediction over clinical, people are quite prone to place confidence in highly fallible interview judgments (Kahneman and Tversky, 1973).

Kahneman and Tversky (1973) and Einhorn and Hogarth (1978) discuss this phenomenon under the term, the illusion of validity. Essentially, interviewers ignore base rate information, do not pay attention to disconfirming evidence, and over-depend on case-specific information in making their judgments. Einhorn and Hogarth (1978) argue that the persistence of judgmental confidence is a function of the frequency and importance of both positive and negative feedback and the effects of experience. In actual employment settings, interviewers tend to receive very little feedback concerning their judgments, and some people have argued (e.g. Webster, 1964) that what evidence they do receive is about their errors. Thus, the feedback loops to interviewers seem tenuous and distorted, which might well act to maintain confidence in the judgments made.

4. *The interview is not valid, but it does other things well.* In this category rest, for the most part, untested assumptions regarding the value of the interview for accomplishing objectives unrelated to the selection decision. One example is selling the candidate on the job. College recruiters often report that much of their time is devoted to this, especially in high demand areas in engineering and business. Interviewers also answer questions from the candidates. Many candidates, but especially those with experience, come prepared with specific questions important for their personal decisionmaking. Finally, many view the interview as an important public relations tool. Interviewers are potential consumers and recruiters, as well as voting citizens, and their perceptions of fair treatment could have important consequences. For these reasons, then, the elimination of the employment interview would probably be very unpopular among both interviewers and job applicants. Of course, whether these objectives are best met by the employment interview rather than by other means is an unanswered research question.

A FINAL WORD

The employment interview continues to be widely used. While many industrial and organizational psychologists are well aware of the findings concerning the limited reliability and validity of this device, few would advocate eliminating the interview or not interviewing candidates to fill jobs in their own organizations (e.g. research assistants, secretaries, etc.). Thus, research on the interview continues and will continue as long as it is a widely used technique. One direction industrial psychologists should move toward is that of converting the findings and results stemming from research into applied guidelines for interviewers and interviewees. There is a dearth of guidelines and suggestions concerning the improvement of interview effectiveness based on research findings. Instead, many guidelines, suggestions, "how to interview" workshops, and techniques are founded on intuition, beliefs, and what seems more comfortable, rather than on research results. There need to be greater efforts made to merge research with application in this domain. There are some exceptions, however. Both Schmitt (1976) and Hakel (in press) have made efforts to translate research findings into practical guidelines. Perhaps these efforts should receive greater attention among practitioners.

REFERENCES

Anderson, C. W. The relation between speaking times and decision in the employment interview. *Journal of Applied Psychology*, 1960, 44, 267–268.

Arvey, R. D. *Fairness in selecting employees.* Reading, Mass.: Addison-Wesley, 1979.

Arvey, R. D. Unfair discrimination in the employment interview: Legal and psychological aspects. *Psychological Bulletin*, 1979, 86, 736–765.

Bigby, D. G. A Bayesian analysis of employment interviewers' errors in processing position and negative information. Unpublished Masters thesis, University of Houston, 1977.

Bolster, B. I. and Springbett, B. M. The reactions of interviewers to favorable and unfavorable information. *Journal of Applied Psychology*, 1961, 45, 97–103.

Callender, J. C. and Osburn, H. G. Development of a test of a new model for validity generalizations. *Journal of Applied Psychology*, 1980, 65, 543–558.

Campion, M. A. Identification of variables most influential in determining interviewers' evaluations of applicants in a college placement center. *Psychological Reports*, 1978, 42, 947–952.

Carlson, R. E. The relative influence of appearance and factual written information on an interviewer's final rating. *Journal of Applied Psychology*, 1967, 51, 461–468.

Carlson, R. E., Thayer, P. W., Mayfield, E. C., and Peterson, D. A. Research on the selection interview. *Personnel Journal*, 1971, 50, 268–275.

Cash, T. F., Gillen, B., and Burns, D. S. Sexism and "beautyism" in personnel consultant decision making. *Journal of Applied Psychology*, 1977, 62, 301–307.

Cohen, S. L. and Bunker, K. A. Subtle effects of sex role stereotypes on recruiters' hiring decisions. *Journal of Applied Psychology*, 1975, 60, 566–572.

Dipboye, R. L., Fromkin, H. L., and Wiback, K. Relative importance of applicant sex, attractiveness, and scholastic standing in evaluation of job applicant resumes. *Journal of Applied Psychology*, 1975, 60, 39–43.

Einhorn, H. J. and Hogarth, R. M. Confidence in judgment: Resistance of the illusion of validity. *Psychological Review*, 1978, 85, 395–416.

Farr, J. L. Response requirements and primacy-recency effects in a simulated selection interview. *Journal of Applied Psychology*, 1973, 57, 228–233.

Farr, J. L. and York, C. M. Amount of information and primacy-recency effects in recruitment decisions. *Personnel Psychology*, 1975, 28, 233–238.

Haefner, J. E. Race, age, sex, and competence as factors in employer selection of the disadvantaged. *Journal of Applied Psychology*, 1977, 62, 199–202.

Hakel, M. D., Dobmeyer, T. W., and Dunnette, M. D. Relative importance of three content dimensions in overall suitability ratings of job applicants' resumes. *Journal of Applied Psychology*, 1970, 54, 65–71.

Hakel, M. D., Hollmann, T. D., and Dunnette, M. D. Accuracy of interviewers, certified public accountants, and students in identifying the interests of accountants. *Journal of Applied Psychology*, 1970, 54, 115–119.

Hakel, M. D. Employment interview. In Rowland, K. M. & Ferris, G. R. (Eds.) *Personnel Management: New Perspectives*. Boston: Allyn & Bacon, in press.

Harlan, A., Kerr, J., and Kerr, S. Preference for motivator and hygiene factors in a hypothetical interview situation: Further findings and some implications for the employment interview. *Personnel Psychology*, 1977, 30, 557–566.

Hastorf, A. H., Schneider, D. J., and Polefka, J. *Person perception:* Reading, Mass.: Addison-Wesley, 1970.

Hollandsworth, J. G., Dressel, M. E., and Stevens, J. Use of behavioral versus traditional procedures for increasing job interview skills. *Journal of Counseling Psychology*, 1977, 24, 503–509.

Hollandsworth, J. G. and Sandifer, B. A. Behavioral training for increasing effective job-interview skills: Follow-up and evaluation. *Journal of Counseling Psychology*, 1979, 26, 448–450.

Huegli, J. M. and Tschirgi, H. An investigation of the relationship of time to recruitment interview decision making. *Proceedings of Academy of Management,* 1975, 234–236.

Kahneman, D. and Tversky, A. On the psychology of prediction. *Psychological Review,* 1973, 80, 251–273.

Keenan, A. Some relationships between interviewers' personal feelings about candidates and their general evaluation of them. *Journal of Occupational Psychology,* 1977, 50, 275–283.

Keith, R. D., Engelkes, J. R., and Winborn, B. B. Employment-seeking preparation and activity: An experimental job-placement training model for rehabilitation clients. *Rehabilitation Counseling Bulletin,* 1977, 21, 259–265.

Kopelman, M. D. The contrast effect in the selection interview. *British Journal of Educational Psychology,* 1975, 45, 333–336.

Landy, F. J. The validity of the interview in police officer selection. *Journal of Applied Psychology,* 1976, 61, 193–198.

Landy, F. J. and Bates, F. Another look at contrast effects in the employment interview. *Journal of Applied Psychology,* 1973, 58, 141–144.

Langdale, J. A. and Weitz, J. Estimating the influence of job information on interviewer agreement. *Journal of Applied Psychology,* 1973, 57, 23–27.

Leonard, R. L. Cognitive complexity and the similarity-attraction paradigm. *Journal of Research in Personality,* 1976, 10, 83–88.

London, M. and Hakel, M. D. Effects of applicant stereotypes, order, and information on interview impressions. *Journal of Applied Psychology,* 1974, 59, 157–162.

London, M. and Poplawski, J. R. Effects of information on stereotype development in performance appraisal and interview contexts. *Journal of Applied Psychology,* 1976, 17, 239–260.

Mayfield, E. C. The selection interview: A reevaluation of published research. *Personnel Psychology,* 1964, 17, 239–260.

Newman, J. M. and Kryzstofiah, F. Self-reports versus unobtrusive measures: Balancing method variable and ethical concerns in employment discrimination research. *Journal of Applied Psychology,* 1979, 64, 82–85.

Osburn, H. G., Timmrick, C., and Bigby, D. Effect of dimensional relevance and accuracy of simulated hiring decisions by employment interviewers. *Journal of Applied Psychology,* 1981, 66, 159–165.

Pearlman, K., Schmidt, F. L., and Hunter, J. E. Validity generalization results for tests to predict a job proficiency and training success in clerical occupations. *Journal of Applied Psychology,* 1980, 65, 373–406.

Rand, T. M. and Wexley, K. N. Demonstration of the effect, "similar to me," in simulated employment interviews. *Psychological Reports,* 1975, 36, 535–544.

Rosen, B. and Jerdee, T. H. The influence of age stereotypes on managerial decisions. *Journal of Applied Psychology,* 1976, 61, 428–432.

Rozelle, R. M. and Baxter, J. C. The influence of role pressure on the perceiver: Judgments of videotaped interviewers varying judge accountability and responsibility. *Journal of Applied Psychology,* in press.

Schlenker, B. R. *Impression Management.* Monterey, Calif.: Brooks/Cole Publishing Company, 1980.

Schmidt, F. L. and Hunter, J. E. Development of a general solution to the problem of validity generalizations. *Journal of Applied Psychology,* 1977, 62, 529–540.

Schmitt, N. Social and situational determinants of interview decisions: Implications for the employment interview. *Personnel Psychology,* 1976, 29, 79–101.

Schuh, A. J. Contrast effect in the interview. *Bulletin of the Psychonomic Society,* 1978, 11, 195–196.

Shaw, E. A. Differential impact of negative stereotyping in employee selection. *Personnel Selection,* 1972, 25, 333–338.

Speas, C. M. Job-seeking interview skills training: A comparison of four instructional techniques. *Journal of Counseling Psychology,* 1979, 26, 405–412.

Springbett, B. M. Factors affecting the final decision in the employment interview. *Canadian Journal of Psychology,* 1958, 12, 13–22.

Stevens, W. and Tornatzky, L. The effects of a job-interview skills workshop on drug-abuse clients. *Journal of Employment Counseling,* 1976, 13, 156–163.

Sydiaha, D. Bales' interaction process analysis of personnel selection interviews. *Journal of Applied Psychology,* 1961, 45, 393–401.

Tucker, D. H. and Rowe, P. M. Consulting the application form prior to the interview: An essential step in the selection process. *Journal of Applied Psychology,* 1977, 62, 283–287.

Tucker, D. H. and Rowe, P. M. Relationship between expectancy, causal attributions, and final hiring decisions in the employment interview. *Journal of Applied Psychology,* 1979, 64, 27–34.

Tullar, W. L., Mullins, T. W., and Caldwell, S. A. Effects of interview length and applicant quality on interview decision time. *Journal of Applied Psychology,* 1979, 64, 669–674.

Ulrich, L. and Trumbo, D. The selection interview since 1949. *Psychological Bulletin,* 1965, 63, 100–116.

Valenzi, E. and Andrews, I. R. Individual differences in the decision process of employment interviewers. *Journal of Applied Psychology,* 1973, 58, 49–53.

Wagner, R. The employment interview: A critical summary. *Personnel Psychology,* 1949, 2, 17–46.

Wanous, J. P. *Organizational entry: Recruitment, selection, & socialization of newcomers.* Reading, Mass.: Addison-Wesley, 1980.

Webster, E. D. (Ed.) *Decisionmaking in the employment interview.* Montreal, 1964.

Wexley, K. N. and Nemeroff, W. F. The effects of racial prejudice, race of applicant, and biographical similarity on interviewer evaluations of job applicants. *Journal of Social and Behavioral Sciences,* 1974, 20, 66–78.

Wexley, K. N., Yukl, G. A., Kovacs, S. Z., and Sanders, R. E. Importance of contrast effects in employment interviews. *Journal of Applied Psychology,* 1972, 56, 45–48.

Wright, O. R., Jr. Summary of research on the selection interviews since 1964. *Personnel Psychology,* 1969, 22, 341–413.

D.

SIMULATIONS AND ASSESSMENT CENTERS

Going for Broker: Our Man Takes Part in Stock-Selling Test
Lawrence Rout

CHICAGO — My "in" basket is brimming with memos and unanswered letters. My desk calendar shows that conflicting appointments haven't been taken care of, and a client may pop in at any moment. Ignoring it all, I call a local industrialist who, I have been told, may be willing to buy some stock.

"You've got to be kidding," he screams when I make my pitch. "Based on your recommendation, my brother lost $97,000 on a $100,000 investment, and now he is going to sue you."

Who me?

Well, sort of. Welcome to the Merrill Lynch account-executive simulation exercise, or, as dubbed by some, the Merrill Lynch stress test. It's a nail-biting three hours filled with alternating despair and satisfaction that leaves many longing for the good old days of calculus finals. Still, whether you leave in frustration or imbued with self-confidence, the exercise can't help but get you keyed up.

"I just can't calm down," says 25-year-old Michael Schrimmer about an hour after the exercise has ended. "It was a real high."

STAKES ALSO HIGH

The stakes are high, too. Those taking part in the simulation, except me, are applicants for the job of account executive, or stockbroker, at Merrill Lynch, Pierce, Fenner & Smith Inc., the nation's largest securities firm. The simulation exercise is designed to gauge how they will perform under conditions similar to those that a real stockbroker faces.

It's a method that is becoming increasingly popular in hiring and promoting. Three years ago, only about 1,000 companies of any sort used simulations; that figure has doubled to about 2,000 today, according to William C. Byham, president of Development Dimensions International Inc., a Pittsburgh-based consulting firm.

Mr. Byham stresses that simulation is only part of a more extensive hiring process. At Merrill Lynch, for instance, the applicants taking the simulation have already undergone a written test and a personal interview.

Neither of those, however, prepares you for the simulation, which works like this:

You have taken over for Frank Jones, a stockbroker who has been transferred to another office. Frank has left you his client book, with individual descriptions of each client's portfolio and investment objectives, a hot-prospect book, and various unanswered letters and memos. There is a constantly changing stock market, news releases every five minutes, research reports and a book describing the stocks and defining the terms used in the game.

THE FIRST HALF-HOUR

Sound complicated? It is, especially when it's all thrown at you at once. "The first half-hour was the part that really unnerved me," says Meg Roggensack of Lancaster, Wis., who took the test here on another occasion. "I felt totally out of it."

This time, nine people take the test at a Merrill Lynch office here one night. A tape recording is played throughout the test, giving forth the sounds of a bustling daytime brokerage office. The ticker-tape clicks, salesmen shout.

After a while, the phones start ringing, as three trained Merrill Lynch stockbrokers, holed up in a back room except when they keep appointments with us, play the roles of Frank Jones's clients. Applicants are told to field their requests after explaining that Frank has been transferred.

Even that can confuse the harried stockbroker candidates who are trying to decipher the reams of material on their desks. Just ask Sylvia DeWitt, a 28-year-old job-seeker from Ames, Iowa. When she took the test and her first caller asked for Frank Jones, Mrs. DeWitt put the receiver down, looked around the room and asked: "Anybody here named Frank Jones?"

Few of her colleagues noticed. They were all absorbed in their own efforts to sell stock to Mr. Jones's former clients.

Approaches differ widely. One applicant was asked by a client whether a particular stock was too risky. "No guts, no glory," he replied. To the same question another candidate said: "I don't really know if this is the stock for you. I would hate to recommend it."

Neither response is necessarily correct or incorrect. "There is no one answer," says Russell Scalpone, a manager in the Los Angeles office of A. T. Kearney Inc., management consultants. "A simulation exercise allows a person a number of different ways of dealing with a situation — he can put his best foot forward."

But it's pretty easy to stumble. One situation we are faced with is a rise in the market price of a stock before an order is completed. When I call the client back to explain, he is upset. "We made a deal," he says. "How come you're backing out?" Helped, no doubt, by the fact that I really don't want the job anyway, I manage to keep cool, mollifying the client with something like "these things happen."

Another candidate explodes under the same circumstances. "What the hell do you want me to do?" he tells the client. "I've only got two hands." That candidate ultimately received a poor rating, and he speculated that the blowup "may have sealed my fate."

The test is designed so that someone without prior knowledge of the stock market isn't operating at a disadvantage. Still, for applicants who actually have no prior knowledge, the test can be unnerving. When the candidate behind me tells someone on the phone that a particular stock is a good buy if the investor wants to "preserve capital; it's got a real good yield," some of the applicants are awed by such professional language. "What's the matter with this guy?" the candidate next to me asks. "He got tired of working for Paine Webber?"

TAPPING THE FUNDAMENTAL

Our clients avoid technical jargon. Lowell Hellervik, president of Personnel Decisions, a Minneapolis-based psychological-consulting firm that helped develop the test, says: "There are relatively simple concepts involved. We did that on purpose so that we would be tapping something very fundamental in the individual."

This idea of looking for something fundamental is instilled in the "evaluators," the three stockbrokers who will eventually rate our performance — the same three people who play the role of our contacts.

The evaluators play three different characters each, and most of them find that the roles hit close to home. "I deal with guys like this all the time," says Anthony Faath, talking about his role as the irate local industrialist. "It's fun to be on the other side for a change."

It's hard work too. The evaluators take detailed notes on each conversation, and since they each play three parts and there are usually nine candidates, they can end up as frazzled as their prospective colleagues.

After the simulation has ended, the evaluators discuss each individual separately, spending as much as a half-hour on each candidate. Their final decisions are based on everything from successful sales to letter writing. Nervous laughter, overblown promises — everything is considered. And since all evaluations are clocked, the assessors are able to determine if a candidate improves as the exercise proceeds.

60% RECOMMENDED

In the end, about 60% of the applicants taking part in the simulations are recommended for hiring. That is 60% of a group already considered the best of account-executive applicants; after the written test and the interview, only about 10% of the 30,000 applicants who will come to Merrill Lynch this year will make it to the simulation.

The evidence is that the test works. In 1977, Merrill Lynch gave it to a group of new account executives who already had been hired but hadn't yet started working. Sixteen months later, the personnel department compared the production of the stockbrokers who did well in the simulation to those who didn't. The result: The former group's production was 25% to 30% greater than the latter's.

The test has been just as valuable in helping candidates decide whether they really like the job. "It never really occurred to me," one candidate said, "that I would be personally responsible for making recommendations about other people's money." Another candidate, in Dallas, got up after an hour and said, "I don't know whether I'm coming or going, so I'm leaving."

As for me, I did well. (The evaluators didn't know my identity, but Merrill Lynch did.) My overall rating was the highest possible — "outstanding potential, definitely recommended for hire." But then, I had to do well. After all, the other applicants' scores would never go beyond the evaluators and the Merrill Lynch files. I was going to have to tell you.

A Critical Look at Some Common Beliefs about Assessment Centers

Paul R. Sackett

The assessment center has become a commonly used, well regarded approach to managerial selection. Numerous descriptive and laudatory articles have appeared throughout the management literature; a much smaller number of data-based articles have been presented. The purpose of this paper is to sound a cautionary note by attempting to differentiate what is commonly accepted as true regarding assessment centers from what has been empirically demonstrated regarding assessment centers.

The paper is structured around what I will call six "tenets of conventional wisdom." These will be listed here and each will then be discussed in some detail:

1. The validity evidence for assessment centers is strong.
2. Assessment centers are more valid than conventional selection devices.
3. As job samples, assessment centers can be justified on content validity grounds.
4. Assessment centers don't illegally discriminate.
5. Research findings regarding assessment centers can be generalized from one organization to another.
6. Rating and reaching consensus regarding candidates is a straightforward, well understood process.

THE VALIDITY EVIDENCE

The cornerstone of the validity evidence for assessment centers remains the AT&T Management Progress Study (Bray and Grant, 1966). In this study, 422 candidates were assessed; the assessment results were then set aside to be used for research purposes only. Five to seven years after assessment, the assessment center predictions of which candidates would reach middle management were compared with the management level actually achieved by the candidates. Dividing the sample into college and non-college subsamples, the correlations between the assessment center prediction and level attained were .44 and .71 respectively.

A number of other validity studies have been reported. Cohen, Moses, and Byham (1974) summarize 18 validity studies and report an average correlation of .40 between assessment ratings and number of promotions received, and an average correlation of .63 with manager's ratings of a candidate's promotion potential. Byham (1970) reviewed 23 studies and reports that only one produced a negative validity coefficient.

It is important to realize that the Management Progress Study is one of only two instances in which complete secrecy as to assessment results was maintained. [An AT&T center for selecting salesmen (Bray and Campbell, 1968) is the other.] Making the results available to the candidate's manager in an operational center makes the interpretation of validity results problematic due to the possibility of criterion contamination. Criterion contamination refers to the lack of independence between the assessment rating and the criterion: promotions received. For example: a candidate returns from assessment with a favorable evaluation; as a result the candidate's manager forms a more favorable impression of the candidate; this impression becomes the basis for a

Sackett, P. R., "A Critical Look at Some Common Beliefs about Assessment Centers." *Public Personnel Management*, Summer 1982, 140–147.

recommendation that the candidate be promoted. In this case, an apparent relationship between assessment center performance and progress in the company would in fact be artifactual. A more subtle example: as a result of favorable assessment ratings, a candidate receives more challenging job assignments; due to these assignments, the candidate's skills develop and the candidate becomes promotable. Again we face the possibility that the promotions received are at least in part a result of being evaluated favorably in the assessment center. The result of such criterion contamination is an overestimate, of undeterminable magnitude, of what the actual validity would be if the assessment results were not used operationally.

Klimoski and Strickland (1977) point out another potential problem in interpreting validity results. They note that most studies have used advancement measures — salary change or promotions — as criteria. They suggest the possibility that assessment centers do not result in better selection decisions, but rather simply identify those individuals who are likely to be promoted using the organization's current standards. A correlation between assessment center evaluations and advancement may simply indicate that the assessment center can tell us what the organization would eventually do anyway. This is not necessarily bad: there may be value in the early identification of candidates with high promotion potential. But it is not evidence that assessment centers are valid predictors of performance. In addition, consider the possibility that an organization is adopting an assessment center due to dissatisfaction with existing promotion procedures. If this is the case, what interpretation should be placed on a positive correlation between assessment ratings and advancement? This could be interpreted as evidence that the assessment center is not useful. On the other hand, if one has enough confidence in the assessment center, one can view promotions as a predictor and assessment ratings as a criterion and view this correlation as a reaffirmation of the firm's promotion procedures.

In summary, only two validity studies are free from the criterion contamination problem, and the use of advancement measures rather than performance measures as criteria makes the results of validity studies difficult to interpret. The above discussion is not intended to suggest that assessment centers are not valid, but rather to point out that the evidence is not so overwhelming as to justify closing the door on the issue of assessment center validity.

MORE VALID THAN OTHER PREDICTORS?

"Perhaps the most dramatic and impressive feature of assessment centers is the greatly increased validity when compared to traditional selection and promotion techniques" (McNutt, 1979, p. 1). This statement represents the conventional wisdom with regard to assessment centers. Often cited as a basis for this conclusion is Byham's (1970) report of 22 studies in which assessment was found to be more effective than other approaches. Details of the studies, e.g. what the other approaches were, were not provided.

Hinrichs (1978) reports an interesting study in which assessment center participants were independently evaluated by management representatives based on information in the participant's personnel files. Eight years later both the assessment center ratings and the evaluations based on personnel files were correlated with a measure of the managerial level attained. The evaluations based on personnel files correlated more highly with the criterion than did the assessment center evaluation.

Other studies also provide reason to question the superiority of assessment over other methods. Campbell, Dunnette, Lawler, and Weick (1970) review a number of studies examining the validity of different approaches to managerial selection. For example, in a large scale validation study done by the Standard Oil Company of New

Jersey, ability test, personality test, and biographical data blank information were used to develop and cross-validate a predictor of managerial effectiveness. The correlation between a prediction of success based on these various sources and managerial effectiveness, measured by a combination of advancement and performance appraisal data, was .70. Several other studies produce comparable findings. One important factor contributing to the success of these studies is that organization specific keys were developed for the various tests. The rigor of this research is in sharp contrast to the "off the shelf" approach to the selection and use of tests.

These results compare favorably with the assessment center validities reported earlier and provide a basis for challenging assertions that assessment centers are more valid than other predictors. Several observations are in order at this point. First, the validity evidence for assessment centers is more consistent than the evidence for other predictors: while virtually all assessment center validity studies have produced positive results, there are numerous instances of testing programs failing to produce positive results. Second, it is recognized that validity is not the sole reason for choosing assessment over other approaches to managerial selection. Developmental value and user acceptability are among the other factors entering into such a decision. It does appear that claims for "greatly increased validity" may be overstated: other carefully developed predictors may be as or more effective at a substantially lower cost per candidate.

USE OF A CONTENT VALIDITY STRATEGY

It is a common belief that, because assessment centers are job samples, they can be justified on content validity grounds rather than requiring complex empirical validation. According to Jaffee and Sefcik (1980), content validity "is inherent in the assessment center process when the situational exercises are developed based on a thorough job analysis" (p. 42). We commonly consider a measure as having content validity when the measure represents a sample of the skills or knowledge needed for the job, e.g. can a typist type, can a lifeguard swim.

A key element of the content validity idea is that the applicant is already expected to possess the skill or knowledge; content validity makes no sense if it is expected that the skill or knowledge will be acquired on the job or in training after hire. As Dreher and Sackett (1981) point out, this requirement that job candidates possess the requisite knowledge and skill may not be met in many applications of the assessment center method. The most common use of assessment is the selection of first level supervisors who commonly go through supervisory training programs after being selected. In this setting, reliance on content validity is clearly inappropriate. While the assessment center may be a very useful selection device, it is being used as an aptitude test rather than as a sample of necessary job skills. In a study by Moses and Ritchie (1976), one group of supervisors received interpersonal skills training, another did not. Both groups then went through a specially designed assessment center; the trained group performed significantly better. Thus, assessment center performance was higher after training. This study illustrates the problem in using a content validity strategy: is it reasonable to assess whether or not a candidate has the level of interpersonal skills needed for a job, if the skills will be acquired or substantially improved in subsequent training?

Even if content validity is conceptually appropriate, the fact that the assessment center is a job simulation doesn't necessarily indicate that the center is content valid. The 1978 Uniform Guidelines on Employee Selection Procedures present rigorous standards for the use of a content validity strategy, including requirements for a thorough job analysis and requirements for a high degree of congruence between the selection procedure and the work situation. For example, a fire department, as part of the selection procedures for the position of fire captain, devised a fire scene simulation in which candidates viewed slides of a fire and made written responses as to the appropriate course of action. The 8th Circuit Court of Appeals, in *Firefighters' Institute for Racial Equality v. City of St. Louis,* found that this part of the selection procedure lacked content validity. The paper and pencil aspect of the simulation was not a close enough approximation of actual work behaviors to show content validity. Thus, extreme care is called for in the design of simulation exercises.

It should be noted that the above observations are currently under dispute. For instance, the court in *Guardians Association of New York City Police Dept. v. Civil Service Commission of the City of New York* concluded that the Guidelines were too rigid. The court objected both to the conclusion that content validity is inappropriate when training follows selection and to the requirement that a high level of congruence exist between the selection device and job behavior, stating that elaborate efforts to simulate actual work settings would be beyond the resources of most employers. Thus, judicial debate regarding content validity continues. The most appropriate conclusion at this time is to simply recognize that a belief that content validity is inherent in assessment centers is an over-simplification of a complex issue.

DISCRIMINATION AND ASSESSMENT CENTERS

One commonly hears statements such as "assessment centers don't discriminate," "assessment centers are court endorsed," or "assessment centers have EEOC approval." The legal status of assessment centers will be reviewed briefly to determine if such statements are warranted.

Considerable interest in assessment centers was generated by the 1973 consent decree between AT&T, the EEOC, and the Department of Labor. As part of the agreement, AT&T agreed to use an assessment center to evaluate college graduate female employees as one mechanism for identifying promotable females. Over a 15-month period, 1634 women were assessed, and 42 percent were evaluated as having management potential. Note that this center was part of an organization specific program to increase minority representation and does not imply any sort of blanket endorsement of assessment centers.

Byham (1979) has reviewed a number of court cases involving assessment centers. *Berry v. City of Omaha* is the only case to date directly challenging the fairness and validity of an assessment center. The major issue raised dealt with the subjectivity of assessor judgments; the court ruled that the center was fair, since adequate assessor training produced reliable judgments. In a variety of other cases, assessment centers were suggested or ordered by the court as an alternative to or supplement to paper and pencil tests. The courts are recognizing the potential value of assessment centers; nowhere is there anything to indicate that assessment centers will not be evaluated with any less scrutiny than is given to other selection devices.

Studies have been published which directly address the issue of discrimination in assessment centers on the basis of race and sex. Huck and Bray (1976) found a high degree of predictive validity for both a group of black female and white female candidates, and Moses and Boehm (1975) found assessment center evaluations to be fair and valid for both men and women. Thus, no evidence of differential validity was found.

It is useful at this point to consider the "shifting burden of proof" model used in fair employment practice litigation: a selection device has adverse impact if it rejects significantly more members of a protected class than of a majority group; if adverse impact is found, the burden shifts to the employer to demonstrate the job relatedness (validity) of the selection device. If an assessment center was found to have adverse impact, the organization would have to demonstrate its validity for all groups. In a study by Huck (1974), 53 percent of white candidates and 29 percent of black candidates were evaluated as having high potential for advancement, indicating adverse impact against blacks. Moses and Boehm (1975) report no adverse impact on the basis of sex; however, the present author has examined data from one center in which 16 percent of males and 10 percent of females were evaluated as having high potential. Note that adverse impact alone is not evidence of discrimination: if race or sex differences in assessment center evaluations correspond to comparable differences in on-the-job performance, the center does not discriminate. In many cases, it is likely that adverse impact may be found due to differences in the applicant population by race or sex. Consider an organization concerned with identifying promotable females; assume that a high proportion of the organization's workforce is male. Assume all interested women are encouraged to go through assessment; at the same time only a small proportion of men are selected for assessment. Due to the differences in candidate identification procedures, it is quite likely that a higher proportion of men than women will be evaluated favorably in assessment, despite the fact that the center may be highly valid.

Thus, while the evidence suggests that a well-designed assessment center does not discriminate, e.g. is equally valid for all groups, it is not unlikely that adverse impact will result, thus forcing the organization to defend the procedure. Organizations are cautioned against a belief that one does not have to be concerned about discrimination if an assessment center is used.

GENERALIZABILITY OF RESEARCH FINDINGS

It is somewhat discomforting to note that, despite the large number of organizations using assessment centers, the bulk of the reported research on assessment centers comes from only a handful of organizations. The main cause of concern is the lack of standardization among centers. Assessment is a complex process and variations exist from organization to organization on countless factors, including the number of exercises, the number of dimensions, the extent of assessor training, and the method of reaching consensus among assessors, to name but a few. A few comparative studies have been done. For example, Thomson (1969) found no difference between ratings made by psychologists and managers; Cohen and Sands (1978) found that the order of assessment center exercises had no impact on performance. However, the impact of most of the above factors on outcomes such as validity or fairness is unknown.

Recent research has also identified some interesting aspects of the judgment process in which differences between centers can be seen. Sackett and Dreher[1] examined the correlations among the dimension ratings made at the conclusion of each exercise in three different organizations. In two of the organizations, the average correlation among ratings of different dimensions rated in different exercises (e.g. delegation in the in-basket compared with oral communication in a leaderless group discussion) was, as expected, near zero. In the third, however, the average of these correlations was .45. In essence, almost any rating, regardless of dimension or exercise, correlates relatively highly with almost any other rating. How these striking differences between organizations affect the validity of the process is an open question.

Whether some assessors have more influence than others in determining the final evaluation of a candidate is another issue of interest. Sackett and Wilson (in press) compared two centers and found negligible difference among assessors in the amount of influence exerted in one center, but fairly substantial differences in the second. Klimoski, Friedman, and Weldon (1980) noted that the role of the assessor team chairperson varies from center to center so they designed a laboratory study to examine the influences of the chairperson. They found that chairpersons with prior contact with the candidate and with formal voting rights exerted more influence on the group than chairpersons who had not observed the candidate's performance and who did not have a formal vote. The impact of differences in influence on the overall effectiveness of the assessment center is unknown.

In summary, it is not clear that research findings can be generalized from one center to another. Centers differ in a multitude of ways, some of which are obvious, e.g. the number of dimensions used. Others are not readily apparent, such as the findings discussed above regarding patterns of correlations among assessment center ratings and differences in influence. What is clear is that comparative research across organizations is needed to determine the impact of these differences from center to center.

THE RATING PROCESS

On paper, the rating process looks quite straightforward. Candidates are observed in a variety of exercises; they may or may not be evaluated at the end of each exercise. After all exercises have been concluded, the candidates are reviewed one at a time, with each assessor independently rating the candidate on each dimension. Differences are then reconciled by discussion; a similar process of independent judgment and reconciliation of differences is then followed for the overall rating.

An examination of ratings made by different assessors was made by Sackett and Hakel (1979). It was found that the overall rating in the center could be predicted with a very high degree of accuracy on the basis of only three dimensions — leadership, organizing and planning, and decision making. When asked to rate the importance of the dimensions, assessors consistently identified these three as the most important. Beyond these three dimensions, there was no agreement among assessors as to the importance of the remaining dimensions. These findings challenge the notion that the careful identification of multiple dimensions through job analysis makes a major contribution to the validity of assessment centers.

Moving from the individual ratings to the process of reaching consensus among assessors, Sackett and Wilson (in press) found that a simple mathematical rule could predict the outcome of the consensus discussion with 94.5 percent accuracy. It was observed that extreme ratings, e.g. 1s or 5s, had more impact on the group decision than mid-range ratings. These findings suggest that mid-range ratings may be used to indicate that an assessor has not had a chance to observe behavior relevant to the dimension or is not confident of his/her rating, rather than indicating that the assessor truly believes the candidate is average. Again, a departure from the intended process is indicated by this research.

Finally, Sackett and Dreher examined the dimensional ratings, ratings made upon the completion of each exercise. One disconcerting finding was that the average correlations among different ratings of the same dimension in different exercises (e.g. leadership rated in the in-basket, a role play, and a leaderless group discussion) were near zero in two different assessment centers. Central to the assessment center approach is the belief that stable behavior patterns exist, which can be categorized as representing the various dimensions. Multiple exercises are used in order to provide multiple opportunities for these behavior patterns to be manifested. These low correlations between exercises are a basis for concern as to what is actually being measured in an assessment center.

Thus, in looking at the rating process, one finds few dimensions contributing to the final evaluation, disagreement among assessors as to the importance of various dimensions, extreme ratings being given more weight in reaching consensus among assessors, and low agreement among the various post exercise ratings of the same dimension. An understanding of "what's going on" in the rating process is not complete;

the dynamics of the assessor group and the processes of individual impression formation and decision making are in need of additional research.

CONCLUSIONS

This paper has attempted to summarize empirical work and conceptual issues relevant to a select set of issues concerning the use of assessment centers. The predominant theme has been one of caution against overly rapid acceptance of some often heard statements about the validity, legal status, and research base underlying the assessment center method. The paper should in no way be interpreted as an attempt to discredit assessment centers; the author is a strong advocate of work sample/job simulation approaches to selection. The intent of the paper is to point out that far less is known about assessment than could or should be known, to encourage comparative research to determine the effects of various differences between centers, and to increase the knowledge base of individuals considering the use of assessment centers.

NOTES

1. Sackett, P. R., and Dreher, G. F. Constructs and assessment center dimensions: some troubling empirical findings for content oriented validation strategies. Manuscript under review, 1981.

REFERENCES

Bray, D. W., and Campbell, R. J. Selection of salesmen by means of an assessment center. *Journal of Applied Psychology,* 1968, *52,* 36–41.

Bray, D. W., and Grant, D. L. The assessment center in the measurement of potential for business management. *Psychological Monographs,* 1966, *80* (17, Whole No. 625).

Byham, W. C. Assessment centers for spotting future managers. *Harvard Business Review,* 1970, *48,* 150–167.

Byham, W. C. Review of legal cases and opinion dealing with assessment centers and content validity. Pittsburgh: Development Dimensions International, 1979.

Campbell, J. P., Dunnette, M. D., Lawler, E. E., and Weick, K. E. *Managerial behavior, performance, and effectiveness.* New York: McGraw-Hill, 1970.

Cohen, B. M., Moses, J. L., and Byham, W. C. *The validity of assessment centers: a literature review.* Monograph II. Pittsburgh: Development Dimension, Press, 1974.

Cohen, S. L., and Sands, L. The effects of order of exercise presentation on assessment center performance: on standardization concern. *Personnel Psychology,* 1978, *31,* 35–46.

Dreher, G. F., and Sackett, P. R. Some problems with the applicability of content validity to assessment centers. *Academy of Management Review,* 1981.

Firefighters' Institute for Racial Equality v. City of St. Lous, 22 EPD 30,570.

Guardians Association of the New York City Police Department, Inc. v. Civil Service Commission of the City of New York, 23 EPD 31,153.

Hinrichs, J. R. An eight-year follow-up of a management assessment center. *Journal of Applied Psychology,* 1978, *63,* 596–601.

Huck, J. R. Determinants of assessment center ratings for white and black females and the relationship of these dimensions to subsequent performance effectiveness. Unpublished doctoral dissertation, Wayne State University, 1974.

Huck, J. R., and Bray, D. W. Management assessment center evaluations and subsequent job performance of white and black females. *Personnel Psychology*, 1976, 2, 13–30.

Jaffee, C. L., and Sefcik, J. T. What is an assessment center? *Personnel Administrator*, February, 1980, 40–43.

Klimoski, R., Friedman, B., and Weldon, E. Leader influence in the assessment of performance. *Personnel Psychology*, 1980, 33, 389–401.

Klimoski, R. J., and Strickland, W. J. Assessment centers — valid or merely prescient. *Personnel Psychology*, 1977, 30, 353–361.

McNutt, K. Behavioral consistency and assessment centers: a reconciliation of the literature. *Journal of Assessment Center Technology*, 1979, 2, 1–6.

Moses, J. L., and Boehm, V. R. Relationship of assessment center performance to management progress of women. *Journal of Applied Psychology*, 1975, 60, 527–529.

Moses, J. L., and Ritchie, R. J. Supervisory relationships training: a behavioral evaluation of a behavior modeling program. *Personnel Psychology*, 1976, 29, 337–344.

Sackett, P. R., and Hakel, M. D. Temporal stability and individual differences in using assessment information to form overall ratings. *Organizational Behavior and Human Performance*, 1979, 23, 120–137.

Sackett, P. R., and Wilson, M. A. Factors affecting the consensus judgment process in managerial assessment centers. *Journal of Applied Psychology*, in press.

Thomson, H. A. Internal and external validation of an industrial assessment program. Unpublished doctoral dissertation, Case Western Reserve University, 1969.

Uniform guidelines on employee selection procedures. *Federal Register*, 1978, 43, 38290–38309.

E.

TESTING

Employment Testing: Old Theories and New Research Findings

Frank L. Schmidt and John E. Hunter

This article contains two messages: a substantive message and a methodological message. The substantive message is this: (a) Professionally developed cognitive ability tests are valid predictors of performance on the job and in training for all jobs (Hunter, 1980; Schmidt, Hunter, & Pearlman, 1981) in all settings (Lilienthal & Pearlman, in press; Pearlman, Schmidt, & Hunter, 1980; Schmidt, Gast-Rosenberg, & Hunter, 1980; Schmidt, Hunter, & Caplan, 1981; Schmidt, Hunter, Pearlman, & Shane, 1979; Sharf, Note 1; Timmreck, Note 2; Schmidt, Hunter, Pearlman, & Caplan, Note 3); (b) cognitive ability tests are equally valid for minority and majority applicants and are fair to minority applicants in that they do not underestimate the expected job performance of minority groups; and (c) the use of cognitive ability tests for selection in hiring can produce large labor cost savings, ranging from $18 million per year for small employers such as the Philadelphia police department (5,000 employees; Hunter, Note 4) to $16 billion per year for large employers such as the federal government (4,000,000 employees; Hunter, Note 5).

The methodological message is this: In the last 10 years the field of personnel selection has undergone a transformation in viewpoint resulting from the introduction of improved methods of cumulating findings across studies. Use of these methods has shown that most of the "conflicting results" across studies were the result of sampling error that was not perceived by reviewers relying on statistical significance tests to evaluate single studies. Reviews in our field were also subject to systematic distortion because reviewers failed to take into account the systematic effects of error of measurement and restriction in range in the samples studied. The real meaning of 70 years of cumulative research on employment testing was not apparent until state-of-the-art meta-analytic procedures were applied. These methods not only cumulate results across studies but correct variance across studies for the effect of sampling error and correct both mean and variance for the distorting effects of systematic artifacts such as unreliability and restriction of range.

Tests have been used in making employment decisions in the United States for over 50 years. Although occasional use has been made of personality tests, and content-validated job knowledge and job sample tests have been used with some frequency, the most commonly used employment tests have been measures of cognitive skills — that is, aptitude or ability tests. Examples include tests of verbal and quantitative ability, perceptual speed, inductive and deductive reasoning, and spatial and mechanical ability. A great deal of new knowledge has accumulated over the last 10 years on the role of cognitive abilities in job performance and in the employment-selection process. In the middle and late 1960s certain theories about aptitude and ability tests formed the basis for most discussion of employee selection issues and, in part, the basis for practice in personnel psychology. At that time, none of these theories had been tested against empirical data. However, they were plausible at face value, and some were accepted by personnel psychologists as true or probably true. Two important events occurred during the 1970s: (a) new methods were developed for quantitatively integrating research findings across studies to provide strong tests of theories, and (b) these methods were used to cumulate the empirical research evidence needed to determine whether these theories were true or false. We now have this evidence, and it shows that the earlier theories were false.

THE THEORIES AND THE RESEARCH EVIDENCE

The Theory of Low Utility

The first theory holds that employee selection methods have little impact on the performance and productivity of the resultant workforce. From this theory, it follows that selection procedures can safely be manipulated to achieve other objectives, such as a racially representative workforce. The basic equation for determining the impact of selection on workforce productivity had been available for years (Brogden, 1949; Cronbach & Gleser, 1957), but it had not been employed because there were no feasible methods for estimating one critical equation parameter: the standard deviation of employee job performance in dollars (SDy). SDy indexes the magnitude of individual differences in employee yearly output of goods and services. The greater SDy is, the greater is the payoff in improved productivity from selecting high-performing employees.

During the 1970s, a method was devised for estimating SDy based on careful estimates by supervisors of employee output (Hunter & Schmidt, in press; Schmidt, Hunter, McKenzie, & Muldrow, 1979). Applications of this method showed that SDy was larger than expected. For example, for entry-level budget analysts and computer programmers, SDy was $11,327 and $10,413, respectively. This means that a computer programmer at the 85th percentile in performance is worth $20,800 more per year to the employing organization than a computer programmer at the 15th percentile. Use of valid selection tests substantially increases the average performance level of the resultant workforce and therefore substantially improves productivity. For example, use of the Programmer Aptitude Test in place of an invalid selection method to hire 618 entry-level computer programmers leads to an estimated productivity improvement of $54.7 million ($68 million in 1981 dollars) over a 10-year period if the top 30% of applicants are hired (Schmidt, Hunter, McKenzie, & Muldrow, 1979). Estimates have also been made of the impact of selection on national productivity. Based on extremely conservative assumptions, Hunter and Schmidt (in press) calculate that the gross national product would be increased by $80 to $100 billion per year if improved selection procedures were introduced throughout the economy.

These findings mean that selecting high performers is more important for organizational productivity than had been previously thought. Research has established that mental skills and abilities are important determinants of performance on the job. If tests measuring these abilities are dropped and replaced by the interview and other less valid procedures, the proportion of low-performing people hired increases, and the result is a serious decline in productivity in the individual firm and in the economy as a whole. The rate of growth in productivity in the United States has slowed markedly in recent years — from about 3.5% to zero or even negative rates. One possible reason for this decline is the decline in the accuracy with which employers sort people into jobs. In response to pressures from the federal government, American employers have substantially reduced the use of valid tests of job aptitudes in making hiring and placement decisions. Many companies have abandoned the use of such tests entirely. Over a period of 8–10 years, this change would manifest itself in lower productivity gains. Consider two examples. Seven or eight years ago, the General Electric Company (GE) responded to government pressure by dropping all tests of job aptitude and "getting their numbers right" in the hiring process. Like many firms, GE has a policy of promoting from within. About two years ago, several plants realized that a large percentage of the people hired under the new selection standards were not promotable. GE had merely transferred the adverse impact from the hiring stage to the promotion stage. These plants have now resumed testing (Hawk, Note 6). Some years ago, U.S. Steel selected applicants into their skilled trades apprentice programs *from the top down* based on total score on a valid battery of cognitive aptitude tests. They then lowered their testing standards dramatically, requiring only minimum scores on the tests equal to about the seventh-grade level and relying heavily on seniority. Because their apprentice training center kept excellent records, they were able to show that (a) scores on mastery tests given during training declined markedly, (b) the flunk-out and drop-out rates increased dramatically, (c) average training time and training cost for those who *did* make it through the program increased substantially, and (d) average ratings of later performance on the job declined (Braithwaite, Note 7).

The theory that selection procedures are not important is sometimes presented in a more subtle form. In this form, the theory holds that all that is important is that the people hired be "qualified." This theory results in pressure on employers to set low minimum qualification levels and then to hire on the basis of other factors from among those who meet these minimum levels. This is the system U.S. Steel adopted. In our experience, minimum levels on cognitive ability tests are typically set near the 15th percentile for applicants. Such "minimum competency" selection systems result in productivity losses 80% to 90% as great as complete abandonment of valid selection procedures (Mack, Schmidt, & Hunter, in press). For example, if an organization the size of the federal government (4,000,000 employees) were to move from ranking on valid tests to such a minimum competency selection system with the cutoff at the 20th percentile, yearly productivity gains from selection would be reduced from $15.6 billion to $2.5 billion (Hunter, Note 5), an increase in labor costs of $13.1 billion per year required to maintain the same level of output. In a smaller organization such as the Philadelphia police department, the loss would be $12 million per year, a drop from $18 million to $6 million (Hunter, Note 4).

The problem is that there is no real dividing line between the qualified and the unqualified. Employee productivity is on a *continuum* from very high to very low, and the relation between ability test scores and employee job performance and output is almost invariably linear (APA, 1980; Hunter & Schmidt, in press; Schmidt, Hunter,

McKenzie, & Muldrow, 1979). Thus a reduction in minimum acceptable test scores at any point in the test-score range results in a reduction in the productivity of employees selected. A decline from superior to average performance may not be as visible as a decline from average to poor performance, but it can be just as costly in terms of lost productivity. The finding that test-score/job-performance relationships are linear means that ranking applicants on test scores and selecting from the top down maximizes the productivity of employees selected. This finding also means that any minimum test score requirement (test cutoff score) is arbitrary: No matter where it is set, a higher cutoff score will yield more productive employees, and a lower score will yield less productive employees. On the other hand, it means that if the test is valid, all cutoff scores are "valid" by definition. The concept of "validating" a cutoff score on a valid test is therefore not meaningful.

Most of the productivity loss in minimum competency selection systems comes from majority, not minority, group members. Minimum competency systems usually reduce standards for all applicants. Since most people hired are majority group members, the cumulative productivity loss from hiring less productive members of the majority group is much greater than the loss due to less productive minority workers.

The usual purpose of minimum competency systems is to eliminate discrepancies in minority and majority employment rates. However, despite the productivity losses, such systems typically merely reduce this discrepancy; they do not eliminate it. On the other hand, selection systems based on top-down hiring within each group completely eliminate "adverse impact" at a much smaller price in lowered productivity. Such systems typically yield 85% to 95% of the productivity gains attainable with optimal nonpreferential use of selection tests (Cronbach, Yalow, & Shaeffer, 1980; Hunter, Schmidt, & Rauschenberger, 1977; Mack et al., in press). However, such selection systems raise a host of legal, social, and moral questions (Lerner, 1977, 1979).

The Theory of Subgroup Validity Differences

This theory holds that because of cultural differences, cognitive tests have lower validity (test-criterion correlations) for minority than for majority groups. This theory takes two forms. The theory of single-group validity holds that tests may be valid for the majority but "invalid" (that is, have zero validity) for minorities. Although it was erroneous (Humphreys, 1973), the procedure adopted by psychologists to test for single-group validity involved testing black and white validity coefficients for significance separately by race. Since minority sample sizes were usually smaller than those for the majority, small-sample single-group validity studies produced a high frequency of white–significant, black–nonsignificant outcomes. Four different cumulative studies have now demonstrated that evidence for single-group validity by race does not occur any more frequently in samples than would be expected solely on the basis of chance (Boehm, 1977; Katzell & Dyer, 1977; O'Connor, Wexley, & Alexander, 1975; Schmidt, Berner, & Hunter, 1973).

The theory of differential validity holds that population validities are different for different groups, but are not necessarily zero for any group. This theory was tested by applying a statistical test of the difference between observed sample validities. Individual studies obtained varying results. Most recent studies have cumulated findings across studies. The first such review was done by Ruch (Note 8), who found that differential validity occurred in samples at only chance levels of frequency. Two more recent reviews claim to have found somewhat higher frequencies: Boehm (1977) found a frequency of 8%, and Katzell and Dyer (1977) reported frequencies in the 20%–30% range. But it has been shown (Hunter & Schmidt, 1978) that the data preselection technique used in these studies results in a Type I bias — rejecting the hypothesis of no difference when it is true — which creates the false appearance of a higher incidence of differential validity. Two more recent studies that avoid this Type I bias have found differential validity to be at chance levels (Bartlett, Bobko, Mosier, & Hannan, 1978; Hunter, Schmidt, & Hunter, 1979). Bartlett et al. (1978) analyzed 1,190 pairs of validity coefficients for blacks and whites and found significant black–white differences in 6.8% of the pairs, using an alpha level of .05. Hunter et al. (1979) found the frequency of differential validity among the 712 pairs with a positive average validity to be 6%. Similar results have been obtained for Hispanic Americans (Schmidt, Pearlman, & Hunter, 1980). Thus the evidence taken as a whole indicates that employment tests are equally valid for all groups (Linn, 1978). The earlier belief in differential validity apparently resulted from excessive faith in the individual small-sample studies in which significant difference occurred by chance.

The Theory of Test Unfairness

This theory holds that even if validity coefficients are equal for minority and majority groups, a test is likely to be unfair if the average test score is lower for minorities. There are numerous statistical models of test fairness, and these differ significantly in their properties (Cole, 1981; Jensen, 1980, chap. 10; Hunter & Schmidt, 1976; Hunter et al., 1977). However, the most commonly accepted model of test fairness is the regression model (Clearly & Hilton, 1968). This model defines a test as unfair to a minority group if it predicts lower levels of job performance than the group in fact achieves. This is the concept of test fairness embedded in the Uniform Guidelines on Employee Selection Procedures (Equal Employment Opportunity Commission, Civil Service Commission, Department of Labor, & Department of Justice, 1978; Ledvinka, 1979). The theory of test unfairness is based on the assumption that the factors causing lower test scores do not also cause lower job performance. The accumulated evidence on this theory is clear: Lower test scores among minorities are accompanied by lower job performance, exactly as in the case of the majority (Bartlett et al., 1978; Campbell, Crooks, Mahoney, & Rock, 1973; Gael & Grant, 1972; Gael, Grant, & Ritchie, 1975a, 1975b; Grant & Bray, 1970; Jensen, 1980, chap. 10; Schmidt, Pearlman, & Hunter, 1980; Ruch, Note 8; Tenopyr, Note 9). This finding holds true whether ratings of job performance or objective job sample measures of performance are used. Tests predict job performance of a minority and the majority in the same way. The small departures from perfect fairness that exist actually favor minority groups.

These findings show that employment tests do not cause "adverse impact" against minorities. The cumulative research on test fairness shows that the average ability and cognitive skill differences between groups are directly reflected in job performance and thus are *real*. They are *not* created by the tests. We do not know what all the causes of these differences are, how long they will persist, or how best to eliminate them. For many other groups in the past, such differences have declined or disappeared over time. But at the present time, the differences exist and are reflected in job performance.

The Theory of Test Invalidity

This theory holds that cognitive employment tests are frequently invalid for all (majority and minority alike). This theory takes two forms. The first subtheory holds that test validity is situationally specific — a test valid for a job in one organization or setting may be invalid *for the same job* in another organization or setting. The conclusion is that a separate validity study is necessary in each setting. The second form of this theory holds that test validity is job specific — a cognitive test valid for one job may be invalid for another job. The conclusion is that a separate validity study is necessary for every job.

Subtheory I: Is validity situationally specific? The empirical basis for the subtheory of situational specificity was the considerable variability in observed validity coefficients from study to study even when jobs and tests appeared to be similar or identical (Ghiselli, 1966). The older explanation for this variation was that the factor structure of job performance is different from job to job and that the human observer or job analyst is too poor an information receiver and processor to detect these subtle but important differences. If so, empirical validation would be required in each situation, and validity generalization would be impossible (Albright, Glennon, & Smith, 1963; Ghiselli, 1966; Guion, 1965).

A new hypothesis was investigated during the 1970s. This hypothesis is that the variance in the outcomes of validity studies within job–test combinations is due to statistical artifacts. Schmidt, Hunter, and Urry (1976) showed that under typical and realistic validation conditions, a valid test will show a statistically significant validity in only about 50% of studies. As an example, they showed that if true validity for a given test is constant at .45 in a series of jobs, if criterion reliability is .70, if the prior selection ratio on the test is .60, and if sample size is 68 (the median over 406 published validity studies — Lent, Aurbach, & Levin, 1971b), then the test will be reported to be valid 54% of the time and invalid 46% of the time (two-tailed test, $p = .05$). This is the kind of variability that was the basis for the theory of situation-specific validity (Ghiselli, 1966; Lent, Aurbach, & Levin, 1971a).

If the variance in validity coefficients across situations for job–test combinations is due to statistical artifacts, then the theory of situational specificity is false, and validities are generalizable. We have developed a method for testing this hypothesis (Pearlman et al., 1980; Schmidt, Gast-Rosenberg, & Hunter, 1980; Schmidt & Hunter, 1977; Schmidt, Hunter, Pearlman, & Shane, 1979). One starts with a fairly large number of validity coefficients for a given test–job combination and computes the variance of this distribution. From this variance, one then subtracts variance due to various sources of error. There are at least seven sources of error variance: (a) sampling error (i.e., variance due to $N < \infty$); (b) differences between studies in criterion reliability; (c) differences between studies in test reliability; (d) differences between studies in range restriction; (e) differences between studies in amount and kind of criterion contamination and deficiency (Brogden & Taylor, 1950); (f) computational and typographical errors (Wolins, 1962); and (g) slight differences in factor structure between tests of a given type (e.g., arithmetic reasoning tests).

Using conventional statistical and measurement principles, Schmidt, Hunter, Pearlman, and Shane (1979) showed that the first four sources alone are capable of producing as much variation in validities as is typically observed from study to study. Results from application of the method to empirical data bear out this prediction. To date, distributions of validity coefficients have been examined for 152 test–job combinations (Lilienthal & Pearlman, in press; Pearlman et al., 1980; Schmidt, Gast-Rosenberg, & Hunter, 1980; Schmidt & Hunter, 1977; Schmidt, Hunter, & Caplan, 1981; Schmidt, Hunter, Pearlman, & Shane, 1979; Schmidt, Hunter, Pearlman, & Caplan, Note 3; Linn, Harnisch, & Dunbar, Note 10). The first four artifacts listed above accounted for an average of 72% of the observed variance of validity coefficients. About 85% of the variance in validities accounted for by artifacts is accounted for by simple sampling error. Corrections for sampling error alone lead to the same conclusions about validity generalizability as corrections for the first four artifacts (Pearlman et al., 1980; Schmidt, Gast-Rosenberg, & Hunter, 1980). Had it been possible to partial out variance due to all seven rather than to only four artifacts, all observed variance would probably have been accounted for.

These findings are quite robust. Callender and Osburn (1980) have derived alternative equations for testing validity generalizability and have shown that these produce identical conclusions and virtually identical numerical results. These findings effectively show the theory of situational specificity to be false. If one looks at the estimated distributions of operational (or true) validities (that is, validities corrected for the effects of criterion unreliability and range restriction; cf. Schmidt, Gast-Rosenberg, & Hunter, 1980), one finds that in 84% of 152 test–job combinations, even the validity value at the 10th percentile is positive and substantial enough in magnitude to have practical value in improving workforce productivity. These findings show that cognitive test validities can typically be generalized with confidence across settings and organizations, and there is no factual basis for requiring a validity study in each situation.

Subtheory 2: Is test validity job specific?   Job differences might moderate the validity of a given test in one of two ways. First, the test could be valid for all jobs but more valid for some jobs than for others. Second, the test could be valid for some jobs but invalid for others. The latter is the moderating effect postulated by the theory of job-specific validity. But sampling error and other artifacts can falsely cause a test to appear to be invalid. Just as sampling error can produce the appearance of inconsistency in the validity of a test for the same job in different settings, sampling error in validity coefficients can cause tests to appear to be valid for one job but invalid for another job.

The first large-sample tests of this hypothesis were recently completed. Based on an analysis of data from almost 370,000 clerical workers, Schmidt, Hunter, and Pearlman (1981) show that the validities of seven cognitive abilities were essentially constant across five different task-defined clerical job families. All seven abilities were highly valid in all five job families. They next examined the validity patterns of five cognitive tests determined on a sample of 23,000 people in 35 highly heterogeneous jobs (for example, welders, cooks, clerks, administrators). Validities for each test varied reliably from job to job. But the variation was small, and *all tests were valid at substantial levels for all jobs.*

This finding has now been replicated and extended to the least complex, lowest-skill jobs. The U.S. Employment Service has conducted over 500 criterion-related validity studies on jobs that constitute a representative sample of jobs in the *Dictionary of Occupational Titles* (U.S. Department of Labor, 1977). In a cumulative analysis of these studies, Hunter (1980) showed that cognitive abilities are valid for all jobs and job groupings studied. When jobs were grouped according to complexity of information-processing requirements, the validity of a composite of verbal and quantitative abilities for predicting on-the-job performance varied from .56 for the highest-level job grouping to .23 for the lowest. These values were larger for measures of success in job training. Thus, even for the lowest-skill jobs, validity is still substantial. These studies disconfirm the hypothesis of job-specific test validity. There is no empirical basis for requiring separate validity studies for each job; tests can be validated at the level of job families. These cumulative analyses of existing studies show that the most frequently used cognitive ability tests are valid for all jobs and job families.

In conclusion, our evidence shows that the validity of the cognitive tests studied is neither specific to situations nor specific to jobs.

The Theory That Criteria of Success in Training Are Insufficient

This theory holds that a test valid for predicting success in training programs may be invalid for predicting performance on the job because training success may or may not be related to job performance. This theory was only recently subjected to a strong test. Earlier tests of the theory compared individual validity coefficients computed on small sample sizes and were therefore methodologically unsound. As a result, the validity coefficients for different abilities for a given job were very unstable because of sampling error. For this reason, tests frequently appeared to be valid for training-success measures but not for job-performance measures, or vice versa. Further, validities for training-success measures showed only low correlations with validities for job-performance measures.

The problem of unstable validity estimates was overcome in a recent massive cumulative study based on a sample of almost 370,000. This study showed that all eight cognitive abilities examined were valid for both training and job-performance criteria. Further, even the relative degrees of validity were similar: The two sets of validities correlated .77 (Pearlman et al., 1980). These findings show that the cognitive tests valid for predicting performance in training programs are also valid for predicting later performance on the job. Further, the more valid the test is for predicting training success, the more valid it is apt to be as a predictor of later performance on the job. When employers select people who will do well in training programs, they are also selecting people who will do well later on the job (cf. Tenopyr, 1981).

CAN PAST MISTAKES BE CORRECTED?

All of the theories discussed above have been incorporated, implicitly or explicitly, in the federal Uniform Guidelines on Employee Selection Procedures (EEOC et al., 1978) and preceding guidelines. As a result, every one of these theories has been incorporated into EEO case law to one degree or another. Recent research findings show these theories to be false. Is it possible to eradicate these false theories from the field of EEO? We believe so, for two reasons. First, in court cases in which defendants have clearly presented and explained the empirical evidence showing that these theories are false, defendants have won. Judges can be educated to the facts. The *Pegues* case* is a good example. Second, the federal government is currently planning to revise and update the Guidelines to be consistent with current research knowledge and professional practice.

RELATION BETWEEN RESEARCH KNOWLEDGE AND SOCIAL POLICY CONSIDERATIONS

Not one of the advances in research knowledge summarized in this paper changes the fact of group differences in average levels of employment related abilities. The differences in ability test scores mean that there is still a serious social problem. The research findings of the 1970s show that we can no longer entertain the belief that the problem is in the tests and that it can be solved by modifying or eliminating the tests. Instead, we must face the problem, which is that some groups of individuals are not acquiring the cognitive skills needed in a modern society to the same degree as others, and we must focus on ways of improving acquisition of those skills. For example, research in educational psychology has shown (not surprisingly) that a major educational determinant of student learning is *time on task* — the amount of time the student actually spends attempting to learn the material (cf. Berliner, 1979). However, it has also been found that minority students report spending *less* time on homework, on the average, than majority students (Sewell, Hauser, & Featherman, 1976; Wiley, 1973). The implications are obvious.

---

*Pegues et al. v. Mississippi State Employment Service et al., 22 FEP 3929 (N.D. Miss., Mar. 7, 1980).

Social policy decisions about how best to attack this problem must be made. No options, including racial or ethnic quotas, need be ruled out in advance of open discussion. But the solution to the problem cannot begin until the problem is faced in an intellectually honest way. It is not intellectually honest, in the face of empirical evidence to the contrary, to postulate that the problem is biased and/or invalid employment tests. Empirical facts must be acknowledged. On the other hand, admitting that the problem is not in the tests does not mandate the conclusion that employment tests should be used in the manner that maximizes economic output. How (and whether) valid and fair tests should be used is a question of social policy (Haney, 1981; Novick, 1981; Tenopyr, 1981).

Even honestly faced, the problem is a complex one. Opposing goods must be carefully weighed; these include the trade-off between maximal economic productivity and living standards on one hand, and social goals such as proportional minority representation in the occupational structure on the other. Further, even after priorities are set, not all means are equally effective in attaining goals. For example, preferential selection systems, based on top-down hiring within each group and using valid tests, increase minority employment faster and at much less economic cost than random selection from among applicants who are above minimum qualifications levels.

STATE-OF-THE-ART META-ANALYSIS

In each empirical research area reviewed in this article, the same pattern of analysis of the literature prevailed across time. In the beginning, individual studies were interpreted as showing conflicting results. There were sporadic reports that tests valid for whites did not appear to be valid for blacks. There were sporadic reports that tests that had been shown earlier to be valid for a given job were found to be invalid for the same job in a new setting. Narrative reviews responded to this situation by arguing that there must be unknown variables causing the apparent situational specificity of findings (Schmidt & Hunter, 1978). However, use of correct methods of cumulating results across studies showed these conflicting findings to be the result of sampling error. That is, these sporadic findings were flukes resulting from the small samples forced on investigators by the limitations of field studies. The use of significance tests within individual studies only clouded discussion in the review studies because narrative reviewers falsely believed that significance tests could be relied on to give correct decisions about single studies. Sampling error can never be detected or corrected in single studies. The only answer to the detection of sampling error is a cumulative analysis of results across studies in which the variance of results across studies is corrected for sampling error (Hunter & Schmidt, Note 11).

In similar fashion, narrative reviews tended to make systematic errors in the interpretation of quantitative results because reviewers did not correct outcome measures for either error of measurement or restriction in range. The estimate of the validity coefficient in employment studies is erroneous if it is not corrected for error of measurement of job performance. (For theoretical purposes, correlations should be corrected for unreliability in the predictor variable [i.e., ability] as well.) Furthermore, there is typically considerable restriction in range resulting from the necessity of basing studies on incumbent populations instead of on applicant populations, and failure to correct for this artifact results in (often severe) underestimation of validities. Thus, state-of-the-art procedures of meta-analysis must correct for systematic distortions such as unreliability and restriction in range as well as the unsystematic effects of sampling error.

We share with Glass (1976) the belief that narrative reviews have been disastrous for the attainment of cumulative knowledge in all areas of psychology. We strongly urge the use of meta-analysis, the quantitative cumulation of results across studies. Glass has advanced one method of meta-analysis. Concurrent to Glass's work, we and our associates developed a related quantitative meta-analysis procedure. Our procedure can be regarded as an extension of Glass's method designed to deal with the distorting effects of artifacts such as sampling error, measurement unreliability, and range restriction while integrating findings across studies (Pearlman et al., 1980; Schmidt & Hunter, 1977; Schmidt, Hunter, Pearlman, & Shane, 1979). Originally developed to integrate employment test validities across studies, this procedure has since been generalized for application to other research areas (Hunter & Schmidt, Note 11; Hunter, Schmidt, & Jackson, Note 12).

At one time in the history of psychology and the social sciences, the pressing need was for more empirical studies to examine a problem. But now large numbers of research studies have been carried out on many research questions. The need today is increasingly becoming, not one for additional empirical data, but one for some means of making sense of the vast amounts of data that have accumulated. Unless we can do this, there is little hope of producing the cumulative, generalizable knowledge essential for theory development. Meta-analysis provides a solution to this problem. Furthermore, the need for meta-analysis goes beyond the theoretical aspirations of science: It is crucial to the solution of social problems as well. The continuing inability to produce cumulative knowledge and general principles may now be leading to widespread disillusionment with psychological research and consequent reductions in research funding by governmental and other bodies ("Cuts Raise New Social-Science Query," 1981).

How can a funding agency continue to support research in an area where researchers maintain that further studies are needed on an issue for which hundreds of studies already exist? Since most of the "conflicting results" are actually due to sampling error, it is incumbent on us to put our house in order.

REFERENCE NOTES

1. Sharf, J. C. Recent developments in the field of industrial and personnel psychology. Paper presented at the conference, *Recent directions in testing and fair employment practices.* Washington, D.C.: The Personnel Testing Council of Metropolitan Washington and BNA Systems, April 23, 1981.

2. Timmreck, C. W. *Moderating effect of tasks on the validity of selection tests.* Unpublished manuscript, University of Houston, 1981.

3. Schmidt, F. L., Hunter, J. E., Pearlman, K., & Caplan, J. R. *Validity generalization results for three occupations in the Sears, Roebuck Company.* Chicago: Sears, Roebuck Company, 1981.

4. Hunter, J. E. *An analysis of validity, differential validity, test fairness, and utility for the Philadelphia Police Officer Selection Examination prepared by Educational Testing Service.* Unpublished manuscript, Michigan State University, 1980.

5. Hunter, J. E. *The economic benefits of personnel selection using ability tests: A state of the art review including a detailed analysis of the dollar benefit of U.S. Employment Service placements and a critique of the low cutoff method of test use.* Report prepared for U.S. Employment Service, U.S. Department of Labor, Washington, D.C., January 15, 1981.

6. Hawk, J. Personal communication, November 20, 1978.

7. Braithwaite, D. Personal communication, January 15, 1976.

8. Ruch, W. W. *A re-analysis of published differential validity studies.* Paper presented at the meeting of the American Psychological Association, Honolulu, September 1972.

9. Tenopyr, M. L. *Race and socioeconomic status as moderators in predicting machine-shop training success.* Paper presented at the meeting of the American Psychological Association, Washington, D.C., September 1967.

10. Linn, R. L., Harnisch, D. L., & Dunbar, S. B. *Validity generalization and situational specificity: An analysis of the prediction of first year grades in law school.* Unpublished manuscript, University of Illinois at Urbana–Champaign, 1980.

11. Hunter, J. E., & Schmidt, F. L. *Cumulating results across studies: Correction for sampling error, a proposed moratorium on the significance test, and critique of current multivariate reporting practices.* Manuscript submitted for publication, 1981.

12. Hunter, J. E., Schmidt, F. L., & Jackson, G. B. Quantitative methods for integrating research findings across studies. Paper prepared as part of the project, *Methodological Innovations in Studying Organizations.* Funded through the American Psychological Association by the Office of Naval Research and the National Institute of Education. Washington, D.C., 1981.

REFERENCES

Albright, L. E., Glennon, J. R., & Smith, W. J. *The uses of psychological tests in industry.* Cleveland, Oh.: Allen, 1963.

American Psychological Association, Division of Industrial and Organizational Psychology. *Principles for the validation and use of personnel selection procedures* (2nd ed.). Berkeley, Calif.: Author, 1980. (Copies may be ordered from Lewis E. Albright, Kaiser Aluminum & Chemical Corporation, 300 Lakeside Drive — Room KB 2140, Oakland, Calif. 94643.)

Bartlett, C. J., Bobko, P., Mosier, S. B., & Hannan, R. Testing for fairness with a moderated multiple regression strategy: An alternative to differential analysis. *Personnel Psychology,* 1978, *31,* 233–241.

Berliner, D. C. Tempus Educare. In P. Peterson & H. Walberg (Eds.), *Research in teaching: Concepts, findings and implications.* Berkeley, Calif.: McCutchan, 1979.

Boehm, V. R. Differential prediction: A methodological artifact? *Journal of Applied Psychology,* 1977, *62,* 146–154.

Brogden, H. E. When testing pays off. *Personnel Psychology,* 1949, *2,* 171–183.

Brogden, H. E., & Taylor, E. K. A theory and classification of criterion bias. *Educational & Psychological Measurement,* 1950, *10,* 159–186.

Callender, J. C., & Osburn, H. G. Development and test of a new model of validity generalization. *Journal of Applied Psychology,* 1980, *65,* 543–558.

Campbell, J. T., Crooks, L. A., Mahoney, M. H., & Rock, D. A. *An investigation of sources of bias in the prediction of job performance: A six year study* (Final Project Report No. PR–73–37). Princeton, N.J.: Educational Testing Service, 1973.

Cleary, T. A., & Hilton, T. I. Test bias: Prediction of grades of Negro and white students in integrated colleges. *Journal of Educational Measurement,* 1968, *5,* 115–124.

Cole, N. S. Bias in testing. *American Psychologist,* 1981, *36,* 1067–1077.

Cronbach, L. J., & Gleser, G. *Psychological tests and personnel decisions.* Urbana: University of Illinois Press, 1957.

Cronbach, L. J., Yalow, E., & Schaeffer, G. A mathematical structure for analyzing fairness in selection. *Personnel Psychology,* 1980, *33,* 693–704.

Cuts raise new social-science query: Does anyone appreciate social science? *Wall Street Journal,* March 27, 1981, p. 54.

Equal Employment Opportunity Commission, Civil Service Commission, Department of Labor, & Department of Justice. Adoption by four agencies of Uniform Guidelines on Employee Selection Procedures. *Federal Register*, 1978, *43*, 38290–38315.

Gael, S., & Grant, D. L. Employment test validation for minority and nonminority telephone company service representatives. *Journal of Applied Psychology*, 1972, *56*, 135–139.

Gael, S., Grant, D. L., & Ritchie, R. J. Employment test validation for minority and nonminority clerks with work sample criteria. *Journal of Applied Psychology*, 1975, *60*, 420–426. (a)

Gael, S., Grant, D. L., & Ritchie, R. J. Employment test validation for minority and nonminority telephone operators. *Journal of Applied Psychology*, 1975, 60, 411–419. (b)

Ghiselli, E. E. *The validity of occupational aptitude tests*. New York: Wiley, 1966.

Glass, G. V. Primary, secondary, and meta-analysis of research. *Educational Researcher*, 1976, *5*, 3–8.

Grant, D. L., & Bray, D. W. Validation of employment tests for telephone company installation and repair occupations. *Journal of Applied Psychology*, 1970, *54*, 7–14.

Guion, R. M. *Personnel testing*. New York: McGraw-Hill, 1965.

Haney, W. Validity, vaudeville, and values: A short history of social concerns over standardized testing. *American Psychologist*, 1981, *36*, 1021–1034.

Humphreys, L. G. Statistical definitions of test validity for minority groups. *Journal of Applied Psychology*, 1973, *58*, 1–4.

Hunter, J. E. *Validity generalization for 12,000 jobs: An application of synthetic validity and validity generalization to the General Aptitude Test Battery (GATB)*. Washington, D.C.: U.S. Employment Service, U.S. Department of Labor, 1980.

Hunter, J. E., & Schmidt, F. L. A critical analysis of the statistical and ethical implications of five definitions of test fairness. *Psychological Bulletin*, 1976, *83*, 1053–1071.

Hunter, J. E., & Schmidt, F. L. Differential and single group validity of employment tests by race: A critical analysis of three recent studies. *Journal of Applied Psychology*, 1978, *63*, 1–11.

Hunter, J. E., & Schmidt, F. L. Fitting people to jobs: Implications of personnel selection for national productivity. In E. A. Fleishman (Ed.), *Human performance and productivity*. Hillsdale, N.J.: Erlbaum, in press.

Hunter, J. E., Schmidt, F. L., & Hunter, R. Differential validity of employment tests by race: A comprehensive review and analysis. *Psychological Bulletin*, 1979, *86*, 721–735.

Hunter, J. E., Schmidt, F. L., & Rauschenberger, J. M. Fairness of psychological tests: Implications of four definitions for selection utility and minority hiring. *Journal of Applied Psychology*, 1977, *62*, 245–260.

Jensen, A. R. *Bias in mental testing*. New York: Free Press, 1980.

Katzell, R. A., & Dyer, F. J. Differential validity revived. *Journal of Applied Psychology*, 1977, *62*, 137–145.

Ledvinka, J. The statistical definition of fairness in the federal selection guidelines and its implications for minority employment. *Personnel Psychology*, 1979, *32*, 551–562.

Lent, R. H., Aurbach, H. A., & Levin, L. S. Predictors, criteria, and significant results. *Personnel Psychology*, 1971, *24*, 519–533. (a)

Lent, R. H., Aurbach, H. A., & Levin, L. S. Research and design and validity assessment. *Personnel Psychology*, 1971, *24*, 247–274. (b)

Lerner, B. Washington v. Davis: Quantity, quality, and equality in employment testing. In P. Kurland (Ed.), *The 1976 Supreme Court Review*. Chicago: University of Chicago Press, 1977.

Lerner, B. Employment discrimination: Adverse impact, validity, and equality. In P. Kurland & G. Casper (Eds.), *The 1979 Supreme Court Review*. Chicago: University of Chicago Press, 1979.

Lilienthal, R. A., & Pearlman, K. *The validity of federal selection tests for aid/ technicians in the health, science, and engineering fields*. Washington, D.C.: U.S. Office of Personnel Management, Personnel Research and Development Center, in press.

Linn, R. L. Single-group validity, differential validity, and differential predictions. *Journal of Applied Psychology*, 1978, *63*, 507–514.

Mack, M. J., Schmidt, F. L., & Hunter, J. E. Estimating the productivity costs in dollars of minimum selection test cutoff scores. Washington, D.C.: U.S. Office of Personnel Management, Personnel Research and Development Center, in press.

Novick, M. R. Federal guidelines and professional standards. *American Psychologist*, 1981, *36*, 1035–1046.

O'Connor, E. J., Wexley, K. N., & Alexander, R. A. Single group validity: Fact or fallacy? *Journal of Applied Psychology*, 1975, *60*, 352–355.

Pearlman, K., Schmidt, F. L., & Hunter, J. E. Validity generalization results for tests used to predict training success and job proficiency in clerical occupations. *Journal of Applied Psychology*, 1980, *65*, 373–406.

Schmidt, F. L., Berner, J. G., & Hunter, J. E. Racial differences in validity of employment tests: Reality or illusion? *Journal of Applied Psychology*, 1973, *53*, 5–9.

Schmidt, F. L., Gast-Rosenberg, I., & Hunter, J. E. Validity generalization results for computer programmers. *Journal of Applied Psychology*, 1980, *65*, 643–661.

Schmidt, F. L., & Hunter, J. E. Development of a general solution to the problem of validity generalization. *Journal of Applied Psychology*, 1977, *62*, 529–540.

Schmidt, F. L., & Hunter, J. E. Moderator research and the law of small numbers. *Personnel Psychology*, 1978, *31*, 215–231.

Schmidt, F. L., Hunter, J. E., & Caplan, J. R. Validity generalization results for two jobs in the petroleum industry. *Journal of Applied Psychology*, 1981, *66*, 261–273.

Schmidt, F. L., Hunter, J. E., McKenzie, R., & Muldrow, T. The impact of valid selection procedures on workforce productivity. *Journal of Applied Psychology*, 1979, *64*, 609–626.

Schmidt, F. L., Hunter, J. E., & Pearlman, K. Task differences and validity of aptitude tests in selection: A red herring. *Journal of Applied Psychology*, 1981, *66*, 166–185.

Schmidt, F. L., Hunter, J. E., Pearlman, K., & Shane, G. S. Further tests of the Schmidt–Hunter Bayesian validity generalization procedure. *Personnel Psychology*, 1979, *32*, 257–281.

Schmidt, F. L., Hunter, J. E., & Urry, V. M. Statistical power in criterion-related validity studies. *Journal of Applied Psychology*, 1976, *61*, 473–485.

Schmidt, F. L., Pearlman, K., & Hunter, J. E. The validity and fairness of employment and educational tests for Hispanic Americans: A review and analysis. *Personnel Psychology*, 1980, *33*, 705–724.

Sewell, W. H., Hauser, R. M., & Featherman, D. L. (Eds.). *Schooling and achievement in American society*. New York: Academic Press, 1976.

Tenopyr, M. L. The realities of employment testing. *American Psychologist*, 1981, *36*, 1120–1127.

U.S. Department of Labor. *Dictionary of occupational titles* (4th ed.). Washington, D.C.: U.S. Government Printing Office, 1977.

Wiley, D. E. Another hour, another day: Quality of schooling, a potent path for policy. *Studies of Educational Processes,* No. 3, University of Chicago, July 1973.

Wolins, L. Responsibility for raw data. *American Psychologist,* 1962, *17,* 657–658.

The Implications of Genetic Testing

Judy D. Olian and Tom C. Snyder

The field of genetic engineering has made significant progress in the last decade and is changing scientific thinking in numerous areas of the biological and physical sciences. Some applications of these scientific advances may directly affect work place practices.

For example, scientists are now able to predict the likelihood of some types of disease, including occupational disease in an adult's life, based on the genetic material at birth. Moreover, a worker's susceptibility to disease from exposure to toxins on the job may be predictable, in part, from the genetic endowment of the individual.[1] These advances may have far-reaching implications for human resource management. Specifically, genetic tests could be used to predict individual susceptibility to occupational disease and to monitor reactions to toxins in the work environment.

There are two potential HRM applications of genetic testing:

☐ Genetic screening (GS) is a one-time testing procedure to determine whether a job applicant carries genetic traits that could predispose them to adverse health effects when exposed to certain chemicals. The usual means of obtaining genetic information is via a blood or urine count.

   Individuals identified as having a specific genetic condition that makes them more susceptible to occupational diseases or to toxins could be screened out of "unhealthy" jobs and placed in environments that do not pose special hazards to them. Hence, GS is analogous to existing pre-employment selection devices in that it provides information on the potential applicant-job match.

☐ Genetic monitoring (GM) is the routine testing of employees working with potentially toxic substances, to detect any changes in the genetic material of the exposed employee. Evidence of genetic impairment could lead to the elimination of the culpable agent from the production process, installation of engineering controls or transferral of affected employees.

Beyond anecdotal accounts of companies using genetic tests[2], the only source of information on GS and GM is a recent survey published by the Office of Technology

Reprinted from the January 1984 issue of *Personnel Administrator,* copyright 1984, The American Society for Personnel Administration, 606 North Washington Street, Alexandria, VA 22314, $30 per year.

and Assessment (OTA).[1] Of the 366 respondents to the survey (including CEOs of Fortune 500 companies, the directors of large utilities and unions), six companies (1.6 percent of the respondents) were presently using genetic tests: 17 (4.6 percent) had used the tests in the past 12 years, while 59 (16.1 percent) were contemplating genetic testing in the next five years.

One of the survey items asked what actions were taken as a consequence of genetic tests. Of the 18 responses to this question, eight had informed the employee of the test results, five had transferred the employee, three had instituted personal protection devices on the job, two had installed engineering controls, and one organization had changed the products it was using. Among those that had checked the "other actions" category, one respondent noted that genetic tests had been used for pre-placement purposes.

These survey results should be interpreted cautiously because of sample and response bias problems. They do appear to indicate, however, that at least among the survey sample there is a growing interest in the introduction of genetic testing into work practices.

EFFECTS ON HRM

GS could be implemented as part of the test battery that job applicants go through. GS devices have yet to be proven as accurate and reliable predictors of hypersusceptibility. However, if future research results in the development of reliable and valid GS devices, genetic data may enhance the quality of the applicant-job matches, e.g., by selecting and placing individuals in jobs that do not present them with unique health problems.

Hiring decisions on the basis of GS results rest on individual characteristics that are beyond personal control. Employers may find it more palatable to use genetic information only after the hiring decision is made, in order to place individuals in job areas which will not affect their hypersusceptibilities. This assumes that employers have the latitude to engage in differential placement, i.e., a sufficient mix of jobs and individuals with a variety of "genetic dispositions" such that an optimal match can evolve. That is probably an unrealistic assumption in the case of small organizations.

GM information could also be used for placement purposes if, for example, tests revealed that continued exposure to certain toxins caused genetic damage and subsequent disease in some workers but not in others. Affected workers could then be transferred out of the area to which they were sensitive.

The most serious HRM quagmire as a consequence of genetic testing would involve the development of equitable and cost-effective placement and transferral policies. What would be the job rights of an individual identified as having a genetic impairment? Would that individual be eligible, automatically, for transfer out of the job? To where? Would the employee's previous level of pay and benefits be retained on the post-transfer job, even if the transfer involved downward movement? If the previous pay and benefit level were retained on the new job, would the employer be vulnerable under the Equal Pay Act or the Civil Rights Act, if the transferred employee's co-workers on the new job sued for equal pay? In organizations in which job transfers are seniority based, what "bumping" rights, if any, would an employee with a genetic impairment have relative to more senior workers awaiting transfer?

Selection and placement activities capitalize on individual differences. Safety management activities are designed to achieve a safe and healthy environment for all workers. GM is an extremely useful tool in that regard. If long-term monitoring indicated that all workers were negatively affected by exposure to certain toxins, possible remedies include personal protection devices, engineering controls or total elimination of the toxin from the work process.

If GM indicated that just some workers were hypersusceptible to certain toxins and if exposure levels were within acceptable OSHA limits, selective out-placement of affected employees might be warranted.

Genetic information may potentially be used in cases involving employer liability for occupationally related diseases. There are numerous cases in which employers are being sued for worker exposure that often occurred decades before the onset of disease (e.g., workers' claims of asbestos exposure against Manville Corp.). Genetic information may provide the data that could alternatively implicate or absolve the employer. For example, GS results that indicate an individual is hypersusceptible to certain toxins may minimize employer liability and damage amounts if workers subsequently contract occupationally related diseases.

Conversely, GM evidence showing systematic debilitation in the genetic material of workers exposed to a toxic agent would weaken an employer's defense in a law suit brought by affected workers. Subsequent disability insurance premiums would be increased as a result of the employer's obvious liability.

Hence, genetic testing could be either a bane or a blessing in disability suits, depending on the circumstances and type of genetic data available to the employer.

LEGAL IMPLICATIONS

Existing laws that cover HRM practices may have implications for genetic testing. Here, we must be somewhat speculative since there are, to date, no directly relevant legal precedents.

The general duty clause of OSHA calls for an employer to provide a "... place of employment free from recognized hazards." Furthermore, two specific standards that regulate the permissible level of toxins in the work environment (lead and vinyl chloride) explicitly call for the removal of employees from their jobs if health impairment will result from continued exposure. GS and GM practices both provide information that will ultimately contribute to the health and safety of workers by facilitating selective placement decisions.

While there are no legal precedents in this regard, the general duty clause of OSHA and the specific standards dealing with employee removal policies could be seen as sanctioning any practice that contributes to worker health. Consequently, if employers failed to take GS and GM information into account, they may be violating the spirit of OSHA.

GS results may trigger discrimination suits under Title VII of the Civil Rights Act because there is substantial evidence showing that genetic impairments differ as a function of ethnicity.[4] Since applicants will have different GS results as a function of race or ethnicity, they will have grounds to register a charge of discrimination, shifting the burden of proof to the employer.

A successful employer defense in this regard requires the showing of "business necessity" or validity of the selection device, data not available given the state-of-the-science. Hence, at present, employers would be unsuccessful in defending the inequality of results of the genetic tests. While genetic data can be collected at the screening stage, human resource managers would be ill-advised to use that data for exclusionary employment decisions.

We should note one caveat in this discussion. Even if employers have valid data in support of GS devices, it is unclear whether the data could be used as part of "business necessity" argument. The courts have accepted the business necessity defense when employers could justify unequal hiring or promotion rates in terms of expected differences in performance.[5] If the business necessity argument were applied to GS practices, it would have to be extended to cover probabilities of contracting disease in addition to expected performance differences.

There is a potential contradiction between Title VII and OSHA in that Title VII would effectively prevent use of GS (because of an inability to defend unequal racial results) while OSHA would require their implementation in the interest of achieving employee health.

A situation analogous to the Title VII–OSHA dilemma exists with regard to the Rehabilitation Act and parallel state laws. The primary question is whether individuals diagnosed as genetically impaired would be considered handicapped. Based on somewhat analogous precedents[6] and on the legal definition, which includes " . . . individuals regarded as having such an impairment," genetically impaired individuals would probably be covered under these laws.

Accordingly, they are entitled to employment protection as long as they are capable of performing the job duties, as presently defined.[6] Since genetic impairment is unlikely to cause performance problems in the short-run, workers with genetic deficiencies will probably be entitled to the job protection afforded by the Rehabilitation Act and similar laws. Hence, the Rehabilitation Act may provide employees with job protection in a manner inconsistent with OSHA.

WORKER'S COMPENSATION

Laws provide for the financial compensation of individuals incurring work related injuries, disease or death. The Worker's Compensation (WC) system is funded by a tax levied against employers, the level of which is based on their experience rating; the more employees drawing WC benefits, the higher the employer's WC contributions.

One of the requirements for eligibility for WC benefits is the establishment of a cause-effect relationship between the work environment and the subsequent illness or injury. It is very difficult to establish direct cause-effect relationships between toxic agents and subsequent occupational disease, largely because of the long latency period between exposure and the onset of disease symptoms.

Moreover, two contradictory legal theories exist with regard to establishing WC liability. One theory ("manifestation") limits employer liability to the active term of the WC policy, even if the disease manifests itself after the WC policy has expired. The other theory ("exposure") covers work-related diseases throughout a worker's life, including instances in which the WC insurance policy has expired.

Under the first approach, employers have an incentive to minimize their potential liability through the use, for example, of GS showing an employee's predisposition to disease. The second approach provides no incentive for GS because the employer is considered liable under any circumstances. Since the Supreme Court has not chosen between the two theories, HRM professionals must decide which approach prevails in their local jurisdiction.

GS and GM are invasive tests that elicit information that can be used to make diagnoses on a wide range of syndromes, both job and non-job related. In light of this, it is extremely important to protect individuals' privacy rights and to ensure against use of the genetic information for non-job purposes. At present, no federal laws provide individuals with such protection. There are only broad recommendations within a National Commission's report[7] encouraging employers to limit themselves to job-related information from applicants.

OSHA guarantees the rights of employees to their medical records, with the exception of information that is deemed damaging to the employee by a physician.[9] That means that under most circumstances, employees will have the right to obtain their genetic test results. In order to avoid inaccurate and unnecessarily stressful inferences from these tests results, employers will need to have a staff trained in genetic counselling.

Nine states provide employees with "the right to know" the labels of chemicals used in the work process. Moreover, legal precedents imply that the courts require disclosure of any medical data available on work place exposure. Employers who intentionally conceal such information, including GM results, from exposed workers run the risk of incurring punitive damages above and beyond WC liability. Several cases in the Manville Corp. asbestos suit illustrate this point.

COURSES OF ACTION

Figures 1 and 2 summarize the alternative courses of action available to employers with regard to GM and GS respectively.

Genetic Monitoring

If valid tests exist for the detection of genetic damage from toxic exposure, the general duty clause of OSHA can be interpreted to require a GM program. Whenever any type of genetic information is collected, employees' privacy rights must be protected and safeguards must be built into the genetic database. Genetic diagnoses must be strictly limited to job-related purposes; moreover, individual employee diagnoses must be available only to the staff of the corporate genetic counseling program the employees and their physicians if the corporate physician deems it necessary. Aggregated information concealing individual identities can be provided to those involved in establishing safety policies (e.g., engineering controls) in the work place. Genetic tests results at the individual level should be handled only by human resource specialists who are an integral part of the professional genetic counseling staff, if such information is ultimately used for employment decisions.

A genetic counseling program staffed by trained genetic counselors, including physicians, is imperative any time employees submit to genetic tests. Genetic information is very complex and is easily misinterpreted by the layman. This can cause unnecessary stress on individuals diagnosed as having certain genetic conditions, the implications of which are unexplained. This happened during the early '70s when many cities instituted tests for the sickle cell trait. Individuals diagnosed as carriers frequently suffered terrible trauma, because they did not understand the difference between the innocuous sickle cell trait and the actual disease.

Genetic counselors must be trained to provide non-threatening yet informative feedback to employees since OSHA now provides workers with access to their own medical records.[8] That same rule provides physicians with the discretionary right to withhold information deemed damaging to employees. Consequently, a genetic feedback and counseling program needs to establish information withholding policies that specify when such actions are legitimate. Employee and union participation in policy formulation and oversight is recommended.

The actions taken on the basis of GM information depend on four criteria: (1) the credibility (or validity) of the test information; (2) the seriousness of the hazard; (3) the feasibility of elimination of the toxin and engineering controls; and (4) the generality of the health hazard.

If there are some doubts about the validity of the test data, it is reasonable to abstain temporarily from dramatic changes in work policies and procedures until further information is available. If the data are valid and indicate serious genetic hazards, employers should explore the feasibility of eliminating the toxin from the work process.

FIGURE 1
Possible Courses of Action

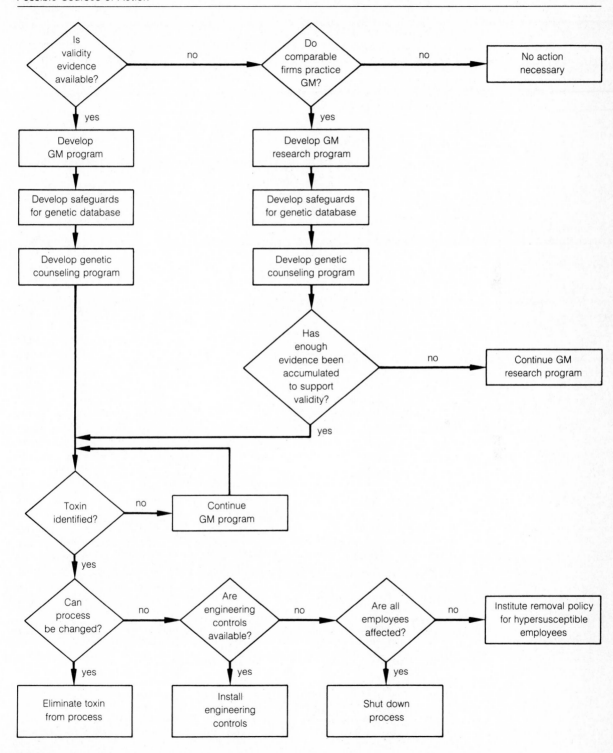

FIGURE 2
Possible Courses of Action

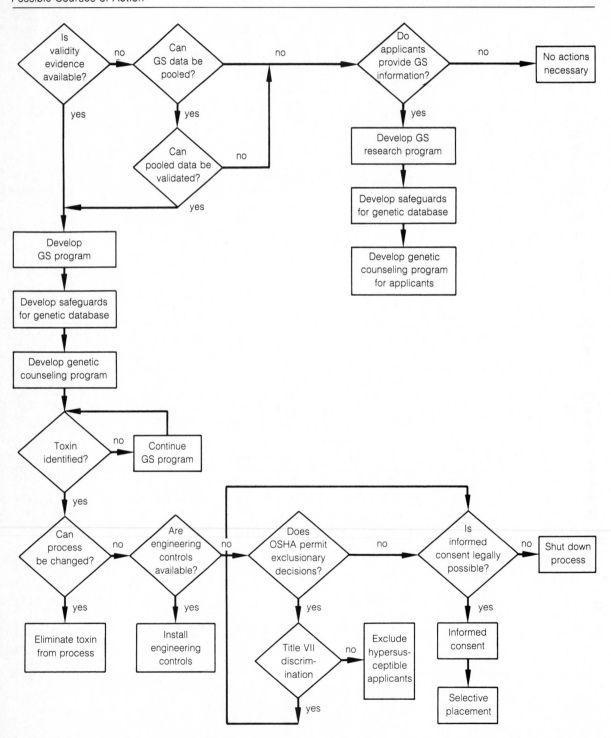

If that alternative is not viable, engineering controls should be installed to minimize the presence of the toxic agent in the work environment. OSHA has encouraged engineering controls even at considerable employer expense.

Only if the total elimination or reduction in the level of the toxin is not feasible is it legitimate to capitalize on individual differences in susceptibility to genetic damage. GM information will reveal whether a toxin affects all employees exposed to it, or damages only an identifiable, hypersusceptible employee subgroup. In the former case, employers have a responsibility to shut down the toxic process. Such extreme measures may not be necessary in the latter case. Hypersusceptible employees can be removed to safe work environments that do not pose special hazards to their genetic makeup. However, the rights of displaced workers must be addressed in any employee removal program. For example, in its lead removal policy,[10] OSHA guarantees the rights of hypersusceptible employees to transfer into "safe" jobs without any loss of pay or benefits for up to 18 months after transfer.

Since it is unrealistic to assume that all employers, particularly smaller firms, will have the flexibility to out-place all hypersusceptible employees, some employees may be faced with the difficult choice of accepting an inferior job or total unemployment versus remaining on the hazardous job, at least in the short-term.

Jennings[10] observes that "Experience has abundantly demonstrated that when faced with the choice between their health and their jobs, many workers unfortunately sacrifice their health rather than give up their jobs." Allowing workers to remain on jobs that are potentially hazardous to their health can only be a temporary solution.

Until transfer opportunities are available, it is advisable for employers to obtain signed voluntary consent agreements from affected employees who choose to stay on hazardous jobs. While these consent agreements will not absolve employers from liability under WC laws and civil disability suits, they may minimize the amount of punitive damages employees are awarded.[3]

If evidence in support of the validity of genetic tests is not yet available, employers should scan the industry to determine whether other, similar firms are conducting GM research programs. Ignorance of scientific advances in the protection of worker health is no defense, since the general duty clause of OSHA obligates an employer to protect the health of workers through measures used by "the prudent man."

If other comparable firms engage in GM, the employer is also obligated to institute a GM research program. Where GM is not practiced by comparable firms, there is no legal requirement to initiate one. Nevertheless, some companies may choose to establish a GM research program as part of a broad-based attempt to find ways to improve the quality of the work environment.

Whenever a GM research program is instituted, the database safeguards suggested above should be introduced. When the research program accumulates evidence in support of the predictive validity of the tests, employers can use GM information for safety and employment policy purposes.

Genetic Screening

As Figure 2 indicates, validity evidence must be available before GS results can be used. Where GS data are elicited, our previous recommendations for database safeguards apply: institute policies that protect applicants' genetic information, employ a staff of professional genetic counselors and provide feedback to applicants.

While OSHA guarantees only the rights of employees, but not applicants, to access their medical records,[8] we still believe it advisable to provide genetic feedback within the previously mentioned constraints, to those applicants explicitly requesting it. Beyond ethical reasons, it improves the employer's image in the eyes of potential incumbents as an accessible, open and employee-oriented company. We emphasize, however, that provision of GS information to applicants is voluntary at this point, contrary to GM feedback to employees.

Even if GS tests are valid, OSHA has a clear bias in favor of elimination of the toxin or installation of engineering controls. If these alternatives are not feasible, under OSHA it is preferable to exclude hypersusceptible applicants rather than to place them, with their consent, in hazardous work environments. In contrast, employment exclusions are problematic under Title VII because, as mentioned, genetic screening results in unequal racial effects which are indefensible unless persuasive validity data are available.

Because genetic impairments occur at low frequencies in the population, it is possible to obtain support for the validity of GS devices only if research is conducted on large groups of high-risk populations. Single employers are unlikely to have a large enough applicant pool on which to establish validity evidence.

Hence, it may be reasonable for multiple employers in a single industry to pool genetic data for validation purposes providing the following conditions are met: (1) preliminary evidence from alternative, credible sources is available in support of the validity of the GS devices in question; (2) strong safeguards are instituted to protect the identity of individual employees and to restrict the use of the genetic database to job-related purposes. Concerns for the protection of individual privacy may be partially alleviated if the pooled database is administered by OSHA or by a responsible union.

When research on a pooled database is not feasible, firms can still collect GS information for basic research purposes. The research program might ultimately yield validity evidence that could prove useful in subsequent selection and placement decisions. Again, the same database safeguards apply here.

REFERENCES

1. Office of Technology and Assessment, *The role of genetic testing in the prevention of occupational disease*; Washington, D.C., Government Printing Office, 1983.

2. See, for example, R. Severo, *New York Times*, February 4–6, 1980; or *U.S. News and World Report*, April 11, 1983.

3. This is suggested in G. Nothstein & J. Ayres. "Sex based considerations of differentiation in the work place: Exploring the biomedical interface between OSHA and Title VII," *Villanova Law Review*, 1981, 26(2), pp. 239–321.

4. See, for example, OTA report (*op. cit.*). Also, see Beutler, E., *Hemolytic anemia disorders of red cell metabolism*, New York, N.Y.: Plenum Medical Book Co., 1978 or Olian, J. D., Genetic screening for employment purposes; working paper, University of Maryland, 1983.

5. See *Burwell* v. *Eastern Air Lines Inc.*, 663 F. 2d at 371, for an elaboration on the business necessity argument.

6. See *OFCCP* v. *E. E. Black, Ltd.*, Bureau of National Affairs, 19 Fair Employment Practices Case, 1624. See also *Sterling Transit Co.* v. *Fair Employment Practice Commission*, 121 Cal. App. 3d 791, 175 California Reporter 548, 1981.

7. See D. Linowes, "Update on privacy protection safeguards," *Personnel Administrator*, June 1980, pp. 39–42.

8. 29 CFR 1910.20.

9. 29 CFR 1910.1025.

10. R. L. Jennings, "Medical removal protection and the sensitive worker." *Annals of the American Conference on Government Industrial Hygienists*, 1982, Vol. 3, pp. 147–150.

F.

SELECTION AND THE LAW

Jobs: The Pursuit of Fairness

Kathy Sawyer

AFFIRMATIVE ACTION: BIRTH AND LIFE OF A 'BUGABOO'

As the Senate argued its way toward passage of the Civil Rights Act one day in 1964, one of its leading liberals, exasperated, tried one more time to reassure the opposition on a critical point.

"I will start eating the pages, one after another," Sen. Hubert H. Humphrey (D-Minn.) vowed, if they contain "any language which provides that an employer will have to hire on the basis of percentage or quota related to color."

That "bugaboo," he assured at another point, "is nonexistent."

Humphrey never ate those words. But 18 years after passage of the historic act and over a decade after the Nixon administration introduced the notion of goals and timetables for hiring blacks and others, American society is still digesting the bugaboo.

Government-enforced employment quotas based on sex, race or other group status have grown into the most explosive, the most despised and, supporters say, one of the most effective of the antidiscrimination initiatives.

They are a key tool — but not the only one — in the audacious package known loosely as "affirmative action."

In the simplest terms, the phrase "affirmative action" means doing something that takes race or sex specifically into account in order to repair the effects of injustice, something beyond simply, passively, not being unjust anymore.

It lies at the heart of the civil rights issue of the decade: access to jobs. And yet Congress has passed no law spelling out what it is.

Instead, a sort of bureaucratic virgin birth occurred in about 1969, when Nixon appointees in the Labor Department made the hiring of white women and minorities a bid specification under federal procurement law, just as bids specify a certain weight of nail or grade of marble.

In place of the brave marchers and anthem singers of the 1960s, this policy has mobilized an army of technocrats and computers against an ancient devil.

Its actual record of achievements, shrouded in righteous rhetoric from all sides,

---

Reprinted with permission from *The Washington Post*, 1982: April 11 (pp. 1, 10), 12 (pp. 1, 8), and 13 (pp. 1, 6).

is a murky one — of small, haphazard successes, crazy ironies and a high price-tag of bitterness and confusion.

Reagan administration officials have spelled out their intentions to ease enforcement and halt the use of quotas. The only clear effect of these and other of their sorties into the minefield of civil rights, so far, is to create potentially serious political problems for themselves and rally a rapid movement back to the barricades. Still, some see the nation at a crossroads on these issues.

Today's hard times and the uneven effects of affirmative action threaten the tenuous political coalition that has fought for equal opportunity. For instance, blacks, especially men, express resentment that white women are reaping greater benefits than they, the original objects of affirmative action.

Redistributing privileges is never easy but the civil rights movement did not invent the idea. Both federal and state governments have for decades made a major exception to the merit standard by affording massive, permanent, special preferences to military veterans at virtually every level.

————

How has affirmative action worked for its intended beneficiaries, those known in the parlance as "protected classes"? In general, of course, they continue to lag far behind white men in terms of earnings and employment.

But evidence shows that the policy has spurred significant advances in certain categories, for certain people, at least for the short term:

▫ White women — the largest of all groups, including white men in total population, and over 43 percent of the workforce — are the biggest gainers. The vaunted "influx of women" into the workforce has consisted essentially of white women, who have taken a share of new opportunities out of proportion to even their large numbers.

▫ Black women, with their "two-fer" status, also seem to have taken relatively good advantage of new openings, although some specialists believe this is changing. Black women have always had a high work rate, traditionally in lower-rung jobs. The rising generation is breaking out of the housemaid role and into better-paying fields and they even out-earn white women in three occupational categories: managerial, clerical and sales.

▫ Black men advanced in certain categories. A study for the Urban League indicates that in the last decade black men have increased by 71 percent in higher-paying jobs (managers, professionals and skilled craft workers), or twice the rate of their overall employment growth. (Blacks and other minorities such as American Indians are 12.6 percent of the workforce, and Hispanics — most of them included in the white count — are about 5.5 percent.)

But their growth stayed focused in professional jobs at the lower end of the earnings scale, including social workers, engineering and science technicians especially, but also including lawyers, according to the Labor Department.

▫ Protected classes have also improved markedly in police work, managerial bank jobs, underground mining and certain other work settings where the affirmative action artillery has been specifically focused.

However, while affirmative action clearly has accelerated the progress of certain young, well-educated, hard-working or otherwise outstanding members of the affected groups, it has not affected broad traditional patterns of inequality.

For instance, the proportion of black men in the labor force has actually declined since 1948, especially among teen-agers, the old and the less-educated. And all working women still earn only about 50 cents on the dollar compared with working *white* men.

Still, in the last half of the 1970s, white men and women were taking more than their share of new jobs. Together they made up 64 percent of labor force growth but took 74 percent of the new jobs, according to the National Commission on Employment Policy.

And more than half of these new jobs were taken by white women, it said, although they made up only one-third of the increase.

———

In light of the controversy over affirmative action in the Reagan era, this series will focus on the achievements and the costs of affirmative action in practice, rather than on the complex and persistent problems of discrimination itself. It will focus primarily on the employment arena (rather than, say, education), based on dozens of interviews around the country with personnel administrators, top executives, hard-hats and secretaries and others on the work-a-day frontlines.

Beyond the numbers, this survey suggests the following conclusions:

☐ Affirmative action measures can achieve long-term progress only in combination with improvements in the pipeline of education and training, an economic climate that creates new opportunities, and the personal commitment of top managers who, after all, still retain considerable control of their workforces.

☐ Despite political and visceral reactions against it, affirmative action has sufficient momentum to survive, at least in the flowchart and paperwork sense. It has withstood a decade of constant legal challenge, and some of its most powerful lobbyists are not civil rights activists but corporate executives, lawyers and consultants who make their living in the field.

"Anybody who says he can't find a qualified woman or minority doesn't know what he's talking about," says former Nixon official Bill Marumoto, a Japanese-American "minority" and a professional headhunter who uses a computerized data bank to help employers fill high-level job vacancies. "It's a science for us now."

☐ A significant peripheral effect of affirmative action (along with other fair employment laws) is that it has helped expose to public scrutiny the rituals by which all personnel decisions are made. Some employers report the changes can actually be good for business.

☐ Under pressure to achieve demonstrable change, some employers have hired unqualified white women and minorities and applied a lower standard in judging their performance on the job. Because of persistent inequities in education and culture, some say this is the only way to induct significant numbers of them into certain occupations any time soon.

But this two-track approach also sets some up for failure, reinforces prejudices, cheapens the success of the truly qualified and aggravates hostility and resentment on all sides. Supporters of affirmative action insist that forcing employers to hire the unqualified was never the policy's intent.

———

Affirmative action is such a prickly pear politically that Congress has given it wide berth, generally acquiescing in whatever was done by a succession of presidents, courts and bureaucrats.

Black economist Thomas Sowell, conservative nemesis of civil rights leaders, describes the process as one in which "nonelected judges, the media and the intellectual establishment" have allowed themselves to be swept along uncritically by emotional rhetoric and "a horror of being classed with bigots."

The system has been molded to a great degree by Republicans — notably the Nixon Labor Department and the Nixon Supreme Court. Arthur Fletcher, a black Nixon appointee, rather than a Great Society partisan, signed the key paper. As he puts it, "We started the counting."

A succession of presidential orders as far back as Roosevelt had called vaguely for positive action by government contractors to end discrimination.

Lyndon Johnson, in 1965, signed a crucial order creating a new bureaucracy to enforce the mandate. And he gave poetic voice to the philosophy of it: "You do not take a person who, for years, has been hobbled by chains and liberate him, bring him up to the starting line of a race and then say, 'You are free to compete with all the others,' and still justly believe that you have been completely fair . . . "

The problem, Fletcher observed recently, was that employers simply ignored the flowery but toothless presidential exhortations. Their attitude was, as a company lawyer told him one day in the mid-'60s, "When the government tells us what affirmative action is, then we'll comply."

"A year later," he said with an extravagant chuckle and a they-asked-for-it tone, "I was an assistant secretary of labor."

The idea was to emulate the cleverest manipulators of government rules — the defense contractors, he said. But in order to link job equity to procurement law, he added gleefully, "*You got to count.*"

In their opening salvo in 1969, known as "the Philadelphia Plan," Fletcher's staff specified that certain Pennsylvania construction contractors would have to have minorities and women working a certain number of man-hours.

"We made sure there were enough hours required that one minority couldn't work 'em all," he said. "That was called 'motorcycle compliance' in those days, where they'd put one black on a motorcycle and run him from one job to another all day long.

"And we got around calling them quotas. If we'd just said 18 percent, that would be inflexible, and it would be a quota. So we set a *range*, of say 18 to 20 percent."

Some civil rights groups have tried to draw elaborate semantical distinctions between this notion of a "range" (known as "goals and timetables") and quotas. But others on both sides argue that this is usually a specious distinction.

To reach that range, Fletcher went on, "We called for a 'good faith effort.' And how do you show that? Simple: you count the man-hours, the cost, the number of personnel it took to make the effort. That's procurement law."

Other top Nixon labor officials have since called the idea a horrid mistake. But Fletcher, now a consultant in the field, says he would do it again. "No court has ever declared our concept unconstitutional."

The far-reaching presidential order is only one of the policy's legal legs. The other is in the Civil Rights Act, which provides vague authority.

The significant difference is that, on this second footing, the courts can order affirmative action only as a remedy after a finding of discrimination. Enforcement of the presidential order requires no such finding.

Moreover, the courts have declared it legal for employers (and unions) to adopt voluntary, private affirmative action measures — including quotas — as a kind of preventive medicine, in order to head off lawsuits.

In 1967, women were added as a protected class, followed by the physically handicapped and Vietnam veterans.

Nobody knows for sure exactly how many workers are covered directly by the federal affirmative action machinery, but Labor Department officials estimate it could be as high as 300,000 employers of perhaps 40 million American workers. Most of the workforce is affected, one way or another.

And every white woman, black, Cuban, Mexican American, Puerto Rican, American Indian, Alaskan Native, Asian or Pacific Islander, Vietnam veteran or handicapped person who works for pay in this country, indeed virtually everyone except able-bodied white men — whether underclass or uppercrust, whether or not hired specifically under the affirmative action banner — may be counted as an affirmative action statistic.

On one side, then, are around 48 million able-bodied white Anglo males in the civilian workforce not covered. On the other, roughly 36 million white women, 10.7 million blacks, 4.8 million Hispanics, 2.4 million American Indians, Asian and Pacific Islanders and Alaskans, 3 million or 4 million white handicapped males and around 7,000 white Vietnam veterans — or a total of 57 million or more are in the protected groups [estimates are based on the latest federal figures, in 1979].

———

Even though statistical formulas are the bedrock upon which affirmative action has been built, the government has never refined the statistics in a way that measures the program's impact very clearly. The picture clicks and changes like a kaleidoscope.

In selected occupational categories or industries that have been specifically targeted by affirmative action enforcers, change is evident.

FIGURE 1

Participation in the Civilian Labor Force, by Race and Sex, from 1910 to 1980

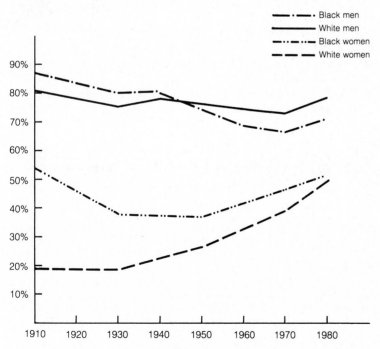

Figures from U.S. Census Bureau and Bureau of Labor Statistics. Lines show the rate of participation for each group, that is the percentage of all black men, etc., who were in the labor force of a given time. Figures include the employed and those seeking work. Age universe has varied over the years. If military labor force were included, this would add about one percentage point to black male participation, and a fraction to each other group. (Figures for 1940 do include military.)

Before the advent of Fletcher and his "goals and timetables," for example, his first target — the highly paid, hidebound iron workers, electricians and other construction workers in the Philadelphia area — had a minority membership of under 1 percent. Today that proportion has risen to 12.1 percent. A dramatic increase, though far short of the government-imposed goal of 19 to 26 percent.

In 1970, there were about 24,000 black police officers. The lastest figures show that has risen to 43,500, or 9 percent of the total.

"You can say there has been a sea change in the workforce," said Barry Goldstein of the NAACP Legal Defense Fund. "What you cannot say is that exactly 10,000 are there because of affirmative action, another 15,000 because of other fair employment laws and other factors" such as a suddenly perceived need, in the wake of the 1960s' urban riots, to recruit more black policemen to patrol the inner cities.

Under pressure from women's groups, the government had targeted the banking industry for special attention. And the proportions of female officials and managers zoomed.

But at the same time civil rights groups hailed these changes as proof that affirmative action works, they also branded such figures as potentially hollow. Huge increases in the category of officials and managers "may indicate that banks are changing women's job titles, not their pay, duties or responsibilities," a report by Working Women warns.

In another targeted industry, the number of female underground coal miners rose from zero in 1973 to 3,295, or 8.7 percent, by late 1980.

Women's groups offer this not only as an example of an effective program but also as a clear illustration of how affirmative action can outstrip the kind of simple "passive nondiscrimination" which requires only that the employer select fairly from among all applicants.

In a more general sampling: among physicians, women are 13.4 percent and minorities are 10.8 percent; among lawyers and judges, women are 12.8 percent and minorities are 4.2 percent, and among editors and reporters, women are 50 percent and minorities are 5.7 percent.

Still, nationwide more than 60 percent of daily newspapers employ no black reporters or editors. And at the rank of city editor and above, only 1 percent are black and other minorities.

———

Opposing sides disagree about exactly what the workforce statistics prove about the impact of affirmative action.

Whatever progress has been made, experts on all sides agree it is impossible to measure how much of it would have occurred as a result of economic and other pressures, without any affirmative action.

Stunningly little specific data or case studies are available. Personnel information is protected as "proprietary" and employers . . . generally refuse to make it public unless forced by a court.

The government has demanded vast statistical recordkeeping by employers but, in 1980, the U.S. Commission for Civil Rights informed top Carter administration equal employment opportunity officials that its researchers had found the data virtually useless in assessing the effects of affirmative action in given organizations since 1973, according to interoffice correspondence.

Some records have been lost over the years as they were shuttled from one government office to another during successive reorganizations; some data tapes were of poor quality, and perhaps three-fourths of employers (mostly small ones) had simply failed to file the most basic form.

Officials responded that they hoped a reorganization of enforcement and a new computerized system at the budget office would improve the situation. But "up-to-the-minute, 100 percent accurate" data might be impossible.

Meanwhile, out in the real world, affirmative action had taken on a life of its own.

REVERSE BIAS VICTORY PROVES A MIXED SUCCESS FOR BLACKS

In some hard hat hall of fame, Brian Weber is surely immortalized as the good ole boy who fought a five-year battle against a quota system favoring blacks. He lost the case, but he popularized the catchy phrase "reverse discrimination."

Take a trip to the Gramercy, La., plant where it started, though, and things look a lot less simple. Black workers there do not view Weber as an enemy or themselves as victors.

Weber has treated them decently, tried to steer some to higher paying job openings and generally has "looked out for some of us," according to some black workers.

As for their "victory," blacks note that the modest training program that inspired the history-making lawsuit has been suspended because of layoffs and that in any case it did not exactly floorboard the engine of progress.

They don't particularly blame the company. Kaiser Aluminum and Chemical Co., Weber's employer, has developed as energetic and enlightened an affirmative action program as any major corporation, by all accounts a model program.

But the problem is this: even at its best, the process seems to spin its wheels in a mire of complexity and contradiction. And wherever you go, from the cool thrum of the high-tech computer companies to banking towers to the heat and clang of a plant floor, the message is that affirmative action does not create good jobs. And it has a difficult time moving people into good jobs.

As the U.S. Civil Rights Commission observed plaintively in a recent memo, supporters of affirmative action need to round up some "success stories" to fight the public perception that the policy is unworkable. Evidence of how success is achieved, or even a clear definition of what it is, they found, is "almost totally lacking."

Based though it is in group rights and statistical formulas, it seems anyone looking for a coping manual on this vast machinery must rely to a great extent on what the folks working the jobs say, the ordinary people who make it work, if it works at all, and who feel the consequences either way.

————

Kaiser's Gramercy plant, on the Mississippi about an hour's drive from New Orleans, is a part of the "billion-dollar strip" of oil, sugar, coal and steel refineries strung along the levee in a pungent haze, their towers belching flame.

Here, along the levee, men prowl the dusk with shotguns, looking for rabbits for supper, and the white teen-ager hanging out at the filling station with friends still answers a white visitor who asks directions to a house with, "That's the nigger section, ma'am."

A wiry black Gramercy worker named Kernell Goudia, 45, embodies both the hope and despair of the historic ruling in Weber. He is a graduate of the training program worked out with the United Steelworkers Union which skipped over Weber in order to admit a less-senior black.

In the case, the Supreme Court ruled, 5 to 2, that where there is a racial imbalance, a voluntary plan giving one race preference over another may be permitted, despite the prohibition against racial discrimination in the Civil Rights Act of 1964.

The court was addressing the sort of barriers faced by blacks such as Goudia (pronounced go-DAY), after his military service. Most vocational schools refused to admit blacks. Black schools taught only the lower-paying skills for "black jobs."

The training program enabled him to move into one of the prized craft jobs, repairing electrical instruments. He lives in a comfortable house with his family, holds a union title and enjoys a certain stature in the plant. But as a black, he says, he stands out.

Goudia and his co-workers measure their progress in terms like this:

"A white worker wouldn't let a black man touch his tools when Kernell was going through the program," co-worker Yahya Muhammed recalled. Muhammed was halfway though the training when it was suspended.

"Now, the rank and file, they've pretty much accepted that we're going to be working with them," Goudia said.

Like many of their counterparts around the country, they blame instead certain union officials and supervisors in particular and society in general.

According to court records in the Weber case, blacks constituted 39 percent of the workforce in the community (and 46 percent of the total population) but held only 15 percent of jobs at the Gramercy plant and 2 percent of the craft jobs. In the higher-paying skilled crafts, five of 273 jobs were held by blacks.

To these black workers, the phrase "reverse discrimination" seems ludicrous.

Since 1974, the special programs at 12 Kaiser plants have graduated 162 white men, 62 white women, 50 minority men and four minority women, according to a company spokesman. Only one still offers the training. "Right now, there are no positions to train for," he added.

In fact, at Kaiser, as elsewhere, concerns have shifted from hiring and promotions to layoffs.

"Opportunities laboriously created in the 1970s may be destroyed during hard times in the 1980s," warns the U.S. Commission on Civil Rights, referring to existing layoff systems based on seniority. To break the "last-hired, first-fired" cycle, the commission has recommended a proportional layoff procedure and other alternatives. But these pit workers already on the job against one another, stir gut resentments and face a tough road through the courts.

Said Muhammed, "We need knowledge. . . . Most blacks I know work three or four jobs. They have to do that to make any money. But they get no legacy of knowledge to pass on. . . . The white man gets it working in his daddy's shop. My daddy ain't got no shop."

Weber, meanwhile, is still in his old job as a laboratory technician. He is not surprised, he said, to hear that the workers have some good things to say about him. "I was a union grievance official for years. I think the black people realized I represented them equally."

Weber, as it happens, is taking political science courses. He said he plans to run for office in his parish.

———

A continent away at Kaiser's white collar headquarters tower in Oakland, Calif., Bonnie Guiton, 40, a chic black woman, works out of an elegant corner executive suite with a sweeping, plate-glass view of San Francisco, the Bay Bridge and the buttery sun as it sets.

In her three years at the company, she has risen to vice president and general manager of Kaiser Center Inc., the headquarters complex.

In contrast to Goudia, she has an impressive string of education, credentials and awards. As recently as 15 years ago, she never would have been considered for a top post at Kaiser. As it is, Kaiser management sought her out.

She grew up in the area. Her mother was a maid, sometimes on welfare, and her father had left home. Guiton's first job was in a government mail room. It wasn't until she was 30 years old and had a daughter that she started college, working her way through as a secretary and ending up with a master's degree.

She became an assistant dean at Mills College in Oakland and later head of the Marcus A. Foster Educational Institute where Kaiser found her.

In recent ceremonies, the chairman of the board pinned a diamond tie pin on the executive whose equal employment opportunity efforts included "hiring Bonnie Guiton and shepherding her career."

Top Kaiser executives tell line managers that future promotions depend in part on how well they implement affirmative action programs, including pursuing an array of minority recruiting activities, establishing contacts with minority schools and community groups, planning management seminars and competitions which give points for affirmative action and adopting voluntary racial quotas for training programs.

"It happened to be a plus that I was black and female," said Guiton. "But I have never felt like an 'affirmative action hire' in that sense. I have to tell you it's been easy for me to feel like a colleague here at Kaiser. I'm treated as an equal."

Every worker has a different perspective. Estelle Wrisley, a white woman who coordinates international traffic for Kaiser, talking to far-flung steamship companies and plant managers, said, "If not for affirmative action, I don't think I would ever have been hired. I had 14 interviews before I was hired, and I was the first woman placed in a position like this."

And Andrea Robinson, a black female Kaiser labor attorney, said with a faint smile, "I think my position is the woman's slot. My predecessor was a woman. . . . My biggest gripe is that we are still called on to be *super* people."

Affirmative action is always going to work some places better than others. "It depends on who the manager is," says Thomas Bowdle, director of equal employment affairs for Kaiser. "One of the best plants we have is in Jacksonville, Fla., and that's after a period of layoffs."

One of the spurs Kaiser uses to promote progress involves summoning managers from around the country to seminars in the coastal resort town of Carmel, Calif. "We want the superintendent from Gramercy to sit down in the same meeting with the one from, say, Trentwood [Spokane, Wash.] and hear how they're handling it up there."

Kaiser's numbers look good: for instance, while its professional and managerial positions increased by 30 percent in the last decade, the participation rate for minorities increased by 232 percent and for women (including minorities) by 404 percent. That still leaves the company with 9 percent minorities (including women) in that category, and 7.5 percent women.

But, just as lousy numbers don't necessarily mean an employer is unfair, the Civil Rights Commission has said, good numbers don't prove an employer offers true equal opportunity.

However, Kaiser goes the extra mile. The company's policy includes such actions as getting a maitre d' fired when a restaurant or country club refuses to serve an integrated group of its employes. "It's the consistency," Bowdle said. "It doesn't improve your numbers, but it creates a value system."

Workers and others across the land seem to agree that each work setting requires a different and sometimes painful process of trial and error which may or may not add up, often in ways no one can chart, to change.

Switch to a different sort of industry and you run into a different need.

Jim Talley, a black graduate of Howard University here, like most of those with electronic engineering degrees, was able to pick his employer instead of the other way around. Interviewed by 30 companies, he had job offers from 15 or 20. "I was determined not to work in a program for blacks. I wanted to be viewed as an engineer, not an 'affirmative action hire.' "

He ended up at Hewlett-Packard Co., one of the oldest and largest of the silicon chip pioneers in the rolling coastal hills of California, known as Silicon Valley because of its concentration of high-tech computer companies.

Federal affirmative action enforcers under the Carter administration had singled out this and other high-tech industries for special pressure and criticism because they hold many jobs of the future. But that didn't work.

In California, for instance, the schools will turn out only one-tenth the number of electronic engineers needed over the next five years, by industry estimates.

"We're too desperate to care about race, color or plumbing," summed up one industry spokesman. A congressional report noted recently that the industry is even going to Japan and Korea to import skilled workers.

So, why aren't more minorities and women taking advantage of these job openings?

"The ones who are motivated to go to college at all tend to go into the higher-paying professions such as law or medicine, or they become teachers or social workers. That's their self-image. Those are their role models," summed up Ken Coleman, a black man who is manager of corporate staffing for Hewlett-Packard.

Isolation from peers can also be a problem, he added. Even educated blacks are sometimes reluctant to follow a company to a place like this one, where the population is only 4 percent black.

In order to overcome various blocks, Coleman and others believe it will take a lot more of the sort of aggressive and early outreach that snared Anthony Watkins, son of a taxi driver in St. Thomas, Virgin Islands. He was recruited by a Howard University professor who was looking for promising science students at black schools which lacked the capacity to train engineers. He took his finds to Howard under a specially funded program.

Now, at 27, Watkins is a production engineer in charge of "i.o." (input-output memory) for the HP 3000 series computer.

The great historical tug and pull of economic growth and contraction has had its effects on the migrations of blacks, just as on other Americans, bringing blacks to Oakland to fill World War II buildup jobs, for instance, or out of the South to the manufacturing plants of the Northeast and now back to the Sun Belt South. But always before, the pattern of discrimination got built into the hiring and promotion structure, civil rights leaders say.

For Hispanics now concentrated in the Southwest, and for blacks in the South — both growth areas — there is a chance to use civil rights laws now in place to start afresh, and prevent recurrence of the old patterns from the ground up, says Eleanor Holmes Norton, former Equal Employment Opportunity Commission head, now a law professor at Georgetown. "But only if the government enforces the laws."

Still, employers who want to avoid real change usually can find a way to do that and still placate the enforcers, specialists say.

Containment and tokenism are among the dodges developed by some employers, according to sociologist Joe Feagin of the University of Texas, a specialist in the subject.

One of the most familiar defenses, tokenism, involves placing women or minorities in "conspicuous and/or powerless positions," or channeling them into job ghettos such as a "department of community affairs," Feagin said, isolating them from one another, from "important organizational networks" and from the path to real power.

Increasing the number of tokens can help reduce the stress and turnover rate, allow support groups to form and improve performance, some say.

On the other hand, using the level of complaints and lawsuits, rather than statistics, as a barometer for distinguishing among fair and unfair employers may not work so well either, according to many workers and specialists. The employers who try hardest to develop good programs may suffer more than their share of lawsuits and bad publicity.

"Maybe it's the consciousness-raising within the organization," suggested Joan Bicocchi, EEO administrator for a New Orleans Coca-Cola bottling plant. Sometimes, she said, echoing statements by numerous others, it boils down to employes' intimidating the boss, "especially if you're a consumer products company where your public image is important."

———

Some degree of federal enforcement is necessary to make affirmative action work, specialists say, but even the most impressive show of muscle sometimes proves futile.

For instance, in the costly, 10-year case of a Uniroyal Inc. plant, hailed as a showcase victory by civil rights groups, the government used its ultimate weapon — debarment of the company from all federal contracts. It won a multimillion-dollar back pay penalty for discrimination and a legal agreement to implement affirmative action measures.

After three years, all this has had no noteworthy effect on employment opportunities for women and minorities in the plant, which is suffering from an industry slump, according to company spokesmen. Federal officials say they cannot deny this, since they have failed to keep track of the company's employment figures.

PERSONNEL OFFICE TRANSFORMED INTO A NEW CENTER OF POWER

The old personnel office, traditionally a backwater of payroll clerks, has been transformed into a power center — hardly surprising in the era of "under-utilization," the "eight-factor analysis," and other refinements of equal opportunity law.

As Thomas N. Bowdle, a stolid, white, former FBI agent turned director of equal opportunity affairs for the Kaiser Aluminum and Chemical Corp., observes: "The development of affirmative action has done more to force companies to focus on how they manage their workforces than anything that's been done."

For the first time on a wide scale, the policy has forced bosses to explain why they fire one person or promote another, noted John Blodger, a black employe relations executive with the Bendix Corp. and an officer of the American Association of Personnel Administrators.

Virtually every major company and institution these days has its "EEO operatives." Ideally, their equal employment opportunity mission is to integrate fairness into routine management procedures. But in practice, their success is more often defined as keeping employers out of trouble with the feds and the courts, guiding them through the maze of rules that can shape key decisions and that might cost them big bucks.

This vast legal machinery also nourishes a support industry of lawyers, data services, statisticians, placement services and others. They speak their own jargon, practice their own insider gamesmanship.

And, they wrestle with questions like:

□ An outside study at a Fortune 500 corporation showed women were less likely than men to have sought and accepted promotion. Will the government hold the company responsible for cultural conditioning that suppressed the aspirations of its female employes and force it to take action?

▫ An American Indian in Albuquerque wants an Internal Revenue Service job and files suit on grounds he has been unjustly excluded by quotas based on race. In light of a federal decision giving preference in job exams to blacks and Hispanics, what position will officials take on an Indian applicant?

▫ You are a university admissions officer with one student slot. Your choice is between the son of a black Park Avenue Ph.D. and the son of a white Appalachian coal miner who never got past third grade. Their test scores are equal. In the spirit of affirmative action, whom do you admit?

Some of these briefcase Solomons maintain that confronting difficult choices is what much of modern management is all about anyway.

However, in such a diverse and creative society, the manifestations can prove quirky:

There was the "white male" denied promotion who went to court to acquire a Hispanic surname so he would be eligible for special preferences.

There are black workers suing city governments with black mayors and a majority black population.

There is the possibility that regulations protecting Asian Americans against discrimination at the hands of a white economic establishment now may hit Japanese employers opening plants in this country (a question to be decided by the Supreme Court).

There is the white woman manager who says she bitterly resents being told she "has to hire a black for the next vacancy," but then remembers how she got her own position as the boss of six men.

There are women who won't work for women, blacks who won't hire blacks, husbands fighting mixed emotions about the special advantages they see going to their professional wives, and a human Rubik's cube of other variations.

If protections against age discrimination are thrown in, it seems, fair employment laws embrace virtually everybody except able-bodied young white males. "If you fall off a bar stool and break your leg, or if you grow old, you're in," Bowdle said.

Their jargon deals in the expanding definitions of discrimination, which emphasize "effects" as well as intent, and "institutional" as well as personal forces.

A critical sticking point here, as in the tug-of-war over the Voting Rights Act, is an apparent reliance on "proportional representation," the notion that in a just society, each race, gender and ethnic group will somehow be represented in proportion to its numbers in every occupational, educational or other setting.

For instance, when it was found that 1.3 percent of the chemical engineers residing in Orange, Tex., were either women or minorities, federal enforcers then required the synthetic rubber plant there to analyze its workforce. Because the plant did not have that same percentage of women and minority chemical engineers, the employer was required to "declare under-utilization," and take action to achieve that proportion.

How does an employer find the percentage of black chemical engineers available in Orange, Tex., or the proportion of female auditors available in Chicago, for instance? Enter the eight-factor analysis. Affirmative action in such cases would have employers divide their work-forces into job categories and do a "utilization analysis" based on such things as the percentage of minorities and women who hold a certain degree relative to their need.

There are seminars and pamphlets and audiovisual films. There are incantations — likely to put a righteous fear into managers — of cases such as AT&T's comeuppance to the tune of $15 million in back pay and $50 million in promotional pay and wage adjustments.

Major corporations have pooled their resources to develop their own EEO data banks. Placement experts track various shapes and colors of job candidates.

Bill Marumoto, a headhunter based in Georgetown and a former Nixon official, has a notebook identifying, for example, some 2,000 marketing employes in the New York-New Jersey area broken down by "EEO code." When a deodorant manufacturer wanted a black candidate for a job as product manager, Marumoto knew where to find him.

In the political "High Noon" brewing over affirmative action, the establishment specialists who work the territory may be the heaviest guns on the side of civil rights groups.

"The Fortune 500 don't want affirmative action killed, just made reasonable," said one civil rights lawyer. "They've learned to live with it. Anyway, some of these executives have built little fiefdoms around it. The personnel office was never so powerful before."

While much attention has focused on the employers' gripes about government contrariness, an increasing number have experienced a rite of passage, specialists say.

After a period of resistance, they went through the initial shock of seeing a woman or black in a staff meeting, and finally began to see some pluses — such as opening up for themselves new pools of previously wasted talent which, in a highly competitive market, can cut costs and increase productivity.

"We like to think of it practically," and Kaiser executive Howard Nelson. "To use a sports analogy, there are some southern schools that wouldn't be playing the kind of ball they are today if they had continued to keep out black players."

At AT&T, it was only after they felt the "spur" of affirmative action that telephone company executives realized "the more efficient and equitable personnel selection and assessment system adopted by AT&T (and its affiliates) puts the telephone company in a much stronger position to compete with other firms . . . ," Dr. Bernard Anderson, a Rockefeller Foundation economist, told a House subcommittee.

Increasing the labor pool can mean less-costly labor. The law sometimes allows an employer to do something he wanted to do anyway, hire women and blacks and blame it on the government, some managers say. The tighter labor market of the future may make this course even more attractive, some specialists believe.

Borne along on an anti-regulation, anti-big-government tide, Reagan officials landed on this treacherous ground at a run, proposing changes in the enforcement machinery, reducing staff and budgets. But now they are squabbling among themselves over how to proceed, their policy signals have been muddled and they have pleased none of the sides. Others, such as Sen. Orrin G. Hatch (R-Utah), have found it wise to tone down their attacks on the issue in an election year.

Most all concerned agree that, for most of its history, the federal enforcement bureaucracy has been chaotic, fragmented, its personnel often poorly trained or overly zealous. It was only late in the Carter administration that there was enough law on the books and federal rationality to make the program credible. "Before that, we had no program," said Day Piercy of Women Employed.

Affirmative action rules for private sector employers now are enforced mostly by the Labor Department's obscure Office of Federal Contract Compliance Programs.

The Equal Employment Opportunity Commission, the Office of Personnel Management, and the Justice Department also play roles in the public and/or private sector.

———

All of this machinery spins around human judgments about who can do a job. The great myth among the "unwashed" is that businessmen used to have some scientific, well-thought-out system for judging qualifications and performance, said Kaiser's Bowdle.

To illustrate, he tells a few stories about white guys who didn't get hired because they didn't go to the right school, wore a funny looking suit or had a southern instead of northern accent.

"The white male who succeeds has had somebody in their career do something for them that fits exactly the description of affirmative action and that doesn't take anything away from anybody."

While white women have numerous hurdles to overcome, ranging from sexual harassment to ingrained notions of their "proper place," specialists say, it is nevertheless easier to integrate white women than black, particularly in the higher white-collar echelons. They cite a variety of reasons from sheer numbers to cultural background.

"A white woman will have the same father as the white male," summed up Kaiser Vice President Nelson.

Many EEO specialists are themselves white women or minorities. Some grumble that it's a no-win job, often lacking real influence, with a hostile management on one hand, dissatisfied employes on the other, and under siege by government enforcers and civil rights groups which, they say, don't even understand how business operates.

Between 1972 and 1979, the number of personnel and labor relations specialists increased from 310,000 to 413,000, according to the Bureau of Labor Statistics. The proportion of women in that category rose from 31 to 45.5 percent and minorities rose from 9 to 10.2 percent.

———

The moral and philosophical arguments over affirmative action, which have flamed up brighter than ever under the Reagan administration, often seem strangely unrelated to practical reality.

At the political extremes, one side claims not to care how well affirmative action tactics work. They believe its use of quotas and preferential treatment is unjust, unconstitutional and un-American.

The other side claims not to care that affirmative action is politically unpopular. They believe the government has a duty to enforce it because it is right, like taxation.

Black conservative economist Thomas Sowell has drawn considerable blood in combat with civil rights forces with his brassy, well-researched assaults on this and other government programs, which he says are only quick fixes that serve in the long run to "undermine self-reliance and pride of achievement" among blacks.

Black leaders, an elite out of touch with their own constituency, he says, have focused the debate on past wrongs, rather than present results.

Sowell also ridicules the theory that statistical representation of a group can be used to measure discrimination, calling it "the noble lie of our time."

His adversaries counter that Sowell, having benefited from government-driven change himself, now selfishly discounts its importance to others. His emphasis on the importance of hard work and education for blacks, they argue, grossly underestimates the monstrous drag of race.

However, even within the ranks of the civil rights community there is disagreement about who the program is supposed to help, tension over who it has helped.

Civil rights attorney Morris Abram and others argue that it ought to have focused on lifting the most disadvantaged.

But Eleanor Holmes Norton, head of the EEOC under Carter, says the "poverty program concept of affirmative action" is wrong.

"Affirmative action is a legal remedy to overcome specific exclusion of specific groups, not something that gives people a little boost up . . . This is not a gratuity. This is not a benefit," she says.

"[This] is a legal remedy for a legal wrong. It must be understood that way or else we don't understand it at all."

Each group lumped under the catch-phrase of "women and minorities" has a very different history, culture and struggle.

Leaders of the fragile coalition, made even more tenuous by the pressures of hard times and unequal progress, are at some pains to downplay the deepening conflicts within their ranks.

Blacks, who speak bitterly of the gains made by white women in a program originally conceived for them, also face competition from growing numbers of illegal aliens, most of them constituents of Hispanic interest groups.

The administration, having alienated blacks, is still reportedly trying to attract Hispanic voters into the Republican fold, appealing to their strong Catholic and family values, supporting some programs aimed at them.

Asian Americans, a relatively tiny group, remain "protected" even though they have earnings higher than the national average.

Liberal Jewish groups already have split from other factions because of their adamant opposition to quotas, which victimized them in the past. And labor groups are opposing the attacks on the seniority system by white women and minorities.

Will the affirmative action effort die of complications? Does America want to give up the experiment?

Clearly many Americans — including some intended beneficiaries — feel they've been conned by double-speak on affirmative action. Some feel misled about its promise, others about its proper bounds.

They've been told that quotas are not quotas but flexible "goals," when plainly in many cases the distinction is meaningless. Some courts have not hesitated to call them by that name.

They've been told that the plan is not to carve each workforce into the ethnic and racial mold of the larger society, even though the "effects test" clearly has become the standard for spotting discrimination.

They've been told that it is unfair to call this "reverse discrimination" unless blacks, for instance, could somehow systematically oppress whites for a century or two. Affirmative action is an attempt to dismantle, not to engage in, such a process. It is "color-conscious" only in order to create the equilibrium of the ideal color-blind (and sex-neutral) society, its defenders say.

"Although particular affirmative action plans may adversely affect particular white men as individuals, they do not unfairly burden white men as a group," the U.S. Civil Rights Commission explains.

But many white men use unprintable words to describe their feelings about that distinction.

Opinion polls have regularly reported that Americans — white, black, female, whatever — are overwhelmingly opposed to quotas. But, clearly, when treated to a certain body of facts, reasonable people have been persuaded that, sometimes, quotas are justified.

At the least, then, the times seem to demand a little honest talk, a more straight-arrow selling job than the public has been given.

Because, despite their aversion to some of the tactics used so far, Americans are also expressing to the pollsters an increasing tolerance of human differences and a significant desire, for whatever motives, to offer a fair chance to everybody.

People seem open to the notion that some sort of positive action, judiciously applied to fit varying situations and sometimes even including quotas, is in the best interests of the society.

"There are lots of idealogues off on a binge right now," said William Taylor of Catholic University, a veteran civil rights activist. "The practical consequences are not all that apparent yet.

"The vested interest in the established peace and good order may assist us. Businesses and others may be unsettled by the prospect of social conflict and chaos. That's sort of a negative optimistic outlook."

Perhaps workers like Kaiser Aluminum's Yahya Muhammed have the clearest view of how things work. "I think it's gonna be better for my kids," said the black New Orleans plant worker, frustrated so far by the illusory promises of affirmative action. "But not because of the system. It's because I'm going to make it better, one way or another."

Moving toward Unbiased Selection
Marilyn K. Quaintance

. . .

REGULATORY MANDATE FOR UNBIASED SELECTION: UNIFORM GUIDELINES ON EMPLOYEE SELECTION PROCEDURES

Evolution of the Uniform Guidelines

Approximately one year after Title VII of the Civil Rights Act of 1964 took effect, the EEOC issued its testing guidelines (August 24, 1966) to assist employers covered by the statute (i.e., private employers with fifteen or more employees, labor organizations with thirty-five or more members, and private employment agencies). The late 1960s and the early 1970s saw issuances regarding testing practices from "three separate federal agencies having responsibility for eliminating employment discrimination, each with its own policies and guidelines or orders and areas of authority" (Novick, 1982, p. 76). The documents published by the EEOC, the Department of Labor's Office of Federal Contract Compliance (OFCC) and the U.S. Civil Service Commission (CSC) are presented in Fig. 1, which is reproduced from A *Professional and Legal Analysis of*

Reprinted with permission from M. Cohen and R. T. Golembiewski (eds.) *Public Personnel Update.*
New York: Marcel Dekker, 1984.

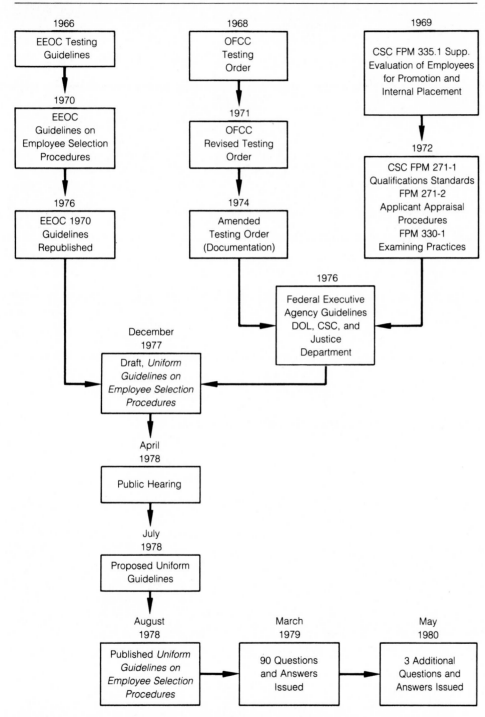

Source: Reprinted from *A Professional and Legal Analysis of the Uniform Guidelines on Employee Selection Procedures,* copyright 1981 by The American Society for Personnel Administration, 606 N. Washington St., Alexandria, VA 22314, $52.50.

the Uniform Guidelines on Employee Selection Procedures prepared by the Ad Hoc Group on Uniform Selection Guidelines.

With the passage of the Equal Employment Opportunity Act in March of 1972, Title VII coverage was extended to include all public employers and private educational institutions. Section 715 of the EEO Act of 1972 created the Equal Employment Opportunity Coordinating Council (EEOCC) to coordinate more closely enforcement activities of the various federal agencies. The EEOC members, who included the Secretary of the Department of Labor, the Attorney General of the Department of Justice, and the Chairpersons of the U.S. CSC, the Civil Rights Commission and the EEOC, directed their staffs to draft uniform selection guidelines. While the project began in February of 1973, a uniform document was not published in the *Federal Register* until November 23, 1976. That document, the *Federal Executive Agency Guidelines (FEA Guidelines)* was endorsed by the CSC and the Departments of Labor and Justice. On November 24, 1976, to demonstrate its opposition to the *FEA Guidelines,* the EEOC republished verbatim its 1970 EEOC testing guidelines. The CRC joined EEOC in opposition to the *FEA Guidelines.*

In early 1977 EEOC Chair Eleanor Holmes Norton directed her staff to reopen negotiations with the Justice Department in order to achieve a uniform set of selection guidelines. After many drafts were circulated among federal enforcement agencies, the "Proposed Uniform Guidelines on Employee Selection Procedures" were jointly published in the *Federal Register* for comment by EEOC, CSC, and the Departments of Labor and Justice on December 30, 1977. After public hearings and meetings with employer and civil rights group representatives, the agencies issued the *Uniform Guidelines on Employee Selection Procedures* on Aug. 25, 1978, to be effective September 25 of that same year. On Sept. 11, 1978, the Office of Revenue Sharing of the Department of the Treasury endorsed the *Uniform Guidelines* and directed all recipient governments to use selection procedures consistent with the guidelines. Two sets of interpretive questions and answers were later published in the *Federal Register* on March 2, 1979 and May 2, 1980.

Description and Coverage of the Uniform Guidelines

The Uniform Guidelines on Employee Selection Procedures were written to interpret Title VII of the Civil Rights Act, as amended by the Equal Employment Opportunity Act of 1972. The *Uniform Guidelines* are *guidelines* not "regulations," since EEOC does not have the authority to issue substantive regulations. The guidelines were written to eliminate discrimination, not to establish standards for test development and validation. The *Uniform Guidelines* are triggered by the presence of adverse impact (i.e., a substantially different rate of selection) for a given racial, sex, or ethnic group.

Nearly all public and private employers are covered by the *Uniform Guidelines* including:

1. Employers with fifteen or more employees who are covered by Title VII

2. Contractors covered by Executive Order 11246, as amended by Executive Orders 11375 and 12086

3. Government employers receiving revenue-sharing funds from the Department of the Treasury who are covered by the State and Local Fiscal Assistance Act of 1972, as amended

4. Government employers receiving grant-in-aid funds under the Intergovernmental Personnel Act of 1970, as amended, who must comply with the *Standards for a Merit System of Personnel Administration* to which the *Uniform Guidelines* were appended

5. Employers receiving funds from the Law Enforcement Assistance Administration under the Omnibus Crime Control and Safe Streets Act of 1968, as amended.

With such broad coverage, it is necessary for most employers to have a clear understanding of the major provisions of the *Uniform Guidelines* and their corresponding requirements for compliance.

Major Provisions of the Uniform Guidelines

Adverse Impact. The term adverse impact evolved from problems in the concept of discrimination. Initially, the concept of discrimination meant evil intention on the part of the employer to discriminate against members of a particular group (Miner and Miner, 1978). Civil rights advocates found that it was difficult to prove evil intention on the part of the employer and, consequently, women and minorities did not make much progress entering the workforce under this definition.

Miner and Miner (1978) have suggested that, for this reason, the definition of discrimination was broadened to encompass *unequal or disparate treatment*. Under this new definition, evidence of discrimination was present if the employer used a different selection procedure for members of different groups (e.g., for whites and blacks) or the same procedure in a differential manner for different groups. Even when employers were forced to equate selection processes and standards for all groups, however, minorities did not make much progress entering the workforce.

As a result, the definition of discrimination was broadened to include *adverse impact theory*. When a selection process has adverse impact on members of a particular racial, sex, or ethnic group, the employer must eliminate the adverse impact (by modifying a procedure, by eliminating a procedure, or by selecting an alternative selection procedure) or otherwise justify the selection process by federal law (e.g., by demonstrating the job-relatedness or validity of the selection procedure having the adverse impact).

The *Uniform Guidelines* require employers to collect data to demonstrate the degree of adverse impact of their selection procedures on various racial, sex, and ethnic groups when those procedures are used to make employment decisions. *Selection procedures* are defined in Sec. 16Q as any of the various measures used as the basis for any employment decision. The guidelines state, "Selection procedures include the full range of assessment techniques from traditional paper and pencil tests, performance tests, training programs, or probationary periods and physical, educational, and work experience requirements through informal or casual interviews and unscored application forms." Other examples of selection procedures include medical examinations, oral boards, and assessment centers (see also Sec. 2C and Questions and Answers 5 and 6). The *Uniform Guidelines* also cover the *total selection process* which means any combination of selection procedures that is used as the basis for *any* employment decision. *Employment decisions* are defined as including, but not limited to, "hiring, promotion, demotion, membership (for example in a labor organization), referral, retention, and licensing and certification, to the extent that licensing and certification may be covered by Federal equal employment opportunity law. Other selection decisions, such as selection for training or transfer, may also be considered employment decisions if they lead to any of the decisions listed above" (see Sec. 2B and Question and Answer 6).

Employers must have available data showing whether the total selection process for a job has adverse impact on any racial, sex, or ethnic group constituting at least two percent of the labor force in the relevant labor area or two percent of the applicable workforce in the case of promotions. Adverse impact calculations are to be made on an annual basis [see Sec. 15A (2)(a)]. Before discussing the nature of these calculations, we shall examine who is covered by the adverse impact data collection system, how the data should be collected, the nature of the data to be collected, and the consequences for failure to collect adverse impact statistics.

Who Is Covered: Definition of Applicant/Candidate. The *Uniform Guidelines* require the collection of adverse impact data for all applicants and candidates. Question and Answer 15 defines an applicant as "a person who has indicated an interest in being considered for hiring, promotion or other employment opportunities. This interest might be expressed by completing an application form or might be expressed orally *depending upon the employer's practice*" (emphasis added). Thus, the *Uniform Guidelines* contain a loose definition of the term "applicant," suggesting that anyone walking into an office and expressing an interest in employment is an "applicant." However, the phrase, "depending upon the employer's practice," suggests that employers can voluntarily tighten up the definition of applicant and make this definition agency policy. Such a definition might read:

> A *bonafide applicant* is a person who personally completed and filed with the employer a formal written application for a specific job for which the employer was accepting applications on the date and at the place of receipt of the application . . . A person who makes formal or informal inquiry about employment opportunities in general or about specific jobs for which the employer is not currently accepting applications is not considered to be a bonafide applicant. Likewise, a person referred to an employer by a third party is not considered to be a bonafide applicant as defined above. [American Petroleum Institute, comments on record keeping regulations, 1978].

Most employers receive unsolicited resumes in the mail. These individuals should receive a form letter, job announcement information, and an application form if the employer is hiring. To be considered an applicant, the individual must complete and return the application form and specify a particular job. Employers who are not hiring may retain resumes in a "recruitment file" (not an applicant file). When a job vacancy occurs, all individuals should be notified by sending a job announcement and an application form.

Question and Answer 15 further state that "a person who *voluntarily* withdraws formally or informally at any stage of the selection process is no longer an applicant or candidate for purposes of computing adverse impact" (emphasis added). For example, if an individual passes the first selection procedure (e.g., a written test), but is not present for the second procedure (e.g., an oral examination), that individual is dropped from calculations of the degree of adverse impact for the total selection process and for any component part of that process. If voluntary withdrawals are heavily minority, the employer may wish to contact a sample to determine why they are not competing further in the selection process. Employers should ensure that neither their practices nor reputation are having a "chilling effect" on minority applicants.

Finally, Question and Answer 15 clarify the distinction between the terms "applicant" and "candidate" as used in the *Uniform Guidelines*. The term "candidate" refers to those situations where the employer is considering current employees for promotion or for training or other employment opportunities, without inviting applications.

How to Collect Adverse Impact Data.   To determine the adverse impact of a given selection decision, the employer must have data regarding sex and racial or ethnic group membership for a particular applicant or candidate. Question and Answer 8 state that the *Uniform Guidelines* have not specified a particular procedure for collecting such data and that "the federal enforcement agencies will accept different procedures that capture the necessary information." Such procedures include a log or applicant flow chart based upon visual observation, identifying the number of persons expressing an interest by sex and by race or national origin, personal knowledge by the employer, or self-identification.

One problem in collecting demographic data is the disparity between self-reports and visual observations. One study showed substantial disagreement between data provided by Hispanics' self-identification and visual observation of Hispanics (Northrup, 1977). Further research corroborated the disparity between self-identification and visual observation data for Hispanics and revealed misclassifications on the basis of sex as well. As long as these disparities continue to appear, it seems that the only legally defensible procedure for employers to follow is to rely on self-identification, even though some faking will undoubtedly occur. Also, research by the Personnel Research and Development Center (PRDC) of the Office of Personnel Management noted that larger proportions of both whites and males did not complete the form. However, another PRDC study demonstrated that the nonresponse rate decreased over time, apparently as applicants became familiar with the system and as they saw that the data were not being misused.

Some formal guidance for race/ethnic/sex data collection procedures has been issued in the *Federal Register* [Guidelines for the Collection of Race, Ethnic Background, Age and Sex Information for Benefits from Federal Programs (including employment) 44 *Federal Register* No. 238, Dec. 10, 1979]. The guidelines require that: (1) data be collected on a separate, detachable portion of the application; (2) the data collection form contain a statement telling applicants the purpose for the data collection and assuring them that the data will not be used for purposes of discrimination; (3) data be cross-matched for compliance purposes; (4) visual observation be used as a back-up if self-identification data are not supplied; and (5) completion of the self-identification data collection form is voluntary. A sample self-identification data collection form attempting to meet these requirements is shown in Fig. 2.

What Data to Collect.   For each applicant and candidate, the employer is responsible for maintaining records by sex and for the following groups: blacks; American Indians including Alaskan natives; Asians, including Pacific Islanders; Hispanics; and whites other than Hispanics (See Sec. 4B). While adverse impact calculations are made on the basis of groups (e.g., all men versus all women; all blacks versus all whites versus all Hispanics versus all Asians versus all American Indians), Question and Answer 87 require employers to collect data by subgroups (black males, black females, white males, white females, etc.) allowing the "identification of persons by sex, combined with race or ethnic group, so as to permit the identification of discriminating practices on any such basis." One reason for this is to provide data for subgroup discrimination charges. A recent Court of Appeals decision found discrimination against black females using subgroup statistics. (*Jefferies v. Harris Co. Community Action Association* 615 F. 2d 1025, CA 5, 1980).

Additionally, Question and Answer 86 require employers to maintain data on race, sex, and ethnic identification, and the effects of the selection procedure for all groups, even those constituting less than two percent of the labor force unless the employer has fewer than 100 employees. This data requirement is imposed on employers even

FIGURE 2
Background Survey Questionnaire

GENERAL INSTRUCTIONS

Please answer each of the questions to the best of your ability. Your responses are voluntary.
Please print entries in pencil or pen. Use only capital letters. Read each item thoroughly before completing the appropriate code number in each box.

Name (Last, First, MI)

Position for which you are applying | Date (Month, Day, Year)

THIS INFORMATION IS REQUESTED SOLELY FOR THE PURPOSE OF DETERMINING COMPLIANCE WITH FEDERAL CIVIL RIGHTS LAW, AND YOUR RESPONSE WILL NOT AFFECT CONSIDERATION OF YOUR APPLICATION. BY PROVIDING THIS INFORMATION YOU WILL ASSIST US IN ASSURING THAT THIS PROGRAM IS ADMINISTERED IN A NONDISCRIMINATORY MANNER.

| 1. Social Security Number | 2. Year of Birth | 3. Do you have any Physical Disability? |
| | 1 9 | 1 - Yes   2 - No |

4. Please categorize yourself in terms of the race, sex, and ethnic categories below. First read definitions of subcategories.

DEFINITIONS

The racial and ethnic categories for Federal statistics and administrative reporting are defined as follows:

ETHNICITY:

Hispanic. A person of Mexican, Puerto Rican, Cuban, Central or South American, or other Spanish culture or origin, regardless of race.

RACE:

American Indian or Alaskan Native. A person having origins in any of the original peoples of North America, and who maintains cultural identification through tribal affiliation or community recognition.

Asian or Pacific Islander. A person having origins in any of the original peoples of the Far East, Southeast Asia, the Indian subcontinent, or the Pacific Islands. The area includes, for example, China, India, Japan, Korea, the Philippine Islands, and Samoa.

Black. A person having origins in any of the black racial groups of Africa.

White. A person having origins in any of the original peoples of Europe, North Africa, or the Middle East.

A. RACE OR ETHNICITY	B. SEX
1 - AMERICAN INDIAN OR ALASKAN NATIVE 4 - BLACK	1 - MALE
2 - ASIAN OR PACIFIC ISLANDER 5 - WHITE	2 - FEMALE
3 - HISPANIC, OTHER THAN WHITE 6 - OTHER _____ *(Specify)*	

Note: This form is an adaptation of OPM Form 1386 (10/79) approved by OMB No. 50–RO–616. The categories under Section A have been redefined to separately classify "Whites" and "Hispanics other than Whites." Adapted by the International Personnel Management Association.

---

though they need not calculate adverse impact for any group constituting less than two percent of the relevant labor market.

Failure to Collect Data.   If an employer neglects to maintain data on the adverse impact of the employer's selection process on women or men or on members of various racial and ethnic groups, as required by the guidelines, then the employer can be charged with adverse impact in the case of underutilization. Underutilization is measured by the applicable workforce or relevant labor market. Applicable workforce refers to internal availability when jobs are filled from within. The relevant labor market is defined as those persons available with the necessary skills to perform the jobs in question (*Hazelwood School District v. United States*, 433 U.S. 299, 1977). The relevant labor market includes all persons who are willing, available, and qualified to perform a particular job (the internal or external labor pool or a combination of both). Sometimes geographical factors influence the size of the relevant labor market (such as commuting patterns or location of employer). Some guidance in assessing the distribution of minorities and women in the relevant labor market has been issued by the OPM former Office of Intergovernmental Personnel Programs (Harris and White, 1981).

Operational Definition of Adverse Impact: Calculation Exercise. Section 16B defines *adverse impact* as "a substantially different rate of selection in hiring, promotion or other employment decision which works to the disadvantage of members of a race, sex or ethnic group." The phrase "substantially different rate of selection" is clarified in Sec. 4D by the presentation of the four-fifths rule. Specifically, "a selection rate for any race, sex or ethnic group which is less than four-fifths (4/5) (or eighty percent) of the rate for the group with the highest rate will generally be regarded by the Federal enforcement agencies as evidence of adverse impact, while a greater than four-fifths rate will generally not be regarded by Federal enforcement agencies as evidence of adverse impact." The four-fifths rule, which was set arbitrarily (not statistically), is a rule of thumb for enforcement personnel. It was believed that this rule would be more easily understood by employers than the concept of statistical significance (i.e., a statistically significant difference between the selection rates for the groups).

The four-fifths rule is best explained by a numerical example. If 100 blacks applied for a job and 90 were accepted, the selection rate for blacks would be .90, or 90% (90 hired/100 applied). If, for the same job, 100 whites applied and all 100 were selected, the selection rate for whites would be 1.0, or 100% (100 hired/100 applied). To apply the four-fifths rule, the highest selection rate (i.e., 1.0) is multiplied times .8 (4/5). In our example, .80 × 1.0 = .80. We shall refer to this product as the *adverse impact threshold* [i.e., the numerical value obtained by multiplying four-fifths (80%, or .8) times the selection rate of the most successful group]. The selection rates for the other groups (blacks, in our example) must equal or exceed this threshold value, otherwise adverse impact is demonstrated. As the selection rate for blacks, .90, is greater than .80, the adverse impact threshold, there is no adverse impact against the blacks. However, had only 70 of the 100 blacks been hired, the selection rate for blacks of .70 (70 hired/100 applied) would have been less than .80, the adverse impact threshold, indicating adverse impact against the blacks.

Table 1 presents another numerical example. Visual comparison of the adverse impact threshold of 29.6% to the selection rate of blacks (23%) shows evidence of adverse impact against the blacks. However, as the selection rate of Hispanics (33%) is greater than the adverse impact threshold (29.6%), there is no evidence of adverse impact against the Hispanics.

If an employer meets the four-fifths rule, is the employer free from further investigation? Not necessarily. Section 4D also states that "smaller differences in selection rate may nevertheless constitute adverse impact, where they are significant in both

TABLE 1
Calculation of Adverse Impact*

	Whites	Blacks	Hispanics
Applied	43	13	6
Hired	16	3	2
Selection rate	37%	23%	33%
	$\frac{16}{43} = 37\%$	$\frac{3}{13} = 23\%$	$\frac{2}{6} = 33\%$

*To determine if adverse impact exists. Highest selection rate: whites at 37%; four-fifths rule: multiply four-fifths (80% or 0.8) times highest selection rate, or 37%. Adverse impact threshold: 37% × .8 = 29.6%.

statistical and practical terms or where a user's actions have discouraged applicants disproportionately on grounds of race, sex or ethnic group."

In our numerical example in Table 1, if one more black were hired, there would no longer be evidence of adverse impact against blacks. The resulting selection rate of 30.8% (4 hired/14 applied) would exceed the adverse impact threshold of 29.6%. Do the *Uniform Guidelines* address such circumstances in which the numbers may be so small that a change of one would result in a different conclusion when calculating adverse impact? Yes. Section 4D suggests that when numbers are too small to be reliable, the employer should continue collecting data over a longer period of time. The employer is also permitted to transport adverse impact data. That is, "evidence concerning the impact which the selection procedure had when used in the same manner in similar circumstances elsewhere may be considered in determining adverse impact."

In certain circumstances, an employer may violate the four-fifths rule: (1) when the differences are very small and not statistically significant, and (2) when special recruiting programs cause the candidate pool to be atypical.

Many authors have acknowledged the complexities involved in establishing an adverse impact data collection system. Bemis (1978) has recommended that such systems be computerized. Kraft (1978) has discussed various problems found in conducting studies on adverse impact in the federal government.

Quaintance (1981) summarized the extent of development of adverse impact data collection systems for federal, state, and local governments. Federal government agencies had only received approval for adverse impact data collection in January of 1980, using a special form developed by the OPM and approved by the Office of Management and Budget (OMB). Consequently, implementation of their systems was understandably delayed. To complicate matters, OMB approval of the adverse impact data collection form used by the federal government expired in January of 1982, with no attempts to have it renewed by OPM. As for progress by state governments, a 1980 survey by the International Personnel Management Association (IPMA) showed that approximately two-thirds of the thirty-two states responding were systematically collecting adverse impact data. The states without such data bases said that they were planning to develop them soon. Only six states had computerized systems for monitoring the adverse impact of their selection procedures. There was little uniformity among states in their methods of data collection (Quaintance, 1981). In some cases, the race and ethnic categories did not correspond to those defined in the *Uniform Guidelines*. One state had even devised its own formula for calculating adverse impact, disregarding the four-fifths rule.

Half of the municipalities responding to IPMA's survey of fifty-eight cities and counties reported that they had studied the degree of adverse impact of their selection procedures on minorities and women. A few larger cities had computerized systems. Several municipalities reported using a test of statistical significance as a back-up to the four-fifths rule.

The Committee on Ability Testing of the National Academy of Sciences supported the *Uniform Guidelines'* emphasis on the close investigation of any selection procedure having an adverse impact. The committee stated, "A healthy suspicion of such selection practices is warranted by the discriminating behavior that has tended to characterize American society. Enforcement of the *Guidelines* has revealed that many employment testing programs did not meet professional standards and were making no verifiable contribution to productivity" (Wigdor and Garner, 1982, p. 146).

The Bottom Line. The *total selection process* is defined as any combination of selection procedures that is used as the basis for any employment decision such as deciding whom to hire, selecting people to promote or demote, or picking candidates for training or the kind of transfer that leads to promotion. Section 4C of the *Uniform Guidelines* calls for an employer to examine initially adverse impact for the total selection process or the *bottom line*. If, for example, an assessment center and an oral examination are used in combination for selection decisions, to examine the extent of adverse impact, the employer would combine the total number in each racial, ethnic, or sex group selected after competing in the total selection process with the total number of each group who had originally applied. Section 4C states that if the total selection process for a job has adverse impact, then the component selection procedures should be evaluated for adverse impact. If, however, the total selection process does not have an adverse impact, "the Federal enforcement agencies, in the exercise of their administrative and prosecutorial discretion, in usual circumstances will not expect a user to evaluate the individual components for adverse impact, or to validate such individual components and will not take enforcement action based upon adverse impact of any component of that process."

Section 4C also describes certain exceptions to the bottom line defense: (1) if a selection procedure for assignments of incumbent employees is a significant factor in the continuation of patterns caused by prior discriminatory employment practices, or (2) if a selection procedure is considered to be non-job-related, based on the weight of court decisions or administrative interpretations. Other exceptions to the bottom line will be made in unusual circumstances, but only as a result of a decision at a high level within the federal enforcement agencies. Investigators and compliance officers are not authorized to make this decision (see Question and Answer 25).

Calculation Exercise. Table 2 presents an example of the calculation of adverse impact for the total selection process for the job of police officer. Applicants participate in a medical examination, a written examination, and an oral examination before the hiring decisions are made. Initially total selection rates are calculated for whites (90 hired/200 applied) = .45, or 45% (the highest selection rate), for blacks (40 hired/100 applied) = .40 or 40%, and for Hispanics (29 hired/80 applied) = .363, or 36.3%. Comparison of the total selection rates for blacks (40%) and for Hispanics (36.3%) with the adverse impact threshold (.8 × 45% = 36%) indicates no adverse impact for either of these two groups. *There is no adverse impact based upon bottom line statistics for either blacks or Hispanics.* However, a review of the adverse impact calculations for the component selection procedures reveals that the medical examination has adverse impact against Hispanics, while the written test has adverse impact against blacks. In this situation, with good bottom line statistics, according to the *Uniform Guidelines*, the employer would not be obligated to investigate the adverse impact of the component selection procedures (unless one of the exceptions specified in Sec. 4C is operational). While the federal enforcement agencies will generally, in their administrative and prosecutorial discretion, not proceed beyond the bottom line, an individual applicant or candidate always has the right to sue an employer under Title VII, charging that a particular component of the selection process is discriminatory.

Adverse Impact of Component Parts. A recent Supreme Court decision (*State of Connecticut v. Winnie Teal et al.*, Docket No. 80–2147, decided June 21, 1982) clearly established the right of plaintiffs to challenge any selection procedure as being discriminatory even in the presence of good bottom line statistics for the total selection process. Four black employees (including Winnie Teal) of the Department of Income Maintenance of the State of Connecticut were promoted provisionally to the position of welfare eligibility supervisor. To attain permanent status, the employees had to participate in a merit selection process. As a first step in the total selection process, all candidates had to take a written paper and pencil examination. Candidates who failed

TABLE 2
Calculation of Adverse Impact and the Bottom Line

Applicants	Medical Examination			Written Examination			Oral Examination			Total		
	Took	Passed	Pass Rate	Took	Passed	Pass Rate	Took	Passed	Pass Rate	Number Hired	Selection Rate	Bottom Line
Whites (200)	200	160	80%	160	128	80%	128	90	70.3%	90	45%	
Blacks (100)	100	85	85%	85	48	56.5%	48	40	83.3%	40	40%	No adverse impact
Hispanics (80)	80	48	60%	48	36	75%	36	29	80.6%	29	36.3%	No adverse impact

For the total selection process:

1. Calculate the *total selection rate* for each group.

$$\frac{\text{hired}}{\text{applied}} = \frac{90}{200} = 45\%; \quad \frac{40}{100} = 40\%; \quad \frac{29}{80} = 36.3\%$$

2. Apply the four-fifths rule to find the *adverse impact threshold.*

$0.8 \times 45\% = 36\%$

3. Compare the *selection rates* of the remaining groups with the threshold.

Black: $40\% > 36\%$; Hispanic: $36.3\% > 36\%$

As both rates are greater than the threshold, there is no indication of adverse impact for the *bottom line.*

For the written examination:

1. Calculate the *pass rates* for each group.

2. Calculate the *adverse impact threshold.*

$0.8 \times 80\% = 64\%$

3. It is concluded that the written examination has an adverse impact on blacks.

For the medical examination:

1. Calculate the *pass rates* for each group.

$$\frac{160}{200} = 80\%; \quad \frac{85}{100} = 85\%; \quad \frac{48}{80} = 60\%$$

2. Apply the four-fifths rule to find the *adverse impact threshold.*

$0.8 \times 85\% = 68\%$

3. Compare the pass rates of the remaining groups with the threshold.

White: $80\% > 68\%$; Hispanic: $60\% < 68\%$

As the selection rate for the Hispanics is less than the threshold, it is concluded that the medical examination has an adverse impact on Hispanics.

For the oral examination:

1. Calculate the *pass rates* for each group.

2. Calculate the *adverse impact threshold.*

$0.8 \times 83.3\% = 66.7\%$

3. It is concluded that the oral examination does not have an adverse impact on any group.

the examination were not allowed to proceed further. Other component selection procedures included consideration of past work performance, recommendations, and seniority. Additionally, the state used an affirmative action plan to ensure large minority representation in its supervisory workforce.

All four plaintiffs failed the written examination which had adverse impact on blacks (blacks' pass rate = 68% of the whites' pass rate). However, the promotion rate for blacks at the end of the total selection process was 169 percent that of the whites' promotion rate. Consequently, there was no adverse impact at the bottom line. In spite of the impressive group statistics, the Supreme Court ruled that the plaintiffs, on the basis of their individual rights under Title VII, had the legal right to challenge the component selection procedure which they believed to be acting as a discriminatory barrier. The presence of adverse impact against blacks on the written examination was taken by the Court to be sufficient evidence of *prima facie* discrimination, so as to shift the burden to the State of Connecticut to defend the job-relatedness of the test. The Court described the principal focus of Title VII as "the protection of the individual employees, rather than the protection of the minority group as a whole." Further, the court stated, "Title VII does not permit the victim of a racially discriminatory policy to be told that he has not been wronged because other persons of his or her race or sex were hired. . . . Every *individual* employee is protected against both discriminatory treatment and against practices that are fair in form, but discriminatory in operation" *Griggs v. Duke Power Co.*, 401 U.S. at 431.

The practical result of this decision is that employers must collect adverse impact statistics for each component selection procedure and be able to demonstrate the job-relatedness of those having adverse impact. Public employers operating under merit systems must be able to demonstrate the job-relatedness of *all* selection procedures in the total selection process including those that do *not* have an adverse impact, since merit legislation mandates the use of valid selection procedures. Quaintance (1981), in her review of adverse impact data collection systems, found a number of states (notably Wyoming, Hawaii, and New Mexico) and municipalities (Stockton, California; Pueblo, Colorado; and Urbana, Illinois, to name a few) were already examining the degree of adverse impact of all of the component selection procedures in the total selection process.

Alternative Selection Procedures. In the presence of adverse impact, one employer option is the adoption of an alternative selection procedure, presumably one that will eliminate the adverse impact. Section 6A of the *Uniform Guidelines* says that when an employer utilizes an alternative selection procedure, that alternative "should eliminate adverse impact in the total selection process, should be lawful and should be as job-related as possible."

Employers are also directed to search for alternative selection procedures whenever undertaking a validity study. Specifically, Sec. 3B states that employers must conduct "an investigation of suitable alternative selection procedures . . . which have as little adverse impact as possible to determine the appropriateness of using or validating them in accord with these guidelines." The employer must demonstrate that a reasonable effort has been made to become aware of alternative selection procedures.

Additionally, whenever an employer is shown an alternative selection procedure with evidence of less adverse impact and substantial evidence of validity for the same job in similar circumstances, Sec. 3B requires the employer to investigate that alternative to determine the appropriateness of using or validating the selection procedure. Employers have referred to this provision of Sec. 3B as sending employers into a "cosmic search for alternatives." Employers argue that once a search for alternatives has been conducted as part of the validity study and a selection procedure has been selected and validated, then it should be used as long as it is current. Alternative selection procedures shown to the employer before then should not have to be investigated.

There is legal support for the position that the burden of searching for and validating an alternative selection procedure is not the employer's. In *Albemarle Paper Company v. Moody* (422 U.S. 405, 1975), the Supreme Court placed the burden of searching for alternatives with less adverse impact and substantial evidence of validity on the plaintiff, not the employer.

Albemarle notwithstanding, employers felt the need to partially reduce the "cosmic search" for alternative selection procedures imposed by Sec. 3B by tightening up the language in the *Uniform Guidelines*. This was accomplished by inserting the phrase "for the same job in similar circumstances" which suggests that alternatives with less adverse impact and substantial evidence of validity for other jobs or used in different situations need not be investigated by the employer.

Why the emphasis on a search for selection procedures to substitute for or to supplement written paper and pencil tests? The answer lies in the conflicting societal goals of productivity and equity. While the contributions of valid tests to an effective workforce are acknowledged, the authors of the *Uniform Guidelines* were also painfully aware that tests have adverse effects on minority opportunities for employment. The Committee on Ability Testing summarized these effects as follows:

> The salient social fact today about the use of ability tests is that Blacks, Hispanics, and native Americans do not, as groups, score as well as do White applicants as a group. When candidates are ranked according to test score and when test results are a determinant in the employment decision, a comparatively large fraction of Blacks and Hispanics are screened out [Wigdor and Garner, 1982, p. 143].

Research Literature on Alternative Selection Procedures. The search for alternative selection procedures has led to a number of literature reviews assessing the current applicability for a number of possible alternatives. Of particular interest in these reviews was the assessment of the procedure's previously demonstrated degree of adverse impact on women and minorities, as well as of the procedure's validity for particular purposes. One of the four issuing agencies (Office of Personnel Management, 1980) undertook comprehensive literature reviews of a variety of alternatives: biodata/application blanks, reference checks, self assessment, interviews, work samples and simulations, miniature training and evaluation, assessment centers, work motivation, probationary period, and college grade point average.

Tenopyr (1981) summarized research findings for a variety of alternatives. Over a two-year period, she found only one published study demonstrating validity for the interview, while during the same period, there were approximately fifty studies indicating the vulnerabilities of interviews. Tenopyr (1981, p. 1123) concluded that the interview "at best . . . introduces randomness to the selection process; at worst it colors selection decisions with conscious or unconscious biases." Tenopyr (1981) also found disappointing results for ratings of experience and education. Not only did these measures have low validity, they also seemed to exclude members of groups who had been denied job opportunities and educational advantages. Scored biodata forms demonstrate respectable validity, but they need large sample sizes to ensure the development of stable weights, a condition that presents an operational problem not readily solved by many employers. Tenopyr (1981) found moderate validity evidence for assessment centers, but called for more criterion-related evidence. She could find neither validity nor adverse impact studies for probationary periods. Based upon her review of alternative selection procedures, Tenopyr (1981, p. 1124) decided that "there are no alternatives better than tests when validity, degree of adverse impact on various groups, and feasibility of use are all taken into account. With few exceptions, most alternatives are less useful than tests. Thus it seems that a practitioner undertaking a search for alternatives will primarily just be going through an exercise to satisfy government requirements."

Reilly and Chao (1982) undertook a comprehensive review of research on alternative selection procedures examining eight categories of alternatives in terms of validity, adverse impact, fairness, and feasibility. Only biodata and peer evaluations were supported as having validities substantially equal to those for standardized tests.

Hunter and Hunter (1983) examined the validity and utility of alternate predictors of job performance for entry level jobs. Their report, based on the results of cumulative research done on various predictors, concluded that for entry level jobs there is no predictor with validity equal to that of ability tests. The validities found were: ability tests (.55), job tryout (.44), biodata (.37), reference check (.26), grade point average in college (.21), experience (.18), interview (.14), training and experience ratings (.13), and education (.10). Fortunately, Title VII of the Civil Rights Act of 1964, as amended, contains a specific provision, known as the Tower amendment, supporting the use of ability tests, as long as they do not discriminate. Title VII states that it is permissible "to give and to act upon the results of any professionally developed ability test provided that such test, its administration or action upon the results is not designed, intended, or used to discriminate because of race, color, religion, sex or national origin."

The feasibility of alternatives is also an often ignored issue. Ashe (1980) noted that no mention is made of costs or other feasibility factors when alternatives are discussed in the *Uniform Guidelines*. One viable alternative, the assessment center, is particularly costly to implement. While a written paper and pencil test may cost from $5 to $25 per applicant, an assessment center can cost from $300 to $4000 or $5000 per individual (see Wigdor and Garner, 1982, p. 144).

Comparisons across alternative selection procedures are difficult because researchers are not certain what constructs each separate procedure measures (Ironson and Guion, 1981). Differences in results across procedures may be due to differences in methodology or to differences in what is being measured.

The general conclusion appears to be that the most valid alternative selection procedure will have the least amount of adverse impact (Reilly and Chao, 1982; Ironson and Guion, 1981). Thus, the *Uniform Guidelines* are somewhat misdirected in placing emphasis on alternatives of questionable validity with less adverse impact. If the guidelines emphasized the adoption of alternatives which would maximize validity, they would best achieve their goal of minimizing adverse impact. The Committee on Ability Testing strongly supported the need to consider validity in employment selection processes. The committee recommended that "the validity of the testing process should not be compromised in the effort to shape the distribution of the workforce." Further, the committee states, "If comparatively valid selection procedures are abandoned as a consequence of administrative pressure, the morale of the workforce and the productivity of the economy will suffer" (Wigdor and Garner, 1982, p. 147).

Job Relatedness/Validity.   Another employer option in the presence of adverse impact is the defense of the selection procedure in question on the basis of its job-relatedness or validity. The Supreme Court in *Griggs* v. *Duke Power Company* clearly articulated this defense by stating, "Nothing in the Civil Rights Act precludes the use of testing or measuring procedures; obviously they are useful. What Congress has forbidden is giving these devices and mechanisms controlling force unless they are demonstrably a reasonable measure of job performance . . . Congress has placed on the employer the burden of showing that any given requirement must have a manifest relation to the employment in question."

The problem arises, however, of deciding what constitutes job-relatedness or validity. Initially, the *Griggs* decision was interpreted as saying that any evidence of job-relatedness could serve as an adequate rebuttal to *prima facie* evidence of discrimination resulting from adverse impact statistics. However, the Supreme Court later clarified the employer's burden in *Albemarle Paper Company* v. *Moody* 422 U.S. 405 (1975). While Albemarle presented criterion-related validity evidence to support the test instruments, the study was flawed due to a small sample size, a subjective criterion based on supervisory judgments, an inappropriate method for grouping jobs, and an unrepresentative sample. After reviewing the validity study, the Court concluded that "the odd patchwork of results would not entitle Albemarle to impose its testing program under the Guidelines."

Section 5A of the *Uniform Guidelines* states that users may rely upon criterion-related validity studies, content validity studies, or construct validity studies. Anastasi (1976) provides complete descriptions of these three concepts. While the *Uniform Guidelines* appear to give equal status to the three validity strategies in Sec. 5A, other sections, including the documentation requirements and some questions and answers, suggest a preference for criterion-related validity. In practice, especially in the public sector, content validity studies are most prevalent as they are substantially less expensive than the other two types of validity evidence and more easily understood.

Evidence of content validity is provided by showing that the behaviors being tested are a representative sample of the behaviors to be exhibited on the job. Criterion-related validity involves correlating performance on the selection procedure with performance on another measure representing training, job, or organizational success. Construct validity involves a demonstrated relationship between underlying traits or hypothetical constructs inferred from a large body of empirical evidence involving behavior and a set of test measures related to those constructs. The Educational Testing Service has sponsored a colloquium of behavioral scientists to explore the meaning of construct validity (Office of Personnel Management and the Educational Testing Service, 1979). The uniform guidelines provide technical standards for criterion-related validity studies (Sec. 14B), content validity studies (Sec. 14C), and for construct validity studies (Sec. 14D).

While the *Guidelines* divide validity into the three categories listed above, the psychological profession has been moving in the opposite direction decrying this rigid compartmentalization (Messick, 1975, 1980; Guion 1977, 1978, 1980; Tenopyr, 1977; and Cronbach, 1980a and 1980b). The proliferation of literature in this area has led Tenopyr and Oeltjen (1982, p. 590) to conclude that the "rigid division of validity into criterion-related, content, and construct is wrong . . . In a sense then all validity is essentially construct validity, and the various strategies by which one assesses goodness of measurement of the attribute in question appear to be inextricably intertwined."

The psychological profession is also at odds with the *Uniform Guidelines* on documentation requirements. Sharf (1982) has said that the extraordinary documentation requirements lead to a "checklist mentality" such that if only one piece of documentation is missing then the validity study will be judged insufficient by enforcement personnel. Novick (1982, p. 96) has stated that too much specificity can be harmful in either government guidelines or professional psychological standards as "typically there are a variety of ways to do acceptable professional work."

In light of the burdensome technical and documentation requirements for validity studies, have any studies effectively withstood charges of discrimination in litigation? Ashe (1980, p. 113) states that "employers can win and are winning testing cases when they've done their homework. See e.g., *EEOC* v. *duPont* 445 F. Supp. 223 (D. Del. 1977) and *U.S.* v. *South Carolina, supra."* Bersoff (1981) also provides some examples including *Guardians Association of New York City* v. *Civil Service Commission of New York* 630 F. 2d 79 (2d Cir. 1980), *cert. denied,* 49 U.S. L.W. 3932 (June 15, 1981).

Method of Using Selection Procedures. Job candidates can either be ranked or given a pass/fail score on a selection procedure, according to Sec. 5G of the *Uniform Guidelines.* If an employer decides to use the ranking basis and that method has a greater impact on hiring and promotional opportunities of members of a particular group than the pass/fail method does (a typical finding, especially on written paper and pencil ability tests), the employer then should have "sufficient evidence of validity and utility to support the use on a ranking basis." Also, Sec. 14C(9) says that if an employer can show by job analysis or otherwise that a higher score on a content valid selection procedure is likely to result in better job performance, the results may be used to rank persons who score above minimum levels. Both of these sections suggest that special kinds of evidence are required to support ranking. In reality, professional psychological standards maintain that any evidence of validity is sufficient to support ranking. Specifically, the *Principles for the Validation and Use of Personnel Selection Procedures: Second Edition* by the Society of Industrial-Organizational Psychologists (Division 14) of the American Psychological Association (American Psychological Assoc. Division of Industrial-Organizational Psychology, 1980, p. 18) state:

> Selection standards may be set as high or as low as the purposes of the organization require, if they are based on valid predictors . . . In usual circumstances, the relationship between a predictor and a criterion may be assumed to be linear. Consequently, selecting from the top scores on down is almost always the most beneficial procedure from the standpoint of an organization if there is an appropriate amount of variance in the predictor. Selection techniques developed by content-oriented procedures and discriminating adequately within the range of interest can be assumed to have a linear relationship to job behavior. Consequently, ranking on the basis of scores on these procedures is appropriate.

Division 14 maintains that the most appropriate method of use for a selection procedure based on either criterion-related or content validity is to rank order the candidates and to select from the top of the list on down. Of course, ranking is a legal requirement in some public merit systems. This method of use maximizes the utility of the selection procedure and its contribution to organizational productivity. Schmidt and Hunter (1981, p. 1130) have stated that:

> The finding that test score/job performance relationships are linear means that ranking applicants on test scores and selecting from the top down maximizes the productivity of employees selected. This finding also means that any minimum test score requirement (test cutoff score) is arbitrary. No matter where it is set, a higher cutoff score will yield more productive employees, and a lower score will yield less productive employees. On the other hand, it means that if the test is valid, all cutoff scores are "valid" by definition. The concept of "validating" a cutoff score on a valid test is therefore not meaningful.

Section 5G also requires the employer to consider the effect on adverse impact of the way in which a selection procedure is used. This consideration is a social policy issue, not a professional one. The Division 14 *"Principles"* do not suggest that the degree of adverse impact be taken into account. However, in an effort to balance society's conflicting goals, the Committee on Ability Testing suggested that "the typical requirements for ranking candidates by test score and selecting according to the 'rule of three' . . . be replaced by a selection system that recognizes the dual interests of equal opportunity and productivity" (Wigdor and Garner 1982, p. 148). The committee thus suggested that employers avoid ranking or quotas.

Another way to increase minority hiring with little cost to productivity is to set up separate rosters for each group and to hire from each (Schmidt and Hunter, 1981). However, such selective certification practices for minorities and nonminorities raise legal, social, and moral questions. Two such selective certification programs have been upheld by state supreme courts: *Maehren et al. v. City of Seattle et al.* No. 44975, Aug. 10, 1979 and *Price et al. v. Civil Service Commission of Sacramento et al.* S. F. 23836, Super. Ct. No. 257623, Jan. 25, 1980. However, the outcome of similar litigation involving constitutional protections of due process in the U.S. Supreme Court is less certain. . . .

Strategies for Compliance

When adverse impact is present, employers are required to adopt a strategy to achieve compliance. The *Uniform Guidelines* recommend five strategies: (1) demonstrate the job-relatedness or validity of the selection procedure; (2) modify the selection procedure to eliminate adverse impact; (3) eliminate the selection procedure; (4) select an alternative selection procedure; or (5) otherwise justify the procedure by federal law (e.g., by evidence of business necessity, a bonafide seniority system, etc.; see Sec. 3A, 3B, and 6). Public employers operating under merit systems must also be able to demonstrate the job-relatedness of all selection procedures in the total selection process, including those which do not have an adverse impact as merit legislation mandates the use of valid selection procedures. Thus, public employers operating under merit system constraints can select but one strategy to achieve compliance under the *Uniform Guidelines,* the first strategy — to demonstrate the job-relatedness or validity of the selection procedures. While the other strategies for compliance would free public merit employers of their Title VII obligations, employers would still remain vulnerable to litigation under their merit statutes or the U.S. Constitution.

The demonstration of job-relatedness for assessment techniques can be an extremely costly proposition, which requires particular kinds of expertise (such as knowledge of job analysis methodologies, psychometrics, industrial psychology, statistics, etc.). Perry (1980) has noted the deficiencies of a number of public sector assessment professionals, who lack training in job analysis techniques, item construction, and other matters, as well as the inability of the public sector to compete with the salaries offered to similar professionals by private corporations. Sharf (1982, p. 173) maintains that "if literally applied . . . the *Uniform Guidelines* offer unattainable standards for even the largest employer and the most expert professionals." What options do small employers have when confronted with limited financial and staff resources?

Cooperative Validity Studies. The *Uniform Guidelines* provide several employer options. Section 8A encourages employers to pool their limited resources in cooperative studies for "research, development, search for lawful alternatives and validity studies in order to achieve procedures which are consistent with these guidelines." The guidelines go on to state in Sec. 8B that in such cases evidence of validity specific to each user will not be required "unless there are variables in the user's situation which are likely to offset validity significantly." (Once again, it is possible that compliance officers will interpret those variables to be sex or race or ethnic group membership, reflecting support for the discredited concept of differential validity.)

Ashe (1980, p. 109) has suggested that cooperative validity studies are likely to be a "strong wave of the 1980's," as they offer large and adequate sample sizes and substantial cost savings. Ashe (1980) indicated that cooperative studies were currently under way by the Edison Electric Institute and the Life Office Management Association.

Similarly, the Committee on Ability Testing of the National Academy of Sciences urged government agencies to "accept the principle of cooperative validation research so that tests validated for a job category such as firefighter in a number of localities can be accepted for use in other localities on the basis of the cumulated experience" (Wigdor and Garner, 1982, p. 148).

Test Transportability. Section 7B of the *Uniform Guidelines* permits use of criterion-related validity evidence from other sources. The evidence must (1) meet the standards of Sec. 14B; (2) contain a fairness study if technically feasible; and (3) involve a similar job to the user's job, as demonstrated through job analysis. Allen (1979) has described in detail the procedures for test transportability under the *Uniform Guidelines.*

The concept of test transportability has been upheld by the U.S. Court of Appeals in the Fourth Circuit (*Friend et al.* v. *Leidinger et al.* No. 77–2351, decided Nov. 29, 1978). The city of Richmond, Virginia was permitted to transport the International Personnel Management Association's B-1(M) firefighter examination. This test is supported by criterion-related validity evidence gathered from jurisdictions in Nevada and California. Richmond demonstrated through job analysis that entry-level firefighter jobs were comparable in Virginia, Nevada, and California. The court stated, "To require local validation in every city, village and hamlet would be ludicrous" (p. 8).

Validity Generalization. The *Uniform Guidelines* have a clear preference for local validity evidence in each situation. This requirement reflects the belief that tests must be demonstrated to have validity for each job (i.e., the doctrine of occupational specificity) and for each situation (i.e., the doctrine of situational specificity). These doctrines resulted partially from the research literature in industrial psychology, which showed conflicting results for the same or similar tests used for different jobs or by different organizations. Recently, however, Schmidt and Hunter (1981), using improved methods of cumulating findings across studies, have challenged both doctrines. They found that most of the so-called conflicting results were due to small sample size and measurement error and restriction of range in the samples studied. Thus, Schmidt and Hunter (1981) concluded that the real meaning of seventy years of cumulative research involving employment testing was obscured; cognitive tests are valid at substantial levels for all jobs and cognitive test validities can typically be generalized with confidence across settings and organizations.

Tenopyr (1981) noted that based on the work of Schmidt and Hunter and their colleagues (Schmidt, et al., 1980; Pearlman, et al., 1980; Schmidt et al., 1981; Wunder and Herring, 1980), and others (Callender and Osborn, 1980), validities generalize to a far greater extent than previously believed.

These findings show that the *Uniform Guidelines'* emphasis on situational and occupational specificity is at odds with professional psychological research. However, as Tenopyr and Oeltjen (1982) have pointed out, the hypotheses of situational specificity and validity generalization are not mutually exclusive. Fleishman and Quaintance (1984) have summarized Fleishman's extensive research indicating situational effects do moderate validities. Fleishman (1975; 1978) explained his findings by suggesting that when the researcher has better control over the measurement of the criterion performance, it is possible to show that different task requirements moderate test validities. Tenopyr and Oeltjen (1982) considered this explanation a plausible hypothesis worthy of further study. More recently, Linn and Dunbar (1982) have suggested that as much as twenty-five percent of the variance might be explained by moderating effects of situational variables.

Nonetheless, it is likely that more and more organizations in both the public and private sectors will rely on validity generalization studies to meet the requirement for the demonstration of job-relatedness of their selection procedures. Organizations which have conducted such studies include: Sears Roebuck, the American Petroleum Institute, the U.S. Office of Personnel Management, ARMCO Steel, the U.S. Employment Service, the Life Insurance Marketing Research Association, the Central Intelligence Agency, and the Philadelphia Electric Company. The concept of validity generalization was upheld in a district court decision (*Pegues et al.* v. *Mississippi State Employment Service et al.* 22 FEP 3929, Northern District of Mississippi, March 7, 1980). . . .

CONCLUSIONS

This chapter has reviewed the legal and regulatory mandates for unbiased selection. The discussion has shown that one mechanism for unbiased selection is the use of written examinations that have been demonstrated to be valid for members of all racial, sex, and ethnic groups. Such job-related examinations ensure equal employment opportunity.

As Schmidt and Hunter (1981, p. 1134) have indicated, racial differences in ability test scores are real, reflecting a serious social problem. They stated, "We can no longer entertain the belief that the problem is in tests and that it can be solved by modifying or eliminating tests." Rather, attention must be directed toward improving the acquisition of skills and abilities by all members of society. Additionally, as Gordon and Terrell (1981) have recommended, test developers may wish to redesign tests to include diagnostic information as to why certain levels of proficiency are not achieved. Score outcomes could well be accompanied by appropriate suggestions for developmental activities.

The discussion has also shown that selection occurs not solely in a legal/regulatory context, but also in a social/political context. Thus, we are confronted by conflicting societal goals: to provide for equal employment opportunity and to achieve equal results or representation of members of all groups in the workforce. Glaser and Bond (1981, p. 1000) have stated that "test use will have to serve broader social values. . . . In the final analysis, the work of behavioral science must encompass both scientific rigor and social responsibility." In this context, employers will have to make choices between maximizing productivity of employee performance (typically achieved through ranking applicants/candidates on the basis of job-related selection procedures such as tests) and increasing opportunities for the disadvantaged (typically by adjusting the method of use of the selection procedure, as was suggested by the National Academy of Sciences' Committee on Ability Testing). Only through careful balancing of the legal, regulatory, professional, political, and social factors can employers achieve our societal goal of moving toward unbiased selection. There is a need for those responsible for the *Uniform Guidelines* revision process to recognize these conflicting forces and to assist employers in achieving our societal goal.

REFERENCES

Allen, L. (1979). Test transportability and the *Uniform Guidelines*. *Public Personnel Management*, Sept.–Oct.: 309–314.

American Petroleum Institute (1978). Comments on recordkeeping regulations. Personal communication.

American Psychological Association Division of Industrial–Organizational Psychology (1980). *Principles for the Validation and Use of Personnel Selection Procedures*, 2nd ed. Berkeley, Cal. Author.

Anastasi, A. (1976). *Psychological Testing*, 4th ed. MacMillan Publishing Company, Inc., New York.

Ashe, R. L., Jr. (1980). Employment practices, test validation and *Uniform Guidelines* — Principles of merit selection. In *EEO for State and Local Public Employers: Laws, Rules and Regulations* (A. M. Koral and R. L. Ashe, eds.). Law Journal Seminars Press, New York, pp. 101–113.

Bemis, S. E. (1978). Systems for measuring and assessing adverse impact. *Public Personnel Management* 1:354–357.

Bersoff, D. N. (1981). Testing and the law. *American Psychologist* 36:1047–1056.

Callender, J. C., and Osborn, H. G. (1980). Development and test of a new model for validity generalization. *Journal of Applied Psychology* 65:543–558.

Cronbach, L. J. (1980a). Selection theory for a political world. *Public Personnel Management* 9:37–50.

Cronbach, L. J. (1980b). Validity on parole: How can we go straight? *New Directions in Test Measurement* 5:99–108.

Fleishman, E. A. (1975). Toward a taxonomy of human performance. *American Psychologist* 30:1127–1149.

Fleishman, E. A. (1978). Relating individual differences to the dimensions of human tasks. *Ergonomics* 21:1007–1019.

Fleishman, E. A., and Quaintance, M. K. (1984). *Taxonomies of Human Performance: The Description of Human Tasks*. Academic Press, Orlando.

Glaser, R., and Bond, L. (1981). Testing: Concepts, policy, practice and research. *American Psychologist* 36:997–1000.

Gordon, E. W., and Terrell, M. D. (1981). The changed social context of testing. *American Psychologist* 36(10):1167–1171.

Guion, R. M. (1977). Content validity, the source of my discontent. *Applied Psychological Measurement* 1:1–10.

Guion, R. M. (1978). Content validity in moderation. *Personnel Psychology* 31:205–214.

Guion, R. M. (1980). On trinitarian doctrines of validity. *Professional Psychology* 11:385–398.

Harris, P. A. and White, K. A. (1981). *Assessing the Distribution of Minorities and Women in Relevant Labor Markets: Information for State and Local Government Employees*. Office of Personnel Management, Washington, D.C.

Hunter, J. E. and Hunter, R. F. (1983). *The Validity and Utility of Alternative Predictors of Job Performance*. Office of Personnel Management, OPRD-83-4, Washington, D.C.

Ironson, G. H. and Guion, R. M. (1981). *Adverse Impact from a Psychometric Perspective: A Case Study in Evaluating Group Differences*. Unpublished manuscript, Bowling Green State University, Bowling Green, Ohio.

Kraft, J. D. (1978). Adverse impact determination in federal examinations. *Public Personnel Management* 7(6):362–367.

Linn, R. L. and Dunbar, S. B. (1982). *Validity Generalization and Predictive Bias*. Paper prepared for the Fourth Johns Hopkins University National Symposium on Educational Research, "Performance Assessment: The State of the Art," Washington, D.C., Nov. 5–6, 1982. (Available from R. L. Linn, the University of Illinois at Urbana-Champaign.)

Messick, S. A. (1975). Meaning and values in measurement and evaluation. *American Psychologist* 30:955–966.

Messick, S. A. (1980). Test validity and the ethics of assessment. *American Psychologist* 35:1012–1027.

Miner, M. G. and Miner, J. B. (1978). *Employee Selection Within the Law.* Bureau of National Affairs, Inc., Washington, D.C.

Northrup, L. C. (1977). *Pilot Study No. 1 for the Collection of Race, Sex, and Ethnic Origin Data in Federal Testing.* Personnel Research and Development Center, U.S. Civil Service Commission, Washington, D.C.

Novick, M. (1982). Ability testing: Federal guidelines and professional standards. In *Ability Testing: Uses, Consequences and Controversies. Part II: Documentation Section* (A. K. Wigdor and W. R. Garner, eds.). National Academy Press, Washington, D.C., pp. 70–98.

Office of Personnel Management (1980). Alternative selection procedures. *Federal Personnel Manual System* FPM Bulletin 331-3, Office of Personnel Management, Washington, D.C.

Office of Personnel Management and the Educational Testing Service (1979). *Construct Validity in Psychological Measurement: Proceedings of a Colloquium on Theory and Application and Employment.* Educational Testing Service, Princeton, N.J.

Pearlman, K., Schmidt, F. L., and Hunter, J. E. (1980). Validity generalization results for tests used to predict job proficiency and training success in clerical occupations. *Journal of Applied Psychology* 65:373–406.

Perry, R. A. (1980). Public sector selection specialist: A survey of state and local government utilization and training needs. *Public Personnel Management* 9(2):86–93.

Quaintance, M. K. (1981). Guidelines compliance: In search of the golden fleece. *Personnel Selection and Training Bulletin,* 2:164–172.

Reilly, R. R. and Chao, G. T. (1982). Validity and fairness of some alternative employee selection procedures. *Personnel Psychology* 35:1–62.

Schmidt, F. L., Gast-Rosenberg, I., and Hunter, J. E. (1980). Validity generalization results for computer programmers. *Journal of Applied Psychology* 65:643–661.

Schmidt, F. L. and Hunter, J. E. (1981). Employment testing: Old theories and new research findings. *American Psychologist* 36:1128–1137.

Schmidt, F. L., Hunter, J. E., Pearlman, K., and Caplan, J. R. (1981). *Validity Generalization Results for Three Occupations in the Sears Roebuck Company.* Unpublished manuscript. Available from F. L. Schmidt, George Washington University, 96 pp.

Sharf, J. C. (1982). Personnel testing and the law. In *Personnel Management* (K. Rowland and J. Ferris, eds.). Allyn and Bacon, Boston, pp. 156–182.

Tenopyr, M. L. (1977). Content-construct confusion. *Personnel Psychology* 30:47–54.

Tenopyr, M. L. (1981). The realities of employment testing. *American Psychologist* 36:1120–1127.

Tenopyr, M. L. and Oeltjen, P. D. (1982). Personnel selection and classification. *Annual Review of Psychology* 33:581–618.

Wigdor, A. K. and Garner, W. R. (eds.) (1982). *Ability Testing: Uses, Consequences and Controversies. Part I: Report of the Committee.* National Academy Press, Washington, D.C.

Wunder, R. S. and Herring, J. W. (January 1980). *Interpretive Guide for the API Test Validity Generalization Project,* API Publication 755:18 pp.

G.

SELECTION

Interview with Virginia R. Boehm

Virginia Boehm is currently president of Assessment & Development Associates, a position she has held since 1982. Earlier in her career, she held human resource management positions at SOHIO, AT&T, and the State of New York. In those organizations, Dr. Boehm gained experience in a variety of personnel areas, including test development, career planning, and management development and assessment.

Dr. Boehm earned her Ph.D. in social psychology from Columbia University in 1966. She is a Fellow of Division 14 of the American Psychological Association, and is the author of numerous papers and presentations on testing, management development, and selection.

1. *Many people view selection and staffing as the heart of the human resource management process. What are the goals of selection and why is it important to an organization?*

The ultimate goals of selection are to maximize organizational productivity and profitability by staffing the organization with the best qualified recruitable candidates for positions. If you have unqualified, or just marginally qualified people, you wind up taking a huge loss in productivity, and/or spend much more than you need to on training; or you simply have to start the hiring process all over again to get better people.

2. *Employee selection has been heavily influenced over the past twenty years by civil rights legislation and federal court decisions. How have employers, in general, responded to these increasing legal constraints? Are the goals of valid selection and equal employment opportunity at odds with each other?*

Employers have in general responded by improving the validity of their selection procedures, something that they should have done anyway because good selection is just plain good business. Some — particularly smaller employers without professional personnel staffs — have unfortunately done the reverse and given up objective selection in a misguided attempt to avoid legal hassles. But overall, the impact has been to improve selection.

No, the goals of equal opportunity and valid selection are not at odds — they are highly compatible. Excluding people from the applicant pool on grounds of race, sex, or other irrelevancies means that you are using a non-job-related component in your selection process. This automatically decreases validity. What's happened to give the impression that validity and equal opportunity are at odds is that people have confused equal opportunity with equal outcomes.

3. *The selection process is usually a joint effort involving both the personnel department and the line manager. What role should each party play in this process? How are responsibilities typically divided in this effort?*

Let me respond to the second part of the question first. There is no "typical" division I know of. It depends on the organization, and on the position within the organization. There are situations where the line organization plays absolutely no role — they in effect order so many bodies for two weeks from Monday and the personnel department hires them and sends them out. And there are other situations where the first the personnel department knows is when a manager calls and says I've hired so and so at salary thus and such, and the personnel department's only role is to process the paperwork.

How should it be divided? That depends on the nature of the position. For an unskilled or other lower-level position, probably the personnel office should in effect handle the entire matter, particularly if the volume of workers in question is high and hiring is a pretty constant activity. At the other extreme, except for executive search activities, the personnel department should do little when it comes to hiring top-level managers until it's time to process the paperwork, unless they are specifically requested by the hiring manager to conduct a particular activity (maybe a reference check). But for most jobs, the personnel office should screen applicants, then pass on the best qualified to the hiring manager for further screening and a final decision.

4. *Do entry level jobs exist in the selection and staffing area for recent college graduates? If so, what background and skills do you suggest that students acquire to be qualified for such positions?*

Yes, there are some opportunities in positions such as Employment Interviewer, Test Administrator, and Personnel Administrator. Computer literacy is essential, as well as good verbal skills and a "smooth" way with people (employment interviewing is as much public relations as it is personnel). A lot of recent college graduates who become interested in personnel because they "like to work with people," get a personnel job and find they are spending more time interacting with a CRT than they are with people! But it's a fact of life that the personnel end of any business involves an enormous amount of record keeping, and government interventions in the area are responsible for a lot of it.

5. *What are some of the differences between selection for managerial and nonmanagerial jobs?*

First, there is usually a difference in the attitude of those doing the hiring. In a nonmanagerial blue-collar or white-collar job, the applicant is viewed as being someone who wants to work with your organization. Often the applicant is not presently employed, and it is felt, rightly or wrongly, that the applicant will accommodate to the organization's needs — come back three or four times for interviews, take tests, fill out forms and in general permit him or herself to be "processed."

The experienced managerial or technical candidate is perceived very differently. Frequently, he or she has been actively recruited by the organization or an outside recruiter. Most such candidates are employed, and if they are not, other organizations are probably interested in them as well. So an important part of the process is selling the candidate on the organization, and consequently the organization will accommodate itself to the candidate. The ironic part of this is that an organization may know less about a managerial candidate prior to hiring the person than they know about a clerk!

Another difference is that the managerial hiring process is less objective than the hiring process for a nonmanagerial person. Probably, most managerial hiring is 90 percent dependent on interviews, and the "chemistry" between the managerial candidate and others in the organization is a critical factor. While some organizations use assessment centers, tests, and other objective devices as part of internal promotion into or up in management, not many do so for external hires. In nonmanagerial hiring, objective selection devices tend to be heavily used and are often used as the first stage in the selection process. In some organizations, nonmanagerial applicants don't even get interviewed until after they pass a test.

6. *You mentioned assessment centers as a possible selection technique. How have they contributed to organizations' ability to validly select managers?*

They have contributed greatly so far as selecting *internal* candidates for managerial positions, particularly at the entry level. When picking a first-level supervisor, an organization is in a situation where the skills the job requires vary sharply from those the candidates have shown on their present job. Without objective selection, the best worker may be selected for the supervisory position and turn out to be a terrible supervisor. The skills needed are very different. Selection of internal candidates for sales and technical management positions is also a natural for assessment centers and for the same reason — the crack salesman may be a disaster as a sales manager.

Assessment centers have also made a contribution in the internal selection of managers at higher levels. While some of the skills are the same as a person moves from supervisory to managerial to executive levels within an organization, there is a change in the mix. An executive gets heavily involved in long term and strategic planning (activities a supervisor is concerned with very little) and less involved with day-to-day supervisory tasks.

Assessment centers have had only very limited use in *external* managerial recruiting, basically for logistical reasons. Unless an organization is filling a large number of positions that require similar skills at the same time, an assessment center that requires any sort of group exercise is just not feasible. What is happening — and I think that there will be more of it — is that individual assessment exercises, in-baskets, interview simulations, etc., are being used in a few places in external managerial staffing.

7. *What are some of the problems that assessment centers experience in practice? How can these problems be overcome?*

Probably the biggest difficulty is that the people who are running them may not really understand what they are doing. An assessment center? Hey, that sounds nifty. Let's have one. So they buy a few exercises off the shelf — or worse yet, make them up themselves — and call it an assessment center. None of the preliminary work, including a job analysis, gets done. Nobody knows how candidates should be selected, how the results are to be used, or how assessors should be selected and trained. So, the assessment center is a fiasco and the personnel department usually gets blamed, even if the decision to have an assessment center came from the line organization.

Another big problem operationally is trying to stretch the assessment center to do something it wasn't designed to do. Assessment centers are expensive and the temptation to get "more bang for the buck" is nearly irresistible. An organization has a perfectly good and effective selection center, and someone thinks it can also be used for career development purposes. They try it and discover that the selection center doesn't really give enough information or the kind of information needed for that purpose, so they start to tinker with the center. Pretty soon, you have total confusion, with candidates unsure why they are attending the center, assessors unsure whether they are evaluators or coaches, information gathered for developmental purposes being used for selection and vice versa, and an assessment center that isn't really usable for either assessment or development.

A third big problem is the "install-it-and-forget-it" syndrome. This is particularly likely to happen if an outside consultant develops and installs an assessment center in an organization, trains people how to run it, trains the first group of assessors, and then walks away. Assessment centers need on-going, constant monitoring and tracking. Assessors need on-going feedback on their performance. The way the rating process takes place needs to be analyzed and problems corrected. Impact statistics need to be kept. And, perhaps most important, steps must be taken to assure that when the center gets a new administrator or new assessors, they are as well trained as the initial batch.

A fourth big operational problem is assessor quality. When the assessment center is new and exiciting, the best managers may actively seek out the opportunity to serve as assessors. Then, after a while, it becomes a ho hum kind of thing — a chore that somebody has to do — and the assessors wind up being people who are seen as easily replaceable on their present job or not involved in anything that's really important. These aren't the organization's brightest and best, to say the least, and even with very good assessor training, it's hard to maintain the standards of the assessment center.

8. *What do you foresee in the future for assessment centers? Will their application be expanded? What limitations exist on their use?*

I'll start with the last part first — the limitations. I already mentioned one limitation, the logistical problems associated with using assessment centers with external candidates. Another limitation is organizational size. Small and some medium-sized organizations can't support an assessment center internally. There may not be sufficient expertise in the personnel department. Also, if the company is small enough, the assessor pool is so small that it is difficult to find assessors who aren't familiar with the candidates' job performance, and this influences the assessment. Another limitation is cost. Is the organization willing to spend that much money on selection? This is related to size again. Development and implementation costs of an assessment center are pretty much the same for large and small organizations. But a large organization can spread this out over a far larger number of candidates so the cost-per-candidate is reasonable. Smaller companies can't do that.

The future? I think that the use of assessment center technology will continue to expand, although the use of standard assessment centers for selection may remain about what it is in the private sector. It's my impression that the number of private sector organizations using assessment centers hasn't changed much during the last three years or so — some have discontinued them, others have started them, but not much change. This is different than in the 1970s, when the number of organizations using assessment centers went from maybe a dozen to over a thousand.

But the use of assessment center technology will expand. As I mentioned earlier, individual assessment exercises are getting incorporated as parts of the selection process. Also, assessment exercises are being used increasingly in training and in career planning efforts that frequently include elements of self or peer assessment and video tape feedback. And, the use of assessment centers as developmental rather than selection devices is growing. Using assessment centers for developmental purposes has been talked about for years, but only recently have there been many programs in this area. Finally, elements of assessment center technology are getting incorporated in interactive computer simulations. This has the potential of being a very exciting growth area.

Back to the use of traditional assessment centers in selection. I said I didn't see much of an increase in the private sector. However, I do see a tremendous increase in the public sector. It looks to me that assessment centers as a selection method are virtually taking over in the selection of supervisory and management personnel in the uniformed services — police and fire. Recent experience indicates that, for selection to these positions where getting sued over the exam is a near certainty, chances of winning the case are much greater if an assessment center, or at least a process that includes assessment exercises, is used.

9. *Do some selection techniques seem to have less adverse impact on protected groups than others? If so, which ones?*

We've been talking about assessment centers. From information I've seen, assessment centers frequently don't have adverse impact on minorities and simply don't have adverse impact on women. The use of biodata is another good way to minimize or eliminate adverse impact. Often, an empirically validated biodata instrument doesn't have adverse impact to start with. And it is also possible to design one that won't illegally discriminate through the initial selection and keying of questions.

But what really seems to determine the extent of adverse impact is not so much the tool as it is the number of previous hurdles candidates have been over during the course of their careers. Entry level selection, for just about any tool and just about any job, tends to exhibit adverse impact on minorities. But, once this hurdle is crossed, selection procedures further up the ladder often have no adverse impact because the screening has already taken place. A mistake some organizations make is to abandon a valid entry level selection device because it has adverse impact. What happens then is that a promotion process — the validity of which is often harder to demonstrate — winds up having adverse impact because the minority and majority incumbents in the lower level job are in effect from different applicant pools.

10. *What is the status of the work sample for nonexempt jobs? Why has it not been used more? Will it become more prevalent in the future?*

Work samples — aside from areas such as typing where they have traditionally been used — simply haven't caught on. The reason is quite simple. They cost more than paper-and-pencil tests, are not substantially more valid in most cases, have a comparable degree of adverse impact on entry-level workers who have not been pre-screened, and require more administrative time and training. While they are a nice idea and look good to applicants, there is no compelling reason to use them. There is only one area where I see an increase in their use and that is where they are also seen as vehicles for providing an applicant with a realistic job preview. Their value as a self-screen can justify the additional cost if it reduces turnover at a later date.

11. *What trends do you see in the environment that will affect selection and staffing in the future?*

That's a global question, so here's a global answer: the role of work in society is changing. The traditional view that working was the major pursuit of adults — particularly males — is on its way out. The average working life of male Americans has dropped several years during the last two decades and will drop still further. It will start to drop for women before too many years as well. Technological changes will mean that we simply don't need to have anything close to full employment to keep the economy going and the society functioning. A large class of permanently unemployed is almost inevitable, which will make competition for what jobs do exist much more stringent. Selection standards will become higher for almost any kind of job because more and more people will become recruitable.

This may sound like an employer's paradise, but it's not. The people who aren't needed in the work force will still have to be supported, and what is saved in labor costs will probably be spent in taxes. It's also a jolt for people. We don't train people for leisure; we equate employment with virtue. Unless we make some pretty abrupt and enormous cultural changes, and make them soon, we're in for massive social unrest. You can see the beginning of this in areas that have depended on the traditional smokestack industries. People who have worked for twenty or thirty years are suddenly out of jobs and the plants they worked in just won't open again. They don't know what to do with themselves and the erosion in their self-esteem is just terrible, even when they can cope financially.

Personnel selection, which has always been a "gate" into the workforce, will become a much narrower gate and the pressures on people who do selection will become enormous. Very highly skilled technical and professional workers will still be in demand. There will be room at the bottom of the occupational structure too, where the work needs to be done and people are more economical than machines. But the middle of the work force — white-collar office, skilled and semiskilled, middle level service and technical — is eroding. Employee selection will be a very different type of activity and, for many young people, the choice will become not "what kind of work shall I do" but whether or not to compete in the labor market at all.

12. *Equal employment and affirmative action are commonly viewed as the largest selection issue of the last decade. What do you think will be the largest issue of the* next *decade?*

The impact of the demise of the employment-at-will doctrine on the selection process. The traditional view has been that in the absence of a written contract employers can dismiss workers for any cause, or even for no cause at all, as long as the intent is not discriminatory or malicious. This view is slowly being eroded by court decisions and state laws. Ads that describe a position as "permanent," statements in employee handbooks, personnel policy manuals, and verbal statements by a recruiter or interviewer are being construed as employment contracts. As jobs become a scarcer commodity, the right of workers to be retained so long as performance meets minimum standards is likely to be increasingly advocated.

This will put additional pressure on selection. Selection errors will become increasingly difficult to correct by termination or demotion, once probationary periods have passed. The focus of equal opportunity and affirmative action, to "screen in" all that have a reasonable probability of job success will clash with a pressure to "screen out" all that have a measurable probability of failure in the foreseeable future. There will be a strong push to develop selection devices with a higher degree of validity, because only the impossible dream — the 100 percent valid and accurate selection device — can simultaneously deal with the "screen in" and "screen out" pressures. It will be an interesting time!

A. _____

Schein

- ☐ What is the traditional selection validation model and what assumptions must hold to support its use?
- ☐ What trends in the society at large do you see influencing the selection process in the next ten years?

Guion

- ☐ Distinguish between the various types of validity.
- ☐ What is job-relatedness and what is its relation to validity?
- ☐ How does the author use the concept of values in his discussion?

Wernimont and Campbell

- ☐ What position are the authors arguing for and what is the evidence they cite?
- ☐ What specific jobs would the consistency theory work best for? Work least effectively for?

B. _____

England

- ☐ Describe how a weighted application blank is developed.
- ☐ How would the validity of the weighted application blank be assessed?

The Effective Manager

- ☐ What are the most problematic types of reference inquiries?
- ☐ Why do you suppose reference checks are mostly positive?
- ☐ What would the disadvantages to the person giving the reference be for being less than candid?

C. _____

Martin

- ☐ Summarize the author's perception of the interview's utility.
- ☐ In your experience as an interviewee can you agree or disagree with the author?

Arvey and Campion

- ☐ Summarize the research findings and conclusions about the interview.
- ☐ How are decisions really made in an interview, according to research?
- ☐ What advice would you give to someone about to interview a group of candidates for an important position?

D.

Rout

- What is an in-basket test?
- How effective do you feel the procedure described would be for selecting stockbrokers?

Sackett

- What problems are discussed regarding assessment centers?
- How can the validity of these procedures be measured?
- How can the assessment center be strengthened as a selection device?
- For what types of jobs would assessment centers be inappropriate?

E.

Schmidt and Hunter

- Summarize the authors' position regarding cognitive tests.
- What "theories" do the authors dismiss and what evidence do they cite?
- How can significant amounts of money be saved by employing the authors' notions?

Olian and Snyder

- What is genetic testing?
- Is genetic screening legal?
- Review the ethical implications of using this type of test.

F.

Sawyer

- Based on the available evidence, has affirmative action been effective in providing job gains for protected classes?
- What is reverse discrimination?
- Approximately what percentage of the work force is protected by various equal employment opportunity legislation?
- What effect has affirmative action had on the power of personnel managers?

Quaintance

- Briefly describe the legal foundations of our current position on discrimination.
- What, specifically, can employers do to comply with the law?
- Why are the *Guidelines* so difficult to interpret and follow in practice?

PART V
TRAINING AND DEVELOPMENT OF HUMAN RESOURCES

A.

ASSESSMENT OF TRAINING NEEDS

Assessment of Training Needs for Supervisors
Karen L. Vinton, Arben O. Clark, and John W. Seybolt

- ☐ Describes a comprehensive training system model for assessing an organization's training needs.
- ☐ Provides guidelines for conducting organization analysis, operations analysis, and person analysis for the purpose of answering where, what, who needs training.

B.

PROGRAM DESIGN AND METHODS

Training and Development Programs: What Learning Theory and Research Have to Offer
Craig Eric Schneier

- ☐ Argues that training and development programs should be designed in accordance with the principles of learning theory.
- ☐ Suggests that the learning principles form a set of contingencies to be managed in each training and development program.

Curriculum Design in Training: An Overview
William J. Rothwell

- ☐ Presents four major approaches to curriculum design.
- ☐ Argues that the contingency approach is the "best" method.

Behavior Modeling Training: Update and Recommendations
Glenn M. McEvoy and Sara A. Sporer

- ☐ Reviews the literature on modeling and applied learning.
- ☐ Details the recent experimental research on behavior modeling training.
- ☐ Discusses implications of this research for practitioners.

C.

CAREER DEVELOPMENT

Managing Career Transition: A Missing Link in Career Development
Meryl Reis Louis

- Discusses limitations of current approaches to career planning and development.
- Offers suggestions for managing the transitions from one position to another.

D.

EVALUATION OF TRAINING AND DEVELOPMENT PROGRAMS

An Objective Evaluation of a Behavior Modeling Training Program
Herbert H. Meyer and Michael S. Raich

- Details the results of an evaluation of a behavior modeling training program for salespeople in a field setting.
- Argues for more "bottom line" evaluations of training programs.

E.

TRAINING AND DEVELOPMENT

Interview with John R. Hinrichs

A.

ASSESSMENT OF TRAINING NEEDS

Assessment of Training Needs for Supervisors

Karen L. Vinton, Arben O. Clark, and John W. Seybolt

If one were to logically formulate an approach to supervisory training, assessing the training needs of supervisory trainee candidates would be an important and fundamental step. Such a logical approach was illustrated by Brown and Wede.[1]

Organizations generally consider training an investment in increased effectiveness through improved participant behavior.[2] This occurs through accommodating personnel growth, preparing employees for newly-created duties and responsibilities and improving performance on present and future jobs.[3] Interest in training is shown by the size of the investment. For example, in the private sector for the year 1976, organizations spent $1.2 billion on management training. Additionally, 3.2 million hours were spent on supervisory training in fiscal year 1977 by the federal government.[4]

Moore and Dutton suggest that effective utilization of training dollars and resources is achieved through first determining the location, scope and magnitude of the training need.[5] Howell adds reinforcement by observing that supervisory behavior is improved most readily when training and development efforts are geared to suit both individual and organizational needs.[2] Moore and Dutton point to dysfunctional consequences from failure to properly evaluate training needs: time and money may be expended on training programs that do not advance the organization toward its goals, the credibility of the training function may be reduced, the training sessions may meet the needs of the training director but not those of the individuals or the organization, and trainees may be receiving information and skill development that they already possess.[5]

McGehee and Thayer describe levels of determining training needs: *organization analysis* to determine where within the organization training emphasis can and should be placed, *operations analysis* to determine what should be the content of training in terms of what an employee must do to perform a task, job or assignment in an effective way, and *person analysis* to determine what skills, knowledge or attitudes individual employees must develop if they are to perform the tasks that constitute their job in the organization.[6]

ORGANIZATION ANALYSIS

Moore and Dutton suggest that since training deals with optimal use of scarce resources and goal achievement, needs analysis data must be considered in the context of organization purpose and management strategy.[5] Goldstein states that training programs often fail because skills learned in training are not successfully transferred to the job.[7] A basic reason for this is that training needs assessments have not considered system constraints that often prevent transfer or learning from training to the job. Since top management creates many of these constraints (implicit and explicit performance standards and subsequent rewards), their input into training needs assessment is essential.[8]

From consideration of purpose and strategy, one should move to an assessment of the adequacy of the human resources of the organization.[6] Human resource planning skills inventories, managerial inventories and replacement charts are of value here. Such planning is useful in the short term (some skills can be developed and put to use rapidly) and the long term (other skills can be acquired through further development and training).

A third consideration in organization analysis, after organization purpose and the availability of human resources, is some measurement of efficiency. A comparison of output with input efficiencies may indicate that tasks are not properly organized in conjunction with other factors of output.[6]

The final factor of the McGehee and Thayer structure for organization analysis is organization climate. To ensure that programs meet the needs of managers, the trainer must consider both the climate of the training environment and that of the manager's work environment.[8] Comparative and trend analysis can be developed from statistics concerning factors such as labor-management conflict, turnover, absenteeism, number and content of employee suggestions, productivity, accidents, illness and on-the-job employee behavior. Measurements can be developed from interviews, surveys and attitude scales. Climate analysis should determine if training might produce changes in behavior that would contribute to organizational goals.[6]

OPERATIONS ANALYSIS

Operations analysis deals with the content of specific jobs and the skills needed to fill job requirements. This logically follows attention to the organizational issues previously noted. McGehee and Thayer suggest that operations analysis should observe a procedure of determining what tasks constitute a job, establishing the best methods for performance of these tasks, and describing the proper supervisory behavior to achieve satisfactory task completion.[6] This approach focuses directly on the operational needs of the organization and provides a comparative anchor for assessment of individual training needs.

Job descriptions provide an initial step toward effective operations analysis. Unfortunately, these tend to be static and fail to reflect changes in technology.[8] They also fail to show position interdependency or set performance standards. Job descriptions for supervisors are complicated by the need for general statements of tasks to permit a discretionary range of activities, many of which do not lend themselves to specific translation into training needs. In addition, criteria for determining effectiveness tend to be subjective and situational. This tends to make the process of determining training needs more difficult and the task-specific (skills) training model less useful.[8]

Performance appraisals can reduce the subjectivity in task identification if conducted in a framework of measurable objectives. Major job responsibilities can be coupled with expected levels of accomplishment to provide a base for monitoring actual levels of accomplishment. Acceptable standards can be further developed through interviews, comparative studies of good versus poor supervisors, tests of job knowledge and performance measures. Task analysis is another technique in which the supervisory job would be broken down into tasks and elements for the purpose of describing the skill components of a competency.[9, 10]

We have made little progress in developing techniques for obtaining operations information through reliable and valid instruments. For example, research studies dealing with assessing training needs for supervisors tend to have had little, if any, emphasis on operations analysis.[3, 11, 12, 13, 14]

Moreover, Wessman concludes that many training and development specialists tend to fail more often than they succeed because of the difficulty in defining what constitutes effective supervisory behavior . . . and the imprecisions of tools and techniques used to diagnose training and development needs.[8]

Training programs run the risk of being limited in value if training needs have not been individualized. In addition, trainees must perceive a personal benefit in the training sufficient to provide motivation to learn and actually change behavior.[6] A variety of techniques is available for assessing individual training needs.

Interviews, both structured and unstructured, can help build a more complete assessment of training needs. A strength of this technique is in the opportunity to clarify statements, questions and responses. Among its major weaknesses are the potential for lack of trust, difficulty in analysis, consumption of time and hazardous use of unskilled interviewers.[15]

Surveys have the advantage of directing the attention of the respondent to agenda items important to the survey administrator. This can also be a disadvantage, since the survey may ignore items that both are relevant to the training needs and about which the respondent may have valuable insights.[1] Surveys provide highly structured, prompt (computer scored) information. However, they are dependent upon expert help in initial construction, analysis and feedback of results. They also build expectations that the results will be used in some way (hopefully to the respondent's advantage).[1]

Some relevant questions concerning surveys need to be asked. Who should be surveyed? Should subordinates be surveyed concerning the training needs of their supervisors? Would peers have input worth the cost of obtaining it? Would the survey form be suitable for getting useful information from superiors of supervisors? Should survey questionnaires be sent to respondents through the mail or administered to all respondents in groups with an expert facilitator present? These questions are not as easy to answer as they may seem at first reading. Calhoon and Jerdee found that first- and second-level supervisors vary greatly in their perception of the training needs for first-level supervisors.[14] They also found that what appeared to be a training problem for first-level supervisors was actually a problem at higher levels of management. This illustrates a potential disadvantage of relying exclusively on survey data.

Survey feedback is a method of using survey information as part of the training process through identifying and solving both individual and organizational problems. Summarized survey data can be given to top management and disseminated as general, but helpful information to the entire organization. Survey feedback has been shown to be a powerful and effective change treatment in and of itself.[16]

Another option in individualizing training needs assessment is what Stewart and Stewart call *behavior analysis*.[17] They describe it as a special case of content analysis where a supervisor's on-the-job actions and statements are monitored and categorized by the trainer. These same authors discuss a diary method, in which the supervisor trainee keeps track of activities performed on a day-to-day basis. This provides insights into what might be used as a more accurate job description and develops feelings concerning those activities for which training would be useful.

Psychological tests, used with professional assistance, can be useful in assessing training needs. They are most useful when reserved for assistance in long-term career development guidance rather than short-term needs.[8, 17]

Performance appraisal, through the use of measurable objectives, provides data in assessing training needs as performance deficiencies are exposed and analyzed. Objective data can also emerge from a close relationship at work between the supervisor and boss as the latter attempts to coach the former toward effective supervisory behavior.[8] This has the weakness of the assumption that the boss is well-informed concerning proper supervisory behavior. Attempts to overcome this weakness can be seen in extending Behaviorally Anchored Rating Scales to assessing training needs.[18]

Supervisory self-assessment is another option. Gordon developed a six-phase program for this purpose. The quality of self-assessment data can be improved if assessees can compare their own performance with that of some predetermined standard.[19]

Finally, assessment centers, used primarily for hiring and promotion,[20] can be adapted to the process of assessing needs for training.[21] Assessment centers are now designed with a strategy to identify those ready for an available (or soon to be available) job opening. To meet the demands of training needs assessment, a diagnostic strategy would have to be developed.[22] The diagnostic approach implies commitments on the parts of the organization, the immediate supervisor and the individual, to pursue a training and development plan. This could present a formidable task considering current "identification programs" that examine dimensions (initiative, judgment) that are difficult to teach.

DEPRESSING DEFICIENCIES

A review of the literature dealing with the assessment of supervisory training needs revealed some depressing deficiencies in the research in this area.

The majority of articles dealing with needs assessment are based on the authors' intuitive approaches. Only six research-based articles were found that deal with the results of studies of supervisory needs analysis.[3, 11, 13, 14, 23, 24] *Training in Business and Industry* is the book that serves as the basis for much of the literature dealing with training needs analysis. Written by McGehee and Thayer in 1961, they recognized, even at that time, the inadequacies of research in this area. Because even inadequate research in the area of the effect of training supervisors is rare, one can only speculate on the effect of improved training:

> Training will not come of age until it abandons intuitive approaches to the solution of training problems. . . . Specifically, an adequate training program depends upon securing *reliable* data as a basis for answering the following questions:
> Who is to be trained? In what are they to be trained? By whom are they to be trained? How are they to be trained? How are the results of training to be evaluated? . . . in order to approach the securing of answers to these questions, we must effectively utilize research techniques and methods of investigation. We cannot rely on the opinions of experts, the enthusiasm of our trainees, the acceptance of top management, and logic alone to answer these questions. Empirical research — decades of research — is necessary.[6] (pp. 22–23)

FIGURE 1
Training System Model

345

*A. ASSESSMENT OF
TRAINING NEEDS*

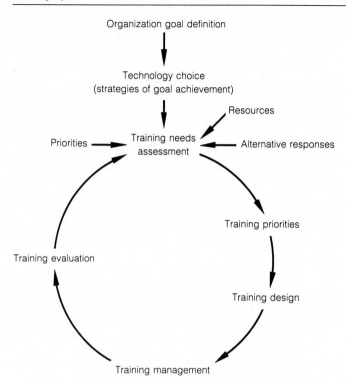

Unfortunately, in the more than 20 years since McGehee and Thayer wrote their book, there have been no real advancements in the field of needs analysis as a scholarly endeavor. The available literature suffers from major deficiencies:

> Little theory development has occurred addressing the issue of how to diagnose performance problems and ascertain that they are caused by some lack of knowledge and that some variant of training represents the optimal solution set. A second failing is that organizational strategic planning considerations have been traditionally ignored or assumed as given. There has been little explicit linkage between organization planning modalities and training needs decisions. Lastly, the data collection procedure itself has been downplayed with consequent blurring of the issues surrounding the acquisition and use of training needs analysis data.[5] (pp. 532–533)

Limitations found by these studies include:

☐ Research does not agree on a universally effective model of supervisory behavior.[13, 14]

☐ Studies are developed to solve problems for particular groups of supervisors and therefore are not readily transferable to other work groups.[3, 13]

☐ The correlations among most elements in training needs analysis and supervisory effectiveness are unknown.[11]

☐ There is generally a poor response to follow-up progress reports of trainees.[3]

☐ Some characteristics used in models of supervisory effectiveness may not be able to be modified through training.[3, 11, 13, 14, 23, 24]

☐ Supervisors and their superiors often do not agree on their training needs. This difference in perceptions has not been adequately researched.[14, 23, 24]

Further, EEO considerations are typically ignored in the training need assessment literature. Affirmative action requires equal employee access to training opportunities and subsequent advantageous changes in status. Legal problems may develop in an organization ignoring this factor:

> To sum it up, defining the training needs of managers is a complex process. The assumption has been that we can define, behaviorally, what constitutes effective management. In reality, however, a generally accepted definition of management itself is lacking. For the conscientious trainer, defining the training and development needs of managers will involve more than a rating of performance on basic management functions. He must consider the level of management and the norms, values and structural aspects of the organization which may significantly influence manager performance. And he must have a working knowledge of several diagnostic techniques.[8] (p. 125).

Clearly, there are significant gaps in the training needs assessment literature. One method to help close these gaps is to develop a framework or model which will allow the training assessor to begin by asking the "right" questions concerning training needs. Based upon the above discussion, it appears that the variables of Figure 2 offer such a model. As the model illustrates, there are at least three broad areas where training needs may surface.

Training problems focused at the organization as the unit of analysis most likely deal with such issues as definition and awareness of organizational objectives, resources and the allocation of those resources. Any training assessment must begin at this level if the training is to be congruent with the organization's mission.

Of course, the external environment of the organization impinges on this level of training and a significant part of any training focused at this organizational level may well be concerned with a better understanding of how to deal with environmental constraints from such factors as union activity, governmental intervention and the general state of the economy facing the organization. If a training need is identified at this organizational level, then an operations analysis is an essential next step.

The operations analysis focuses on the specific job to be accomplished and the required behaviors of successful completion of that job. This analysis builds upon the organization analysis in that it operationalizes in very specific terms exactly how the organizational objectives are to be realized and how resources are (should be) actually allocated. A training need might arise at this level after it has been determined to redesign a job and incumbents, who previously had not been required to perform certain tasks, are now educated to do so.

Finally, there is person analysis. At this level, the assessment considers whether the job incumbents are actually doing their assigned jobs. Of course, this assessment must be preceded by organizational analysis and operations analysis to first determine whether or not the jobs *should* be done. If it is determined that the jobs should be done, then questions concerning the job incumbents' knowledge, skills and attitudes become relevant and need to be assessed. Here, a training need can be identified by comparing current levels of actual performance with optimal levels of performance (which are defined through the operations analysis).

At this point, training is either desirable or not. If it is desirable, then the training cycle should begin. It is critical to remember that at this point the training needs assessment is *not* completed. It has just gone through one iteration. To evaluate any training program, and to assess any future training needs, the cycle of organization-operation-person analysis is critical. It should be an ongoing process.

To neglect any one of the three levels of analysis is to invite training failure, in that the wrong training may well be given to the wrong people at the wrong time for the wrong reasons. Following this assessment cycle model forces the practitioner to focus on all levels that might have impact on training needs, thus avoiding the expensive and time-consuming pitfalls of providing unnecessary training.

FIGURE 2
Supervisory Training Needs Assessment Model

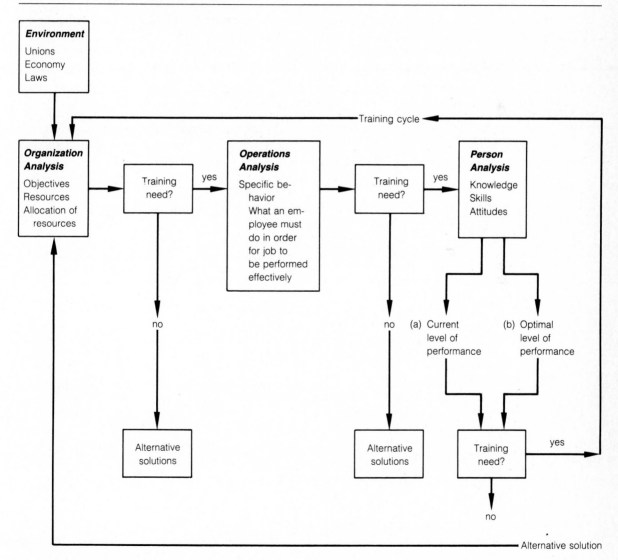

Obviously, this model is a rudimentary one. However, its focus on the few major levels of analysis needed to perform an adequate training needs assessment hopefully will move us from the state of just talking about such assessments to actually beginning to complete such assessments in a more systematic way than has generally been the norm.

REFERENCES

1. Brown, F. Gerald, and Wedel, Kenneth R., *Assessing Training Needs*. Washington, DC: The National Training and Development Services Press, 1974.

2. Howell, D. L., "Supervisory development for small business firms," *Personnel Journal*, July 1970, pp. 570–576.

3. Braun, Alexander, "Assessing supervisory training needs and evaluating effectiveness," *Training and Development Journal*, February 1979, pp. 3–10.

4. "ASTD national report for training and development," American Society for Training and Development, January 5, 1979, and May 31, 1977.

5. Moore, Michael L., and Dutton, Philip, "Training needs analysis: review and critique," *Academy of Management Review*, Vol. 3, 1978, pp. 532–545.

6. McGehee, William, and Thayer, Paul W., *Training in Business and Industry*, New York: John Wiley & Sons Inc., 1961.

7. Goldstein, Irwin L., "Training in work organizations," in Rosenzweig. Mark R., and Porter, Lyman W. (eds.), *Annual Review of Psychology*, Vol. 31, 1980.

8. Wessman, Fred, "Determining the training needs of managers," *Personnel Journal*, February 1975, pp. 109–113.

9. Becker, Stephen P., "Competency analysis: looking at attitudes and interests as well as technical job skills," *Training*, December 1977, pp. 21–22.

10. Zemke, Ron, "Task analysis: figuring out what people need to learn," *Training*, December 1977, pp. 16–20.

11. Roach, Darrell E., "Diagnostic forced-choice scale for first line supervisors," *Personnel Journal*, March 1971, pp. 226–230.

12. Roach, Darrell E., "Factor analysis of rated supervisory behavior," *Personnel Psychology*, Vol. 9, 1956, pp. 487–498.

13. Milich, Robert Peter, "Supervisory development: determining training needs of supervisors," MS thesis, University of Utah, June 1973.

14. Calhoon, Richard P., and Jerdee, Thomas H., "First-level supervisory training needs and organizational development," *Public Personnel Management*, May–June 1975, pp. 196–200.

15. Steadham, Stephen V., "Learning to select a needs assessment strategy," *Training and Development Journal*, January 1980, pp. 56–61.

16. Baumgartel, Howard, "Using employee questionnaire results for improving organization," *Kansas Business Review*, Vol. 22, 1959, pp. 2–6.

17. Stewart, Valerie, and Stewart, Andrew, *Managing the Manager's Growth*, Great Britain: Gower Press, 1978.

18. Schneier, Craig E., and Beatty, Richard W., "Integrating behaviorally-based and effectiveness-based methods," *The Personnel Administrator*, July 1979, pp. 65–76.

19. Gordon, David E., "Appraising training needs," *Personnel Journal*, July–August 1965, pp. 349–353.

20. Steiner, Richard, "New use for assessment centers — training evaluation," *Personnel Journal*, April 1975, pp. 236–237.

21. Fitz-enz, Jac, Hards, Kathryn E., and Savage, G. E., "Total development: selection, assessment, growth," *Personnel Administrator*, February 1980, pp. 58–62.

22. Boehm, Virginia R., and Hoyle, David F., "Assessment and management development," in Moses, Joseph L., and Byham, William C. (eds.), *Applying the Assessment Center Method*, New York: Pergamon Press, 1977.

23. Wood, Wendell F., "Identification of management training needs," thesis, Purdue University, 1956.

24. Culbertson, Katherine, and Thompson, Mark, "An analysis of supervisory training needs," *Training and Development Journal*, February 1980, pp. 58–62.

B.

PROGRAM DESIGN AND METHODS

Training and Development Programs: What Learning Theory and Research Have to Offer

Craig Eric Schneier

There is little debate among those interested in training and development in organizations that the principles of learning are basic to their programs' design and implementation. This view is evidenced by the fact that training has been equated with learning (e.g. Blumenfeld and Holland, 1971), and that many proponents of Organizational Development, notably those favoring laboratory training techniques, have stressed "learning to learn" as a primary objective (e.g. Golembiewski, 1972).

Recently, various authors have used learning theory and research effectively in their discussions of training and development programs. Such concepts as anxiety, punishment, and reinforcement are used to help evaluate training experiences. Schrank (1971) has used some learning theory research to help emphasize the degree of similarity between the teacher-pupil role and the supervisor-subordinate role. He has also shed some light on the importance of the teacher's role in determining the pupil's learning success. At least one learning theory, operant theory, has recently been explored as to its application to a wide variety of training and development problems (Murphy, 1972; Beatty and Schneier, 1972).

Despite this sampling of useful ideas generated from learning theory and a widespread recognition that training and development programs are primarily learning processes, there is still much validity in the following remarks by Goldstein and Sorcher (1972, p. 37):

> Management training — in its several underlying philosophies, its specific conceptualizations and its concrete techniques — is a human learning process. Yet almost without exception, there has been remarkably little reliance in the development and implementation of management training on this vast and relevant body of research literature.

We agree with the statement that there are principles of various learning theories and findings from empirical research that are still relatively unknown and/or not utilized by specialists in training and development. While there is considerable disagreement among the experts as to which one of the several learning theories best explains the human learning process, many principles which logically follow from the various theories are supported by a considerable body of research. Obviously, not all of this research was performed with managers, or even with adults in work situations, but so much of it has been substantiated time and again that the findings are generally agreed upon in the literature.

This article will state some of these principles and findings which are thought to be useful in all phases of training and development programs. The statements will be grouped under the learning environment, the role of the teacher/trainer, characteristics of the learner, basic processes in the human learning activity, reinforcement and punishment, retention and transfer of learning, and practice.*

It will be stressed that these seven categories form the interdependent considerations in the design, implementation, and evaluation of effective training and development programs, that they represent the sources of possible contingencies to be dealt with in each unique learning situation, and that they form the conceptual base for many important organizational training and development programs, such as MBO, skill training, and performance appraisals.

PRINCIPLES AND FINDINGS FROM LEARNING THEORY AND RESEARCH

1. The Learning Environment

1. Objectives and success criteria for the learning program should be specified and communicated to all learners before the program begins (see V-7).

2. Tests of the learner's progress should be scheduled. If a learner is not ready for a test, he should continue practicing. The learner should have an idea of the types of questions or activities that will be on the test. The "ordeal" aspect of testing should be eliminated.

3. Tasks should be broken into component behaviors that can be learned directly. The behaviors should be sequenced in order of increasing difficulty toward a final target behavior (see V-5).

4. The value of teaching machines and programmed learning devices lies in their ability to help sequence learning, to allow the learner to progress at his own pace, and to help control attention by focusing the learner on the stimuli; their value does not lie in their gadgetry or hardware.

5. To measure learning, note observational changes in the frequencies of desired behavioral responses, not necessarily in the strength of responses, in intentions, or in attitudes. Baseline frequencies of behavior must, therefore, be established prior to the learning situation in order to note the differential effects of learning.

6. "Whole" presentation is usually better than "part" presentation. Therefore, give the learner a "feel" for the total task initially.

7. Learning can and does take place in every context, not only in specified

---

*For a more detailed explanation of these principles and findings, the reader is referred to any of the works on learning cited in the references.

locations and in formal programs. Undesirable and desirable behaviors learned in these "informal" settings should be noted.

II. The Role of the Teacher/Trainer

1. Teachers learn a great deal about their learners when they are actually teaching and given responsibility. Having students act as teachers in some situations increases their ability to learn, as well as their empathy for other teachers.

2. The teacher conditions emotional reactions in the learning program, as well as behavioral responses and should, therefore, attempt to condition favorable reactions to himself and to the subject matter.

3. The teacher establishes objectives, methods, sequences, and time limits in learning programs with varying degrees of participation by the learner. The teacher's knowledge of the learner, the situation, and the content of the learning program is vital for specifying both the proper methods and the appropriate degree of learner participation in each learning program.

III. The Characteristics of the Learner

1. People not only learn at different rates, but each person brings a different emotional state or temperament to the learning situation (see II-2). Assessment of temperament facilitates a more effective choice of teaching strategies.

2. The motivational level of the learner is relevant to the type and amount of stimuli to which he will respond. Whether he finds the learning intrinsically or extrinsically rewarding (i.e. instrumental for internally mediated or externally mediated rewards), should be considered. The needs the learner has unsatisfied as he enters the learning program are also relevant.

3. Each learner's prior conditioning or learning background will influence the amount, frequency, and type of reinforcement and punishment which will be most effective, as well as the method of stimuli presentation (e.g. visual, auditory).

4. Individual learners should be encouraged to learn the skills or behaviors of which they are capable and in which they are interested. They should be able to specialize and demonstrate expertise in at least one area in order to take pride in their accomplishments.

IV. Basic Processes in the Human Learning Activity

1. Interest and attention come from successful experiences. These, in turn, facilitate learning as they are seen as rewarding experiences.

2. Attention and curiosity in learning are best facilitated by the use of moderate (not too high nor too low) levels of arousal, curiosity, or anxiety.

3. Learning can occur when the learner merely observes. Active participation is not always necessary, unless motor skills are being taught.

4. Learners should not leave the learning setting after giving incorrect responses. Final responses should always be correct.

5. There are several ways to learn: trial and error, perception-organization-insight, and modeling another's behavior, are all effective under certain conditions.

6. Learning usually progresses to a point and then levels off. This leveling (a "plateau" in a "learning curve") may be due to the fact that incorrect responses are being reduced or that small simple steps in learning were learned rapidly and now as the small steps are combined into complex tasks, learning slows. Incentives added in the "plateau" stage are helpful.

7. If motor responses are to be learned, verbal guidance, practice, and a favorable, supportive environment are helpful. If ideas or concepts are to be learned, active participation and the formation of meaningful associations between the new material and more familiar material are helpful.

8. Learning can be inhibited and therefore proper responses decreased if too much repetition or fatigue is evidenced (see VII-3).

9. Avoidance learning occurs when fear is felt and a response is made to eliminate the fear. This fear-avoiding response is often reinforced, and it therefore has little chance of being eliminated, as it is needed to avoid aversive stimuli (see V-2). To eliminate avoidance behaviors, the aversive stimuli must be removed.

10. Incidental learning is learning that remains dormant until the occasion for its demonstration arises (e.g. curiosity is stimulated or reinforcement is powerful enough to elicit the response) (see VI-1).

11. Imitation requires that the learner is directly reinforced for matching a model's behavior. "Matched dependence" occurs when the learner models a model. "Same behavior" occurs when two learners respond to the same stimulus, not to each other. Vicarious learning is matching the behavior of another without receiving direct or immediate reinforcement from the model.

12. Complex human learning includes a proper degree of discrimination and generalization. Discrimination requires distinguishing between quite similar stimuli which require *different* responses. Generalization requires noting that similar, but not exactly the same stimuli often require the *same* response.

13. Attitudes can be learned and reinforced in much the same way as behavior is reinforced.

V. Reinforcement and Punishment

1. The "Law of Effect" states that behavior that is reinforced will increase in probability of future occurrence. A reinforcer is, therefore, any object or event that *strengthens* the probability of future occurrence of behavior.

2. Punishment occurs when the probability of a response is *weakened* by an object or event. Punishment leads to escape and avoidance behaviors, as well as frustration.

3. Secondary reinforcers (e.g. money) are those objects or events which are linked to or instrumental for receiving other primary reinforcers (e.g. food) and so also take on reinforcing properties themselves. The many effective secondary reinforcers should be identified and used.

4. Undesired behaviors can be extinguished if they are simply not reinforced and not punished, but ignored.

5. "Shaping" behavior occurs when desired responses are observed which are approximates of a target behavior, and are reinforced. The responses are continually reinforced as they become closer and closer to the target, until the target is imitated.

6. For punishment and reinforcement to be effective, they must be dispensed immediately and be appropriate in intensity for the particular response they follow.

7. Knowledge of results of performance is basic to learning and is often a reinforcer. It provides necessary feedback for corrective action, and should be related to goal levels which are predetermined standards of performance communicated to and understood by the learner.

8. A harder, more intense response will not be elicited unless a more intense, more powerful reinforcer is given.

9. If reinforcement is dispensed on a variable ratio schedule (after a random and changing number of responses unknown to the learner), behavior will be most difficult to extinguish. The variable ratio is thus more effective in sustaining desired responses than either a continuous reinforcement schedule (each desired response rewarded) or fixed interval reinforcement schedule (reinforcement given after the passage of an interval of time, e.g. weekly).

10. Social reinforcement (e.g. approval, status given by others) can be effective in controlling behavior, depending upon the environment and personal attractions.

11. The personality and position of the reinforcing/punishing agent influences the effectiveness of the reinforcement or punishment he dispenses. Therefore, it is not only that he dispenses rewards, but his manner, sincerity, and tone in these instances that is noticed by the learner.

VI. Retention and Transfer of Learning

1. In transferring learning, the teacher/trainer should be aware of latent learning and offer reinforcement to prompt the demonstration of such learning.

2. Time does not cause forgetting per se; it merely allows for interfering learning processes to occur between what was learned and the time recall is desired.

3. Retroactive inhibition refers to the interference of new material on the ability to recall older material. Proactive inhibition occurs when old material interferes with the learning of new material. At times, therefore, it is wise to almost over-learn or repeat some material many times.

4. Some learned material is not recalled, as it is repressed in the subconscious of the learner because its overt demonstration is deemed to be harmful to the learner.

5. Identical stimuli presented in the learning and application settings should result in positive transfer. The learning of principles that apply across situations also aids in transfer of learning.

6. Transfer is aided if responses are given in situations which are similar to those which will be encountered in the post-learning environment.

7. Transfer is aided if the learner is able to demonstrate generalization (see IV-12).

8. Retention is strengthened if a variable-ratio reinforcement schedule is followed (see V-10).

VII. Practice

1. The learner must be encouraged (i.e. reinforced) to take practice seriously.

2. Practice should include responses to different stimuli than those encountered in learning, but which may be encountered in actual application (see IV-12).

3. Distributed, rather than massed practice with frequent short rests, is usually optimal.

USES OF THE PRINCIPLES AND FINDINGS

It is obvious that while not all of these findings and principles from learning theory and research are applicable to each type of training and development program, some are of obvious use. Depending on the type of program, exigencies of time and cost, and the characteristics of the trainees and trainers, some will be more relevant than others. Furthermore, the seven categories are not meant to be entirely separate. Many items necessarily overlap. The most important aspect of the categories is their *interdependent* nature. Program developers can benefit from some consideration of each category.

As with so many aspects of organizations, the effective design and implementation of training and development programs depend largely on the recognition of the contingencies the data from the seven categories present to the specialist. In each particular instance, the categories come together in a unique way to form a complex learning situation or set of contingencies to be managed. The use of a particular type of training program can depend upon the characteristics of the trainees, which can depend upon the learning environment and learning content, which may depend upon the role of the trainer, and so on. It can thus be seen that each of the seven categories may influence, or be contingent upon, any or all of the others in any given learning situation. The training and development specialist's success in facilitating learning will, therefore, depend in large part on his ability to properly *diagnose* a situation and then develop the most effective learning strategies for that situation. In the diagnostic phase of the facilitation of learning in organizations, the seven categories represent the possible sources of data which can be gathered regarding a training situation (e.g. data regarding the environment, the trainer, the trainees, etc.) (see Figure 1).

After the diagnosis is completed, the actual *design* of a particular program or learning strategy can begin. The statements in each category can be scanned for their relevance to a specific type of strategy, such as programmed instruction, lectures, modeling, etc. For example, if a "skill" training program is required, statements concerning practice, knowledge of results, and reinforcement schedules would be helpful. Following design, the *implementation* of the strategy can be aided by the statements, as they suggest points to be noted which can deter or facilitate implementation in a particular situation. For example, as category three notes, certain characteristics of the learner are vital considerations which would make some strategies more effective than others. The last stage in training and development work is *evaluation* of the strategy and possible *redesign*. This stage can be aided as the seven categories again present the sources of probable success or failure.

The principles and findings from learning theory and research have been presented as an initial list compiled to help those engaged in training and development programs become aware of the scope of the learning literature which is applicable to their programs. The list is also designed for use in the following stages of training and development work: diagnosis of the learning situation, design of the learning strategy, implementation of the strategy, and evaluation and possible redesign. The seven categories are offered as possible sources of data which combine to form each particular training and development situation. Data gathered from the seven categories can facilitate a more rigorous diagnostic effort on the part of the training and development specialist. This diagnosis aids in tying the unique learning situation faced by the specialist to the learning strategy most amenable to that situation. Particular statements within the categories can also be scanned as to their obvious use as guides in imple-

FIGURE 1

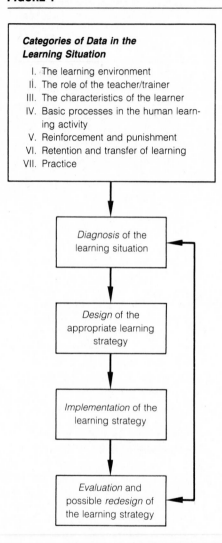

*Categories of Data in the
Learning Situation*

   I. The learning environment
  II. The role of the teacher/trainer
 III. The characteristics of the learner
 IV. Basic processes in the human learn-
     ing activity
  V. Reinforcement and punishment
 VI. Retention and transfer of learning
VII. Practice

Diagnosis of the
learning situation

Design of the
appropriate learning
strategy

Implementation of the
learning strategy

Evaluation and
possible *redesign* of
the learning strategy

menting specific programs such as MBO, skill training, performance appraisals, and the many other training and development programs which are designed to facilitate learning in organization settings.

REFERENCES

Bass, B., and Vaughan, J. *Training in Industry: The Management of Learning.* Belmont, California: Wadsworth, 1968.

Beatty, R. W., and Schneier, Craig Eric. "Training the Hard-Core Unemployed through Positive Reinforcement." *Human Resource Management*, Winter 1972, 11(4), pp. 11–17.

Berrelson, B., and Steiner, G. *Human Behavior.* New York: Harcourt Brace, 1967.

Blumenfeld, W. A., and Holland, M. C. "A Model for the Empirical Evaluation of Training Effectiveness." *Personnel Journal*, Aug. 1971, 50(8), pp. 634–40.

Bugelski, B. R. *The Psychology of Teaching*, second edition. Indianapolis: Bobbs-Merrill, 1971.

Goldstein, A. P., and Sorcher, M. "Changing Managerial Behavior by Applied Learning Techniques." *Training and Development Journal*, Mar. 1973, 27(2), pp. 36–9.

Golembiewski, R. T. *Renewing Organizations; The Laboratory Approach to Planned Change*. Itasca, Ill.: Peacock, 1972.

Hilgard, E. R., and Bower, G. H. *Theories of Learning*, third edition. New York: Appleton Century Crofts, 1966.

Logan, F. A. *Fundamentals of Learning and Motivation*. Dubuque, Iowa: Wm. Brown, 1970.

Murphy, J. "Is It Skinner or Nothing?" *Training and Development Journal*, Feb. 1972, 26(2), pp. 2–9.

Schrank, W. R. "Three Experiments in Education." *Personnel Journal*, Sept. 1971, 50(9), pp. 702–4.

Skinner, B. F. *The Technology of Teaching*. New York: Appleton Century Crofts, 1968.

Staats, A. W., and Staats, C. K. *Complex Human Behavior: A Systematic Extension of Learning Principles*. New York: Holt, 1963.

Curriculum Design in Training: An Overview
William J. Rothwell

In a time of increasing technological change, decreasing rate of productivity growth and burgeoning numbers of the young, white-collar and highly educated workers in the labor force, training is needed as never before. It fights skill obsolescence, stimulates productivity, motivates those who value professional growth above high salaries and bridges the gap between academic theory and organizational practice. Continuous training is a key to remaining competitive — whether for nations, organizations or individuals. And a key to successful training is a well-planned curriculum.

But what is a curriculum? What are the most common theories of curriculum design? How can each of these be applied in an organizational setting? By examining each of the major theories of curriculum design, we can familiarize all practitioners with the state of the art in this most critical facet of training.

Despite the mysterious aura that sometimes surrounds the term, a curriculum is nothing more than a plan of instruction. It is ambiguous because (depending on con-

Reprinted from the November 1983 issue of *Personnel Administrator*, copyright 1983, The American Society for Personnel Administration, 606 North Washington Street, Alexandria, VA 22314, $30 per year.

text) it may refer to one course, a series of related courses, the collective instructional offerings of one institution or of one profession, or the totality of an individual's education. At the very least, it denotes an organized framework of learning goals, activities, subject matter and evaluation methods that have been integrated to form a coherent whole. There are, of course, many ways of organizing; hence, there are many different methods of curriculum design.

There are as many theories as there are theorists of curriculum design. However, for our purposes we can classify the theories into four major curriculum design approaches: the school approach, the systems approach, the andragogical approach and the contingency approach. Let's examine each one.

The School Approach

Ralph Tyler, principal theorist of the school approach, has had a profound and continuing influence on the curriculum design process in public education at all levels in the United States. His most important work,[1] originally written as a syllabus for a University of Chicago seminar, summarized the curriculum design process as one dependent on the answers to four basic questions. The so-called Tyler Rationale emphasizes (1) the development of instructional objectives; (2) the specification of instructional strategies; (3) the careful planning of instruction; and (4) the rigorous evaluation of learning outcomes. Those influenced by this approach contend that the curriculum design process is dependent on the needs of the learner, the needs of the society, the logic of the subject matter, the designer's philosophy of education and a psychology of education.

The school approach has had the least influence on the practices of progressive training departments. But since its effects on public education have been great, it has established a way of thinking about learning that does affect training. Indeed, when higher management or trainees evaluate training, they may unconsciously use the Tyler Rationale.

It has been interpreted, in practice, to mean a content-centered approach to curriculum design. It emphasizes the subject matter of training, organized by an instructor-expert into a logical, hierarchical sequence from least to most difficult.

To apply the approach, a trainer would need to identify employee training needs. These needs can be determined by many different methods.[2] Next, the trainer determines what will be taught, how it will be taught, when it will be taught, and how the success or failure of the instruction can be judged during training (formulative evaluation) and following training (summative evaluation).

In practice, this approach may be rather informal yet prescriptive. Needs assessment may be determined through a Delphi procedure, a course may be designed around what supervisors believe employees should know, and evaluation may be based on employee or supervisory opinions about the course. Trainees may then be told they must attend certain training courses.

The Systems Approach

The systems approach to curriculum design has had the most profound impact on training. Highly technical, it stresses rationality, efficiency and structure. It is the culmination of work that extends back to Franklin Bobbitt and, more recently, to the behavioralists of the 1960s.[3] Robert F. Mager, the most prominent writer in training, is a chief spokesman of this school.

Each step in the curriculum design process of this approach is integrated and interrelated. The intended result is specific, observable behavioral change. The approach is quite appropriate for those occupations in which critical job performance is dependent on actions that may be observed. For example, most industrial and clerical workers can be trained quite well by using it.

But it is less easily applied to the professionals because the critical factors in professional job success are primarily unobservable mental actions. Many training theorists contend that the systems approach can be applied to training the more creative professional and managerial employee, but the focus should be shifted from an emphasis on job *behaviors* to observable job *results*.[4]

In the systems approach, the emphasis is on design and on the results of a carefully planned sequence of activities. The learner and the instructor are equally important, and the true focus is on the cognitive (fact-based, rational) rather than on the affective (feeling-based).[5]

While the order of the curriculum design process varies somewhat among the various systems theorists, it can be more or less summarized as follows:

The instructional designer:

- ▢ Identifies training needs
- ▢ Specifies training goals
- ▢ Examines the knowledge, skills, abilities and personalities of the learners
- ▢ Derives specific behavioral objectives
- ▢ Designs tests related to each objective
- ▢ Develops a strategy for meeting each behavioral objective
- ▢ Prepares instruction based on all preceding steps
- ▢ Evaluates the learning sequence to improve the final product
- ▢ Re-evaluates the learning sequence based on the first evaluation

An independent source:

- ▢ Evaluates the instructional product

The first step of this process is reached through job (or task) analysis, and the second through the development of performance standards. Behavioral objectives must be carefully written to link with the performance standards. Unlike the school approach, the systems approach necessitates design by someone thoroughly versed in the technical intricacies of job and task analysis, behavioral objectives, research on instructional strategies and evaluation techniques.

The Andragogical Approach

Andragogy refers to adult instruction. It is different from pedagogy, which refers to the instruction of children. The andragogical approach, based on the little we know of adult learning, is as much philosophical stance as it is a methodology of curriculum design. In this respect, it differs from the school and the systems approaches, which only *imply* their philosophies about learners.

Cyril O. Houle and Malcolm Knowles are undoubtedly the modern leaders of this approach,[6] but Carl Rogers is its spiritual forefather.[7] It is unlike the school approach to curriculum design, which emphasizes the arrangement of content-matter by an expert; it is unlike the systems approach, which emphasizes highly-structured planning and technique.

Instead, the andragogical approach stresses the central place of the learner in the design of instruction. It applies participative management to training. For this reason, advocates of this approach believe that learners must be involved in decisions about training objectives, content, strategies and evaluation techniques.

The role of the trainer is to facilitate decisions. The primary assumption is that learners will know their training needs better than instructional experts ever can. Trainees should, then, be given the opportunity to reach their potential by meeting learning objectives they have helped to establish.

This approach allows learners to meet both affective (feeling-based) as well as cognitive (fact-based) training needs. The instructional sequence does not depend on the arrangement of subject-matter, but rather proceeds "from field experience to theory and principles to foundational knowledge to skill practice to field application."[8]

The andragogical approach seems much more suited than other approaches to meeting the needs of experienced professionals, because it provides for the integration of training and career development. It allows learners the freedom to create the personal, idealized image of what they would like to be and to work toward realizing this goal. It thus encourages employees to take the responsibility for their own development.

Unlike the school or systems approaches, which primarily impose training on employees lower in the organization, the andragogical approach allows training to be designed from the bottom up. Each employee negotiates with a supervisor an individual learning contract for a specified time. These contracts are congruent with MBO plans or other methods of performance contracting. They may be written on special forms, or on blank sheets of paper.

From all learning contracts in the organization, the training director can then develop courses internally to meet the most common and frequently identified needs. More specialized training needs, on the other hand, can be met for individuals through other sources, such as local universities, short seminars, professional conferences and so forth.

The Contingency Approach

Like the andragogical approach in many respects, the contingency approach differs in its greater stress on the environment and on the culture in which training takes place. Leonard Nadler is perhaps the foremost advocate of this approach.[9]

While eclectic, it differs from the other approaches in its assumption that learning is not restricted to the individual. Rather, it assumes that organizations and work groups can also learn collectively. For this reason, it considers learning on the organizational level as most important, and this process is facilitated by organization development. Next in importance is learning at the level of the work group, and this process is facilitated by organizational dynamics. At the lowest level of priority is training for the individual.

The contingency approach advocates initiating any change effort at the top of the organization and moving downward. Learning is inherently change-oriented; hence, that which facilitates learning should begin where the power is — at the top. Cultural and social conditions in an organization can prevent an individual's application of principles learned in training. Therefore, these conditions must be treated before training can be successful.

In applying this approach, it is first necessary to diagnose system-wide problems in the organization, collect information about these problems, articulate them, plan the means by which to solve them (training is but one of many ways), provide feedback to the participants in this effort, and examine and evaluate the effort. These stages, otherwise recognizable as the stages of an OD intervention, are also stages in guiding a learning activity for an entire organization.

As a result of this intervention, it will then be possible to specify those problems at the level of the individual employee which can be solved by (1) feeling-oriented training, or (2) fact-oriented training. Feeling-oriented training centers on attitudes, values and beliefs; fact-oriented training centers on information related to the employee's job. Two curricula can then be designed for meeting these needs.

STRENGTHS AND WEAKNESSES

No curriculum design approach is entirely satisfactory for meeting all training needs. Hence, any organization will most likely have many training curricula. A summary of the major approaches to curriculum design is presented in Figure 1.

The school approach is useful for conveying information. But, at a time characterized by a virtual explosion of information, the school approach is probably inadequate even to keep employees abreast of changes in their occupations. Another weakness of the approach is its tendency to prescribe what the learner should know rather than to encourage the learner to make that judgment.

The systems approach is quite technical. It does result in very carefully planned instruction, but it restricts the amount of learner participation in the program design. Well-suited to occupations in which critical job performance depends on observable behaviors, it is less suited to those in which job success depends on judgment.

FIGURE 1
Approaches to Curriculum Design

	School Approach	*Systems Approach*	*Andragogical Approach*	*Contingency Approach*
Chief spokesperson(s)	Ralph Tyler	Robert F. Mager	Malcolm Knowles Cyril O. Houle	Leonard Nadler
Assumptions	Effective training must be prescribed.	Effective training results from technique.	Effective training results from learner participation.	Effective training must be preceded by learning for the organization.
Trainer-designer	Expert in the subject of the training.	Expert in designing training.	Expert in adult learning. A facilitator.	Change agent.
Sequence of activities in curriculum design	1. Conduct needs assessment. 2. Decide what will be taught. 3. Decide how to teach it. 4. Evaluate.	1. Identify needs, goals, learners, objectives. 2. Decide how to teach subject. 3. Evaluate during instruction. 4. Evaluate following instruction.	1. Allow learners to identify needs, goals, objectives. 2. Allow learners to select methods. 3. Help learners meet their needs. 4. Evaluate results of learning objectives.	1. Identify organizational learning needs and facilitate their achievement. 2. Design feeling and fact training. 3. Use andragogical approach for individual needs.

The andragogical approach applies participative management to instructional design and thus, presumably, fosters employee commitment to learning goals. However, it is an approach that makes management evaluation of training difficult for the organization as a whole. For this reason, it may lead to a certain amount of uncertainty about organization-wide learning priorities.

The contingency approach is, finally, the best of methods but also the most difficult and time consuming to use. In acknowledging the importance of organizational culture, it combines a change effort for the organization and training for the individual. But change efforts are usually long-term and subject to unexpected outcomes. The approach suffers from these possible disadvantages, which make it extremely difficult to evaluate.

As knowledge workers dominate the labor force,[10] employers of all kinds must necessarily become learning-oriented to preserve the skill levels of their employees. For this reason, curriculum design — the planning of instruction — is becoming an area of increasing importance. All HR practitioners should understand the current theories of curriculum design, and they should focus additional attention on this most critical facet of training.

REFERENCES

1. Tyler, R., *Basic Principles of Curriculum and Instruction*. Chicago: University of Chicago Press, 1949.

2. Brown, G., and Wedel, K. W., *Assessing Training Needs*. Washington: National Training and Development Service, 1974. Moore, M., and Dutton, P., "Training needs analysis," *Academy of Management Review*, Vol. 3, July 1978, pp. 532–45.

3. Bobbit, F., *The curriculum*. Boston: Houghton Mifflin, 1918.

4. See for example, Warren, M. W., *Training for Results*, second edition. Reading, MA: Addison-Wesley, 1979.

5. See for example, Bortz, R. F., *Handbook for Developing Occupational Curricula*. Boston: Allyn & Bacon, 1981. Gagne, R. M. and Briggs, L., *Principles of Instructional Design*, second edition. New York: Holt, Rinehart and Winston, 1979. Dick, W., and Carey, L., *The Systematic Design of Instruction*. Glenview, IL: Scott, Foresman, 1978.

6. Houle, C. O., *The Design of Education*. San Francisco: Jossey-Bass, 1972. Knowles, M., *The Adult Learner: A Neglected Species*, second edition. Houston: Gulf, 1978.

7. Rogers, C., "Toward becoming a fully functioning person," in A. W. Combs (ed.), *Perceiving, Behaving, Becoming: A New Focus for Education*. Washington, D.C.: Association for Supervision and Curriculum Development.

8. Knowles, *The Adult Learner*, p. 259.

9. Nadler, L., *Developing Human Resources*, second edition. Austin, TX: Learning Concepts, 1979.

10. Ginzberg, E., "The professionalization of the U.S. labor force," *Scientific American*, March 1979, pp. 48–53.

Behavior Modeling Training: Update and Recommendations

Glenn M. McEvoy and Sara A. Sporer

It would be difficult to find a skills training technique that has generated as much excitement and interest over the last ten years as behavior modeling (also called behavioral role modeling, interaction modeling, or applied learning). Behavior modeling training (BMT) appears to have a great deal of promise for training supervisors in areas that have always been highly problematic — namely, interpersonal skills and effective handling of "people problems." However, BMT is still relatively new, and much remains to be learned about it if BMT is to avoid becoming just another passing fad in training.

Significant research has been conducted over the last few years that relates to the use of BMT in practice. Appropriate and productive applications of BMT are more likely if practitioners are aware of this current research, and if they understand the theoretical foundations underlying behavior modeling. The purpose of the present paper is to provide this necessary background. Specifically, the paper:

□ Describes BMT and its theoretical foundation

□ Recommends improvements in current BMT practice based on the most recent research

WHAT IS BEHAVIOR MODELING TRAINING?

The first documented application of BMT to industrial training was developed by Mel Sorcher at General Electric in the early 1970s (Goldstein & Sorcher, 1974). Sorcher's initial efforts focused on supervisory skill development, particularly as the skills applied to dealing with employees from culturally disadvantaged backgrounds. The skill areas determined to be important for supervisors at GE were:

1. Orienting a new employee
2. Motivating the poor performer
3. Correcting inadequate work quantity and quality
4. Reducing absenteeism and turnover
5. Handling employee complaints
6. Discussing personal work habits with an employee
7. Discussing formal corrective action with an employee
8. Giving recognition to the average employee
9. Overcoming resistance to change
10. Delegating authority
11. Conducting a performance review

The majority of subsequent BMT applications in other organizations have involved training supervisors in skill areas similar to those listed above. Typically, a 2–4 hour training session is necessary for each skill area taught.

BMT usually involves a brief discussion of key learning points, a filmed model

---

This reading was prepared specifically for inclusion in the present book.

FIGURE 1
Steps in Behavior Modeling Training

Learning points
Filmed model
Role play
Social reinforcement
Transfer of learning

demonstrating the learning points, trainee rehearsal through role play, social reinforcement from the trainer and other trainees, and some steps to insure transfer of training back to the work environment. Figure 1 summarizes this sequence.

In some BMT programs, learning points are specific to the particular situation. An example would be the following learning points associated with "handling employee complaints" (Latham & Saari, 1979):

- ☐ Avoid hostile or defensive reactions
- ☐ Listen openly to complaint
- ☐ Restate complaint to assure understanding
- ☐ Recognize and acknowledge others' viewpoint
- ☐ State own position nondefensively
- ☐ Set specific date for follow-up meeting

Other applications (e.g., Porras et al., 1982) utilize more general learning points applicable to each skill area, such as:

- ☐ Describe the problem behavior and its effect on organizational performance
- ☐ Listen actively to subordinate's perspective
- ☐ Problem solve participatively
- ☐ Follow-up and provide reinforcement for correct behaviors

A "model" is filmed (or videotaped) exhibiting the correct behaviors in a role play situation. This model, along with the learning points, provides the major cognitive inputs for trainees. Organizations can develop their own modeling displays or purchase commercially developed ones.

At this point in the BMT sequence, the trainees move from cognitive learning to skills practice. The practice sessions typically involve trainee role playing of subordinate-supervisor episodes similar to the ones depicted in the modeling display. The trainee who plays the supervisor's role then receives feedback and reinforcement regarding his or her performance vis-a-vis the key learning points. Each trainee is allowed to role play as the supervisor at least once. In some applications, these "rehearsals" are videotaped so that trainees can view and evaluate their own performance.

The last step of the BMT sequence involves provisions for transfer of the trainees' learned skills back to the work environment. In some cases, trainees make a public commitment or a verbal contract to practice the learned skills on the job. In other cases, subsequent training sessions start with a review of all of the trainees' experiences stemming from their use of the newly learned skills on the job. In still other instances, the trainees' managers have been taught in advance to recognize and reinforce the new skills demonstrated in the work setting. When deliberate arrangements for transfer of learning are not made, trainees typically revert to the less effective behavior patterns they exhibited prior to BMT (Russell, Wexley & Hunter, 1984).

THE UNDERLYING MODELING PROCESS

The fundamental logic underlying BMT is the common-sense notion that much of an individual's behavioral repertoire is acquired through the observation and imitation (i.e., "modeling") of others. Such vicarious learning explains how someone without any hands-on experience using computers can sit down at a terminal, and after observing another, take reasonably proficient first steps toward operating a computer program. There can be no doubt that modeling is a powerful learning process. The question is: how can a trainer best harness knowledge of the modeling process for use in planned training situations?

Psychologist Albert Bandura studied the modeling process in detail and suggested that it consists of four subprocesses: attention, retention, motor reproduction, and motivation or reinforcement (Bandura, 1977). Figure 2 summarizes the process.

It is immediately obvious that there is a relationship between the modeling process depicted in Figure 2 and the steps involved in BMT (Figure 1). The nature of this relationship is as follows:

- *Attention processes* result from the interaction of the modeling stimulus and trainee characteristics. Trainee attention is enhanced if the model is distinctive, attractive, engaging, powerful, competent, and demographically similar to the trainee. Attention is further enhanced if the trainee is alert, aroused, motivated to learn, and has been positively reinforced in the past for paying attention. Attention processes are facilitated in BMT through the use of an appropriate model and the inclusion of key learning points.

- *Retention processes* involve symbolic coding, symbolic rehearsal, and motor rehearsal. Symbolic coding is simply the mental process by which trainees reduce the complex behaviors observed in the model to verbal symbols in the brain. Symbolic rehearsal consists of trainees imagining or visualizing themselves performing the same behaviors as the model. These retention processes are enhanced in BMT through the presentation of learning points (symbolic coding) and through role playing (rehearsal).

- *Motor reproduction processes* involve the actual practice of newly learned behaviors. In BMT this is achieved through role playing a situation similar to the one presented in the modeling display. For successful reproduction of new behaviors, trainees must have the physical capabilities necessary to perform the skill, and they must receive accurate feedback (either from themselves or from observers) regarding performance.

FIGURE 2
The Process of Modeling

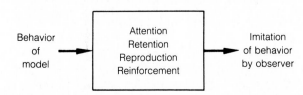

▫ *Reinforcement processes* involve three possible sources of motivation. Trainees may receive reinforcement either from others or from themselves for successful behavior replication. Observers of modeled behavior may also obtain so-called "vicarious reinforcement" by watching a highly regarded model receive positive reinforcement (e.g., praise from a manager) for engaging in correct behaviors on videotape. Reinforcement processes are thus incorporated into BMT in both the modeling and role playing stages.

RECENT RESEARCH ON BEHAVIOR MODELING TRAINING

Early research on BMT applications focused primarily on establishing the effectiveness of the technique for eliciting desired employee learning and behavioral change. Most of this research is adequately summarized in several sources (e.g., McGehee & Tullar, 1978; Robinson, 1982). Overall, the literature suggests that BMT is quite effective as measured by favorable trainee reactions, learnings achieved, and behavioral changes in role play situations similar to those in the training workshops. The evidence is somewhat less persuasive in terms of BMT's ability to induce measurable and sustainable changes in performance and effectiveness back in the work environment.

Nonetheless, BMT has withstood the test of evaluation research much better than most training techniques. As a result, the focus of BMT research shifted in the early 1980s to an exploration of ways to improve an already demonstrably effective training method. Findings from recent research can be discussed following the general modeling process described earlier: attention, retention, reproduction, reinforcement, and transfer (the latter is added to this listing due to its critical importance in training). The topic of reinforcement, however, will not be addressed directly because little recent research on this aspect of BMT has been conducted.

Attention Processes

A recent successful BMT program in a large forest products company provides several key insights into ways to enhance attention processes (Porras & Anderson, 1981; Porras et al., 1982). "Success" in this case was measured by improvements in productivity, absenteeism, turnover and subordinate ratings of satisfaction for those supervisors trained using BMT. Attentional processes were enhanced through:

▫ Involvement of supervisors in a critical incident analysis of their jobs and diagnosis of major organizational problems prior to the design of the BMT

▫ Support of the training program by top management (high level managers attended many of the training sessions and a key executive introduced each training module via videotape)

▫ Use of higher level managers as models, both in modeling displays and as trainers

This last suggestion must be viewed cautiously because a more recent study found no difference in a training program using line managers compared to one using professional trainers as models (Russell et al., 1984). However, there can be no doubt about the importance of using competent, attractive, credible, high status models in a BMT program.

A model that meets with success in a modeling display is likely to strengthen observers' "outcome expectations" (i.e., heighten observers' expectations that positive outcomes will follow if they perform the new skills). Further, a model who displays apprehension, yet completes a difficult task, has been found to be more effective than a model displaying no apprehension in a difficult situation (Manz & Sims, 1981). Apparently, such apprehension allows observers to more fully identify with the model.

As noted earlier, attention results from the interaction of modeling stimuli and observer characteristics. Little is known about what individual characteristics enhance attention processes. However, one recent study found that BMT was more effective for individuals exhibiting positive self-image, high degree of self-actualization, feelings of control and competence, and little role overload or job stress (Porras & Hargis, 1982). Overall, this pattern suggests that individuals with a generalized sense of mastery of their work situations may respond more effectively to BMT. This tentative conclusion is in stark contrast to the conventional wisdom in organizational change efforts which has long held that individuals must be "hurting" (i.e., feel a strong need to change or, in a sense, feel "incompetent") before change efforts are likely to be successful.

Retention Processes

Until recently, little research had been done on the retention stage of the modeling process. While the use of learning points is known to facilitate symbolic coding, there are questions about what type of learning points — and from what source — are most effective. Further, almost no work was done prior to 1980 on symbolic rehearsal as a means of improving retention and learning in BMT programs.

Several of these issues have been addressed in a recent stream of research conducted by Phillip Decker (Decker, 1980, 1982, 1984; Mann & Decker, 1984). In both laboratory and field studies, Decker has examined whether formalized retention processes facilitate BMT and what the effects are of the *source* of learning points (trainer or trainee) and the *type* of learning points (descriptive or rule-oriented). Descriptive learning points provide summary statements of the model's key behaviors. Rule-oriented learning points state the principles underlying the model's behavior. Decker also had some experimental BMT subjects close their eyes and imagine themselves engaging in the behavior exhibited by the model while keeping the learning points in mind (symbolic rehearsal). The outcome variables in most of his studies were reproducibility of behaviors and generalizability of learnings to novel contexts. These were measured by a trainee's ability to successfully role play supervisory situations that were first similar to, then slightly different from, those situations modeled in the BMT sessions.

Decker's results suggest the following:

- Both formalized retention aids (e.g., learning points) and symbolic rehearsal improve reproducibility of behaviors and generalizability of learnings
- Rule-oriented learning points tend to facilitate generalizability while descriptive learning points enhance reproducibility
- Trainee-generated learning points are ineffective; however, it may be advantageous to ask trainees to rewrite trainer-generated learning points in their own language and in such a way as to be most pertinent to their own individual situations (Latham & Saari, 1979)

Motor Reproduction Processes

This phase of modeling corresponds most closely to the role play step in BMT. Little research has been directed at examining what characteristics of the role play process facilitate learning. However, one recent study (Decker, 1983) suggests the following:

- One or two observers in a role play situation is preferable to ten observers
- Videotaping the role play for feedback to trainees improves reproducibility of learned behaviors

Smaller groups of observers are apparently able to elicit the same increased commitment to behavior change as large groups of observers, but without incurring the increases in trainee evaluation apprehension typical in large-group settings. This suggests that after presentation of the learning points and modeling display, training groups should be broken down into smaller subgroups for role playing. Such separation would increase training costs because trainers would be needed for each subgroup. Offsetting this cost, however, would be a reduction in total training time due to more rapid completion of the role play step.

It also appears that feedback from trainer and peers is more effective when supplemented with trainee videotaping. Most of the recent successful field studies in BMT have utilized videotape feedback. Thus, taping appears to be well worth the added time and expense. Under certain circumstances, such videotapes could also serve as modeling displays for subsequent BMT sessions.

Transfer

A critical problem in all training is the transfer of learning back to the work environment. For many reasons (including measurement difficulties) the vast majority of training programs fail to evaluate the degree of successful transfer of learning. BMT has done better than most training programs in this regard. Consequently, several recent studies suggest ways of facilitating transfer. The possibilities include:

- Verbal or written contracting is done at the end of each training session, with trainees committing publicly to practice the new skills during the next week. The following training session begins with a discussion of successes and/or failures in applying the new learnings. Successes are reinforced and failures diagnosed (Latham & Saari, 1979; Porras & Anderson, 1981; Porras et al., 1982).

- The last training module is dedicated solely to "skill generalization" — how the general principles learned in previous training sessions may be applied to a wide variety of supervisory situations (Porras et al., 1982).

- Subordinates of supervisors are trained simultaneously in reciprocal skills (e.g., how to express complaints to your supervisor, how to clarify instructions, how to cooperate in changing situations, etc.) utilizing BMT techniques. With both supervisor and subordinate trained to use more effective and complementary behaviors, the skills learned are likely to be mutually reinforced and maintained on the job (Sorcher & Spence, 1982).

- Managers of supervisors are trained simultaneously in recognizing and reinforcing appropriate new behaviors on the job. This can, of course, start during training if the managers are involved as trainers. Part of a supervisor's annual performance evaluation can be based on the degree to which BMT skills are utilized on the job (Latham & Saari, 1979; Meyer & Raich, 1983; Porras & Anderson, 1981).

- Self-perception theory predicts that new behaviors will be integrated into behavioral repertoires only if they are consistent with a supervisor's self-image. Cases of initial inconsistency require "strong medicine." Possibilities here include: 1) the provision of negative models (obtaining negative outcomes) along with the positive ones in order to attack well-entrenched, undesirable behaviors; 2) significant amounts of time devoted to structured mental practice (i.e., symbolic rehearsal) of new behaviors to overcome inconsistencies with self-perceptions; and 3) frequent multiple follow-up activities involving goal-setting and reinforcement for behavioral change (Russell et al., 1984).

Supervisory training using behavior modeling has withstood the test of evaluation research rather well. As a result, BMT has become quite popular in practice and a "second round" of experimental research among academics has been stimulated in the last five years. This recent research has been aimed at understanding more fully the various steps of BMT and at fine-tuning BMT to make it an even more effective training technique. Taken together, this research yields the following recommendations for changes in BMT programs:

- Initial training needs assessment should involve the target group of supervisors
- Active support and involvement of higher levels of management are required — they are the on-the-job "models" for supervisors
- Appropriate choice of videotape models is critical, and the modeling display must grab the trainee's attention
- Learning points that emphasize underlying behavioral principles should be utilized — they are more likely to result in generalizability of learning
- Formal retention aids — such as symbolic rehearsal or trainee reformulation of learning points (symbolic coding) — should be built into BMT design
- Small group role play rehearsals with videotaping are preferable to larger groups without videotaping
- Numerous devices for facilitating transfer must be built into BMT design if enduring on-the-job changes in behavior are to be achieved

These recommendations are based on a limited number of experimental studies and therefore must be viewed with some caution. However, the theoretical underpinnings of BMT seem sound, and much corroborative research has been done in the field of psychology on the various aspects of the modeling process. Therefore, we can have some degree of confidence in our current level of understanding of behavior modeling and its application as a potent training device. More research will, of course, result in even greater insights into BMT. Such research presents a golden opportunity for cooperation between academics and practitioners to simultaneously advance our understanding of BMT theory and enhance its effectiveness in practice.

REFERENCES

Bandura, A. 1977. *Social learning theory.* Englewood Cliffs, N.J.: Prentice-Hall.

Decker, P. J. 1980. Effects of symbolic coding and rehearsal in behavior-modeling training. *Journal of Applied Psychology*, 65: 627–634.

Decker, P. J. 1982. The enhancement of behavior modeling training of supervisory skills by the inclusion of retention processes. *Personnel Psychology*, 35: 323–332.

Decker, P. J. 1983. The effects of rehearsal group size and video feedback in behavior modeling training. *Personnel Psychology*, 36: 763–773.

Decker, P. J. 1984. Effects of different symbolic coding stimuli in behavior modeling training. *Personnel Psychology*, 37: 711–720.

Goldstein, A. P. & Sorcher, M. 1974. *Changing supervisor behavior.* New York: Pergamon Press.

Latham, G. P. & Saari, L. M. 1979. Application of social-learning theory to training supervisors through behavioral modeling. *Journal of Applied Psychology*, 64: 239–246.

Mann, R. B. & Decker, P. J. 1984. The effect of key behavior distinctiveness on generalization and recall in behavior modeling training. *Academy of Management Journal*, 27: 900–910.

Manz, C. C. & Sims, H. P. Jr. 1981. Vicarious learning: The influence of modeling on organizational behavior. *Academy of Management Review*, 6: 105–113.

McGehee, W. & Tullar, W. L. 1978. A note on evaluating behavior modification and behavior modeling as industrial training techniques. *Personnel Psychology*, 31: 477–484.

Meyer, H. H. & Raich, M. S. 1983. An objective evaluation of a behavior modeling training program. *Personnel Psychology*, 36: 755–761.

Porras, J. I. & Anderson, B. 1981. Improving managerial effectiveness through modeling-based training. *Organizational Dynamics*, 9(Spring): 60–77.

Porras, J. I. & Hargis, K. 1982. Precursors of individual change: Responses to a social learning theory based on organizational intervention. *Human Relations*, 35: 973–990.

Porras, J. I., Hargis, K., Patterson, K. J., Maxfield, D. G., Roberts, N. & Bies, R. J. 1982. Modeling-based organizational development: A longitudinal assessment. *The Journal of Applied Behavioral Science*, 18: 433–446.

Robinson, J. C. 1982. *Developing managers through behavior modeling*. Austin, Texas: Learning Concepts.

Russell, J. S., Wexley, K. N. & Hunter, J. E. 1984. Questioning the effectiveness of behavior modeling training in an industrial setting. *Personnel Psychology*, 37: 465–481.

Sorcher, M. & Spence, R. 1982. The InterFace Project: Behavior modeling as social technology in South Africa. *Personnel Psychology*, 35: 557–581.

C.

CAREER DEVELOPMENT

Managing Career Transition: A Missing Link in Career Development

Meryl Reis Louis

The purpose of this article is to call attention to the critical limitations of current approaches to career planning and development, and to propose a more effective approach. The issues raised here should be particularly relevant both for managers responsible for developing key subordinates and for individuals concerned with managing their own careers. In addition, these issues have a direct bearing on the research, design, and implementation of formal career-development programs.

CURRENT APPROACHES TO CAREER DEVELOPMENT

Historically, two major approaches to career planning and development have been taken in business and education. The first is a focus on helping individuals identify career paths that match their interests and abilities. The time horizon in career pathing is long-range; sequences of jobs or types of jobs are plotted during an individual's work life on the basis of assessments made by the individual and others of his or her potential and capabilities. Guidelines for pursuing a chosen career path are recommended.

The second focus in career development has been on the specific activities involved in finding a job. The time horizon here is short-range, with emphasis on resources and strategies for landing a "suitable" job.

I believe that the critical middle range between finding a job and moving along a career path has not been adequately addressed in career development — especially lacking is guidance in adapting to the new job and the organization. Inattention to such middle-range activities has resulted in serious limitations in the practice of career planning and development. I will briefly discuss six such limitations and then describe an enriched approach to career development.

LIMITATIONS IN CURRENT APPROACHES

Limitation 1: Future vs. Present Focus

Current career-development approaches tend to reinforce a preoccupation with the future at the expense of the present. Jobs are currently being evaluated in terms of their long-term contribution to the pursuit of the chosen career path; in other words, an orientation toward work in which the present job is seen only as a stepping stone to the next one is being reinforced. A 1980 *Fortune* article entitled "On a Fast Track to the Good Life" illustrates such an orientation among a group of 25-year-old college graduates: "They plan to get what they want by driving hard and fast up the career path." "A key tactic . . . is to keep moving."

It is not surprising that such an attitude has developed when one considers the kind of advice individuals receive early in their careers. For example, Arjay Miller, former dean of the Stanford Business School, told his students to "Get to a high visibility position as fast as you can." And, in what is generally considered a useful guide to career pathing, *Business Week* (drawing heavily from Eugene Jennings' *Routes to the Executive Suite* in its October 12, 1974 article "Plotting a Route to the Top"), gave success seekers the following advice:

> Don't lose valuable career time; avoid being blocked by immobile people.
> Become a crucial subordinate to a mobile superior.
> Always favor increased exposure and visibility (relabeled visiposure).
> Be prepared to practice self-nomination. Leave the company at your
>   convenience, not that of another.
> Define the corporation as a market; time your moves.

The "ticket punching" mentality this kind of advice may foster sidetracks commitment to the organization and to one's job. This is the dysfunctional consequence of an over-concern with future-oriented career pathing.

In addition, a preoccupation with appearance over experience, with "how it looks on the résumé," sometimes results from overemphasis on such a focus. For example, the same *Fortune* article cited above quotes one young man as saying, "Switching jobs looks good on résumés. It shows restlessness and ambition. I'm not going to stay with a company just because I love it."

Limitation 2: "Career" vs. Job Focus

A second limitation stems from the overuse of "career" as a way of thinking. "Career," a term that was not frequently used by nonacademics a decade ago, is really an abstraction: a concept attributed to the set of events, activities, experiences, and decisions that occur over the course of an individual's work life. "Career" is not what one lives, but rather how one *thinks about* what one has lived or will live. As with other concepts, it is useful for generalizing from the experience of an individual and of many individuals, but the misuse of concepts may produce some undesirable results. For instance, a too-heavy focus on one's "career" may lead to detachment and hence alienation from one's day-to-day work experiences. Focus on a career and a career path must be balanced by attention to the job and immediate work experiences. Preoccupation with a "career" can shift attention away from a satisfactory present-day job situation, as the following case illustrates:

> A 29-year-old junior executive wrestled with the problem of career versus job goals. He was relatively happy in his present job, but worried because he didn't see how it fit in with his long-range career plans. He felt that he would have

better prospects in the long run if he returned to the industry where he had his initial training — mining engineering. Yet his present job was satisfying, he was doing quite well, and he liked the people. His family liked Oregon and didn't want to leave.

Limitation 3: Premature Career Pathing

Career pathing presumes that with guidance, one can determine what one really wants to do. However, Edgar Schein's work on career anchors suggests that only with substantial experience do one's "true" work preferences emerge. What this implies is that career pathing for those in the early stages of their career is, at best, premature and may have long-term negative consequences for these individuals and the organizations in which they work.

The blame for premature pathing, broadly speaking, rests not only or even primarily with formal career-development programs: To some extent, it is built into our educational institutions and is perpetuated through peer, family, and other pressures. According to the same *Fortune* article, career-oriented college graduates "have deliberately planned their career moves far in advance and are making a beeline to attain them." The stigma attached to acknowledging that you don't know what you want to do after graduation remains to this day. This stigma, and the career counseling remedies prescribed for such uncertainty, reflect unsupported assumptions about the development of work and other life orientations. It may be that formal career pathing should be undertaken only after the individual has been in the workforce for five or more years.

Limitation 4: The Linear Assumption

Imbedded in current career-pathing efforts is a "linear assumption," or an "up or out" mentality. "Up or out" is a phrase used in many organizations to describe manpower practices. Marilyn Morgan, in *Managing Career Development*, suggests that until the mid-to-late 1960s, success was consensually defined in terms of progression up the corporate ladder. Success was associated with holding a sequence of jobs, each offering greater responsibility and authority than the previous job within a single occupation. However, as Michael Driver has discovered, many people gravitate toward other types of career profiles. For example, a steady state or flat profile may characterize the histories of successful professionals such as doctors and lawyers, and Driver has increasingly found a spiral profile reflecting serial immersion in different occupational/professional pursuits. This suggests that the assumption that careers either are or ought to be linear is no longer appropriate.

From an organizational perspective, the linear assumption collapses under a number of structural and environmental pressures. These pressures include a leveling off of the number of new and old positions available and the increasing competition for these positions produced by the baby-boom cohort. As a result, managers need to reexamine their criteria for "acceptable" and "successful" career profiles. The advent of lateral transfer programs and technical career ladders is evidence that some organizations are supporting an expanded portfolio of career profiles. However, it appears that the linear assumption continues to influence the framing of career issues. For instance, recent studies by the U.S. Office of Personnel Management are grounded in an implicit "mobility is good" and "plateauing is bad" assumption, revealing the traditional linear view of career success. Caution must be taken to avoid slipping back into the linear-assumption mind set.

Limitation 5: Work Life vs. Total Life

Current approaches to career development have not adequately considered the total life space of the individual, yet the nonwork aspects of a person's life may critically affect and be affected by his or her work life. In my five-year study of M.B.A. graduates, I found that family and life-style considerations contributed significantly to most of the major work-life decisions (for example, to change jobs or decline a promotion) of both single and married graduates. A case in point is that of a young man who left a prestigious accounting firm in Los Angeles for a position with a regional firm in Oregon. He accepted the new position despite a decrease in salary and responsibilities because " . . . my wife and I wished to own our own home and to have a better quality of life than was obtainable in Los Angeles."

The study also revealed that among the minority of M.B.A. graduates who at the outset adopt a single-minded devotion to work, most make a concerted effort to rebalance work and other life activities by their third year in the workforce. For example, it occurred to one individual that during his two years with his company his only really "free" time was that spent on airplanes traveling to and from business meetings. He found the realization "sobering," and reports having begun a "realignment" program of delegating more work to key subordinates and recultivating neglected friendships away from the job. The increasing prevalence and societal impact of dual-career families also underscores the need to consider the work/family interface in connection with career development.

Career-development efforts therefore need to reflect current views of the relationships among work and other life considerations. In particular, assumptions about individuals for whom career-development programs are designed may no longer be appropriate. Work and other life priorities of today's employees may no longer mirror the priorities of those of the 1950s and 1960s. To repeat, the total life space of an individual may impose constraints on and/or provide resources for career-development efforts. Family and extra-work spheres represent potential staging areas for developmental experiences that could feed work-life capabilities. Extra-work spheres simultaneously represent areas in which the "developed" worker can play out and/or utilize skills for which the organization currently has no channel — either because of manpower bottlenecks, cutbacks in business, or skill-mix problems. For a number of reasons, then, it is essential that career-development efforts be expanded to encompass the total life space of the individual.

Limitation 6: The Individual vs. the Organization

Despite the urgings of such experts on organizational careers as Douglas and Francine Hall and Edgar Schein, career-development activities have not been meshed with organizational interests — that is, career development has been oriented toward the individual without adequate consideration of the organization. In the future, costs and benefits to the organization in terms of resources, mission, and unit productivity must be assessed in designing career-development programs.

In addition, broad organizational structures, policies, and practices must be examined as webs of potential opportunities for, and roadblocks to, human development. A decade ago, organization-development specialists sought to separate themselves from traditional personnel functions so they could more effectively negotiate resources, access, and credibility. It may now be similarly advisable for career-development design groups to do the same. Underlying any such shift in reporting relationships should be a basic reconceptualization of the issues to encompass both organizational and individual needs. More than mere marketing of career development is at stake. Narrow-vision career-development programs based predominantly on individual interests are as likely to fail as those in which there is inadequate consideration of the realities of the organizational settings in which they are implemented.

In summary, current approaches to career development tend to emphasize the future at the expense of the present, the individual over the organization, and the career over the job. Current career-development efforts may lead to premature pathing and overemphasize a linear career profile assumption. Finally, career development tends to overlook relevant aspects of an individual's nonwork life.

These limitations reflect trends in the practice of and the thinking about career development rather than any inherent deficiencies in the idea itself. They are best viewed as imbalances that can be rectified through judicious self-reflection, reexamination of premises and values, and a refocus of career-development efforts.

Nearly exclusive attention to long- and short-range concerns (to career pathing and job finding, respectively) and inattention to such middle-range concerns as managing job transitions has no doubt contributed to these imbalances. As a strategic change, it is therefore recommended that a middle-range focus on managing the post-job-finding transition period be added to the portfolio of career-development approaches.

ADDING TRANSITION MANAGEMENT TO CAREER DEVELOPMENT

Transition refers to the period during which an individual adjusts to a different setting and/or work role. Promotion and job rotation, as well as change of organization or profession, typically entail some transition. A transition period is associated with any major job or role change, whether the individual is in the early, middle, or late stage of his or her career. The experience is demanding, often requiring the newcomer to alter his or her work-related thoughts, feelings, and behaviors. Such adaptation is critical for success in the situation and in the job. In particular, subsequent job attitudes and behaviors (that is, commitment to the organization, productivity, job tenure, and intentions to stay or leave) are a function of experiences during the early or transition period in the new setting. The substantial impact of the transition period and the fact that more and more employees are making major job and role changes involving transition underscore the need to expand career development to include transition management.

For a variety of reasons, then, it is strongly recommended that transition management be covered as part of regular career-development activities in industrial, educational, or counseling settings (for example, employee development, supervisory training, and college placement). With an understanding of transition issues, supervisors and managers would be better equipped to help integrate and develop new personnel. Individuals who are well versed in the realities of transitions would be better able to plan for and adapt to new settings after changing jobs.

What specifically does transition management entail, and what does one need to know about transitions in order to manage them?

Following are some basic issues and action steps designed to help newcomers and the people with whom they work — supervisors, career counselors, placement and personnel department representatives, and co-workers — better understand and manage transition, both in the new job and in future jobs. (These issues and steps are summarized in Figure 1).

THE "TYPICAL" TRANSITION EXPERIENCE

To begin with, it is helpful to know something about the "typical" transition experience. Although no two transitions are identical and no two individuals experience transition in precisely the same way, most transitions have several characteristics in

FIGURE 1
Managing Career Transitions: Issues and Actions

1. *Appreciate "typical" transition experience:*
   Feelings (of being overwhelmed and surprised).
   Contrasts between old and new job.
   Obsolete frame of reference.

2. *Define "ideal" transition:*
   Specific to the individual.

3. *Analyze the transition situation in terms of:*
   The newcomer.
   The supervisor.
   The predecessor.
   Key personnel.
   The new position.
   The job change.

4. *Highlight potential problems and resources:*
   Specific to the transition and the newcomer.

5. *Review essential transition tasks:*
   Master job basics.
   Build role identity.
   Build relationships.
   Update frame of reference.
   Map players/networks.
   Locate self in networks.
   Learn vernacular.
   Assess unit functioning.

6. *Set priorities:*
   Based on analysis of situation, knowledge of essential tasks, and appreciation of personal preferences.

7. *Select strategies on the same basis used in 6, above.*

common. Awareness of these characteristics helps reduce self-imposed and dysfunctional pressures to "hit the deck running," to be fully functioning on Day One in the new job. Such awareness also provides reassurance, letting newcomers know that it's normal to feel as they do, and that no amount of preparation would prevent certain experiences.

What are the characteristics of a "typical" transition experience?

First of all, a new employee typically feels *overwhelmed:* There is so much that is new, all happening to the newcomer at once, with no quick, efficient way to organize all of it and no time in which to assimilate it. There are dozens of faces, names, titles, and work roles to interconnect. Impressions and reactions are forming and reforming in response to physical features of work settings, people, tasks, and the individual's own anticipations of settings, job, and experience.

It is also quite normal during a transition to experience *surprise*. Surprise of some sort seems to be an inevitable part of any transition experience. There is always something significant that was unanticipated or perhaps inaccurately anticipated; for example, surprise may result from the job itself (its tasks and/or work conditions), the people, the department or organization, or the newcomer's own preferences and predispositions.

In addition to being surprised by differences between anticipation and reality, newcomers recognize differences between the new job setting and the previous one, especially the most recent one. This is normal, but it nevertheless distracts the new-comer from getting on with the business of learning about the new setting. This "leave-taking" process — a process of letting go of the old setting, and rolling forward into the new one — can be compared to closing out ledger books account by account, but without knowing until the process is actually occurring what the titles of the accounts to close will be. What stands out in the contrast between new and old settings is an individual matter, as is the relative standing of each setting on any single dimension of contrast. Once again, it is normal for the newcomer to notice differences between new and old settings. In fact, he or she tends to describe the new setting in comparative terms during the first few months on the job.

Finally, newcomers discover as part of the transition experience that old habits don't work. Their job-related frames of reference are in at least some ways obsolete, having been formed in and tailored to the old setting. The newcomer's sense of what's essential, what's taboo, and what's appropriate at work typically does not fit the new setting — and most newcomers do not realize this until they have made a few mistakes.

To sum up, a newcomer is likely to experience a variety of surprises and contrasts, the feeling of being somewhat overwhelmed, and the recognition that his or her frame of reference is somewhat obsolete during a "typical" transition into an unfamiliar set-ting. The duration and intensity of the transition experience depend on a variety of factors (which will be discussed below). However, even in the smoothest of transitions, newcomers report having this same basic pattern of experience.

THE "IDEAL" TRANSITION

Although there are some experiences shared by every newcomer during a transition period, each differs in his or her preference and needs. Therefore, it is useful to help newcomers define for themselves "the ideal transition."

What is the ideal transition? Is it the most challenging one or is it the one that is completed most quickly, most comfortably? Knowledge of one's preferences generated through this exercise directs the newcomer to seek out particular tasks, people, and information during the early period on the job. The newcomer who likes to have ample time to get oriented to the new job before undertaking the first major project would manage the transition quite differently, all else being equal, than would the newcomer for whom it is most important to have a challenging assignment the first week. In other words, what one personally considers "ideal" in a transition will directly affect how that transition is managed.

Appreciation of personal preferences and needs is also critical for individuals seek-ing to guide employees undergoing transition. For these would-be helpers, the as-sumption that one's own preferences are universal — that, for instance, everyone wants an opportunity to "sink or swim" by going it alone — may undermine the best of in-tentions to be helpful.

ANALYZING THE TRANSITION SITUATION

When embarking on a job or role change, it is useful to take stock of those factors that help determine how closely the transition will approximate one's "ideal." At the outset conditions may appear favorable, unfavorable, or mixed, and whether any given con-dition turns out to be a help or a hindrance depends on a number of factors. However, by mapping specific conditions early on in the transition, the newcomer can better prepare for and exert greater influence on potentially critical areas.

It is advisable, when conducting a personal analysis of the transition situation, to examine selected features of (1) the newcomer, (2) the boss, (3) the predecessor, (4) other key personnel, (5) the new position, and (6) the job change. Following is an outline of the types of features to examine in each of these areas.

Among the relevant aspects of the *newcomer*, one would want to take stock of one's preparation (for example, experience and/or training) for the new position and one's expectations about the job and the organization. Additionally, one should conduct a candid self-assessment of such dimensions as patience, tolerance for ambiguity, preferences for structure, preferred modes of communication, and interpersonal skills. How one's family is affected by a job change also has direct bearing on the transition.

In analyzing the *boss's* potential contribution to the transition, it makes sense to assess how clearly he or she communicates expectations about priorities and standards, his or her understanding of and support for the newcomer's position, and his or her reputation for consistency. Of course, the degree of the supervisor's contribution cannot be ascertained until the newcomer is formally on the job, and much is a matter of judgment. Nevertheless, it is useful for the newcomer to "size up" the boss and note any areas that stand out as potential problems.

Concerning one's *predecessor*, it is useful to address the following questions: Will the predecessor be present to help orient the newcomer? Why is the predecessor leaving? How competent is the predecessor? And what is his or her reputation with subordinates, supervisor, important clients, and counterparts in other departments?

Similar issues should be considered with respect to subordinates and other *key personnel*. In addition, it is important to consider how they view the newcomer. For instance, was a key subordinate hoping to get the newcomer's job? What do key personnel know about the newcomer?

Another area to assess in diagnosing the transition is the *new position*. For example, what is the history of the position? Will the position be a good experience for the newcomer? How does it fit in with the newcomer's longer-term career plans? Other questions should focus on the condition of the new work unit in terms of backlog and resources and the kind of reputation the organization has.

Finally, aspects of the *job-change situation* need to be considered. For example, at what point in the work cycle of the new unit will the newcomer arrive? What was the impetus for and how sudden was the newcomer's decision to leave and his or her choice of a new position?

Early on in the transition situation, then, the newcomer should analyze its main features — an undertaking that can provide a picture of its overall favorableness by high lighting potential problem areas and resources. Typical considerations in analyzing it are summarized in Figure 1.

ESSENTIAL TRANSITION TASKS

In negotiating a transition, a newcomer must accomplish several basic tasks to become a fully functioning member of the department or organization. The same basic transition tasks have been identified by people in civilian and military organizations; by people in finance, marketing, production and other functional areas; by people at different levels in the organizational hierarchy; by people in small, medium, and large organizations; by people in public and private work organizations; and by people making a major job change within the same organization or moving to a different organization. Among the commonly identified transition tasks are:

□ Mastering the basics of the job — which include the formal procedures, technology, and the required tasks and activities.

□ Building an image or role identity. This signals to others with and/or for whom the newcomer works whether, for instance, the newcomer intends to maintain the status quo or shake things up a bit.

▫ Building relationships, first of all with immediate superior(s) and then with peers or subordinates with whom the newcomer must work. It is through these relationships that the needed flow of information and cooperation is ensured and specific expectations are negotiated.

▫ Constructing a current frame of reference, one that reflects how and why things are done as they are in the new situation. What's essential, what's taboo, and what's appropriate in the new setting — in essence, the core values, basic assumptions, and norms that constitute the frame of reference.

▫ Mapping the relevant players. This involves learning names, faces, and roles as well as how people fit together in terms of the formal organizational tasks, the informal power sources, and the social networks.

▫ Locating oneself in task and social networks. Newcomers must see where they fit in role and work-flow networks and how their jobs relate to the units' overall mission so they can function effectively.

▫ Learning the local language and decoding the special symbols used by the work group and organization. In fact, being able to speak and understand the technical, organizational, and social vernacular is often an indication that the transition is nearing completion and the newcomer is becoming an insider.

▫ Assessing how well the job is being done and the general state of affairs in the unit. This final task is essential for most newcomers, particularly those in positions above the most basic blue-collar levels. Decisions about where to direct one's efforts, what to pay attention to, and when and whom to ask for information will often reflect one's sense of how well things are running in the department.

Of these basic transition tasks, only the first two — learning basic job activities and developing role identity — bear directly on the job for which the individual was hired. Yet as this list indicates, transition entails a much broader set of tasks. Learning a new job is typically no small matter, and learning the ropes of a new "system" with its players, pecking order, norms, values, and symbols is no less demanding or essential for effectiveness in the job. While assistance in learning basic job activities is routinely offered through career development, similar assistance in accomplishing other transition tasks, in learning "the system," is lacking. It is time to focus attention on these other transition tasks and, more broadly, on transition aspects of careers to help individuals and organizations better manage transitions. (Included in Figure 1 is a summary of these essential transition tasks.)

CONCLUSION

In summary, what is involved in adding career-transition management to career-development practices is an appreciation of:

1. The characteristics of "typical" transition experiences.
2. Individual differences in "ideal" transitions.
3. Features to consider when analyzing transition situations.
4. Essential tasks newcomers must accomplish to complete a transition.

The newcomer who is aware of these issues can better set priorities, seek and organize information, understand his or her own experience, and otherwise manage the process of "getting up to speed" or "learning the ropes." With such a framework, the supervisor can help facilitate the effective and efficient transition of newcomers and develop them into productive members of the organization.

Inclusion of a transition management perspective within career development could also help overcome some of the limitations in current career-development practices discussed earlier. Explicitly incorporating transition management into career-development activities could shift the focus from the future to the present, from appearance to day-to-day experience, and from "career" to the job at hand, and bridge the gap between organizational and individual issues.

D.

EVALUATION OF TRAINING AND DEVELOPMENT PROGRAMS

An Objective Evaluation of a Behavior Modeling Training Program

Herbert H. Meyer and Michael S. Raich

Review articles by psychologists on the subject of training have generally highlighted the need for more and better evaluation research (Goldstein, 1974; Hinrichs, 1976). The need for objective evaluations of training results is almost always cited as being especially critical. Campbell et al. (1970) concluded after a survey of training practices in large companies: "The major question at this point concerns how long organizations will follow a policy that is best characterized as spending millions for training but not one penny for training evaluation." (page 49)

Kirkpatrick (1978) surveyed over 100 firms that indicated that they had made systematic efforts to evaluate the results of their training programs. Of these, he found that over 75% said they measured participant reactions toward or feelings about the training, less than half attempted to measure what had been learned in the way of specific knowledge or skills, less than 20% attempted to measure behavior changes, and only about 15% made any attempt to measure on-the-job results of the training. Actually, in this latter group, the majority said that their results evaluations were largely subjective — that is, they used supervisory ratings of the trainees as their results criteria.

"Behavior modeling" has become increasingly popular as a training method in the last 10 years for improving interpersonal skills (Goldstein and Sorcher, 1974). Most of the formalized attempts to measure the results of this type of training have focused on measuring or judging behavior changes (Burnaska, 1976; Byham et al., 1976; Moses and Ritchie, 1976). A search of the literature revealed only one study where an attempt was made to measure changes in job performance as a result of behavior modeling training (Smith, 1976). McGehee and Tullar (1978) pointed out flaws in the research design of that study, and of other studies attempting to measure the results of behavior modeling training, for that matter.

Recently we were presented with an opportunity to conduct a controlled and objective evaluation of a behavior modeling program to improve the effectiveness of sales-

Reprinted with permission from *Personnel Psychology*, Winter 1983, pp. 755–761.

persons. A large retailer decided to experiment with this approach in training sales associates. The sales training staff in this company decided to conduct a pilot test of a behavior modeling program in two departments, Large Appliance and Radio/TV, within 14 of their stores in one large metropolitan area.

THE TRAINING PROGRAM

The supervisors of the sales associates were trained as trainers in this behavior modeling program. The program focused on specific aspects of sales situations, such as "approaching the customer," "explaining features, advantages and benefits," "closing the sale," and the like. The usual behavior modeling procedure was followed by presenting guidelines or "learning points" for handling each aspect of a sales interaction, followed by the presentation of a video taped situation where a "model" sales associate followed the guidelines in carrying out that aspect of the sales interaction with a customer. The trainees then practiced the same situation in role playing rehearsals. Their performance was reinforced and shaped by their supervisors who had been trained as instructors.*

THE STUDY DESIGN

The 14 stores in one large metropolitan area that participated in this study were matched into seven pairs as best we could for their size, type of location, market characteristics, and the like. Actually, there were enough stores in the area to permit fairly accurate matching. For example, two of the stores of similar size and performance characteristics were in intercity areas. Two others with similar characteristics were in relatively affluent suburban areas. Others were in similar shopping malls, and the like. Stores with unusual characteristics, such as declining sales, recent changes in management, or where other conditions existed which could have affected their overall performance, were not included in the study.

The behavior modeling training program was then introduced in seven stores, one in each of the matched pairs, and not in the other seven stores. Other kinds of ongoing sales training programs were provided in the "control group" stores, but the behavior modeling approach was used only in the seven "experimental group" stores. A total of 58 sales associates received the behavior modeling training in the experimental group stores, and there were 64 sales associates in the same departments in the control group stores.

As in most sales organizations, detailed records of the sales for each individual were kept on a continuous basis. Fortunately, these records included not only total sales, but hours worked on the sales floor. We found considerable variation in the total hours worked by individual sales associates due to illness, leaves of absence, vacations, and assignments off the floor. Thus, we could compute an index of average-sales-per-hour for each person. Actually, since all participants received commissions on sales, and the value of various products sold varied greatly, their average commissions per hours worked seemed to be the best performance measure for this study.

The training program was conducted in the fall of 1979. An analysis of the reliability of sales records indicated that we would have to combine results for several months in order to obtain a reasonably reliable criterion measure. We found, for example, that month-to-month correlations for individual sales records averaged about .40, whereas correlations for six-month periods were about .80. (Averages were com-

---

*This program was developed and conducted by a consulting firm specializing in retail sales, the Mandev Training Corporation of Miami, Florida.

puted from r to z transformations.) Therefore, we decided to compare sales records for the participants in this study for the first six months of 1979 (before the behavior modeling training was introduced) with results achieved in the first six months of 1980 (after the training was concluded). All sales promotions and other programs in the stores were identical, since these were administered, with the accompanying advertising and other inducements, on an area-wide basis.

We also evaluated certain subjective aspects of the program results. In the experimental group we asked the participants to give us their opinions of the behavior modeling training. In both groups, we asked them to appraise the value of any sales training they had had in the company at any time. Since supervisors served as trainers, we also asked the participants to describe the degree to which their supervisors exhibited such behaviors as: "praise you for things you have done well," "provide suggestions for performance improvement in a constructive and tactful manner," "help you to develop your selling skills," "show concern for you as an individual," and "create a climate that encourages you to do your best." We expected the training and service as trainers to have an impact on the degree to which these supervisors might have demonstrated behaviors of that kind. This survey of participant attitudes, incidentally, was conducted about nine months after the behavior modeling training had been given.

STUDY RESULTS

Of the original 58 who participated in the behavior modeling training, 50 were still working as sales associates one year later. Four of the remaining eight had been promoted in the interim and the other four had left the company.

In the control group stores, only 49 of the original 64 were still working as sales associates during the entire six-month followup period one year later. Of the remaining 15, only one had been promoted and the other 14 had left the company. Thus, it appeared that the behavior modeling program may have had a substantial positive effect on turnover, since only about 7% of the trained sales associates left during the ensuing year, whereas about 22% of the counterpart sales associates in the control group stores left the company during that same period. (This result had not been predicted.)

Figure 1 presents the changes in average per-hour commissions for participants in both groups from the six-month period before the training was conducted to the six-month period after the training had been conducted in the experimental group stores. As can be seen, the average per-hour earnings for sales associates in the experimental group stores increased over the year from $9.27 to $9.95. On the other hand, the average per-hour earnings of the comparable sales associates in the control group stores declined over the year from $9.71 to $9.43. In other words, the trained sales associates increased their average earnings by about 7%, whereas the sales associates who did not receive the behavior modeling training experienced a 3% decline in average earnings. This difference was significant at the .01 level.

The nature of the turnover in the two groups probably attenuated the effects of the modeling training on the sales performance records we used as the criterion for this study. This company's experience has shown that the poorer performers are more likely to leave the company and the better performers are more likely to get promoted. Only four of the experimental group left the company before the six-month followup period was completed, whereas 14 of the control group participants left the company. Also, only one of the control group participants was promoted, whereas four of the participants in the training group were promoted. Two of the latter group, for example, showed very high gains in sales during the first three months of the followup period and then were promoted. Since they did not have sales records for the entire six-month followup period, we did not include their records in the "after" figures reported.

FIGURE 1
Changes in Per-Hour Commissions

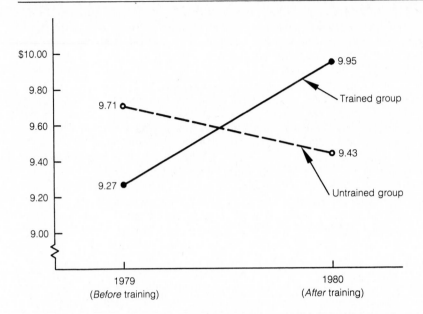

As is usually found in training programs of any kind, the sales associates who had participated in the behavior modeling training expressed very favorable attitudes toward this program. On the average, they estimated that this training would result in about a 30% increase in their personal sales. (They must have been subsequently disillusioned, since the actual average increase in their sales was less than 10%). The survey conducted about nine months after this training program had been conducted also showed that sales associates in the experimental group stores expressed more favorable attitudes toward their previous sales training in general than those in the control group stores. Of those who participated in the behavior modeling training, 96% rated the sales training courses they had had in the company as either "good" or "very good." On the other hand, in the control group stores only 58% rated the company's sales training programs as either "good" or "very good." With regard to the supervisory behaviors we expected to be changed by the training and experience the supervisors had in conducting behavior modeling training, the results were disappointing. Ratings of the supervisors in the experimental group were more favorable on these behaviors than for supervisors in the control group stores, but these differences were not statistically significant.

DISCUSSION

The most important outcome of this study was that it provided objective evidence to show that the behavior modeling approach to sales training did actually result in increased sales. The program also appeared to have an important secondary effect on turnover. Significantly fewer of the sales representatives who participated in the behavior modeling training program quit their jobs in the ensuing year than did their counterparts in the matched stores where that training program was not given. Since all sales representatives are given considerable training, which represents an expensive investment of time and money, it appears that the behavior modeling training contributed to cost savings in addition to increased sales results.

Of even greater interest than the actual results of this study, however, was probably the fact that it was possible to carry out an objective, "bottom line" appraisal of the effectiveness of the training program. The most important performance criterion measures for evaluating the program, actual sales performance records, were readily available. This would seem to be the case for almost all sales jobs. Therefore, it would seem that in many cases, sales trainers, with relatively little extra effort, should be able to obtain more than just subjective opinions about the effectiveness of their sales training programs.

The use of objective data as the criterion in a study of this kind does, of course, often entail some problems. We found, for example, that month-to-month variations in sales performance were considerable due to changing work schedules, sales promotions which meant that performance of almost all sales representatives was at optimal levels, and similar influences that affected individual results. It required a six-month period to balance out these various influences. We also found that it took some vigilance to insure that the records we needed for this study were kept in a consistent and conscientious manner in each store. These problems, however, were not great in relation to the usefulness of the study results. The evidence that the training program had a measurable effect on sales was certainly more convincing in demonstrating the value of the program than would be merely the opinions of participants that the training was worthwhile.

REFERENCES

Byham, W. C., Adams, D. and Kiggins, A. (1976). Transfer of modeling training to the job. *Personnel Psychology*, 29, 345–349.

Burnaska, R. F. (1976). The effects of behavior modeling training upon managers' behaviors and employees' perceptions. *Personnel Psychology*, 29, 329–335.

Campbell, J. P., Dunnette, M. D., Lawler, E. E., III and Weick, K. E. (1970). *Managerial behavior, performance, and effectiveness.* New York: McGraw-Hill.

Goldstein, A. P. and Sorcher, M. (1974). *Changing supervisor behavior.* New York: Pergamon.

Goldstein, I. L., (1974). *Training: Program development and evaluation.* Monterey, Calif: Brooks/Cole.

Hinrichs, J. R. (1976). Personnel training. In M. D. Dunnette (Ed.), *Handbook of industrial and organizational psychology.* Chicago: Rand-McNally.

Kirkpatrick, D. L., (1978). Evaluating in house training programs. *Training and Development Journal*, Sept 6–9.

McGehee, W., and Tullar, W. L., (1978). A note on evaluating behavior modification and behavior modeling as industrial training techniques. *Personnel Psychology*, 31, 477–484.

Moses, J. L. and Ritchie, R. J. (1976). Supervisory relationships training: A behavioral evaluation of a behavior modeling program. *Personnel Psychology*, 29, 337–343.

Smith, P. E. (1976). Management modeling training to improve morale and customer satisfaction. *Personnel Psychology*, 29, 351–359.

E.

TRAINING AND DEVELOPMENT

Interview with John R. Hinrichs

John Hinrichs is currently president of Management Decision Systems, a human resources consulting firm. He has held this position since 1976. For thirteen years prior to this, Dr. Hinrichs held a variety of managerial positions with IBM corporation. His responsibilities focused on personnel research, with a particular emphasis on training, development, and job redesign.

Dr. Hinrichs earned his Ph.D. from Cornell in industrial and labor relations in 1962. He has been a visiting associate professor at Cornell and has been invited to write chapters in the *Annual Review of Psychology* and *Handbook of Industrial and Organizational Psychology*. He is a Fellow of the American Psychological Association and a member of the Board of Governors of the Center for Creative Leadership.

1. *Much money is being spent these days on training and development. What return are most organizations expecting on this "investment" in human resources? How do organizations know if they are meeting their training goals?*

Actually, it's almost impossible to answer this question with any degree of precision. It all depends on how you define training, what you include in your estimates, and how you delineate the population about which you are talking. One of the few estimates of this done recently was in the October 1983 issue of *Training* magazine in their so called "U. S. Training Census and Trends Report for 1983." Their conclusions are based upon 611 surveys returned in a study of industrial firms with more than 50 employees. One of the problems is that they had an extremely low response rate and their obtained sample deviates rather markedly from the total population of industrial firms in the United States. However, based upon this admittedly somewhat unrepresentative sample, they project direct dollar expenditures in 1983 of $733 million on training hardware, $714 million on off-the-shelf programs, $584 million on custom programs and one billion 35 million dollars on services, for a grand total of $3.067 billion.

This is clearly not the total amount being spent on training in this country, however. Their figures do not include salaries — both of trainees and trainers — and benefits. They do not include overhead or offset costs (lost work time by employees who are involved in training). They also do not include in-house training or on-the-job training. And from what we can tell, they do not include any government or military training where the expenditures for training are tremendous. Clearly, the total amount of money spent on training in the United States is significantly higher than $3 billion a year.

Another estimate is included in Wayne Cascio's book on *Costing Human Resources*. He states that the cost of training increased from an estimated overall bill of $100 billion in 1976 to $137 billion in 1981. There is no indication of where those numbers come from, but they must include all of the intangibles which I mentioned. In any event there is a lot of money being spent on training in the United States.

Obviously, organizations expect some return from this investment. In the private sector they are looking for more effectiveness in competing, improved production methods, and increased efficiency. They are hoping for a tangible return in dollars and cents. They are also looking for more fully developed personnel — people who can do the job effectively, who have the skills available for new activities when needed, and who are growing or developing. As a by-product of this, they are hoping for a more satisfied workforce which perceives that their skills are being developed and used fully.

So, in addition to immediate returns of more effective, efficient, and competitive operations, organizations view training and development as an investment in their capacity to meet future needs. Organizations know that they are achieving these goals when they are able to operate effectively — their customers are satisfied, the product is going out the door, the organization functions smoothly and adapts to changing conditions, and they are able to deal with new technology that has come along.

2. What kinds of activities are training and development professionals involved in on a day-to-day basis?

Here, too, it's hard to come up with a precise answer because many training people do a lot of different things, some of which are not particularly tied to training. In 1983 the American Society for Training and Development (ASTD) published the results of a competency study done among training professionals, and that's probably the best indication of what trainers do. They identified the primary focus of training and development as "identifying, assessing, and — through planned learning — helping develop the key competencies of knowledge, skill, attitudes which enable individuals to perform current or future jobs." In doing this they came up with fifteen training and development roles. These are evaluator, group facilitator, individual development counselor, instructional writer, instructor, manager of training and development, marketer, media specialist, needs analyst, program administrator, program designer, strategist, task analyst, theoretician, and transfer agent.

3. Where do organizations typically fall down in their training programs — at the assessment, design, or evaluation phase? What are the reasons for this?

I think the primary place where they fall down is that the vast majority of organizations are very small and they just don't devote any time at all to training. It's kind of hit or miss.

The other area where they fall down is that most of the training that is done is trial-and-error training. Trial-and-error can be a very persuasive learning technique, but it is also very expensive and inefficient. Most training takes place on the job. Employees are thrown in and the nearest person to them is asked to train those people. The trainer has no knowledge, capability, or experience in training, and he or she will often impart the wrong ways of doing a job. Without a proper approach to training, they perpetuate their own inefficiencies and lack of skill throughout the organization.

Contrast American organizations with Japanese, which typically devote considerable attention to training. Sharp manufacturing in Memphis, for example, gives two weeks of orientation training to new hires on the assembly line. United States companies wouldn't do that at all. Most would just throw new hires on the line and let somebody show them the job.

Japanese firms also give employees very extensive training in production, plus a lot of other topics. It's a very thorough orientation, and they do it as an investment in the future for these people. American organizations, on the other hand, typically view training as a cost rather than as an investment — the real commitment of most U.S. organizations to the human resource is rather limited and covers a short time perspective rather than long term.

In terms of the specifics in the question, the assessment process is also problematic. There is a lot of lip service to assessment in the training profession, but actually very little is done in any systematic fashion. The training field is replete with fads, "me-too-ism," and tradition. There are some very good techniques available for needs assessment, but they tend not to be applied.

One of the problems here is that training can serve as a kind of placebo for managers. If they perceive they have a problem or if some indicators tell them there is a problem in their operation, the quick answer is either throw money at it or put in a training program to solve the problem. Once that decision is made, managers are comfortable with it; they say "Well, we've done something" and tend to forget about it. And they don't really worry about whether it's the right response. As a result, training often is installed for the wrong reasons, and has the primary purpose of making managers feel comfortable that something is being done.

There is also relatively limited evaluation of training. Evaluation implies a research mentality, and operating managers don't have research mentalities. They're off and onto the next topic, rather than reviewing what they've done in the past. But there really does need to be some evaluation research done on training so we understand what we're doing well and what we could do better the next time.

4. *In the articles preceding this discussion, much emphasis is placed on assessing training needs. How would the assessment process differ when training for improvement of current performance versus training the employee for a future job?*

When assessing needs for training for improvement of current performance, the issue is one of clearly identifying the critical requirements for successful completion of the job. This immediately suggests some form of job analysis and needs assessment. One has to first identify families of jobs with similar characteristics required of them and identify what those characteristics are — the requirements to do the job. The methodologies for this are fairly standardized. They include job study and observation; interviewing of incumbents, managers and subordinates; questionnaires; and the evaluation of operating data. The purposes are to identify what is done on key jobs or job families and then make a bridge to what are the person-oriented attributes required to carry out those activities. Then the job analysis makes a systematic assessment of each of these attributes and determines which should be enhanced through attention to the selection and placement process. In other words, which are involved primarily around basic inborn attributes, abilities and characteristics of the individual; which are relatively difficult to influence through training and development; and which *can* be developed through training efforts? One then has a picture of what the needs are for training and can form a framework for making logical decisions about what training to institute.

When you are dealing with the issue of training an employee for a future job, one may have a job-related picture of the attributes required for that job from the job analysis procedure and know that that's a logical progression for an individual. In that case it's a matter then of training in the developable characteristics required for that job. For other types of future jobs — maybe ones that don't currently exist — it's a matter of keying the organization's strategic and product plans with human resource plans. If it's known that certain technologies are going to be involved in the future, or that certain markets are going to be opening up and that these are new to the organization, one has to do some logical, systematic assessment of characteristics required to operate in those environments. It may be possible to look at other organizations which are already in those environments or using those technologies (though that's probably not very likely). In general it will be just a logical process which should be followed in deciding upon the training and development efforts for future jobs in the organization.

In this area the identification of whether or not a person has those attributes can often be accomplished through various simulations and assessment center procedures. One has to build a simulation of the future job and evaluate the individual's competency in performing these simulations.

5. *How does one demonstrate the cost effectiveness of training and development programs? Is it necessary to do so?*

This question deals with the most sophisticated and comprehensive of training effectiveness evaluations. Generally, these kinds of analyses are not done. Training evaluation can be done in general at four levels. The first level deals with reaction: "How did you like the training program?" This is the most prevalent kind and the easiest to deal with. But, it tells us essentially nothing about the real return which an organization or individual may be achieving from training.

The second level deals with the learning which occurs in the training program. Typical in this are achievement tests — tests of knowledge gained.

The third evaluation level deals with behavior and a determination of whether or not the individuals applied the training skills back on the job. This becomes more difficult, but there are some studies done in this area. Usually it entails some observation of trainees after they return to the job.

The highest level of training evaluation, and the one which this question really addresses, is the results achieved — "How much did it cost?" versus "What positive benefits did we get out of it as a total organization?" Basically, this fourth level of evaluation looks at the productivity of the training and the basic framework is the familiar productivity ratio of outputs over inputs. On the output side, one has to identify and quantify in monetary terms what it is that the training accomplishes. Some of these are intangibles and some are very tangible. There may be such things as increased units produced per employee, reduction in rejects or scrap, fewer warranty returns of a product, reduced down time and attendant costs associated with that, reduced absenteeism or turnover, fewer employees required to do a job, and so forth. Dollar estimates can be put around these types of outcomes. On the input side, the numerator of the productivity ratio deals with the direct cost of training in terms of supplies, time, salaries, production losses, and so forth. These need to be aggregated in as logical a fashion as possible. Then one can claim a positive cost effectiveness of training and development when the numerator of the ratio is greater than the denominator — where outputs exceed inputs. This is the measure of the return on the investment on training.

Obviously, there are often a lot of intangibles in this process; it is an imprecise process at best. Many of the benefits of training may be long term, such as employee attitudes, general organizational effectiveness, good public relations, or customer satisfaction. It's just about impossible to collect quantitative cost or return data on factors like these, but it may be desirable to put some item into the ratio to cover such factors.

6. What contribution can assessment centers make to the training and development process? Also, what about career planning? How does it fit?

Assessment centers and other simulations can make quite a contribution to the training and development process. First of all, they can serve as job samples, simulating the activities required in a job an individual is being considered for, either in initial hiring or replacement. For example, the most typical example is in management assessment. The assessment center process is intended to mirror many of the activities required in actually functioning in a managerial job such as group relationships, communication skills, presentation skills, decision making, and so forth. Individuals participate in the simulations and are evaluated in how competently they display the key attributes required in those aspects of managerial behavior. These evaluations are netted down into decisions about selection and placement.

Second, assessment centers allow differential decisions about the kinds of developmental experiences from which individuals can benefit. Assessment centers provide a valid and useful set of information for determining development and training needs both at the individual level and in an aggregate for an organization or organizational unit.

Another often mentioned benefit of assessment centers is that development itself occurs through participation in the center. It is clear that a great deal of learning can take place. Similarly, there is often some benefit to the assessors in gaining some experience and insight into the evaluation process. When there is feedback from individuals, the learning from participation in the center itself can be significant.

Career planning has been receiving a great deal of attention in organizations recently. I see it as a response to a basic human need which most people have for personal growth and progression. Organizations are trying to optimize their utilization of human resources, and individuals want to grow and progress. The response is some form of career planning. Often a formalized career planning program is intended to help retain key staff by providing growth and satisfaction. There are valid business reasons for engaging in career planning. It is not just a philanthropic exercise on the part of organizations. However, many organizations are getting into it without really understanding why or what the implications are of embarking on career planning efforts.

7. Where is the training and development process going? What will be its functions in the future? What techniques are likely to become more popular? What will a training program of the 1990s look like and what type of people will staff it?

One of the key things that's influencing the training and development function right now is the introduction of instructional technology. Training is becoming much more multi-media and involving. We're seeing less dependence on old-fashioned lecture techniques. This is partly because the new technology exists, but more because people today don't like to be lectured to, and they're used to multi-media and involving situations. Training is becoming much more individualized, and the technology is helping to make this possible. Interactive computer, video discs, and self-study programs of various kinds have become much more prevalent than they have been in the past.

In the future, there will be more technical training because of the growing complexity of technology. Also there is going to be more need to train in management skills so that the technology is well managed and the interface between people and technology operates efficiently. Training is going to be more dispersed with the capability of rapid information transfer. It's going to be more modularized and focused at the specific needs of individuals — more like the ability to operate on a shopping list of personal needs and respond to them selectively through the use of media. I think basically there is going to be more training responding to the changes and complexities that are taking place. Trainees are going to be less dependent on the trainer and more driven by technology. Such things as video discs will make much of this possible.

In the future, there will be more capability of remote training so that master trainers can be used more effectively in networks. Because of that, I think there will be fewer training people. The ones that are in training will have a greater degree of professionalism and competence. One of the major functions of the trainer will be to ensure that trainees utilize the training technology effectively and that it is tailored to their specific needs.

I think those in the training field currently have some tremendous challenges ahead of them. Too many of the people in the training function are old-line trainers, and they're just not going to be able to handle it in the future. A lot of them are going to be looking for work! The field needs more imaginative people; people more rooted in practical business concerns; people who are able to adapt to change; and people who are willing to grab hold of new technology and grow with it and see the potential for vastly expanding their influence and enhancing their results.

PART V: FOR DISCUSSION AND REVIEW

A.

Vinton, Clark, and Seybolt

- ☐ What is the primary purpose of an organization analysis? an operations analysis? a person analysis?
- ☐ Briefly describe the training system model discussed.
- ☐ In what way, if any, does training needs assessment for supervisory jobs differ from other jobs?

B.

Schneier

- ☐ What is the difference between punishment and negative reinforcement?
- ☐ How would you design a training program to maximize transfer of learning?
- ☐ What is the role of practice in learning?

Rothwell

- ☐ How does the "systems approach" to curriculum design differ from the "school" approach?
- ☐ Do you agree or disagree with the author's statement that the contingency approach to curriculum design is the "best" method? Why?

McEvoy and Sporer

- ☐ How does the Traditional Training Model differ from the Behavioral Modeling Approach to training (BMT)?
- ☐ In what ways might BMT not be appropriate for training managers?

C.

Louis

- List and describe the essential tasks that would be associated with an "ideal" transition experience.
- How does transition management overcome the limitations of traditional approaches to career planning and development?
- What transitions would be most difficult to manage?

D.

Meyer and Raich

- Why do you think organizations spend a great amount of money on training programs, but spend very little money evaluating these training programs?
- What makes an effective evaluation plan?

PART VI
MAINTAINING AND IMPROVING SATISFACTION, COMMITMENT, AND PERFORMANCE

A.

THE USE OF NONFINANCIAL REWARDS

Making Sense of Quality of Work Life Programs
Herman Gadon

- ☐ Defines quality of work life and describes various examples of organizational programs.
- ☐ Explains why quality of work life programs are currently enjoying popularity in American organizations.

What's Creating an "Industrial Miracle" at Ford
Business Week

- ☐ Describes the "Employee Involvement" program at Ford and its effect on absenteeism, productivity, and product quality.

The Work Ethic Is Underemployed
Daniel Yankelovich

- ☐ Argues that there has not been a decline in the work ethic, but rather that workers believe that they will not benefit from increasing their productivity.

B.

THE USE OF FINANCIAL REWARDS: COMPENSATION AND BENEFITS

Government Influences on Compensation
Richard I. Henderson

- ☐ Briefly reviews the history of government impact on social issues through legislation.
- ☐ Outlines legislation relevant to compensation programs and policies in organizations.

Job Evaluation and the Wage-Salary Structure
Marc J. Wallace, Jr., and Charles H. Fay

- ☐ Describes common methods of job evaluation.
- ☐ Offers guidelines for using the results of job evaluation and market data to build an organization's wage-salary structure.

394

*PART VI
MAINTAINING
AND IMPROVING
SATISFACTION,
COMMITMENT,
AND PERFORMANCE*

Whatever Happened to Incentive Pay?
Edward E. Lawler

 Reviews the problems with piece-rate incentive plans.

 Explains how societal changes relate to the declining popularity of piece-rate incentive plans.

Comparable Worth: Implications for Compensation Managers
Frederick S. Hills

□ Defines the concept of "comparable worth."

□ Projects the potential impact that comparable worth legislation would have on organizations, labor markets, and society.

The Creative Flowering of Employee Benefits
J. H. Foegen

□ Details common and "exotic" examples of benefits offered by organizations and demanded by employees.

C.

WITHDRAWAL FROM WORK, HOURS OF WORK, AND SAFETY

Dealing with Premature Employee Turnover
John W. Seybolt

 Presents a model of the turnover process, including primary causes and moderators.

 Presents the results of a study designed to test the model.

□ Discusses implications of the model in terms of differing strategies for dealing with turnover.

Taking a Look at Flexitime
Philip I. Morgan and H. Kent Baker

□ Details the advantages and disadvantages associated with flexitime programs.

□ Suggests guidelines for implementing an effective flexitime program.

Safety and Health Programs
Hermine Zagat Levine

□ Presents the results of a survey describing organizational safety practices.

□ Provides guidelines for developing or improving an overall safety program.

D.

COMPENSATION AND MOTIVATION

Interview with Francis W. Miller

A.

THE USE OF NONFINANCIAL REWARDS

Making Sense of Quality of Work Life Programs

Herman Gadon

General Motors is doing it, and so are Ford, Chrysler, Motorola, Honeywell, Westinghouse, Digital Equipment, Hewlett-Packard, AT&T, Bethlehem Steel, Polaroid, and General Electric. The list grows so that it is hard these days to find anyone who isn't doing it.

What is IT? IT includes quality circles, participation teams, alternative work schedules, wellness in the workplace, union-management productivity committees, job restructuring, and socio-technical systems. There are more terms, all loosely collected under a heading which is today known as quality of work life. What's in a name? Names are symbols that can capture imaginations and signal new directions. They can portend new intent and make credible what was previously distrusted. General Motors found this out in the late 1960s after it began its first experiment with organization development (OD). Influenced by Rensis Likert from the Institute for Social Research at the University of Michigan and his approach to systems change, GM began a program in 1968. The name Organization Development created resistance. In a public address a GM executive said "we first used the term 'OD' and this was disastrous . . . so we changed the program's title to 'quality of work life' and this became accepted."

The phrase *quality of work life* has entered the mainstream of our language. It graces a large body of literature, dignifies conferences, and is found in national labor-management collective bargaining agreements in the auto, steel, communications, and electrical industries.

The origin of the phrase is uncertain. One of the earliest references to quality of life, as connected to work, occurred in 1973 at the Forty-Third American Assembly on the Changing World of Work at Columbia University's Arden House. The select participants assembled there concluded in their final remarks that "improving the place, the organization, and the nature of work can lead to better work performance and a *better quality of life* in the society."[1] Also in 1973, a special task force of the Secretary of Health, Education, and Welfare asserted that much work in America was unneces-

396

*PART VI
MAINTAINING
AND IMPROVING
SATISFACTION,
COMMITMENT,
AND PERFORMANCE*

sarily brutish, impersonal, menial, unrewarding, and inefficient. This was a sweeping indictment of American institutions, including private organizations, public bureaucracies, and trade unions, for affronting individual dignity in the workplace and wasting human resources. It was also an appeal to American managers to recognize and meet new challenges ahead.

The response has been gradual but growing in volume and importance. Today quality of work life is seen as a new field, even movement, whose significance is marked by the appearance of consultants, professional groups, and public and private study centers, such as the Center for the Quality of Work Life at UCLA; Work in America Institute in Scarsdale, New York; the American Productivity Center in Houston, Texas; The American Center for Quality of Work Life in Washington, D.C.; and Quality of Work Life Councils in Maryland, Massachusetts, Michigan, and New York.

QWL — WHAT IT IS

QWL has become an umbrella term for a host of activities. They include new efforts in the areas of personal and professional development, work redesign, team building, work scheduling, and total organizational change. Commonly used terms in each category are these:

Personal and Professional Development: M.B.O. (management by objectives), management development, career counseling, mental health counseling (employee assistance programs), and physical health improvement (wellness in the workplace).

Work Redesign: job enlargement, job enrichment, work flow reorganization, and socio-technical systems.

Team Building: quality circles, participation teams, task forces, project groups, and joint labor-management productivity committees.

Work Scheduling: flexible working hours (flextime), staggered working hours, compressed workweeks, job sharing, and part-time work.

Total Organizational Change: parallel organization (cross-hierarchical representative system which coexists with the traditional organization), gain sharing (Scanlon and Rucker Improshare Plans which are participatory systems with all personnel sharing in the gains of increased productivity), and work councils and codetermination (employee representation in policy making assemblies, commonly found in Europe, but rare in the U.S. [for example, U.A.W. President Fraser's membership on Chrysler's Board of Directors]).

The programs share the belief that people will respond creatively, productively, and with satisfaction to conditions which confer:

□ Personal dignity and respect, reflected in provisions for individuals to influence events that affect them;

□ Some reasonable measure of self-control or autonomy;

□ Personal recognition for contributions made to organizational effectiveness;

□ Rewards commensurate with performance, including opportunities to develop, to face challenge, and to experience variety, as well as to receive more pay, promotions, and favorable assignments;

□ Identification with work groups and organizations that are sources of pride and support; and

☐ Job security, protection from arbitrary treatment, and decent working conditions.

The concepts are not new. They have been proposed for many years as the basis for more productive and more satisfying organizations. Elton Mayo, celebrated for his part in the well-known Hawthorne experiments at Western Electric in the 1930s, suggested as much. So did inheritors of his legacy, including Douglas McGregor (Theory X, Theory Y), Abraham Maslow (an ascending order of needs satisfactions), the Tavistock group in London, England, made up of Eliot Jacques, Fred E. Emery, Eric L. Trist, and A. K. Rice (socio-technical systems), and the MIT group made up of Kurt Lewin, Alvin Zander, Dorwin Cartright, Douglas McGregor, Alex Bavelas, Charles Myers, Paul Pigors, Douglas Brown, and Joseph Scanlon (force field analysis, group dynamics, and the Scanlon Plan). For nearly fifty years, numerous others like those above have been writing about, experimenting with, and studying the effects of the themes which are the basis of all quality of work life activities. It is during the last ten years that the ideas have finally had a substantial effect on organizational practice.

WHY IT IS NOW

Organizations throughout the world are under competitive pressures from which the United States was largely insulated for many years after World War II. With our capital base, infrastructure, and organizations intact, United States products, managerial practices, and technology spread throughout the world. The epithet "ugly American," which grew through the '50s, reflected our success, as well as our lack of sensitivity to other people. Today we are not the only ones who are clicking cameras in foreign cities, ensconced in major resorts, taking cruises, and suffering insults. We now share these fruits of success with travelers from Japan and West Germany. The competition explains in large part our present interest in organizational structures and processes which are intended to increase productivity, quality, and satisfaction at work. Once known for our superior practices, we are now associated with shoddy workmanship and poor performance.

Why did it happen? The economic bases of most of the rest of the industrialized world had been ravaged by World War II. For all practical purposes, U.S. organizations operated with little competition for twenty years. In the middle 1960s the first signals of potential danger were masked by the commitment of resources to the Vietnam War. We were an economy that was pushed by demand for "butter" as well as "guns," and appeared to provide both. In these circumstances the developing weaknesses in our internationally competitive position were not readily apparent.

In fact, we were spending relatively less than organizations in other countries on capital improvements and on organizational innovations. Whereas other countries were being honed to a fine competitive edge in a process of recovery, we were lulled into a false sense of security by the apparently overwhelming size of our advantage. Therefore, we did not upgrade our industrial equipment or improve our technologies or experiment with new organizational forms and practices as rapidly as did our developing international competitors.

Driven by a labor shortage and by a social change which stressed more democratic values throughout their societies, European countries developed organizational variations which increased output and worker satisfaction. From this source came semi-autonomous work groups, flexible working hours, work councils, codetermination, and worker-managed enterprises. Japan's reputation for cheap, poorly made merchandise limited the appeal for its goods in the markets of the world. The need to export pushed

398

PART VI
MAINTAINING
AND IMPROVING
SATISFACTION,
COMMITMENT,
AND PERFORMANCE

Japan into a compulsive attention to quality. Quality circles are one outcome, the term entering our language as another association with the Japanese miracle.

The end of the Vietnam War exposed our weaknesses. The steel industry was one of the first to suffer seriously from international competition. In a defensive effort, the United Steel Workers of America, AFL-CIO, and the major steel producers agreed to suspend strikes between contracts and to submit unresolved differences to arbitration. The industry could not afford to risk further permanent losses of customers to foreign sources, as had followed previous work stoppages. The union and management also made the first tentative efforts to cooperate to increase productivity through joint productivity committees.

In 1974, the oil embargo by OPEC nations forced upon us, and the U.S. automobile industry in particular, awareness of our vulnerability to foreign competitors. In addition, as in Europe, a shift in values had taken place in the United States. An emphasis on equity, freedom of choice, and fulfillment had emerged, from the expectations of a younger and better educated work force. Since the late 1960s, Daniel Yankelovich[2] has documented this change through surveys conducted at regular interviews. American firms needed more output from people who wanted to be treated differently. GM's experience in the early 1970s in Lordstown, Ohio, at a plant built to produce its new line of Vegas at low cost, represents a classic clash of new worker values with unchanged attitudes of management. Workers simply wouldn't perform as expected. Rallying around cries for consideration, dignity, and humanity, young workers struck and forced GM to change its perceptions of what would motivate its employees. Perhaps Lordstown was a necessary confrontation before GM could make a full-scale commitment to improving the quality of work life.

Nothing succeeds like success. But the other side of this coin is that pain must precede change. American managers paid only passing attention to the experiments, theories, and experiences concerning quality of work life which had been underway, and written and talked about, since the early 1940s. Why should they have? What they did worked. Change meant adjustments that would require new learning and redeployment of assets. Change is also always accompanied by uncertainty, and there was little incentive to risk that. When the stakes became high enough, U.S. managers began a search for new methods of management. In this response they are no different from managers anywhere. The pressures for change must be felt before change will take place.

QWL — IT DOES WORK

Quality of work life programs have two objectives: to increase productivity and to increase the satisfaction of employees. It is difficult to unequivocally attribute effects on productivity and morale to specific activities. As a consequence, evaluations of the effectiveness of QWL programs tend to use considerable anecdotal evidence. Since surveys seem to provide a fairly reliable index of attitudes, some companies rely on them to justify their QWL efforts. Still, it is with less certainty that results, even in this area, can be traced to single factors in complex organizations, affected as they are by many variables.

Finding cause and effect relationships between programs and the desired results of satisfaction and productivity is elusive. Yet there are rigorous studies that have made efforts to isolate dependent and independent variables and to explain their connections. One such study was undertaken by a research group at Case Western Reserve for the National Science Foundation.[3] Looking for productivity and attitude effects in programs of socio-technical systems (16 firms), job restructuring (27 firms), participative management (7 firms), and organizational change (7 firms), the investigation team reported overwhelmingly positive results. Criteria were costs, productivity, quality, withdrawal, and attitudes. Similarly positive results are reported by rigorous studies of the effects of flexible schedules and of Scanlon Plans.[4]

What matters most to participants in QWL programs is the achievement of objectives *they* deem important. Many measures therefore become criteria of success or indicators of problems which require attention. Criteria include output/labor ratios, numbers of rejects, turnover, absenteeism, complaints, ability to resolve conflicts, and frequency of communications across organizational boundaries. Consensus reached to use any particular indices will increase the likelihood of commitment and provide guidelines to desirable behavior. What the measures are is less important than agreement to use them.

It has been observed that managers in Europe, in contrast to American managers, are more likely to go ahead with plans solely because they make sense. American managers, on the other hand, seem to require considerable quantitative proof before they act.[5] Attention to reasonable objectives and ways of measuring achievement of them can inspire confidence and generate commitment, but insistence that risk be removed by accumulating large quantities of statistical proof may simply be a thinly disguised effort to prevent anything from happening.

For managements that are ready to make the emotional commitment of time, energy, and resources to improving productivity and satisfaction, quality of life programs offer many choices. Those that seem to provide the most substantial and enduring results, helping the organization to cope better with changing circumstances, take the total organizational culture into account. Two comprehensive studies suggest strongly that companies that are better managed and use their human resources most effectively reflect the characteristics that are associated with QWL programs in all their policies and practices.

This conclusion appears in a major report by McKinsey & Company, Inc.,[6] the culmination of a "four year R&D effort to reexamine Management and Organization Effectiveness." In a summary statement, the report observed:

"We have surfaced perhaps hundreds of interesting devices (for example, reviews, team structures); we think *each* is important as an example of a climate support; on the other hand *none*, or no small set, constitutes a panacea; it is to a great extent the large number of supportive devices *per se* that underpins the observed self-renewing, innovative climates."

Fred Foulkes[7] reaches a remarkably similar conclusion. While acknowledging the difficulty of evaluating organizational effectiveness, he concludes from his data: "the personnel policies and practices of the companies studied seem to be, for the most part, quite effective . . . From the experiences of the companies studied there can be no doubt about the importance of the integrity of their managements and the climate of the organizations. The critical question is not whether a climate of trust and confidence is important, but rather how such a climate is created and maintained. This field survey has shed much light on this important issue. It has suggested that the combination of certain top management attitudes, values, philosophies, and goals and certain substantive policies — including the effective management of environmental factors and company characteristics; employment security; promotion from within; an influential and proactive personnel department; satisfactory compensation and benefit programs; effective feedback mechanisms, communication programs, and complaint procedures; and careful selection, development, and evaluation of managers — will produce such a climate."

The cluster of characteristics which McKinsey and Foulkes associate with outstanding performance has also been linked with the characteristics associated with outstanding performance of Japanese management. William Ouchi calls this cluster

400

*PART VI
MAINTAINING
AND IMPROVING
SATISFACTION,
COMMITMENT,
AND PERFORMANCE*

"Theory Z." Richard T. Pascale and Anthony G. Athos refer to it as the "Art of Japanese Management." It is worth pointing out that these studies emphasize the importance of *leadership,* as seen in the commitment, visibility, and example of top management in supporting an organizational culture which encourages superior results.

Although concepts which lie behind America's present interest in quality of work life have been widely circulated for more than forty years, it has taken changing circumstances, in international competition and attitudes toward work, to force a large-scale reconsideration of existing organizational practices.

Because QWL is a response to environmental pressures, the efforts to cope with them that QWL represents will continue. The label may change, as labels are wont to do, but the momentum of change will not. We have become acutely aware of the world's limited resources, heightened by the rising clamor of nations to share more of them. The good life will be pursued in the marketplaces of the world, and our access to it will depend substantially on our ability to compete successfully. Quality of work life is not, therefore, a passing fancy, or even an appeal to better, more humane values. It is a practical way of addressing our material and psychological needs in a harshly competitive world.

NOTES

1. J. M. Rosow, ed., *The Worker and the Job* (New York: The American Assembly, Columbia University, 1974).

2. Daniel Yankelovich, *New Rules* (New York: Random House, 1981).

3. S. Srivastra, et. al., *Job Satisfaction and Productivity* (Cleveland: Department of Organizational Behavior, Case Western Reserve University, 1975); T. G. Cummings and E. S. Molloy, *Improving Productivity and the Quality of Work Life* (New York: Praeger, 1977).

4. H. Gadon and A. Cohen, *Alternative Work Schedules* (Reading, Mass.: Addison-Wesley, 1978); James W. Driscoll, "Working Creatively with a Union: Lessons from the Scanlon Plan," *Organizational Dynamics,* Summer 1979: 61–80; Alternative Work Schedules Experimental Program, Interim Report to the President and Congress (Washington, D.C.: United States Office of Personnel Management, 1981); S. D. Nolen, "Does Flextime Improve Productivity?" *Harvard Business Review,* September-October 1979: 17–22.

5. H. Gadon and N. Foy, "Work Participation, Contrasts in Three Countries," *Harvard Business Review,* May-June 1976: 71–83.

6. McKinsey & Company, Inc., *Findings from the Excellent Companies* (Internal Monograph, 1981).

7. F. K. Foulkes, *Personnel Policies in Large Non-union Companies* (Englewood Cliffs, N.J.: Prentice-Hall, 1980).

What's Creating an "Industrial Miracle" at Ford

Business Week

At Ford Motor Co.'s Edison (N.J.) plant, the high-pitched whir of power tools rings out along the assembly line where workers install fenders and hoods. They have 55 seconds to fit, bolt, and drill as each car hull glides by, and they move with a rote-like rhythm. It is easy to let defects slip by when the job is so monotonous and the line keeps moving. U.S. auto makers have always emphasized uninterrupted production over quality, and only rarely would even a foreman dare shut down a line to catch a mistake. But the Edison plant has reversed those priorities. Each work station is equipped with a "stop button," and the workers themselves often halt the line 10 to 20 times a day when a problem prevents them from doing their jobs. A foreman hurries to the trouble area, helps the worker correct a malfunctioning machine or a defect in the car, and usually within 30 seconds the line is moving again.

The innovation at Edison — other Ford plants are now installing the stop concept — is only the most visible symbol of a near-revolution in labor-management relations that started five years ago and has since become entrenched. Ford and the United Auto Workers have established what may be the most extensive and successful worker participation process in a major, unionized company. Thousands of teams of workers and supervisors at 86 of Ford's 91 plants and depots meet weekly to deal with production, quality, and work-environment problems. Employee Involvement (EI), as the process is called, has reduced production costs and absenteeism and played a major role in what one outside expert calls "an industrial miracle" in improving product quality.

It was to improve quality that the Edison plant took the radical step of allowing hourly workers to stop the line. The idea would have shocked Henry Ford, who once remarked that "the assembly line is a haven for those who haven't got the brains to do anything else." But Edison management and UAW Local 980 decided that if assemblers were "treated like adults," as Foreman Frank Cunningham puts it, permitting them to stop the line to correct defects would pay off. "For the first time in their lives they had the authority to control quality at the source, and their response was fantastic," says Philip I. Staley, the plant manager. Within four months after the stop buttons were installed in 1982, defects had dropped to less than one per car, down from 17.

"ZOMBIES BEFORE"

As many as 20,000 to 34,000 hourly employees — 20% to 30% of Ford's work force — have some direct involvement in an EI project during the course of a year, Ford estimates. This is an extraordinary level of participation for a voluntary process. "It's been like a firestorm," says W. Patrick Dolan, a consultant who has helped set up EI at some 25 Ford plants. He adds: "We can see now that rank-and-file workers were walking around like zombies before we started EI."

Participation still has opponents, particularly among first-line supervisors and UAW committeemen, and EI efforts simply collapsed at a few plants. But at many other plants, union and management roles are being stretched far beyond the traditional

---

402

*PART VI
MAINTAINING
AND IMPROVING
SATISFACTION,
COMMITMENT,
AND PERFORMANCE*

"management decides, union reacts" relationship. Managers are consulting union officials and workers on a wide range of issues, such as work scheduling and technology changes, before making decisions. And while many UAW officials still worry that EI reduces members' dependence on the union, participating leaders contend otherwise. "It's democracy in the workplace," says David A. Curson, chairman of UAW Local 898 at Ford's Rawsonville (Mich.) plant. "It makes the people more aware of their own self-worth and intelligence, and it makes them better union members."

Neither Ford nor the UAW make any effort to measure the economic results of EI, believing that "playing the numbers game," says Peter J. Pestillo, Ford's vice-president for labor relations, would kill the process. Plant managers think that EI has had the most impact on quality and cite improvements in warranty repairs above 40% for many products. An independent research firm reported that a survey of 6,500 buyers of 1984 Ford cars showed that "things gone wrong" had declined 55%, compared with a 1980 survey.

EI's impact on productivity is less clear. Hours worked per vehicle at Ford declined 27% from 1980 to 1983, largely because of new technology. To prevent EI from undermining the union's role as the bargaining agent, the teams are prohibited from discussing collective bargaining issues, such as wages and work rules, that most affect productivity. The teams, however, often reduce production costs, by suggesting changes in equipment or production flow, which in turn increases efficiency.

STAYING COMPETITIVE

The more cooperative relationships fostered by EI have enabled local unions to negotiate work-rule changes with a direct impact on efficiency. At Edison, Local 980 in 1983 agreed to eliminate 220 jobs, saving $8 million, to keep the plant competitive. Says Local 980 Chairman Earl D. Nail: "We're learning to accept automation, and we're working toward a goal of no layoffs except by attrition."

Ford was a latecomer to worker participation compared with General Motors Corp., which started its quality-of-work-life (QWL) process with the UAW in 1973. Some GM plants today are just as innovative in labor relations as any Ford plant. But participation is not as pervasive in GM, knowledgeable observers say. The union charges that some GM managers have used QWL in manipulative ways. Last year, Ford changed practices at about 10 plants where abuses had been reported by the UAW.

Worker participation is only one of several mechanisms by which Ford and the UAW have changed their labor climate. EI was established in 1979 negotiations. Japanese competition and the 1980 and 1981–82 recessions then brought large job losses that forced both sides to reassess their relationship. In late 1981, Pestillo says, "we made the corporate policy decision that a trained work force is an asset to the company and that labor would no longer be treated as our most variable cost." This led to major job-security and training provisions in the 1982 contract. Also in that year, Ford and the UAW initiated Mutual Growth Forums, quarterly meetings at which managers brief UAW officials on business developments.

The combination of these elements makes a powerful lever for changes to increase Ford's competitiveness. In 1979, for example, the Rawsonville plant began losing products, such as brakes and fuel pumps, to companies that could supply them to Ford assembly plants at lower prices. Some 3,000 jobs disappeared. In 1980, Local 898 at Rawsonville and plant management began an EI process and now have 90 teams at work.

EI "opened up lines of communications," Curson says, enabling the two sides to collaborate on cutting costs and outbidding competitors. Last March the members of Local 898 ratified a precedent-setting agreement that calls for experimentation with new forms of work organization, such as production teams, and, in a major cost-cutting move, consolidates 24 skilled trades into 14. In return, all 2,582 full-time, hourly workers at Rawsonville are guaranteed 32 hours of work per week for three years — the most comprehensive job guarantee in the auto industry.

MINOR MAINTENANCE

Plant management can no longer use temporary layoffs to balance production needs with employment. Instead, it will use part-time workers to fill in during production surges. But the 100% job-security protection gives management flexibility to make the plant competitive, says Dennis J. Cirbes, the plant's industrial-relations manager. "People had a strong reluctance to make changes that would allow us to be more efficient and competitive when they feared losing their jobs," he says.

Collaboration has also saved jobs at the Indianapolis steering gear plant, the site of Ford's first participation program. Productivity has increased by 8.5% annually since 1980, and a year ago the plant underbid its old competitor, TRW Inc., to supply the steering gear mechanism for the Taurus, a midsize car that Ford will introduce in 1985. Among other things, UAW Local 1111 agreed to let machine operators perform minor maintenance chores that had always been the job of skilled tradesmen. This and other changes in work practices, says Plant Manager Arland E. Phelps, reduce the labor cost of producing the Taurus gear by 15%, or $4 million.

Winning the Taurus bid will save roughly 300 jobs at the Indianapolis plant and add about 200 new ones, depending on production volumes. "We have a common objective of wanting to stay in business," Phelps says, "and so we've been making the union more of a partner in what we're doing. We share data with them, instead of doing things [unilaterally] and making them react." He adds: "We're not to the point of jointly running the organization, but we're moving in that direction."

At Ford's Chesterfield trim plant in Mt. Clemens, Mich., 35% of the 1,500 hourly workers belong to EI "circles," as they are called — a particularly high level of involvement. Moreover, 70% to 75% of workers in a department typically turn out when Plant Manager William R. Brooks calls meetings for ideas about reorganizing the workplace to produce a new product. A visitor can sense participation in the plant's atmosphere. Not confined to team meetings, it is becoming a way of life. This is Pestillo's goal for the entire company.

WILLED INTO BEING

UAW officials and managers at Chesterfield informally settle a wide range of issues that previously would wind up in the grievance system. This eliminates the legalistic climate that exists in plants where the union and management spend much time defending their "rights" under the contract. Brooks no longer insists on asserting management's right to make various decisions instead of consulting with the union. "That right doesn't mean anything if you've got a bunch of unhappy people who aren't going to give you 100% on the job," Brooks says. "We bend the rules all the time."

The future of EI, however, is not entirely settled. Negotiations for a new national contract, which begin on July 24, will create strong tensions that could hurt the process in some plants. Moreover, leadership changes in the union and the company could weaken the commitment to participation. EI started fast and matured quickly at Ford, largely because Pestillo and Donald F. Ephlin, a UAW vice-president and former director of its Ford Dept., personally promoted and willed it into being. Last year, Ephlin became the UAW's chief negotiator at GM and was replaced at Ford by Stephen P. Yokich, a more conventional unionist. Company and union sources say Yokich has

404

PART VI
MAINTAINING
AND IMPROVING
SATISFACTION,
COMMITMENT,
AND PERFORMANCE

come to accept EI because the members want it, but he is not a crusader as Ephlin was.

On the company side, Chairman Philip Caldwell and possibly other top managers who are partisans of EI may retire next year. Dolan, the management consultant, worries that their successors might be less committed. "There's a question whether some of Ford's financial management people have been involved in EI at all or even understand it," Dolan says.

"Some fear is always warranted when there is a change in leadership," Pestillo says. "But it would be hard for the new guys to go back to the old ways and give up everything we've gained." At the Indianapolis plant, UAW member Gilbert Lynch expresses what many rank and filers feel: "EI might be called something different in the future, but I can assure you it's here to stay."

The Work Ethic Is Underemployed

Daniel Yankelovich

Americans hold two beliefs about why the Japanese are outdoing us in autos, steel, appliances, computer chips, and even subway cars. The first is that our productivity has become stagnant. The second is that this has happened because our work ethic has deteriorated badly.

The first belief is, alas, true. Since 1965, the country's productivity has improved at ever smaller rates. It now shows no growth at all, and may even be falling. But despite these signs and additional evidence that people are not working as hard as they once did, it is emphatically not true that our work ethic has become weaker. If by work ethic — a very slippery term — we mean endowing work with intrinsic moral worth and believing that everyone should do his or her best possible job irrespective of financial reward, then recent survey research shows that the work ethic in the United States is surprisingly sturdy, and growing sturdier.

To understand the findings, we need to keep in mind the sharp distinction between work *behavior* — what we actually do in the work place — and the work *ethic* — a set of psychological and moral beliefs.

A 1980 Gallup study for the United States Chamber of Commerce shows that an overwhelming 88 percent of all working Americans feel that it is personally important to them to work hard and do their best on the job. (This should not be confused with Gallup findings that fewer Americans are enjoying their work — a separate issue. See "Newsline," April 1982.) The study concludes that a faulty work ethic is *not* responsible for the decline in our productivity; quite the contrary, the study identifies "a widespread commitment among U.S. workers to improve productivity" and suggests that "there are large reservoirs of potential upon which management can draw to improve performance and increase productivity."

In a subtler examination of American attitudes toward work, a 1982 pilot study for the nonprofit Public Agenda Foundation explores three conceptions of what might be called the "unwritten work contract" — the assumptions that each individual makes about what he or she will give to the job and expects to get in return. The first conception is one that historians recognize as the dominant attitude toward work throughout human history: the view that people labor only because they would not otherwise have the resources to sustain themselves. A second conception regards work as a straight economic transaction in which people relate effort to financial return: The more money they get, the harder they work; the less money they receive, the less effort they give. The third conception views work as carrying a moral imperative to do one's best apart from practical necessity or financial remuneration. The Public Agenda considers the implications of its findings so important that it intends to replicate the pilot study — from which national figures can only be surmised — among a larger cross-section of the work force within the next few months.

The study found that nearly four out of five people in the work force (78 percent) embrace the third conception, aligning themselves with the statement: "I have an inner need to do the very best job I can regardless of pay." Fewer than one out of 10 working Americans (7 percent) embrace the idea of work as a mere "business transaction" whereby one regulates one's effort according to the size of one's paycheck, and an additional 15 percent regard work as a necessary but disagreeable chore ("Working for a living is one of life's necessities. I would not work if I did not have to").

Other surveys reveal similar findings. In 1977, for example, the respected Quinn and Staines Quality of Employment Survey conducted by the University of Michigan's Survey Research Center discovered that three out of four Americans (75 percent) would prefer to go on working even if they could live comfortably without working for the rest of their lives. It is revealing of the expanding commitment to the value of work that eight years earlier, significantly fewer Americans (67 percent) had expressed the same attitude.

Yet at the same time that the work ethic, in the sense defined above, has actually been growing stronger, most Americans also believe that people are working less. A 1981 Harris study for Sentry Insurance reveals that:

- 78 percent of all working Americans feel that "people take less pride in their work than they did 10 years ago."
- 73 percent believe that "the motivation to work hard is not as strong today as it was a decade ago."
- 69 percent feel that our workmanship is worse than it was.
- 63 percent simply believe that "most people do not work as hard today as they did 10 years ago."

Polls by Harris and Gallup, and my own research firm, show that business leaders hold similar views.

These beliefs do not prove that Americans are actually working less effectively than in the past. But it is difficult to discount such widespread impressions among both working people and business leaders. One bit of direct evidence on the declining performance of the American worker allows us to go beyond these impressions. For a number of years, the University of Michigan asked a sample of workers to keep a diary of activities on the job. Analysis of these diaries reveals that between 1965 and 1975 the amount of time workers actually worked declined by more than 10 percent. If extrapolated to all American workers, the researchers say, this one factor alone, quite apart from such considerations as insufficient investments or aging equipment, could account for the slowed tempo of productivity growth in the decade from 1965 to 1975.

*PART VI
MAINTAINING
AND IMPROVING
SATISFACTION,
COMMITMENT,
AND PERFORMANCE*

How, then, are we to reconcile these two sets of seemingly incompatible facts? Why do Americans endorse the ideal of giving one's best to the job while their actual performance reveals a slackening effort? What forces have produced this self-defeating situation at the precise moment when economic competition from Japan, Korea, Taiwan, Germany, and other nations threatens to outpace us and drag down our standard of living?

The answer lies, I believe, in the deeply flawed reward system, both psychological and financial, that now rules the American work place. To grasp this argument, we need to understand just what most work is like today. The Public Agenda study asked people the amount of control they exercised over how hard they worked and over the quality of the products they made or services they performed. A huge majority (82 percent) stated that they had some degree of discretion and control over the effort they gave to their job, and an even larger majority (88 percent) said that they had control over the quality of the work or service they performed (72 percent, a great deal of control; 16 percent, moderate control). This finding illuminates a little-noted but important fact about the modern work place: Most working Americans have it in their power to decide whether they will satisfy only the minimum requirements of their job or exert the extra effort that makes the difference between ordinariness and high quality, between adequacy and excellence.

When the Public Agenda asked people whether they were using this freedom of choice to fulfill their "inner need to do the very best job" they can, fewer than one out of five (16 percent) said they were. All others acknowledged that they could improve their effectiveness — if they really wanted to. And many claimed that they could be twice as effective as they are now.

Why aren't they? The answer could hardly be plainer. When Gallup's Chamber of Commerce study asked workers whom they thought would benefit from the improvements in their productivity, only 9 percent felt that they, the workers, would. Most assumed that the beneficiaries would be others — consumers or stockholders or management. This finding accords with the finding of Yankelovich, Skelly, and White several years ago that a majority of college students no longer believe that working hard pays off. Some interpreted this finding to mean that the work ethic was eroding. It signifies, rather, the growing doubt that hard work will bring the rewards people have come to cherish. When Gallup's Chamber of Commerce study asked people whether they would work harder and do a better job if they were more involved in decisions relating to their work, an overwhelming 84 percent said they would. One need not take this finding literally to appreciate the vast sea of yearning that underlies it.

We arrive, then, at the heart of the matter. The questions of who benefits from increased productivity, and how, are the critical factors, not the work ethic. If the American work ethic has gone to seed, there is not much anyone can do about the problem of productivity. But if, as I contend, our work *ethic* is actually thriving while our work *behavior* falters, then the prognosis for action is excellent — once we grasp the reasons for the discrepancy and confront the task for remedying it.

In principle, most Americans are willing to work harder and turn out a higher-quality product; indeed, their self-esteem demands that they do so. That they are not doing it points directly to a serious flaw in management and in the reward system under which they perform their jobs. Why should workers make a greater effort if (a) they don't have to and (b) they believe that others will be the beneficiaries of such efforts? It is ironic that a political administration so finely tuned to encouraging the business community should pay such scant attention to stimulating the average American to work harder.

As our competitive posture in traditional industries such as steel and automobiles grows ever more grim, workers and trade unions are starting to pay more attention to productivity. But in many labor circles productivity is still regarded as a code term for speedups that benefit management and threaten job security. The mismatch between the national goal of improved productivity and the inadequate system of rewards now in operation could hardly be more obvious.

Lest anyone dismiss the idea that a more thoughtful approach to rewards can pay off, a large body of experimental data proves otherwise. Psychologist Raymond Katzell has reviewed 103 experiments designed to test whether an improved incentive system — including both money and greater control over one's work — would lead to higher individual productivity. It did in 85 of the experiments.

Perhaps more to the point is the Japanese experience in this country. The Japanese distinguish between the "soft" factors of production (the dedication of the work force) and such "hard" factors as technology, capital investment, and research and development. They recognize that the soft factors are just as important as the hard ones and that, indeed, the two are interdependent. It is this understanding that underlies Japan's spectacular success not only in their homeland but also in the plants they own and manage in the United States. One Japanese strategy, for example, is to bring together both workers and managers to solve the problem of how new technology can be introduced to the advantage of both. Such participation does not just assure workers of job security; it enables them to devise with management a system that also provides job satisfaction. The Japanese success in this country is evidence that the American belief in the work ethic is not just rhetoric. Without the work ethic, the Japanese would have had to rely solely on the hard factors, by themselves not enough to spur productivity.

Ironically, the Japanese seem to have a better grasp of how to capitalize on our work ethic than we do. In the American approach to work, the relevant institutions — business management, labor unions, government, professional economists — do not have a firm grasp of the soft factors and how they interact with the hard ones. Unwittingly, most "experts" hold an obsolete image of the work force as a pool of "labor" responsive solely to economic imperatives, driven by the fear of unemployment, and inspired by the promise of consumer goods — the familiar carrot-and-stick psychology that worked in the past when workers and work were different. The leaders who run our institutions do not really understand today's work force: tens of millions of well-educated Americans, proud of their achievements, zealous of their freedoms, motivated by new values, with substantial control over their own production, and ready to raise their level of effort if given the proper encouragement.

B.

THE USE OF FINANCIAL REWARDS: COMPENSATION AND BENEFITS

Government Influences on Compensation
Richard I. Henderson

With the arrival of agriculture and the widespread domestication of animals, the production of specialized tools and utensils, and the rise of commerce between cities came the enactment of laws, regulations, and injunctions to control the working hours and rewards available for effort exerted on the job. These laws came from custom and tradition and from government and religious jurisdictions. Although religious and government leaders occasionally were rivals for ultimate authority, they normally worked together to regulate the activities of the members of their society.

The earnings of most workers provided few luxuries and basically permitted mere survival. Agricultural workers were entitled to some share of the food they produced and access to fuel and shelter materials. Any earnings available after taking care of food, clothing, shelter, and modest entertainment were effectively removed through some form of government taxation or through levies and tithes imposed by religious leaders.

Similar to their scavenging, hunting, and gathering forebears, the farmers and most craftworkers from the dawn of written history until relatively recent times had their work hours controlled by hours of daylight, variations in weather, and climatic changes. As more workers became involved in craft activities and the production of buildings, goods, and services, government and religious leaders recognized the need to regulate working hours. Regulated time off from work allowed for both the replenishment of physical energy and the nourishment of social and spiritual needs. To sustain these needs, early societies established sacred or holy days as well as a weekly day of rest.

Except for possible death during wars or for the occasional periods of plague and famine when large numbers of people perished because of illness or lack of food, agricultural society was a society of certainty, conformity, and uniformity.

By the fourteenth century, however, the rising commercial revolution and the final disintegration of the medieval society in Europe introduced change and disorder into

Richard I. Henderson, *Compensation Management: Rewarding Performance*, 4th Ed., 1985. Reprinted by permission of Reston Publishing Company, a Prentice-Hall Company, Englewood Cliffs, NJ 07632.

the world of work. No longer were earnings set by custom and tradition. By the four-teenth and fifteenth centuries, European workers were negotiating wages, and the early craft guilds (forerunners of the modern unions) were major forces in setting wage rates. As socially controlled "just price" wage rates began to crumble, rulers began to assign specific wage rates for specific occupations to block escalation of wage demands.[1]

A combination of dramatic events was responsible for these changes. Concurrent with a move toward commercial endeavors and increased production of luxury items, the Black Death struck western Europe in 1348. By the time the plague had subsided, the population of Europe had been reduced by one-third. This tremendous loss of population, coupled with increased demands for goods, caused many of the remaining farm laborers to migrate to the cities to seek jobs in the trades and crafts. This move-ment led to a shortage of farm workers. The need for workers both in the city and on the farm gave workers an opportunity to demand higher wages.[2]

By the sixteenth century, widespread trade and competition for the consumer's money provided an impetus for the rise of the cottage industry. Working in their own homes, families produced goods required by commercial traders at prices lower than those demanded by the urban guilds. Competition for supplying the goods and services resulted in a decline in the prices paid to nonfarm workers of this period.

With the decline in the price of labor and increases in the cost of food and shelter, sixteenth-century workers in England experienced a decline in their standard of living. Commercial workers who had given up their share of the food and the shelter available in the agricultural community for the wages available in a commercial society were unemployed and destitute in many cases. In attempting to improve the plight of the nonfarm worker, Parliament passed a minimum wage act in 1562.[3]

In the seventeenth and eighteenth centuries the cottage industry that had been centered in homes in rural areas moved into the homes of the workers in the towns and cities. The individuals responsible for meting out work to these home-workers set rates of pay for pieces produced. Because of the decentralization of work activities and the lack of any mechanism for wage standardization, the piece rates set by business enterprises for cottage industry work were extremely low.

With the invention of the steam engine and other technology that led to the de-velopment of factories for spinning and weaving fabrics independent of water as a source of power, a major change occurred in the way masses of people earned their livelihood through work. Within a hundred years after the beginning of the Industrial Revolution, working conditions had become so bad that, by the latter part of the nine-teenth century, the term "sweated" was applied to conditions under which many En-glish workers toiled. "Sweating" applied to "(1) a rate of wage inadequate to the necessities of the workers or disproportionate to the work done; (2) excessive hours of labor; and (3) unsanitary state of houses in which work is carried on."[4]

Demands for improvement in working conditions, fewer hours of work a week and shorter working weeks, and improved pay had already been proposed early in the nineteenth century. A major breakthrough occurred in the United States in 1840 when President Martin Van Buren issued an executive order that established the 10-hour day for workers on government contracts.[5] At this time, a 13-hour day and a 6-day work-week were the norm for most industrial workers. From 1840 until 1866, the 12-hour workday was accepted practice for industrial workers.

Ira Steward, a Boston machinist, provided a philosophical base for an eight-hour day when he stated that wages were determined by worker habits and that because wages depended on wants, the surplus provided by the advancing technology through the establishment of an eight-hour day should result in increased wages for workers.[6]

Following the Civil War, eight-hour leagues were established throughout the United States extolling the benefits of the eight-hour day. Some states passed eight-

410

*PART VI
MAINTAINING
AND IMPROVING
SATISFACTION,
COMMITMENT,
AND PERFORMANCE*

TABLE 1

Average Weekly Hours for American Nonagricultural Workers

1850	1860	1870	1880	1890	1900	1910	1920	1930	1940	1980
65.7	63.3	60.0	58.8	57.1	55.9	50.3	45.5	43.2	41.1	35.3

Source: J. Frederic Dewhurst et al., *America's Needs and Resources* (New York: Twentieth Century Fund, 1955) p. 1073; 1980 statistics in U.S. Department of Labor, Bureau of Labor Statistics, *Employment and Earnings, April 1981* (Washington, DC: Government Printing Office, 1981) p. 117.

hour laws, and the federal government passed an eight-hour law for federal employees. However, all these statutes were weak and provided for only minimal enforcement.[7]

Although many groups continued to champion an eight-hour day, the 12-hour day was still an integral part of the life pattern of many workers in the United States into the 1920s. Efforts toward shortening the workweek did, however, result in a reduction of the length of an average workday to 9.5 hours by 1890. (See Table 1.)

The first major reduction in hours worked weekly by industrial workers resulted from state laws passed to protect women and children.[8] From the 1890s until the 1920s, practically every state had laws limiting the number of hours worked by women or children.

The strong efforts to reduce working hours in the United States that followed the Civil War were accompanied by pressures to increase hourly earnings. The Iron Law of Wages theory formulated by the economist David Ricardo in 1817 stated that "the *natural price* of labour is that price which is necessary to enable the labourers, one with another, to subsist and to perpetuate their race without increase or diminuation."[9] This theory outlined in clear terms the wage payment practices followed by most employers from earliest times until fairly recent years.

As early as the fifteenth century, however, urban laborers in England were enjoying a substantial improvement in their standard of living. Food was abundant and cheap, and most laborers were able to pay for their weekly board and lodging with the pay from two days of work a week or less. This opportunity for a better life for the working masses disappeared by the 1550s and did not return until the late nineteenth century.

With the movement to improve working conditions and reduce hours worked, considerable attention was focused on the establishment of minimum wage rates and higher hourly wages. Initial efforts were focused on the pay provided to women and children. Although the earnings received by the male industrial worker were extremely low, payments received by women and children were even lower.

In 1896 the province of Victoria in Australia enacted the first minimum wage law in a modern industrial state. New Zealand and England soon followed with minimum wage legislation covering workers in certain industries. In 1912 Massachusetts passed the first minimum wage legislation in the United States. The Massachusetts law was enacted to protect women and children. By 1923, 14 more states had passed minimum wage laws aimed at protecting women and children.[10] In 1923 in the case of *Adkins* v. *Children's Hospital,* the Supreme Court overturned a District of Columbia statute, stating that it was unconstitutional to deprive individuals of their freedom to take whatever job they chose on such conditions as were acceptable to them. This Supreme Court ruling gave judicial sanction to minimum wage legislation.

LEGISLATION INFLUENCING COMPENSATION PRACTICES

Since the 1930s, the enactment of a broad spectrum of federal laws has had a significant impact on the compensation practices of organizations. With each new government intervention, opportunities for individual initiative and management activities have become more restrictive.

Today, senior management is aware that to survive and grow in a government-regulated environment, an organization must have competent staff members who are able to hire, train, develop, and reward employees within the limits set by government regulations, labor budgets, and employee demands. These ever-increasing pressures shed new light on the value of compensation managers and the requirements they must meet. In order to do their jobs, these human resource managers and staff officials must know not only the wording but also the intent of the many pieces of legislation that direct their daily activities in so many ways. The combination of overly restrictive government codes, unwise enforcement, and ineffective management can adversely affect both the organization and society in general.

The design and the management of a workable compensation system require a solid understanding of the federal, state, and local laws that either directly or indirectly influence how much employees are to be paid, how they are paid, the type and quantity of benefits they receive, and the incentives to be offered. In addition, these laws affect the recruitment, selection, and hiring of new employees; the classification of jobs; the appraisal of performance; and the training, transfer, promotion, termination, and retirement of all employees. The breadth and the depth of the impact of these laws can be more fully appreciated when the laws are grouped into five major categories:

1. Wage and hour legislation
2. Income protection legislation
3. Antidiscrimination legislation
4. Tax treatment legislation
5. Wage and price control legislation

WAGE AND HOUR LEGISLATION

The pressures throughout the entire nineteenth century for some kind of limits on hours worked, minimum rates of pay, and extra pay for hours worked beyond a specific standard continued into the twentieth century. By the 1920s, the pressures had become intense enough for the federal government and state governments to begin writing laws that would restrict hours worked and set rates of pay for significant numbers of American workers. Following are major wage and hour acts introduced as a result of these efforts.

1926: Railway Labor Act. This act grants railway and airline employees the right to bargain collectively with their employers on questions of wages, hours, and conditions of work. When a majority of workers vote to have a union, all employees must pay union dues. Right to work laws do not apply to this act.

1931: The Davis-Bacon Act. The first national legislation on minimum wages came with this act, which required construction contractors and their subcontractors receiving federal funds in excess of $2,000 to pay at least the prevailing wages in their area. The secretary of labor was granted the authority to determine the prevailing wages — the minimum wage that must be paid for work on covered government projects or purchases. (It has been common practice for the secretary of labor to review existing relevant union contracts and use the negotiated wage rates as the "prevailing wages" for a specific locale, but recent rulings permit the secretary of labor more latitude in

412

*PART VI
MAINTAINING
AND IMPROVING
SATISFACTION,
COMMITMENT,
AND PERFORMANCE*

establishing prevailing wages. Often, only 30 percent of workers in the locale have been used as the representative sample for determining the "prevailing wage.") Amendments to the act provided for employee benefits and required contractors or subcontractors to make necessary payments for these benefits.

1933: National Industrial Recovery Act (NIRA).   The federal government's next step toward enacting a national minimum wage law was the passage of the National Industrial Recovery Act. This attempt to establish a national minimum wage, as had been the case with previous state efforts, was foiled by the U.S. Supreme Court in 1935, which ruled that the law was unconstitutional.

1935: National Labor Relations Act.   This act provides employees with the right to bargain collectively for wages, benefits, and working conditions.

1936: Walsh-Healy Public Contracts Act.   The federal government again moved into minimum wage regulations with this act. The act requires the payment of the prevailing wage as established by the secretary of labor in all government-let contract work exceeding $10,000, and also requires that time-and-a-half be paid for work exceeding 8 hours a day and 40 hours a week.

1938: Fair Labor Standards Act (FLSA).   This legislation enabled the federal government to become deeply involved in regulating minimum wages for all employees engaged in interstate or foreign commerce or in the production of goods for such commerce, and for all employees in certain enterprises. In addition, this act established overtime wage requirements and defined specific exempt occupations. From 1938 until the present time, amendments to the act have enlarged the number of work groups covered by the law and have steadily increased the minimum wage. This act, as amended, not only sets a floor or base wage for most employees, but also allows the minimum wage to act as an index for wage increases received by practically all workers. The act requires employers in covered enterprises to pay time-and-a-half the regular rate received by nonexempt employees for all hours worked in excess of 40 hours a week. Employers must maintain and keep for 2 years records of time worked for all nonexempt employees. These files must be readily available for examination by U.S. Department of Labor officials. (The employer has some discretion in defining a workweek, but it must be fixed and be within a regularly recurring period of 168 hours, for example, from midnight Tuesday until midnight of the following Tuesday. Some provisions, however, allow businesses to operate under a 336-hour work period or 80-hour pay period. In an 80-hour pay period, a business may give compensatory time off at the rate of 1½ hours off for each hour worked in excess of 8 within the same time-card period.)

The minimum wage began at 25¢ an hour, and by 1981 reached $3.35 an hour. This act also established a ceiling over a working week in which any hours worked over the ceiling must be paid at the rate of time-and-a-half. In 1938 the ceiling was 44 hours, in 1939 it was lowered to 42, and by 1940 it had risen to the 40-hour ceiling that is still in effect. In 1982, 61.3 million workers were covered by the minimum wage requirements of the FLSA. Table 2 lists the changes in minimum wages between 1938 and 1981.

Provisions of the FLSA permit payment of subminimum wages for the following groups, if approved by the wage-hour administrator:

1. Learners in semiskilled occupations.
2. Apprentices in skilled occupations.

1938	1939	1945	1950	1956	1962	1964	1967
0.25	0.30	0.40	0.75	1.00	1.15	1.25	1.40

1968	1974	1975	1976	1978	1979	1980	1981
1.60	2.00	2.10	2.30	2.65	2.90	3.10	3.35

3. Messengers in firms primarily engaged in delivering letters and messages.
4. Handicapped persons, including those employed in a sheltered workshop.
5. Students in retail or service establishments, in agriculture, or in institutions of higher education.
6. Employees who receive over $30 per month in tips (up to 40 percent of the minimum wage requirement may be covered by tips).

In addition to . . . executive, administrative, professional, and salesperson exemptions . . . the FLSA also contains provisions that exempt the following employees from its overtime requirements (although specific qualifications must be met):

Certain highly paid commission employees of retail or service establishments.

Auto, truck, trailer, farm implement, boat, or aircraft salesworkers.*

Partsmen and mechanics servicing autos, trucks, or farm implements.*

Employees of railroad and air carriers, taxi drivers, certain employees of motor carriers, seamen of U.S. vessels, and local delivery employees paid on approved trip rate plans.

Announcers, news editors, and chief engineers of certain metropolitan broadcasting stations.

Domestic service workers residing in the employer's residence.

Employees of motion picture theaters and farm workers.

The child labor provisions of the FLSA are as follows:

1. Minimum hiring age is 14 to 16, depending on the kind of work to be performed and whether or not the employer is the child's parent.
2. Employees must be 18 to work in hazardous occupations.

Information on the Fair Labor Standards Act and its amendments and on the maintenance of records necessary to comply with the act is available from the U.S. Department of Labor, Employment Standards Administration, Wage and Hour Division, Washington, D.C., or its nearest regional office. This department is responsible for the administration and enforcement of the act. Prentice-Hall, Inc., and the Bureau of National Affairs, Inc., both provide looseleaf materials that describe in detail the

---

*These two groups must be employed by nonmanufacturing establishments primarily engaged in selling these items to ultimate purchasers.

414

*PART VI
MAINTAINING
AND IMPROVING
SATISFACTION,
COMMITMENT,
AND PERFORMANCE*

law, its interpretation, and the impact various court rulings have had on the enforcement of the act.

State Laws on Minimum Wages.   Over the years, most states have passed their own minimum wage legislation. These laws cover employees who are exempt from FLSA regulations. Currently, Alaska is the only state with a minimum wage ($3.85 per hour) higher than the federal requirement. The lowest minimum wage that has been adopted is $0.50 per hour in Puerto Rico. Most states have adopted the $3.35 per hour minimum. It is important to understand that when state labor laws are more rigorous than federal laws, they supersede the federal statutes.

1947: Portal-to-Portal Act.   This act exempts employers from calculating time in transit to the work site as part of hours worked for calculating pay and overtime rates. For some jobs there is considerable variation in the time of arrival at the employer's premises and arrival at the work site (e.g., it may take a miner one hour or even more to arrive at the excavation site after entering the external entrance to the mines). This exemption only holds when make-ready time is not counted as work hours.

1966: Service Contract Act.   The Service Contract Act ensures that service workers on federal contracts of $2,500 or more receive wages and benefits equivalent to those prevailing in the area where work is performed, but no less than federal minimum wage. It provides additional coverage beyond the Davis-Bacon and Walsh-Healy acts.

INCOME PROTECTION LEGISLATION

Throughout the twentieth century, federal and state governments have been increasingly involved in providing economic protection for workers who suffer an earning loss owing to circumstances beyond their control. Such efforts have resulted in the establishment of programs that provide workers' compensation, Social Security, unemployment security, pension control, and, looming on the horizon, government-sponsored health care.

1911: Workers' Compensation.   As the United States moved into an industrial economy at the close of the nineteenth century, the increase of industrial accidents and personal injury suits caused by rapid industrialization underscored the inadequate protection provided to disabled workers. This led to the enactment in 1911 of the first enduring workers' compensation laws. Today, workers' compensation covers over 85 million American workers.

Each of the 50 states currently has its own workers' compensation laws and administrative agencies. Although the provisions of the laws vary among the states, they do have six common objectives:

1. To provide sure, prompt, and reasonable income and medical benefits to victims of work-related accidents, or income benefits to their dependents, regardless of fault.

2. To provide a single remedy and reduce court delays, costs, and work loads arising out of personal injury litigation.

3. To relieve public and private charities of financial drains incident to uncompensated industrial accidents.

4. To eliminate payment of fees to lawyers and witnesses as well as time-consuming trials and appeals.

5. To encourage maximum employer interest in safety and rehabilitation through an appropriate experience-rating mechanism.

6. To promote frank study of causes of accidents (rather than concealment of fault), and thereby to reduce preventable accidents and human suffering.[11]

In 1972, a report by the National Commission on State Workmen's Compensation Laws made 84 recommendations for improving existing workmen's compensation laws, identifying 19 as essential. Since that time, most of the states have enacted massive reforms in their workers' compensation laws, but by 1983 only one state — New Hampshire — had enacted legislation to meet all reform recommendations of this commission. Continuing congressional interest in setting up minimum national standards for state compensation laws has been the primary impetus for improving job-related accident and illness benefits. Improvements have covered areas such as increased weekly benefits and expanded medical coverage. New rehabilitation provisions provide additional maintenance benefits for a disabled employee participating in a retraining program. Improved liability litigation systems, broader definition and expanded coverage with regard to occupational diseases, and subsequent injuries programs (those that provide liability protection to employers who hire workers who have suffered a prior injury) further protect workers.

Most states require all employers to carry workers' compensation insurance with private, state-approved insurance companies. Normally, each state has some form of minimum provision regarding the size of the business before insurance coverage is compulsory. In states in which coverage is not compulsory, employers may elect not to carry such insurance, but they are then liable to employee lawsuits under punitive conditions.

Some states have their own insurance programs. When this is the case, employers may have to insure with the state, or they may have the option of using the programs of private insurance companies. Most states also permit self-insurance. Usually, only large companies take advantage of this option because they can spread the risk over a large number of employees. These self-insurers will normally develop a protective service similar to that established by an insurance company.

1935: The Social Security Act.   This act was established to provide American workers with protection from total economic destitution in the event of termination of employment beyond their control. Employers and employees contribute equally to the benefits provided by this act, as amended. Self-employed persons must pay out of their own pockets an established amount to gain Social Security protection. This government-imposed tax has escalated in recent years and will increase rapidly in the coming decade. Table 3 lists existing and proposed Social Security tax rates, wage bases, and maximum payments. Two avenues are open to employers for minimizing this tax burden: first, they may reduce the total size of the work force; and second, they may reduce the amount of employee turnover. Under present regulations, employers must pay for each employee up to the established total contribution. This payment is mandatory even if an earlier employer has already made contributions toward this amount. However, with the increased size of the wage base, the second option has become less important.

Although Social Security is basically a retirement program, it also established the Federal Old-Age, Survivors, Disability, and Health Insurance System. Social Security currently covers over 90 million workers and provides benefits to over 36 million retired or disabled workers and their dependents. In addition, the original law established the federal and state unemployment compensation system. Amendments to this act also provide for Medicaid and Medicare programs. Because of the concern over the eco-

416

*PART VI
MAINTAINING
AND IMPROVING
SATISFACTION,
COMMITMENT,
AND PERFORMANCE*

TABLE 3

Existing and Proposed Social Security Tax Rates, Wage Bases, and Maximum Payments for Employers and Employees

Year	Tax Rate	Wage Base	Maximum Tax
1979	6.13	$22,900	$1,403.77
1980	6.13	25,900	1,587.67
1981	6.65	29,700	1,975.05
1982	6.70	32,400	2,170.80
1983	6.70	35,700	2,391.90
Employee-1984	6.70	37,800	2,532.60
Employer-1984	7.00	37,800	2,646.00
1985	7.05	Will be set by Social	Depends on set
1986	7.15	Security Administration	wage base
1987	7.15	by approximately Nov. 1	
1988	7.51	of preceding year	
1989	7.51		
1990	7.65		

nomic stability of the Social Security system, Congress in 1983 enacted the Social Security Reform Bill, which made significant changes in the Social Security program.

Unemployment Compensation. Title IX of the Social Security Act of 1935 imposed a federal payroll tax on employers. Because all states that established a state unemployment compensation plan would be given credit for almost all of the tax paid by the employers, by 1937 all states had unemployment compensation laws. When workers become unemployed through no fault of their own, the state provides them with certain weekly benefits. Each state (as well as the District of Columbia, Puerto Rico, and the Virgin Islands) has its own unemployment insurance (UI) laws that define the terms and benefits of its unemployment program. Although these programs are legislated and administered by the states, they follow federal guidelines prepared by the Employment and Training Administration, Unemployment Insurance Service, U.S. Department of Labor.

The federal government requires each employer to pay a federal unemployment tax (FUTA) of 6.2 percent on the first $7,000 earned by each employee. The employer usually pays 5.4 percent of the tax directly to the state employment security agency or to some other designated state agency when the state is in compliance with federal mandates. This 5.4 percent rate may be adjusted up or down by the state, depending on its past unemployment insurance payment experience with the particular employer. In 1983, employers in the state of Alaska paid the highest estimated per employee federal and state unemployment tax of $642, while Texas had the lowest liability of $119 per employee. The 50-state average was $300 per employee.[12] By 1983, four states (Alabama, Alaska, New Jersey, and Pennsylvania) had passed legislation requiring employees to also contribute to the unemployment insurance fund. Employee contribution to unemployment in the state of Pennsylvania is $1.00 per $1,000 of salary.

In January 1984, employers in 13 states, the District of Columbia, Puerto Rico, and the Virgin Islands were required to pay a federal payroll tax surcharge ranging from $12 to $77 per worker in 1983 because these jurisdictions had defaulted on federal unemployment loans. The penalty paid by the employers depended on the amount of the default in their respective jurisdictions.

Each state establishes minimum and maximum amounts of weekly benefits, the total number of weeks that an unemployed person may receive such benefits (which may extend for a maximum of 26 weeks), the qualifying relationship between past earnings and benefits received, and the waiting time after termination of employment before receipt of the first benefit payment. Because of the economic crisis of the 1970s, Congress enacted the *Federal-State Extended Unemployment Compensation Act of 1970*, which made available 13 weeks of extended benefits (EB) during periods of "high" unemployment. Then, on December 31, 1974, the Federal Supplemental Compensation (FSC) program was created through the *Emergency Unemployment Compensation Act of 1974*, and the program was further extended through the *Emergency Unemployment Compensation Extension Act of 1977*. Depending on the state's unemployment rate, this program provides an additional 8 to 16 weeks of benefits to those who have exhausted both their regular (UI) and extended benefits (EB). These laws provide for special unemployment benefits programs relating to local as well as national conditions. For example, some jobless benefits are extended beyond the normal 16-week period to as much as 65 weeks and include those individuals who in the past had not been covered by unemployment benefits.

1974: Trade Act.   The Trade Act was passed to assist employers and employees who have been hurt by foreign competition. For workers who have lost their jobs or have had their hours cut because of import competition, the act provides retraining and relocation assistance and a cash allowance equal to the amount of the weekly unemployment benefits for which the worker is eligible. No benefit is paid until the worker has exhausted all other jobless benefits. The benefits can last up to 26 weeks.

Unemployment compensation in the United States took a new form with the introduction of a *short-time compensation plan*. Although short-time compensation programs have been used by several European nations since the 1920s, the United States did not implement this type of program until 1978, when the state of California adopted its Work Sharing Unemployment Insurance program (WSUI). The program works this way: employers forced to cut production during a downturn in business reduce the number of hours worked by all affected employees instead of laying off a certain number of workers. Employees who have their hours reduced can then apply to the state for unemployment compensation assistance to make up the difference between their normal pay and the reduced pay. The unemployment assistance is provided on a pro rata basis. A person who works 3 days instead of the normal 5 days is eligible to receive two-fifths or 40 percent of the maximum benefits available to the worker for a given week of unemployment benefits.

Pensions

At the present time, about 50 percent of the nonfarm American work force receive some form of retirement protection from employers through either private pension, deferred profit-sharing plans or thrift/savings plans. In recent years, these private retirement protection programs have come under increasing federal regulation. The main federal agencies that review and regulate private retirement programs are the Labor Department's Office of Pension and Welfare Benefits Programs (PWBP) and the Internal Revenue Service (IRS) of the Treasury Department.

IRS policies and regulations restrict the types of pension plans a business can develop, the benefits involved, and the manner of funding and operating the plans. These IRS policies and regulations cover a range of activities from pension financing procedures to pension policies that discriminate in favor of highly compensated employees with respect to both coverage and benefits. (A plan is discriminatory unless the contributions for the benefit of lower paid groups covered by the plan are comparable to contributions for the benefit of higher paid employees.)

418

PART VI
MAINTAINING
AND IMPROVING
SATISFACTION,
COMMITMENT,
AND PERFORMANCE

In addition, IRS policies and regulations and interpretation of legislation through federal tax court rulings have, over the years, further restricted the rights of management in the operation of their pension programs. The major pieces of legislation that influence private pension and welfare plans are reviewed below.

1959: Welfare and Pension Plan Disclosure Act. This act grants the U.S. Department of Labor review and regulatory influence over private pension plans. As amended, it applies to welfare and pension plans covering more than 25 participants in industries affecting commerce. Welfare plans are those providing medical, surgery, or hospital benefits or care and benefits in the event of sickness, accident, disability, death, or unemployment (not including benefits provided under workers' compensation). The term *pension plan* covers profit-sharing plans providing benefits upon retirement.

Pension Reform. During the late 1960s and into the 1970s, a number of pension plans of U.S. businesses became insolvent, and many workers employed by those businesses as well as retired workers found their pension plans to be in jeopardy or, in some cases, worthless. Senator Jacob Javits of New York, a leader in pension plan reform, pointed out that private U.S. pension plans were based on "three dangerously obsolete assumptions":

1. An employee will stay with one company most of his working career.
2. The company can and should use the plan as a "club" to keep the employees.
3. The company will stay in business forever in substantially the same form as when it installed the plan.[13]

1974: Employee Retirement Income Security Act. To protect pension plans from failures and obsolete assumptions, leading political figures and government officials introduced several proposals for reforming private pension plans. Their efforts resulted in the Employee Retirement Income Security Act of 1974 (commonly known as ERISA or the Pension Reform Law). This law establishes fiduciary responsibilities, reporting and disclosure, employee participation and coverage, vesting, funding, limitations on benefits, lump sum distributions, plan termination insurance, and other requirements. In addition, this law established a task force to study the three vesting alternatives of the bill further and to determine the extent of discrimination, if any, among employees in various age groups. The task force is also mandated to study the means of providing portability of pension rights and other problems resulting from the law. Portability opportunities are provided through the Pension Benefits Guaranty Corporation (PBGC). By the end of 1976, more than 10,000 corporate pension plans covering more than 350,000 employees had been terminated because of the additional demands placed on employers by ERISA.[14]

1980: Multiemployer Pension Plan Amendment Act. Further efforts to improve the operation and financial viability of private pension plans occurred with the passage of an amendment to ERISA — the Multiemployer Pension Plan Amendment Act of 1980. Generally, multiemployer pension plans are established and maintained through collective bargaining between employee representatives and more than one employer. According to the PBGC, in 1980 multiemployer plans accounted for only 2 percent of the approximately 106,000 defined benefits plans. . . . A major problem with multiemployer pension funds is the possibility that an employer member may withdraw from the pension fund. Since few, if any, multiemployer pension plans are fully funded, the withdrawal of any employer member, whether voluntary (buy out) or involuntary (bankruptcy), shifts increased liability to all remaining members.

The Multiemployer Pension Plan Amendment Act broadened the legal definition of a defined benefits plan, putting virtually all multiemployer pension plans into the defined category. The major changes made by the act include

1. Increased employer liability for unfunded benefits.
2. Reduced benefit guarantees.
3. Faster amortization of unpaid past costs.
4. New requirements aimed at improving the financial condition of financially distressed plans.

Combining Private Programs with Social Security.   Many companies integrate the benefits provided by their pension plans with those available through Social Security. In 1975, more than 7 million retirees received over $14.8 billion from private pension plans; by 1979, almost 19 million retired workers received over $60 billion in Social Security benefits.[15] Because of the great increases in the Social Security premiums paid by employees and employers, along with the escalator clauses for retirement benefits and the increased availability of Medicare, Medicaid, and other supplementary benefits, the need for coordinating the benefits of private pension plans with Social Security increases.

Some businesses are now providing early retirement programs that offer enlarged pension payments until the retiree reaches the age of 65, at which time, with the start of Social Security payments, the pension payments are reduced. This is but one example of the opportunities available for combining the benefits derived from these two different retirement programs.

With increased government supervision over funding requirements and over the kinds and security of benefits, some employers may even be forced to abandon private pension plans and look for other forms of benefits with fewer governmental restrictions.

National Health Insurance.   Most businesses now provide some form of health and welfare benefits, including some combination of the following:

1. Life insurance and death benefits.
2. Sickness and accident benefits.
3. Hospitalization and surgical benefits.
4. Medical care, excluding surgery and hospitalization.

The employer, the employee, and the private insurance companies collaborate in providing these benefits. In some cases the employee makes a contribution, and in other cases the business pays the total cost of the premium.

1973: The Health Maintenance Organization (HMO) Act.   This act requires employers who are subject to the Fair Labor Standards Act and who have 25 or more employees to whom they are now providing health insurance to offer an HMO option if it is available in the area in which the employees reside. HMOs are health-care organizations that provide medical care at a fixed monthly fee.

Over the past decade, Congress has worked on various forms of national health insurance legislation, but up to this time nothing has been enacted. However, the federal government will probably continue to play a large role in financing health care services. Federal intervention in this area will further extend government influence over programs related to health care.

420

*PART VI
MAINTAINING
AND IMPROVING
SATISFACTION,
COMMITMENT,
AND PERFORMANCE*

Garnishment of Wages. Another government law that protects the income of the worker is the Federal Wage Garnishment Law, which limits the amount of an employee's disposable earnings that may be garnished in any one week and protects the worker from discharge because of garnishment for any one indebtedness. A *garnishment* is a court action or equitable procedure by which earnings of an individual are required to be withheld for the payment of a debt.

The garnishment law identifies *earnings* as compensation paid or payable for personal services, including wages, salary, commission, bonus, and pension or retirement program payments. *Disposable earnings* consist of that part of the earnings remaining after the deduction of any amount required by law, such as the withholdings of federal, state, and local income taxes and federal Social Security tax.

Government Welfare Legislation. Current welfare programs directly influence the wage structure of U.S. businesses. Any government program that provides a person with the option of accepting some form of financial benefit, other than that gained from employment, indirectly and subtly establishes a minimum wage for any business offering a job to that individual.

The present welfare system began during the depression years of 1929 to 1939. Since its inception, the public welfare system has focused attention on government-sponsored programs such as (1) aid to families with dependent children, (2) aid to the permanently and totally disabled, (3) old-age assistance, (4) medical assistance programs, (5) food programs, (6) rent subsidies, and (7) training programs for persons with low incomes. These programs have frequently been accused of fostering idleness and laziness, but, conversely, proponents just as emphatically state that it is the responsibility of society to be receptive to and to satisfy the basic needs of all its citizens.

In recent years, some states have made major improvements in their welfare programs by finding jobs for those who can work.[16] These states have taken the position that any job is acceptable as long as it meets state and federal standards for wages and working conditions. In addition, these states have improved the provision of welfare services to those who cannot work.

In the past two decades, there have been various state and federal experiments with some form of guaranteed annual income to replace the various welfare programs. Guaranteed annual income would provide cash grants to families having incomes below certain prescribed minimums. Such unresolved issues as benefit levels, the rate of reducing benefit payments relative to outside earnings, and work requirements have blocked the replacement of the current welfare system by the guaranteed annual income plans.

ANTIDISCRIMINATION LEGISLATION

Beginning with the first ten amendments to the Constitution of the United States — the Bill of Rights — all who reside in the United States are guaranteed certain rights under law. Beginning in the 1960s, a number of laws and executive orders have been passed to bring civil rights to the workplace. These laws and executive orders also relate to civil rights legislation passed after the Civil War.

1866, 1870, 1871: Civil Rights Acts. The Thirteenth Amendment to the constitution of the United States abolished slavery, while the Fourteenth Amendment gave the right to vote to former slaves and forbade any state to deny them equal protection under the law. These amendments were supported by the Civil Rights Acts of 1866, 1870, and 1871. The primary thrusts of these acts were (1) to provide equal rights under the law, (2) to ensure property rights, (3) to prohibit state laws from depriving a person of rights, and (4) to prohibit conspiracies to interfere with civil rights.

Section 1 of the Civil Rights Act of 1866 and the provisions of the Civil Rights Acts of 1870 and 1871 have been codified as Title 42, Chapter 21, sections 1981–1983 of the United States Code.

Section 1981, Title 42, U.S. Code, precludes job discrimination on the basis of race. A discrimination suit filed under section 1981 does not require that administrative remedies be exhausted, as does Title VII of the Civil Rights Act of 1964. Section 1981 also provides for recovery of compensatory or punitive damages, and the only existing statute of limitations to filing a claim is the statute in the state in which the action is brought. This section does not require an employer to be engaged in interstate commerce.

1963: Equal Pay Act.   This amendment to the Fair Labor Standards Act is the first federal antidiscrimination law relating directly to females. It applies to all employees and employers covered by the Fair Labor Standards Act, including executives, administrators, professionals, and outside salespersons. The act requires equal pay for equal work for men and women and defines equal work as work requiring equal skill, effort, and responsibility under similar working conditions.

When applying various tests of equality, federal enforcement officials review the whole job. It is possible to see if jobs are the same or closely related in character only by analyzing job content and the kinds of activities required in the performance of the job and the amount of time devoted to these activities. Jobs requiring equal skill, effort, and responsibility are seldom identical in every respect. In determining job comparability, it is necessary to consider degrees of difference in skill, effort, and responsibility involved in job performance.

The U.S. Supreme Court has ruled that substantially different or dissimilar working conditions relate primarily to two subfactors — *surroundings* and *hazards. Surroundings* measure such conditions as the frequency of exposure to and intensity of toxic chemicals or fumes encountered on the job. *Hazards* take in the physical environment and its impact on the increased chance of an accident and the possible severity of an injury from such an accident (e.g., falling off a high platform or working near moving parts).

Under the Equal Pay Act, employers can establish different wage rates on the basis of (1) a seniority system, (2) a merit system, (3) a system that measures earnings by quantity or quality of production, and (4) a differential based on any factor other than sex. (These conditions are often referred to as the four affirmative defenses of the Equal Pay Act.) Shift differentials are also permissible under the Equal Pay Act. All these exemptions must apply equally to men and women.

Because of merit system exemptions from equal pay, a number of court rulings have defined what are or are not acceptable performance appraisal programs.

1964: Civil Rights Act — Title VII.   Title VII of the Civil Rights Act of 1964, also known as the Equal Employment Opportunity Act of 1964, as amended, continues to have an impact on the hiring, training, compensation, promotion, and termination practices of organizations. The act requires the Equal Employment Opportunity Commission (EEOC) to investigate charges by an employee that the employer has been guilty of unlawful employment practices. Such practices include failure to hire, failure to provide employment opportunities, or failure to promote any individual because of the individual's race, color, religion, sex, or national origin. The immediate effect is that

422

*PART VI
MAINTAINING
AND IMPROVING
SATISFACTION,
COMMITMENT,
AND PERFORMANCE*

organizations must develop records and procedures that define employment standards on the basis of job requirements. They must also identify working conditions and the manner in which a job is performed. (As of July 1, 1979, administration of the Equal Pay Act and the Age Discrimination in Employment Act were transferred from the DOL to the EEOC.)

Employers have the right to insist that a prospective applicant meet job qualifications, but the qualifications must be well defined and relate directly to success in job performance. Only bona fide occupation qualifications (BFOQ) can be used to discriminate among job applicants. This also holds true for promotional opportunities, but organizations must permit freedom of movement or access to higher rated jobs to all employees.

Organizations found guilty of race, sex, and age discrimination in their past hiring or promotional practices have been subject to attorney's fees and court costs in addition to extensive award payments to parties whose rights have been violated. The awards have covered a broad gamut of activities that range from back pay for as much as seven years, to immediate promotional opportunities, to adjustments in profit sharing and pension plans. Normally, the award is based on what the claimant would have received, according to his or her seniority with the company, had the discriminatory practices not existed.

In addition to these punitive actions, organizations are agreeing to remedial action to remove vestiges of past discrimination. These actions often result in the setting of numerical goals and timetables to remedy present effects of past discriminatory practices. To achieve these goals and timetables, organizations are implementing Affirmative Action programs — results-oriented programs that specifically spell out hiring and promotion goals designed to increase minority and female employment in job classifications in which members of these groups are currently underutilized. Job classifications identified for Affirmative Action programs are (1) officials and administrators, (2) professionals, (3) technicians, (4) protective service workers, (5) paraprofessionals, (6) office and clerical workers, (7) skilled craftworkers, and (8) service maintenance workers.

Opportunities for advancement — for greater use of the potential available within each individual — have been the focal point of much of the effort of the Affirmative Action programs. Any such program committed to eliminating discriminatory promotional practices must have current and valid job requirements, including up-to-date job descriptions and specifications as well as work standards and procedures. Concurrent with the development of this type of job information program, an inventory of the education, the experience, and the skills (EES) of each employee must be developed.

The personnel EES inventory must then be divided into race, gender, and possibly age groups. These inventories can then be related to each job or classification category, indicating available EES qualifications and potential areas of discriminatory practices where there are indications of significant underutilization or a concentration of minorities and females. (*Underutilization* refers to having fewer minority members or women in a particular job category than would reasonably be expected by their presence in the relevant labor market, job categories, classifications, or grade levels.)

By matching available EES with the EES necessary for advanced jobs or classes, the business is able to identify training and development requirements. By laying such an Affirmative Action foundation, it can then develop goals and timetables that will improve the use of minorities and females.

Training and development programs that focus on improving upward mobility for employees must not only have well-designed job description, classification, and grading programs but also well-ordered job progressions that relate to lateral transfers and vertical promotions.

1965, 1967: Executive Order 11246 (1965), as Amended by Executive Order 11375 (1967). These orders ban discrimination because of race, color, religion, sex, or national origin by any employer with a government contract of more than $10,000. The orders are enforced by the Labor Department's Office of Federal Contract Compliance Programs (OFCCP). OFCCP regulations require Affirmative Action programs of all employers with 50 or more employees and government contracts of $50,000.

1972: Age Discrimination in Employment Act. This act prohibits discrimination in hiring individuals between 40 and 65 years of age. It covers employers with 20 or more employees, labor organizations with 20 or more members in an industry involved in interstate commerce, employment agencies, and public employers.

1972: Equal Employment Opportunity Act. This act empowered the Equal Employment Opportunity Commission to prevent any person from engaging in any unlawful employment practice as described in Title VII of the Civil Rights Act of 1964. It also empowered the commission to investigate unlawful employment practices on the part of state government, government agencies, and political subdivisions.

1973: Rehabilitation Act. The act prohibits employers performing under a federal contract or subcontracts exceeding $2,500 from discriminating against handicapped persons. Handicapped persons are those having physical or mental impairments that substantially limit one or more major life activities. This act further requires private contractors with federal contracts of $50,000 or more or those hiring 50 or more employees to develop a written Affirmative Action plan. The goal of such a plan is to take affirmative action to employ and advance qualified handicapped individuals.

1974: Vietnam Era Veterans Readjustment Act. This act protects the rights of employees to return to their former jobs after engaging in military service. The employee must have made application for reemployment within 90 days after discharge or not more than one year if hospitalization continues after discharge.

An employee qualified to perform the duties of a previously held position must be returned to that position or to a position of like seniority, status, and pay and must be entitled to participate in all benefits offered by the employer that would have been gained by the employee if the employee had been on furlough or leave of absence.

1978: Age Discrimination in Employment Act Amendments. The Mandatory Retirement Age amendment to the Age Discrimination in Employment Act covers most employees. Beginning January 1, 1979, it prohibits forced retirement of any employee under 70 years of age. College professors and top business executives are exempt from this law, as are employees who have certain bona fide occupational qualifications. The law does not preclude the discharge or layoff of older employees because of unsatisfactory performance. However, an organization must be able to substantiate that such actions are based on job performance. The law also requires certain revisions in pension and profit sharing plans and in medical and life insurance plans. Differences are allowed if based on a bona fide seniority system or a bona fide benefit plan.

1978: Pregnancy Discrimination Act. Congress enacted the Pregnancy Discrimination Act as a result of its unwillingness to accept the ruling of the Supreme Court in the case of *Gilbert v. General Electric*, 13 FEP Cases 1657 (1976). In this case, EEOC and Gilbert contended that General Electric had an insurance disability plan that excluded pregnancy-related disabilities and that this was a violation of the Civil Rights Act. The

424

*PART VI
MAINTAINING
AND IMPROVING
SATISFACTION,
COMMITMENT,
AND PERFORMANCE*

Supreme Court, meanwhile, ruled that discrimination on the basis of pregnancy was not sex discrimination, but discrimination based on the person's condition, and that no existing law prohibited discrimination against someone on the basis of the condition of the individual. This act is an amendment to the Civil Rights Act of 1964. It prohibits employers from excluding from employment opportunities (disability insurance, medical benefits, leave, accrual of seniority, etc.) any applicant or employee because of pregnancy or related conditions. Disability by, or contributed to, any of these conditions shall be treated the same as disabilities caused by or contributed to by any other medical condition.

This law was further broadened in the case of *Newport News Shipbuilding and Drydock Co.* v. *EEOC,* 29 FEP Cases 200 (1982), in which the court ruled that the employer unlawfully discriminated against its male employees on the basis of sex by limiting pregnancy-related benefits to employees' wives, while affording more extensive insurance coverage to employees' spouses for all other medical conditions requiring hospitalization. Male employees were thus treated less favorably than female employees because the husbands of female employees received hospitalization coverage for all conditions and the wives of male employees received the same coverage except for pregnancy-related conditions.

Pension Discrimination and Insurance Company Practices. Pension premium payments and retiree pension annuities became a discrimination issue because of insurance company practices requiring that the amount of both premiums paid and benefits received must relate to actuarial calculations. Since women as a group live longer than men as a group, either the contributions to the pension plans have to be greater or, if the contributions are the same, the benefits provided to female retirees must be less than those received by male employees of the same status. In the case of *Manhart, et al.* v. *City of Los Angeles, Department of Water and Power, et al.,* 13 FEP Cases 1625 (1976), the court ruled that the employer violated Title VII by requiring female employees to make larger contributions to the retirement plan than male employees. The court further stated that since not all women live longer than all men, each woman must be considered an individual, and since Title VII protects individuals, not classes of individuals, female employees must be treated the same as male employees.

In 1983, a court ruling further clarified this issue in *Arizona Governing Committee* v. *Norris,* 32 FEP Cases 233 (1983). The court ruled that Title VII prohibits an employer from offering its employees the option of receiving retirement benefits from one of several insurance companies selected by the employer, all of which pay a woman lower monthly retirement benefits than a man who has made the same contribution. This ruling, in essence, requires insurance companies to use unisex actuarial tables for calculating pension premium payments and retiree annuities.

Comparable Worth Issue

During the latter part of the 1970s and into the 1980s, federal court decisions involving the Equal Pay Act frequently ruled in favor of the defendants and against individuals, claiming that the defendants were discriminating against women jobholders in pay practices. These decisions and other pressures brought about by women and minority groups led the EEOC and the Office of Federal Contract Compliance Programs (OFCCP) to investigate the actions they could take through their authority relative to Title VII of the Civil Rights Act and Executive Order 11246, respectively, to eliminate pay discrimination in jobs segregated by sex or race.

In the late 1970s and early 1980s, there have been approximately 100 state and local government initiatives on comparable worth. Fifteen states currently include comparable worth standards in their equal pay laws. Some states require pay equity for state employees only, while others include private-sector employees. No legislation yet enacted identifies and defines any method for determining comparable worth. In 1983, Minnesota appropriated $15.9 million to begin making corrective salary adjustments in line with a 1982 amendment to the state's civil service law that established a policy of equitable compensation for male and female job classifications. In New York, the state, in negotiation with its Civil Service Employees Association, provided $500,000 for a pay equity study. Ohio has also ordered a similar study. . . .

TAX TREATMENT LEGISLATION

Most tax reform legislation has had little impact on the majority of workers. Rather, most tax legislation has related to the deferral and sheltering of income from current income tax payments and has focused principally on stock options and other estate-building benefits for executives. Each year Congress becomes more and more concerned about which components of the compensation package should be exempted from tax payments on earned income. The following legislation and government actions have influenced the take-home pay (after-tax income) of employees for over a century.

1861: Tax Revenue Act This act was the first income tax legislation and was passed to assist in financing the Civil War. It imposed tax at the rate of 3 percent on income in excess of $800.

1872: The income tax act was repealed.

1894: A tax was imposed on personal income derived from various services, but was ruled unconstitutional by the Supreme Court.

1913: The Sixteenth Amendment to the Constitution was passed, granting Congress the right to levy and collect taxes on income from whatever source.

1913: Income Tax Law This law imposed a 1 percent tax on personal income over $20,000 and rose to 6 percent on income over $2 million.

1939: Internal Revenue Code Existing tax laws were codified, making it possible to amend existing laws, and eliminated the requirement to rewrite them.

1950: Tax Revenue Act This act established rules for the favorable tax treatment of what were termed "Restricted Stock Options."

1954: Internal Revenue Code This code repealed the Internal Revenue Code of 1939 and established present tax laws. It modified requirements for restricted stock options.

1962: Self-employment Individual Tax Retirement Act This act allows individuals to contribute up to 15 percent of their self-employment income to a retirement plan. The maximum amount to be contributed is $7,500. The Tax Equity and Fiscal Responsibility Act of 1982 raised the contribution to 25 percent and the maximum amount of contribution to $30,000.

1964: Revenue Act In this act, restricted stock options were replaced with qualified stock options. It lowered maximum marginal tax rates to 70 percent.

1969: Tax Reform Act This legislation reduced the maximum income tax rate on earned income to 50 percent, raised the maximum tax rate on capital gains to 35 percent, introduced a 10 percent minimum tax on preference income, and established provisions for taxing income set aside for retirement purposes.

426

*PART VI
MAINTAINING
AND IMPROVING
SATISFACTION,
COMMITMENT,
AND PERFORMANCE*

1975: Tax Reduction Act The Tax Reduction Act Employee Stock Ownership Plan was introduced. The act allows corporations to claim 11 percent investment tax credit if an extra 1 percent is contributed to an employee stock ownership plan.

1976: Tax Reform Act This act eliminated qualified stock option plans as of May 20, 1981, and sanctioned group legal plans, liberalized tax treatment of deferred payments, increased minimum tax on preference income to 15 percent, and increased the holding period for capital gains. It also redefined legal, tax-exempt benefits received by employees. The changes in tax exemption relate to (1) the elimination of sick pay as a tax-deductible, employer-sponsored disability benefit; (2) the elimination of tax-deductible, employer-paid attendance to more than two foreign conventions in one taxable year and limitations on travel and subsistence rates to these conventions; and (3) the ability to offer prepaid legal services that are tax-deductible to the employer and nontaxable to the employee.

1978: Revenue Act This act lowered the capital gains maximum tax to 28 percent, continued favored treatment of deferred income, reduced the impact of minimum tax, introduced a second alternative maximum tax, and prohibited discrimination in favor of highly compensated employees relative to certain benefits. Provisions of this act also affect various types of benefits employers provide to their employees. The major benefits-related provisions are

1. Benefit options selected in a cafeteria-flexible benefits plan need not be included in gross income.

2. A payroll reduction plan can be established that is more flexible and has greater tax advantages than an IRA. . . .

1981: Economic Recovery Tax Act (ERTA) The passage of this act reduced individual tax rates by 5 percent on October 1, 1981; 10 percent on July 1, 1982; and 10 percent on July 1, 1983. It reduced maximum tax rates on all income to 50 percent, which in turn reduced the maximum capital gains tax rate to 20 percent from 28 percent as of June 10, 1981. Individual tax rates will be "indexed," which will automatically adjust personal income tax brackets to changes in the Consumer Price Index starting in 1984. It excluded from taxation the first $75,000 of income for Americans employed abroad and housing expenses for these employees in excess of $6,059, a threshold based on a formula tied to the salaries of federal workers. It extended current prohibition against IRS regulations on taxation of fringe benefits to December 31, 1983 and included a provision for recipients of stock options to pay tax at capital gains rate on the difference between the option price and the actual price of the stock at the time of the sale. Options must be exercised in the sequence in which they were made available; the employer is not permitted to deduct the option cost as a business expense.

1982: Tax Equity and Fiscal Responsibility Act (TEFRA) Provisions of this act established a single, consolidated, alternative minimum tax that replaced minimum add-on tax and alternative minimum tax provisions and reduced qualified retirement benefits for highly paid employees by limiting defined benefits to the lesser of average 3-year-high compensation or $90,000, and defined contribution to the lesser of 25 percent of compensation or $30,000. Other restrictions were also placed on qualified retirement benefits. The act placed strict requirements on top-heavy plans (any plan maintained by a corporate or noncorporate endeavor under which more than 60 percent of the accrued benefits of a defined benefits plan are provided for key employees). It liberalized Keogh plan requirements for the self-employed; changed various rules affecting employee and survivor benefits; modified Social Security "integration" rules for defined contribution plans; and established new requirements for group term life insurance.

In the coming years, Congress will scrutinize even more closely the wide range of nontaxable benefits employers offer to their employees. Many of these current benefits will be considered earned income and will add to the tax burden of each worker. As these changes take place, employers and employees will take a much closer look at their benefits programs and make changes that will increase the effectiveness of the benefits while reducing tax burdens to both employers and employees.

NOTES

1. Barbara Nachtrieb Armstrong, *Insuring the Essentials* (New York: Macmillan, 1932), pp. 17–19. Just price theory was first proposed by Plato and Aristotle 300 years before Christ. They suggested that a person is foreordained to occupy the same status in life as his or her parents. This theory resurfaced in the middle ages when the Catholic Church, under pressure from wealthy noblemen and landholders, established just wage schedules for skilled artisans, who were in short supply and demanding higher pay. The Church recognized the artisans' birthright and right to more pay by placing them in a higher social group than other workers of that time.

2. C. Harold King, *A History of Civilization* (New York: Scribner's, 1956), pp. 504–33.

3. Armstrong, *Insuring the Essentials*, p. 14.

4. Ibid., pp. 34–35.

5. Ray Marshall, "The Influence of Legislation on Hours," in Clyde E. Dankert, Floyd C. Mann, and Herbert R. Northrop, eds., *Hours of Work* (New York: Harper & Row, 1965), pp. 36–53.

6. Ibid, p. 43.

7. Ibid., pp. 44–45.

8. Ibid.

9. David Ricardo, *On the Principles of Political Economy and Taxation*, 3rd ed. (London: John Murray, 1821), p. 93.

10. Armstrong, *Insuring the Essentials*, pp. 42–65.

11. *Analysis of Workers' Compensation Laws*, 1980 edition (Washington, DC: U.S. Chamber of Commerce, January 1980), p. vii.

12. Eugene Carlson, "States' Unemployment Plans Can Sting Contributing Firms," *Wall Street Journal*, March 13, 1984, p. 33.

13. "Compensation Currents: Pension Debate Under Way," *Compensation Review*, Third Quarter 1971, pp. 2–3.

14. Eugene J. Keogh, "Why Does the Corporation Need to Know About Private Retirement Plans?" 1977 Regional Conference Proceedings, Scottsdale, Ariz., American Compensation Association; and Charles N. Stabler, "A Closer Look: The New Pension Law May Cut Profits Less Than First Thought," *Wall Street Journal*, October 1, 1974, pp. 1, 18.

15. U.S. Department of Commerce, Bureau of the Census, *Statistical Abstract of the United States* (Washington, DC: Government Printing Office, 1981), pp. 340, 344.

16. "How a State with Lots of Poor Is Getting People Off Welfare," *U.S. News and World Report*, October 1, 1973, pp. 33–35.

428

PART VI
MAINTAINING
AND IMPROVING
SATISFACTION,
COMMITMENT,
AND PERFORMANCE

Job Evaluation and the Wage-Salary Structure

Marc J. Wallace, Jr., and Charles H. Fay

. . . It is not enough for the compensation analyst to collect wage and salary data and use it directly as the wage salary structure. First of all, the survey data will not consist of a single wage for any job, but will be made up of a broad range of wages reflecting location, size, industry, employee demographics such as seniority and performance levels, and other factors. Second, it is not possible for any organization to collect wage and salary data for all jobs in the organization. Most jobs in any organization have some characteristics unique to that organization. Secretaries in one organization may be expected to operate automated data retrieval equipment requiring special training; in another organization, secretaries may have to deal with no higher a technology level than the electric typewriter. There are also jobs in many organizations for which there is no market; that is, the job is truly unique to that organization. The so-called administrative assistant is a job for which this is frequently the case. The variety of abilities, skills, company-related experiences, and specific training often required belies the generality of the title.

Third, even if single rates (with adjustments for location, and so on) were available for all jobs in the company through surveys, such rates would not satisfy internal equity demands. The value of an engineer to company A and company B relative to the value of a lawyer to those two companies could vary significantly, depending on environmental pressures. If company A has a history of discrimination cases but its products are very successful, and company B has few legal problems but has significant quality control problems, the relative worth of lawyers and engineers may vary considerably.

Thus, lack of information and internal equity considerations require that market data alone not be used to build the wage and salary structure. In fact, the structure is usually built on internal equity considerations and then adjusted to meet market forces. These internal equity decisions, when formalized, become the process known as job evaluation, that is, what jobs are worth to the organization: which jobs are of similar value, which are worth more, and which are worth less. After describing current approaches to job evaluation, we will show how the results of job evaluation are merged with market data to achieve the final wage-salary structure.

JOB EVALUATION

The immediate purpose of job evaluation is to create a hierarchy of jobs based on their value, or worth, to the organization doing the evaluation. Most job evaluation techniques do not have as their initial result the wage and salary structure, but rather a ranking of jobs by classification, or a ranking in some other format. The jobs then must have prices attached to them within the structure of their ranking.

Job evaluation is the process by which one tries to ensure internal equity — that jobs of comparable worth receive comparable wages. It is not, on the whole, concerned with value of the job in the external market.

Job Families

When undertaking a job evaluation, the compensation analyst first must decide the scope of jobs to which the job evaluation process will be applied, and thus, the number of job-worth structures that will be constructed. There are several arguments for having a single job-worth structure, but most of them are based on one of two factors. First, an organization ends up with a simple wage and salary structure in that one job is paid in one range, and a second job in another range. In the end, jobs are paid in common units, dollars; and the job-worth structure should be common to all jobs too. If different structures are developed, say for managers and supervisors, points of overlap, between lower managers and upper-level supervisors, for example, may create problems. The compensation analyst will, in any case, have to combine the two or more job-worth systems into a common wage-and-salary structure.

Aside from difficulties from the organization's point of view, employees may not feel internal equity goals are met when they compare their pay to the pay of others whose jobs are valued under a different system, or to the pay they receive when they are moved to a different job which is valued under a different system. This is a litigious age, and an employer may find it difficult to justify valuing one set of jobs on one basis while valuing another on a second basis, particularly if the two systems result in an adverse effect on any legally protected group.

Countering these arguments, proponents of multiple job-worth structures point out that most organizations do have separate pay systems, for example, exempt versus nonexempt, or union versus nonunion, and for a variety of practical reasons often wish to recognize those differences in the job-worth structure. If the compensation analyst does decide on separate job-worth structures, he or she will use a variety of criteria to help determine which jobs should be clustered into *job families*. The job-worth structures will then be constructed for those job families.

Criteria.   The criteria used for clustering are those related to administering wage and salary systems, and those which make building the worth structure easier. Criteria related to ease of job evaluation include:

1. common skills
2. common occupational qualifications
3. common technology
4. common licensing
5. common working conditions.

Criteria related to administering the final wage and salary system include:

1. common union jurisdictions
2. common work place
3. common status with respect to the law (for example, exempt versus nonexempt)
4. common career paths
5. organizational tradition
6. special compensation arrangements (for example, sales personnel and executives).

Typical job families used in job evaluations based on these criteria include sales, managerial, supervisory, production, technical, and clerical, though other categories are sometimes used.

430

*PART VI
MAINTAINING
AND IMPROVING
SATISFACTION,
COMMITMENT,
AND PERFORMANCE*

Sources of Value

A second major decision to be made by the compensation analyst (with agreement by the organization) is the source of value in jobs. Some job evaluation techniques require that these sources of value be made explicit, but all job evaluation requires that the organization think about what aspects of a job have value to the organization. These sources of value are known as compensable factors. . . . In practice, compensable factors may be classified into job inputs (what employees bring to the job) and job outputs. Inputs include experience; education; effort; responsibility for people, assets, or work-flow; and ability to function under various working conditions. Job outputs include work outcomes such as production, profit, or results.

Job Analysis

Having decided on the sources of job value, the compensation analyst must get job descriptions that will allow him or her to estimate the degree to which jobs possess the factors that create value. This is generally done through job analysis. It is important to differentiate job analysis and job evaluation. Job analysis is a systematic study of the tasks making up a job, the employee skills required to do the job, time factors, situation-specific factors such as the technology used, certain physical aspects (for example, lighting and temperature), information flows, interpersonal and group interactions, and historical traditions. From good job analysis procedures, job descriptions can be written. One reason it is important for the compensation analyst to make decisions about sources of value before selecting a job analysis technique or getting job descriptions is to ensure that the job analysis procedure speaks to those dimensions of jobs which give them value to the organization.

Ordinarily, the compensation analyst will not be the individual doing the job analysis. Because job analysis is the basis for many personnel processes — such as performance appraisal, selection, and training — each of which requires knowledge of different aspects of jobs to different degrees, most organizations have specially trained job analysts who can coordinate the analysis with the needs of other personnel specialists. Thus, the compensation analyst will have as input a series of job descriptions to work with.

A typical job description the compensation analyst might get is shown in Exhibit 1. This description, after a general summary of the job, lists the key tasks performed by the employee and the amount of time devoted to each task. A task-statement data sheet at the end of the description notes the equipment used, the knowledge, skills, and abilities required for each task, and the level of difficulty or consequence of error associated with each task.

Further information is provided on supervisory responsibilities, supervision received, external contacts, and equipment used on the job. Finally, different aspects of working conditions are noted and the variety of training (both formal and on-the-job) is listed. Similar data sheets would be provided to the compensation analyst for all jobs in the job family under evaluation.

Job Evaluation Techniques

Hundreds of job evaluation techniques have been developed over the years. The great majority of them belong to four general types. These types can be differentiated by looking at two major lines along which job evaluation systems vary. The first question concerns the directness of the evaluation, whether a job being evaluated is compared to some other job directly (that is, ranking), or whether it is measured against some

EXHIBIT 1
Job Description

431

*B. THE USE OF FINANCIAL
REWARDS: COMPENSATION
AND BENEFITS*

Date Issued: _____

Job Title: Secretary II

Summary of Job:

Under general supervision independently performs assigned administrative and secretarial duties. Maintains log of executive staffs' activities and whereabouts. Executes special assignments as requested by various staff personnel.

Job Tasks:

Task 1: 10% — Keeps records of special activities for various staff representatives.

Task 2: 60% — Performs general secretarial duties for all four members of executive staff (correspondence, reports, and telephone duties).

Task 3: 10%— Communicates and answers telephone. Supplies appropriate information when possible and directs caller to appropriate other if not.

Task 4: 10% — Executes special assignments as requested.

Task 5: 10% — Maintains staff appointment calendars and itineraries. Coordinates trip details and schedules with travel department.

Supervisory Responsibilities: None

Supervision Received: Direct 25% — General 25%

External Contacts: Customers, operating managers, travel department

Equipment Used: Telephone, IBM Selectric, Electronic Calculator, Copier, Dictaphone.

Employee: _____

Supervisor: _____

Working Conditions

Hazards: None

Work Environment: Comfortable

Noise Level: Below normal office exposure

Lighting: Excellent

Temperature: Controlled 70–72 degrees

Miscellaneous: —

Job Training

A. Required Experience: (Include other jobs) 2–3 years secretarial exposure

B. Formal Educational Experience: Time in semesters/quarters

Vocational Courses: —

High School Courses: Shorthand, typing

College Courses: —

Continuing Education: —

C. Internal Training Programs: Telephone etiquette/message-taking

Task Statement: 1–5

1. Equipment Utilized: Typewriter, telephone, Dictaphone®, calculator, copier

2. Knowledge Required: Filing, business forms, telephone etiquette, general business experience

3. Skills Required: Typing, shorthand, and mathematical

4. Abilities Required: As indicated, and good at thinking on his/her feet.

5. Time Spent and Frequency of Performance: —

6. Level of Difficulty/Consequence of Error: Varies by particular task/basically error-free

Source: Adapted from R. Beatty, N. F. Crandall, C. H. Fay, R. Mathis, G. T. Milkovich, and M. J. Wallace, Jr., *How to Administer Wage-Salary Programs and Perform Job Evaluations.* New York: Penton Learning Systems, 1980.

432

PART VI
MAINTAINING
AND IMPROVING
SATISFACTION,
COMMITMENT,
AND PERFORMANCE

EXHIBIT 2
Four Approaches to Job Evaluation

	Whole Job	*Specific Job Factors*
Job vs. job	Ranking method	Factor comparison method
Job vs. standards	Classification method	Point method

Source: Adapted from R. Beatty, N. F. Crandall, C. H. Fay, R. Mathis, G. T. Milkovich, and M. J. Wallace, Jr., *How to Administer Wage-Salary Programs and Perform Job Evaluations.* New York: Penton Learning Systems, 1980.

standard to produce a rating, with the rating then being compared with the ratings of other jobs. The second question concerns the specificity of the evaluation, whether the comparison is made on the basis of the whole job, or whether specific factors in jobs are compared. These characteristics suggest a classification table for the four major types of job evaluation as depicted in Exhibit 2. We shall look at all four types: first at the two whole job systems, then at the two systems utilizing specific job factors.

Ranking. The ranking of jobs is the simplest evaluation system available. When there are fewer than twenty jobs, ranking is probably an acceptable method. It is simple, fast, and inexpensive. There are two ways of ranking jobs. The first is a forced ranking, done either by one individual or a committee. In either case, one job is chosen as having most value to the organization, a second as having next most value, and so forth, until one job is chosen as having the least value to the organization. There are several problems inherent in this technique. There are no standards for comparison. Job A may be seen as more valuable than job B because it requires much more responsibility; job B may be seen as more valuable than job C because of educational differentials, and so on. This lack of standards makes rankings particularly vulnerable to bias when most of the job incumbents are women or minorities. In addition, forced rankings do not allow for jobs having equal value. Nor are changes in job value readily accommodated by the ranking method. Ranking does not indicate how much *more* value job A has than job B, and value differentials are essential if internal equity is to be preserved. Most individuals appear to have trouble ranking many jobs: most can agree on which jobs have most value and which have least, but the mid-level jobs are difficult to differentiate.

To get around this, proponents of ranking techniques have used paired comparisons, in which each job is compared to every other job and the job of most value in each pair is noted. The score for a job is the number of times it is considered the most valuable; ranks are based on these scores. There are two drawbacks to the paired-comparison technique. First, there is still no guarantee that comparisons are made on the same basis. A second equally serious drawback is that as the number of jobs to be ranked rises arithmetically, the number of paired comparisons to be made rises geometrically. The formula showing the number of comparison decisions to be made is $CD = N(N-1)/2$, where N is the number of jobs to be ranked. Thus, with seven jobs to be ranked, the analyst must make $(7)(6)/2 = 21$ comparison decisions; with twenty jobs to be ranked, the number of comparison decisions rises to $(20)(19)/2 = 190$! On the whole, then, ranking is simply not a very satisfactory method of evaluating jobs.

Classification. The classification method of job evaluation is a job-to-standard comparison technique that solves a number of the problems inherent in simple job ranking. The compensation analyst using the classification method first decides into how many categories, or classification steps, the job value structure is to be broken. A typical number of classes is around eight; the number might vary from five to fifteen.

The second step in the classification method is writing definitions for each class. These definitions are the standards against which the jobs will be compared. Exhibit 3 shows a part of a classification system developed for clerical workers. Notice that although several factors are used to define class levels, a job is compared to these standards on the whole-job basis, not on a factor-by-factor basis. The compensation analyst compares the jobs to be evaluated with the class definitions, placing jobs in appropriate classifications.

Although classification does provide specific standards for comparison and does accommodate changes in the value of individual jobs, it too has some drawbacks. There is still not much detail in the standards, and a rigid relationship between job factors of value is assumed. In Exhibit 3, for example, it is assumed that no clerical job will exist that entails complex work and supervisory responsibility but has no public contact. As a result, many jobs in a large organization using a classification method are likely to be forced to fit into the classes when it comes to job evaluation. The fact that some jobs do not exactly fit their classes may lead to some disagreement about the equity of the final value structure.

A related problem is tied to the decision as to how many classifications there should be. If there are too few classes for the number of jobs in an organization, it will be difficult to differentiate job value, and thus wage levels, sufficiently. If there are too many, the drafting of class definitions will be difficult, and the results of placing particular jobs in certain classes will be more open to dispute. On the positive side, a classification system can be constructed simply, quickly, and inexpensively. It is also an easy system to understand (if not to get agreement on); organizations that have open pay plans may find that a classification system helps in its communications with its employees.

The Factor Comparison Method. In factor comparison, jobs are compared against other jobs on the basis of how much of some desired factor they possess. It therefore ranks certain aspects of jobs rather than whole jobs. It is also one of the most complex of job evaluation systems and requires considerable training if it is to be done well.

The first step is for the compensation analyst to get job descriptions that will allow him to make judgments about factors the jobs possess. Traditionally, five factors are used in the factor comparison method: the mental, physical, and skill requirements of the job, the responsibility entailed by the job, and the working conditions.

From the entire set of jobs to be evaluated, the compensation analyst then selects ten to fifteen key jobs. . . . For factor comparison, the primary requirements are two: key jobs must show considerable variation on the five factors, and there must be well-defined market rates, which the organization considers legitimate.

To start the actual evaluation process, each job is ranked on each factor. This stage

EXHIBIT 3
Clerical Worker Classification System

CLASS I	Simple work, no supervisory responsibility, no public contact
CLASS II	Simple work, no supervisory responsibility, public contact
CLASS III	Work of medium complexity, no supervisory responsibility, public contact
CLASS IV	Work of medium complexity, supervisory responsibility, public contact
CLASS V	Complex work, supervisory responsibility, public contact

PART VI
MAINTAINING
AND IMPROVING
SATISFACTION,
COMMITMENT,
AND PERFORMANCE

EXHIBIT 4

Factor Comparison Method
Step 1 — Vertical Ranking

	Factors				
Key Jobs	Mental Requirements	Physical Requirements	Skill Requirements	Responsibility	Working Conditions
Job A	1	5	2	3	3
Job B	2	4	4	1	6
Job C	3	6	1	6	4
Job D	4	1	6	2	1
Job E	5	3	5	5	2
Job F	6	2	3	4	5

Note: The rank of 6 is highest.

Source: Adapted from: R. Beatty, N. F. Crandall, C. H. Fay, R. Mathis, G. T. Milkovich, and M. J. Wallace, Jr. *How to Administer Wage-Salary Programs and Perform Job Evaluations.* New York: Penton Learning Systems, 1980.

is conventionally done vertically; an abbreviated version is shown in Exhibit 4. The vertical ranking is identical to whole-job ranking except that factors are used.

The next stage is to take the market rate for each of the key jobs and apportion that rate across factors. An example of this apportionment is shown in Exhibit 5. In this stage, the compensation analyst is deciding how much of the salary associated with a specific key job is being paid for mental requirements, how much for physical requirements, and so on. This allocation is made for each key job. When allocations have been made for all key jobs, the dollar figures for each factor are ranked across jobs.

EXHIBIT 5

Factor Comparison Method
Step 2 — Allocation of Wage Across Factors
Step 3 — Ranking of Allocations Across Jobs

	Factors					
Key Jobs	Mental Requirements	Physical Requirements	Skill Requirements	Responsibility	Working Conditions	Current Market Rate (Dollars/Hour)
Job A	.40 (1)	2.00 (5)	0.40 (1)	0.75 (3)	0.30 (4)	3.85
Job B	1.75 (2)	1.50 (4)	1.95 (3)	0.20 (1)	2.20 (6)	7.60
Job C	2.15 (3)	2.05 (6)	2.70 (5)	4.10 (6)	0.35 (3)	11.35
Job D	3.00 (4)	0.25 (1)	2.80 (6)	0.40 (2)	0.10 (1)	6.55
Job E	3.20 (5)	1.35 (3)	2.50 (4)	2.50 (5)	0.25 (2)	9.80
Job F	4.10 (6)	0.75 (2)	1.80 (2)	2.10 (4)	0.70 (5)	9.45

Note: The rank of 6 is highest.

Source: Adapted from: R. Beatty, N. F. Crandall, C. H. Fay, R. Mathis, G. T. Mikovich, and M. J. Wallace, Jr. *How to Administer Wage-Salary Programs and Perform Job Evaluations.* New York: Penton Learning Systems, 1980.

These rankings are shown in Exhibit 5 in parentheses. For example, job F has more allocated to mental requirements than any other job, so it receives the highest rank of 6.

The purpose of this ranking becomes clearer in Exhibit 6. In Exhibit 6, a comparison of the two rankings is presented. The vertical rankings are based on the factors' importance to the jobs, or on the extent to which they form a basis for the jobs' value. The allocation rankings indicate the relative pay currently given the jobs for each factor. If the jobs are truly key jobs, there should be little or no difference between the two sets of numbers. The reconciliation shown in Exhibit 6, then, is basically a validity check on whether the jobs chosen are truly key jobs. It can be seen in the exhibit that generally there is no difference in the two sets of rankings, except with respect to skill requirements for job C. The current market rate allocated to those skills is considerably higher than the skill requirements would indicate. It may be that these skills are currently in short supply or that union pressure has forced up wages. Regardless of the reason, job C is not a key job, and must be discarded from the evaluation for the time being. The elimination of job C brings the rest of the rankings into exact agreement.

The compensation analyst is then ready to set up a job evaluation scale to be used in evaluating the other jobs in the organization. An example of such a scale constructed from the data from Exhibit 5 is shown in Exhibit 7. The data from Exhibit 5 have been rearranged to show ascending dollar values for each factor. The amount allocated to each factor for key jobs is indicated by the anchoring of value levels by the key jobs. It is for this reason that the validation of key jobs in the previous stage is so important. As another check, the compensation analyst will take an additional set of key jobs and value them using the scales. That is, key job G will be compared on each factor with respect to jobs A through F and a value level determined. Total value assigned to the job will be summed, and that value will be compared with market data. There should be a close match for the additional set of key jobs. If there is, the compensation analyst

EXHIBIT 6

Reconciliation of Vertical Ranking and Allocation of Wages Ranking

Key Jobs	Mental Requirements	Physical Requirements	Skill Requirements	Responsibility	Working Conditions
Job A	V-1	V-5	V-2	V-3	V-3
	A-1	A-5	A-1	A-3	A-4
Job B	V-2	V-4	V-4	V-1	V-6
	A-2	A-4	A-3	A-1	A-6
Job C	V-3	V-6	V-1	V-6	V-4
	A-3	A-6	A-5	A-6	A-3
Job D	V-4	V-1	V-6	V-2	V-1
	A-4	A-1	A-6	A-2	A-1
Job E	V-5	V-3	V-5	V-5	V-2
	A-5	A-3	A-4	A-5	A-2
Job F	V-6	V-2	V-3	V-4	V-5
	A-6	A-2	A-2	A-4	A-5

Factors

Source: Adapted from: R. Beatty, N. F. Crandall, C. H. Fay, R. Mathis, G. T. Milkovich, and M. J. Wallace, Jr. *How to Administer Wage-Salary Programs and Perform Job Evaluations.* New York: Penton Learning Systems, 1980.

EXHIBIT 7
Job Evaluation Scale for Additional Jobs

Job Value	Factors				
	Mental Requirements	Physical Requirements	Skill Requirements	Responsibility	Working Conditions
.00					Job D
.20		Job D		Job B	Job E/Job A
.40	Job A		Job A	Job D	
.60					
.80		Job F		Job A	Job F
1.00					
.20		Job E			
.40		Job B			
.60					
.80	Job B		Job F		
2.00		Job A	Job B	Job F	
.20					Job B
.40					
.60			Job E	Job E	
.80			Job D		
3.00	Job D				
.20	Job E				
.40					
.60					
.80					
4.00					
.20	Job F				
.40					

Source: Adapted from: R. Beatty, N. F. Crandall, C. H. Fay, R. Mathis, G. T. Milkovich, and M. J. Wallace, Jr. *How to Administer Wage-Salary Programs and Perform Job Evaluations.* New York: Penton Learning Systems, 1980.

can then use the scales, with the additional key jobs as further anchors of value to evaluate the rest of the jobs in the organization.

Factor comparison does have some advantages over both ranking and classification systems. It is much more reliable than either because of the two rankings made. It also speaks to internal and external equity issues at the same time. However, there are some major drawbacks to the use of this system. To use it requires extensive training. As dollar values change, particularly in periods of inflation, the whole system needs to be changed. More seriously, market rates tend to change differently for different jobs. These differential changes require extensive reworking of the system. Some compensation analysts argue that not all jobs can be analyzed accurately in terms of the five factors traditionally used. Finally, as the example of job C indicates, the reconciliation of internal and external equity issues is incomplete. In the balance, the factor comparison system of job evaluation is cumbersome and not appropriate when labor markets have any instability. As a final note, consider yourself in the position of a compensation analyst trying to explain to a worker why a job is valued as it is under this system.

The Point Factor Method. The point factor method, or one of its variations, is the most commonly used job evaluation method, and the one that seems most sensible for use by most organizations. The first step in the point factor method is to choose the factors that will be used to rate each job. Some typical compensable factors are education, experience required, need to work independently, physical demands, visual/mental demand, responsibility for equipment, responsibility for material, responsibility for safety of others, supervisory responsibility, working conditions, accident and health hazards, contact with public, and manual dexterity. In fact, any aspect of a job for which a company is willing to pay can be a compensable factor.

Having chosen the compensable factors, the compensation analyst must define each factor in some detail and then develop a scale for each factor. A sample factor scale, for education, is shown in Exhibit 8. Notice that besides the definition of the factor itself, there is a definition for each level of the scale. There is no optimal number of scale levels, nor do all factor scales have to have the same number of levels.

The compensation analyst then decides how many points will be used in the system as a whole. Although this is an arbitrary number, we recommend the use of 1000 since it is easy to work with and provides enough points to make meaningful differentiations. The total number of points must be allocated across factors. Given the factors education, experience, physical demands, responsibility, and working conditions, the analyst might decide to have education worth 300 points, experience worth 300 points, responsibility worth 200 points, and physical demands and working conditions each worth 100 points. This weighting of factor value cannot be done in an entirely arbitrary fashion. Rather, the analyst will look at key jobs in the organization and will decide how much each of the factors contributes to the value (note, not the wage) of the job to the organization. Although only rough estimates can be made, it is clear that in most organizations education is of much more value than the ability to tolerate poor working conditions.

When points have been assigned to each factor, the points assigned to each level of a factor must be determined. Our education scale, for example, has been weighted fairly heavily: 300 points out of 1,000. The analyst must now decide how many points to assign each level. The highest level of a scale is always assigned the full number of points allocated to the factor; thus, a graduate degree would be assigned 300 points. The lowest level on a factor scale is usually assigned some points, since an eight-grade education is not equivalent to no education at all. For the job family we are considering, it seems equitable to value an eighth-grade educational level at 20 points. Scale levels between the base level and the top level can be assigned points on the basis of rational argument, or levels can be assigned such that the differences between levels are (in

EXHIBIT 8
Point Factor Method Compensable Factor Scale

Education — 300 points

This factor measures the amount of formal education required to satisfactorily perform the job. Experience or knowledge received through experience is not to be considered in evaluating jobs on this scale.

Points

20	Level 1	Eighth-grade education	
90	Level 2	High school diploma or eighth-grade education and four years of formal apprenticeship	
160	Level 3	Two-year college degree or high school diploma and three years of formal apprenticeship	
230	Level 4	Four-year college degree	
300	Level 5	Graduate degree	

438

PART VI
MAINTAINING
AND IMPROVING
SATISFACTION,
COMMITMENT,
AND PERFORMANCE

terms of points assigned) equal. We have assigned equal intervals to this scale; thus the intermediate levels are assigned 90, 160, and 230 points.

A similar process is carried out for each factor scale. Jobs are then compared to scales and points assigned to the job for each factor. Factor points are totaled, and the resulting scores may be compared to show the relative value of each job.

The advantages of the point factor system lie in its reliability and its immunity to the fluctuations in market rates. Changes in jobs may be accommodated. Once created, the scales are relatively easy to use. The points assigned to jobs not only give differences in value, but also indicate the size of those differences. On the other hand, the point method is expensive and time-consuming to develop. The accuracy of the scales may be questioned, for although they are based on the judgment of the compensation analyst, there is no way to "prove" that they accurately reflect value. However, some statistical checks (for example, against employee perceptions) can be used to support factor scales. Finally, we should note that the analyst has only a set of points reflecting the internal equity value of a set of jobs, and not a wage and salary structure. It remains for these values to be translated into such a structure.

Administering the Job Evaluation Process

The discussion of job evaluation so far has been written as if it were a one-person job, that is, as if the compensation analyst handled all aspects of the process. In fact, nothing could be further from reality, especially in larger organizations.

Even in using the simple whole-job ranking method, a committee usually does the ranking. Compensable factors are usually developed by a committee consisting of management, compensation specialists, and representatives of at least some of the jobs in the job family being evaluated. When a job family is represented by a union, there will usually be an official of the union on the committee.

The same kind of participation takes place when jobs are actually being evaluated. The inclusion of some job-knowledgeable people on the committee is useful, because written job descriptions may be misleading to individuals not familiar with the way the jobs are actually done. Finally, it is important for all decisions of the job evaluation committee (or of the compensation analyst) to be written down in a job evaluation manual. In this way, consistency between committee members and consistency over time can be ensured. The manual also provides important documentation in the event of a comparable worth lawsuit.

Miscellaneous Job Evaluation System

There are a variety of commercial job evaluation systems in use in many types of organizations. The leading systems in terms of popularity are the Hay system, the NMTA's National Position Evaluation Plan, EVALUCOMP, the PAQ, and Management Compensation Services' Project 777.

The Hay System. The Hay system is essentially a point factor system that evaluates jobs with respect to "know-how," "problem-solving," and "accountability." It is aimed at evaluation of upper-level jobs in organizations, both professional and managerial. Hay utilizes standardized "Guide Charts" but does customize them to fit the needs of individual clients.

National Position Evaluation Plan. The National Position Evaluation Plan has evolved from the old National Electrical Manufacturers Association (NEMA) job evaluation system. Sponsored by eleven management/manufacturers associations, the plan is offered under the umbrella group known as NMTA Associates. The plan is a point-factor system with four units, each utilizing common criteria, which can be used to evaluate all jobs in an organization. Unit I is used to evaluate manufacturing, warehousing, service, distribution, and maintenance jobs. Unit II evaluates nonexempt clerical, technical, and administrative jobs. Unit III is used in evaluating exempt professional, technical, administrative, sales, and supervisory jobs. Executive jobs are evaluated using unit IV. The commonality of criteria used in the units is a strength of the NMTA Associates plan, since it allows for a single hierarchy of job evaluation points for all jobs in an organization.

EVALUCOMP. EVALUCOMP is a job evaluation plan for office personnel, technicians, professional and scientific personnel, and all levels of management. Developed and offered by the American Management Associations, EVALUCOMP differs from traditional job evaluation systems in that no effort is made to construct an internal hierarchy of jobs on the basis of job characteristics. Rather, an extensive description of each job is provided (to allow for matching) along with EVALUCOMP wage survey data. Users of the system can ensure external equity, but unless adjustments are made on some consistent basis, internal equity may not be achieved.

The Position Analysis Questionnaire (PAQ). The PAQ, developed by Ernest McCormick and his associates, is a job analysis technique that captures more than 150 aspects of a job. PAQ results can be regressed against market data to provide the dollar value of each level of each of these aspects. Additional jobs can then be analyzed with respect to level of these aspects and valued using weights from the regression equation. Like EVALUCOMP, the PAQ does not speak to internal equity so much as external equity, and its value as a job evaluation system is therefore limited.

Project 777. A third market-based system is Management Compensation Services' Project 777 and supplements such as MR/MA (multiple regression/multifactor analysis). Salary survey data for executives is related to sales, number of employees, net income, stock value, and other relevant organizational variables. By matching organizations, a compensation specialist can maintain external equity. Because of restrictions on participants, however, use of Project 777 is limited. (A participant must be a manufacturer with sales in excess of $100 million per year, not a division or subsidiary of another organization.) Again, internal equity is not served except by accident, and it is questionable whether such systems should be considered job evaluation systems.

BUILDING THE WAGE AND SALARY STRUCTURE

At this point, if the compensation analyst used the point factor method, he or she has the number of points assigned to the jobs in the organization and, on the basis of wage and salary surveys . . . has reliable market data for a variety of key jobs. What is needed is to construct a wage structure from these two data sets. Although a wage structure might be constructed which provides a specific range of wages for each job in the organization (including a starting, midpoint, and high wage figure) such a structure is inadvisable for several reasons.

1. In a company with many jobs the structure would be unwieldy and possibly unworkable.
2. Neither job evaluation nor wage survey data are sufficiently precise, reliable (having agreement between sources), or stable (over time) to justify such a structure.

440

PART VI
MAINTAINING
AND IMPROVING
SATISFACTION,
COMMITMENT,
AND PERFORMANCE

3. Internal equity issues are unlikely to be served by such a structure, because of the problems noted in 2. Aggregation is likely to smooth over small inconsistencies in survey and evaluation rankings.

In brief, neither survey nor job evaluation data are good enough to create one salary range per job. Therefore, organizations create wage structures with a number of ranges, into which are aggregated all the jobs in the organization. This structure will have several characteristics controlling its construction; these are the questions the compensation analyst must keep in mind when building the structure:

1. How many classes (or ranges) is the structure to have?
2. How far apart should the midpoints of those ranges be?
3. How wide should each range be?
4. How much should the ranges overlap?

To answer these questions, the compensation analyst will also have to know the answer to some additional questions:

5. How is the organization going to relate to the market with respect to pay levels? Will it exceed, fall short of, or match the market?
6. On what basis is the organization going to make individual pay decisions? Will all incumbents receive the same salary, or will there be differentials for seniority, performance, or some other factor?

Number of Ranges

The number of ranges to be used depends on several things. A major determinant is the number of jobs evaluated, their hierarchical level in the organization, and their reporting relationships. That is, a supervisor and subordinate would not ordinarily be in the same pay range. The more layers an organization has, the more pay ranges it will require. Career development issues also influence the number of ranges. When an individual is promoted to a new job, a raise is expected; career paths can typically be mapped by moves between ranges.

Range Parameters

The distance between midpoints will be largely determined by the number of classes. When the number of ranges has been determined, the compensation analyst can look at job evaluation points assigned to various jobs and see if there are obvious breaks. Another method is to divide the total number of job evaluation points possible (under the example used for the point factor system there were 1000) by the number of ranges decided on. Thus, if it were decided to have ten ranges, range 1 would consist of all jobs receiving between one and 100 points; range 2 would consist of all jobs receiving between 101 and 200 points, and so on.

The midpoints would be based on salary survey data for the jobs in the range in this case; thus, the distance between midpoints would be derived from marketplace differentials.

The Range Spread

The width of a given range, or the rate range spread, can be determined in different ways. One way is to look at market rate data of jobs falling within the classification and to base rate ranges on those data. A second way is to use a percentage band (usually between 5 percent and 20 percent) above and below the midpoint of each range. When this is done, the smaller percentages are used on lower ranges, and the larger percentages for the upper classes.

The midpoints and ranges chosen will depend on the policies of the organization reflected in questions 5 and 6. The organization must decide if it is going to exceed or fall below the market, or just match it. To implement this policy, the organization will choose a survey statistic (median, upper quartile, lower quartile) and consistently use that statistic for each key job surveyed. It may choose to adjust these figures in a consistent fashion; for example, it may say, "We will pay 15 percent above the median salary reported for this class."

Individual pay policies will influence range spreads. If the organization is going to pay for performance, then a wider range is needed to reflect differentials than if no merit pay is given. The same is true of seniority payments. In the typical organization, employees are brought into the lower end of a range and move to the midpoint in two or three years if performance is satisfactory; movement thereafter is less rapid. Promotion policies also influence range spreads. If most people in a job will be promoted to the next level within three years or fired, the range need not be broad.

Range Overlap

Many of the same issues governing range width influence ideal range overlap. As with range spread, there is no "right" overlap. The problems that occur when overlap exists include:

1. A promoted employee who was at the top of the old range must be placed above the base of the new range, or receive a cut in salary.
2. Supervisors may have employees working for them who make more money than they do. This can cause morale problems.

However, to avoid overlap completely creates an alternative problem: jobs will have artificial constraints on pay ceilings. All other factors being equal, organizations with more classifications can expect more overlap; each organization will have to judge the degree of overlap acceptable on the basis of the issues noted. An example of a typical wage structure is shown in Exhibit 9.

In building the wage structure, the compensation analyst must relate job evaluation points and wage survey data. Salary data for key jobs in each point range are noted. Some analysts average out salary data to arrive at a midpoint. Others use more complex statistical techniques to derive not only the midpoint but also the minimum and the maximum of the range. Actual range construction is an art; it is an iterative process in which the compensation analyst tries to meet the constraints of internal policy and still allow the organization to provide external equity.

ADJUSTMENTS TO THE STRUCTURE

From time to time, adjustments will need to be made to the structure. Inflation drives labor prices upward, jobs change in their relative value to the organization, and jobs themselves change as technology changes. Employees entering jobs change as well. The wage structure will have to be adjusted to meet these changes. In some cases, the compensable factors and their weightings will be questioned; in other cases, scale values will need to be changed. These kinds of changes will make it necessary to reevaluate all jobs. A more normal situation will be the need to reevaluate selected jobs.

442

PART VI
MAINTAINING
AND IMPROVING
SATISFACTION,
COMMITMENT,
AND PERFORMANCE

EXHIBIT 9
Wage Chart

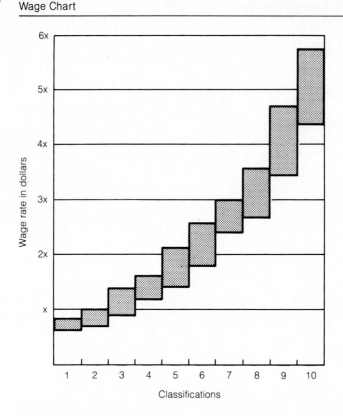

Adjustments that should be made are adjustments to movements in labor markets and to major changes in the organization. Adjustments that should be avoided are general cost of living adjustments, whether they are simple across-the-board adjustments or formal programs tied to the Consumer Price Index.

Finally, the structure should be taken seriously, but not as a straightjacket. Job evaluation is a tool, and wage survey data are estimates and averages. Building the structure is a matter of judgement, not a precise science. If done carefully, the structure should handle almost all jobs and the base salary for all but a few employees. There will always be a few employees who require special treatment. The compensation analyst, recognizing the uniqueness of these situations, should handle them outside the wage and salary structure and not distort the structure to accommodate these few cases. In short, adjustments to the structure should not be confused with individual employee adjustments.

Whatever Happened to Incentive Pay?

Edward E. Lawler

Historically, the popularity of incentive pay has gone hand-in-hand with the popularity of the scientific management approach to work design. The 1920's and 1930's saw a tremendous growth in the installation of piece-rate and other individual incentive plans. For the last several decades, however, the popularity of incentive plans has been in steady decline. Fewer and fewer new ones have been adopted, and many of those that are in place are being eliminated. The impact of this trend has appeared in the attitudes of the American workforce: A 1983 study by the Public Agenda Foundation found that only 22% of American workers say there is a direct link between how hard they work and how much they are paid.

The movement away from incentive pay has had its costs, for there is considerable evidence that pay can be a particularly powerful incentive. Research shows productivity increases of between 15% and 35% when incentive pay systems are put into place. And there is some evidence that the absence of such pay is a *dis*incentive. The Public Agenda Foundation survey reports that 73% of American workers attribute their *decreased* job efforts to a lack of incentive pay. Given such effectiveness, the declining popularity of incentive pay systems is, at first glance, hard to understand. After all, there is a desperate need for management approaches that will increase productivity. So why not return to pay for performance?

There are important reasons for the decline of certain kinds of incentive pay — in particular, piece rates — that need to be considered before we turn to what can be done to make better use of pay as an incentive.

PROBLEMS WITH PIECE-RATE PAY

The literature on incentive plans is full of vivid descriptions of the counterproductive behavior that piece-rate incentives produce. In many respects, this is caused not so much by the inherent nature of these incentives in themselves, but by the way they have been utilized in organizations. Nevertheless, it is difficult to separate the problems of implementation from the general nature of incentive pay. Here is a brief review of the major problems with piece-rate incentive plans:

Beating the System

Numerous studies have shown that, when piece-rate plans are put into place, an adversarial relationship develops between the designers of the system and the workers who participate in the plans. Employees play all sorts of games in order to get rates set in such a way that they can maximize their financial gains relative to the amount of work they do: They work at slow rates in order to mislead time study experts who come to set production standards; and they hide new work methods or productive procedures from the time study experts so that standards will not be changed. Additionally, informal norms tend to develop concerning how productive workers should be. In effect, workers set informal limits on their production, and anyone who goes beyond the limit may be socially ostracized (and sometimes even physically abused).

Reprinted by permission from *New Management* 1984, 1, 4, copyright the Dean and Faculty of the Graduate School of Business Administration, University of Southern California.

444

*PART VI
MAINTAINING
AND IMPROVING
SATISFACTION,
COMMITMENT,
AND PERFORMANCE*

Unfortunately for the organization, the informal standard is usually set far below what the workers are capable of producing.

Other games include:

producing at extremely low levels (when employees consider the official standards too difficult to reach), and

using union grievance procedures to eliminate rates that are too difficult.

Finally, in order to gain leverage in negotiating piece-rates, employees may even organize unions so that they can deal from a more powerful base.

Often, unions are able to negotiate rates that allow workers to perform below standards — while being paid at a rate that represents their previous high level of performance. Thus, organizations end up with the undesirable combination of high pay and low performance.

Divided Work Force

Since many staff and non-production jobs do not lend themselves to production standards, an organization often ends up with part of its workforce on incentive pay and part of the workforce not on it. This leads to a we/they split in the workforce that can be counterproductive, and it leads to noncooperative work relationships. This split is not a management/worker split, but a worker/worker split. In its most severe form, this gulf can lead to conflict between the production people on incentives and those who are not — the people in materials handling, maintenance, and other support functions on whom production workers depend. This split can also lead to dysfunctions in the kind of career paths people choose — individuals may bid for, and stay on, incentive jobs even though these don't fit their skills or interests. The higher pay of incentive jobs also causes individuals to be inflexible when asked to change jobs temporarily, and causes them to resist new technology that might require a rate change.

Maintenance Costs

Because incentive plans are relatively complicated and need to be constantly updated, a significant investment needs to be made in the people whose job it is to maintain them. This maintenance problem is further complicated by the adversarial relationship that develops between employees and management. Since employees try to hide new work methods and to avoid changes in their rates (unless, of course, their rates are being raised), management needs to be extremely vigilant in determining when new rates are needed. In addition, every time a technological change is made, or a new product introduced, rates need to be adjusted.

Finally, there is the ongoing cost of computing wages relative to the amount and kind of work employees do. All this activity requires the efforts of engineers, accountants, and payroll clerks. Added together, the support costs of a piece-rate incentive system are thus significantly greater than those associated with alternative systems.

Organization Culture

The effect of dividing the workforce into those who are and those who are not on incentive pay — combined with the adversarial process of rate setting — can create a negative organizational climate. It produces a culture characterized by low trust, lack of information sharing, poor support for joint problem solving, inflexibility due to individuals protecting their rates, and the absence of commitment to organizational objectives.

In short, incentive pay is, at best, a mixed blessing. Although it may improve work performance, the counterproductive behavior that it generates, the maintenance costs, the splitting of the workforce, and the poor climate that it creates, may make it a poor investment. Hence, many organizations have dropped incentive pay (or decided not to adopt it) because they feel the negative effects outweigh potential productivity advantages. The decreasing popularity of incentive pay, however, cannot be understood solely from this perspective. Some important societal changes have taken place since Frederick Winslow Taylor first wrote about scientific management. These changes have also led to the declining popularity of piece-rate pay.

SOCIETAL CHANGES

The United States has changed dramatically since the first installations of incentive pay. The society, workers, and nature of the work itself have all changed. Let us see how these changes relate to the decline in incentive pay:

Nature of the Work

In the early 1900's, many manufacturing jobs involved the production of relatively simple, high-volume products. Today, the United States is moving rapidly toward a service-knowledge-information-high technology-based economy. Many of the simple, repetitive jobs in manufacturing have been automated (or exported to less-developed countries). Instead of the traditional simple, stand-alone jobs that one individual could do, many jobs today involve the operation of complex machines, continuous process technologies, or the delivering of services which require the integrated work of many individuals.

Work in the United States today, therefore, is less amenable to individual measurement and to the specification of a "normal level" of individual production than it was in the past. Instead, performance can only be measured reliably and validly when a group of workers or an entire plant is analyzed. In many knowledge-based jobs, it is even difficult to specify what the desired product is until it has been produced. Work of this nature simply does not lend itself to incentive pay. Moreover, many jobs in services as well as manufacturing are subject to rapid technological change. This change conflicts directly with incentive pay because stability is needed to set rates and to justify start-up costs.

Finally, even in those situations where there might be simple, repetitive, stable jobs that would lend themselves to piece-rate pay, corporations are making these jobs more complex and creating conditions in which employees will be intrinsically motivated to perform them well. For example, in many companies, self-managing teams are being given responsibility for large chunks of work. Thus, the process of enriching jobs has made them less likely candidates for incentive pay because, first, a different kind of motivation is present and, second, the enrichment process has made the simple, measurable, repetitive, and individual nature of the jobs disappear. All told, then, the nature of jobs in the United States is less and less amenable to individual incentive pay.

Nature of the Workforce

When incentive pay was introduced in the United States, the manufacturing workforce was primarily composed of poorly-educated, immigrant workers who were entering factories for the first time. Today, workers are more highly educated and there is evidence to indicate that they have different values and different orientations toward their jobs

446

*PART VI
MAINTAINING
AND IMPROVING
SATISFACTION,
COMMITMENT,
AND PERFORMANCE*

than did their parents. For example, over 20% of today's workers have a college education and this, combined with a number of other social changes, has produced workers who are interested in influencing workplace decisions, who desire challenging work, and who seek to develop their skills and abilities. Piece-work pay plans tend not to fit the desires and interests of such workers.

Nature of the Society

During the last ten years, the United States has seen an expansion in employee rights, employee entitlements, and the kinds of legal avenues that are open to employees when they feel unfairly treated in the workplace. This has made incentive pay plans subject to grievances and to legal challenges which make them difficult and expensive to maintain.

In addition, the nation has seen increased international competition and the export of jobs to other countries. The consequent fear of job loss can lead to production restriction: Employees reduce production because they are afraid that, if they produce too much, they will work themselves or their co-workers out of a job. Hence, the long-term, macro need to be productive for purposes of international competitiveness gets lost in the short-term, individual struggle to maintain jobs.

CURRENT SITUATION

The net effect of these changes seems to have been to push the society toward pay practices that are more egalitarian and in which there is a smaller percentage of pay "at risk," that is, based on individual performance. Overall, the United States has become a society in which the profits of *companies* are at risk as a function of performance, but the pay of *individuals* is affected only at the extremes of performance. An employee only loses when the company is in such poor shape that it has to lay him or her off, and the employee only gains when growth is such that the employee has the opportunity to be promoted. The society seems to have evolved to where employees consider that they are *entitled* to a fair wage and extensive fringe benefits simply because they are employed. This kind of thinking is represented in union contracts that have eliminated piece-rate pay, and in companies that have offered high base wages to all employees in order to stay nonunion.

FUTURE DEVELOPMENTS

Looking to the future, there are no indications of social or workplace changes in the offing that are likely to tip the scales in favor of incentive pay. Indeed, if anything, the trends that have led to the abandonment of incentives seem to be continuing. There is, however, one important trend which seems to call for the increased use of pay as a motivator — the lack of growth in national productivity and the worsening international competitive situation.

Given the international situation, it would seem foolish to abandon such a potentially powerful incentive as pay for performance. Just this point was made by the 1983 White House Conference on Productivity at which the increased use of pay as a motivator was recommended. The Public Agenda Foundation study also supports pay for performance: It found that 61% of workers surveyed want their pay tied to performance. Yet, my analysis so far has suggested that piece-rate and similar forms of incentive pay may be inappropriate. Moreover, the typical merit increase plan also has many drawbacks and is seldom an adequate motivator (because it fails to effectively tie significant amounts of pay to performance). What, then, is the answer?

There probably is no *single* answer, but for some companies a good strategy is to use some combination of profit sharing, gain-sharing, and stock ownership. In proper combination, these approaches can dramatically increase the motivation of everyone in the organization. Not surprisingly, the use of these plans is showing a dramatic increase, and every indication is that they will continue to grow in popularity. Let us look at each of these three promising methods:

Gain-Sharing Plans

The Scanlon Plan is the oldest and best known gain-sharing plan. More recently, a number of companies have adopted the Improshare plan and others have developed their own plans. The idea behind them all is to define a business unit — typically a plant or a major department — and to relate pay to the overall performance of that unit. Monthly bonuses are paid to all employees in a unit based on a pre-determined formula.

Typically, bonuses are paid when there is a measurable decrease in such costs as labor, materials, and supplies.

The Scanlon Plan was formulated by Joe Scanlon, a union leader in the 1930's, and has been in place in some companies for over 30 years. Until recently, it was used primarily in small, family-owned manufacturing organizations. During the 1970's, however, an interesting and important trend developed: Such large companies as General Electric, Motorola, TRW, Dana, and Owens-Illinois began Scanlon-like gain-sharing in some of their manufacturing plants. This tendency of large corporations to subdivide into smaller units, each with its own bonus plan, seems to be spreading. The reasons for this are many and relate directly to the kinds of changes in the work force and the society discussed above. Gain-sharing plans seem to fit current conditions better than piece-rate plans for five reasons:

First, gain-sharing does not rely on individual performance measurement. This is important in workplaces where performance can only be measured objectively at the group or plantwide level, and where technology does not lend itself to the identification of individual output.

Second, gain-sharing is typically developed and administered in a participative fashion. That is, employees have a say in the design of the plan and are able to participate in its ongoing maintenance and administration. This tends to significantly decrease the adversarial relationship between employees and management, and to fit better with a society in which workers want to be involved in business decisions.

Third, gain-sharing affects everyone in the work force: managers, production employees, and support people. Thus, it encourages the cooperation and teamwork that tends to produce an increase in overall organizational performance. The ability to include everyone in a plan can be an important advantage in almost all workplaces — since it means that the performance of the many can be increased, and not just the performance of a few.

Fourth, gain-sharing meets the needs of organizations for increased productivity. Gain-sharing can positively affect organizational productivity because it creates a good fit between organizational performance and the payout to the individual — that is, situations are unlikely to develop where a bonus is paid and the organization performs poorly. Because the connection between individual performance and reward is less direct in gain-sharing, it may be a less powerful motivator than *individual* piece-rate incentives; nonetheless,

448

*PART VI
MAINTAINING
AND IMPROVING
SATISFACTION,
COMMITMENT,
AND PERFORMANCE*

in those workplaces where *cooperation* is the key to performance (e.g., where process production techniques are used), gain-sharing often leads to higher productivity.

Fifth, gain-sharing requires less administrative support than individual piece-rate plans. While it still requires some administration, it does not require the setting of individual standards for each job, nor the calculation of pay for individual workers based upon their performance.

Thus far, gain-sharing has largely been limited to manufacturing organizations, but recently a few service organizations (such as banks and hospitals) have begun to experiment with it. My guess is that over the next five to ten years there will be increased use of gain-sharing plans, although a great deal remains to be learned about how they should be installed in nonmanufacturing environments.

Profit Sharing and Stock Ownership

Profit sharing and employee stock ownership are better known, older, and more widely-practiced than gain-sharing. However, by themselves, they typically are less effective as motivators. This is particularly true in large organizations where the link between individual performance and corporate performance is poor, and the connection between individual performance and stock price is virtually nonexistent. Thus, particularly in large organizations, these pay systems are desirable primarily because of their symbolic value. Such approaches effectively tell all workers that they are part of a single organization and that their joint efforts are needed. Stock ownership, in particular, can emphasize the importance of long-term organizational performance (and, in very small organizations, they may make gain-sharing plans unnecessary because they have the same effect). In most organizations, however, these two systems should be thought of as symbolic and as balancing supplements to gain-sharing. The one exception is with top managers. For them, profit sharing and stock ownership plans should be thought of as the *major* motivators of performance.

MULTIPLE SYSTEMS

Installing *multiple* pay systems that reward performance is potentially the most effective approach to improving organizational productivity and profitability. Yet, it is surprising how slow most organizations have been to use multiple bonus plans. Particularly in large organizations, many workers have lost a sense of the business and of their involvement in ongoing operations. As a result, they often become mere bureaucrats routinely carrying out tasks with little appreciation or concern for how their performance relates to the overall success of the business. Indeed, this type of relationship between individuals and organizations has contributed to both the stagnation in national productivity growth and, in many cases, to the manufacture of poor quality products.

Gain-sharing, profit sharing, and stock ownership are financial ways of getting people involved in their organizations. Such managerial approaches as quality circles, self-managing work teams, and individual job enrichment can also do this. But experience shows that the two tracks work best when they run parallel. Everything that is known about incentives clearly points out that motivation is greatest when people have both a psychological stake *and* a financial stake in the organization's success. The absence of a relationship between the success of the organization and the pay of the employee causes an important part of the business experience to be missed for the individual worker. Organizations that are "shot through with" a variety of participative and managerial systems produce this necessary link.

Comparable Worth: Implications for Compensation Managers

Frederick S. Hills

When at the helm of the Equal Employment Opportunity Commission (EEOC), Eleanor Holmes Norton said that the issue of comparable worth in pay administration would be the EEOC topic of the 1980s. Although Norton is no longer at the EEOC, the courts continue to consider the issue (see box below for legal background and recent relevant court cases). It is not at all surprising, therefore, that the issue of comparable worth is getting more and more attention from management. Indeed, the American Society for Personnel Administration (ASPA) and others representing business interests are monitoring the topic carefully.

DEFINING COMPARABLE WORTH

The real meaning of comparable worth, however, is at best unclear in the literature. I reviewed many articles on the topic and found that no one has yet defined the concept. What does seem to emerge, though, is that comparable worth is determined by its juxtaposition against language in the Equal Pay Act (EPA) of 1963. That is, the EPA says that organizations cannot discriminate in pay between the sexes on jobs that (1) are "substantially equal" in terms of skill, effort, and responsibility and (2) performed under similar working conditions. Presumably, under the comparable worth concept, jobs do not have to be "equal" in terms of skill, effort, responsibility, and working conditions.

The distinction between equal and comparable worth can best be demonstrated by comparing a multiple-hurdles model with a compensatory model through the use of job evaluation. In a multiple-hurdles model, there are N dimensions on which we can assess a job, and to be assessed as equal, jobs must be equal in every one of the dimensions (skill, effort, and so forth). A compensatory model would allow for one dimension to have a greater value than another across jobs, but if in the final analysis two or more jobs had equal total scores, they would be comparable. In job evaluation language, we could depict two jobs, in two situations, as in Figure 1.

Under the EPA wording, situation 1 depicts a case in which the jobs are equal and pay differences on the basis of sex would be clearly illegal. Under situation 2, the jobs are not equal in an EPA sense, but they are comparable in that evaluation of job skills in both jobs total 310 points even though the total is arrived at through different combinations of points for compensable factors. Given the present wording of EPA and the present pressure by advocacy groups to change the application of EPA to cover comparable worth as well as equal worth, it is no surprise that job evaluation is now being viewed as the most effective administrative mechanism to eradicate male/female wage differentials. For example, the EEOC commissioned the National Academy of Sciences to investigate the feasibility of a "universal" job evaluation system for all of industry. The results of this investigation are currently available but seem to provide less-than-clear guidance for compensation managers.

In this article, we define comparable worth as existing when the total dimensional requirements of two jobs have equal total weights even if all the component requirements are not the same. There is a very real paradox here, however — that is, that the

---

450

PART VI
MAINTAINING
AND IMPROVING
SATISFACTION,
COMMITMENT,
AND PERFORMANCE

FIGURE 1

Comparative Job Evaluation of Two Jobs in Two Situations

	Situation 1 (points)		Situation 2 (points)	
Dimension	Job A	Job B	Job A	Job B
Skill	100	100	100	80
Effort	80	80	80	120
Responsibility	120	120	120	100
Working conditions	10	10	10	10
Total points	310	310	310	310

intention of job evaluation, in part, has always been to equate unequal jobs for pay purposes, but it has generally done so only within job families. Thus our view is compatible with current job evaluation schemes so long as one is dealing with a single job family. However, once one begins to cross job families, our definition is inconsistent with most job evaluation plans. Part of this occurs because the compensable factors themselves vary across job families, and there may be no a priori way to equate factors. It is no surprise, then, that comparable worth advocates want a universal job evaluation plan that would apply to all jobs in all industries.

The comparable worth issue is controversial. In an article tracing the EPA's legislative history, former director of the Office of Federal Contract Compliance Programs Lawrence Lorber concluded that Congress specifically meant the Act to assure equal pay for equal, not comparable, work. He further concluded that current views advocating comparable worth, if enforced, would be in direct violation of the working and legislative intent of the Act. His key conclusion, however, is that, given the legislative intent behind the Equal Pay Act and the embodiment of that intent in the Civil Rights Act of 1964 through the Bennett Amendment, the EEOC has no authority to impose comparable worth standards on business and industry. (See box.)

In short, it is Lorber's contention that it will literally take an act of Congress for comparable worth to become the law of the land. (The Supreme Court rejection of the comparable worth doctrine in *Gunther* seems to reinforce this assertion — also in box.)

However, if there is the remotest possibility that comparable worth legislation will be enacted — indeed, if the issue of comparable worth is to be the topic of the 1980s — it is important to ascertain the possible impact that official sanction of this concept might have on compensation policy.

THE BACKGROUND ISSUES

Because comparable worth is intimately tied to concepts of employment discrimination, labor market discrimination, job evaluation, and job pricing, one must understand these concepts in order to understand the effect that adoption of the comparable worth concept might have on industry and society. In this section, therefore, we examine these concepts to set the stage for our discussion of the impact of comparable worth.

EMPLOYMENT DISCRIMINATION AND LABOR MARKET DISCRIMINATION

The employment discrimination concept covers discriminatory treatment by employers toward protected groups — for example, females and minorities. Employment discrimination can and does arise when employers fail to grant the same opportunities to

The Bennett Amendment, the Court, and Comparable Worth

The Bennett amendment to Title VII of the Civil Rights Act of 1964 requires that sex-based pay discrimination cases must conform to Equal Pay Act (EPA) standards. That is, for a sex-based pay discrimination charge to be made, the jobs in question must be substantially equal in terms of skill, effort, and responsibility and must be performed under similar working conditions. Under EPA, there are four legitimate exceptions: Pay differentials are acceptable if they result from a pay system based on (1) quality or quantity of production, (2) a seniority system, (3) a merit system, or (4) any factor other than sex. As noted below, recent court interpretations have restricted the interpretation of the Bennett amendment to the "justifiable exceptions."

Two recent noteworthy cases have addressed this issue. In the *County of Washington v. Gunther* (U.S.S.C. No. 80–429, June 8, 1981), the Supreme Court ruled that jobs did not have to be equal for a pay discrimination suit to be filed under Title VII. The Third Circuit Court of Appeals reached a similar decision in *IUE v. Westinghouse Electric Corp.* (3rd Cir., August 1, 1980). Both cases dealt with the issue of whether the Bennett amendment to Title VII limited sex-based pay discrimination suits only to cases in which the jobs were equal (the EPA standards) or whether the Bennett amendment restrictions applied only to the four EPA exemptions. In both cases, the courts ruled that the Bennett amendment restrictions to Title VII dealt with the four justifications for pay differentials and did not limit Title VII cases to the "equal" job constraints of the EPA.

The final paradox of the *Gunther* case is that Title VII cases do not require male and female employees to be in equal jobs — yet the Supreme Court specifically renounced a comparable worth doctrine, preferring instead to rule only on the restrictions of the Bennett amendment. Thus the narrow issue of how the EPA relates to Title VII was resolved and the comparable worth issue was left undecided.

protected groups that they normally grant to white males in, for example, such areas as recruitment, selection, and promotion. Each time white males are afforded more opportunities than protected groups, members of the protected classes obviously suffer.

More opportunities are open to white males — principally for one of two reasons: Either the protected group member has fewer attributes or credentials than the white male (for example, he or she may have a lower education level or be younger), or the employer puts a different value on the attributes, depending on which group possesses them — that is, the white male and the protected group member have equal attributes or credentials, such as education, but the employer weights them differently for the two.

The distinction between, on the one hand, differences in the two groups' attributes and, on the other, differences in weighting these attributes has important implications for employment discrimination and for pay discrimination. More specifically, if there are differences in the two groups' attributes or credentials, and if the protected group member falls short on the attribute that the employer has set as a prerequisite for the job, adverse impact discrimination will result and protected group members will have fewer opportunities to be selected, promoted, and so forth. Under current dis-

452

PART VI
MAINTAINING
AND IMPROVING
SATISFACTION,
COMMITMENT,
AND PERFORMANCE

crimination laws, adverse impact in an organization makes it guilty of illegal discrimination unless it can demonstrate that there is a business necessity for using such attributes or credentials as predictors of performance on the job.

On the other hand, assigning different weights to the same attributes, depending on whether they are held by white males or by protected group members, is analogous to disparate, or unequal, treatment discrimination — which is illegal in any case.

In one sense, the conflict between the two laws — the Equal Pay Act and Title VII of the Civil Rights Act (CRA) — and the EEOC is focused sharply by this distinction between adverse impact and disparate treatment discrimination. Under the EPA and the CRA (because of the Bennett amendment) adverse impact is not illegal discrimination with regard to pay. More specifically, only disparate treatment discrimination in wage payments is illegal under EPA and CRA. Thus adverse impact discrimination is seemingly applicable to all areas of employment discrimination *except pay.* (However, depending on one's interpretation of the *Gunther* case, one might argue that pay issues too can now be examined under an adverse impact doctrine.)

The concept of labor market discrimination (LMD) is broader in scope. LMD exists, presumably, because employers have collectively discriminated often enough over time that certain labor markets take on race/sex characteristics. Managerial markets, for example, are generally all white male; certainly the nursing labor market tends to be female (and also white); and custodial labor markets tend to be black. Thus LMD and employment discrimination are not entirely discrete concepts but, rather, highly analogous concepts approached from two different perspectives: that of the single employer or that of aggregations of individual employer behavior over time.

JOB EVALUATION

As most managers know, job evaluation is the process by which organizations determine the relative worth they place on various jobs. While there are many methods of conducting job evaluations, we will briefly trace through one method, the point method, because it is easiest to work with for later discussion. Use of the point method of job evaluation requires the firm to go through several steps.

First, the organization must decide which jobs are to be included in the evaluation plan. (We will return to this shortly.) Second, the firm must decide upon a set of compensable factors and their relative weights. That is, it must decide which job components are to be rewarded. Third, having established the compensable factors, decisions must be made as to the weighting of the degrees (or points) within each factor. Finally, once these steps have been taken, the organization can evaluate the jobs by means of current job descriptions developed through job analysis. The outcome of the job evaluation process is an ordering of jobs, by point value, for the firm. The next step, typically, is to conduct a wage and salary survey of "key jobs" in the relevant market and then to use the key job data and point (job evaluation) data to establish a wage structure for jobs within the firm. Thus the outcome is a structure of wage rates that reflects both the relative value of jobs within the firm and the market value of those jobs (or at least relevant key jobs).

We noted earlier that the first step in this process is to select the jobs to be evaluated. For analyzing comparable worth issues, this is no small issue. Some firms use one job evaluation plan for all jobs while other firms use separate evaluation plans for different job clusters — for example, managerial jobs, office jobs, or shop jobs. The arguments for using more than one plan are multiple, including the observation that not all compensable factors are relevant for all jobs (noncomparability of jobs) and the observation that since these different job groups will ultimately be tied to different labor markets, one should use different evaluation plans from the start.

As indicated earlier, firms ultimately must relate the relative worth of jobs back to the labor market. This is normally accomplished by conducting wage/salary surveys in the relevant labor and/or product markets. The observed wage rates for key jobs "anchor" wage rates in the wage structure for all jobs that have been evaluated. This process, known as job pricing, will reflect "equitable" rates relative to the labor market. Having done this for all job classes, the firm will then have a series of intrafirm wage structures that, it would argue, are equitable, relatively objective, and nondiscriminatory.

Some writers have argued, of course, that this may not be the case at all. The principal alternative argument is that internal wage rates are in fact discriminatory at this point because the established wage structures reflect earlier employment discrimination that has become institutionalized in labor market discrimination. Thus job-evaluation and the job-pricing processes reinforce and perpetuate labor market discrimination. Without a doubt these assertions are valid to some extent. This chicken-and-egg argument cries for resolution in a sensible way.

COMPARABLE WORTH: ONE SOLUTION

One antidote for pay discrimination that is currently being advocated is to pay jobs that are of comparable worth the same amount. Thus, it is argued, if a firm has two jobs, both worth 1,000 points, the pay rate for those two jobs should be the same regardless of the labor market in which the job is found.

Again, one must be careful to distinguish between comparable worth and equal worth at this point. At the beginning of this article we noted that the Equal Pay Act of 1963 requires, by law, equal pay for men and women performing jobs that are equal in terms of skill, effort, and responsibility, and that are performed under similar working conditions. There are four exceptions to this requirement: Pay differences between the sexes can be justified if the pay plan is based on (1) a seniority system, (2) a merit system, (3) a system that measures earnings by quantity or quality of production, or (4) a differential based on any factor other than sex. For example, the EPA makes it clear that a firm can legally pay different rates for two jobs that are weighted equally (for instance, each is worth 1,000 points) if they are in different labor markets with different associated wage rates. (Figure 2 illustrates this legal wage differential.)

This differential is legal under EPA because it is based on the relationship of jobs within clusters to two separate labor markets (Market A and Market B). From the firm's perspective this differential is justified on two grounds: First, under exception four, this differential is based on a factor "other than sex" — for example, different labor markets. The second — and more forceful — argument is that the differential is also probably legal because EPA says the work must be equal. It is important to remember that there was much debate in Congress about whether to use the word "equal" or "comparable" in the Act. Legislative intent was clearly in favor of the "equal" terminology.

In the situation being discussed, to determine whether the work *is* equal or not, the firm would have to examine how each job was valued at 1,000 points. If we refer back to Figure 1, we find two hypothetical situations with different combinations of points for two jobs. In one, the jobs would probably be considered comparable and equal (situation 1); in the second, the jobs would be comparable but not equal (situation 2). Most jobs in different occupational groupings will probably not be worth nearly equal points for each factor; the likelihood is small, therefore, that they would be found to be "equal" in an EPA sense.

Simply stated, Figure 1 illustrates the difference between equal work and com-

454

*PART VI
MAINTAINING
AND IMPROVING
SATISFACTION,
COMMITMENT,
AND PERFORMANCE*

FIGURE 2
Hypothetical Wage Lines for Two Job Clusters

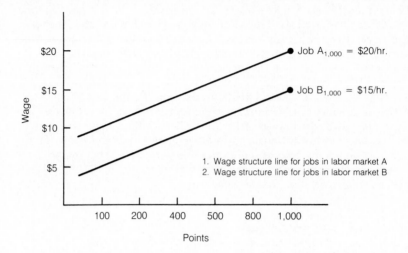

1. Wage structure line for jobs in labor market A
2. Wage structure line for jobs in labor market B

parable work. And again, probably partly because of the inability of EPA to eradicate pay differentials over the past 18 years, advocacy groups are solidly in favor of substituting the concept of comparable work for the EPA's concept of equal work.

Let us now analyze the likely impact such a change would have on organizations' compensation practices.

IMPACT ON COLLECTIVE BARGAINING

The adoption of comparable worth would affect compensation management and pay practices in at least two major ways. First, in the absence of an exception dealing with seniority systems, such as that contained in EPA, any pay differential among jobs of equal point worth would be illegal if the seniority system could be shown to have adverse impact on females. Thus pay differentials that were fostered by seniority clauses would be null and void. This impact is more than financial; in one sense it would result in an equal pay plan for all jobs at any particular point value. Unfortunately, such a change would also potentially have an impact upon employees' motivation to stay with the firm. That is, because those with more seniority could no longer be rewarded with higher wage payments, the incentive for individuals to remain with the organization over the long term might be weakened.

Second, and probably more significant in terms of bargaining practices and the wage bill, the collective bargaining process may end up as the principal determinant of a large array of wage rates. There are two ways in which this can happen. First, let us take the situation in which an organization has unionized jobs that are worth from 200 to 400 points. Of course, the employer probably also has many nonunion jobs that are worth from 200 to 400 points. If, as most unions claim, they are able to get for their members wages that are higher than those of other employees (at least in the short run), then there would be a pay differential in favor of the union wage structure. (See Figure 3.)

Under EPA provisions, of course, such a differential is legal, since the difference results from "a factor other than sex" — that is, the institutional forces of collective bargaining. But, under comparable worth, such differentials would be illegal in the

FIGURE 3
Hypothetical Wage Structures for Union and Nonunion Positions

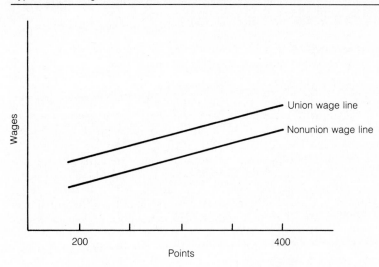

absence of an exceptions clause. All 400-point jobs should be paid the same, all 200-point jobs the same, and so on.

The second way in which the collective bargaining process might affect a large array of wages is through its effects on higher-level jobs in the organization. To clarify this point, let's examine a hypothetical situation. Suppose an organization has supervisory, managerial, and professional employees in addition to a unionized shop. Because of the unionized shop, wages for shop workers are high (relatively speaking), and this necessitates paying their first-line supervisors (who all happen to be male) at higher-than-normal market rates. As a result, these first-line supervisors of unionized workers may receive a higher pay rate than those of the firm's other supervisors (both male and female).

Again, under EPA this practice would currently be quite legal since the differential is made on the basis of "a factor other than sex" — that is, the institutional process of collective bargaining. However, under the comparable worth concept the system would not hold up because, once again, certain jobs are paid more than other jobs of equal point value. Clearly, the impact of collective bargaining would now be felt throughout the entire management wage structure — at considerable cost to the firm's wage bill and, ultimately, to the consumer.

DIFFERENT OPERATING SITES

The arguments presented above also apply to firms with more than one operating site. Consider that a firm in a large metropolitan area has two nearly identical production facilities, one on the far east side of the metropolitan area, the other on the far west side. These two plants might be as much as 40 or 50 miles apart; one might employ predominantly female labor while the other employs predominantly male labor. What would happen if there were local market differences in pay (discriminatory or otherwise) that resulted in the male market commanding a higher wage than the female market? Again, a situation would arise in which different wages would be paid for comparable work at the two sites. Having to equalize wages would again impact on

456

*PART VI
MAINTAINING
AND IMPROVING
SATISFACTION,
COMMITMENT,
AND PERFORMANCE*

the wage bill and would also have an impact on wages in the local labor market. This would surely obtain unless any enabling legislation for comparable worth made an exception for different operating sites, as EPA currently does.

IMPACT ON LABOR MARKETS

Previously we noted that the micro-concept of employment discrimination was analogous to the macro-concept of labor market discrimination. The rationale for that argument was that certain groups (that is, men, women) get assigned to particular occupations, and those occupations tend to become known as "women's work" or "men's work." The process through which this occurs, of course, is much too complex to address adequately in an article as short as this. Suffice it to say not only that sex stereotyping is associated with occupations, but also that wage differentials are usually associated with occupations. In short, the average wage in female-dominated occupations tends to be less than the average wage in male-dominated occupations. What is perplexing about this is that some, although certainly not all, of this differential may be justifiable. That is, there may indeed be differences in supply-and-demand forces across occupational labor markets that would justify a portion of the differential. Further, at least in theory, there should be human capital and/or productivity differentials that are justifiable. What the justifiable proportion is, of course, is an empirical question that needs answering.

In any event, the point to be made for our purposes is that if comparable worth is implemented as policy, it may in fact send labor markets into disequilibrium — because one purpose of comparable worth would be to pay solely in terms of job evaluation (point) worth regardless of supply and demand, human capital, or productivity factors. Such a disregard for market forces will undoubtedly be costly to employers, consumers and, most likely, ultimately to occupational structures.

THE UTILITY OF COMPARABLE WORTH

Given the various influences on labor costs, collective bargaining processes, and labor markets that implementing comparable worth practices have, the question to be answered is, would it be worth it or are there better alternatives? There obviously is no "guaranteed correct" answer to this question — and yet, given the ramifications of such a policy charge, we as a society ought to consider other remedies. It is also appropriate to suggest that continued concentration on employment discrimination may be the long-run viable solution.

To make this point clearer, it is useful to reiterate the distinction between pay discrimination and employment discrimination. As currently defined, pay discrimination occurs when the Equal Pay Act of 1963 is violated. This is, when a firm fails to pay equal rates for jobs of equal skill, effort, and responsibility that are performed under similar working conditions, pay discrimination (subject to the exemptions in the Act) is present.

Employment discrimination, however, covers issues of recruitment, selection, training, performance review, promotion, lay-off, and discharge. The point is this: Yes, it is a fact that women earn less than men. It is also a fact that this is due, in large part, to the fact that women do not get recruited for the best jobs; they do not get selected for the best jobs; they frequently don't qualify for, or don't get, the training necessary for higher-paying jobs; and so forth. In a world of employment discrimination, pay will, on average, be less for women than for men.

Note: For some time, economists have studied the issue of the extent of employment discrimination versus differences in human capital variables and related matters.

In fact, at least one study has suggested that much of the sex-related pay differential can be explained away by human capital and other variables.

We would suggest, however, that continued rigorous enforcement of employment discrimination laws is the best way to combat the pay differentials between men and women. That is, we think that the greatest strides to eradicate these pay differentials can be made through EEOC efforts to enforce the Civil Rights Act of 1964 and through the Department of Labor's enforcement of Executive Order 11246, which requires affirmative action. Of course, this process will be slower than the immediate change that would come from a comparable worth interpretation of pay. At the same time, it is true that all of the machinery to accomplish what needs to be accomplished is now available. The alternative solution, implementing comparable worth policies, would as suggested here be exceedingly costly to all parties — and, in addition, may not even be feasible because of the questionable ability to develop a universal job evaluation plan.

The Creative Flowering of Employee Benefits

J. H. Foegen

You'd think that by this time, every conceivable employee benefit would have been thought of; a composite employer would finally have provided everything possible. Such, however, is definitely *not* the case — nor, on second thought, is it ever likely to be. The human imagination is too fertile.

The recent history of benefits dates to World War II, when they were instituted as a way to get around government wage controls. Among large firms, basic benefits are assumed as a matter of course. A 1979 Bureau of Labor Statistics study, representing 21 million professional, administrative, technical, and clerical employees, showed that 100 percent of these had paid vacations, 99 percent paid holidays — usually from 9 to 11 a year — 97 percent health insurance, 96 percent life insurance, and 87 percent pensions.[1]

Beyond these basics are a host of exotic benefits. There are babysitting allowances at a Texas insurance company, manhunt-overtime at Illinois prisons, and maternity benefits for unmarried employees.[2] A Manhattan haberdashery provides offtrack betting breaks; another firm gives workers in their tenth year with the company airline tickets good for a trip anywhere in the world. General Electric contracts have included "to hell with it" clauses, providing extra days off when workers don't feel like working.[3]

Basic or exotic, all must be paid for. Even in the unlikely case of employees and unions being content with what they have, inflation pushes costs ever higher. The cost of a paid vacation, for example, rises with wages, which in turn are often tied to consumer prices. Benefits already average over 37 percent of payroll; among 983 firms reporting in a well-known national survey, the range was from under 18 percent to over

458

*PART VI
MAINTAINING
AND IMPROVING
SATISFACTION,
COMMITMENT,
AND PERFORMANCE*

65 percent. The average amounted to $2.96 per payroll hour, or $6,084 per year per employee. For 186 firms submitting data since 1959, benefits amounted to 24.7 percent of payroll in that year, 31.1 percent ten years later, and 41.4 percent in 1980.[4] As benefits expand to include such things as vision care and exercise facilities, the figure is expected to reach 50 percent by 1990.[5]

Understandably, employers are trying hard to contain such increases. Some try to be less generous in bargaining. Others look to "freebie fringes," benefits which are welcomed by employees but require relatively modest additional outlays. As two-earner families become more numerous, companies try to minimize overlap by permitting individual choice under "cafeteria" plans.

Try as they might, however, employers' containment efforts face formidable obstacles, not the least of which is human nature; people never have enough. Another powerful force, habit, is reinforcing. Both wages and benefits have been expanding for a long time, and employees are used to it. Years ago, a pay increase was rare; as applied to both pay and fringes, it's now expected every year. Employees have become "benefit junkies." Where unions exist, their "more and ever more" philosophy adds fuel to a fire that is already burning furiously. Even with no union, competitive conditions force employers to meet or exceed other firms' benefit packages; if they don't, it will be more difficult to get and keep good people. Furthermore, today's sophisticated workers recognize the tax avoidance feature of many benefits; if the company provides them, employees' after-tax income is relieved of significant burdens. (Employers, of course, often get a deduction; it's a win-win situation — except of course, for government.)

THE MEDICAL FRONTIERS

Regardless of cost, coverage, and containment efforts, benefits continue to accumulate. A sample of what's going on in two major areas, medical services and paid leave, demonstrates just how far the frontiers have been pushed back. Some corporations, for example, make company-paid facelifts available to executives and their wives; the perquisite can be expensive, but it's unique, and carries substantial status overtones.[6] While it's hard to image facelifts being made generally available, unusual benefits have a tendency to catch on. As the population ages, and the emphasis on youth remains strong in the national psyche, company-paid facelifts may yet become common.

Prepaid dental insurance is rapidly becoming more common and coverage is broadening to include such benefits as adult orthodontia. Plans enrolled 70 million in 1980, twice as many as in 1975; the American Dental Association expects 99 million to be enrolled by 1985, although rising costs are already requiring fixed payment schedules and employee contributions in some cases.[7]

While not a traditional medical benefit, sex-change operations are already covered by some employer insurance.[8] Although the incidence of such operations is likely to be low, the costs, when incurred, can be substantial.

With pregnancy now considered a "temporary disability" for insurance purposes, can abortion coverage under group policies be far behind? In fact, it too is already provided in some instances.[9]

Chiropractic services are not covered routinely under group medical policies, but a start has been made. Coverage has been negotiated by the United Rubber Workers Union with some of the firms with which it bargains.[10]

Group insurance policies usually include spouses and dependent children along with employees themselves. A logical extension of this idea, and one already available in Puerto Rico, is to include workers' parents.[11] A precedent has been set by unions getting cost-of-living pension increases for retired members. As the work force ages and retirees live longer, *two* generations of retirees in households will become more common. When and if such a benefit becomes widely available, it would take some of the financial burden off hard-pressed Medicare.

Mental health is also getting more attention. The biggest concern so far is alcoholism, but in-house counsel is being provided to deal with an increasing number of personal problems. Among them are: saving a marriage, buying a used car, dealing with stress, and coping with everything from finances and tennis elbow to weight loss or smoking. Metropolitan Life began its counseling program sixty years ago; ITT, JC Penney, Dow Jones, and Union Carbide are among current providers. Although critics charge that such programs meddle in the private lives of employees, companies like them because they have the potential to improve productivity and are visible proof of companies' concern for their workers.[12] Some companies deal with the problem of confidentiality by using outside firms to do their counseling. During the past few years, about one hundred independent mental health organizations have been formed to service corporate clients. Such diagnostic health service firms sometimes act as surrogate Employee Assistance Programs, and sometimes as supplements to in-house programs, providing literature, interviewing, offering basic treatment, and making referrals, all for agreed-upon fees. In addition to providing more privacy, such firms can supply a "supermarket of specialists," something otherwise impossible for smaller companies.[13]

Even isolation at work can be a mental health problem with which companies have to deal. Since 1978, trains can be operated by a crew as small as two, with one crew member at each end of the train. A twenty-year employee says that a 125-mile run is "like being alone in a small office for six to twelve hours. It's hairy." Another called his situation "akin to a person in solitary confinement." To compensate workers, the United Transportation Union has bargained a palliative — "lonesome pay." Up to $11.07 per run is now possible, plus a bonus, all in addition to regular pay. Also, a two-way radio is provided to enable the two crew members to communicate.[14]

The significance of premium pay for working in isolation goes beyond railroads. As robots make major inroads into manufacturing, other things being equal, the probability is that the fewer human workers remaining will often work alone.

Though still rare in this country, many German employers pay for death notices in local papers when employees die.[15] An increasing number of U.S. firms provide "well pay," extra wages to those neither absent nor late for a certain period. Presumably, this benefit focuses attention on preventive medicine as well as on good attendance. Such an incentive is part of a four-part "positive incentive plan" at Parsons Pine Products, Inc. of Ashland, Oregon; it also includes "retro pay" (a bonus based on reductions in premiums from the state's industrial accident fund), "safety pay" (two hours extra wages for remaining accident-free for a month), and a profit-sharing bonus.[16]

Well-pay often includes "no-smoke pay"; at least 3 percent of all U.S. companies, and 6 percent of Canadian ones, pay workers to stop smoking, according to the Dartnell Institute of Business Research in Chicago. Cybertek Computer Products, Inc. of Los Angeles has offered employees $500 "health bonuses" if they quit for a year. In Spokane, Norweco's non-smokers have collected an extra $10 a month. And at Neon Electric Corporation in Houston, reformed smokers have received a 50-cent-an-hour raise after not smoking for six months. In addition to the obvious health benefits, less smoking can reduce fires, maintenance, and cleanup costs, boost productivity, and cut absenteeism.[17] One survey says that some 30 percent of U.S. businesses have smoking policies in hundreds of offices around the country.[18]

CREATIVE REASONS FOR TIME OFF

Not surprisingly, the medical area is not the only one in which imaginative innovation continues to push back benefit frontiers. Another frontier is paid leave. As with medical

460

*PART VI
MAINTAINING
AND IMPROVING
SATISFACTION,
COMMITMENT,
AND PERFORMANCE*

benefits, the basic benefits have long been entrenched: vacations, holidays, sick leave. New twists, however, keep appearing. Reflecting changing social mores, for example, one union in Nevada has bargained what it calls "funeral leaves for pair-bonded relationships." As interpreted, "pair-bonds" can include unmarried couples, even of the same sex.[19]

Extended leaves, for both personal growth and social service, are gaining popularity. Wells Fargo & Co. has offered the former, for up to three months, to employees in any job who have fifteen years seniority and a serious interest to pursue. It has also provided up to six months of social service leave for work on "worthwhile" projects. Xerox has been offering leaves of up to a year for a long time; over 185 employees have participated. Employees in good standing, and with at least three years seniority, can receive full pay and benefits while on leave and return to the same job, or one with an equivalent salary. A few other large firms, such as Control Data and IBM, also offer such benefits.[20]

A small but growing number of employers give paternity leave to new fathers, as a logical outgrowth of maternity leave and the concern for sexual equality on the job. The Ford Foundation gives eight weeks at full pay, followed by up to eighteen weeks without. Procter & Gamble gives six months without pay. So far, however, men are not rushing to take advantage of the opportunity. At AT&T, fewer than one hundred have stayed home since the company adopted a policy of giving six-month leaves in April 1979. Security Pacific Bank reports fewer than a dozen a year.[21]

Educational leaves are granted by many companies; they also reimburse all or part of tuition for courses completed successfully. *Paid* educational leave, however, is something else; the worker gets not only time off the job with right of return, but also regular wages while going to school. The United Auto Workers Union reports that taking educational time off to attend union-run courses on politics, economics, and so on, works well under about seventy contracts in Canada, but the idea has yet to really take hold in the U.S.[22]

Some Japanese workers enjoy vacation trips with all accommodations paid for by the company.[23] Again, both logic and imagination are at work. First, bargain only the time off, next get the firm to pay for it, and finally have the company grant not only the time off and the wages, but also expenses incurred while gone. These can be substantial, of course; more money is spent while on vacation than while working.

In an interesting about-face, situations already exist in which employees might have to take more time off, whether they want to or not. To create more jobs in Denmark, the government considered making it illegal for employees to work more than 100 overtime hours a year. Overtime worked would have to be compensated with time off. Up to 12,000 jobs were said at stake.[24]

Sometimes, the impetus for forced time off is dictated by security reasons. For example, "Banks require vacations because they know that internal theft schemes often fall apart if the perpetrator isn't on hand to take care of the niggling details such schemes require."[25] With computers ever more numerous, and with more people knowing how to operate them, the security aspect of leave is bound to become more general.

Benefit proliferation has yet to run its course. Not by any means has the human imagination been wrung out of this costly and complex part of compensation. While they may not *like* the rising costs and increasing hassles that new benefits often entail, good managers won't be surprised at such developments; change is a universal, after all, in benefits as elsewhere. At the same time, good managers don't *want* to be taken unawares. Alert to what's happening on the benefits frontier, they can have constructive reactions ready. At times, they may even take the initiative themselves, to their own and their employer's advantage.

1. Bureau of Labor Statistics news release, June 27, 1980.

2. See the author's "Far-Out Fringe," *Personnel*, May-June 1967.

3. See the author's "Is It Time To Clip the Fringes?" *Personnel*, March-April 1972.

4. "Employee Benefits 1980," Chamber of Commerce of the United States, Washington, D.C., 1981.

5. *Wall Street Journal*, June 20, 1980: 1.

6. *Wall Street Journal*, March 28, 1980: 22.

7. *Wall Street Journal*, June 20, 1980: 1.

8. Lad Kuzela, "Fringes Becoming Benefits of Doubt," *Industry Week*, January 22, 1979: 45.

9. Kuzela: 45.

10. *Wall Street Journal, February 5, 1980:*

11. *Wall Street Journal*, June 20, 1980: 1.

12. Roger Ricklefs, "In-House Counsel," *Wall Street Journal*, August 13, 1979: 1.

13. "More Help for Emotionally Troubled Employees," *Business Week*, March 12, 1979: 97.

14. *Wall Street Journal*, August 6, 1980: 17.

15. *The German Tribune*, February 4, 1979: 14, from *Die Zeit*, January 12, 1979.

16. *Business Week*, June 12, 1978: 143.

17. *Business Week*, May 29, 1978: 68.

18. "Smoking Policies," *Industry Week*, February 22, 1982: 101.

19. *Wall Street Journal*, June 20, 1980: 1.

20. Marilyn Much, "Few Firms Offer the Ultimate 'Perk,'" *Industry Week*, November 13, 1978: 83.

21. *Wall Street Journal*, April 21, 1981: 1.

22. *Wall Street Journal*, May 29, 1979: 1.

23. Kuzela: 45.

24. *Wall Street Journal*, March 13, 1980: 33.

25. Hal Lancaster and G. Christian Hill, "Anatomy of a Scam," *Wall Street Journal*, February 26, 1981: 1.

C.

WITHDRAWAL FROM WORK, HOURS OF WORK, AND SAFETY

Dealing with Premature Employee Turnover
John W. Seybolt

Premature turnover of valued employees is costly. Minimal replacement costs exceed $3,000 for the lowest level employee.[1] Although most organizations are not concerned with turnover of all their employees, there should be great concern when valued employees leave prematurely. The study reported here suggests that a model of work-role design might be appropriate to study this turnover. The model is used to investigate specific facets of employees' work roles at different points of their organizational careers to illustrate how turnover might be better predicted and thereby controlled. Work-role design is defined in terms of three concepts: the job itself, the kinds of interactions at work, and organizational policies which affect the employees. Five stages of organizational career stage, or tenure, were empirically developed and proved to be useful in explaining differences in relationships between various employee attitudes toward jobs. The study found that at different organizational career stages different facets of the work-role design become more or less important to employees in terms of their satisfaction and their turnover intentions.

The present approach, using the variables mentioned above, can help managers examine in sequence those facets of job satisfaction which predict turnover intentions, and ultimately the specific factors of the work-role design which are better predictors of those satisfactions. From the results that are discussed, it is apparent that issues of both work-role design and organizational career stage should be considered when attempting to remedy conditions leading to premature employee turnover.

For the organizational manager who has determined that turnover is a problem, there are several models in the research literature which help focus on the possible causes of turnover.[2] Generally, the models agree that the best single predictor of actual turnover is turnover intentions. Thus, in a practical way, it makes sense to examine the turnover intentions of present employees and the predictors of these intentions, then dealing with those predictors to stem the tide of premature turnover. It is also generally agreed that employee dissatisfaction has strong impact on turnover intentions. Of course, there is not just one overall satisfaction at work, but there are many satisfactions with different facets of the work place, and each of these can be important in determining turnover intentions. In addition, it is wise to look beyond comments of employee dissatisfaction to the factors in the work place which affect those attitudes. One thrust of research which appears useful here is the job and work-role-design literature.

For the past five to ten years, there has been a significant focus on job design and redesign and the impact of the job on individual employees.[3] This research has focused on the work itself as a cause of differential levels of satisfaction, motivation, absenteeism and turnover. Recently, there has been some work trying to broaden this concept of job design to include more of the work environment which employees face. This expanded environment, labeled work-role design, includes such factors as the job and work itself, the type of interactions at work (including feedback and role-clarity issues), and the nature of the organizational policies and how they impinge on the employee (most specifically the consistency and equity of those policies).[4]

There is also mounting evidence that different individuals react to their work in different kinds of ways. For example, it has been found that individuals who have what might be called high needs for growth at work tend to react differently (more favorably) than do individuals with lower growth needs at work to jobs which have been redesigned to encourage growth.[5] Another factor which could be important here is the length of tenure the employee has in an organization, which might be called the employee's organizational career stage. It has been found, for example, that individuals perceive their jobs differently the longer they have been in their employing organization.[6]

THE MODEL

From the above discussion, it appears that a practical approach to dealing with premature employee turnover may be to follow the steps listed below:

- ☐ Categorize the organization's employees according to their organizational career stage, or length of tenure, and examine the work-related attitudes of these different groups.
- ☐ Focus on the turnover intentions of these groups, both in terms of absolute level of these intentions and the relative levels of the intentions.
- ☐ Dealing first with those groups with the highest levels of turnover intentions, examine the various dissatisfactions which are predictors of these levels of turnover intentions.
- ☐ Having singled out the facets of dissatisfaction which best predict turnover intentions, examine the factors in the work-role design which best predict those most important facets of work dissatisfaction.
- ☐ Having identified those work-role-design factors which tend to best predict the important dissatisfactions, try to design specific programs to deal with those factors which are the most crucial.

Utilizing this approach may help avoid a shotgun approach to employee turnover, trying to deal with all employees as one large mass. It will force a focus on specific factors in the work-role design which are critical to employee turnover, factors which can be isolated and dealt with separately.

From these questions, the model shown in Figure 1 was delineated. The specific variables of this model have been derived from the research literature on work design and job satisfaction. In work-role design, three general factors appear to be important: the job itself, interactions at work, and organizational policies.

464

*PART VI
MAINTAINING
AND IMPROVING
SATISFACTION,
COMMITMENT,
AND PERFORMANCE*

FIGURE 1
Factors in Turnover

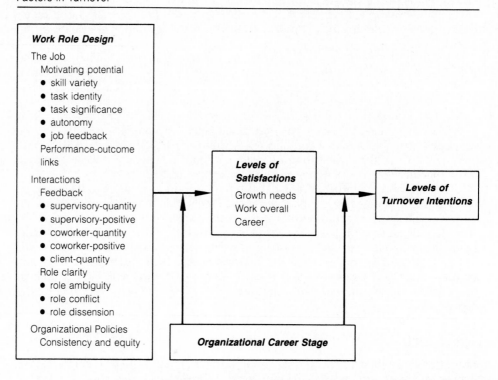

The job is defined in terms first of its motivating potential. Jobs are considered to have high motivating potential if they have the following five characteristics: skill variety, task identity (doing complete tasks at work), task significance, autonomy, and feedback from the job itself. A second facet of the job which has been found to be important in the prediction of satisfaction, motivation, and turnover is the performance-outcome linkage, derived from expectancy theory of motivation.[7] This facet is employees' perceptions that high levels of performance lead to certain valued outcomes for themselves. In the present instance, these outcomes are defined as several "growth-related" outcomes (opportunities to learn new things, using skills and abilities, opportunities to make independent decisions, and having responsibility).

Interactions at work can include such factors as feedback and role clarity. Feedback has been defined here in terms of supervisory feedback and coworker feedback (both quantity in general and amount of positive feedback) and client feedback (in terms of quantity). Role clarity has been defined in terms of role ambiguity (uncertainty as to what one's role entails), role conflict (where the various role requirements for an individual are incompatible), and role dissension (lack of agreement with supervisor over work-role duties). Regarding the last factor important to work-role design, organizational policy, one of the critical issues appears to be the level of consistency and equity of the policy across work groups within the organization.

It is not extremely useful to talk of the second major variable of the model, job satisfaction, in general terms. It appears more promising to focus on its various facets; for the present work, three facets of satisfaction were examined: satisfaction of growth needs (learning opportunities, use of skills, decision making, amount of responsibility); overall work satisfaction; and satisfaction with one's career.

To examine the usefulness of this approach, a nursing staff in a large, West Coast hospital was studied. The staff was experiencing what had been determined by the nursing director to be unacceptably high turnover levels. There were 647 female registered nurses included in the attitude survey study, which was designed to identify factors in the work-role design which were good predictors of satisfactions and ultimately turnover intentions. The analysis performed used Pearson Product Moment correlational techniques. The data was interpreted using an arbitrary cutoff value of r greater than or equal to .40. While many of the correlations were statistically significant at the level of p less than .01, it was felt that correlations of .40 or higher could certainly be considered to have practical significance as well, since such a correlation would imply that at least 16 percent of the variance in one variable could be explained by the other variable of concern.

The staff was divided into groups according to their hospital career stage. Because the average tenure for a staff nurse at this hospital was two to three years, the stages were defined as follows:

- entry level: less than six months;
- early career: from six months to one year;
- mid career: from one to three years;
- advanced career: from three to six years; and
- later career: over six years.

It was anticipated that the staff members would react differently to their work roles based to some degree on their tenure in the hospital and that hospital career stage would moderate relationships between work-role design, satisfaction, and turnover intentions.

The turnover intentions of each group were examined. The following is the ranking of the five groups of staff nurses in order of the highest to lowest turnover intentions (the scaling is a seven-point Likert type, with a high score meaning very likely to turn over; a low score meaning very likely to stay; 4 = neutral score):

- early, $\bar{x} = 3.55$
- mid, $\bar{x} = 3.17$
- advanced, $\bar{x} = 2.96$
- entry, $\bar{x} = 2.50$
- later, $\bar{x} = 2.36$

From this initial result, it is clear that for the first six months there is not much concern with turnover intentions for this hospital, most probably since it generally takes about that long to become acclimated to such an organization and job. Formal orientation programs were barely terminated by this time. It is also unlikely that the later-career employees (those with more than six years' employment) will cause severe turnover problems. However, even with these groups, while turnover intentions are generally low, it may well happen that a valued employee leaves. Therefore, it is helpful to continue with the model as presented here to investigate potential predictors of turnover even among these groups. For the early-career and mid-career groups, turnover intentions may well be a problem. For this reason the analysis using the present model focused on these groups first, to attempt to isolate turnover intention predictors. The discussion which follows will examine each career-stage group individually, beginning with that one with the highest turnover intentions.

466

*PART VI
MAINTAINING
AND IMPROVING
SATISFACTION,
COMMITMENT,
AND PERFORMANCE*

Early Career. For this group, the relationship between turnover intentions and the satisfaction facets in general were the highest of all groups (see Table 1). Of the relationships, the highest was between overall work satisfaction and turnover intentions. It is perhaps the most useful to examine the relationships between overall work satisfaction and the work-role-design variables for this group. Two of the work-role-design factors reached the .40 cutoff in their relationships with overall satisfaction: performance-outcome linkage and the quantity of coworker feedback (see Table 2). Thus, for this group, the work-role-design factors most likely to affect turnover intentions are performance-outcome links and coworker feedback. This might lead one to the following questions:

□ What can be done to ensure that staff members at the six-month to one-year point in their hospital careers experience growth (learning opportunities, using abilities, having responsibility, making decisions) as a result of performing well on the job?

□ What can be done to help increase the amount of coworker feedback to these staff members?

Mid-Career. For this group, the second most prone to turnover intentions, the satisfaction facets were not as good predictors of turnover intentions as they were for the early-career groups. However, two of the correlations were moderately high, overall work satisfaction and growth need satisfaction (see Table 1). Examining the work-role-design factors and their relationships to these two satisfaction facets, it was found that none of the correlations reached the .40 cutoff for overall work satisfaction. For growth satisfaction, however, there were two correlations which reached the cutoff, autonomy and role dissension (see Table 2). Given that these are the factors most likely to affect the turnover intentions of this group, two questions that might be asked are:

□ Are staff members in this group allowed enough freedom to make their own decisions and to do their work fairly independently?

□ Has enough care been taken to ensure that expectations are known and shared by this group of staff members?

Advanced Career. For this group, the turnover intentions were slightly lower than for the previous two groups. The correlations between turnover intentions and the satisfaction facets also tended to be fairly low (see Table 1). The highest correlation was

TABLE 1

Relationships between Turnover Intentions and Satisfaction at Different Career Stages

	Career Stages				
Satisfactions	*Under 6 Mos.*	*6 Mos.–1 Yr.*	*1–3 yrs.*	*3–6 yrs.*	*Over 6 Yrs.*
Growth	.34	.46	.37	.29	.26
Overall	.46	.64	.41	.33	.42
Career	.49	.49	.31	.52	.43
	$\bar{x} = .43$	$\bar{x} = .53$	$\bar{x} = .36$	$\bar{x} = .38$	$\bar{x} = .37$
N =	55	61	140	130	195

Note: all correlations are significant at p < .01.

TABLE 2
Career Stage Results: Relationships between Work Role Variables and Satisfaction

	Growth Need Satisfaction					*Overall Satisfaction*					*Career Satisfaction*				
	6 Mo.	6 Mo. -1 Yr.	1-3 Yrs.	3-6 Yrs.	6+ Yrs.	6 Mo.	6 Mo. -1 Yr.	1-3 Yrs.	3-6 Yrs.	6+ Yrs.	6 Mo.	6 Mo. -1 Yr.	1-3 Yrs.	3-6 Yrs.	6+ Yrs.
The Job															
Motivating potential															
Skill variety	.54					.46			.42						
Task identity														.41	
Task significance				.42					.41						
Autonomy	.63	.53	.53	.55	.44	.48			.40			.46	.43		
Job feedback	.44			.46		.43								.43	
Performance-outcome link		.50					.41					.62			
Feedback															
Supervisor quantity	.44									.45					
Supervisor positive										.48					.41
Coworkers quantity	.43	.40					.51				.43				
Coworkers positive	.43														
Patients quantity															
Role Clarity															
Lack of role ambiguity															
Lack of role conflict						.43									
Lack of role dissension			.45	.45	.49						.40		.41		
Organizational Policy															
Consistency										.49					.49
N =	55	61	140	130	195	55	61	140	130	195	55	61	140	130	195

468

PART VI
MAINTAINING
AND IMPROVING
SATISFACTION,
COMMITMENT,
AND PERFORMANCE

for career satisfaction. At this advanced career stage in the hospital, career satisfaction becomes more critical in the determination of turnover than at other stages in one's hospital career.

The work-role-design factors most highly correlated with career satisfaction were task significance and job feedback (see Table 2). Indeed, this was the only group for whom task significance was a good predictor of any satisfaction facet, and for this group it consistently remained a fairly good predictor. Implications of this finding may be that at this point there is a question in staff members' minds concerning the true meaning of their work and a need for feedback from the job itself to show them what it all means. Possible questions to ask for this group might be:

- Now that they have been here a relatively long time, is there any sense of excitement that their work is important? What can be done to rekindle that excitement if it is gone and show that the work is important?
- Are these people able to see the results of their work or is there a smokescreen in the way? Have they been "promoted" to so much paperwork that they cannot see how well they are doing with their primary charges (in this case, the patients)?

Entry Level. For this group there seems to be less turnover intent than for most other groups. This makes intuitive sense since they are generally still learning the ropes at this point in their careers. The correlations between turnover intentions and the satisfaction facets were moderate (see Table 1). Two of the correlations were quite similar, those for overall satisfaction and for career satisfaction. At this early time it appears that the employees are looking at the overall job and its career implications as they think (if they think) about turnover.

The work-role-design factors which are the best predictors of career satisfaction are autonomy, the amount of supervisory positive feedback, and the lack of role dissension (see Table 2). Those factors which best predict overall work satisfaction are skill variety, autonomy, job feedback, and role conflict. Clearly, the job, feedback and role clarity are all important for this very new group of employees as they consider possible turnover. At this stage some questions which might be asked are:

- Have the new people been given room to grow (autonomy)?
- Have expectations been explicitly shared (role dissension)?
- Are the new employees able to see how well they are doing on the job?
- Have these new employees been given adequate, positive feedback for a job well done, even in their new jobs where they may not be doing a lot of productive work at this time?
- Are conflicting cues being given — first telling these new employees to do one thing and then telling them to do another?
- Are the new employees given a good variety of tasks to do or is their "orientation" forcing them into temporary, perhaps tedious jobs?

Later Career. Ostensibly, these individuals are the least likely to leave. They had the lowest turnover intentions as a group, as well as a low relationship in general between turnover intentions and the facets of satisfaction. The two best predictors of turnover intentions for this group were career satisfaction and overall work satisfaction (see Table 1). Interestingly, growth satisfaction had much less to do with turnover intentions for this group than for any of the other groups. As a side note, it is interesting to note the changing relationships between growth satisfaction and turnover intentions for the different groups. The relationship was moderate for the entry-level group, rose for the early-career group, then steadily declined through the mid-career, advanced-career, and later-career groups. Thus, it appears that employee concerns over growth needs at work may be most crucial at a fairly early point in their organizational careers but may recede after that.

For the later-career group, the work-role-design factors of importance seem to be supervisory feedback and lack of role dissension (see Table 2). Both of these factors reached the .40 cutoff for career satisfaction. None of the factors reached the cutoff for overall work satisfaction. The possible implications of this are that these individuals have seen it all and there is not much left to faze them. But if they think of turnover, the reason most likely has to do with their supervisor, whether they share and agree with supervisory expectations, and whether they get supervisory feedback. Some questions which might be asked here are:

- Is enough time spent with long-term employees giving them feedback or is it assumed they know how well they are doing?
- Is this group kept up-to-date on changing expectations in the organization? Have they gotten into the we've-always-done-it-this-way syndrome?
- Have they had the career movement that they deserve? (These feedback and role-clarity issues may mask a promotion question — "We've been here a long time. Why haven't we been promoted?")

CONCLUSIONS

The turnover intentions of employees at different times are affected by different work-role-design factors. To help prevent premature turnover, it is wise to focus not on the whole organization but on different groups of employees. Organizational career stage or tenure appears to be a useful variable. Certainly, as one's career in an organization gets longer, the work-role-design factors change in importance in terms of satisfaction and turnover intentions. For the organization discussed here, the scenario seems to read as follows:

- The Raw Recruits: the less-than-six-month group. The employees are new to the job and probably still in the orientation phase. They're learning the job and are somewhat overwhelmed by conflicting demands. They need feedback to make sure they are doing the job well.
- The Young Turks: the six-month-to-one-year group. These employees are ready to move. They know the job (or think they do) and now focus on the payoffs for working well. This is the only group for whom payoff for good work is so important. Interestingly, the performance-outcome link was not critical for any other group, while it was the most important factor for this group. They want to charge ahead, and if they see no payoff they'll be the first to think of leaving. At this point, the relation between satisfaction and turnover intentions is also the highest of any group. If members of this group are dissatisfied, they will tend to be more prone to leave than members of any other group. Unfortunately, this group is often neglected. The orientation is over, and they're left alone to flounder, not yet respected as the old guard.
- The Skeptics: the one-year-to-three-year group. These employees have the lowest relationship between turnover intentions and job satisfaction. If they think of turnover, it is probably because they do not agree with their

470

PART VI
MAINTAINING
AND IMPROVING
SATISFACTION,
COMMITMENT,
AND PERFORMANCE

supervisor's expectations. If disillusioned, it may well be because they first saw no performance-outcome links and now are unsure of their supervisor's expectations.

☐ The Burn-Out Candidates: the three-to-six-year group. These employees have been around long enough to know all the ropes. Their turnover thoughts probably come as a result of the notion, "Is this all there is?" They are wondering about the significance of their work, to which they have dedicated such a large chunk of their careers. They need to be shown that their work is important and have to get feedback from doing the work itself.

☐ The Old Guard: the over-six-year group. These individuals are the pillars of the organization. They not only know the rules, they probably were instrumental in forming those rules. At this point, turnover is less likely, but if it does occur, it may well focus around supervisors' interactions. At this point, it is the supervisor who really makes the difference.

Is this study generalizable? While the process definitely appears to be so, the specifics may well vary across organizations and occupations. First, the sample discussed here is a group of female registered nurses. They are one of the most, if not the most, mobile of occupational groups in the country. They have generally high levels of turnover. Because their tenure in organizations tends to be rather short, the career stages discussed here may well be of too short a duration to be generalizable to other organizations. Katz, for example, has suggested three career stages spanning the employee's organizational life.[8]

Second, the work-role-design factors may change in their relative importance for turnover intentions. For instance, a recent study in a major oil company showed that the important variables for managers were very different than those for technicians, which in turn were very different from those for clerical workers.[9]

Third, in considering turnover, one should focus on the mobility of the employees involved. Generally, it is issues of satisfaction and mobility (and one's perception of one's mobility) which have the greatest impact on turnover. In the present example, the mobility of the staff was extremely high since the nurses were all professional RNs in a highly prestigious hospital in an area where there were many other hospitals paying as well as or more than this hospital. Thus, in a sense, their mobility was not a limiting factor. In other organizations and occupations, mobility is a critical issue which cannot be ignored.

Even with these concerns, the process discussed here makes practical sense. To find out about turnover of present employees, one can begin by focusing on their turnover intentions. Then one can move to various facets of satisfaction, and from there to work-role-design factors which influence those satisfactions most important to turnover intentions. In this way, supervisors can act quickly to deal with turnover intentions before they become actual turnover statistics. By focusing on specific work-role-design factors for different career-stage groups, one is able to eliminate a more haphazard approach which often ends up having missed the target completely.

REFERENCES

1. For example, see E. E. Lawler, *Motivation in Work Organizations* (Brooks-Cole, 1973).

2. For example, see W. H. Mobley, R. W. Griffeth, H. H. Hand, and B. M. Meglino, "Review and Conceptual Analysis of the Employee Turnover Process," *Psychological Bulletin* (May 1979), pp. 493–522.

3. For example, see J. R. Hackman and G. Oldham, *Work Redesign* (Addison-Wesley, 1980).

4. R. Katz, "Time and Work: Toward an Integrative Perspective," in B. M. Staw and L. L. Cummings, *Research in Organizational Behavior*, vol. 2 (JAI Press, 1980), pp. 81–127.

5. Hackman and Oldham, op. cit.

6. Katz, op. cit.

7. V. Vroom, *Work and Motivation* (Wiley, 1964).

8. Katz, op. cit.

9. J. W. Seybolt and S. Ross, "The Impact of Work Role Design on Job and Career Decisions," *Proceedings: 12th Annual Meeting of the American Institute for Decision Sciences* (1980).

Taking a Look at Flexitime

Philip I. Morgan and H. Kent Baker

"Working 9 to 5 — what a way to make a living. Barely getting by, it's all taking and no giving." These words of a popular song describe the typical workday for many people — 9 a.m. to 5 p.m., five consecutive days each week.

Apart from tradition, there is nothing that makes this schedule sacred. In fact, some companies are breaking with tradition and, using a system called flexitime, changing the work hours to better suit the workers and firm.

Flexitime, also referred to as flex-time, flexible hours, and even alternative work scheduling, is a relatively recent development. By allowing people to restructure their work hours, flexitime, it is believed, helps reduce absenteeism, tardiness, and turnover and increases job satisfaction, morale, and productivity. Although the concept has gained substantial management and employee support, a company's needs and objectives should be carefully evaluated before its management jumps on the flexitime bandwagon. There are advantages and disadvantages to flexitime, and before implementation a firm needs to know the conditions favoring its adoption and how to implement the system.

GROWTH OF FLEXITIME

Flexitime was first used in 1967 in Munich, Germany, at the Messerschmidt Research and Development Center. Although originally intended to ease the parking problem around the plant and reduce traffic congestion, it had unexpected positive side effects on employee attitude in terms of increased job satisfaction. Flexitime quickly spread

---

472

*PART VI
MAINTAINING
AND IMPROVING
SATISFACTION,
COMMITMENT,
AND PERFORMANCE*

to other European countries and to the United States. Today, some form of flexitime is used in about 40 percent of the labor force in Switzerland, 30 percent in West Germany, and 20 percent in France. Since it was first introduced in the United States by Control Data Corporation in 1972, companies such as Northwestern Mutual Life and Nestle and many government agencies have adopted flexitime.

Flexitime refers to a policy of replacing the traditional fixed work hours with a more flexible schedule set by employees within certain prescribed limits. These limits typically include a *core time* and *flexible time*. During core time, such as 9:30 a.m. to 3:00 p.m., all employees are required to be at work. Flexible time is a period before or after core time when employees can exercise their option to start or leave work. The prescribed band is usually between 7:00 a.m. and 9:30 a.m., and 3:00 p.m. and 6:00 p.m.

Many companies are also experimenting with a system related to flexitime called the compressed work week. Typically, the compressed work week consists of a four-day, 40-hour week, Tuesday through Friday or Monday through Thursday. Under this system workers reach agreement with their supervisors to work the requisite number of hours per day, per week, or even per month. Of course, times can vary from organization to organization and even between departments depending upon job requirements.

ADVANTAGES

Although some studies on flexitime report mixed results, most demonstrate increased benefits accruing from its adoption. Flexitime benefits the organization in two main areas: employee satisfaction and increased organizational effectiveness.

Some of the personal benefits of using flexitime are:

☐ Employees can set their own work hours to avoid traffic tie ups and other commuter problems.

☐ Employees can adjust the work hours to match their own energy rhythms, which helps to reduce stress and burn out. For example, employees who work best in the morning can schedule most of their work hours early in the day.

☐ Employees are better able to attend to personal business, such as shopping, banking, or dealing with public agencies, during regular work days.

People also prefer flexitime and the compressed work week because they provide them with more personal leisure time. For example, by working a four-day work week, workers can take a three-day weekend. Thus, flexitime and the compressed work week complement today's leisure-oriented society. Flexible work schedules also allow two-career parents to better manage the needs of their families. One parent can see the children off to school while another can be home when they return at day's end.

Some employees like the four-day work week because it eliminates both travel time and "dead time," that is, nonworking time spent on the job simply because they have to be there. In fact, some believe that they get more done because their concentration is improved.

By using flexible working hours, supervisors can plan and make better use of employees' time. Management also reports that there appears to be less time wasted. Perhaps flexitime workers tend to become more task-oriented since it is no longer necessary for them to stretch tasks to fill working hours.

In addition to these personal benefits, flexitime benefits the organization. For instance, a 1978 survey by Stanley Nollen and Virginia Martin of organizations using flexitime found that flexitime generally raised employee morale; reduced lateness in

84 percent of the cases; reduced absenteeism in more than 75 percent of the organizations; reduced turnover in more than 50 percent of the cases; cut employee commuting time in more than 75 percent of the cases; and increased productivity in almost 50 percent of the companies using it. Similar results were obtained three years earlier. This implies that the benefits of flexitime are fairly stable over time.

DISADVANTAGES

Flexitime also has its disadvantages. For example, it tends to increase overhead costs. Because the office is open longer (usually from 7:00 a.m. to 6:00 p.m.), lighting and heating costs can escalate. The extra time requirement also makes the supervisor's job more difficult, not only increasing the work day but adding to the need for careful planning. Because of the monitoring problem, it may even be necessary to purchase automatic clocks or pay supervisors and others "overtime." The rearrangement of transportation, revision of rules and facilities to accommodate different work flow patterns, and the adjustment of support services including food, medical, and communications facilities, can also prove costly.

Then, too, flexitime may be incompatible with the kind of work involved. Flexitime can play havoc with assembly line operations involving multiple shifts, machine-paced work requiring continuous worker coverage, and work needing mutual interdependence between work groups or extensive communications and interfacing.

Thus, the decision to start flexitime should not be made lightly.

There are potential negative consequences as well in adopting a compressed work week. For example, productivity of some employees may decline as they find they cannot remain at peak productivity during consecutive nine- or ten-hour days. Studies show that employees may willingly work long hours intermittently to earn time off but balk at doing it on a regular basis.

CONDITIONS FAVORING FLEXITIME

After studying 11 different companies having flexitime, a professor at Loyola University identified three conditions that favor the successful implementation of flexitime programs. Professor Petersen recommends that managers and supervisors do the following:

Set clear, appropriate goals for the flexitime program. Although flexitime may result in numerous benefits, including improved productivity and morale and decreased absenteeism and turnover, it is important to keep expectations realistic. It is easy to "oversell" the idea. Consequently, the actual results may not meet inflated expectations.

Consider the makeup of the workforce. Flexitime is generally more successful when used in the office. If it is to be used with factory workers, consideration should be given to whether the technology will allow the degree of independence necessary for a flexitime program. The employees' ages, life styles, and leisure time pursuits should also be considered. For example, Professor Petersen found that preference for traditional working hours increased with age and that male workers prefer four-day 40-hour work weeks, whereas female employees were evenly split in their preferences.

Consider the permissible degree of flexibility. Flexitime sometimes involves relinquishing power and control. How much is relinquished depends on the maturity of the workforce and its ability to handle the new freedom. There is a tendency among supervisors to increase the use of controls upon implementation of the flexitime system, although Professor Petersen reported finding the greater the degree of flexibility, the greater the benefits.

474

*PART VI
MAINTAINING
AND IMPROVING
SATISFACTION,
COMMITMENT,
AND PERFORMANCE*

IMPLEMENTING A FLEXITIME PROGRAM

Several steps can be taken to ensure the successful installation of a flexitime program. The following are critical.

1. Obtain the support of top management. Before implementing a flexitime program, supervisors should ensure that there is support for flexitime among top managers. Trying to set up a flexitime program without it dooms the project to failure from the start.

2. Solicit employee involvement at all levels. It is important to involve employees at all levels when introducing any form of organizational change, for their participation not only increases the range of inputs into the decision making process but ensures their commitment to the change because the decision was shared. In the case of flexitime, employee and union participation should be invited in the planning, design, and operation of the program.

3. Appoint a project director. It is advisable to appoint a flexitime project director to oversee all aspects of the program. This person needs to have the respect of both management and the workers.

4. Appoint a committee or task force. Depending on the size of the organization, a committee or task force should also be appointed to coordinate work assignments and hold meetings to explain the procedures necessary to implement the program. Two-way communication, especially in the beginning, will do much to allay fears and suspicions and minimize resistance to the effort.

5. Train supervisors. A training program should be used to acquaint supervisors and others about their responsibilities in the new system. Some companies have also had success publishing a small flexitime manual or handbook covering the key points of the program.

6. Run a pilot test of the program. Before implementing a flexitime program companywide, it is advisable to run a small pilot test in order to identify likely problems. This way, too, it is possible to assess whether flexitime will be suitable to the organization before too much time and money are committed.

7. Develop guidelines, policies, and procedures. As problem situations with flexitime arise and are settled, the solutions should be formalized and written into the company rules and procedures. For example, an employee may become "sick" during the day that he planned to charge as time-off hours. Can he charge that time to sick leave or must he use the time-off hours that he signed up for? The answer must be clearly written up as an organizational policy; otherwise, inconsistencies in administering the flexitime program may arise and lead to charges of inequity.

8. Set up procedures to monitor work schedules. Consideration should be given to how to monitor each employee's hours under the new system. Some companies use the honor system, allowing their employees to keep track of their own hours; others use a time clock to enter starting and stopping times. Experience with employees will dictate which system can best be used and under what circumstances. If the honor system is used, some employees may believe rightly or wrongly that other employees are taking advantage of the flexitime program. Supervisors must be alert to resolving these perceived inequities.

9. Build evaluation into the program. Some means of measuring how well the program meets objectives will have to be developed. Productivity, turnover, and absenteeism can be easily measured, but not so employee morale and job

satisfaction. For measuring those, questionnaires gauging employee attitude towards the flexitime system may be administered.

Some caution is in order here. Failure of productivity to increase may not be a sufficient reason to scrap the flexitime program. Improvement in worker morale resulting from perceived more control over the work environment may be enough to make the program worthwhile.

HOW ABOUT A FLEXIYEAR?

A logical extension of the flexitime programs is the flexiyear. About 20 companies in Germany and Austria are experimenting with this concept. For example, Beck-Feldmeier KG, Munich — a large retail store — has its employees decide on the number of hours that they want to work annually. The company employs full-time workers who work 173 hours per month and part-time employees who work between 60 and 160 hours. This means that it is possible for each employee to work three months on and three months off, only a couple of days per week, or any other schedule that suits his or her needs and those of the company.

There are many advantages to adopting a flexiyear approach as opposed to a weekly schedule. For example, in seasonal occupations it may enable employers to offer employees greater job security, since it is easier to guarantee a worker a certain amount of work over a year than over a week. With a flexiyear, though, supervisors have to begin to think of time as a key resource that they manage.

CONCLUSION

Flexitime and flexiyear are innovative approaches that give workers more control over their work and often result in improved productivity and heightened motivation and satisfaction. These programs are not panaceas. They require careful thought to be administered properly. But once people have tried flexitime, few want to return to the old system. This suggests that the positive aspects of adopting a flexitime system typically outweigh the negatives.

Safety and Health Programs
Hermine Zagat Levine

Promoting employee safety and health can be a cost-effective policy for management. Such a policy can cut down on absenteeism, keeping employees on the job and producing. Thus it is not surprising that an overwhelming majority (48 of 54, or 89 percent) of the respondents to CONSENSUS questions on safety and health reported that their companies had formal written safety policies. Slightly fewer — 45 of the 54, or 83 percent — have formal safety training programs.

In spite of this effort, all but one of the respondents reported having at least one minor accident within the past five years.

476

PART VI
MAINTAINING
AND IMPROVING
SATISFACTION,
COMMITMENT,
AND PERFORMANCE

THE CONSENSUS QUESTIONS

To find out the state of companies' safety and health programs, CONSENSUS asked readers of the January-February 1983 *Personnel* to respond to pertinent questions. (See page 11 in that issue.) We also sent questionnaires to 100 human resources managers asking the same questions in greater detail. Here's what they told us.

SAFETY POLICIES

As the first step toward creating a safe workplace, management must let employees know that the company *wants* them to use safe work procedures and practices. A formal, written safety policy statement is the most straightforward way of doing this; 48 of the 54 respondents, some 89 percent, use such a statement.

For example, the employee relations manager of a medium-size New York State consumer goods manufacturer summarized his company's policy in this way: "It is the company's policy to provide the maximum degree of safety for its personnel and property and to comply with all OSHA [Occupational Safety and Health Administration] and N.Y.S. Labor Department Regulations."

Many respondents include their statement of policy in their safety manuals, which also spell out the company's safety rules and regulations.

SAFETY TRAINING PROGRAMS

Policy statements tell employees what is expected; training programs show them how to accomplish that. A safety training program, therefore, is the next logical step in an overall safety program.

A large majority — 45 of the 54, or 83 percent — of the respondents have safety training programs. Of these, 36 train all employees — including new hires, transferees, and supervisors. In addition, eight companies specified that they train new hires; the same number specified that they train supervisors; and two specify that they train transferees.

The type of training varies for different levels of employees and/or for different functions. Here are some examples:

> All employees receive training as required based on accident statistic rates, locations, and type of accident. *(Pat Spears, personnel manager for Racal-Vadic)*

> We are currently training those employees who work with chemicals, solvents, and so forth, on proper use, handling, and safety. *(Personnel manager, small midwestern manufacturer)*

INSTRUCTORS

Many companies report that safety training is conducted by several types of instructors. The most popular choice is the employees' own supervisor — 30 companies use supervisors. A medium-size industrial manufacturer indicates, for example, that "supervisors hold monthly tailgate meetings."

Also popular as instructors are personnel staff members (27 companies) and trained in-house staff (22 companies). Outside safety advisors conduct training courses for 15 respondents — such advisors are provided by the company's insurance carrier in several instances; by state agencies in others.

While many companies provide training "as needed," others find it advantageous to schedule such sessions on a regular basis. Sixteen companies schedule sessions once a month; five conduct them once a year; and five conduct them when an employee is hired or newly transferred. Some companies use various schedules.

For example, Albert T. Metzger, the manager of safety/training-GPD, for McCormick & Company, Inc., states that the company has a "Yearly Safety Day with outside speakers, displays of on-the-job and off-the-job safety equipment. Specific subjects [are] discussed at monthly department meetings."

He also notes that the company schedules "periodic meetings" about specific safety problems. For example, the company is currently conducting an "in-house back-care seminar."

Other companies conduct programs on a weekly, biweekly, or quarterly basis.

SYSTEM FOR IDENTIFYING HAZARDS

No safety program is effective if it doesn't identify hazards before accidents occur. It's no wonder, then, that all but three of the respondents have systems for identifying safety problems and potential hazards. Such systems include one or more of the following: regularly scheduled routine workplace inspections (47), job safety analyses (23), and special inspections (9).

Routine inspections may be conducted by a member of the safety department — such as a safety engineer or safety director — members of the safety committee, or insurance company representatives.

Special inspections are frequently conducted after an accident or when accident statistics indicate that a specific area or operation is hazardous.

Job safety analyses, on the other hand, are usually made when a new job is launched or when an operation seems to be posing an unexpected hazard. For example, a large consumer goods manufacturer uses its job operation instruction breakdown not only to explain the important steps in the job, but also to spell out "anything in a step that might make or break the job, injure the employee, or cause injury to others, damage equipment, or make the work easier to do."

PROTECTIVE EQUIPMENT

Many operations, particularly in manufacturing and construction, require the use of safety equipment. A surprising 51 of the 54 respondents (94 percent) have operations that require such equipment.

In such operations, the company has both a legal (under OSHA or the state equivalent) and moral obligation to make sure that employees use the equipment. Most companies make this the supervisor's responsibility. Others make the worker him- or herself responsible; some of these indicate that failure to comply with the requirements is grounds for disciplinary action. Compliance may also be part of performance review.

Companies frequently post rules or warning notices in areas posing dangers that require protective equipment. Plant or facility managers or safety officers frequently make regular rounds or spot checks to make sure employees are complying with rules.

Because protective equipment may be expensive, companies may supply equipment (20), subsidize the purchase (7), or do both (22). (Two of the 51 companies that require protective equipment didn't answer this question.)

In most cases companies supply such required equipment as respirators, hard hats,

478

PART VI
MAINTAINING
AND IMPROVING
SATISFACTION,
COMMITMENT,
AND PERFORMANCE

safety gloves or other apparel, and/or earplugs. On the other hand, they may only subsidize the cost of safety shoes or safety glasses. For example, Ipsen Industries' policy on safety shoes and safety glasses is this:

Safety Shoes: Employees who spend a considerable amount of time in the manufacturing areas of the plant are urged to purchase safety shoes. You will be allowed a rebate once a year of ½ the cost of a pair of safety shoes up to a maximum rebate of $25.00. Further information may be obtained from the personnel department.

Safety Glasses: The company provides nonprescription safety glasses, at company expense, for all employees whose job requires them to enter restricted plant areas where they must wear safety glasses. If you wear prescription glasses and are required to enter restricted areas, the company will provide your first pair of prescription safety glasses. Eye examinations and all replacements of prescription safety glasses which occur more often than once a year will be your responsibility unless the replacement is caused by work-related damage. See the personnel department for details.

MOTIVATION

Employees must continuously be reminded to work safely. Employers use a variety of techniques to get this message across. Posters or notices on the bulletin board are the most popular; 50 of the 54 respondents, some 93 percent, use this method.

Other popular means of communication include employee publications (37), safety films (34), safety contests (21), and special incentives (21). Other motivation methods include insurance company programs, safety committee meetings, periodic meetings with supervisors, signs and banners, annual hearing tests, employee suggestion award systems, individual communication, and videotapes. One company notes that it provides "negative motivation — for example, loss of job."

ACCIDENT RECORDS

Because OSHA and equivalent state agencies require nearly all employers to keep accident records and because most employers believe that this is an effective tool to help prevent future accidents, all 54 respondents reported that they keep such records. Such records may simply be the forms required by government agencies or graphs and statistics covering a number of years' experience for internal use.

The records are kept by the personnel department in 35 of the 54 responding companies, by the benefits department in two, and by others, such as the safety and/or health department, the claims department, the medical department, or the risk management department, in the 17 other responding companies.

Most frequently, it is the supervisor's responsibility to report the accident to the recordkeeper — 43 companies place this responsibility on the supervisor. However, 23 companies place some or all of the responsibility on the worker involved to report the accident. Eight respondents require the personnel department to report accidents, and six call for the medical department or the plant nurse to carry out this responsibility.

ACCIDENT OCCURRENCES

A remarkable 53 of the 54 respondents reported that their firms had had at least one minor accident within the past five years. Thirty-eight of these (72 percent) reported that minor injuries were involved; 23 said serious injuries were involved; and nine reported that one or more employee deaths resulted.

Accidents, even minor ones, call for remedial action. Some remedies used by respondents include eliminating the cause, working with the employee and supervisor, changing processes, providing more training, conducting investigations by safety officers or engineers, enforcing rules more strictly and setting up incentive programs.

A medium-size manufacturer requires supervisors to include suggested remedies in their accident reports. Welk Brothers Metal Products Inc. makes future employment contingent on employee's compliance with safety rules.

Of the accidents that occurred, 14 companies reported that one or more were serious enough to warrant investigations by regulatory agencies.

In nine of the investigations, the companies were found to be not responsible for the accident. In three instances, companies were found responsible and penalized, while in two instances the companies were found responsible but not penalized. Only one company appealed verdicts in which it had been found responsible; here the courts' decisions were split between those that upheld the agencies' verdicts and those that dismissed the verdicts.

OTHER INSPECTIONS BY GOVERNMENT AGENCIES

Forty-three respondents report that their firms have been inspected by government agencies at times other than when accidents have occurred. Such inspections are generally routine or in response to employee complaints. Most companies reported no special problems arising from these inspections, although some admit being assessed small fines for minor violations. One southern medium-size manufacturer reports "Numerous OSHA and NIOSH [National Institute for Occupational Safety and Health] inspections and many court battles over harassment by agencies."

On the other hand, several companies reported that they have used agency consultation services to prevent or remedy health or safety hazards.

FIRST AID EQUIPMENT AND MEDICAL SERVICES

Effective safety programs rely on such backup services as first aid equipment and medical personnel. Fifty-one of the respondents have first aid equipment on hand, ranging from basic first aid kits to a fully equipped ambulance with trained personnel. Among the equipment kept on company premises are blankets, stretchers, wheel chairs, eyewash equipment, oxygen, and nonprescription drugs.

In several cases, respondents note that outside medical supply services maintain their first aid equipment.

Forty-eight respondents have trained first-aiders on the premises at all times; 43 have people trained in cardio-pulmonary resuscitation (CPR), 26 have nurses on staff, and eight have doctors — five of them part-timers. A number of companies have emergency medical technicians, and one, a small manufacturer, reported having 21 industrial medical technologists on staff.

As for medical services, 43 companies report that they are situated near a hospital; 36 are located near a clinic, and 20 have a doctor on call. Other companies depend on community groups, such as fire departments or ambulance services, to provide emergency medical services. One respondent, a small government agency, reports having a plant hospital.

Many companies go one step further: 48 respondents provide first aid or CPR training to employees — many through the American Red Cross. Many make such training available to any employee who wishes it. Others limit it to supervisors — one

480

*PART VI
MAINTAINING
AND IMPROVING
SATISFACTION,
COMMITMENT,
AND PERFORMANCE*

makes CPR training mandatory for all supervisors. The company with trained industrial medical technologists provides this type of training once a year and offers follow-up "monthly skills practice and techniques training."

HEALTH-RELATED PROGRAMS

Providing ways for employees to learn and practice good health habits is another way that companies can attack the problem of absenteeism. Only a very few respondents, however, report using such techniques. Among the 54 survey respondents, for example, only four have onsite exercise facilities, such as tennis and volley ball courts, jogging tracks, exercise machines, aerobics classes, weight rooms, or shower facilities. Many companies, of course, don't have space for such facilities on premises, but only seven others subsidize employees' use of outside health or exercise facilities, and these are usually limited to executives or selected groups of employees.

Even such simple projects as weight-reduction classes or stop-smoking clinics have not been widely adopted — only 14 respondents have such programs.

On the other hand, some companies place great emphasis on such activities. Albert T. Metzger, for example, reports that his company "sponsors an annual Health Fair Day" during which employees receive diabetes and sickle cell anemia checks, pap smears, eye tests, and blood pressure checks.

VERDICTS ON OSHA

Before the Reagan administration took office, OSHA was subjected to a great deal of criticism from industry. Because of that, the agency under Reagan appointee, Assistant Labor Secretary Thorne G. Auchter, has changed its policies — cutting down on required records and the number of safety and health standards that are enforced and promulgated.

In response to the question on the effectiveness of OSHA, 30 or 56 percent of the 54 respondents gave the agency high marks; 17 or 34 percent said it wasn't effective, and three had mixed feelings. One of the latter, a medium-size western manufacturer, said; "They provide incentives for safe work programs; however, their contacts are mainly punitive in nature only."

On the positive side, Metzger of McCormick & Co. said, "I think that if we didn't have OSHA or other regulatory agencies to monitor the work environment, some companies would be lax in their safety programs."

As for the changes in direction, 23 respondents (43 percent) felt the agency is now more effective; 13 (24 percent) felt that the changes had made no difference; the rest of the respondents didn't know, felt it was too soon to tell, or didn't answer.

Positive reactions include these:

They seem more concerned with the "spirit" of the law as opposed to the letter, that is, the height of handrails, the color of aisle markings, and so forth. *(Personnel manager of a small industrial manufacturer)*

They appear to be more cooperative and willing to work with business and its problems where they used to act like cops only — "find them and fine them" [seemed to be the motto]. *(Section manager/salaried personnel of a medium-size consumer goods manufacturer)*

Here are some negative reactions:

Confusion over authority and direction of programs makes it difficult to know what to expect. *(Emma L. Waters, personnel manager, Swift & Company R&D Center)*

I believe having the ability to call trustworthy employers on receiving complaints from employees frees the OSHA inspector for other problems. *(Fountain L. Ray, Jr., supervisor, safety and health, Rockwell International)*

THE WINDUP

Results of this survey indicate that respondents are paying a great deal of attention to the safety of their employees, but little to promoting good health habits. This may be because the results of safety promotion are more immediately apparent than those of encouraging good health habits. Over the long run, however, companies should probably think seriously about the cost effectiveness of such health-related activities as stress-reduction classes, weight-reduction groups, and stop-smoking clinics or simply encouraging participation in sports, jogging, or some other kind of exercise activities.

D.

COMPENSATION AND MOTIVATION

Interview with Francis W. Miller

Francis Miller is executive director of the American Compensation Association (ACA), a position he has held for the last nine years. ACA is an 8,000-member professional organization headquartered in Scottsdale, Arizona. Before assuming his present position, Mr. Miller was director of compensation at Honeywell Information Systems.

Mr. Miller is a member of the board of directors of the American Society of Association Executives. He is both an Accredited Personnel Diplomat and a Certified Compensation Professional. He holds a master's degree in economics from the University of Minnesota.

1. *What is the American Compensation Association* (ACA) *and how does the journal* Compensation Review *fit into the goals of the ACA?*

ACA is a nonprofit association of professionals who design, implement, and manage employee compensation and benefits programs for their respective organizations. It has been in existence since 1959 and is primarily noted for providing comprehensive educational seminars for those seeking instruction in both the theoretical and practical aspects of the field. ACA's membership includes practitioners from all levels of compensation management — in manufacturing, finance, health care, utilities, government, education, and service industries. *Compensation Review* publishes timely and useful compensation information and supplements/reinforces the educational process.

2. *What objectives should a compensation system in an organization attempt to achieve? How well do you believe compensation systems in practice attain these objectives?*

There is no question that the design and development of pay programs have grown increasingly complex over the last several years. The classical objectives of a compensation program are to attract, retain and motivate employees. In addition, a good compensation program should provide internal equity and external competitiveness, productivity incentive, ownership protection, and administrative efficiency, as well as being in compliance with the many laws and regulations.

The compensation profession is better educated, more experienced, and more innovative than at any time in history. And pay programs generally, although not perfectly, reflect this increased level of expertise.

3. *The Equal Pay Act and the current public discussion of "equal pay for jobs of comparable worth" have created pressures for organizations to change their compensation policies and practices. How have organizations responded to these pressures?*

I think very well! In many firms the compensation professional has assumed a leadership role. The technology exists for designing and administering a sound pay program that is bias-free. If the typical professional has that as his or her goal, the actual product of these programs should be far more equitable than it has ever been in our history.

4. *What is your sense of the comparable worth controversy? What would be the pros and cons of pay systems based on the notion of comparable worth?*

The concept of comparable worth is gaining appeal. I believe it will be a dominant issue for the balance of the 1980s and perhaps even into the 1990s. Because of the political possibilities, I see the initial thrust to be primarily in the public sector. There is no question, however, that it will spread inexorably to the private sector. It is very difficult to argue this concept in the abstract. It is also very difficult to get agreement on a simple definition of what constitutes comparable worth. ACA's position, and one that I support fully, is that the challenge to the compensation professional is to strike a balance between the external market forces and internal pay relationships. Neither internal equity nor the external market is a valid criterion in and of itself. If organizations are to manage their human resources effectively while at the same time compete in the marketplace, they must balance both factors.

5. *Pay is not the only motivator of individual performance. How can compensation systems be integrated with other forms of motivation such as job enrichment, MBO, promotion, positive reinforcement, and so forth?*

I believe one of the key factors that differentiates the journeyman compensation professional from the learner is his or her ability to think in terms of systems as opposed to components. Organizations are so complex that the subsystems must be designed so that they provide an integrated, coherent result. It is important that the compensation professional work closely with the other functions in the human resource area because so many of the programs are interrelated. There also is a need for humility! A good example is the progress that has been made in cafeteria-type benefit programs. We have learned that we can increase value-motivation by letting the employee make some of the decisions.

6. *What are the most important pieces of legislation affecting compensation practices?*

One would have to mention the Wage-hour Law, the Equal Pay Act, the Civil Rights Act, ERISA, ERTA, and TEFRA. In the next few years I look for significant legislation concerning comparable worth, the taxation of employee benefits, medical cost control, social security, and federal and military pensions.

7. *How do executive compensation programs differ from those applied to other positions? What are the components of an executive compensation plan?*

The basic components of an executive pay program are salary, benefits, short-term incentives, long-term incentives, and perquisites. The principal difference is that the cash compensation is typically comprised of salary plus bonus. There also is a greater

484

*PART VI
MAINTAINING
AND IMPROVING
SATISFACTION,
COMMITMENT,
AND PERFORMANCE*

emphasis on capital accumulation with executive plans. The short- and long-term incentives and the "perks" are also unique to the executive pay program.

8. *The range of employee benefits and their cost effectiveness have been much discussed in the recent literature. What important trends do you see in the field of employee benefits? What is the potential of the "cafeteria-style" benefit programs you mentioned earlier?*

There have been a number of recent important trends such as the widespread addition of 401k salary reduction plans; an increase in the number of employee stock ownership plans; a rapid drop in "first dollar" medical benefits as reflected by an increased use of "front-end" deductibles and decreased use of 100 percent reimbursement for hospital room and board; a shorter averaging period for final average pension plans; an increased use of capital accumulation plans; more dental plans; and a continuing liberalization of both vacation and holidays. In terms of "cafeteria-style" benefit programs, as I mentioned earlier, this is a refreshing trend which I see continuing to accelerate. Most larger and more sophisticated firms now offer partial — if not full — cafeteria plans. I see the movement continuing into middle and smaller sized firms.

9. *What is a Certified Compensation Professional (CCP) and how does one become accredited?*

The ACA certification program was inaugurated in 1976. Already almost a thousand people have been certified and there are over three thousand in the "pipeline." Fourteen separate courses are offered through ACA. The courses are designed for those seeking competency in all the functional areas that comprise the profession; for example, executive compensation, sales compensation, and so forth. To become certified a person must pass six examinations, five of which are required and one of which is elective. The tests must be completed within a five-year period. It is not necessary to be a member of ACA to become certified, nor is it necessary to take any seminars. The examinations are available to everyone.

10. *What role does the computer play in compensation administration today?*

Computer literacy is now a "must" for every compensation professional. ACA is so convinced of this that we have invested over $100,000 in portable computers which we transport around the country to teach computer literacy. We offer a seminar that is two and a half days long and each person has his own personal computer for the full two and a half days. Another indicator of computer impact is the extensive array of software packages designed specifically for the compensation professional.

11. *There are a number of human resource professional associations. Do you see these as being competitive?*

Definitely not. As a matter of fact, it is just the opposite. I have been very active and supportive of an organization called the Council of Human Resource Management Associations. This consists of some eight organizations in this field, including ACA, American Society of Personnel Administration (ASPA), American Society of Training Directors, Employment Managers Association, International Personnel Management Association, College and University Personnel Association, and College Placement Council. We meet about twice a year and share trends and information which helps each of us do a better job. We also work cooperatively where it makes sense to do so. For example, ASPA and ACA have teamed up on several major projects. We exchange a mailing list among the organizations when we have catalogs or other information which we think might be of interest to those members. In addition, I consider myself to be personal friends with each one of the other participants.

12. *What experience, education, and skills are necessary to be a compensation manager today? Will these qualifications change in the future? Are there entry level positions available in compensation for recent college graduates? If so, what are they?*

I believe that over time the requirements specified to become a Certified Compensation Professional will generally be accepted as a starting point — a foundation. The compensation manager today must be smarter, better educated, and have broader perspectives and skills than ever before in history. In the old days it was not uncommon for Human Resource positions to be filled with relatives and/or executives who had failed in some other functional capacity. This is rarely the case today. Jobs are so demanding, and technical obsolescence so real, that only the swift will survive! The common characteristic of all the survivors will be a perpetual drive to keep abreast of the latest developments in the field.

Certainly most firms (especially larger ones) have entry level positions in the compensation and human resource field. Many firms rotate assignments to broaden the person's background. I would encourage any college graduate interested in entering the human resource field to select a company with progressive policies. This is the best guarantee for accelerated career development.

PART VI: FOR DISCUSSION AND REVIEW

A.

Gadon

- □ What specifically is QWL?
- □ What are the assumptions common to the various QWL programs?
- □ Explain why QWL programs are currently popular with American corporations, despite being in existence for over 40 years.

Business Week

- □ What is "Employee Involvement" and how does it differ from QWL programs?
- □ What effects has EI had on product quality and employee attitudes at Ford?
- □ Are EI and QWL programs fads or are they here to stay?

Yankelovich

- □ Summarize the author's position. Do you agree or disagree with him? Why?
- □ What would be required to improve productivity and better employ the work ethic?

486

*PART VI
MAINTAINING
AND IMPROVING
SATISFACTION,
COMMITMENT,
AND PERFORMANCE*

B.

Henderson

- □ What did the 1938 Fair Labor Standards Act (FLSA) establish?
- □ What factors led to the passage of the 1974 Employee Retirement Income Security Act?
- □ What practices or organizations are covered by Title VII of the 1964 Civil Rights Act (CRA)?

Wallace and Fay

- □ What is the purpose of job evaluation?
- □ How does job evaluation ensure internal equity?
- □ How do the ranking method and the point method of job evaluation differ?

Lawler

- □ Why does the author say that incentive pay is a mixed blessing?
- □ Explain how societal changes have resulted in the declining popularity of piece-rate pay.
- □ What conditions in an organization would facilitate an effective incentive pay system?

Hills

- □ What is comparable worth? How is it different from equal pay for equal work?
- □ Would the development of a universal job evaluation plan eliminate the problem of comparable worth?
- □ What would disadvantages and problems with comparable worth be?

C.

Seybolt

- □ Discuss the causes of turnover.
- □ How do the causes of turnover vary for different groups of workers?

Morgan and Baker

- □ Why would organizations resist implementing flexitime programs?
- □ What are some organizational conditions that should facilitate the successful implementation of a flexitime program?
- □ How could the dollar costs of flexitime be determined?

Levine

- □ How might an organization take a positive position with respect to its overall safety program?
- □ How can a safety program be evaluated?

PART VII
PERSONNEL/HUMAN RESOURCE MANAGEMENT IN THE CONTEMPORARY ENVIRONMENT

A.

DISCRIMINATION AND EQUAL EMPLOYMENT OPPORTUNITY

Women in Management: A Research Review
James R. Terborg

- ☐ Reviews the literature pertaining to the entry and socialization of women into management roles.
- ☐ Suggests areas where the research evidence on women in management is inadequate.

The Pregnancy Discrimination Act: Compliance Problems
John P. Kohl and Paul S. Greenlaw

- ☐ Details what organizations should do to comply with the law.
- ☐ Reports the results of a survey on organizational compliance.
- ☐ Offers suggestions on improving compliance.

Sexual Harassment: Critical Review of Legal Cases with General Principles and Preventive Measures
Robert H. Faley

- ☐ Reviews sexual harassment court cases with the goal of understanding how sexual harassment has been legally defined.
- ☐ Details principles and preventive actions organizations should become familiar with.

Workforce of the Future: The Problems and Opportunities of Maturity
Edward J. Harrick and Paul E. Sultan

- ☐ Discusses the potential impact of an aging work force on P/HRM.
- ☐ Reviews the literature on the older worker.

B.

HEALTH AND WELLNESS, EMPLOYEE ASSISTANCE PROGRAMS, AND STRESS

Physical Fitness and Employee Effectiveness
John J. Hoffman, Jr., and Charles J. Hobson

- ☐ Describes three basic categories of corporate fitness programs.
- ☐ Reviews the research evidence relating fitness to outcome measures, such as performance and satisfaction.

Improving Corporate Performance through Employee-Assistance Programs
Julian L. Carr and Richard T. Hellan

- ☐ Describes common types of employee assistance programs.
- ☐ Enumerates the benefits to both the individual and the organization accruing from employee assistance programs.

Stress: Can We Cope?
Time

- ☐ Addresses a universal and pervasive problem: the stress epidemic.
- ☐ Presents a general review of the stress literature and research, with practical implications.

C.

EMPLOYEE RIGHTS AND TERMINATION-AT-WILL

Privacy Regulation
James Ledvinka

- ☐ Addresses the issue of who should control employee information.
- ☐ Discusses the use of lie detectors in an employment context.

Erosion of the Employment-at-Will Doctrine
Emily A. Joiner

- ☐ Explains the employment-at-will doctrine.
- ☐ Details common-law challenges to at-will terminations.
- ☐ Discusses the future of the employment-at-will doctrine.

D.

COSTING OF HUMAN RESOURCE MANAGEMENT

The Financial Impact of Employee Attitudes
Wayne F. Cascio

- ☐ Argues for determination of the financial impact of attitudes on employee behavior and organizational effectiveness.
- ☐ Presents the behavior costing approach, its advantages and disadvantages, and underlying assumptions.

Quantifying the Human Resources Function
Jac Fitz-Enz

- ☐ Argues that human resource managers must speak to the "bottom-line" and that human resource departments must show their contribution to profits.
- ☐ Offers suggestions for demonstrating how a human resource department can measure its effectiveness.

E.

LABOR RELATIONS

Lifeboat Labor Relations: Collective Bargaining in Heavy Seas
Arnold Weber

- ☐ Reviews the basic characteristics of the American labor management system during the 1970s.
- ☐ Discusses environmental changes that challenge existing assumptions and practices of collective bargaining.
- ☐ Projects future trends in collective bargaining agreements.

The 1982 Union Wage Concessions: A Turning Point for Collective Bargaining?
Daniel J. B. Mitchell

- ☐ Addresses the debate that concessions bargaining during 1982 signalled a fundamental change in collective bargaining.
- ☐ Argues that the 1982 concessions had the potential for making fundamental changes in collective bargaining.

F.

PERSONNEL RESEARCH

Personnel Research
William H. Holley and Kenneth M. Jennings

- ☐ Describes personnel research and explains its importance.
- ☐ Provides a brief overview to six types of personnel research activities.

G.

LABOR UNIONS

Interview with Ronnie J. Straw

A.

DISCRIMINATION AND EQUAL EMPLOYMENT OPPORTUNITY

Women in Management: A Research Review

James R. Terborg

This article reviews recent literature on the psychological processes surrounding the integration of women into management. Reviews of research published prior to 1974 and discussions of related issues can be found in Gordon and Strober (1975), Hoffman and Nye (1974), O'Leary (1974), and Terborg and Ilgen (1975).

The present review focuses on two broad topics: the entry of women into management and the socialization of women once they have gained entry. These topics and the treatment of issues within topics were organized to follow a developmental progression that begins with choice of a career and ends with conflicting role demands that are encountered by women managers. This categorization provides a logical framework within which to consider the diverse literature on women in management and allows for the identification of important areas where little data currently exist. Specifically, the section on entry deals with the relationship between self-concept and career choice, problems associated with blocked career pathways, the validity of sex stereotypes as an explanation for hiring discrimination, and factors affecting women's choices of organizations within which to work. The section on socialization deals with three process stages corresponding to anticipatory socialization, encounter and accommodation, and role management. The review ends with a set of summary statements and a set of recommendations for further research.

ENTRY

Self-Concept and Career Choice

Theory and research on career choice points to the importance of a person's self-concept as a determinant of vocational preferences. Other things being equal, people will choose careers that are consistent with their beliefs about themselves (Korman, 1970).

The existence of a "male managerial model," however, perpetuates societal norms

From the *Journal of Applied Psychology* 62, 6, 1977, pp. 647–664. Copyright 1977 by the American Psychological Association. Reprinted by permission of the publisher and author.

that women should not or cannot be successful in management. McClellend (1965) and O'Leary (1974) both report that women as a group describe themselves as different from or even opposite to men as a group on presumed requisite management traits. Schein (1973, 1975) has shown that these beliefs are strongly held by male and female managers as well. Maccoby and Jacklin (1974), in an extensive review of sex differences, conclude that self-confidence is one achievement-related characteristic that consistently differentiates the sexes. Performance expectancies and self-evaluations of abilities are lower among women than men. Although these differences can be affected by situational characteristics (Lenney, 1977), the prevalence of low self-confidence among women may have long-range effects with regard to their career choice.

Some research on career and vocational choice with women has shown that the rejection of stereotyped sex roles may be an important factor in later career decisions. Almquist (1974) and Vogel, Broverman, Broverman, Clarkson, and Rosenkrantz (1970) found that women who chose nontraditional careers (i.e., jobs that historically have been occupied by men) were raised in families in which the mother worked full time. These authors proposed that highly differentiated sex role beliefs concerning male and female behaviors would be less likely to develop when the mother worked because both parents would share in support of the family and in household duties. Attitudes concerning the role of women in our society also were related to occupational interests as measured by the Strong-Campbell Interest Inventory (Tipton, 1976). Female college students with traditional sex role attitudes scored high on conventional sex-typed occupations, whereas those with more liberal attitudes had little in common with such occupations.

Blocked Career Pathways

The rejection of sex role stereotypes and the development of self-concepts consistent with managerial positions do not guarantee entry into these positions. Research indicates that pressures are exerted by vocational counselors and family members that discourage women from fulfilling their career aspirations in nontraditional occupations.

Schein (1971) noted that she was advised to contact Dr. Joyce Brothers for employment rather than to consider a career as a psychologist in industry. In a more serious vein, Weisman, Morlock, Sack, and Levine (1976) found that counseling given to women who were denied entry into medical school was different from that given to men who were denied entry. Men were encouraged to reapply to more schools or to consider a PhD program in a related field. Women were warned of the difficulties that would lie ahead if they chose to persist in medicine and were encouraged to change their career aspirations to more sex-role-accepted professions such as nursing. It should be noted that there were no ability differences due to sex between the rejected student groups so that this can be ruled out as a reason for differential counseling.

The consequences of these continued practices might be to lower the self-concepts of the affected women and to perpetuate sex-typed occupations. Of interest, however, were the findings that women who supported the women's rights movement showed a higher degree of persistence in having a medical career than women who did not support the women's rights movement (Weisman et al., 1976). These findings are consistent with those reported by Tipton (1976) concerning occupational interests.

Ahrons (1976) had 289 high school counselors rate several occupational concepts (e.g., nurse, engineer, career women, career man) using the sematic differential technique. Counselors of each sex reported high similarity among the male occupational concepts and among the female occupational concepts with the exception of the career women concept, which was dissimilar from all others. Ahrons concluded that counselors with such biases may discourage women from choosing nontraditional careers.

Lack of support and encouragement for women choosing nontraditional careers also exists within the family. Goodale and Hall (1976) reported that high school students of both sexes had similar aspirations for college and career choice, yet male students indicated significantly more parental interest and pressure in the pursuit of their aspirations.

Stereotypes as an Explanation for Job Entry Discrimination

Discrimination at the entry level refers to non-job-related limitations placed on an identifiable subgroup at the time a position is filled. Rejection of subgroup applicants for non-job-related reasons, failure to recruit subgroup applicants for certain positions, and lower starting salaries represent some forms of this type of discrimination (Terborg & Ilgen, 1975).

The existence of various stereotypes has been frequently invoked as an explanation for the following findings: Compared to men, women are rated less desirable for management positions, are extended fewer job offers, and receive lower salaries (cf. Bowman, Worthy, & Greyson, 1965; Cecil, Paul & Olins, 1973; Cohen & Bunker, 1975; Dipboye, Fromkin, & Wiback, 1975; Haefner, 1977; Rosen & Jerdee, 1974a, 1974b; Schein, 1973, 1975; Terborg & Ilgen, 1975; Ullrich & Holden, Note 1). There are several issues that should be resolved, however, before the pervasive effects of stereotypes are accepted. These include the possibility that stereotypes are not operating at all but that many women are not qualified for management positions, the manner in which job applicants are depicted in experimental situations, the effect of situational variables on the saliency of stereotypes, and the distinction between sex role stereotypes and sex-characteristic stereotypes. Each of these is discussed below.

Most working women probably are not qualified for management positions. This is not meant to suggest that women lack potential for the job, but that the cumulative effects of past discrimination have prevented women from gaining necessary skills and experience. Goetz and Herman (Note 2) and Deaux (Note 3) found that even when job level was controlled, women were in positions of less responsibility, power, and influence.

Assuming that these findings are typical, the results reported by Ullrich and Holden (Note 1) are not surprising. They surveyed employees in the U.S. Forest Service and asked them to rate the existing capability of men and women to handle top-level positions in the organization. Women were rated less capable than men. This was attributed to stereotypes and sex bias because the effect was found only among respondents who were men. Schein (Note 4) pointed out, however, that these men may have been reflecting reality because the women in that organization had little managerial experience. Thus, the differential ratings would not necessarily be the result of stereotypes.

The manner in which job applicants are depicted presents another problem. In some studies, respondents are asked to evaluate the "typical woman" or the "typical manager," etc. In other studies, respondents may only be told that the applicant for a white-collar job is a woman. O'Leary (1974) and Brigham (1971) warn that the use of different instructional sets to elicit stereotypic profiles or evaluative responses may produce different results. For example, Brigham (1971) stated that asking about the "typical black" and the "typical white" confounds race with socioeconomic status. When these are varied systematically, socioeconomic status accounts for more response variance than race. Similarly, asking about the "typical woman" and the "typical manager" confounds sex with occupation because most managers are men. Consider the different profiles that might be provided to the instructional set of "typical woman" and "typical woman MBA." The "typical woman MBA" may elicit the same profile and evaluative response as the "typical man MBA." General stereotypes do not apply to *all* subgroups or to *all* individuals within a subgroup just as general attitudes do not predict specific behaviors toward a particular object (Ajzen & Fishbein, 1973; Brigham, 1971; Feldman & Hilterman, 1975).

The situation represents another variable that has been found to affect the predictive validity of stereotypes. Rosen and Jerdee (1974c) reported that stereotypes had little impact on personnel decisions when specific rules were operative. Similarly, Terborg and Ilgen (1975) found that attitudes toward women as managers were related to subsequent behaviors only in situations in which little information about the woman was provided. Knowledge of stereotypes will only be useful when relevant situational conditions that facilitate and minimize the expression of stereotypes are specified (Terborg, Peters, Ilgen, & Smith, 1977).

One situational condition that merits further investigation concerns the availability of job-related information. Evidence indicates that predictors such as biographical data and assessment center ratings, which have been validated on men, also predict managerial performance for women (Huck & Bray, 1976; Moses & Boehm, 1975; Nevo, 1976). Such information could reduce the discriminatory effects of stereotypes.

Finally, it may be valuable to make a distinction between sex role stereotypes and sex-characteristic stereotypes. Sex role stereotypes refer to widely held beliefs concerning appropriate male and female behavior. For example, it may be acceptable for a supervisor who is a man to verbally chastize a recalcitrant subordinate, whereas the same behavior by a woman supervisor may be perceived as out of role and unacceptable. The ability of the person to display the behavior is not an issue.

Sex-characteristic stereotypes refer to widely held beliefs concerning sex differences on various personality traits. The implication is that women are not able to be aggressive, are too emotional, etc. The validity of sex differences on such characteristics, especially as they relate to managerial job performance, has been questioned (Maccoby & Jacklin, 1974). Further, even on characteristics where there are sex differences, the overlap in distributions is so large that valid individual predictions from group characteristics are impossible.

What is important is that these two types of stereotypes may be differentially affected by manipulations and that they may be differentially related to evaluative responses. For example, Bowman et al. (1965) found that even when women were perceived as capable, they were not judged desirable for management because of anticipated resistance by co-workers. Although this study was not designed to answer the question, it is possible to speculate that sex-characteristic stereotypes were not in operation, but sex role stereotypes were in operation.

Choice of an Organization

The acceptance of a job with a particular company is the result of a dual-decision process: Members of the organization evaluate the job applicant and the job applicant evaluates the organization.

Terborg and Ilgen (1975) suggested that one subtle but effective means for denying women entry into an organization would be to offer lower starting salaries to women applicants. The intention of such an offer would be to get the applicant to decide against that company. The organization would appear to comply with Equal Employment Opportunity Commission guidelines concerning minority employees because an offer was extended. Economists and others (cf. Rosen & Jerdee, 1975b; Treiman & Terrell, 1975) have countered with the argument that lower salaries offered to women are justified for economic reasons and do not represent discrimination. The logic is that women as a group are less likely to provide a return on the company's recruitment and training costs because women terminate employment sooner than men. Simply stated, women are worth less from a cost–benefit standpoint.

The fallacy of this argument is twofold. First, studies using aggregate data have found that women do not take more sick leave, terminate sooner, etc., than men (East, 1972; Hoffman & Nye, 1974). Second, even if women did display such behaviors in certain situations, the reason may reside in the lower salaries women are paid. If women perceive their rewards as inequitable, then they should be less likely to remain with the organization. Similar findings have been reported for men (Dansereau, Cashman, & Graen, 1973; Lawler, 1971). Thus, although some women may display the behaviors that seem to justify their lower salaries, they may be victims of unfair employment practices. Women still lag behind men in salaries (Treiman & Terrell, 1975); however, this may be changing in some occupations. Recent statistics compiled by the College Placement Council on 1976 college graduates show that in technological fields women are being offered higher salaries than men.

On factors other than salary, the reviewed literature contained no studies that examined the processes associated with a woman's job choice. Some research has been done with male accountants (cf. Lawler, Kuleck, Rhode, & Sorensen, 1975), but little is known about variables affecting how *women* make job choice decisions and the accuracy of those decisions.

SOCIALIZATION

Regardless of whether a woman is hired from outside the organization or promoted from within, she faces a new environment and must learn to behave effectively in that environment. New employees of either sex must be socialized properly if they are to fit with the established functioning of existing work units and if they are to develop into contributing members of organizations.

Factors Affecting Socialization

Based on the work of Feldman (1976), Graen (1976), Hall (1971), Katz and Kahn (1966), Van Maanen (1975), and Wanous (1977), the following discussion identifies factors relevant to socialization and considers them in the same temporal order as that encountered by newcomers.

The first stage in socialization occurs prior to the time the individual enters the organization, or, in the case of a promotion, advances to a new position. Relevant factors in this anticipatory socialization period are (a) information the individual has concerning the functioning of the organization and the duties required of a person in the position and (b) the degree to which the individual and members of the organization share in the belief that exchanges of resources will be mutually rewarding for all involved. If employment decisions made at this stage are based on faulty information or unrealistic expectations, then the newcomer and members of the organization may encounter difficulty achieving effective socialization (Feldman, 1976; Wanous, 1977).

The second stage involves the newcomer's encounter and accommodation with the technological and social aspects of the job (Feldman, 1976; Van Mannen, 1975). Through initiation to job duties and co-workers, newcomers learn what tasks are to be performed, priorities associated with the tasks, and specific methods used in doing the tasks (Katz & Kahn, 1966). The technological demands of the job dictate work flow and specify necessary skills and abilities. Co-workers who have an interest in, and dependency on, the newcomer communicate prescriptions and proscriptions for job behavior. Over time, evaluations are made concerning the adequacy of the newcomer's behavior and performance. Deviations from the expected pattern may result in additional pressures on the newcomer to conform, alterations in the content of the communicated expectations, or some combination of both (Graen, 1976).

The final stage deals with role management, or the newcomer's ability to cope effectively with conflicting behavior and performance demands (Feldman, 1976; Van Mannen & Schein, 1977). Schedules associated with homelife and the family, and personal attributes of the newcomer, such as idiosyncratic needs, values, and motives, exert pressure on the individual concerning allocation of time, energy, and resources. These non-job-related sources may make demands that conflict with those communicated by job-related sources. Inability to cope with these conflicts is a barrier to effective socialization.

The development of the newcomer into a contributing member of the organization is a by-product of successful socialization. This comes about through attainment of meaningful goals by independent effort and the use of one's skills and abilities (Hall, 1971). Newcomers must be provided with opportunities to achieve and master new skills. This fosters a positive self-image and provides the employee with the means for repeated goal attainment.

Breakdowns in socialization may inhibit employee development. Possible consequences of socialization breakdowns are dysfunctional behaviors, lack of skill use, lowered self-image, and termination of employment. Newcomers enounter resistance when opportunities are denied, expectations and behaviors from one source are in conflict with expectations and behaviors from another source, or skill and training are deficient. This places stress not only on affected new employees but on other components in the larger system as well (cf. Alderfer, 1971).

Anticipatory Socialization

The reviewed literature contained no studies that were designed to identify specific problems that women entering management positions might encounter. It would be valuable, however, at this socialization stage to briefly consider some research on men that suggests potentially important variables.

Wanous (1977) reviewed research on realistic job previews and concluded that the exchange of job-related information between members of the organization and the job applicant is predictive of later socialization success. Similarly, Gomersall and Myers (1966) were able to reduce new employee absenteeism and training time with a program designed to (a) reduce the newcomer's fear of failure, (b) facilitate the newcomer's ability to cope with "hazing" practices, and (c) enhance the newcomer's communications and interpersonal relations with supervisors and co-workers.

A valid job analysis would seem to be a preliminary step in this job information exchange process. This may require careful attention in the selection and training of job analysts because Arvey, Passino, and Lounsbury (1977) found that female job analysts, when analyzing an administrative job, produced lower scores than male job analysts on several dimensions of the Position Analysis Questionnaire (McCormick, Jeanneret, & Mecham, 1972). But the position analyzed was not particularly sex typed, and one is left to speculate concerning sex of analyst and sex of incumbent effects for positions that traditionally have been occupied by males.

Encounter and Accommodation

The second stage in the socialization process concerns the newcomer's initiation to her work group, and reactions to the newcomer's behavior and performance by relevant co-workers.

The formation of group bonds through which the newcomer obtains social and technological support is an important part of this socialization stage (Hall & Hall, 1976a; Van Maanen & Schein, 1977). Research suggests that the formation of these bonds is affected by newcomer characteristics. Taylor (in press) reports that if the newcomer is different from the group on sex or race, the newcomer will be viewed as a "solo" or "token" by the group. This serves to exclude the token newcomer from formal and informal work contacts, and elicits extreme evaluations, in either direction, from group members. Evan (1963) examined training group size, but not sex or race, and found that isolates (one- or two-person training groups) had greater turnover than nonisolates (three-or-more-person training groups). There were no ability differences between the isolate or nonisolate groups. To the extent that we can generalize from these two studies, it would appear that the newcomer's ability to establish links with existing group members is an important step toward effective socialization.

The evaluation of a woman's behavior and performance by relevant others in her work unit is another important factor at this socialization stage. A common theme in the literature centers on the lack of congruency between perceptions of the traditional feminine sex role and a woman's behavior and performance in a nontraditional, masculine sex-typed job. The review of this literature will consider data pertinent to (a) evaluations of behaviors emitted by women subordinates and women supervisors, (b) ratings of performance levels attained by women on masculine tasks, and (c) affective responses to women supervisors by subordinates of both sexes.

Two studies that examined sex role behavior by women subordinates were conducted in laboratory settings using scenarios of various job situations as stimulus materials. Rosen and Jerdee (1975a) found that women were perceived as out of role when they used a threatening approach in filing a job grievance. Such complaints by women were judged to be more serious than similar threats by men. In another study, Rosen and Jerdee (1974a) found that requests for time off from work because of family problems were judged more acceptable when coming from a woman than a man.

Three laboratory studies were designed to examine out-of-role behavior by women supervisors. Rosen and Jerdee (1973) manipulated leader sex and type of behavior using the in-basket technique. A reward style of behavior was rated more effective when displayed by a man. There were no sex of leader effects for threat or helping behaviors. A friendly, dependent leader behavior was rated as more effective for either sex when used with subordinates of the opposite sex. Similar results were obtained when college students or bank supervisors were used as subjects. Jacobson and Effertz (1974) had men and women students act as leaders on a task that involved the reproduction of a pattern of dominoes. They found support for their hypotheses that followers would be more critical of leaders who were men than women because more was expected of men in this leadership position, and leaders would be more critical of followers who were women than men because more was expected of women in this follower position. Finally, Bartol and Butterfield (1976) had college students rate the effectiveness of four different leader behaviors as a function of leader sex. Short paragraphs describing behaviors of (a) initiating structure, (b) consideration, (c) production emphasis, and (d) tolerance for freedom were prepared. Moderate support was found for the hypotheses that men would be rated more effective as leaders than women in the initiating structure condition, and women would be rated more effective as leaders than men in the consideration condition.

Research designed to examine whether performance evaluations are affected by employee sex has produced inconsistent results. Hagen and Kahn (1975) found that competent women were evaluated negatively only in conditions of competition. Under conditions of observation and cooperation, raters positively evaluated a competent woman's performance. Similarly, Hamner, Kim, Baird, and Bigoness (1974) and Bigoness (1976) reported that given equal levels of objective performance, job applicants who were women were rated superior to job applicants who were men. When job incumbents were examined, however, Terborg and Ilgen (1975) and Hall and Hall (1976b) found no differences in rated performance. Finally, in the only field studies conducted, Epstein (1970) reported that career women received more praise than men for lower performance, but Deaux (Note 3) found no difference in rated performance of retail store department managers due to manager sex.

The findings of Hagen and Kahn (1975) and Epstein (1970) could be explained by the role congruency notion if one assumes that not being competitive and the display of low performance are consistent with a woman's traditional role. But the findings of Hamner et al. (1974) and Bigoness (1976) suggest that some other process may be operating. Superior performance when unexpected may result in a more positive evaluation than superior performance when expected (Leventhal & Michaels, 1971; Weiner, Note 5). If women are not expected to perform well, and research suggests that men see women managers as operating under constraints beyond their control (Terborg & Ilgen, 1975), then when they do perform well, their performance may be attributed to extra effort, and so forth. Thus, they may be perceived as more worthy of a reward. Evidence also suggests that this attribution process may be influenced by the raters' attitudes toward women in management. Garland and Price (1977) found that men with favorable views toward women managers attributed success to factors such as ability and effort and avoided attributions to luck and task difficulty. Measures of performance level or reward allocation were not taken, however, so it is not known whether differential attributions would have influenced these other measures.

A strong warning needs to accompany these results. Except for the studies of Epstein (1970) and Deaux (Note 3), all of these findings were based on laboratory studies, and as with much of the work in this area, the external validity needs to be determined.

Studies designed to examine subordinate affective responses to men and women supervisors produced inconsistent results. The single laboratory study is presented first. This is followed by a discussion of (a) four field studies that did not adequately control for job type, job function, subordinate characteristics, etc., and (b) four field studies that did consider some of these additional factors. Finally, alternate explanations for the results are discussed.

Bartol (1974), in a detailed experiment that used an 8-week management game task, examined subordinate satisfaction with leader behavior as a function of leader sex, leader need for dominance, and sex composition of work group. Satisfaction was positively correlated with leader need for dominance for either sex. Also, all-male work groups were more satisfied than mixed-sex work groups regardless of leader sex. There were no all-female work groups.

Hansen (Note 6) analyzed field data collected as part of a larger study on employee attitudes. No attempt was made to control for job level, job type, etc. She found no sex-of-supervisor differences on subordinate ratings of support behaviors and goal facilitation behaviors, but subordinates of both sexes were less satisfied if their supervisor was a woman. Correlations between leader behavior and subordinate satisfaction were generally lower for groups with women supervisors, and there was some indication that this was due to low satisfaction reported by women subordinates working for women supervisors. Finally, a subset of women supervisors reported having less job autonomy than men supervisors. If subordinates also perceived this, then this could explain the lower correlations.

In a series of three studies, Petty and his associates (Petty & Lee, 1975; Petty & Miles, 1976; Petty, Odewahn, Bruning, & Thomason, Note 7) examined correlations between subordinate perceptions of leader behavior (i.e., initiating structure and consideration) and various measures of subordinate satisfaction. Supervisor job level was the only variable controlled besides sex of supervisor and sex of subordinate.

Petty and Lee (1975) examined employees in nonacademic divisions of a large university. They found that the correlation between subordinate ratings of consideration behaviors and subordinate satisfaction was significantly greater for divisions with supervisors who were women as opposed to men. There also was a negative correlation between subordinate ratings of initiating structure and satisfaction for a subset of men under women supervisors ($n = 10$). Petty and Miles (1976) found similar results using subordinates of directors in social service organizations. The correlation between consideration behaviors and satisfaction with supervision was significantly greater for subordinates of supervisors who were women than for subordinates of supervisors who were men. In contrast, the correlation between initiating structure behaviors and satisfaction was significantly greater for subordinates of men supervisors than for subordinates of women supervisors. Sex of subordinate also was important. A correlation of .83 was obtained between initiating structure and satisfaction with supervision when both subordinates and supervisors were men ($n = 5$); however, the correlation was $-.33$ ($n = 23$) when subordinates were men and supervisors were women. In the final study, an attempt was made to collect data from a larger sample (Petty et al., Note 7). The first two studies had cell sizes as small as 5 and 10. The smallest cell size in the third study was 68. In addition, the authors attempted to separate production emphasis items from the Initiating Structure scale of the Supervisor Behavior Description Questionnaire (SBDQ; Fleishman, 1957) and participation items from the Consideration scale of the SBDQ. Data were collected from employees in mental health organizations. The results obtained in this study were in sharp contrast to those of the other two. Satisfaction with supervision was positively correlated with all leader behaviors except production emphasis. There were no differences between correlations due to supervisor sex or subordinate sex. Correlations between leader behaviors and satisfaction with work produced similar results.

These four studies provide some evidence that subordinates working for supervisors who are women respond differently than subordinates working for supervisors who are men. These studies, however, do *not* show that supervisor sex is the primary cause of these subordinate affective responses because adequate controls were not included in the designs.

The final four studies in this area did consider some of the necessary controls. Roussell (1974) examined effects of department head sex on teacher ratings of department climate in 10 high schools. The teachers, three men and three women, were randomly selected from the four largest departments in each of the schools. The department heads, 25 men and 15 women, had few biographical differences — women were slightly older and had more experience in education — and had no differences on teacher ratings of power, aggressiveness, suggestibility, or professional knowledge. The climate results showed that departments headed by men were rated high on dimensions labeled *esprit* and *intimacy* and that departments headed by women were rated high on the dimension labeled *hindrance*. Consistent with the findings of Hansen (Note 6), correlations between department head power, aggressiveness, etc., and teacher ratings of climate were generally lower in departments headed by women than by men. Department function and characteristics of teachers in departments were not controlled.

Goetz and Herman (Note 2) examined subordinates of department managers in a large retail store chain. Although employees working for women managers were more satisfied with supervision than employees working for men, these sex effects, as noted by the authors, were largely due to confounding with other determinants of subordinate reactions such as commissioned versus noncommissioned sales, sex composition of work unit, etc. Osborn and Vicars (1976) similarly reported the disappearance of sex of supervisor effects once employee demographics and leader demographics were considered.

Finally, Adams (Note 8) collected data from 276 subordinates of eight white women and 10 white men who were store managers in a large retail chain. Dependent variables included subordinate ratings of leader consideration and initiating structure and subordinate satisfaction with supervision. Store managers were selected on the basis of geographic location, store size, education level, and tenure. Subordinate education and tenure were statistically controlled. In contrast to the findings reported by Petty and Lee (1975) and Petty and Miles (1976), Adams found little support for differential results due to sex of manager or sex of subordinate. There were no differences in correlations between supervisor satisfaction and leader behaviors. Almost all correlations were significantly different from zero, and all were positive. Only one mean difference was found, with store managers who were women being rated more considerate than store managers who were men. This was found for subordinates of either sex.

In their attempts to explain the above findings, most authors have limited their arguments to one of two overlapping positions. First, sex role stereotypes exist, and second, successful performance by a woman is unexpected and therefore noteworthy. It would be valuable to consider other processes that could help explain these differential reactions to women in management positions. If stereotypes are as pervasive as some assume, then why are the results in this area so inconsistent?

One possibility involves the methodological issue of laboratory experiments versus field studies. In laboratory experiments, strangers interact with other strangers, or with pencil-and-paper stimulus others, for brief periods of time in contrived settings. Consequently, the manipulated variable of sex may be one of the few things the subject has with which to make a discrimination. Cues about the situation are weak compared to the cue of leader sex. On the other hand, the results from field studies are difficult to interpret because of the impact of situational variables. Schriesheim and Murphy (1976) reported that job stress, unit size, and role clarity moderated relationships between leader behaviors of initiating structure and consideration and subordinate satisfaction. To the extent that such situational variables are confounded with sex, we would expect to find sex effects unless these other variables are controlled. Data supporting the congruency explanation were most often found in laboratory experiments or in field studies that did not have adequate controls. The one field study that made an explicit attempt to control for major situational variables had only one effect due to sex (Adams, Note 8). More carefully designed research in both the laboratory and the field must be conducted before some closure can be made on the congruency explanation.

Another explanation that merits further research is what Staines, Tavris, and Jayaratne (1973) call the "queen bee syndrome." The queen bee is a woman who has attained success and status in a man's world and views other women as competitors for her position. If women managers display different behaviors toward women subordinates than toward men subordinates in the same job situations, then findings of low satisfaction among women subordinates of women supervisors could be explained. Although past studies show no behavioral differences across sex of supervisor, respondents frequently are asked to rate their supervisor "on the average." This method would not uncover differential behavior directed toward individual subordinates. Use of the methodology employed by Graen (1976) in his vertical-dyad-linkage model of leader behavior would be able to determine better whether the queen bee syndrome is a viable explanation. Graen (Note 9) has not found any evidence in support of this position in his own work.

Another consideration deals with the upward influence women supervisors have in making resources available to their work unit. Research shows that women managers often are found in dead-end jobs (Day & Stogdill, 1972), low status jobs (Goetz & Herman, Note 2), and other positions outside of the career path (Lyle & Ross, 1973). If Hansen's finding that women managers have less autonomy is replicated, then dissatisfaction and resistance toward women managers by their subordinates may not be due to the sex or behavior of the manager. Rather, women as a result of their present low status positions are unable to wield influence. If this is correct, then we would expect to find similar subordinate reactions to managers who are men and who also lack upward influence. Work by Pelz (1952) and more recently by Graen and his associates (Cashman, Dansereau, Graen, & Haga, 1976; Graen, Cashman, Ginsburgh, & Schieman, in press) provides strong support for the influence explanation.

The existence of inconsistent results should also be examined with regard to possible confusion among the women's role set. It was stated earlier that co-workers who have an interest in, and dependency on, the newcomer possess and communicate expectations concerning appropriate actions, qualities, and performance levels that are associated with a position or job. Because these expectations deal with a position and not with individual members who occupy that position, then sex of role incumbent should not drastically influence progress at this socialization stage. Similarly, the display of identical behaviors and performance levels should result in identical evaluations of that role incumbent. The process, however, is much more complex as evident from the proliferation of inconsistent results.

Perhaps, due to the high visibility of women, their role set includes a different membership than that of men. The interest of personnel in related departments or units may be aroused by the presence of a woman, especially if she is the first woman manager. Second, although the sent role for men may be expected to vary as a function of position, when considering women incumbents the sent role may vary as a function of sex, position, and a Sex × Position interaction. In those instances in which sex stereotypes are operative, women may be evaluated along the dimensions of sex and position while men are evaluated according to position. Consequently, the behavior and/or performance of women can be out of role by sex and in role by position, in role by sex and out of role by position, out of role by sex and position, and in role by sex and position. Of course, the same argument can be made for men in feminine sex-typed jobs, but our concern here is with women in management.

A further complication arises when we distinguish behavior from performance. Successful performance by women may be unexpected, and for that reason they are evaluated positively. But they may be evaluated negatively if the behaviors are discrepant from accepted sex roles.

Role Management

Effective socialization at this final stage involves the newcomer's ability to resolve conflicting demands at home and at work. Relevant factors include personal attributes of the newcomer, such as idiosyncratic needs, values, and motives, and demands placed by homelife and family responsibilities.

Several studies were found in the literature that relate to personal attributes. Miner (1974) found that there were no differences between sexes on motivation to manage within a sample of store managers and school administrators. Motivation to manage was assessed with a projective technique that measured competitiveness, assertiveness, and uniqueness. Further, as would be expected, managerial motivation was related to managerial performance for women. In a different study, Miner (1965) found that the motivation of women changed with training and experience in a manner similar to that observed for men. Similar findings were reported by Morrison and Sebald (1974). Female executives were similar to male executives on self-esteem, motivation, and mental ability. Also, similar profile patterns emerged when male executives were compared with male nonexecutives and female executives were compared with female nonexecutives. Results in agreement with those just reported have been found by several investigators using different dependent variables in different settings (cf. Bartol, 1976; Brief & Aldag, 1975; Brief & Oliver, 1976; Deaux, Note 3; Matteson, McMahon, & McMahon, 1974). Although evidence can be cited to the contrary (Reif, Newstrom, & St. Louis, 1976; Schuler, 1975), it seems to be the exception. These results coupled with the relationship between self-concept and occupational choice suggest that in the aggregate women who gain entry into management jobs and who experience the associated pressures have motives similar to men who encounter equivalent experiences.

A possible exception is the fear of success motive, which is assumed to be present in most women but in few men (Horner, 1972). Women with high fear of success are assumed to be inhibited in their performance on achievement-oriented tasks. Replication of Horner's original work would certainly be important for understanding women managers' behavior. O'Leary (1974) reviewed some of the literature in this area and concluded that problems associated with the measurement of this motive made it premature to speculate about the prevalence, stability, and behavioral consequences of this construct. Zuckerman and Wheeler (1975), in a more recent and comprehensive review than provided by O'Leary, reached a similar conclusion.

Research also has examined the influence of homelife and family responsibilities as barriers to effective socialization. Hawley (1971) found that women's perceptions of sex stereotypes held by men were strongly related to these women's own role expectations and role behaviors. To the extent that these perceptions place home and family duties primarily in the domain of the "feminine role," then working women may experience pressures from relevant others, and perhaps their own self-concepts, to sacrifice their professional careers for family responsibilities. Mathews, Collins, and Cobb (1974) found that such responsibilities were frequently mentioned as reasons why women terminated training for the job of air traffic controller. Men who terminated rarely mentioned these responsibilities as reasons. Similar results with a self-report measure of role conflict as the dependent variable instead of turnover were reported by Gordon and Hall (1974) and Hall and Gordon (1973). Finally, Jerdee and Rosen (Note 10) found that even among women who were already employed in low-level jobs, the potential loss of income and the family's demands for personal time were seen as barriers to obtaining needed training so that they would be qualified for higher level management positions.

It appears then that although women can add the role of business career, they have difficulty shedding the role of housewife and mother, which results in experienced role conflict on two levels. First, conflicts can arise because of the incompatibility between the woman's self-perception of her role and the role sent to her by relevant others. Second, the taking on of additional roles may create role overload. Here, the roles are not necessarily incompatible, but it is difficult to allocate sufficient time and energy to all of the multiple roles.

Hall (1972) examined these conflicts among working women and focused on the methods they used to cope with the added stress. He found three different coping strategies. These involved (a) changing the demands of a role, which was termed *structural role redefinition*, (b) setting priorities on meeting role demands and otherwise learning to live with the added conflict, which was termed *personal role redefinition*, and (c) attempting to meet the demands of all the multiple roles, which was termed *reactive role behavior*. In general, structural role redefinition was positively related to satisfaction with one's career, and reactive role behavior was negatively related to satisfaction. The results were complicated, however, by other variables such as full-time versus part-time employment. As McGrath (1976) points out, such coping strategies will be successful only if they are directed toward the source of the conflict. Similarly, Hall (1972) found that structural role redefinition would be the best strategy in the long run.

SUMMARY

Research interest on women in management is a relatively recent occurrence, with much of the literature in this area being published since passage of the Equal Employment Opportunity Act of 1972, which amended the Civil Rights Act of 1964. The preceding review indicates, however, that considerable data already exist in some topic areas and that in those areas meaningful conclusions can be stated.

Based on aggregate data, women describe themselves and are described by men as having self-concepts that are not suitable for management. Also, women who do choose nontraditional careers fail to receive support for their choice or are actually discouraged from pursuing their choice by members of the family and by vocational counselors. It is not known, however, whether those women who choose nontraditional careers have different self-concepts from women who choose traditional careers because no research on career choice has been reported. It does appear that women who pursue nontraditional careers reject sex role stereotypes and that, once in those positions, they have needs, motives, and values that are similar to men who also are in those positions. Whether this similarity is the result of self-selection, experience, or both is not known given available research.

Although considerable evidence exists that is consistent with a stereotype explanation, it is difficult to make any firm conclusions. Many studies have not included independent assessments of stereotypes, the operationalization and measurement of stereotypes are open to criticism, and effects of situational variables on the stereotype–behavior relationship are largely unexplored.

Research on reactions to the behavior and performance of women managers and to those of women in nontraditional jobs has produced inconsistent results. Some evidence suggests that behavior that is consistent with accepted sex role behavior is evaluated more positively than when it is out of role; that is, women leaders are perceived better than men if they are high on consideration behaviors rather than initiating structure behaviors. Many of these results, however, are based on laboratory studies in which sex of stimulus person may have been the only cue that was varied. When performance was evaluated, no consistent results were found.

Field studies of subordinate reactions to leader behaviors suggest that effects associated with the sex of the leader are not directly related to sex per se, but to the situations of the leaders. When relevant variables such as type of job, sex composition of subordinates, tenure, etc., are controlled, there seem to be few differences in how subordinates react to women or men leaders. It is important to note, however, that these studies suggest that women in management have not attained similar or equal positions as men in management, since sex appears to covary with important situational variables.

Research on factors affecting the management of work and family role demands by women managers indicates that although women can add the role of a business career, they have difficulty shedding the role of housewife or mother. This can result in various role conflicts that may limit the expression and use of women who are unable to cope effectively with these conflicts.

One additional observation should be stated. In many of the studies, and even in the summary conclusions just presented, the results are discussed in the context of women compared to men. Although this is necessary for semantic clarity, such conclusions fail to point out the importance of individual differences so that exceptions to the above can always be made in specific cases. In this research area, it is too easy to attribute wrongly the findings of aggregate data to individuals. We should be careful not to conclude the existence of sex effects when these differences may really be due to variables that covary with sex. Rather, sex should be considered a surrogate variable that correlates imperfectly with other causal variables.

Recommendations for Further Research

More research needs to be done in the general area of career choice, vocational counseling, and vocational development. For example, Do women who choose nontraditional careers have self-concepts or childhood experiences (i.e., mother worked full time) that are different from those who do not choose such careers? and Do these self-concepts or childhood differences relate to later success in the chosen career? It is also important to determine the extent to which a person's self-concept, needs, and values are modified by job experience. If a person's self-concept of value system changes over time, then these variables may be less important for later success than was previously thought. Related to this are questions concerning the causes, occurrences, and consequences of vocational counseling that discourage women from pursuing career choices in nontraditional areas. Little is known about how prevalent such counseling is, the reasons that counselors use to make their recommendations, the validity of the reasons, and the effects of the counseling on affected women. Finally, women may begin a career in management at a different stage of vocational development than men. Although many men may be at the "establishment" stage, women may still be at the "exploration" stage. Consideration of the vocational development model proposed by Super and his colleagues (Super, Crites, Hummel, Moser, & Warmath, 1957) would be a beginning.

Research must be designed that examines more closely the effects of stereotypes on discriminatory behaviors. The distinction made earlier between sex-characteristic stereotypes and sex role stereotypes should be examined empirically. The effects of sex-characteristic stereotypes may be highly situational, dependent on the manner in which job applicants are depicted, and predict only a subset of discriminatory behaviors. Sex role stereotypes, on the other hand, are primarily due to socialization processes. Thus, these stereotypes may require different strategies in order to diminish their effects and may predict a different subset of discriminatory behaviors than sex-characteristic stereotypes. Specifically, research should be designed to examine the effects of these two forms of stereotypes on the evaluation of behavior and performance. Additional research would include manipulations of type of behavior displayed, which could be stereotypically masculine, feminine, or neutral; type of task, which again could be stereotypically masculine, feminine, or neutral; and level of performance. Such designs would be valuable for understanding inconsistent results that were reported earlier on this topic. Finally, sex role stereotypes and sex-characteristic stereotypes must be assessed accurately if knowledge concerning their effect on women in management is to advance. The Women as Managers Scale developed by Peters, Terborg, and Taynor (1974) is one possible measurement device. Although the scale has been criticized as being transparent and easily faked (cf. Rosen & Jerdee, 1975b; Yost & Herbert, Note 11), supportive validity data have been reported (cf. Garland & Price, 1977; Ilgen & Terborg, 1975; Terborg & Ilgen, 1975; Terborg, Peters, Ilgen, & Smith, 1977). Scale items in the Women as Managers Scale do confound sex role stereotypes and sex-characteristic stereotypes, however.

Longitudinal field research is especially needed on the entire socialization process. First, no research was found on how women collect and evaluate information when they make a choice concerning a particular organization within which to work. This may be important if the availability of role models, the past use of women in the organization, and the number of women employed at management levels are found to be variables that predict later socialization success. Second, for women in management, there was no research that specifically examined relevant variables at the anticipatory socialization stage. The utility of realistic job previews, orientation training, and team building should be determined empirically. Third, investigations should be conducted on the importance and formation of group bonds among newcomers and incumbents. Research on men has shown that these bonds are important sources of social and technological support, which ease the newcomer's initiation to both job demands and the work group. This research may be particularly important if women managers who are isolates encounter greater difficulty in the establishment of such support networks. Fourth, structured career development programs should be evaluated. Berlew and Hall (1966), Graen (1976), Hall (1971), and Livingston (1969) point toward the crucial role of the newcomer's first supervisor and the careful sequencing of early job assignments for men who begin management careers. Fifth, field studies on leadership suggest that women managers often are found in low status, low power, dead-end positions even though they may be at the same level in the organization as men. It is not known, however, why this occurs. Discrimination may not be the primary reason if (a) women do not commit themselves to a career as early as men, (b) women are unaware of job-switching techniques due to a lack of role models, or (c) women are unwilling to relocate in order to progress up the career ladder. These are some possible reasons that need empirical verification. Hall's work on role conflicts that working women experience and, more importantly, how to deal effectively with these conflicts, needs to be continued. Are part-time management positions and job sharing effective methods of role restructing for women with families? What role does the husband have in reducing or eliminating sources of conflict? These are just a few questions that need to be pursued. Finally, in our discussion of the socialization process, attention should be directed to discover more subtle forms of discrimination. Schein (Note 4) reminds us that we cannot ignore the fact that sexual attraction or fear of sexual attraction may be important for understanding how women will be received in management and other professional areas. Similarly, not having access to the informal network of liaisons and contacts represents a subtle but perhaps effective method of discrimination.

Research also must not ignore the effects of women in management on aspects that do not relate directly to women. Men may face a reevaluation of their own socialized role of "family provider." Resentment by men who are passed over for promotions by less tenured women may occur. Conflicts arising from dual-career families will certainly develop. The point is that others are affected by the integration of women into management and they should be considered.

A final recommendation concerns some methodological issues. The usual request for longitudinal field research deserves to be mentioned and needs no further elucidation. More attention must be focused on the measurement of behaviors. The repeated correlation of self-report predictors with self-report criteria must be discouraged. The effects of situational and other variables that covary with sex and also covary with other variables of interest need to be identified and controlled. Finally, archival data present potentially rich sources of information that have been previously unexplored.

REFERENCE NOTES

1. Ullrich, M. F., & Holden, J. D. *Attitudes toward equal employment.* Paper presented at the meeting of the American Psychological Association, Washington, D.C., September 1976.

2. Goetz, T. E., & Herman, J. B. *Effects of supervisor's sex and subordinate sex on job satisfaction and productivity.* Paper presented at the meeting of the American Psychological Association, Washington, D.C., September 1976.

3. Deaux, K. *Self-evaluations of male and female managers.* Manuscript submitted for publication, 1976.

4. Schein, V. E. *Women managers: How different are they?* Paper presented at the meeting of the American Psychological Association, Washington, D.C., September 1976.

5. Weiner, B. *From each according to his abilities: The role of effort in a moral society.* Paper presented at the meeting of the American Psychological Association, Honolulu, September 1972.

6. Hansen, P. *Sex differences in supervision.* Paper presented at the meeting of the American Psychological Association, New Orleans, September 1974.

7. Petty, M. M., Odewahn, C. A., Bruning, N. S., & Thomason, T. L. *An examination of the moderating effects of supervisor sex and subordinate sex upon the relationships between supervisory behavior and subordinate outcomes in mental health organizations.* Manuscript submitted for publication, 1976.

8. Adams, E. F. *Influences of minority supervisors on subordinate attitudes.* Unpublished manuscript, University of Illinois, Department of Psychology, 1976.

9. Graen, G. Personal communication, December 1976.

10. Jerdee, T. H., & Rosen, B. *Factors in influencing the career commitment of women.* Paper presented at the meeting of the American Psychological Association, Washington, D.C., September 1976.

11. Yost, E. B., & Herbert, T. T. *The ATWAM scale: A forced choice scale for measuring attitudes toward women as managers.* Unpublished manuscript, University of Akron, Department of Management, 1976.

REFERENCES

Ahrons, C. R. Counselor's perceptions of career images of women. *Journal of Vocational Behavior,* 1976, 8, 197–207.

Ajzen, K., & Fishbein, M. Attitudinal and normative variables as predictors of specific behaviors. *Journal of Personality and Social Psychology,* 1973, 27, 41–57.

Alderfer, C. P. Effect of individual, group, and intergroup relations on attitudes toward management development program. *Journal of Applied Psychology,* 1971, 55, 302–311.

Almquist, E. M. Sex stereotypes in occupational choice: The case for college women. *Journal of Vocational Behavior,* 1974, 5, 13–21.

Arvey, R. D., Passino, E. M., & Lounsbury, J. W. Job analysis results as influenced by sex of incumbent and sex of analyst. *Journal of Applied Psychology,* 1977, 62, 411–416.

Bartol, K. M. Male versus female leaders: The effect of leader need for dominance on follower satisfaction. *Academy of Management Journal,* 1974, 17, 225–233.

Bartol, K. M. Relationship of sex and professional training area to job orientation. *Journal of Applied Psychology,* 1976, 61, 368–370.

Bartol, K. M., & Butterfield, D. A. Sex effects in evaluating leaders. *Journal of Applied Psychology,* 1976, 61, 446–454.

Berlew, D. E., & Hall, D. T. The socialization of managers: Effects of expectations on performance. *Administrative Science Quarterly,* 1966, 11, 207–224.

Bigoness, W. J. Effect of applicant's sex, race, and performance on employer's performance ratings: Some additional findings. *Journal of Applied Psychology*, 1976, *61*, 80–84.

Bowman, G. W., Worthy, N. B., & Greyson, S. A. Problems in review: Are women executives people? *Harvard Business Review*, 1965, *43*, 52–67.

Brief, A. P., & Aldag, R. J. Male–female differences in occupational values within majority groups. *Journal of Vocational Behavior*, 1975, *6*, 305–314.

Brief, A. P., & Oliver, R. L. Male–female differences in work attitudes among retail sales managers. *Journal of Applied Psychology*, 1976, *61*, 526–528.

Brigham, J. C. Ethnic stereotypes. *Psychological Bulletin*, 1971, *76*, 15–38.

Cashman, J., Dansereau, F., Graen, G., & Haga, W. J. Organizational understructure and leadership: A longitudinal investigation of the managerial role-making process. *Organizational Behavior and Human Performance*, 1976, *15*, 278–296.

Cecil, E. A., Paul, R. J., & Olins, R. A. Perceived importance of selected variables used to evaluate male and female job applicants. *Personnel Psychology*, 1973, *26*, 397–404.

Cohen, S. L., & Bunker, K. A. Subtle effects of sex-role stereotypes on recruiter's hiring decisions. *Journal of Applied Psychology*, 1975, *60*, 566–572.

Dansereau, F., Cashman, J., & Graen, G. Instrumentality theory and equity theory as complementary approaches in predicting the relationship of leadership and turnover among managers. *Organizational Behavior and Human Performance*, 1975, *13*, 46–78.

Day, D. R., & Stogdill, R. M. Leader behavior of male and female supervisors: A comparative study. *Personnel Psychology*, 1972, *25*, 353–360.

Dipboye, R. L., Fromkin, H. L., & Wiback, R. Relative importance of applicant sex, attractiveness, and scholastic standing in evaluation of job applicant resumes. *Journal of Applied Psychology*, 1975, *60*, 39–43.

East, C. The current status of the employment of women. In M. E. Katzell & W. C. Byham (Eds.), *Women in the work force: Confrontation with change*. New York: Behavioral Publications, 1972.

Epstein, C. F. *Women's place*. Berkeley: University of California Press, 1970.

Evan, W. M. Peer-group interaction and organizational socialization: A study of employee turnover. *American Sociological Review*, 1963, *28*, 436–440.

Feldman, D. C. A contingency theory of socialization. *Administrative Science Quarterly*, 1976, *21*, 433–452.

Feldman, J. M., & Hilterman, R. J. Stereotype attribution revisited: The role of stimulus characteristics, racial attitude, and cognitive differentiation. *Journal of Personality and Social Psychology*, 1975, *31*, 1177–1188.

Fleishman, E. A. A leader behavior description for industry. In R. M. Stogdill and A. E. Coons (Eds.), *Leader behavior: Its description and measurement*. Columbus: Ohio State University, Bureau of Business Research, 1957.

Garland, H., & Price, K. H. Attitudes toward women in management and attributions for their success and failure in managerial position. *Journal of Applied Psychology*, 1977, *62*, 29–33.

Gomersall, E. R., & Myers, M. S. Breakthrough in on-the-job training. *Harvard Business Review*, 1966, *44*, 62–72.

Goodale, J. G., & Hall, D. T. Inheriting a career: The influence of sex, values, and parents. *Journal of Vocational Behavior*, 1976, *8*, 19–30.

Gordon, F. E., & Hall, D. T. Self-image and stereotypes of femininity: Their relationship to women's role conflicts and coping. *Journal of Applied Psychology*, 1974, 59, 241–243.

Gordon, F. E., & Strober, M. H. *Bringing women into management*. New York: McGraw-Hill, 1975.

Graen, G. Role-making processes within complex organizations. In M. D. Dunnette (Ed.), *Handbook of industrial and organizational psychology*. Chicago: Rand McNally, 1976.

Graen, G., Cashman, J., Ginsburgh, S., & Schiemann, W. Effects of linking-pin quality upon the quality of working life of lower participants: A longitudinal investigation of the managerial understructure. *Administrative Science Quarterly*, in press.

Haefner, J. E. Race, age, sex, and competence as factors in employed selection of the disadvantaged. *Journal of Applied Psychology*, 1977, 62, 199–202.

Hagen, R. L., & Kahn, A. Discrimination against competent women. *Journal of Applied Social Psychology*, 1975, 5, 362–376.

Hall, D. T. A theoretical model of career subidentity development in organizational settings. *Organizational Behavior and Human Performance*, 1971, 6, 50–76.

Hall, D. T. A model of coping with role conflict: The role behavior of college educated women. *Administrative Science Quarterly*, 1972, 17, 471–486.

Hall, D. T. *Careers in organizations*. Pacific Palisades, Calif.: Goodyear, 1976.

Hall, D. T., & Gordon, F. E. Career choices of married women: Effects on conflict, role behavior, and satisfaction. *Journal of Applied Psychology*, 1973, 58, 42–48.

Hall, D. T., & Hall, F. S. What's new in career development? *Organizational Dynamics*, 1976, 5, 17–33. (a)

Hall, F. S., & Hall, D. T. Effects of job incumbents' race and sex on evaluations of managerial performance. *Academy of Management Journal*, 1976, 19, 476–481. (b)

Hamner, W. E., Kim, J. S., Baird, L., & Bigoness, W. J. Race and sex as determinants of ratings by potential employers in a simulated work-sampling task. *Journal of Applied Psychology*, 1974, 59, 705–711.

Hawley, P. What women think men think. *Journal of Counseling Psychology*, 1971, 3, 193–199.

Hoffman, L. W., & Nye, F. I. *Working mothers*. San Francisco, Calif.: Jossey-Bass, 1974.

Horner, M. Toward an understanding of achievement-related conflicts in women. *Journal of Social Issues*, 1972, 28, 157–175.

Huck, J. R., & Bray, D. W. Management assessment center evaluations and subsequent job performance of white and black females. *Personnel Psychology*, 1976, 29, 13–30.

Ilgen, D. R., & Terborg, J. R. Sex discrimination and sex-role stereotypes: Are they synonymous? No! *Organizational Behavior and Human Performance*, 1975, 14, 154–157.

Jacobson, M. B., & Effertz, J. Sex roles and leadership: Perceptions of the leaders and the led. *Organizational Behavior and Human Performance*, 1974, 12, 383–396.

Katz, D., & Kahn, R. L. *The social psychology of organizations*. New York: Wiley, 1966.

Korman, A. K. Toward a hypothesis of work behavior. *Journal of Applied Psychology*, 1970, 54, 31–41.

Lawler, E. E. *Pay and organizational effectiveness: A psychological view*. New York: McGraw-Hill, 1971.

Lawler, E. E., Kuleck, W. J., Rhode, J. G., & Sorenson, J. E. Job choice and post decision dissonance. *Organizational Behavior and Human Performance*, 1975, *13*, 133–145.

Lenney, E. Women's self-confidence in achievement settings. *Psychological Bulletin*, 1977, *84*, 1–14.

Leventhal, G. S., & Michaels, J. W. Locus of cause and equity motivations as determinants of reward allocation. *Journal of Personality and Social Psychology*, 1971, *17*, 229–235.

Livingston, J. S. Pygmalion in management. *Harvard Business Review*, 1969, *47*, 81–89.

Lyle, J. R., & Ross, J. L. *Women in industry*. Lexington, Mass.: Heath, 1973.

Maccoby, E. E., & Jacklin, C. N. *The psychology of sex differences*. Stanford, Calif.: Stanford University Press, 1974.

Mathews, J. J., Collins, W. E., & Cobb, B. B. A sex comparison of reasons for attrition in a male dominated occupation. *Personnel Psychology*, 1974, *27*, 535–541.

Matteson, M. T. Attitudes toward women as managers: Sex or role differences? *Psychological Reports*, 1976, *39*, 166.

Matteson, M. T., McMahon, J. F., & McMahon, M. Sex differences and job attitudes: Some unexpected findings. *Psychological Reports*, 1974, *35*, 1333–1334.

McClelland, D. C. Toward a theory of motive acquisition. *American Psychologist*, 1965, *20*, 321–333.

McCormick, E. J., Jeanneret, P. R., & Mecham, R. C. A study of job characteristics and job dimensions as based on the Position Analysis Questionnaire (PAQ). *Journal of Applied Psychology*, 1972, *56*, 347–368.

McGrath, J. E. Stress and behavior in organizations. In M. D. Dunnette (Ed.), *Handbook of industrial and organizational psychology*. Chicago: Rand-McNally, 1976.

Miner, J. B. *Studies in management education*. New York: Springer, 1965.

Miner, J. B. Motivation to manage among women: Studies of business managers and educational administrators. *Journal of Vocational Behavior*, 1974, *5*, 197–208.

Morrison, R. F., & Sebald, M. Personal characteristics differentiating female executives from female nonexecutive personnel. *Journal of Applied Psychology*, 1974, *59*, 656–659.

Moses, J. L., & Boehm, V. R. Relationship of assessment center performance to management progress of women. *Journal of Applied Psychology*, 1975, *60*, 527–529.

Nevo, B. Using biographical information to predict success of men and women in the Army. *Journal of Applied Psychology*, 1976, *61*, 106–108.

O'Leary, V. E. Some attitudinal barriers to occupational aspirations in women. *Psychological Bulletin*, 1974, *81*, 809–826.

Osborn, R. N., & Vicars, W. M. Sex stereotypes: An artifact in leader behavior and subordinate satisfaction analysis. *Academy of Management Journal*, 1976, *19*, 439–449.

Pelz, D. C. Influence: A key to effective leadership in the first-line supervisor. *Personnel*, 1952, *9*, 3–11.

Peters, L. H., Terborg, J. R., & Taynor, J. Women as managers scale (WAMS): A measure of attitudes toward women in management positions. JSAS *Catalog of Selected Documents in Psychology*, 1974, *4*, 27. (Ms. No. 585)

Petty, M. M., & Lee, G. K. Moderating effects of sex of supervisor and subordinate on relationships between supervisor behavior and subordinate satisfaction. *Journal of Applied Psychology*, 1975, 60, 624–628.

Petty, M. M., & Miles, R. H. Leader sex-role stereotyping in a female dominated work culture. *Personnel Psychology*, 1976, 29, 393–404.

Reif, W. E., Newstrom, J. W., & St. Louis, R. D. Sex as a discriminatory variable in organizational reward decisions. *Academy of Management Journal*, 1976, 19, 469–476.

Rosen, B., & Jerdee, T. H. The influence of sex-role stereotypes on evaluations of male and female supervisory behavior. *Journal of Applied Psychology*, 1973, 57, 44–48.

Rosen, B., & Jerdee, T. H. Influence of sex role stereotypes on personnel decisions. *Journal of Applied Psychology*, 1974, 59, 9–14. (a)

Rosen, B., & Jerdee, T. H. Effects of applicant's sex and difficulty of job on evaluations of candidates for managerial positions. *Journal of Applied Psychology*, 1974, 59, 511–512. (b)

Rosen, B., & Jerdee, T. H. Sex stereotyping in the executive suite. *Harvard Business Review*, 1974, 52, 45–58. (c)

Rosen, B., & Jerdee, T. H. Effects of employee's sex and threatening versus pleading appeals on managerial evaluations of grievances. *Journal of Applied Psychology*, 1975, 60, 442–445. (a)

Rosen, B., & Jerdee, T. H. The psychological basis for sex role stereotypes: A note on Terborg and Ilgen's conclusions. *Organizational Behavior and Human Performance*, 1975, 14, 151–153. (b)

Roussell, C. Relationships of sex of department head to department climate. *Administrative Science Quarterly*, 1974, 19, 211–220.

Schein, V. E. The woman industrial psychologist: Illusion or reality? *American Psychologist*, 1971, 26, 708–712.

Schein, V. E. The relationship between sex role stereotypes and requisite management characteristics. *Journal of Applied Psychology*, 1973, 57, 95–100.

Schein, V. E. Relationship between sex role stereotypes and requisite management characteristics among female managers. *Journal of Applied Psychology*, 1975, 60, 340–344.

Schriesheim, C. A., & Murphy, C. J. Relationships between leader behavior and subordinate satisfaction and performance: A test of some situational moderators. *Journal of Applied Psychology*, 1976, 61, 634–641.

Schuler, R. S. Sex, organizational level, and outcome importance: Where the differences are. *Personnel Psychology*, 1975, 28, 365–376.

Staines, G., Tavris, C., & Jayaratne, T. E. The queen bee syndrome. In C. Tavris (Ed.), *The female experience*. Del Mar, Calif.: CRM Books, 1973.

Super, D. E., Crites, J., Hummel, R., Moser, H., & Warmath, C. *Vocational development: A framework for research*. New York: Teachers College Press, 1957.

Taylor, S. E. Structural aspects of prejudice reduction: The case of token integration. In J. Sweeney (Ed.), *Psychology and politics*. New Haven, Conn.: Yale University Press, in press.

Terborg, J. R., & Ilgen, D. R. A theoretical approach to sex discrimination in traditionally masculine occupations. *Organizational Behavior and Human Performance*, 1975, 13, 352–376.

Terborg, J. R., Peters, L. H., Ilgen, D. R., & Smith, F. Organizational and personal correlates of attitudes toward women as managers. *Academy of Management Journal*, 1977, 20, 89–100.

Tipton, R. M. Attitudes towards women's roles in society and vocational interests. *Journal of Vocational Behavior*, 1976, 8, 155–165.

Treiman, D. J., & Terrell, K. Sex and the process of status attainment: A comparison of working women and men. *American Sociological Review*, 1975, 40, 174–200.

Van Maanen, J. Police socialization. *Administrative Science Quarterly*, 1975, 20, 207–228.

Van Maanen, J., & Schein, E. H. Career development. In J. R. Hackman & J. L. Suttle (Eds.), *Improving life at work: Behavioral science approaches to organizational change*. Santa Monica, Calif.: Goodyear, 1977.

Vogel, S. R., Broverman, I. K., Broverman, D. M., Clarkson, F. E., & Rosenkrantz, P. S. Maternal employment and perception of sex roles among college students. *Developmental Psychology*, 1970, 3, 381–384.

Wanous, J. P. Organizational entry: Newcomers moving from outside to inside. *Psychological Bulletin*, 1977, 84, 601–618.

Weisman, C. S., Morlock, L. L., Sack, D. G., & Levine, D. M. Sex differences in response to a blocked career pathway among unaccepted medical school applicants. *Sociology of Work and Occupations*, 1976, 3, 187–208.

Zuckerman, M., & Wheeler, L. To dispel fantasies about the fantasy-based measure of fear of success. *Psychological Bulletin*, 1975, 82, 932–946.

The Pregnancy Discrimination Act: Compliance Problems

John P. Kohl and Paul S. Greenlaw

Although nearly four years have passed since President Carter signed the pregnancy Discrimination Act of 1978 (PDA), which requires employers to treat pregnancy-related illnesses on an equal basis with all other medical conditions, a recent study revealed that many organizations are still not fulfilling the requirements of the Act. While some managers are purposely not complying, others are simply unaware or uncertain about what they have to do.

The PDA affects three types of employee benefit plans: hospitalization and major medical programs, temporary disability plans, and sick leave provisions. This article will first briefly review what firms should be doing to comply with the Act. Then we will report the major findings of the study on what firms are doing and, on the basis of those results, offer some suggestions to business and government managers on how to improve compliance.

PDA REVISITED: A BRIEF REVIEW

When Congress passed the Civil Rights Act of 1964, it failed to consider whether employers' benefit provisions covering pregnancy and pregnancy-related illnesses that differed from benefits covering other medical conditions constituted a form of sex discrimination that was proscribed by the Act. In retrospect, such an omission appears to be logical, reflecting then-current social norms that differ significantly from those of the late 1970s and early 1980s. This omission has led court cases to address two primary issues: the loss of seniority rights that frequently occurred when women temporarily leave the marketplace because of pregnancy, and the treatment of maternity as different in kind from other medical conditions. Two cases, *Geduldig v. Aiello* (417 U.S. 484), 1974, and *General Electric Co. v. Gilbert et al.* (429 U.S. 125), 1976, eventually reached the Supreme Court, and one, *Gilbert*, provided the major impetus for Congressional action to pass the PDA.

THE *GILBERT* CASE

The *Gilbert* case played such a critical role in motivating Congress to enact the PDA — in the hearings it was frequently referred to as "the Gilbert bill" — that we will briefly review the facts behind it and the implication of the decision.

The facts of the case: Under GE's employee benefit plan all hourly workers received nonoccupational sickness and accident benefits that were equal to 60 percent of their straight-time earnings to a maximum of $150 per week. Benefits began on the eighth day of total disability and continued for a maximum of 26 weeks. However, the plan did not cover absences due to pregnancy. Instead, pregnant females were placed on mandatory unpaid maternity leaves with a resultant loss of earnings and other employee benefits.

The immediate termination of medical benefits and coverage for nonpregnancy disabilities, as well as for those related to the pregnancy, was a major factor in the challenge of this program in the courts. One plaintiff, Emma Furch, lost her baby shortly after being placed on leave. Two weeks later she suffered a pulmonary embolism unrelated to her pregnancy. GE denied her disability claim, arguing that her maternity leave eliminated her eligibility for extended medical benefits under the company's plan.

The Supreme Court eventually ruled that GE's plan was not discriminatory and invited Congress to specify more precisely what it means to "discriminate . . . because of . . . sex" under Title VII of the Civil Rights Act. Without such specification, the Court declined to expand the concept of sex discrimination beyond normal interpretations.

Congress responded to this challenge and passed the Pregnancy Discrimination Act of 1978, which was signed into law on October 31, 1978.

PDA EXAMINED

The PDA, which amends the Civil Rights Act of 1964, specifies that sex discrimination includes (but is not limited to) discrimination on the basis of "pregnancy, childbirth, or related medical conditions." Under the Act firms originally had 180 days, or until April 29, 1979, to bring their affected benefit programs into compliance with the law. (The deadline was later extended to October 30, 1979 or "when existing union contracts expired" — whichever was later.) Although some of the "key dates" associated with PDA are no longer applicable, the following is a brief summary of key PDA requirements that affect personnel managers today.

First, as an amendment to the Civil Rights Act of 1964, PDA affects only firms with 15 or more full-time employees. Second, while the Act forbids discrimination against applicants on the basis of "pregnancy, childbirth, or related medical conditions," its primary effect is on firms with hospitalization and major medical plans, temporary disability benefits, or sick leave for current employees. *The law requires all such affected firms to treat pregnancy and pregnancy-related illnesses on an equal basis with all other medical conditions.*

Third, the law requires employers to maintain equality of benefits. Thus, since the deadlines mentioned above, employers have had the option of eliminating all affected plans, reducing all affected coverages, or maintaining all coverages, as long as they treat pregnancy and pregnancy-related coverages on an equal basis with all other medical conditions.

A number of examples may serve to clarify this point: Under the Act, it would be illegal for an employer to refuse to grant sick days for morning sickness, or even childbirth itself, if such sick days are granted for such other medical conditions as operations or accidents. Similarly, it is illegal to give only six weeks of "time off" for childbirth if longer periods of recuperation are permitted for other illnesses and sicknesses. The key concept to remember is "equal coverages" for pregnancy. In addition, if a firm counts time missed for a gall bladder operation or appendectomy toward promotion or retirement credit, then it must also do so for time missed because of pregnancy and pregnancy-related illnesses. *Any differentiation constitutes a form of sex discrimination that is prohibited under the Act.*

However, what firms are required to do by law frequently differs from what they actually are doing, as we found out in our study of organizational responses to the PDA.

ORGANIZATIONAL COMPLIANCE (AND NONCOMPLIANCE) WITH PDA

To learn more about what organizations and personnel managers/owners were actually doing as a result of PDA, a field study of 41 organizations, 27 manufacturing firms, and 14 organizations, in a metropolitan area of the Northeast was conducted.

The researchers decided to investigate the impact of five variables — organizational size, presence of a union, interface with the federal government, percentage of females in the workforce, and type of industry — on organizational compliance with PDA. (In doing so, multivariate statistics were used.) Noncompliance with the Act was determined on the basis of two criteria: (1) technical noncompliance on key dates and (2) noncompliance with the intent of the law. This latter category included two types of firms: those who simply refused to hire women, and those who have not had any claims that would have been covered by PDA, but who had stated policies that would break the law if such claims should arise.

The study, which was conducted by personal, face-to-face interviews with personnel managers or owners, produced a number of interesting results.

Results of the Study

The major finding was that there was a high correlation between organizational size and compliance with the Act. In Figure 1, the numbers of small, medium, and large

FIGURE 1
PDA Compliance by Key Dates by Firm

	October 31, 1978	April 29, 1979	October 31, 1979	July, 1981*
Firms with less than 100 full-time employees (n = 22)	0	12	12	12
Firms with 100 to 500 full-time employees (n = 10)	1	5	6	8
Firms with more than 1,000 full-time employees (n = 9)	3	8	9	9
Totals (n = 41 firms)	4	25	27	29

*Time at which interviews of the firms studied took place.

firms that were in compliance with PDA on key dates is shown. However, these numbers do not tell the entire story.

As of July 1981 — the time at which the interviews took place — only 55 percent of firms with fewer than 100 employees were in compliance, while all those who employed more than 1,000 employees had implemented the law's requirements. At that time, 80 percent of medium-sized firms were obeying the law. As one can see from the graph, differences between the compliance rates of small, medium, and large firms persist on nearly all the key dates.

The study produced a number of surprises as well. For example, there was no relationship whatever between the percentage of females in the workforce and the employer's compliance or noncompliance with the Act. This is surprising because throughout the Congressional hearings, the issue of compliance costs were of primary concern: Estimates of such costs ranged from between $150 million to almost $2 billion annually. Although it was intuitively plausible that the probable higher costs for a firm that employed a large number of female employees might discourage that employer from obeying the law, nothing in the findings supports this assumption. On the other hand, there would appear to be a number of explanations for this lack of correlation between compliance decisions and the percentage of female employees in the workforce.

First, service organizations, on the average, employ higher percentages of females than manufacturing firms and because some service firms provide fewer benefits for all their employees, compliance is relatively inexpensive. One service organization, for example, reported that the only benefit provided was a group hospitalization plan — paid for by the employee. Another provided only two weeks of sick leave after ten years of service.

A second explanation may be that in many female-intensive industries, overall payroll costs may be lower despite the inclusion of favorable benefit programs under PDA because wages for females are generally lower than those for men; thus higher benefits may be offset by lower wages.

Another surprise was that the presence of a union had little effect on whether the organization complied with the Act although unions were its greatest supporters throughout the Congressional hearings on PDA; after all, the Act would, and did result in a free benefit that the unions did not have to bargain for. In retrospect, a number of reasons might account for this finding.

First, many union locals may not adhere to the views expressed by their parent organizations. Second, many unions are male-dominated by tradition, and may not be "positively inclined" toward PDA's provisions. In fact, the two firms in the study that had no female employees were 100 percent unionized, and the unions were not pressuring them to extend equal rights to women.

In line with these findings and their implications, we would like to make recommendations for personnel managers and government agencies.

IMPLICATIONS FOR MANAGERS IN BUSINESS AND GOVERNMENT

A number of conclusions and suggestions can be derived from this study. First, many firms continue to disobey this particular law. Because some of this failure to comply stems from the fact that many firms do not know what is required, we hope that this article will resolve some of their questions. On the other hand, much failure to comply is deliberate: Firms who perceive they can disobey the law frequently do. In point of fact, there is a great deal of noncompliance, particularly among smaller organizations.

Second, even larger firms have adopted a strategy of "gradualism" toward compliance — and such a strategy may be warranted. The Newport News Shipbuilding and Dry Dock Company, for example, is still in court fighting the Equal Employment Opportunity Commission's (EEOC) interpretation of PDA's dependent coverage. In a free society, such challenge of interpretation is healthy, and perhaps at times necessary because larger, more visible firms may find that such court challenges are the only means of finding out just what the law requires them to do.

Third, many smaller firms expressed grave concerns about the costs of PDA; on the other hand, only one of the 41 organizations studied ever mentioned the benefits to the worker or organization. Personnel managers and owners may need to reconsider the Act's requirements in terms of its benefits to the employer, such as increased worker satisfaction, decreased turnover, and retention of trained and loyal personnel. In the 1980s, more and more women will enter or reenter the work force. Benefit provisions such as those provided by PDA are not only necessary — *they are fair* and may far outweigh their costs.

Fourth, an adversary relationship between business and government continues and was in evidence throughout this study. Part of the blame must be laid upon regulatory agencies. EEOC did little to promote acceptance of PDA when, just nine days before the mandatory compliance date, it issued controversial finalized questions and answers about the meaning of the Act. Regulatory agencies and their managers would do well to initiate reasonable timetables that make sense to assist, not hinder, organizations in their attempts to comply with the law.

Finally, regulatory agencies may need to redirect some of their efforts towards an educative strategy. This is not to say that they should neglect their obligations to enforce compliance with the law. However, many firms, particularly smaller ones, may be unaware or uncertain about what they should be doing. Although it is certainly cost effective to make sure that large firms comply with the law, smaller firms may be the ones that are most in need of such regulation as PDA. After all, in the Congressional hearings it was disclosed that many large organizations already had some form of coverage — even if it proved to be inadequate later — while many smaller firms have little, if any, coverage. Federal agencies may need to expend more resources in explaining not only what must be done, but in spelling out the benefits that accrue to firms that comply.

Having learned that even four years after its passage, compliance with the PDA is far from universal, we have recommended some actions that managers in both business and government can take to improve the relationship between government regulatory agencies and business firms. In addition we hope that this article will better inform business organizations of all sizes about the law's requirements and that it will help improve compliance not only with PDA, but with all aspects of meaningful government regulation.

Sexual Harassment: Critical Review of Legal Cases with General Principles and Preventive Measures

Robert H. Faley

By many accounts, the employment-related sexual harassment of women by men is a pervasive problem in American organizations today (Collins and Blodgett, 1981; Renick, 1980; U.S. Congress, 1981). Despite statutes and presidential orders forbidding policies and procedures which foster a sex-segregated work climate, nearly 75% of working women are still employed in "women's" jobs or in job categories or workplaces that are segregated on the basis of sex, yet controlled by men (Women's Bureau, 1975).

Considering the potential of such environments, it is not surprising that surveys of working women during the past five years have reported the incidence of sexual harassment to be quite high. MacKinnon (1979) reports on several, including one in which 70% of the women interviewed reported sexual harassment experiences; in another 49% said sexual harassment existed on their jobs. Forty-two percent of the women responding to a recent House of Representatives' confidential survey of federal employees reported they had been sexually abused at work by supervisors or co-workers. Interestingly, 15% of the men surveyed also reported some form of sexual harassment.

The first nationwide questionnaire on the topic was published in *Redbook* magazine in 1976. Of the 9,000 women who responded, over 90% reported personal incidents of sexual harassment. In a better prepared and more recent (1980) survey, jointly conducted by *Redbook* and *Harvard Business Review*, the overwhelming majority of respondents perceived sexual harassment to be a very serious problem.

If harassment is as common as this literature suggests, then organizations dealing with the problem need to understand what legally constitutes sexual harassment, as well as the extent of their liability for their employees' sexually harassing behavior. However, organizations cannot hope to achieve this understanding without first acquiring a knowledge of the judicial interpretations of the statutes involved (called case

Reprinted with permission from *Personnel Psychology* 35, 1982, pp. 583–600.

law). Such knowledge will increase organizations' awareness of the types of evidence the courts consider necessary to rebut liability for acts of workplace harassment. This knowledge will also enable organizations to plan remedial action consistent with legal compliance.

To help those dealing with sexual harassment become more aware of these legal pronouncements, this paper reviews sexual harassment complaints brought before the federal courts under Title VII of the Civil Rights Act of 1964, as amended. Title VII is the most important general statute on sex discrimination and, as such, prohibits discrimination based on sex by employers in the terms or conditions under which they employ a workforce. Most courts consider it consistent with the intent of Congress to interpret the Act liberally, and therefore, coverage under Title VII is very broad.

The review is divided into two major parts. Part I examines the important cases that address the specific issues necessary to a thorough understanding of sexual harassment at the workplace. Part II presents the general principles and preventive measures that can be distilled from the information contained in these cases.

PART I: PRECEDENT-SETTING COURT CASES

Each court case included in this part of the review addressed at least one of the three major issues involved in the courts' delineation of the sexual harassment case law. These issues are: (1) the gender-based nature of sexual harassment at work, (2) the direct and indirect employment-related consequences that result from the harassment, and (3) the extent of employer liability for the sexually harassing acts of their employees. Several cases that did not meet this standard were also included because they either addressed an important corollary issue or provided additional useful information. In all, 52 Title VII cases reported through April 1982 were examined; 29 are discussed.[1] Of these, 24 are district court and 5 circuit court opinions. No case dealing with sexual harassment at work has yet been heard by the Supreme Court.

The Gender-Based Nature of Sexual Harassment

Not until ten years after the enactment of the Civil Rights Act of 1964 did the federal courts hear the first case in which sexual harassment was the primary complaint. These initial complaints were unsuccessful in their attempts to establish sexual harassment as sex discrimination under the Act.

In these first cases the courts interpreted harassment based on one's sexuality as a "personal matter" (e.g., *Miller v. Bank of America, Corne v. Bausch & Lomb, Inc., Barnes v. Train*). Defendants generally claimed that for sexual harassment to be prohibited by Title VII, the "primary variable" of the class discriminated against had to be the gender of the class member. Because both genders were similarly situated (i.e., liable to sexual advances), defendants reasoned plaintiffs' claims were not gender-specific. These defendants argued that the matter before the court was not one of gender (which would make it a Title VII violation), but one that could essentially be considered isolated and unauthorized sexual misconduct by one employee towards another. This, they argued, was outside the purview of the Act.

Relief was eventually granted in *Williams v. Saxbe*. The *Williams* court ruled that it was not necessary to a prima facie showing of sex discrimination that the person offended by the behavior be defined by a characteristic peculiar to one gender. The behavior in question only had to create an "artificial barrier to employment that was placed before one gender and not the other, even though both genders were similarly situated" (p. 1093). A comparable ruling came in *Barnes v. Castle*. The *Castle* court contended that Title VII prohibited non job-related conditions of employment which were disparately applied to men and women. This was a direct application to sexual harassment case law of the business necessity test Justice Burger articulated in *Griggs v. Duke Power Co.* Thus, employment practices which created a standard of sexual requirements for one gender but not the other were prohibited by Title VII.

Since *Williams*, the courts have consistently decided that it is enough that gender is a factor contributing to the discrimination in a substantial way for the discrimination to be a violation of Title VII (e.g., *Meyers v. I.T.T. Diversified Credit Corp.* or *Heelan v. Johns-Manville Corp.*). Therefore, any written or unwritten policy or procedure that is applied on the basis of gender alone is a necessary condition to a finding of sex discrimination under Title VII.

Employment-Related Consequences of Sexual Harassment

In addition to establishing that sexually harassing behaviors took place, plaintiffs have also had to prove that the behaviors adversely affected the conditions of their employment. This could be accomplished by showing either a direct relationship between the behaviors and employment-related consequences or that the behaviors were indirectly related to the nature of employment through their detrimental effect on the work environment. The courts call either relationship an "employment nexus." Each nexus may be considered based on a discrimination "theory," the direct relationship here called the Tangible Benefits Theory, the indirect the Atmosphere of Discrimination Theory.

Tangible Benefits Theory. The Tangible Benefits Theory deals with the prohibition in Title VII against specific, overt, discriminatory acts. In such cases, it is important that the plaintiff be able to clearly establish a relationship between the objectionable conduct and the employment repercussions that flow from it. If not, the courts have determined such behavior, however regrettable, constitutes isolated sexual misconduct between two employees rather than sexual harassment.

A case in point is the district court decision in *Bundy v. Jackson.*[2] This court ruled that Bundy's male supervisors did not discriminate against her, even though she was able to prove that they had made sexual advances. The court noted that the sexual advances apparently were taken seriously by neither her nor her supervisors. Moreover, the court observed that her supervisors took no action against her either personally or professionally, and that Bundy apparently filed the complaint to obtain a promotion. In similar actions (*Hill v. BASF Wyandotte Corp.; Davis v. Bristol Laboratories; Neely v. American Fidelity Assurance Co.*), the plantiffs alleged that they were sexually harassed by their employer when, in fact, the court found there was no nexus between the sexual behavior and the conditions of their employment. In *Neely*, the court not only found for the defendants but also awarded them the right to recover damages against the plaintiff for all court-related costs.

Another example of the Tangible Benefits Theory can be seen in the circuit court decision in *Tompkins v. Public Service Electric & Gas Co.* The plaintiff was able to establish that continued job success and advancement were dependent upon her agreeing to the sexual demands of her supervisors. She was also able to show that after an initial complaint to her employer she was subjected to adverse employment evaluations, disciplinary layoffs, and threats of demotion by various other supervisory personnel.

Atmosphere of Discrimination Theory. The Atmosphere of Discrimination Theory is based on an employee's Title VII right to work in an environment free from the psychological harm flowing from an atmosphere of discrimination. Under this theory, plaintiffs do not have to show that a specific discriminatory act had tangible employment-related consequences (such as demotion or termination). What plaintiffs must establish is that the debilitating impact of the sexual misconduct on their work environment indirectly affected the conditions of their employment.

The first district court decision in which the Atmosphere of Discrimination Theory was the major basis for the cause of action occurred in *Brown v. City of Guthrie.*[3] Although the plaintiff could not show a direct employment nexus, she was able to establish that the sexually harassing acts of her supervisor (such as lewd comments, innuendos, and gestures) substantially affected her emotional and psychological stability. This harassment, she argued, contributed to a work environment which was so unbearable that she was forced to resign.

In arriving at its decision, the court in *Brown* became the first judicial body to cite the interim amendments on sexual harassment to the EEOC "Guidelines on Discrimination Because of Sex" (henceforth Guidelines). Quoting Section 1604.11(a) of the Guidelines, the court noted that harassment on the basis of sex is a violation of Title VII when "such conduct has the purpose or effect of substantially interfering with an individual's work performance or creating an intimidating, hostile, or offensive work environment" (p. 1631). Concurring with the Supreme Court opinion in *Griggs,* the *Brown* court concluded that the administrative interpretation of Title VII by the EEOC was entitled to "great deference."

Another ruling based on the Atmosphere of Discrimination Theory occurred in the circuit court decision in *Bundy.* The district court erred, according to the circuit court, when it refused to include the Atmosphere of Discrimination Theory as a basis for relief under Title VII. This was founded on the erroneous assumption by the district court that sexual harassment not leading to loss or denial of tangible employment benefits fell outside the scope of discrimination as defined in Title VII. The circuit court interpreted "terms and conditions of employment" protected by Title VII to mean more than tangible compensation and benefits. The court here, as in *Brown,* cited the interim amendments to the EEOC Guidelines to support their opinion. Although the circuit court decision in *Bundy* occurred subsequent to it, the court did not mention the *Brown* ruling in its decision.

Since the *Brown* and *Bundy* decisions there have been additional cases in which the courts have cited the Atmosphere of Discrimination Theory as grounds for a Title VII suit, as well as the EEOC Guidelines as supportive of that action. For example, in finding for the plaintiff, the court in *Walter v. KFGO Radio* quoted that section of the Guidelines proscribing sexual behavior which created an "intimidating and hostile work environment."

Although often used, the Guidelines are not always a necessary condition for a favorable ruling based on the Atmosphere of Discrimination Theory. Without reference to the Guidelines, the court in *Morgan v. Hertz Corp.* ruled that sexual harassment is established where the harassment "principally takes the form of being subjected to suggestive and indecent comments and direct questions of a sexual nature" (p. 999).[4]

Absent proof of a direct or indirect employment nexus, relief will not be granted by the courts. As was stated in *Heelan,* "Title VII should not be interpreted as reaching into sexual relationships which may arise during the course of employment, but which do not have a substantial effect on that employment" (p. 255). "There is nothing in the Act which could reasonably be constructed to have it apply to verbal or physical sex advances by another employee even though he is in a supervisory capacity, where such complained of acts or conducts have no relationship to the nature of employment" (*Corne,* p. 291). Purely personal encounters without employment repercussions are not covered by the Act.

In addition to a factual showing that the objectionable acts were applied on the basis of gender alone, and that employment-related consequences flowed from them either directly or indirectly, a third issue must be addressed by the plaintiff. This issue concerns the extent of the employer's responsibility for the sexually harassing behavior of its employees. This issue has not yet been clearly resolved by the courts.

Early court decisions explicitly held an employer responsible for the sexually harassing acts of its supervisory personnel. However, as sufficient evidence of this liability, these courts required the plaintiff to show, through the employer's actions (or inaction), that the employer was aware of and condoned the harassment (*Bell v. St. Regis Paper Co., Tompkins, Miller, Williams, Corne*). For example, in *Williams*, the court stated, "If this was a policy or practice of plaintiff's supervisor, then it was the agency's policy or practice" (p. 1099). However, the court ruled only after a preponderance of the evidence supported the plaintiff's allegations that the employer condoned its subordinate's actions. Another example occurred in *Heelan*. This court reasoned (based on *Costle*) that it was unnecessary for the plaintiff to prove that her employer endorsed the sexual harassment. "In no other area of employment discrimination do the courts require such proof" (*Heelan*, p. 2). Although the *Heelan* court apparently meant this to imply that an employer was responsible for the acts of its subordinates acting as "part" of the employer, it appeared that proof of the employer/employee relationship was a necessary but not sufficient condition for a ruling against the employer. For, in both *Costle* and *Williams* as well as in *Heelan*, the court noted that where a supervisor contravened employer policy without the employer's knowledge (and where the wrong, once known, was promptly rectified), the employer may be relieved of responsibility under Title VII.

It was not until the Ninth Circuit Court's reversal of the district court decision in *Miller* that there was better agreement between the words and actions of the courts dealing with the employer liability issue. In that decision the circuit court, defining employer to include "any agent of such," found that the Bank could not rebut liability simply because it had an established policy against sexual harassment. As the court stated, "It would be shocking to most of us if a court should hold, for example, that a taxi company is not liable for injuries to a pedestrian caused by the negligence of one of its drivers because the company has a safety training program and strictly forbids negligent driving" (p. 463). According to the court, congressional intent under Title VII was not to absolve employers of liability for the actions of their subordinates acting within the scope of their job duties. Application of such a standard, the *Miller* court argued, would create an enormous loophole for employers. In its opinion, "An employer whose internal procedures would have redressed the alleged discrimination can avoid litigation by employing those procedures to remedy the discrimination upon receiving notice of the complaint or during the conciliation period" (p. 464).

A recent district court decision (*EEOC v. Sage Realty Corp.*) has interpreted Title VII to hold employers liable even for sexually harassing acts toward their employees by the public that result from conditions of employment. A sexually provocative uniform resulted in lewd comments and innuendoes by customers toward a Sage Realty employee. When she complained that she would no longer wear the uniform, she was fired. Because the employer could not show a job-related reason for requiring employees to wear such a uniform, and because the uniform was only required to be worn by female employees, the court ruled that the employer, in effect, was responsible for the sexually harassing behavior. A suit based on similar grounds occurred in *Marentette v. Michigan Host, Inc.* The *Marentette* court agreed with the decision in *Sage* but found for the defendant because the plaintiff was not able to establish an employment nexus.

The *Brown* court also addressed the perplexing issue of the extent of employer liability for the behavior of its supervisory employees. Here, the court spoke of two different tests of employer liability. The first is based on decisions similar to the ones in *Castle, Heelan,* and especially the circuit court decision in *Miller.* These decisions stress that an employer can be held liable for sexual harassment by its supervisory employees, regardless of whether such acts violate the employer's policy, regardless of whether the employer knew of or condoned such acts, and regardless of whether the plaintiff could prove either. The second, and more stringent test, relies on decisions similar to those in *Price v. Lawhorn Furniture Co., Munford v. Barnes & Co.,* and *Garber v. Saxon Business Products, Inc.* These rulings state that the plaintiff must establish employer policy or acquiescence in the wrong. The employer can only be held liable for acts about which it was notified but took no action. The *Brown* decision did little to resolve the dual-test controversy, since the evidence presented by the plaintiff clearly demonstrated employer liability under the more stringent test.

The extent of employer liability for sexually harassing acts under either test is clearly stated in the 1980 interim amendments to the EEOC Guidelines. The Guidelines affirm that an employer "is responsible for its acts and those of its agents and supervisory employees with respect to sexual harassment regardless of whether the specific acts complained of were authorized or even forbidden by the employer and regardless of whether the employer knew or even should have known of their occurrence" (p. 25025). Furthermore, the Guidelines state that an employer is liable for the sexually harassing acts of its nonsupervisory employees if the employer (or its agents or supervisory personnel) knew or should have known of the harassing conduct. But unlike employer liability for sexual harassment by supervisory personnel, the Guidelines state that employer liability for sexual harassment by nonsupervisory personnel can be rebutted if the employer takes immediate and appropriate corrective action once it learns of the harassment.

Confusion over the extent of employer liability, although clarified somewhat by the decisions in *Miller, Brown,* and *Bundy* and the Guidelines, continues. It likely will only be fully resolved after being addressed in a Supreme Court decision sometime in the future.

PART II: GENERAL PRINCIPLES AND PREVENTIVE MEASURES

Part II of the review builds on the information presented in the court cases. General principles derived from the court cases are discussed, and future trends and preventive measures examined. Also discussed is the role of professionals in the development of future research. A plan of action to combat sexual harassment at the workplace consistent with the preventive measures articulated in the circuit court opinions in *Castle* and *Bundy* is presented.

General Principles

What can be distilled from the court cases and Guidelines? First, there is a developmental pattern to the court decisions regarding sexual harassment similar to the fashioning of case law involving other types of discrimination. Judicial movement is characterized by little initial relief for plaintiffs and very narrow interpretations of the statutes involved. Once additional cases are heard and precedent builds, more liberal interpretations result. Accordingly, reliance on early decisions involving sexual harassment without consideration of the latest court opinions can be misleading.

For example, initial harassment complaints heard by the courts dealt exclusively with clearly overt behaviors (e.g., requests for sexual favors). More subtle behaviors, less directly under the employer's control (e.g., crude jokes and remarks), were considered outside the scope of Title VII action by these courts. However, more subtle behaviors have since come to be included in a broad definition of sexual harassment now accepted by the courts.

Most courts generally agree that sexual harassment is confined to discrimination based on one's sexual desirability. They also agree that the repeated assertion of an employee's sexual identity over his/her identity as a worker is the usual manifestation of harassment in the workplace. Proscribed behaviors include unsolicited, nonreciprocal, verbal and physical sexual advances, requests for sexual favors, and other sexual contact (e.g., leering, gestures, touching, pinching, etc.), as well as crude jokes, remarks or other offensive language of a sexual nature. In the extreme, harassment can involve severe economic and psychological retribution and even rape. In addition to a list of behaviors established through case law precedents, court decisions since April 1980 have also relied on the amended EEOC Guidelines for a general summary of groups of behaviors considered sexually harassing.

Another example of growth in the case law concerns the court's view of sexual harassment as sex discrimination within the scope of Title VII. Since both genders are liable to sexual harassment, early courts ruled that Title VII could not be the basis for a suit. They argued that Title VII required proof that the harassment was gender-specific.

Later decisions are now regarded by all courts as more accurate interpretations of what Title VII proscribes. These rulings consider the sole use of gender, and not gender itself, as a necessary condition for a finding of sexual harassment as sex discrimination under Title VII.

Sex-exclusive conditions of employment by either sex, heterosexually or homosexually, are viewed as actionable (*Wright v. Methodist Youth Services; Costle*). A male or female supervisor, for example, who harasses only subordinates of the opposite gender (or only of the same gender) puts before each gender a condition of employment that is not put before the other, and is thus liable. On the other hand, where a supervisor who is bisexual places these conditions on both genders, a finding of discrimination under the Act could not be made (see *Williams*, footnote 6 or *Bundy*, footnote 7). Here the insistence of sexual favors would not constitute sex discrimination because it would apply to male and female subordinates alike.

In terms of the employment nexus criteria articulated by the courts, the scope of Title VII action with respect to sexual harassment was enlarged considerably with the introduction of the Atmosphere of Discrimination Theory. Prior to *Brown*, only instances in which plaintiffs could establish a direct relationship between harassing acts and outright employment consequences were considered evidence of the employment nexus. Where employees have been harassed, yet no formal employment decisions (such as demotion or termination) could be shown to flow as a consequence of the harassment, the employees were without recourse to the courts. These employees had to either endure the harassment or terminate their employment. However, with the decision in *Brown* (and later *Bundy*), if an employee could show that the conduct had the indirect effect of substantially interfering with his/her work performance by creating an intimidating, hostile, or offensive work environment, relief could be granted.

Brown and *Bundy* are also very important because they were the first cases in which the EEOC "Guidelines on Discrimination Because of Sex" (which included the interim amendments on sexual harassment) were given "great deference." Subsequently, the Guidelines have been of considerable use, as both the basis for complaints by plaintiffs and decisions by the courts.

An important matter which still remains unresolved involves the types of evidence necessary for determining the responsibility of an employer for the sexually harassing behavior of its supervisory and other personnel. When supervisors are the source of the problem, two case law tests exist. The first requires that plaintiffs make a prima facie showing of sexual harassment by supervisory personnel for employer liability to follow. A second, more stringent test, places a greater burden on plaintiffs. This test requires plaintiffs to establish, in addition to a prima facie showing, that the employer either condoned the harassing acts by its actions or at least acquiesced by lack of action. However, this test is inconsistent with other Title VII decisions and the amended EEOC Guidelines. Neither of these require the plaintiff to prove the defendant employer endorsed the discriminatory behavior by its supervisory personnel, only that there had been a discriminatory effect.

The extent of employer liability for harassment by other than supervisory employees has not yet been the central issue of a Title VII suit. Although coworker harassment occurred in *Kyriazi v. Western Electric Co.*, it was confounded with supervisory acquiescence in the wrong.

Some guidance in this area may be gotten, however, by examining court decisions involving other types of discrimination (e.g., race). These decisions are clear in making no distinction between supervisors and coworkers in terms of employer liability. In fact the general rule in these decisions has been that employers are responsible for their acts and those of all their employees, whether the acts were authorized or forbidden by the employer, or whether the employer knew or should have known of their occurrence (*U.S. v. City of Buffalo, Murray v. American Standard, Inc., Anderson v. Methodist Evangelical Hospital, Ostapowicz v. Johnson Bronze Co., City of Los Angeles v. Manhart*).

However, this general rule is inconsistent with the extent of employer liability for the effects of harassment by persons other than supervisors outlined in the amended EEOC Guidelines. In these cases, the Guidelines state employers can only be held liable when it can be proven they or their supervisors knew or should have known of the conduct. Furthermore, employers could rebut liability under these circumstances by showing they took immediate and corrective action upon learning of the conduct. Confusion over whether the same standards of liability should apply to employers when supervisors or persons other than supervisors are the source of the harassment will remain until more cases are heard where these issues are central.

Future Trends

Whatever the judged degree of employer liability, future trends concerning sexual harassment violations will likely take the form of increased complaints involving the Atmosphere of Discrimination Theory. This appears consistent with the rulings in *Brown* and *Bundy*, and the "great deference" they and subsequent decisions have shown the amended Guidelines containing the EEOC's expression of the theory.

Brown may have also opened a potential floodgate for complaints involving employees other than supervisory personnel, especially if the courts ignore the part of the Guidelines which differentiates between the extent of employer liability for harassment by supervisors and coworkers. As evidence of the potential for coworker complaints, the recent survey of federal civil service employees revealed the typical harasser to be a coworker not in a direct supervisory line position. Since coworkers are rarely in a position to formally disturb another worker's job, these suits will almost exclusively be based on the Atmosphere of Discrimination Theory.

Suits involving the public as the harasser may also increase. The decisions in *Sage Reality* and *Marentette* can be read to imply that employers can be held responsible for the sexually harassing acts of the public toward their employees that result from employer-imposed working conditions. The Guidelines would also apply in these cases, as the public would be captured under the liability rubric as "other persons."

While presently most victims of sexual harassment are women, the source of harassment can be either gender. Thus, the initiation of complaints by men may be another new trend: the increase in the number of women in supervisory positions certainly enhances that possibility. And since the court in *Williams* noted that a finding of discrimination could apparently be made if the supervisor was the same sex as the subordinate, the future may also see litigation involving homosexual-based harassment. The House of Representatives survey of federal employees points to the potential magnitude of same-sex harassment as a problem. It revealed that the majority of males who complained of sexual harassment were speaking of harassment from same-sex supervisors and coworkers. With the recent decision in *Wright* that plaintiffs have a Title VII right to sue where the source of the harassment is a same-sex supervisor, direct case law precedent now also exists in this area.

Regardless of whether a supervisor, coworker, or the public is involved in the harassment, legally actionable behavior may be any means of harassment. This includes directly tampering with an employee's job to casting aspersions on an employee's virginity or placing an obscene cartoon on her desk as occurred in *Kyriazi*, or to continual lewd comments or sexual innuendos as occurred in *Brown*. It is important to remember that a supervisor or coworker's actions need not be explicit or obnoxious in their presentation to be a violation of Title VII.

Preventive Measures

It would be naive for any organization to believe that sexual harassment could never occur within its walls. The absence of complaints does not necessarily mean that an organization has nothing to worry about. It may only mean that sexually abused workers don't know how to raise a complaint or they fear retaliation. Under these circumstances, if a complaint were to surface and proceed to court, past Title VII rulings make it clear that the employer would have difficulty establishing an advantageous position for defense.

What measures, then, can employers take to prevent incidents of sexual harassment at their workplace? First, a comprehensive *affirmative* policy is necessary. As a start, employers should review their policies and procedures and eliminate sex-segregating ones which potentially foster a debilitating work environment. These include, among others, sex-segregated job categories and sex-based differential pay rates for jobs with substantially similar responsibilities and skills. In addition to these actions, the knowledgeable employer should develop a formal mechanism that promptly, fairly, and confidentially handles complaints of sexual harassment, yet also serves to protect those accused from unfounded or frivolous complaints.[5] This could be anything from establishing a completely separate apparatus to giving responsibility to a part of the department already set up to address other complaints of discrimination.

As a part of this mechanism, an employer should provide a means for raising the subject of sexual harassment with its employees. This could be done, for example, by posting the firm's policy expressing strong disapproval of sexual harassment and by establishing for all employees an unambiguous code of conduct against which to evaluate complaints. The subject could also be raised in other ways, such as at regularly scheduled meetings or in special training sessions.

Good two-way communication between employer and employee at all levels of the organization is essential if a program to combat sexual harassment is to be effective. Increased communication should help improve employer sensitivity to those claiming sexual harassment. This, in turn, should encourage internal settlements and eliminate the need for employees to go to outside agencies, such as the EEOC, to resolve complaints. Employers can also show their seriousness about the gravity of the matter by developing appropriate remedial sanctions for employees who violate a person's civil rights through sexual harassment. These may include warnings, notes placed in personnel files, demotions, immediate suspension, or dismissal. A mere statement of policy without sanctions for violators is likely to be looked at by the courts as ineffectual policy, at best. As a further reflection of concern, employers should disseminate information to employees about their rights to raise a complaint of sexual abuse. This should include information on how to initiate the complaint, covering the types of information that will be considered necessary to establish the nature of the complaint. In-house redress procedures should be stressed as the most workable alternative. As was stated in *Miller,* litigation can be avoided where a company's legitimate complaint procedures promptly redress the alleged discrimination.

The most significant thing an employer can do is to take the problem of sexual harassment seriously by showing by its actions a genuine concern for the sensitivity to the issues. The courts have consistently ruled in other Title VII lawsuits that employers who take actions consistent with this policy will be dealt with less severely (*Parham v. Southwestern Bell Telephone Co.; EEOC v. Garland Bank and Trust Co.; Furnco Construction Corp. v. Waters*).

The Role of Professionals

Psychologists and other professionals can assist employers in several ways with their efforts to deal with harassment. In addition to the guidance they might provide employers who wish to set up programs to combat sexual harassment, professionals can also help to clarify the extent of sexual harassment in organizations. At present, there is no reliable account of how extensive sexual harassment actually is.[6] For example, in the recent *Redbook/Harvard Business Review* survey, men and women agreed on the seriousness of the problem, but not on how often it occurred. Many more men than women felt the amount of sexual harassment at work was greatly exaggerated.

Our lack of a clear and comprehensive portrait of the magnitude of harassment on the job is the result of two interrelated problems in the way sexual harassment has so far been researched. First, results are often the product of poorly developed research instruments. Survey terminology is rarely defined adequately (if at all). Questions are often written in such a way as to "load" the answers in one direction or the other. Also, since surveys are more reactive measures, respondents are able to introduce their own biases into the data. For example, it has been argued that women exaggerate the extent of sexual harassment at work because they have more to lose if harassment is not taken seriously. Alternatively, men may perceive less harassment because to do otherwise would present an unfavorable image of themselves.

The problems inherent in the use of obtrusive measures point out the need for better prepared, less reactive measurement strategies and techniques. These include the collection of data from personnel files, court cases or other archives. However, these alternative strategies present their own set of problems (cf., Runkel and McGrath, 1972). They also place an increased ethical burden on researchers not placed on them by obtrusive strategies.

The other major reason we lack a clear portrait of the extent of sexual harassment in organizations is due to the selection and rate of response of participants in the research. It is impossible to know about either those who were not included in or did not respond to a survey. And it is obvious that those most interested and involved are more likely to respond. Survey samples often include groups of individuals that are convenient, rather than carefully specified and systematically sampled respondents representative of the population of interest. Coupled with low response rates (often less than 25%), poor sampling strategies compound the problems that plague the research surrounding sexual harassment. Unfortunately, many courts have given credence to these surveys without first attempting to check the validity of their results. This is surprising considering the extensive use of professionals as expert witnesses in other Title VII actions.

The second, and perhaps more important area in which professionals can have an impact, is in helping to increase our understanding of what sexual harassment is and how it affects employment. We need a more complete definition of sexual harassment. We also need a better specification of the hypothetical linkages which locate sexual harassment within a testable theoretical framework. Little is known about the antecedents of harassment or the precise relationship between harassment and other organization variables (e.g., job performance, turnover, or morale). An increase in our knowledge in these areas could help better define the problem for organizations and ease the burden on the courts. Information about the effects of harassment on productivity would make explicit to employers the monetary costs of ignoring the problem. A knowledge of the conditions or events that typically precede harassment, or the characteristics of harassers, would help better define for the courts what constitutes an intimidating, hostile work environment in Atmosphere of Discrimination suits. However, although professionals may assist in determining *what* an offensive work atmosphere looks like, it will always remain the courts' prerogative to determine *when* a work environment stops being bearable and becomes hostile and humiliating.

In summary, neither the preventive measures discussed above nor the assistance of professionals can guarantee an employer that sexual harassment will not occur, or that complaints and litigation will not follow. They both can help create, however, a climate within the organization that discourages such conduct. Employees must be made to realize that making sexual requirements a condition of employment is wrong, illegal, and against company policy, and will be dealt with accordingly within the organization. A comprehensive and genuine policy against sexual harassment will carry the message to all employees that such behavior will not be tolerated at the workplace. Improper personal relationships must not be allowed to interfere with work performance or employment decisions.

NOTES

1. A reference list of all cases is available from the author.

2. *Bundy* has been reversed on appeal, based in part on the Atmosphere of Discrimination Theory.

3. Although the maintenance of a debilitating work environment due to harassment was a factor in the decision in *Kyriazi v. Western Electric Co.*, the main focus of that action dealt with the illegal use of sex as a basis for dismissal. *Kyriazi* also occurred prior to the publication of the sexual harassment amended EEOC "Guidelines on Discrimination Because of Sex."

   Also occurring earlier than the published Guidelines was *Dacus v. Southern College of Optometry*. The *Dacus* court held that an atmosphere of discrimination involving sexual harassment was evidence of the intent and willingness of the employer to discriminate against its female employees. The proof of sexual harassment, however, was used only to substantiate sex-based compensation differences, the major cause of the suit.

4. Although not Title VII cases, two other decisions merit attention. The court in *Woerner v. Brzeczek* decided that a suit based on proof of a "long and pervasive

course of sexual behavior contributing to an intolerable work environment" was actionable on Fourteenth Amendment grounds, and would have been even more so under Title VII (p. 899). The court quoted the *Bundy* decision in arriving at its ruling.

In a related state district court decision (most state anti-discrimination statutes are based on Title VII and adjudicated similarly), the court in *Caldwell v. Hodgeman* deferred to the decisions in *Bundy* and *Kyriazi* in concluding that the plaintiff had established a complaint based on the Atmosphere of Discrimination Theory.

5. The importance of handling complaints properly was the subject of a recent decision involving a suit brought on Fourteenth Amendment grounds. What effect *Huff v. County of Butler* will have on Title VII suits is difficult to anticipate.

6. The survey of federal employees conducted by the Merit Systems Protection Board comes closest to being a reliable study. However, it dealt with harassment in the public sector and generalizability of these results to other than federal employees is somewhat limited.

REFERENCES

Anderson v. Methodist Evangelical Hospital. 4 FEP Cases 987, 1972.

Barnes v. Costle. 15 FEP Cases 345, 1977.

Barnes v. Train. 13 FEP Cases 124, 1974.

Bell v. St. Regis Paper Co. 16 FEP Cases 1429, 1976.

Brown v. City of Guthrie. 22 FEP Cases 1627, 1980.

Bundy v. Jackson. 19 FEP Cases 828, 1979.

Bundy v. Jackson. 24 FEP Cases 1155, 1981.

Cadwell v. Hodgeman. 25 FEP Cases 1647, 1981.

City of Los Angeles v. Manhart. 17 FEP Cases 395, 1978.

Collins, E. G. C. & Blodgett, T. B. Sexual harassment: Some see it . . . some won't. *Harvard Business Review,* 1981, *59,* (March-April, 76–95).

Corne v. Bausch & Lomb, Inc. 10 FEP Cases 29, 1975.

Dacus v. Southern College of Optometry. 22 FEP Cases 963, 1979.

Davis v. Bristol Laboratories. 26 FEP Cases 1351, 1981.

Equal Employment Opportunity Commission. Discrimination because of sex under Title VII of the Civil Rights Act of 1964, as amended; adoption of interim interpretive guidelines. *Federal Register,* 1980, *45* (72), 25024–25025.

Equal Employment Opportunity Commission v. Garland Bank and Trust Co. 9 EPD 9875, 1974.

Equal Employment Opportunity Commission v. Sage Realty Corp. 22 FEP Cases 1660, 1980.

Furnco Construction Corp. v. Waters. 17 FEP Cases 1062, 1978.

Graber v. Saxon Business Products. 15 FEP Cases 344, 1977.

Griggs v. Duke Power Co. 3 FEP Cases 175, 1971.

Heelan v. Johns-Manville Corp. 20 FEP Cases 251, 1978.

Hill v. BASF Wyandotte Corp. 27 FEP Cases 66, 1981.

How do you handle . . . sex on the job? *Redbook,* 1976, *146* (January, 74–75).

Huff v. County of Butler. 27 FEP Cases 63, 1981.

Kyriazi v. Western Electric Co. 18 FEP Cases 924, 1978.

MacKinnon, C. A. *Sexual harassment of working women.* New Haven, Conn. and London: Yale Press, 1979.

Marentette v. Michigan Host, Inc. 24 FEP Cases 1665, 1980.

Meyers v. I.T.T. Diversified Credit Corp. 27 FEP Cases 995, 1981.

Miller v. Bank of America. 13 FEP Cases 439, 1976.

Miller v. Bank of America. 20 FEP Cases 462, 1979.

Morgan v. Hertz Corp. 27 FEP Cases 990, 1981.

Mumford v. Barnes & Co. 17 FEP Cases 107, 1977.

Murray v. American Standard, Inc. 7 FEP Cases 787, 1973.

Neely v. American Fidelity Assurance Co. 17 FEP Cases 482, 1978.

Ostapowicz v. Johnson Bronze Co. 13 FEP Cases 517, 1976.

Parham v. Southwestern Bell Telephone Co. 2 FEP Cases 1017, 1970.

Price v. Lawhorn Furniture Co. 24 FEP Cases 1506, 1978.

Renick, J. C. Sexual harassment at work: Why it happens, what to do about it. *Personnel Journal,* 1980, 8, 658–662.

Runkel, P. J. & McGrath, J. E. *Research in human behavior: A systematic guide to method.* New York: Holt, Rinehart and Winston, 1972.

Tompkins v. Public Service Electric & Gas Co. 16 FEP Cases 22, 1977.

United States v. City of Buffalo. 19 FEP Cases 776, 1978.

United States Congress, House, Committee on Post Office and Civil Service, *Sexual Harassment in the Federal Government (Part II),* 96th Cong., 2nd sess., 25 September 1981.

Walter v. KFGO Radio. 26 FEP Cases 982, 1981.

Williams v. Saxbe. 12 FEP Cases 1093, 1976.

Woerner v. Brzeczek. 26 FEP Cases 897, 1981.

Women's Bureau, U.S. Dept. of Labor, *Handbook of women workers.* 91 (Bulletin No. 197, 1975).

Wright v. Methodist Youth Services. 25 FEP Cases 563, 1981.

Workforce of the Future: The Problems and Opportunities of Maturity

Edward J. Harrick and Paul E. Sultan

The demographics of the U.S. workforce, the economic status of the federal Social Security system, and the employability of older workers are phenomena that will profoundly affect the composition of the workforce in the years ahead. Therefore all managers, but particularly human resources managers, should take a long look at these factors — and the way in which they interact — to determine their possible effect on long-range planning.

We present here an in-depth look at these phenomena and their implications.

SOCIAL SECURITY IN CONTEMPORARY SOCIETY

The U.S. public is besieged with news releases and analyses about the pending "bankruptcy" of the Social Security system. The reasons for public sensitivity and alarm about these unfolding events is not difficult to understand. Some of the alarming figures are presented in the box below.

There is no doubt that the Social Security system is the centerpiece of the security networks that were created for our contemporary society. The unsettling news of the system's pending insolvency is yet another indication of our economy's poor performance. To even the casual observer, it is obvious that the insecure nature of our retirement future is directly linked to the inadequate nature of our present job connection. The U.S. culture has not made overt moves to reduce the length of the workweek from the 40 hours identified as the "norm" in 1938. The distribution of the social dividend of time has been reflected in how we have divided what former Secretary of Labor W. Willard Wirtz has described as the three "time traps" of the human life cycle. The first time trap is in youth, which is given over to education. We have delayed young people's entry into the labor force by our attention to extended education, which, in turn, has increased the average number of years of U.S. schooling by one grade level every ten years. The second time trap is work. And the third time trap is retirement. And here, more than on labor-force entry, the change in life style has been dramatic. In 1947, 48 percent of the workforce that was 65 and older was still in the labor force. This declined to only 22 percent in 1974. Until the current concerns about retirement resources, it had been projected that this figure would decline to 19 percent by 1990. Since 1962, when Social Security recipients were offered the option of taking "early" retirement at age 62 and receiving 80 percent of the benefits they would have been eligible for at age 65, reports cited in the *Congressional Record* state that some 70 percent of those eligible to retire have taken advantage of this option. And studies indicate that some two-thirds of those exercising that option felt it was "necessary" because of personal health or because they had negative perceptions about their work experiences and what the future held in store for them.

But studies have also shown that many who opt for early retirement live to regret this decision. Close to half of all retirees indicate a desire to work if some amenities are introduced into the job environment. One senses, then, that pushing the elderly out of the labor market has been encouraged by a number of forces: a culture hoping to facilitate the upward mobility of the "more vigorous" youthful components in the

Some Facts about Social Security and the Elderly

Today, approximately 5,000 persons had their 65th birthday, and some 3,400 persons aged 65 or older died; theoretically, therefore, the pool of individuals eligible for support from the Social Security system increased by 1,600 in just one day. The ranks of the "elderly" have increased in the past by about 500,000 per year and, more recently, by about 600,000 per year.

Today, the Social Security system sent out over one million checks (some 35 million per month), reflecting some $500 million in payments to retirees and other claimants. Social Security is the major source of income for two-thirds of all beneficiaries over age 65. And of those 5,000 persons who could retire today at 65, the men can anticipate a life expectancy of 14 years, and the women can look forward to close to 20 years. And until today, the average retiree could anticipate receiving an income stream of about $42,000 during his or her lifetime — some six times the average amount each beneficiary paid in, plus interest.

The Social Security system, with its history of providing some $1 trillion of benefits in its first 40 years, lifted millions out of poverty and implanted in the U.S. psyche a sense that their retirement futures were indeed secure. In 1959, 38 percent of the elderly lived in poverty categories, while today only 13 percent live in poverty. The Social Security system, throughout its history, has provided a safety net for 95 percent of those over 65; it has also insured 80 percent of adults who were between 21 and 65 years of age against disability costs. It covered 95 percent of children and mothers if the family breadwinner died. Indeed, some 4.6 million of Social Security's 36 million beneficiaries were children, not the elderly. The fiscal pay-as-you-go foundation for the system, while always a subject of debate, has had a solid performance record. It has never defaulted in its obligations; it has never borrowed a dime. And in its 41-year history, the safety net of social insurance has woven in additional strands of protection. And retirement benefits have never been reduced, only increased.

labor force, public policy that recognized the desirability of retirement, an economy that seemed able to support adequate retirement benefits at increasingly younger ages, corporate structures hoping to avoid the awkward ambiguity of negotiated retirement, and the "taste" for leisure of many employees themselves.

All of this, we must quickly learn, is now changed. First, there is a minimal or zero amount of this social dividend available now, and prospects for revitalizing the economy have yet to be put to its test. In Phase I of the revitalization effort, we witness the unfolding contest between egalitarian and "efficiency" idealogues. Even if the magic of Reagonomics (which promises larger public revenues along with contracted tax rates) is realized, the gestation of capital growth to increase the Gross National Product will take time. Second, the demographic realities are awesome if we adhere to the policy option of allowing retirement at age 62 and encouraging it at age 65. It has been estimated that 2 million Americans will be retiring in 1982, and over the next five years the cumulative total will accelerate to 18 million persons. Some 25 million people in the United States are now 65 years of age or older, and this will increase, by most accounts, to 30 million in 20 years and to 43 million by 2020. By 2020, 15 percent of the U.S. population will be elderly, up from 11 percent in 1980. In 1950, 14 workers supported each Social Security recipient; in 1960 the ratio was five to one; today it is about three to one. By the year 2025, the National Commission on Social Security estimates a two-to-one ratio.

DEMOGRAPHICS AND SOCIAL SECURITY

A 1980 study by *Fortune* reminds us that the population of revenue-producing workers under 65 will stagnate in the years ahead because the baby boom of the 1950s was followed with the comparatively barren 1960s and 1970s. In *Fortune's* estimation, "when the last of the boomers will be over 65, the combined payroll tax rates needed to finance benefits will be at least 25 percent of taxable payroll and could be as high as 36 percent." But if one follows what the Social Security Administration labels as its pessimistic projection and assumes that the fertility rate will continue to fall as it has in all industrialized countries for the last 150 years and that life expectancy will continue to improve at a rapid pace (as it has recently), those factors would combine to lift the number of beneficiaries per 100 workers from 31 today to 68 in 2030. And to 84 per 100 workers in 2050! It strains one's credulity to see how a ratio of support costs that approaches one-to-one could be absorbed, no matter how robust our future egalitarian ideology nor how much growth we can reasonably anticipate in the labor-productivity ratio.

Two responses are triggered by these dramatic realizations. At the macro-policy level, events are closing in on an administration that must redefine mechanisms for solvency. It is most improbable that any further increase of Social Security tax rates above the combined employee and employer contribution of 15 percent to be in place by 1990 can be contemplated; creating greater revenues by raising the payroll tax base is also running into opposition. It seems equally improbable that, with the press of tax reductions, any assignment of costs to general tax revenues can be made. If these premises are correct, the major option remaining involves "tinkering" with the benefit levels. The fact that the notion of adjusting such benefit rates can now be discussed at all suggests that the U.S. public is coming to terms with realities.

The reconciliation of life style to these new realities, we submit, will have profound implications for the personnel function. It will touch the nerve ends of the highly sensitive issues of "employability standards" that are so critical to stretching out the job careers of those in the workforce.

Several proposals before Congress are designed to do just that. President Reagan had proposed that the 80 percent of benefits now available for those retiring at 62 be reduced to 55 percent, making that retirement option much less palatable. Critics of this option have angrily charged that the government has broken its 40-year contract with the workforce. Representative Bob Traxler of Michigan notes that those exercising this option would lose an average of $50,821 over the course of their retirement. He asks why a person who retires in 1982 should be so penalized when a person who retires in 1981 is not. Senator Lawton Chiles of Michigan has proposed, as part of his reform package, that eligibility begin at age 68 rather than 65, making more explicit the obligation to work.

In reflecting on the feasibility of these changes at the plant level, one is haunted with the early estimates that those who "choose" early retirement did not have much choice; they viewed their own faltering health or the faltering capacity of their current jobs as factors in their decision. Medical reports of the recent advance in longevity provides an account of the robust "young-old" category that is not easily reconciled with the self-assessments of retiring workers. But the issue of the economy's health and its capacity to sustain its "ingestion" of the mature worker is a technical engineering reality rather than a biological issue. And here, the issue is joined.

There is yet another major element in most reform packages that would give a further spur to extended workforce participation. This involves the removal of earnings "caps" for Social Security recipients to protect them from losing benefits for earning more than allowed. While some protest the incongruity of support payments for aging professionals drawing attractive salaries, it is pointed out that such talent might well relieve the skill shortage in our future and that the earned income would be taxed at regular rates.

Other inducements to encourage the continued employment of the mature worker, from a macro-policy view, include relieving those who are over 65 and working and their employers from paying Social Security taxes. This would create a cost advantage, from the employer's view, of employing such people. Senator Chiles has planned a modest reduction in the payroll tax rate as an offset made possible by later retirement eligibility; this is also designed, of course, as a mechanism to encourage employment of the mature worker. But the key "reform" — and the only mechanism that promises any long-term stability for the system — involves the extension of the "time trap" of work. This is a reality we cannot avoid. Nor can this challenge be neglected by a company's human resources function.

THE NEED FOR CORPORATE RESPONSIVENESS

One corporate reflex might well be to anticipate the increasing levels of litigation in a society already running the high fever of legal challenge. A defensive or reactive posture involves securing the paper trail that deals with individual performance: the formulation and documentation of performance criteria, frequent conferences on productivity targets, and more assiduous attention to variances in absenteeism, turnover, and other performance indicators.

Such a "defensive" posture seems reasonable in view of the very real prospect that mature workers will be making every effort to keep their jobs — if only because they have no other support system available to them. Being "eased" out of a job at any level will trigger anxieties and resistance. The more protracted our economy's state of depression, the more strident will be employees' efforts to protect what they view as a "property right" in their jobs. The skirmishes at the state level that involve penalties for the social hardship involved when a firm goes out of business — or moves — will take a new form with people struggling one-to-one to keep their jobs. But all of this, we submit, is likely to make a difficult situation even worse. Positive responses involve reactivating some traditional personnel agenda items, and some that are innovative.

MATURE WORKERS: GOOD OR BAD FOR THE ORGANIZATION?

We believe that positive action by the organization is in its own self-interest; it need not be taken simply because of persuasive evidence that people at age 62 or 65 are fully capable of adequate job performance. In the past several years, advances have been made in the fight against killer afflictions that attack the mature individual. While there is some criticism that medical technology has helped people avoid death without fully restoring "life" or rehabilitating the afflicted, evidence abounds that most 65-year-olds are fully capable of sustained work. It is not until people reach age 70 that researchers find evidence of what we perceive as the early signs of senility and, even here, normal bodily and mental functions are generally sustained to age 75.

We suffer two major prejudices: First, we think of the aging process as uniquely linked to chronological rather than biological age. But there is a substantial diversity of human capability at all ages and this is most evident among the elderly. Second, there are deeply entrenched stereotypes or myths about the traits of the elderly, which are burlesqued with monotonous regularity on television. A person may seem to be operating at different "age" levels at one and the same time in terms of his or her mental capacity, physical health, endurance, creativity, and/or productivity.

In recent Congressional testimony, employers consistently testified that they were pleased with older employees who remained on the job. Such companies as Polaroid and Bankers Life and Casualty report that their older employees were among their most loyal and productive workers. Of course, a self-selection process is involved — that is, employees who feel less well, or who are less motivated, are frequently the most anxious to retire. The more competent and more motivated employees are usually the ones with more intense interest in continuing to work.

But there is the pervasive stereotype of the poor, older employee as faltering, frail, forgetful, having a poor attendance record, and so forth. Employers testified this is a pure myth.

K. Warner Schaie, director of the Andrus Gerontology Research Institute at the University of Southern California reports information from a 21-year longitudinal study of age changes as they influence competence and learning ability. He noted no evidence that normal aging resulted in systematic across-the-board poor health, higher accident rates, lower productivity, reduction in learning ability, or poorer results from retraining.

Productivity and the Older Worker

Productivity will continue to be a major management concern during the next two decades. The evidence correlating productivity with age, however, is unclear. Harold L. Sheppard, in reviewing data on elderly workers, concludes that there is no consistent pattern that links superior productivity with any age group.

A recent U.S. Department of Labor study of 1,000,000 workers from 30 states revealed that the "frequency of occupational injuries declines steadily up to age 64 and then drops even more sharply for workers 65 and over." Previous studies had reported a mixed pattern of work accidents with age. This study — comprehensive and well-designed — provides convincing data to prove that older workers are less accident-prone than younger workers.

Not surprisingly, a variety of studies attest to the fact that younger workers have higher rates of turnover than older workers. And reducing turnover obviously reduces the costs of recruiting, orientation, and training.

Many other subjective but positive testimonies attest to the fact that older workers excel in many areas. Some argue that long-term employees are extremely loyal and more devoted to their organization than other employees. Others suggest that the test of time reflects the mature employees' fidelity to the company or interest in productive and profit-generating job activities. Yet another view holds that elderly employees possess greater wisdom to complement their higher levels of skill. The older group of employees is thus uniquely qualified to share or "pass on" perspectives and job skills to junior or younger workers. This last observation is most important. An organization that can link its senior and junior employees in an atmosphere of openness is one that can more fully cultivate the full range of its workforce's talents.

It seems appropriate to conclude that older workers are productive and contributing members of industry. Firms have many reasons to provide options and opportunities that will encourage older workers to remain in the organization's employment.

The Challenge to Employers

There are several convincing responses to this challenge. First, let us remember that just as there is a burgeoning of the aging workforce, so there is a pending decline in the number of youthful entrants to the workforce. Over the 15-year period from 1980 to 1995 the absolute decline in 16-to-24-year-olds in the workforce will number 3.5 million — dropping from 25.3 million to 21.8 million.

It is also clear that we, as a nation, are confronted with the enigma of skill shortages and with serious pockets of unemployment. Up until now, we have had little success in devising effective skill-transfer mechanisms in spite of widespread use of vocational centers and professional programs. On the other hand, the mature worker is likely to be the repository of many of the skills that the youthful segment of the labor force must learn. Thus the pairing of mature and young employees in formal or informal skill-development programs is a promising mechanism for raising performance standards on the job.

Another issue involves the myriad opportunities for changing the configuration of work schedules so that mature workers may enjoy larger slices of leisure without compromising their income flow in any serious way. Workers who find retirement an elusive prospect may well find satisfaction in mini-sabbaticals or extended vacation periods that replicate, in some small way, "retirement." These policy options can also involve work sharing. The increasing presence of women in the workforce is yet another reality that might provide the opportunity for some husband and wife job-sharing programs. There are almost as many women 65 years old and older in the labor force as there are men of this age.

A fourth policy set involves job redesign. The challenge of Japanese Quality Circles, drawing on what we now recognize as a vast reservoir of employee intelligence, suggests that a radical improvement in work process is now in order. The delayed recognition of this fact, and the need to give speedy attention to modernization, creates a fresh opportunity to provide for more humane connection points of employee-to-employee, employee-to-supervisor, and employee-to-the-machine processes. With the recognition that we are now more often than not dealing with a "thinking" rather than simply a "working" labor force, the opportunities for innovation are apparent.

Still another policy option involves an expanded program of employee education, an exercise that can extend to all of the current working-age categories. A regular rhythm of course work and job assignment rotation can broaden and deepen understanding of the dynamics of the production process and create that sense of poise and self-confidence essential for both personal and industrial growth. The resulting increase in versatility of skills will of course increase job adjustment opportunities for individual employees. A fluid and trouble-free accommodation of labor to changing job requirements will involve the marriage of coping skills with industry needs.

There are, in addition, expanding programs that involve uses of the mature worker in self-directed job factories, and in job search and placement activities. Reassigning personnel and using group techniques to buttress confidence are essential in restoring employee self-confidence, particularly in the face of shattering economic realities.

CONCLUSION

It seems clear that change, adjustment, and new accommodations to the "time traps" will dominate our future. Population shifts are occurring today, and major shifts will continue. More older people and fewer young ones are, and will be, available for labor force participation. Stress and pressure points are being applied to our national Social Security system. We believe, contrary to Department of Labor predictions, that labor participation rates for older Americans are likely to stabilize or increase rather than decline over the next 20 years. The challenge to industry is, of course, to anticipate those changes and their inevitable anxieties, and to make the accommodations that are essential for both corporate and employee health.

B.

HEALTH AND WELLNESS, EMPLOYEE ASSISTANCE PROGRAMS, AND STRESS

Physical Fitness and Employee Effectiveness

John J. Hoffman, Jr., and Charles J. Hobson

The growth in interest in physical fitness among U.S. organizations has been staggering. According to the President's Council On Physical Fitness, since 1973 the number of companies offering some kind of employee physical fitness program has increased tenfold from a mere 75 to a rather impressive 750.[15] More than 400 major corporations, including Xerox, Johnson & Johnson, Kimberly-Clark, Sentry Insurance, IBM, Prudential Insurance, Control Data and General Foods offer employees some type of fitness program.

Although the real surge in interest in physical fitness among corporations hasn't taken place until the past decade, the idea of company-sponsored physical fitness has been around for quite some time. In fact, it goes back as far as the 19th century when John H. Patterson instituted a physical fitness program at National Cash Register.[18] This program, which consisted of daily 10 minute exercise breaks, is believed to have been the first one of its kind in the United States. Patterson was convinced by a doctor that he could get more productivity out of his employees if he encouraged daily exercise. Ironically, NCR does not have an employee fitness program at the present time.

Other companies, however, have picked up where NCR left off and have developed their own employee fitness programs, some of which are more elaborate than others. Perhaps the most elaborate physical fitness program currently in existence is that of Kimberly-Clark, which operates a $2.5 million in-house employee fitness center with a full-time staff of 15 health personnel.[11]

TYPES OF PROGRAMS

Needless to say, not all company-sponsored fitness programs are as elaborate as that of Kimberly-Clark. Fitness programs run the full spectrum from fairly simple, such as subsidizing membership in the local Y.M.C.A.,[9] to elaborate, such as Kimberly-Clark's.

Reprinted from the April 1984 issue of *Personnel Administrator*, copyright 1979, The American Society for Personnel Administration, 606 North Washington Street, Alexandria, VA 22314, $30 per year.

Although there are about as many different types of fitness programs as there are companies that sponsor them, they can be classified into one of three basic categories: (1) company sponsorship of outside programs; (2) company sponsored and organized using an outside facility; and (3) company sponsored and organized with an in-house facility.

Company subsidization of an outside program is the simplest form of sponsorship and one that is popular with many companies. It doesn't require any capital investment and doesn't really need a minimum number of participants to make it worthwhile. This type of program simply involves company subsidization (full or partial) of an employee's membership in some fitness-related club or facility (i.e. Y.M.C.A., health spa, racket club, etc.).

While the company has no control over actual employee usage of the facility and thus, physical fitness, the potential is there for the company to reap the proposed benefits of having a physically fit employee. An advantage of this type of program is that the sponsoring company does not incur any liability for possible injury that the employee may receive while exercising.

A company sponsored and organized outside facility requires more extensive company involvement in the fitness program. Although the programs vary with each company, the basic structure is that the sponsoring company secures an outside fitness facility for a specified period of time and makes it available for employee use. The method of exercising done during these periods can either be individual and informal or structured and led by a designated instructor.

These programs usually involve a greater financial commitment from the company and require a minimum number of participants in order to be feasible. However, the company has a much better measure of actual employee usage when evaluating the effectiveness of such a program.

A company sponsored and organized in-house facility is the most extensive type of program and is the one gaining the most in popularity in U.S. organizations. It involves companies providing fitness facilities for employee usage at the worksite. Obviously, it requires a capital outlay by the company and also needs a minimum number of participants.

There are, however, some definite advantages associated with this type of program. In-house facilities provide the greatest opportunity for employee participation. It also enables company personnel to monitor the participation and progress of its employees. Some business executives, however, are somewhat wary of such in-house facilities because they fear the potential liability that could result from employee injuries.

There is much variation in the type of in-house fitness facilities that companies have. The Mitre Corp., an engineering firm, invested $10,000 to convert the basement of its Bedford, MA headquarters into a fitness center complete with showers, lockers and weightlifting equipment. At the other extreme, Xerox pumped $3.5 million into *one* of its seven exercise centers. The Xerox facility in Leesburg, VA includes a putting green, soccer field, swimming pool, two gyms, four tennis courts, two racketball courts, a weight room and 2,300 acres of wooded running area.

METHODS OF PARTICIPANT MOTIVATION

As there is great diversity in the types of fitness programs that companies institute, there are many methods used to motivate employees to participate in such programs. Once again, the motivational method must be structured to fit the particular situation of each individual company, thus no two methods of motivation are exactly alike. Most methods, however, can be categorized into one of three basic groups — purely voluntary, monetary or mandatory.

▫ Purely voluntary — This is the simplest, least costly, and definitely optimal method of motivation. It does, however, require an ideal situation if implementation is to be possible. Under the purely voluntary method, employees participate in the fitness program simply because they *want* to participate in pursuit of their own self-interest.

Implementation of this type of method requires employees who are highly self-motivated and well-disciplined. The theory behind the voluntary method of motivation is that once employees have been exposed to the potential personal benefits of physical fitness, they will take it upon themselves to get in shape. The primary motivating force is the personal benefits that can be derived from participating in a fitness program. The fact that subsequent benefits may also accrue to the organization is a secondary consideration in this situation.

Needless to say, not all corporations would find success with this method of motivation because the essential self-motivated work force is not always found. Recently, another interesting twist has been introduced that may greatly enhance the voluntary participation method of motivation. Several firms have extended the availability of their fitness programs to include the employees' families. By doing so, they hope to increase the level of participation in the programs.

▫ Monetary — As you move further down from top-to-bottom on Maslow's hierarchy of needs, you will find that some, if not most, people can be substantially motivated by monetary compensation. With this in mind, several companies have instituted various types of financial reward systems to encourage and stimulate participation in their fitness programs. Some companies offer bonuses to employees who achieve and/or maintain a desired level of fitness. Others simply pay employees for time spent working out at the company fitness center. Another fairly innovative idea that has been introduced recently encourages not simply participation, but rather achievement. Under this method, employees are paid a predetermined fee for each mile they run, push-up they do, pound they lose, etc. This relatively new concept may have some real potential since it rewards actual achievement rather than superficial participation.

▫ Mandatory — The third method of motivation is one that is fairly controversial. It involves making physical fitness mandatory for all employees. In Japan, for instance, all employees are required to participate in daily sessions of calisthenics in order to promote physical fitness. This type of program does not seem feasible in the United States, at least at the present time.

It is conceivable, however, that corporations could make physical fitness a prerequisite for employment. Only physically-fit employees would be hired in the future. Even more extreme, the existing workforce would be given a certain amount of time in which to get themselves in shape if they wish to remain employed. This is definitely rather extreme and controversial at the present time. However, once solid, statistically significant evidence on the effects of physical fitness on employees has been obtained and if that evidence shows a positive correlation between employee fitness and organizational efficiency, the notion of physical fitness as a prerequisite for employment becomes much more palatable.

EXPECTED BENEFITS

As was mentioned earlier, businesses are not jumping on the fitness bandwagon purely as a result of a sudden rush of paternalistic concern for the well-being of employees. Instead, they feel that there are some definite benefits that can be reaped by the corporation as a result of promoting physical fitness among employees. Fitness advocates strongly contend that physical fitness has a positive impact on important employee variables such as performance, absenteeism, satisfaction and stress. In addition, company sponsorship of physical fitness can substantially reduce company health-care costs. Finally, many businesses now believe that having a physical fitness program can be an important recruitment and retention tool.

RESEARCH EVIDENCE

In evaluating the methodological soundness of research it is useful to consider the typology of research designs introduced by Campbell and Stanley.[2] They described three basic types of designs: experimental, quasi-experimental and pre-experimental.

Briefly, experimental designs represent the most rigorous from a methodological perspective. Random selection of subjects, random assignment of subjects to experimental groups, careful control of experimental conditions, precise administration and manipulation of the independent variable (supposed causal variable) and accurate measurement of the dependent variable (the outcome measure of concern) allow one to realistically address the causal relationships between variables.

Quasi-experimental designs differ from experimental ones basically in the lack of random assignment of subjects to groups. Thus, alternative explanations for an observed relationship between the independent and dependent variable cannot be eliminated. Finally, pre-experimental designs (such as one-shot case studies and single group, pretest/post-test approaches), because of their excessive simplicity are beset with a number of serious methodological problems which preclude adequately addressing causal relationships between two variables.

Unfortunately, much of the research relating physical fitness to the various outcome measures is of the pre-experimental variety. Thus, in such instances, we simply do not know, in any scientific way, whether fitness is causally related to these other variables. In terms of more specific shortcomings in the research, one frequently finds such problems as: (1) the lack of adequate control groups for comparison purposes; (2) self selection of subjects, i.e., only those with the motivation and interest in fitness participated; (3) the lack of statistical significance testing to determine the probability of chance findings.

PERFORMANCE

Advocates of the fitness movement strongly contend that improved fitness leads to improved job performance. There are various schools of reasoning behind this contention, ranging from very sophisticated (such as exercise increases the flow of oxygen to the brain which, in turn, allows for clearer thinking and improved alertness) to rather simplistic (such as "an employee who feels better, works better"). In any case, proponents of physical fitness are quick to include improved productivity as one of its benefits.

To date, few methodologically sound studies on fitness and job performance have been completed. Some research of questionable vigor has been undertaken in Europe[5,22,25,14,4,10] which seems to indicate that fit workers are more productive. On the basis of these results however, no firm causal statements are possible.

Unfortunately, the remainder of the research dealing with fitness and performance is entirely of the pre-experimental variety and thus fraught with all of the associated interpretational problems. For instance, a recent study of office workers at a large insurance company measured supervisory ratings of employee performance at two different intervals.[27] Between measurements, members of the test group took part in a structured physical fitness program while members of the control group did not. While the study indicated that the average level of supervisory ratings increased for the test group, the findings were based on questionnaires that were voluntarily submitted by the employee. As a result, the number of employees responding to the second measurement was substantially less than that of the first. It is logical to assume that those who received higher performance ratings the second time would be more willing to respond to the questionnaire than those who received lower ratings. Thus, the results of this study are uninterpretable and cannot be considered as evidence in support of the fitness-performance relationship.

In summary, while the literature in this area generally supports the notion that fitness is positively related to performance, the bulk of the research is of questionable methodological soundness and thus no firm conclusions can be drawn concerning causality.

ABSENTEEISM

One of the strongest contentions offered by advocates of the fitness movement is that improved employee fitness results in reduced absenteeism. This claim is based on the logic that employees who exercise feel better and are in better physical condition. As a result, they are less likely to miss work. A great deal of pre-experimental type literature supports this contention. Brief examples include:

- A study of two groups of employees at the headquarters of Metropolitan Life found that 100 employees who participated in a fitness program averaged 4.8 sick days per year as compared to 6.2 days absence per year for members of the control group who did not exercise.[32]
- Officials of the Battelle Memorial Institute report that a recent study indicated that employees who used the fitness facilities at the firm's Columbus, OH laboratories averaged 2.8 days less absenteeism than those who did not. The firm reported that the total savings associated with the reduced absenteeism was approximately $150,000 per year.[13]
- Internorth, Inc. of Omaha, NE contends that a recent company study found a positive correlation between fitness and absenteeism.[12] Employees who participated in aerobic exercise classes at Internorth were absent from work an average of one day a year while nonparticipants averaged six days absence per year.[33]
- A study conducted at two large insurance offices indicated that an analysis of company attendance records found that subjects who actively participated in a fitness program had essentially the same absenteeism rate before participation in the program began as did other employees. However, during six months of participation in the fitness program, they developed a 22 percent advantage relative to other employees.[29]
- Northern Natural Gas officials have reported that participants in its aerobic program lost significantly fewer work days because of illness than non-participating employees.[11]

☐ A Johnson & Johnson survey indicated that employees who participated in its fitness program took fewer sick days than non-participants did.[30]

More rigorous studies on the fitness-absenteeism link were generally not available. However, more scientific research originating in Europe[5,23,21,15] does seem to support the contention that fit employees are absent less frequently. Since these studies also fall short of the requirements for vigorous experimental and quasi-experimental designs, we cannot at this time conclusively assert that fitness causes less absenteeism. A general trend in this direction is certainly evidenced, yet causality has not been demonstrated.

SATISFACTION

Proponents of physical fitness maintain that exercise and its subsequent effect on fitness has a positive effect on the level of employee job satisfaction. The basis for this contention is that exercising results in a more positive self-image which, in turn, has impact upon job satisfaction. People who feel better about themselves will usually have a greater amount of satisfaction with the work they do. Fitness advocates maintain that exercise will improve overall job satisfaction and result in greater organizational efficiency.

Folkins and Sime[8] have reviewed the fairly extensive research relating fitness training and various mental health variables, i.e., mood and self-concept. They asserted, "In general, studies of physical fitness effects on psychological health are poorly designed [and] only about 15 percent of the studies reviewed qualified as true experiments." However, on the basis of these studies, the authors concluded that the findings suggest that fitness training leads to improved mood and self-concept.

To the extent that overall improvements in mood and self-concept generalize to job satisfaction, one would expect fitness training to increase satisfaction. No rigorous experimental research bearing directly on this issue is available. There have been some pre-experimental studies in this area however. For instance, Johnson and Johnson conducted a survey of employees and found that those who participated in a regular fitness program were more satisfied with their jobs than were nonparticipants.[30] The interpretational problems with this type of study have already been addressed.

Thus, in summary, while fitness training does seem to cause improved mood and self-concept, and one might reasonably hypothesize that it would also improve job satisfaction, to date we cannot draw any firm conclusions about this particular relationship.

STRESS

At present there is a growing body of experimental and clinical research supporting the notion that physical fitness can lead to significant reductions in job stress.[19,27] Regular, rigorous physical activity has been shown to reduce muscle tension, anxiety, blood pressure, heart rate and incidence of heart attacks — all stress related symptoms.

Schuler[27] has argued that we are currently faced with an epidemic of job stress in this country which is costing billions of dollars per year in lost hours and health costs. Given these staggering figures, it seems rather obvious, based upon the extensive research available, that fitness programs could be expected to significantly reduce job stress and thus have favorable impact on the bottom line.

HEALTH CARE COSTS

Employee health care costs represent a sizeable sum of money for businesses each year. Premature employee death ($25 billion) and employee illness and disability ($3 billion) combine to cost companies approximately $28 billion a year.[11] In other terms, U.S. businesses pay an estimated $60 billion a year for employee health insurance plans.[31]

While few scientific studies are available, there is a growing body of anecdotal case studies supporting the idea that fitness programs can lead to reductions in health care costs. For instance:

□ An insurance employee study found that exercise subjects had a diminished rate of health care visits, lower expenditures for prescription drugs, fewer colds and fewer absences from work. The study noted, however, that the reduced health care utilization may have been attributable to seasonal factors.[29]

□ Several insurance companies have begun to offer lower group health insurance premiums to those corporate clients that have implemented a structured employee physical fitness program. A survey conducted by Fitness Systems found that no firm with a fitness program cited an increase in insurance costs, while 15 percent actually noted a reduction in insurance costs.[15]

□ A model has been created by Marvin Kristein, an economist at the National Institute of Health in Bethesda, MD which shows that the average white-collar company would save about $466,000 in annual medical costs for each group of 1,000 employees by promoting good health and thereby helping them reduce disease factors in their lives.[32]

Given the well documented improvements in fitness attributed to sustained exercise, it seems only a matter of time before conclusive experimental and clinical evidence is forthcoming supporting the causal relationship between fitness and reduced health care costs.

RECRUITMENT RETENTION

The final benefit proposed by advocates of physical fitness programs deals with the aspects of recruitment and retention. They maintain that firms that sponsor an employee fitness program can use it as a selling point to attract potential employees or to retain those currently under hire. Fitness proponents point out that this can be an extremely attractive fringe benefit, especially at the executive level.

Unfortunately, there are virtually no scientific studies of the relationship between fitness programs and enhanced recruiting or retention. For the time being we can only refer to a growing number of anecdotal case studies. For example:

□ As Dr. Robert Dedmon, vice-president of medical affairs at Kimberly-Clark points out, the in-house fitness center has been a big recruiting aid. "It's been swell for us in recruiting. Other considerations being equal, the availability of the program has helped to sway the decisions of young people about joining us."[15]

□ An in-house fitness center can also help with retention of key employees. A bank examiner at Boston Federal noted that his friends at other Boston banks were "very jealous" of Federal's fitness center.[33]

□ *Time* magazine recently commented, "A corporate fitness program is the hottest perk since the executive washroom." The same article quoted a Xerox executive as saying, "Before I'd change jobs, I'd ask an employer if he had a gym."[9]

Thus, while no sound scientific data are currently available, it seems reasonable to hypothesize that a probable relationship would emerge. Certainly such rigorous research is warranted.

Much of the literature is pre-experimental and thus definitive causal relationships have not been well established. However, physical fitness does seem to be related to a number of important aspects of employee effectiveness. More specifically, there is strong evidence that physical fitness leads to improved mood and self-concept (related to job satisfaction) and reduced job stress. There is some support for the hypothesized relationships between fitness and job performance and absenteeism. Finally, there is growing recognition of the probable relationships between fitness and health care costs and recruitment/retention. Thus, on the basis of the available research, we strongly recommend physical fitness as a way to improve both personal and organizational effectiveness.

FUTURE RESEARCH

Obviously, the foremost research recommendation must center on the need for more methodologically rigorous research; i.e., more frequent use of experimental and quasi-experimental designs. Only in this manner will we be able to expand our scientific understanding of the effects of physical fitness.

A second recommendation concerns the need for effective cost/benefit evaluation of fitness programs in the manner suggested by Cascio.[3] Using this approach, one estimates the dollar costs to the company of implementing and operating a fitness program and the dollar benefits of the associated outcomes (improved performance, satisfaction, absenteeism, etc.). These costs and benefits can then be compared to determine if a company's fitness expenditures are justifiable in terms of their dollar return. Given the likely relationships between fitness and a number of economically important employee effectiveness criteria, we would predict that cost/benefit analysis of fitness programs would dramatically demonstrate their value.

In conducting cost/benefit analyses, one must take into consideration the different time frames for realization of expected benefits. Pyle[23] has developed a timetable charting the emergence of these expected benefits. He contends that evaluative measures of fitness programs can be broken down into three basic time frames — short-term (three to four months), intermediate (one year), and long-term (minimum three to five years).

In the short-term, the primary value of a fitness program is to the individual participant who benefits by an improved overall physiology, especially reduced risk of coronary failure and minimization of various other health hazards.

During the intermediate time frame, some benefits begin accruing to the company in terms of reduced absenteeism and improved employee morale. However, the major portion of the benefits during the first year are still realized by the individual participant who develops an improved self-image and self-confidence as well as further improvement on the physiological factors realized in the short-term.

It is not until the longer term, Pyle maintains, that corporate management truly begins to reap the benefits of employee fitness programs. It is during this time frame that increases in productivity and overall organizational effectiveness can be noticed. In addition, the fitness program will now have had sufficient time to produce significant impact on corporate health care costs. It is during this period, Pyle claims, that a cost/benefit analysis should be conducted to get a true evaluation of the effectiveness of the fitness program.[23] An effective cost/benefit analysis of employee fitness must build in this long-term perspective in order to accurately assess the true dollar impact of a program.

A third research recommendation deals with the need for comparative evaluation of the risks and benefits associated with various forms of physical activity. There are two major reasons why this research is important.

First, some types of exercise have a much greater potential for injury than others. For instance, basketball and touch football have a much greater incidence of sprained ankles and broken wrists, than jogging and weightlifting. If a company were to advocate activities such as basketball or football, they could find their increase in health care costs due to injuries would more than offset the reduction in costs resulting from the benefits of exercise.

A second, more "scientific" reason why the type of exercise must be given serious consideration is that different types of exercise have different effects on physiological variables, especially stress. Carl Browman of the State University of New York points out that static exercise has a substantially different impact on stress than dynamic exercise. Static exercise, such as push-ups and weightlifting, seems to trigger a fatigue response that relaxes a person. Dynamic exercise, on the other hand, which includes running and swimming, produces a generalized stress effect.[17]

Finally, a fourth research recommendation concerns the need for evaluation of alternative methods to motivate participation. If one assumes that fit employees are "better," more effective employees, it becomes important to determine how to maximally motivate program involvement. Research is particularly needed in evaluating the relative efficacy of various monetary incentives to encourage fitness.

RECOMMENDATIONS FOR MANAGEMENT

On the basis of this review, it seems safe to conclude that physical fitness is related to important aspects of employee effectiveness. Thus, in general, we advocate the implementation and operation of fitness programs. However, with respect to optional methods of motivating participation and the most beneficial physical activity, specific research-supported recommendations cannot be made at this time. We simply don't know, as our research base is extremely limited. We encourage any organization implementing or operating a fitness program to rigorously measure and evaluate its effect to increase scientific knowledge on the topic. In addition, we recommend a thorough cost/benefit analysis to fully justify fitness program expenditures. On the basis of the available research, we would predict that in most instances, organizations would derive substantial dollar benefits from successfully operated fitness programs.

Finally, in those instances where management has decided to begin a new fitness program, several key ingredients are necessary for successful implementation and operation.

Company commitment is vital to the success of any employee fitness program. Top management's belief in and support of fitness promotion will greatly increase the potential for success. This support must be real. The best way to express this support is to have top executives participating in the program. Furthermore, the commitment must be long-standing; it cannot fade with the initial enthusiasm. If it does, the program will be doomed to failure.[1]

In conclusion, it must be emphasized that there was an overwhelming general consensus of support for fitness programs in the research. This attitude is best expressed by Darwin E. Smith, chairman of Kimberly-Clark: "Kimberly-Clark has a substantial investment in its employees. To us, it is simply good business sense to keep them feeling well, which not only keeps them on the job but even helps them do a better job. If our program is successful, we can look forward to increased productivity. Also, we may have found a partial solution to the continually mounting costs of direct medical care. . . . "[11]

REFERENCES

1. A. J. Brennan, Health promotion in business: Caveats for success. *Journal of Occupational Medicine*, 1981, 23, pp. 639–642.

2. D. T. Campbell & J. C. Stanley. *Experimental and quasi-experimental designs for research*, Chicago: Rand McNally, 1963.

3. W. F. Cascio, *Costing human resources: The financial impact of behavior in organizations*, Boston: Kent Publishers, 1982.

4. K. H. Cooper, Aerobics. (Paper presented at the National Conference on Fitness and Health, Ottawa, Ontario), Dec. 1972.

5. S. Donoghue, The correlation between physical fitness, absenteeism and work performance. *Canadian Journal of Public Health*, 1977, 68, pp. 201–203.

6. Employee physical fitness enhances work efficiency. *Office*, 1981, 94, p. 176.

7. Fitness: Extending the benefits (Kimberly-Clark). *Management Review*, 1982, 71, pp. 45–46.

8. C. H. Folkins & W. E. Sime, Physical fitness training and mental health. *American Psychologist*, 1981, 36, pp. 373–389.

9. From boardroom to locker room. *Time*, 1979, January 22.

10. F. Heinzelmann & D. C. Durbeck, Personal benefits of a health evaluation and enhancement program (Paper presented at the NASA Annual Conference of Clinic Directors, Health Officials and Medical Program Advisors, Cambridge, MA) October, 1970.

11. C. W. Higgins & B. U. Philips, How company-sponsored fitness programs keep employees on the job. *Management Review*, 1979, 68, pp. 53–55.

12. B. A. Jacobs, Wellness goal-trim workers and costs. *Industry Week*, 1980, 206, pp. 90–91.

13. J. S. Lang, America's fitness binge. *US News & World Report*, May 3, 1982, pp. 58–61.

14. W. Laporte, The influence of a gymnastic pause upon recovery following post office work. *Ergonomics*, 1966, 9, pp. 501–506.

15. R. Levy, Fitness fever: Everybody into the company gym. *Dun's Review*, 1980, November, pp. 115–118.

16. V. Linden, Absence from work and physical fitness. *British Journal of Industrial Medicine*, 1969, 26, p. 50.

17. G. Mirkin & M. Hoffman, *The sports-medicine book*, Boston: Little, Brown & Co., 1978.

18. National Cash Register's pioneer physical fitness program. *Dun's Review*, November 1980, pp. 155–166.

19. J. E. Newman & T. A. Beehr, Personal and organizational strategies for handling job stress: A review of research and opinion. *Personnel Psychology*, 1979, 32, pp. 1–44.

20. C. A. Owen, E. F. Beard, A. S. Jackson & B. W. Prior, Longitudinal evaluation of an exercise prescription program with periodic ergometric testing: A 10-year appraisal. *Journal of Occupational Medicine*, 1980, 22, pp. 235–240.

21. J. T. Pauley, J. A. Palmer, C. C. Wright & G. J. Pfeiffer, The effect of a 14-week

employee fitness program on selected physiological and psychological parameters. *Journal of Occupational Medicine*, 1982, 24, pp. 457–463.

22. V. Pravosudov, The effect of physical exercises on health and economic efficiency. (Paper presented at the pre-Olympic Scientific Congress, Montreal, Canada), 1976.

23. R. L. Pyle, Performance measures for a corporate fitness program. *Human Resources Management*, 1979, *18*, pp. 26–30.

24. W. Raab & S. B. Gilman, Insurance-sponsored preventive cardiac reconditioning centers in West Germany. *American Journal of Cardiology*, 1964, *13*, pp. 670–673.

25. P. Reville, Sports for all. (Strasbourg Council for Cultural Cooperation, Council of Europe, Chapter III), 1970.

26. B. Richardson, Don't just sit there . . . exercise something. *Fitness for Living*, 1974, *49*, May–June.

27. R. S. Schuler, Definition and conceptualization of stress in organizations. *Organizational Behavior and Human Performance*, 1980, *25*, pp. 184–215.

28. G. F. Shea, Profiting from wellness training. *Training and Development Journal*, 1981, October, pp. 32–37.

29. R. J. Shepard, M. Cox & P. Corey, Fitness program participation: Its effect on worker performance. *Journal of Occupational Medicine*, 1981, *23*, pp. 359–363.

30. C. Tuhy, New stay-well centers. *Money*, 1981, *10*, pp. 87–88.

31. M. Waldholz, Businesses are forming coalitions to curb rise in health care costs. *Wall Street Journal*, June 11, 1982.

32. *Wall Street Journal*, Ounce of prevention is worth a pound of cure, or so say proponents of "wellness movement," September 15, 1981.

33. *Wall Street Journal*, Employers try in-house fitness centers to lift morale, cut cost of health claims, November 10, 1981.

Improving Corporate Performance through Employee-Assistance Programs

Julian L. Carr and Richard T. Hellan

Over the last thirty years a great amount of business research and program development has centered on improving the performance of organizations and the individuals who make them up: MBO programs, improved organizational structure, incentive programs, and participative management. None of them, however, has addressed the needs of the individual employee as directly as the rapidly emerging Employee Assistance Programs (EAPs).

Why the increased interest in these programs? There seem to be several reasons:

□ Turnover, absenteeism, and sub-par job performance cost American industry substantial sums each year;

□ Both management and labor leaders realize more needs to be done to assist the problem drinker and other problem employees;

□ The increasing complexity of our society creates a wide range of problems that each of us must deal with, from child rearing to marital troubles. Research indicates they can create a major impediment to successful performance on the job. This article will set forth some background data on personal assistance programs and will present data to illustrate the benefits of employee assistance programs. Finally it will suggest ways to implement an EAP in your organization.

A BIT OF BACKGROUND

Today's broadly defined assistance programs began with the work in occupational alcoholism programs. From a handful of occupational alcoholism programs begun in the 1940s, there have emerged not only varying schools of thought regarding the treatment of alcoholism in industry, but also a diversification of occupational programs. As recently as 1959, only about fifty American companies were operating occupational alcoholism programs. By 1975, 700 such programs had been implemented in public and private work environments.

Broader development of the occupational program concept began in 1972 when the Occupational Programs Branch of the National Institute of Alcoholism and Alcohol Abuse (NIAAA) endorsed the "broad brush" approach as the best strategy for occupational alcoholism programs. After surveying 300 companies which had a written policy on alcoholism and employee assistance, the Occupational Programs Branch found that the small percentage of successful programs shared a number of features on which the broader concept of the employee assistance program was based.

HOW EAPs FUNCTION

By its very title, the "employee assistance program" signals a change in both application and technique from the traditional occupational alcoholism program. A program of employee assistance extends services to all "troubled" employees. It makes identification, referral, and counseling elements of the program available to any employee with a personal problem that is affecting work performance — not just the employee who has an alcohol problem. In the traditional occupational alcoholism program the supervisor had to look for symptoms of alcoholism and then diagnose the problem. Now, through an employee assistance program, the supervisor is responsible only for identifying declining work performance, a role for which he is much better suited than that of "alcoholism counselor." When a pattern of poor work performance is identified, and the supervisor's normal steps to intervene do not produce results, the supervisor confronts the employee with this pattern and then offers the employee assistance program. The goal of this offer is to reverse the pattern of declining performance.

One example of a very successful "broad brush" employee assistance program was developed by the Utah Copper Division of Kennecott Copper Corporation in 1970. Planned and implemented by the personnel department, the program caught on quickly. The Kennecott program, INSIGHT, employed a program director and a psychiatric social worker who provided initial counseling to employees in their own homes. Employees were referred by the program director either to other INSIGHT counselors or to the appropriate social service agency for resolving their problems. The referred employee's participation in the program was voluntary, although he or she was made aware that disciplinary action would follow if work performance continued to fall below company standards.

Although the Kennecott program now functions along different lines because of a change in the program's directorship, it demonstrates the practicality and effectiveness of employee assistance programs. Similar employee assistance programs were operating prior to 1972 at Hughes Aircraft Company, Employers Insurance Company of Wausau, and Illinois Bell Telephone Company.

Today's employee assistance programs are designed along much the same lines and can be found in both the public and private sectors.

Those programs that apply the "broad brush" or "troubled employee" approach, whether they are in-house company efforts or programs run by private consulting firms, are designed to provide services to all employees who have personal problems that may interfere with job performance and productivity. Typically, however, these programs avoid involvement with employee problems that relate specifically to management. If a female employee, for example, explains to a counselor that she is being treated unfairly in regard to promotion, and if the counselor, after evaluation, concurs that personal problems are not the issue, then the employee would be informed that the assistance program is not the proper resource for attempting to resolve her problem and she would be referred to another source.

MANAGERS BREATHE EASIER

Rough estimates reveal that 10 to 12 percent of the American work force experiences serious personal problems: a significant number of those suffer from alcoholism or other chemical dependence. On the basis of its analysis of six areas of behavior identified as sources of economic costs, the NIAAA estimated that in 1974 alcoholism and alcohol abuse alone cost American business and industry about $9.35 billion in lost production of goods and services.

Studies of employee assistance programs show that they reduce costs. Kennecott Copper, for example, conducted a study midway through the thirty-second month of its EAP operation. Absenteeism, weekly indemnity costs, and hospital, medical, and surgical costs were calculated during a six-month period preceding their participation in the employee assistance program and these figures were compared with calculations from the six-month period following their involvement. The comparison showed that after an average of 12.7 months in the program, attendance improved by 5.2 percent, weekly indemnity costs decreased by 74.6 percent, and hospital, medical, and surgical costs decreased by 55.4 percent!

Not only does an employee assistance program reduce cost, but also it is an effective tool for dealing with difficult, sensitive problems. By using declining work performance or a particular disruptive incident as the sole criterion for supervisor referral of an employee to the program director, management is able to maintain high work standards and consistent management practices. While the employee knows that his participation in the program is voluntary, he also knows that continuing poor work performance will result in disciplinary action and, in many cases, the loss of his or her job. In an effective employee assistance program, supervisors are trained to identify patterns of declining performance and to refer employees to the counseling services of the program. Never must the supervisor become involved in the employee's personal problem — or even know the nature of the problem. Rather, the supervisor's focus can be on job performance, attitude, and productivity.

Many companies are beginning to institute such programs in response to management's increasing awareness of its own social responsibility. By offering assistance to employees who have personal problems, the company contributes to the individual employee's well-being, his ability to function productively and happily in his home and community as well as on the job.

An employee assistance program, then, reduces absenteeism and other symptoms of employees' personal problems and utilizes their skills more efficiently in the work place. In addition, it lets the employee know that the company cares about his or her personal and emotional well-being.

IMPLEMENTING AN EAP

Most employee assistance programs operate on the same basic premises: Supervisors identify poor work performance and refer the employee to a counselor or program coordinator who suggests follow-up counseling or treatment to help the employee resolve his or her problem. Of course, there are significant variations in particulars such as supervisor training, promotion of the program within the company, and counseling services. Likewise, the effectiveness of a program will depend on the way these particular elements operate. The constant, strong support of all levels of management, expertise in designing and maintaining the program, and ongoing evaluation are essential if the program is to carry out what it promises.

When planning a program, the following questions must be addressed:

☐ How will we insure that the program does not interfere with the role and functions of management?

☐ How will we promote the program within the company and keep it visible?

☐ How can confidentiality be assured? Will employees who use the program be certain that their problems remain private — that their use of the program, in fact, is not known to other employees?

☐ How will we insure that employees will become familiar with the program before personal problems result in reduced work performance?

☐ What sort of interface will the program have with other programs and departments within the company, such as our benefits program?

In the end, an employee assistance program must be tailored to the needs of the company. A successful program will reflect the research, training, experience, and knowledge of individuals who have pooled their resources to arrive at a program which is unique to the company it serves. Given the tremendous impact it can have on a company and the individual employees, it must not be undertaken lightly. Top management should treat it as they would any other key strategic program: by providing support, funding, and proper personnel, and by insisting on sound planning and on-going review and control. Firms that have implemented programs, such as Monsanto, General American Life Insurance Company, and Pet Incorporated, indicate the returns will be rewarding.

Stress: Can We Cope?

Time

> *"Rule No. 1 is, don't sweat the small stuff. Rule No. 2 is, it's all small stuff. And if you can't fight and you can't flee, flow."*
>
> — University of Nebraska Cardiologist Robert Eliot, on how to cope with stress

It is the dawn of human history, and Homo sapiens steps out from his cave to watch the rising sun paint the horizon. Suddenly he hears a rustling in the forest. His muscles tense, his heart pounds, his breath comes rapidly as he locks eyes with a saber-toothed tiger. Should he fight or run for his life? He reaches down, picks up a sharp rock and hurls it. The animal snarls but disappears into the trees. The man feels his body go limp, his breathing ease. He returns to his darkened den to rest.

It is the start of another working day, and Homo sapiens steps out of his apartment building into the roar of rush hour. He picks his way through the traffic and arrives at the corner just in time to watch his bus pull away. Late for work, he opens his office door and finds the boss pacing inside. His report was due an hour ago, he is told; the client is furious. If he values his job, he had better have a good explanation. And, by the way, he can forget about taking a vacation this summer. The man eyes a paper-weight on his desk and longs to throw it at his oppressor. Instead, he sits down, his stomach churning, his back muscles knotting, his blood pressure climbing. He reaches for a Maalox and an aspirin and has a sudden yearning for a dry martini, straight up.

The saber-toothed tiger is long gone, but the modern jungle is no less perilous. The sense of panic over a deadline, a tight plane connection, a reckless driver on one's tail are the new beasts that can set the heart racing, the teeth on edge, the sweat streaming. These responses may have served our ancestors well; that extra burst of adrenaline got their muscles primed, their attention focused and their nerves ready for a sudden "fight or flight." But try doing either one in today's traffic jams or board-rooms. "The fight-or-flight emergency response is inappropriate to today's social stresses," says Harvard Cardiologist Herbert Benson, an expert on the subject. It is also dangerous. Says Psychiatrist Peter Knapp of Boston University: "When you get a Wall Street broker using the responses a cave man used to fight the elements, you've got a problem."

Indeed we have. In the past 30 years, doctors and health officials have come to realize how heavy a toll stress is taking on the nation's well-being. According to the American Academy of Family Physicians, two-thirds of office visits to family doctors are prompted by stress-related symptoms. At the same time, leaders of industry have become alarmed by the huge cost of such symptoms in absenteeism, company medical expenses and lost productivity. Based on national samples, these costs have been estimated at $50 billion to $75 billion a year, more than $750 for every U.S. worker. Stress is now known to be a major contributor, either directly or indirectly, to coronary heart disease, cancer, lung ailments, accidental injuries, cirrhosis of the liver and suicide — six of the leading causes of death in the U.S. Stress also plays a role in aggravating such diverse conditions as multiple sclerosis, diabetes, genital herpes and even trench mouth. It is a sorry sign of the times that the three bestselling drugs in the country are an ulcer medication (Tagamet), a hypertension drug (Inderal) and a tranquilizer (Valium). Concludes Dr. Joel Elkes, director of the behavioral medicine program at the University of Louisville: "Our mode of life itself, the way we live, is emerging as today's principal cause of illness."

Concern over the "stress epidemic" has prompted what may be called a mass fight-and-flight reaction. New fields have sprung into being: behavioral medicine, to battle stress-related illness; psychoneuroimmunology, to explore the way emotional states affect the body's defenses. Major corporations have established elaborate stress-management programs to help harried executives cope. And around the country, but especially in mellow-minded California, says Psychiatrist Mardi Horowitz of the University of California at San Francisco, "everyone is massaging, jogging and hot-tubbing to reduce this cumulative stress."

No one really knows if there is more stress now than in the past, but many experts believe it has become more pervasive. "We live in a world of uncertainties," says Harvard's Benson, "everything from the nuclear threat to job insecurity to the near assassination of the President to the lacing of medicines with poisons." Through television, these problems loom up under our very noses, and yet, says Psychologist Kenneth Dychtwald of Berkeley, Calif., the proximity only frustrates us: "We can't fight back with those people on TV."

The upheaval in society's most basic values adds greatly to the general level of anxiety. Even our pleasures are often fretful. When Psychiatrist George Serban of New York University conducted a nationwide poll of 1,008 mostly married men and women aged 18 to 60, he found that their greatest source of stress was the changes in society's attitudes toward sex, including sexual permissiveness and "the new social roles of the sexes." While stress might have once taken the form of an occasional calamity, it is now "a chronic, relentless psychosocial situation," says Dr. Paul Rosch, director of the American Institute of Stress in Yonkers, N.Y.

Curiously, Rosch notes, today's pressures have created a breed of thrill seekers who, often to their own detriment, prefer excitement over tranquility. Life in the fast lane becomes a dangerous habit for them. "Skydivers get hooked on the jump," he says, "executives purposely arrive at the airport at the last possible minute. People today have become addicted to their own adrenaline secretion."

For all its present vogue, "stress" has only recently been admitted into the medical vocabulary. For years, doctors considered the term too unscientific to be taken seriously. "The moment you used the word, you were dismissed as a thinking individual," says Dr. Harold Ward, director of the stress medicine laboratory at the University of California at San Diego. One reason was the lack of an adequate definition for the concept. According to the late Dr. Hans Selye, the Austrian-born founding father of stress research, stress is simply "the rate of wear and tear in the body." But others persist in using the term to refer to any external stimulus that causes wear and tear, or to the resulting internal damage. This has led to considerable confusion. As one researcher has put it, "Stress, in addition to being itself, and the result of itself, is also the cause of itself."

Medical interest in the phenomenon began on the battlefield, where the devastating effects of chronic stress are unmistakable. During the Civil War, for example, palpitations were so commonplace that they became known as "soldier's heart." During World War I, the crippling anxiety called shell shock was at first attributed to the vibrations from heavy artillery, which was believed to damage blood vessels in the brain. This theory was abandoned by the time World War II came along, and the problem was renamed battle fatigue. By then the great Harvard physiologist Walter Cannon, along with Selye, had proved that psychological strain itself could cause dramatic hormonal changes and hence physiological symptoms. Selye showed that when the fight-or-flight response becomes chronic, as it does in battle, long-term chemical changes occur, leading to high blood pressure, an increased rate of arteriosclerosis, depression of the immune system and a cascade of other problems. "Humans have a fairly robust capacity to withstand a massive dose of acute stress," says Dr. Fred Goodwin, director of intramural research at the National Institute of Mental Health (NIMH). "Where we fall down is in our ability to mobilize for recurrent stressful episodes." Today the physiology of stress is being worked out in extraordinary detail. Says Neurochemist Jack Barchas of Stanford: "We have learned that even subtle behavior can markedly influence biochemistry."

War makes everyone anxious. But because most other kinds of stress are subjective, researchers have found it difficult to say just why a given situation is threatening. "I would die if I had to sit in a space capsule," says Boston University Psychiatrist Sanford Cohen. But while working with the early astronauts some 20 years ago, Cohen observed that "John Glenn just saw it as a job and went about it in a businesslike manner." Notes Benson: "A snowstorm is not stressful to a skier, but it is to someone who has an appointment across town."

In the early 1950s, University of Washington Psychiatrist Thomas Holmes determined that the single common denominator for stress, even for an astronaut, is "the necessity of significant change in the life pattern of the individual." Holmes found that among tuberculosis patients, for example, the onset of the disease had generally followed a cluster of disruptive events: a death in the family, a new job, marriage. Stress did not cause the illness, Holmes emphasizes — "It takes a germ" — but tension did seem to promote the disease process. Holmes discovered that merely discussing upsetting events could produce physiological changes. An experiment in which sample biopsies were taken before and after discussions of certain subjects showed that "we caused tissue damage just by talking about a mother-in-law's coming to visit," says Holmes. The example, he notes, is not facetious: "A person often catches a cold when a mother-in-law comes to visit. Patients mentioned mothers-in-law so often that we came to consider them a common cause of disease in the U.S."

In an attempt to measure the impact of "life change events," Holmes and Psychologist Richard Rahe, working together in the 1940s and '50s, asked 5,000 people to rate the amount of social readjustment required for various events. The result is the widely used Holmes-Rahe scale. At the top is death of a spouse (100 stress points), followed by divorce (73), marital separation (65), imprisonment (63) and death of a close family member (63). Not all stressful events are unpleasant. Marriage rates 50; pregnancy, 40; buying a house, 31; and Christmas, 12. Holmes went on to show that in a sample of 88 young doctors, those who totaled 300 or more units on the scale had a 70% chance of suffering ulcers, psychiatric disturbances, broken bones or other health problems within two years of the various crises; those who scored under 200 had only a 37% incidence of such infirmities. The scale proved to be an effective prognosticator as well: by tallying up the life stress of healthy college football players, Holmes and Rahe were even able to predict which ones would be injured during the next season.

The impact of major life events on health has been reconfirmed many times. A study published earlier this year in the British medical journal *Lancet* reported that the incidence of fatal heart attacks rose sharply in Athens in the days following the 1981 earthquake there. Stanford Neurochemist Barchas has found that a high score on the Holmes-Rahe scale is linked to elevated levels of the hormones associated with stress: adrenaline (which scientists have rechristened epinephrine), norepinephrine and beta-endorphin. An Australian study of bereavement has shown that eight weeks after the death of their spouses, widows and widowers have diminished immune responses, leaving them more vulnerable to infection and cancer.

Some experts do not agree that the Holmes-Rahe scale is the best measure of personal stress. By conducting a series of surveys, Psychologist Richard Lazarus, of the University of California at Berkeley, has become convinced that the everyday annoyances of life, or "hassles," contribute more to illness and depression than major life changes. Lazarus cites a poem by Charles Bukowski to illustrate his point:

> . . . *It's not the large things that*
> *send a man to the*
> *madhouse . . . no, it's the*
> *   continuing series of*
> *small tragedies*
> *that send a man to the madhouse*
>   *. . .*
> *not the death of his love*
> *but a shoelace that snaps*
> *with no time left . . .*

The snapped-shoelace factor ties in with a number of recent studies. In a survey of 210 Florida police officers, Psychologists Charles Spielberger and Kenneth Grier of the University of South Florida found that far more stressful than responding to a felony in progress or making arrests while alone was the day-to-day friction of dealing with what the officers saw as an "ineffective" judicial system and "distorted" press accounts about their work. In other stress surveys, police sergeants in Houston groused about paper pushing more than physical danger; teachers ranked administrative details second only to inadequate salary; air traffic controllers, whose high rate of hypertension and ulcers has been attributed to job pressure, complained more about such mundane matters as management, shift schedules and "irrelevant" chores than the strain of guiding heavy air traffic. Such traffic, however, does take a toll on people living close to airports. Blasted daily by noise, people near Los Angeles International Airport have been found to have higher rates of hypertension, heart disease and suicide than residents of quieter areas.

The relentless stresses of poverty and ghetto life have also been associated with higher health risks. Studies of poor black neighborhoods in Detroit and Boston have correlated hypertension, which is twice as common among American blacks as among whites, with overcrowded housing and high levels of unemployment and crime. Research conducted in Massachusetts by Epidemiologist David Jenkins, now on the faculty of the University of Texas Medical Branch in Galveston, showed that the two areas with the highest mortality rates in the state were the Boston black ghetto of Roxbury and the working-class white enclave of South Boston, which had been locked in a bitter feud over school busing. Mortality rates in these two "death zones" are elevated not only for hypertension-related ailments like stroke, but for all causes of death. Even the rate of cancer among Roxbury men was 37% above the state average.

Whether or not daily stresses and hassles do more damage than life-change events may, in the final analysis, be a moot point. A single event can cause smaller changes that touch every aspect of existence. Divorce, for example, "is not an isolated event," observes U.C.S.F. Psychiatrist Leonard Pearlin. "It is accompanied by some social isolation, a reduction in income and sometimes the problems of being a single parent. These become the chronic strains of life."

Joblessness has a similar ripple effect. The greatest source of stress is not the actual loss of the job but rather the gradual domestic and psychological changes it imposes. These can be devastating, says Sociologist M. Harvey Brenner, professor of health services administration at Johns Hopkins. Brenner has found that over a period of about 25 years beginning in the late 1940s, for each 1% increase in the national unemployment rate, there were 1.9% more U.S. deaths from heart disease and cirrhosis, 4.1% more suicides, and an upturn in the number of first-time admissions to state mental health facilities (up 4.3% for men, 2.3% for women).

To be sure, not everyone falls to pieces because of the loss of a job or even a spouse. While surveying unemployed workers in the Detroit area, University of Michigan Researcher Louis Ferman found one hard-luck victim who had been successively laid off by the Studebaker Corp. in 1962 when it was about to fold, a truck manufacturer that went under in the 1970s, and more recently during cutbacks at a Chrysler plant. By all accounts, "he should have been a basket case," says Ferman, "yet he was one of the best-adjusted fellows I've run into." Asked his secret, the man replied, "I've got a loving wife and go to church every Sunday."

Such examples have convinced stress scholars that far more important than the trials and tribulations in one's life is how one deals with them. Consequently, much research into stress and preventive medicine has focused on what psychologists call "hardiness" or coping behavior. Certain population groups are known to enjoy remarkable good health and longevity: Mormons, nuns, symphony conductors and women who are listed in *Who's Who*. This suggests that something in the way these people live, possibly even such abstractions as faith, pride of accomplishment or productivity, plays a role in diminishing the ill effects of stress. "The most significant observation," says Rosch of the American Institute of Stress, "is that widows die at rates three to 13 times as high as married women for every known major cause of death. Why? How does this work?"

Psychologists point to a number of personal factors that seem to be helpful in coping. Among them: the sense of being in control of one's life, having a network of friends or family to provide what researchers call "social support," and such personality factors as flexibility and hopefulness. At Johns Hopkins, Dr. Caroline Bedell Thomas has correlated psychological factors with the long-term health records of 1,337 medical students who graduated between 1948 and 1964. One of the strongest prognosticators of cancer, mental illness and suicide, she found, was "lack of closeness to parents" and a negative attitude toward one's family. A 1978 study of 7,000 people in Alameda County, Calif., confirmed the importance of social support. Epidemiologist Leonard Syme of Berkeley, Calif., who conducted the study, found that even after adjusting for such factors as smoking and histories of major illnesses, people with few close contacts were dying two to three times faster than those who regularly turned to their friends.

Animal studies also support the notion that company prevents misery. Squirrel monkeys become more agitated if alone when confronted with a boa constrictor than when several monkeys confront the snake together. Mice that are injected with cancer cells and then isolated develop tumors more rapidly than those who remain with their cage mates.

The warm family support given to Barney Clark was considered by his doctors to have been crucial to his remarkable endurance after receiving the artificial heart. Lonely heart attack patients have been shown to live longer when given a pet. Herpes sufferers seem to be helped just by participating in a self-help group. Says U.C.S.F. Psychiatrist Horowitz: "These self-help groups, for everything from single parents to rape victims, are very useful. They replace the small-town systems that we've lost."

Studies of former Viet Nam prisoners of war have revealed that communication with fellow captives, sometimes involving complex tapping codes, was a vital factor in their survival. In a book to be published this fall, one former P.O.W. relates that even while he was being beaten by his captors, he could hear other prisoners tapping out the supportive message "God bless you, Jim Stockdale."

Other studies of prisoners and hostages have also pointed up the importance of maintaining a sense of control over one's environment. NIMH Psychologist Julius Segal was astonished to learn that one of the American hostages in Iran achieved this by saving a bit of food from his meals and then offering it to anyone who came into his cell. That simple coping strategy had the effect of turning the cell into a living room, the hostage into a host welcoming visitors.

Research with animals has shown that when stressful stimuli can be regulated, they are rendered less damaging. University of Wisconsin researchers exposed monkeys to loud, irritating noise but allowed half of them to interrupt the sound by pulling on a chain. Though both groups of monkeys were exposed to the same noise, those with access to the chain showed lower levels of stress-related hormones in their blood. Being in control seemed to make the difference.

The same appears to be true of workers. Robert Karasek, an industrial-engineering professor at Columbia University, has found that people who have little control over their jobs, such as cooks, garment stitchers and assembly-line workers, have higher rates of heart disease than people who can dictate the pace and style of their work. Telephone operators, waiters, cashiers and others whose work makes substantial psychological demands but offers little opportunity for independent decision making are the worst off. This combination of high demands and low control, concludes Karasek, appears to raise one's risk of heart disease by "about the same order of magnitude as smoking or having a high cholesterol level."

In recent years doctors have come to recognize another psychological factor that drastically increases an individual's susceptibility to heart attacks and other stress-related illnesses: Type A behavior. First identified by San Francisco Cardiologists Meyer Friedman and Ray Rosenman, Type A has two main components, both of which can be recognized by giving standardized personality tests or conducting careful interviews with the patients. Says Friedman: "First, there is the tendency to try to accomplish too many things in too little time. Second, there is free-floating hostility. These people are irritated by trivial things; they exhibit signs of struggle against time and other people."

Type A has been accepted as a bona fide risk factor for heart disease by the American Heart Association and the National Heart, Lung and Blood Institute. Studies have shown that Type A's respond differently to stress than do calmer people classified as Type B's. When Dr. Redford Williams at Duke University asked a group of male undergraduates to perform a mental arithmetic task (serial subtraction of 13 from 7,683), the Type A students produced 40 times as much cortisol and four times as much epinephrine as their Type B classmates. The flow of blood to their muscles was three times as great, though there was no difference in their level of performance. "The Type A man is responding as though he were in an emergency or threatening situation," says Williams. The jolt of cortisol and epinephrine, he speculates, "could be causing more fat to be released into the blood, which may later be deposited around the heart."

Mort Ciment, 59, was what Friedman would call a typical Type A. Excitable to begin with, he worked as a Los Angeles commodities trader, a job he likens to "being in a mad cage." When the market was really moving, he says, "there was terrible tension. You'd leave to go to the bathroom, come back and find the position horribly changed." When he got home, he admits, "my nerves were singing, and I'd take it out on the nearest person."

All that ended three years ago when Ciment had a heart attack. A quadruple bypass saved his life, and a chastened Ciment resolved to slow down. He quit his job to become a stockbroker in a lower-keyed office, and now devotes more time to hobbies. "Lining a coffin with gold," he says, "doesn't do the body any good."

Like thousands of other overwrought Americans, Ciment got professional help in learning to reduce and manage the stress in his life. At the California Institute for Behavorial Medicine in Beverly Hills, he underwent psychological counseling to change his Type A mind-set, began an exercise program and learned to modify his diet. Programs like the one he attended have been booming in recent years. By one estimate, there are now more than 300 stress-management enterprises offering their services to hospitals, clinics and even corporations around the country, up from 120 last September. "Stress management has become a multimillion-dollar-a-year business," says Rosch of the American Institute of Stress.

Hospitals took the lead in treating stress by establishing clinics to help those for whom reducing tension was a matter of life and death: heart attack victims and severe hypertensives. Some of the advice offered to such patients is just plain common sense: quit smoking, lose weight, cut down on salt and caffeine (2½ cups of coffee will double the level of epinephrine in the blood), take vacations regularly and exercise. In some cases drugs are used, typically beta blockers like Inderal, which interfere with the action of certain stress hormones. But the core of most stress-management programs, and what makes them distinctive, is teaching patients how to relax.

The guru of therapeutic relaxation is Cardiologist Benson. Back in 1968 he was persuaded by practitioners of Transcendental Meditation to study the effects of the technique on the body. To his surprise, Benson found that TM could elicit dramatic physiological changes, including decreased heart rate, lower blood pressure and reduced oxygen consumption. Meditation, says Benson, sets off "a built-in mechanism that is the opposite of the fight-or-flight response." Practiced ten to 20 minutes once or twice daily, it has been shown, by Benson and others, to produce a lasting reduction in blood pressure and other stress-related symptoms. Thus it is a natural antidote to tension.

TM is only one of several techniques that can be used to produce what Benson has termed the "relaxation response." The effect can be achieved just by following four simple steps: assume a comfortable position, close your eyes, concentrate on a single word, sound or phrase, and cast off all other thoughts. Instead of using the traditional mantra of TM, Benson's patients are encouraged to select a sound or image that appeals to them personally. One of his Jewish patients focuses on the word shalom; a Greek chants *"Kyrie eleison"* (Lord have mercy upon us); a Catholic recites the prayer "Lord Jesus have mercy"; others evoke the response by listening to soothing tapes of ocean waves. "As long as one can become passively unaware of the outside world," says Benson, "the method is not important."

In fact, techniques like muscle relaxation, biofeedback, self-hypnosis, rhythmic breathing and exercise can also elicit the relaxation response. These methods are now widely used at U.S. hospitals and clinics to treat such stress-related problems as migraine and tension headaches, Raynaud's disease (a circulatory disorder that causes painfully cold hands and feet), gastric ulcers and colitis. "Ten or 15 years ago, we thought there was no therapy for stress," says Stanford Psychiatrist Stewart Agras. "Now we know that relaxation is not a gimmick; it works."

At New York City's Columbia-Presbyterian Center for Stress and Pain-Related Disorders, Dr. Kenneth Greenspan claims to be able to reduce the severity and frequency of migraines in 80% of sufferers. The principal weapon: biofeedback. The patient is connected by sensor wires to a machine with a small screen that feeds back information on such physiological indexes of stress as blood pressure, tension in the facial muscles or, most frequently, the temperature of one's fingers — the colder, the tenser. By loosening their muscles, breathing deeply or letting their thoughts drift, patients learn that they can control their stress response; they can make their blood pressure drop or the temperature in their hands rise by as much as twelve to 14 degrees. After six to ten sessions, at $150 each, patients are weaned from the machines and are able to elicit the relaxation response at home without mechanical prompting. "All biofeedback does is make you more aware of what's going on in your own body," says Psychologist Lyle Miller, who uses the technique at Boston University's biobehavioral sciences clinic. "There is a significant amount of voluntary control over so-called involuntary responses, as the yogis have demonstrated for centuries."

As biofeedback and other relaxation techniques gain acceptance, doctors are testing them against all sorts of ills. Duke Psychologist Richard Surwit has shown that biofeedback and progressive muscle-relaxation exercises can help diabetics maintain steadier glucose levels. At Children's Orthopedic Hospital in Seattle, Dr. William Womack helps youngsters contend with the strains of growing up. Kurt Russell, 16, was immobilized by migraines for days at a time until Womack taught him a self-hypnosis technique. Now symptom-free, the teen-ager travels twice a day to a peaceful place in his mind. "You imagine yourself in the woods or skiing," says Russell. "It's pretty neat."

Some of the most remarkable work in relaxation has been done with cancer patients, who often suffer excruciating anguish over the uncertainty of their future and the horrors of treatment. Chemotherapy can be especially devastating. Patients become so apprehensive that they may feel nauseated just at the thought of treatment, says Psychologist Thomas Burish of Vanderbilt University. "One woman even vomited in a drugstore when she saw the nurse who administered her therapy." Burish has helped cancer patients control their anxiety and nausea through biofeedback and progressive muscle-relaxation training. While the technique is not a cure, he says, "patients do gain a positive feeling of being in control again. It is one of the few things they can do to help themselves."

Regaining that sense of being in control is the principle behind another psychological technique designed to aid cancer patients. Devised by Fort Worth Radiologist Carl Simonton, the method requires the patient to imagine his tumor cells being hunted down and devoured by white-knight-like defender cells. Bizarre as it seems, the technique has helped "significant numbers" of terminally ill patients survive beyond all expectations, says Psychiatrist Cohen of Boston University. "How they do it, we do not know."

The relaxation boom has found a warm welcome in America's citadels of stress: large corporations. The reason, experts agree, comes down to the bottom line. By encouraging workers to reduce the strains on their hearts, backs and psyches, corporations can begin to lower the $125 billion or more annually spent on total health care for employees, a figure that has been rising by 15% a year. In addition, Benson points out, many firms are finally beginning to appreciate the long-established fact that too much stress makes workers inefficient. In 1908 Yale Psychologist Robert Yerkes, along with J. D. Dodson, demonstrated that pressure improves performance, but only up to a point;

after that, efficiency drops off sharply. Relieving the strain with relaxation breaks, Benson concludes, "actually enhances performance."

About one out of five of the *Fortune* 500 companies now have some sort of stress-management program. Many are restricted to top executives, though studies have shown that the most stressed workers are in middle management. In addition to facing the pressures of climbing the corporate ladder, these workers are caught in a perilous bind: lots of responsibility but little control. Those who have surmounted these obstacles and made it to the top "have the fewest problems," says Dr. Gilbeart Collings, corporate medical director of New York Telephone Co.

Corporate efforts to reduce stress range from the commonplace alcoholism program to on-premise exercise facilities, meditation classes and company-sponsored biofeedback. At the Equitable Life Assurance Society in Manhattan, employees with frequent stress-related health complaints participated in an in-house biofeedback program and reduced their average number of visits to the company medical office from two dozen annually to fewer than six. According to Psychologist James Manuso, who ran the project, Equitable saved $5.52 in medical costs for every dollar invested.

At New York Telephone, a program involving periodic health exams for all employees and meditation lessons for those with stress-related symptoms has helped cut the corporate hypertension rate from 18% — about average for U.S. firms — to half that amount. New York Telephone estimates that it is saving $130,000 a year from reduced absenteeism alone.

Results like these have created an enormous demand for stress-management programs, and a small army of entrepreneurs has rushed in to fill the vacuum. New York Telephone's Collings reports getting "three or four offers a week to conduct relaxation programs." Not all of them are bargains. In an effort to bring some order to the booming and chaotic field, Rosch (whose respected American Institute of Stress is nonprofit) is establishing a data bank with information on the cost and effectiveness of stress-management programs. The result, he hopes, will be "a kind of *Who's Who* in stress. Right now there's no sense of pedigree."

Rosch and others point out that no single approach to relaxation is right for everyone. "Meditation may be good for somebody with hypertension," says Rosch, "and bad for someone with a peptic ulcer." One person may need psychotherapy to get at the roots of his Type A behavior, while another needs nothing more than regular exercise and vacations. Just as responses to stress vary widely according to age, sex, temperament and other factors, so do the requirements for treatment to offset it.

What no treatment programs attempt to do, however, is eliminate stress entirely. Nor should they. Hans Selye made a career of studying the ill effects of stress, but he nevertheless believed it was "the spice of life." Falling in love, catching a ride on an ocean wave, seeing a great performance of *Hamlet* — all can unleash the same stress hormones as do less uplifting experiences, sending the blood pressure soaring and causing the heart to palpitate madly. But who among us would give them up? "A certain amount of stress is a positive and pleasurable thing," says Neurochemist Barchas. "It leads to productivity in the human race."

As the relaxation boom spreads, as corporate America learns its mantras and chronic worriers unwind their minds, the point, then, is not to escape the effects of stress, which are inescapable in any case, but to channel and control them. Between the fight-or-flight spasms of too much tension and the dullness and dormancy of too little, the challenge for each person is to find the level of manageable stress that invigorates life instead of ravaging it.

— **By Claudia Wallis. Reported by Ruth Mehrtens Galvin/Boston
and Dick Thompson/San Francisco**

C.

EMPLOYEE RIGHTS AND TERMINATION-AT-WILL

Privacy Regulation

James Ledvinka

Privacy legislation concerns the proper treatment of employee information. In a sense, it concerns the question of whether the employer or the employee should control that information. Currently, federal privacy regulation is mostly limited to public sector employment, so it merits less attention than other regulatory areas do. Nevertheless, its impact is growing. Many state governments regulate the use of employee information, and Congress has been deliberating over more comprehensive legislation. . . .

The concern over privacy is not a transitory phenomenon. It has its roots in the Bill of Rights and the Fourteenth Amendment to the U.S. Constitution. For instance, the Fourth Amendment's protection against unreasonable search and seizure could be read to prohibit government from unreasonably searching employee records. The Fifth Amendment's protection against self-incrimination could be read to prohibit government from examining any source of information that might be interpreted as incriminating, personnel file information included. Likewise, the notion of due process of law embodied in the Fifth and Fourteenth Amendments might be used to challenge any government action that deprives a person of privacy.

A number of diverse laws govern privacy. All are concerned in one way or another with the question of who should control information about employees or applicants. In a sense, this is a question of *who owns the information*. While there are some federal laws, most of the regulatory activity has been carried out by the states.

There are two reasons that privacy is relevant to federal regulation. One is that federal legislation to regulate privacy is continually being considered by Congress. The other is that privacy regulation tends to conflict with other federal regulatory mandates. Additionally, some organizations have made concerted efforts to comply with what they perceive to be the demands of government privacy regulation, and those management steps are worth examining.

Privacy regulation can be separated into two major areas: (1) the use of lie detectors and other devices to detect deception, and (2) the management of personnel records.

From James Ledvinka, *Federal Regulation of Personnel and Human Resource Management* (Boston: Kent Publishing Company, 1982), pp. 244, 253–258. © 1982 by Wadsworth, Inc. Reprinted by permission of Kent Publishing Company, a division of Wadsworth, Inc.

LIE DETECTORS

The use of lie detectors by employers is now prohibited in seventeen states and the District of Columbia. Two other states require an employer to obtain the written consent of the employee before administering a lie detector examination. Those laws vary in scope and in their specific prohibitions, but their net effect is to make it illegal for employers to extract any information from employees or applicants that those persons do not want to provide voluntarily.

More recently, the U.S. Congress has considered legislation to make the use of polygraphs, voice analyzers, and other such deception-detection devices illegal in all states. The ultimate fate of such proposals is uncertain. However, they are regarded favorably by organized labor. Labor considers a polygraph examination to be a humiliating experience. On the other hand, employers have testified against such legislation. Employers want to avoid losing the right to use any method they might regard as a possible solution to their growing theft and security problems.[1]

The decisive factor, however, may be the widespread finding that all such forms of deception detection are disturbingly inaccurate.[2] The problem is with the "false positive" — the individual who is actually telling the truth but is falsely identified by the lie detector as lying. Employers may be grateful for any improvement over chance in identifying the culprit, but opponents point to the enormous personal costs of being a false positive. Considering that risk, they insist on very high accuracy, something that is not possible given the current state of the art.

Regardless of what happens to proposals for federal legislation, state regulation of lie detectors seems here to stay, and there is a reasonable chance that other states will pass laws in this area.

EMPLOYEE RECORDS

In this area too, most of the regulation of private employers has been carried out by the states rather than by the federal government. However, the federal government does regulate itself, granting privacy rights to federal employees. The state laws vary, but they generally give employees in private industry the right of access to their files, the right to monitor the information that goes into them, and the right to limit the information that is released from them. Some states single out medical records for specific regulatory attention.

The federal law governing employment is the Privacy Act of 1974, which requires federal agencies to open their personnel files for employee inspection. Specifically, the Privacy Act gives federal employees the right to (1) determine what information is being kept about them, (2) review that information, (3) correct or amend that information, and (4) prevent the use of information for any purpose other than that for which it was collected.[3]

Other federal laws have an impact on privacy in the private sector. For instance, the Fair Credit Reporting Act controls the information that gets into credit reports that employers might request on employees or applicants, and the Family Educational Rights and Privacy Act controls student records at universities. However, those federal laws do not control private sector personnel actions.

The major significance of privacy regulation is not the existing laws but the laws that may be passed in the future. One section of the Privacy Act of 1974 established the Privacy Protection Study Commission, which recently released a report including recommendations for further privacy legislation.[4] In 1975, a bill (aptly numbered House Resolution 1984) was introduced in Congress that would, essentially, extend the provisions of the Privacy Act to cover private industry.[5] While the Privacy Protection Study

Commission stopped short of recommending that, it did recommend legislation to forbid the use of lie detectors by employers and to strengthen the provisions of the Fair Credit Reporting Act.[6]

Several legal issues are involved in the consideration of comprehensive privacy regulation.[7]

The right of access to personnel information

The opportunity to respond to derogatory information

The right to remove or correct erroneous information

The right to be notified that information is to be released to a third party

The right to know how the information is being used within the employer's organization

The right to require that the employer take reasonable precautions to insure that the information is reliable and not misused

While it is by no means certain that those rights will be enacted into law, the prospect seems to be greater than the prospects for other new regulations. Privacy is a concept that has appeal across the political spectrum. While political conservatives are less fond of new government regulation than political liberals are, personal privacy is a cornerstone of conservative belief. Indeed, most of the privacy bills currently pending in Congress have been introduced by a conservative legislator. So it is conceivable that conservatives might make an exception to their general opposition to federal regulation in the case of laws limiting intrusion into private affairs.

CONFLICTS BETWEEN PRIVACY AND OSHA REGULATION

... The Occupational Safety and Health Act gives its regulatory agencies broad rights of access to information regarding health and safety. Mostly, this involves medical information, which is considered to be among the most personal employee information. That fact has already caused problems for some companies. Prior to the passage of OSHA, du Pont Chemical had voluntarily kept health hazard evaluation records on its employees for many years. After the passage of OSHA, the National Institute of Occupational Safety and Health (NIOSH) requested that information from du Pont. Du Pont was willing to release it with employee identification deleted, but NIOSH was unwilling to accept it in that form. When NIOSH issued a subpoena for the documents, du Pont asked for the consent of the employees involved, and 631 refused. When du Pont went to court, the court upheld NIOSH.[8] A similar decision was made in a case involving General Motors.[9] With increasing attention being given to occupational disease, and with the resulting need for medical information on employees, it seems likely that such conflicts will continue.[10]

Management Responses

The Privacy Protection Study Commission report included a set of recommendations for employers. Seven of the recommendations were:

Limit the collection of information to that which is relevant to specific personnel decisions

Give employees access to their personnel records

Inform employees and applicants about how their records will be used

Allow employees to correct inaccurate information

Limit the release of information to third parties without the employees' consent

Limit the internal use of employee records

Limit the external disclosure of employee information [11]

Even in the absence of federal regulation, private sector employers seem to be making a number of voluntary changes in their use of employees' records. Perhaps the most notable change has come in the use of reference information, information about an applicant from the applicant's former employer. There is no law regulating the use of references, but the growing concern over privacy and the threat of lawsuits by applicants and former employees is apparently leading employers to be more cautious, both about providing reference information to other employers and about using reference information provided by other employers. This concern seems well placed. Among the steps that observers recommend are,[12] for *users* of reference information:

Ask for specific, job-related information only

Do not use subjective information

Obtain written consent from candidates before checking references

and for *providers* of reference information:

Document all information released

Release specific, objective information only

Obtain written consent from employees before releasing information

Do not give information over the telephone

Do not blacklist employees

Do not answer the question of whether you would rehire the employee — if your answer is "no," you would not want to be held responsible for the other party taking your advice

The effect of those recommendations is to objectify reference information. That in turn should improve the employer's EEO compliance as well as reduce the employer's vulnerability to lawsuits alleging the misuse of employee information.

A FINAL WORD

The most significant general statement that can be made about federal regulation is that it is *about problems.* Each regulatory area *attacks* problems and *creates* problems. In the heat of debate, people seem to forget that it does both. Those who approach regulation from a pro-regulation public policy perspective are quite conscious of the social problems that underlie regulation, but they are less sensitive to the management problems that regulation creates. Likewise, those who approach regulation from a management perspective are painfully aware of the management problems caused by regulation, but they often seem oblivious to the social problems that regulation is designed to attack.

Yet it is important for those concerned with each side of the regulatory model to be aware of the perspective of those concerned with the other side. If the regulators become more aware of the perspective of the manager, the result might be more effective regulation. And if the manager becomes more concerned with the perspective of the regulators, the result might be greater chances for survival in a highly regulated environment. Better yet, this mutual awareness might result in more voluntary efforts by employers to solve social problems without the compulsion of government regulation and in more voluntary efforts by regulators to recognize that a due concern for the management problems of the organizations they are regulating may do more than anything else to solve the social problems that the regulations were created to solve.

NOTES

1. Jerri L. Frantzve, "The Polygraph Bill (S.1945) — A Legislative Development of Significance to Industrial/Organizational Psychologists," *The Industrial-Organizational Psychologist* 15, No. 4 (1978):10–11.

2. See Paul R. Sackett and Philip J. Decker, "Detection of Deception in the Employment Context: A Review and Critical Analysis," *Personnel Psychology* 32 (1979):487–506.

3. See John D. Rice, "Privacy Legislation: Its Effect on Pre-Employment Reference Checking," *The Personnel Administrator* 23, No. 2 (1978):46–51.

4. Privacy Protection Study Commission, *Personal Privacy in an Information Society* (Washington, D.C.: Government Printing Office, 1977).

5. Ibid.

6. Philip G. Benson, "Personal Privacy and the Personnel Record," *Personnel Journal* 57 (1978):376–80, 395; also see John C. Fox and Paul J. Ostling, "Employee and Government Access to Personnel Files: Rights and Requirements," *Employee Relations Law Journal* 5 (1979):67–83.

7. See Rice, "Privacy Legislation."

8. *E. I. du Pont de Nemours v. Finklea*, 442 F. Supp. 821 (S.D. W. Va. 1977).

9. *General Motors v. Finklea*, 6 Occupational Safety and Health Cases 1976 (S.D. Ohio 1978).

10. See Fox and Ostling, "Employee and Government Access."

11. Ibid.; Benson, "Personal Privacy."

12. See Rice, "Privacy Legislation."

Erosion of the Employment-at-Will Doctrine

Emily A. Joiner

When an employer hires someone for an indefinite period, the relationship is considered to be "at will," and either employer or employee may terminate the relationship at any time. This doctrine was part of a shift to contract theory in the common law of employment relations which, in turn, was part of the industrial revolution. In 1884 a Tennessee court interpreted employment at will as follows: "All may dismiss their employee(s) at will for good cause, for no cause, or even for cause morally wrong without being thereby guilty of legal wrong." This common-law doctrine has been accepted by virtually every state for over a century. The one exception is South Dakota, which has a statute holding that employment at a "yearly rate" is presumed to be for at least one year, and an employer is required to prove sufficient grounds for termination any time before the end of one year.

Although employers and employees are considered people of free will who enter an employment relationship with relatively equal bargaining power, the overall result of employment at will is to limit employers' duties to their employees. The first major departure from the at-will doctrine was the National Labor Relations Act of 1935, which prohibited firing employees to discourage them from unionizing. More important to today's employers, however, is the increasing number of state court decisions in favor of employees who have filed wrongful discharge suits. These decisions reflect a growing awareness of the social need for job protection. Through these decisions, workers are winning something like a property right to their job, something that cannot be taken away except through a fair process.

STATUTORY CONSTRAINTS

Most employees in the workforce today (between 50 and 75 million) are subject to the right of an employer to terminate without cause. Increasingly, however, this right has become subject to numerous statutory restrictions. Federal restrictions include such antidiscrimination-in-employment laws as Title VII of the Civil Rights Act of 1964, and discharges based on military obligations and occupational safety and health concerns. Various state laws protect employees from discharges for filing workers' compensation claims, refusing to commit perjury before a legislative committee, performing jury duty, suing for abusive or wrongful discharge, or serving in the National Guard. In addition, there are a number of federal and state statutes that prohibit termination stemming from an employee's assertion of a claim under a particular statute. One area of particular concern has been whistle-blowing. In addition to various federal and state laws that protect the whistle-blower, more and more judges are deciding in favor of whistle-blowers — even when their conduct is not specifically covered by an antiretaliation statute.

COMMON-LAW CHALLENGES UNDER CONTRACTS AND TORTS

Despite the considerable number of federal and state regulations, an employer retains the right to terminate at will as long as a dismissal is for a reason other than those prohibited by law. This has given rise to a growing number of common-law challenges to at-will terminations. Jack Stieber of Michigan State University estimates that private industry discharges 1,000,000 employees each year without a fair hearing. He also estimates that between 100,000 and 200,000 employees are unfairly terminated each year, and that about half could regain their jobs if they had access to impartial arbitration. The typical employee termination under these conditions is a white male, lower- or middle-level supervisor under 40. He has a fair knowledge of corporate procedures and documents, and is generally able to afford a lawsuit.

Common-law challenges fall into two categories: contracts and torts. Contract law has upheld unjust termination suits in which the court found an implied contract that limited the employer's right to terminate at will or in which there was an implied covenant of good faith and fair dealing. An implied contract can be an oral promise from an employer to the effect that an employee cannot be discharged as long as he or she does the job, a personnel policy in an employee handbook, or simply the meaning construed from a memorandum from employer to employee. The New Hampshire Supreme Court established an employer's duty to good faith and fair dealing in 1974 when it ruled that, "a termination motivated by bad faith or malice or based on retaliation is not in the best interest of the economic system or the public good." Good faith rulings that have caused considerable distress among employers are those that have taken length of service as justification that the employer must have cause for termination.

Tort law exceptions are based on the idea that important public policies must be protected by making it unlawful for employees to be terminated for reasons contrary to those policies. These public policy exceptions are less clearly defined and are of narrower scope than contract law exceptions, but they can open a Pandora's box because punitive damage may be awarded under tort law. Employee suits have been upheld in which employees were terminated, in violation of public policy, for refusing to commit perjury, filing a workers' compensation claim, serving on a jury, engaging in union activity, refusing to participate in a price-fixing scheme, and whistle-blowing. These rulings supported employee behavior that was consistent with existing statutes.

Tort law has upheld other exceptions — involving employees fired for political activities, for continuing to date former employees who had gone to work for competitors, or for reporting employees who were involved in crime and agreeing to assist in investigations and trials. There have also been favorable employee rulings in discharge suits involving fraudulent, oppressive, or malicious (tortious) breach of contract; where employers unfairly break promises on which employees have relied (promissory estoppel); and where employers fail to exercise reasonable care in performing obligations to employees (negligence).

Company Location Makes a Difference

Although many states have found exceptions in favor of employees, others continue to rule in favor of the existing at-will doctrine. Examples of judgments that have upheld employers include cases involving disputes over internal management systems, excessive use of sick leave, conflicts between work and after-hours schooling, and failure to utilize contractual or administrative remedies such as grievance procedures. As of August 1983, there were only six states in which no wrongful discharge suits had been filed. Thirty-nine percent of the states have found contract law exceptions and 55 percent have found tort law exceptions, but in cases in which the exception was based on public policy expressed in statutes or on promissory estoppel, the total is approximately 70 percent. California, Idaho, New Hampshire, Oregon, and Washington lead in favorable employee rulings in wrongful discharge suits; Connecticut, Illinois, Michigan, and Montana are close behind. States that have rejected exceptions to the at-will doctrine are Georgia, Louisiana, Mississippi, North Carolina, Tennessee, Virginia, and New York.

California has been one of the most liberal states, finding exceptions in the areas of implied contracts, implied duty of good faith and fair dealing, public policy, and promissory estoppel. A landmark decision from the California Supreme Court was in *Tameny v. Atlantic Richfield*, 1980: It marked the first time a court ruled that an employee could seek punitive damages from a company.

Federal cases are few, but an employee can sue in a federal court if the organization is engaged in interstate commerce, if it does a large amount of business with the federal government, or if the cause of action involves a federal law. Federal courts, like state courts, have taken a situational view and have hesitated to look beyond state laws in deciding cases. The U.S. Supreme Court ruled in 1972 that an unwritten common law may exist in a particular employment setting and protect an otherwise at-will worker. On the other hand, another federal court upheld an employer who fired an executive for consulting an attorney to represent him in a salary dispute.

CONSEQUENCES TO EMPLOYERS CAN BE SERIOUS

Very often, an employer that loses a discharge suit must pay punitive damages. Terminations that violate local statutes may result in compensatory damages of back-pay, lost benefits, actual damages, attorney's fees, employer fines, and reinstatement or front-pay to compensate an employee until he or she obtains a comparable position. Penalties for breach of implied contract may include back pay and lost benefits, but not reinstatement. In cases of tort-law infringement, an employee may recover actual and exemplary damages, but the major cost to the employer comes from punitive damages. These are used to make an example of a guilty company and can result in huge monetary awards and considerable adverse publicity. (One survey of California cases in this area reported an average award of $400,000.) Hiring and training new employees is another cost the employer must consider. Additionally, once an employer is involved in a lawsuit, company records can be tied up by the court — which can cause considerable inconvenience and inefficiency.

IMPROVING THE ODDS AGAINST LITIGATION

Not surprisingly, employers have become increasingly concerned with ways of protecting themselves from litigation and, if sued, ways of improving their chances in court.

Employers should be aware that several courts have deemed a company's statements, whether oral or written, sufficient to establish an implied contract of employment. (Interviewers and supervisors need to be made aware that oral statements about job security may be just as binding as written statements, and may even take precedence over them.) One of the first things a company can do is review employee handbooks, personnel manuals, employment applications, company brochures, advertisements, and any other written documents to be sure they do not contain any references that might give support to a lawsuit. Or it can ask prospective employees to sign a statement that specifies that employment is at will; this tactic, however, is sure to discourage some would-be employees. Periodic audits of personnel files can be made to eliminate any outdated or unnecessary papers. Most important, companies need to be fully aware of all aspects of their own policies and must apply them and abide by them consistently with all employees.

In-house grievance procedures and progressive discipline systems are two of the best methods a company can use to protect itself from unfair discharge lawsuits. These systems give an employee the opportunity to have his or her "day in court" with the company rather than with a judge. When there is a legitimate problem, the facts and steps taken by the company before termination will be documented. This written record can become an important asset to the company in court. Similarly, it can be to the employer's advantage if an employee has not taken advantage of an available grievance system.

Inflated, inaccurate performance appraisals can be used very effectively by an employee in court. Job descriptions should be kept current; an employee fired for not doing the job may have basis for a claim if the job description doesn't reflect the duties actually involved. Companies may want to consider establishing procedures for "rightful termination." The first step would be to have all terminations reviewed by an impartial person, preferably someone in personnel management. Severance pay could be given in exchange for a release from future claims. Companies could also conduct exit interviews to clear up any misconceptions on either side, provide outplacement counseling, and avoid giving bad references by declining to do more than confirm dates of employment.

The above suggestions cannot guarantee immunity from losing a suit. But if carefully administered, they can help create a healthy employee relations environment that should be able to keep to a minimum the number of suits brought against a company.

RECENT DEVELOPMENTS

Rulings involving the at-will doctrine under common law create uncertainty because they are based on such indefinite concepts as public policy, good faith, and fair dealing. This creates an uncomfortable climate for employers because it is difficult to plan strategy based on contradictory decisions and hazy precedents. Legislative action, while it would impose additional regulations, would serve to establish concrete guidelines for employers to follow. The United States is one of the few industrialized countries without federal legislation concerning unjust dismissals. A bill called the Corporate Democracy Act was introduced in 1980. Title IV of the bill, called "Rights of Employees," was proposed to amend the National Labor Relations Act. It dealt with protecting the security of employment and defined "just cause." It was referred to seven House committees and died before any formal action was taken.

State legislation is more likely to be passed. Although none has succeeded to date, measures introduced in 1982 in Michigan, Pennsylvania, and Wisconsin would have extended statutory protection from unfair dismissal or given discharged employees recourse to an impartial panel. Michigan enacted the Whistleblowers' Protection Act in 1981, and Nevada passed a law in 1983 that protects volunteer firemen from discriminatory discharge.

The most recent state development is in California. Two bills have been introduced in response to the growing number of wrongful discharge suits. One bill would allow recourse to an arbitrator who would apply a "just cause" standard. The other would allow claims for breach of the implied covenant of good faith and fair dealing to be heard in court. Punitive damages would not be allowed under either bill. Though neither bill is expected to pass, their introduction shows recognition that the present method of resolving discharge disputes — through lengthy litigation under ill-defined standards of proof — is unsatisfactory.

The United Nations International Labor Organization passed a "Convention on Termination at Will" in June 1982 that expanded employee protections and provided remedies for unjust dismissal internationally. Although the United States labor delegation supported it, the government and employer delegations did not. Conventions that are ratified become in effect formal treaties under national law; however, the

United States rarely ratifies them. Former Labor Secretary Ray Marshall has stated that the policy of the United States to allow employment at will has hindered employers' ability to increase workers' productivity, which impedes competition in the international marketplace.

WHAT WILL HAPPEN IN THE FUTURE?

Considerable speculation continues on where the erosion of the at-will doctrine and the accompanying furor are leading. Future changes will be effected through three channels: employers, legislation, and the courts. For employers, there are two possible courses. One is the hard-line approach in which employees are required to sign disclaimers waiving their rights to contest discharges, and in which any recourse through grievance procedures or personnel policies are withdrawn. But this approach is counterproductive and would not in any case be an absolute defense against a lawsuit. The second approach is to accept the current trend and plan for the future by improving employee relations and personnel management, especially through the implementation of grievance and discipline systems. Theodore J. St. Antoine of the University of Michigan points out that the experience of Japan and West Germany and experiments in the United States suggest that increased job security and employee participation may significantly improve productivity and reduce negative employee attitudes.

The legislature could become an extremely important arena in the battle over the at-will doctrine. Employers looking for a "just cause" standard to follow will support legislation rather than rely on the murky waters of judicial opinion; however, Jack Stieber, who favors legislative action, feels that employers will strongly oppose further dilution of the doctrine. Professor St. Antoine feels there will be little demand for legislative action unless the number of suits increases dramatically. It is unlikely that federal legislation will be passed soon but some state legislation will probably be enacted by the end of the 1980s. Although management may initially protest such law, companies already practicing good employee relations will not be hurt, and those who are not will have to adopt practices they should have been following anyway.

If legislation is not imminent, case law will become even more important. One of the most important issues to be resolved is the scope of tort liability. A case pending before the California Supreme Court could solidify that state's case law on wrongful discharge based on implied covenant of good faith and fair dealing and treat such discharges as torts subject to punitive damages. If the suit is upheld, even more wrongful discharge suits are expected to be filed.

CONCLUSION

Employers have good reason to exercise caution in dismissing employees. There has been significant change since the 1884 ruling that dismissal could be "for cause morally wrong." Today's courts are in the process of expanding employee rights, especially when it appears to them that the individual employee has been treated unfairly in some way. Even so, some observers believe that the termination-at-will doctrine is very much alive and well, and that employers can expect to win at least half the suits brought against them. But how many million-dollar losses can a company afford?

More and more, employers are realizing that a good employee relations program means happier and more productive employees. Today's progressive manager will prepare to change with the times by developing proper preventive and protective measures, and by adopting an attitude of fairness in employee relations.

D.

COSTING OF HUMAN RESOURCE MANAGEMENT

The Financial Impact of Employee Attitudes

Wayne F. Cascio

A number of studies in behavioral science have examined the relationship between job attitudes and absenteeism, turnover, tardiness, job performance, strikes, and grievances (see Mobley, Griffith, Hand, and Meglino, 1979; and Porter and Steers, 1973 for reviews). Attitudes are internal states that are focused on particular aspects of or objects in the environment. They include three elements: *cognition*, the knowledge an individual has about the focal object of the attitude; the *emotion* an individual feels toward the focal object; and an *action* tendency, a readiness to respond in a predetermined manner to the focal object.

Job satisfaction may be viewed as a multidimensional attitude; it is made up of attitudes toward pay, promotions, co-workers, supervision, the work itself, and so on. Management is interested in employees' job satisfaction principally because of the relationship between attitudes and behavior. Other things being equal, it is assumed that employees who are dissatisfied with their jobs (hold negative attitudes about various aspects of the work environment) will tend to be absent or late for work, or to quit more often than those whose attitudes are positive. Work force productivity therefore suffers. To explain the connection between attitudes and behavior, we must look at the precursors of attitudes: each individual's beliefs (Ajzen and Fishbein, 1980). Attitudes are a function of beliefs.

Generally speaking, a person who believes that a particular behavior will lead mostly to positive outcomes will hold a favorable attitude toward that behavior. A person who believes that the behavior will lead mostly to negative outcomes will hold an unfavorable attitude. According to this approach, any behavior can be predicted from a person's attitude toward it, provided that the measure of attitude corresponds to that measure of behavior (that is, they are evaluated in similar terms). A review of the attitude-behavior literature supports this position (Ajzen and Fishbein, 1977). Experimental evidence in the organizational behavior literature also indicates that improved job satisfaction can reduce absenteeism, turnover, tardiness, and grievances (Marrow, Bowers, and Seashore, 1967).

From Wayne F. Cascio, *Costing Human Resources: The Financial Impact of Behavior in Organizations* (Boston: Kent Publishing Company, 1982), pp. 81–94. © 1983 by Wadsworth, Inc. Reprinted by permission of Kent Publishing Company, a division of Wadsworth, Inc.

From our perspective, the important questions are these: what is the financial impact of the behavioral outcomes associated with job attitudes, and can we measure the costs associated with different levels of job satisfaction and motivation? There is a strong need for behavioral scientists to be able to speak in dollars and cents terms when they argue the merits of human resource development programs designed to change attitudes or improve job satisfaction. . . . Methods for attaching costs to absenteeism and turnover are fairly well developed. Measures of employee attitudes are even more finely developed (Smith, Kendall, and Hulin, 1969; Taylor and Bowers, 1972). The purpose of this chapter is to show how the two types of measures, financial and attitudinal, can be synthesized to produce an estimate in dollars of the costs and benefits of human resource development programs designed to improve employee attitudes.

Let us begin by presenting a model of financial assessment (Exhibit 1) that was developed by Mirvis and Macy (1976). The exhibit depicts several different development programs (x_1 to x_5). There are three distinct accounting activities necessary for evaluating these programs. The first is a *cost model* needed for identifying the firm's direct costs and losses in productive time attributable to the development effort. The second is an *effectiveness model* used for measuring and validating the effects of a project on the work environment and employees' attitudes, behaviors, and performance, and expressing these effects in financial terms. The third is a *synthesizing model* to compare the costs and benefits of a program. Both social and financial goals can then be contrasted with project costs in order to identify the most cost-beneficial development program. That is, programs are judged successful if expenditures are outweighed by the present value of future benefits.

MEASURING THE COSTS OF DEVELOPMENT PROGRAMS

. . . Let us distinguish three broad classes of costs: fixed, variable, and opportunity costs. Fixed costs include salaries, wages, and benefits associated with employees' lost time and the resulting unabsorbed overhead costs. Variable costs include, for example,

EXHIBIT 1
Cost-Benefit Model for Human Resource Development Programs

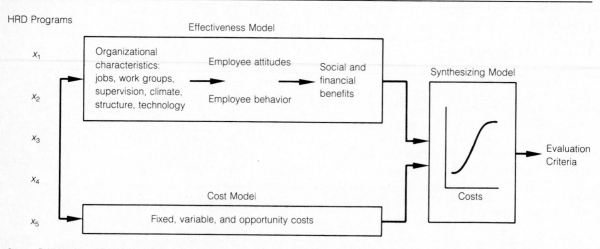

Source: P. H. Mirvis and B. A. Macy. "Accounting for the costs and benefits of human resource development programs: An interdisciplinary approach."
Accounting, Organizations, and Society, 1976, *1,* 181.

consultants' fees and expenses associated with their activities. These costs vary depending on the type of program and the intensity and duration of the development activities. They should be reported in deflated dollar terms. The work site also incurs variable costs in the form of lost worker productivity and overtime. Finally, opportunity costs reflect the profit contribution of the employees' lost time. We can also conceive of an additional opportunity cost, the "opportunities foregone" (Rothenberg, 1975) that might have been realized had the resources allocated to the program been directed toward other organizational ends.

On the other side of the ledger we can distinguish fixed, variable, and opportunity savings resulting from successful development programs. Fixed savings might be realized if some of the service demands placed on the personnel, industrial relations, safety, and quality control departments were reduced. Variable savings might include improved marginal productivity through increased product quality and quantity, limited overtime, reduced consumption of supplies and materials, and less unscheduled maintenance. Wages and other expenses due to absenteeism, accidents, and grievances (including the expense of maintaining a replacement work force) might also decrease. Finally, opportunity savings might be realized if the work time of supervisors that was spent in replacing absent employees or turnovers could be put to more productive use (Mirvis and Macy, 1976). Behavioral-economic measurement provides the methods for documenting these cost savings. Conceptually the synthesis of costs and effectiveness measures seems straightforward. Indeed, two studies have proposed methods for undertaking such calculations. Let us examine the limitations of each method in order to illustrate the complexity of the problem. We will then present a third approach that circumvents many of the shortcomings of the first two methods.

EARLY ATTEMPTS TO ESTIMATE THE FINANCIAL IMPACT OF ATTITUDES

Human Asset Valuation

Myers and Flowers (1974) present a simple framework for measuring human assets. Job performance is viewed as the end product of a five-part flow process: knowledge, skills, health, availability, attitudes, job performance. The individual's knowledge enables him or her to direct his or her skills, and the individual's health enables him or her to apply them. The individual must be available when needed and must have the desire to apply his or her talents and energy toward productive effort. The five dimensions are not additive, so that if any one of them is lacking, the others are rendered ineffective. Before deciding to improve one dimension, therefore, consideration must be given to the level of the others. Thus it may not be cost-effective to improve the job knowledge of an employee if his or her attitude is poor. The first priority may well be to improve attitudes before attempting to improve job knowledge.

According to Myers and Flowers (1974) job attitudes are a symptom of the other four human assets as these are interpreted by each individual's personal value system. Therefore a quantitative, reliable measure of attitudes is probably the best single measure of how well all five assets are being utilized. However, attitude survey results should not be lumped together indiscriminately. Each attitude score should be weighted by the individual's job grade level and company tenure. The higher the job grade level and the longer the tenure with the firm, the higher the weight attached to that individual's score. Myers and Flowers (1974) attempt to quantify attitudes by multiplying salary dollars times weighted attitude scores to measure the potential dollar value increases that would be associated with improved employee attitudes (see Exhibit 2).

This approach is a traditional approach to human asset valuation; it assigns a value to individuals rather than to their behavior. Employees' salaries are equated with their

EXHIBIT 2
Human Asset Valuation Approach to Dollarizing Attitudes

Unit: Digital Assembly

Individual	Annual Salary	Job Grade	Tenure	Attitude Weight	Attitude Score	Weighted Attitude Score
1. Tom Hill	$ 25,000	18	15	6	1.05	6.30
2. Cindy Fleming	15,000	12	6	3	1.12	3.36
3. Ben Williams	33,000	23	22	9	1.25	11.25
4. Judy Francis	15,000	12	6	3	1.26	3.78
5. Amy Fox	27,000	19	15	7	1.16	8.12
	$115,000			28		32.81

$$\text{attitude index} = \frac{(\Sigma \text{ weighted attitude score})}{(\Sigma \text{ attitude weights})} = \frac{32.81}{28} = 1.17$$

dollarized attitudes = attitude index $\times$ annual payroll = 1.17 $\times$ $115,000 = $134,550

gain = $134,550 − $115,000 = $19,550

gain per person = $3,910

value to the organization, and it is assumed that attitudinal improvements make employees more valuable to the organization. As Mirvis and Lawler (1977) have noted, this approach suffers from three shortcomings. First, the effects of improved attitudes on job behavior are not stated. We don't know whether attitudinal improvement implies higher employee productivity, lower absenteeism, reduced turnover, or some combination of these. Second, whether the actual savings associated with any behavioral changes will equal their estimated value improvement (that is, validation of predicted savings) is ignored by this approach. Finally, Myers and Flowers (1974) present no data on the relationship between the attitudes they measure and individuals' behaviors. At best, this framework provides a way for organizations to judge the impact of organizational investment on employee morale. It provides no clues to the direct financial impact of job satisfaction and motivation.

The Unit Cost Approach

The unit cost approach to assigning dollar values to attitudes was developed by Likert (1973) and Likert and Bowers (1973). Rather than trying to assign a value to the overall worth of an employee to an organization, this method attempts to determine the short-term costs of employee behavior. It does this by correlating standardized attitude scores with unit cost. It then predicts changes in unit cost from anticipated changes in attitudes and argues that the cost change represents the economic impact of the attitudes.

There are also problems with this approach, as Mirvis and Lawler (1977) have noted. This first problem stems from the choice of unit cost as a performance criterion. Cost per unit includes fixed costs (those incurred regardless of the number of units or level of service produced) and variable costs (those directly related to the level of activity). Only variable costs can be affected immediately by such employee behaviors as increased productivity and reduced absenteeism and turnover. Furthermore, both cost components are influenced by inflationary trends. The inclusion of fixed costs and inflationary trends in the criterion measure builds in a significant amount of variance that has nothing to do with changes in attitudes.

A second problem with this approach is that it ignores the processes that intervene between changes in attitude and changes in unit cost. That is, previous research suggests that improvements in job satisfaction should reduce levels of absenteeism and turnover, which in turn should result in lower unit cost. Simply relating attitudes to unit costs and bypassing the intervening processes ignores this sequential effect. The resulting relationship and financial consequences might well be over- or understated.

A third problem with the unit cost approach is its assumption of a constant attitude-behavior relationship over time. In fact, improvement in attitude scores could be accompanied by stronger or weaker predictive relationships to behavior. Predicted savings based on a constant relationship would understate the resulting benefits if the relationship was stronger than had been assumed, and it would overstate the benefits if the relationship was weaker than had been assumed. A final problem with this approach is that it relies on analysis at the work-group level, but much of the behavior change would occur at the individual level. Unless organizations are extremely large, relationships derived at the group level may be unreliable indicators of individual-level change.

In view of the shortcomings of the human asset valuation and unit cost approaches, we do not recommend that they be used. An awareness of their shortcomings is instructive, however, especially as a yardstick for measuring progress in methods proposed subsequently. The most recent of these approaches, behavior costing, was developed by Mirvis and Lawler (1977).

THE BEHAVIOR COSTING APPROACH

Behavior costing is based on the assumption that attitudinal measures are indicators of subsequent employee behaviors. These behaviors can be assessed using cost accounting procedures, and they have economic implications for organizations. Only short-term direct costs associated with the behaviors are used. This approach clearly builds on the unit cost approach of Likert and Bowers (1973).

The conceptual framework underlying behavior costing stems from expectancy theory, which emphasizes that employees' behavior at work is the result of choices about whether to appear at the work place ("participation-membership," March and Simon, 1958) and of choices about how to behave at work ("work strategies," Lawler, 1973). This framework assumes that employees will be more likely to come to work than be absent or quit if they obtain satisfaction from their jobs. And they are likely to give more effort and choose more effective job performance strategies if they expect to be rewarded either intrinsically or extrinsically for their efforts (Vroom, 1964).

These ideas suggest that attitudinal indexes of employee satisfaction and job involvement should be the best predictors of participation-membership since they reflect perceptions of the rewards associated with being at work (Lawler, 1973). Employee intrinsic motivation should be the best predictor of job performance, since it reflects some of the performance outcomes contingent on doing a good job: competence, achievement, and self-realization.

A Test of the Theory

These theoretical ideas were tested empirically on a sample of 160 tellers from 20 branches of a midwestern banking organization. The tellers (average age, thirty) were predominantly female (94 percent). They served as cashiers, handling customer deposits, withdrawals, and other transactions.

Attitude measures were taken from the Michigan Assessment of Organizations (Survey Research Center, 1975), and reflected intrinsic satisfaction (sex items), organizational involvement (two items), and intrinsic motivation (three items). For example:

Intrinsic satisfaction: please indicate how satisfied you are with the following aspects of your job: (1) the chances you have to do the things you do best; (2) the chances you have to learn new things; (3) the opportunity to develop your skills and abilities.

Organizational involvement: is what happens in this branch really important to you?

Intrinsic motivation: when you do your job well, do you feel you've done something worthwhile? Do you get a feeling of personal satisfaction from doing your job well?

Measures of participation-membership behavior and work performance were collected monthly after administration of the attitude questionnaire. Using standardized definitions and measures of behavioral outcomes (Macy and Mirvis, 1976), the following data were collected:

short-term absence or illness: unauthorized absences of less than three consecutive days, including short-term illness and absence for personal reasons.

voluntary turnover: voluntary employee departure from the bank, excluding terminations, maternity leaves or turnovers, and transfers.

teller balancing shortages: the number of shortages in tellers' balances (overpayments to customers).

Results of the Teller Study

Over a three-month period there was no statistical measure of relationship (correlation, r) between absenteeism and turnover, and there were few significant correlations between absenteeism and shortages (median $r = -0.06$) or turnover and shortages (median $r = 0.15$). The absenteeism measure reflected some stability across months 1, 2, and 3 ($r_{12} = 0.61$, $r_{23} = 0.71$, $r_{13} = 0.52$). However, no one who was absent the first month was absent the next two months. In contrast, the number of teller balancing shortages was more stable ($r_{12} = 0.82$, $r_{23} = 0.71$, $r_{13} = 0.59$).

Each behavior has a cost to the organization. . . . With respect to teller shortages, the direct cost was estimated to be $8.23 per shortage. This figure includes the cash outlay minus recoveries, and is reported in constant dollar terms. Each incident of absenteeism was estimated to cost $66.45, of which $23.04 (salary) was a variable cost (since the supervisor must either find a suitable replacement or extend the existing staff). The total cost of each turnover incident was estimated at $2,522.03 of which $293.95 (direct hiring costs) was variable.

The distinction between variable and total costs is important, for a reduction in absenteeism and turnover will result in variable-cost savings only. A reduction in fixed costs or realization of opportunity costs depends on subsequent reallocation of fixed costs or staff workloads. Thus fixed and opportunity costs were not included in the financial estimates.

Exhibit 3 shows the relationship between teller attitudes and absenteeism, turnover, and balancing shortages three months later. Correlations between attitudes and turnover are low, negative, and significant (that is, statistical relationships of that magnitude would occur, on the average, fewer than five times out of a hundred by chance alone). This is consistent with results found in other research (Mobley et al., 1979).

EXHIBIT 3
Relationship between Attitudes and Behavior (Lagged Three Months)

Attitudes	Behaviors (Measured in July)		
(Measured in April)	Absenteeism	Turnover	Shortages
Intrinsic satisfaction	−0.81[a]	−0.20[b]	0.10
Job involvement	0.08	−0.29[a]	−0.12
Intrinsic motivation	−0.26[a]	−0.16[b]	−0.23[a]

[a] $p < 0.01$
[b] $p < 0.05$

Source: From P. H. Mirvis and E. E. Lawler, III, "Measuring the Financial Impact of Employee Attitudes," *Journal of Applied Psychology,* 1977, 62:4. Copyright 1977 by the American Psychological Association. Reprinted by permission of the publisher and author.

Notice also the significant negative correlation between tellers' intrinsic motivation and shortages three months later. Finally, the high negative correlation between satisfaction and absenteeism is probably an artifact. July is a primary vacation month for the tellers and some took additional, unauthorized days off. The findings suggest that the most dissatisfied employees took this extra time off. Further, individual absences varied over time, and the correlations between attitude measures and absenteeism fluctuated over the three-month reporting period. Thus the cost savings attributable to reduced absenteeism may be particular to the measurement period.

We are now in a position to relate the attitudinal measures to financial results and to estimate the potential benefits resulting from improvements in employee attitudes. The statistical approach for doing this was developed by Likert (1973). As an example, let us relate tellers' intrinsic motivation scores ($M = 6.11$, SD, $= 0.96$)* and the average balancing shortages ($M = 3.07$, $SD = 1.74$). To estimate the potential savings from a 0.5 standard deviation improvement in motivation, the steps are as follows:

1. present cost level = average balancing shortage × cost per incident
   = 3.07 × $8.23
   = $25.27 per employee per month

2. planned attitudinal improvement = 0.5 *SD*

3. estimated behavioral improvement = (planned attitudinal improvement in *SD* units) × (SD of balancing shortages) × ($r_{mot., shortages}$)
   = .5 × 1.74 × −0.23
   = −0.20

4. new behavioral rate = present mean shortage + estimated behavioral improvement
   = 3.07 + −0.20
   = 2.87 per employee per month

5. new cost level = new behavioral rate × cost per incident
   = 2.87 × $8.23
   = $23.62 per employee per month

*M = mean, SD = standard deviation, a measure of the variability of dispersion of scores about their mean.

EXHIBIT 4
Costs per Month per Teller

Attitude	Change	Cost (in dollars)			
		Absenteeism	Turnover	Shortage	Total
Intrinsic satisfaction	+0.5SD	2.40	10.17	25.98	38.55
	0	5.44	17.04	25.27	47.75
	−0.5SD	8.48	23.93	24.55	56.96
Job involvement	+0.5SD	5.74	7.08	23.62	36.44
	0	5.44	17.04	25.27	47.75
	−0.5SD	5.14	27.01	26.91	59.06
Intrinsic motivation	+0.5SD	4.45	11.55	24.41	40.41
	0	5.44	17.04	25.27	47.75
	−0.5SD	6.43	22.54	26.13	55.10

Source: From P. H. Mirvis and E. E. Lawler, III, "Measuring the Financial Impact of Employee Attitudes," *Journal of Applied Psychology,* 1977, 62:6. Copyright 1977 by the American Psychological Association. Reprinted by permission of the publisher and author.

A similar procedure was used to estimate the cost levels associated with the other attitudes that were measured (see Exhibit 4). For most measures, more positive attitudes are associated with lower costs. The cost figures are conservative for they reflect only the variable costs per teller for one month. For the bank tellers as a whole ($N =$ 160) over a one-year period, an improvement in teller satisfaction of 0.5 standard deviations was estimated to result in direct savings of $17,664. Potential total savings were estimated to be $125,160.

Advantages of the Behavior Costing Approach

Behavior costing has three important advantages associated with it. First, it is a practical method for relating attitudes to costs that can be used in a wide variety of organizations. Moreover, it has the potential to increase significantly the impact and usefulness of attitudinal data. By focusing attention on employee satisfaction and motivation, results of the behavior costing approach could stimulate changes designed specifically to improve satisfaction and motivation.

A second advantage of this approach is that it relates attitudes to future costs. Thus organizations could use it as a way of diagnosing future costs, and as a basis for initiating programs designed to reduce those costs. This makes it possible for managers to estimate the cost savings and potential benefits associated with improved morale and group functioning.

Conceptually, behavioral cost measures should be most sensitive (in comparison to other indicators) to changes in employee satisfaction and motivation (Lawler and Rhode, 1976). A third advantage of the behavior costing approach (the attitude-costs model presented in this chapter), therefore, is that it provides a method for an empirical test of that hypothesis. It yields the financial measure most related to employee attitudes. Traditionally human resource accounting has valued employee service at gross book value (the original investment expense), net book value (the original investment minus depreciation), and economic value (the anticipated financial return of the investment). In contrast, behavior costing shifts the emphasis from assigning a value to employees to assessing the economic consequences of their behavior (Mirvis and Lawler, 1977).

Despite its advantages, behavior costing also has a number of difficulties associated with it. One important issue concerns validation of the predicted cost savings. This can only be done by observing what happens when attitude changes actually occur. To test the validity of the cost figures presented earlier, Mirvis and Lawler (1977) collected data one year later from the same tellers. At that time the tellers' personal motivation had increased to 6.25 or 0.145 standard deviations. Actual shortages had decreased to $21.71 per month, somewhat below the anticipated level, but in the predicted direction. This kind of evidence suggests that the changes in attitude caused the changes in behavior, but since behavior costing is based upon correlational analyses, other causal explanations are possible.

Two additional problems in predicting behavioral rate changes and costs from attitudinal data stem from the nature of the attitude-behavior relationship. The first problem has to do with the appropriateness of the time lag. Mirvis and Lawler (1977) used a three-month lag, but they also examined one- and two-month lags. Relationships between attitudes and behavior were found in all cases, but the relationships were stronger in the three-month lag. The superiority of the three-month lag is consistent with findings in the economic literature (Katona, 1975), but findings in the organizational literature suggest that a variety of time lags produce significant effects (Taylor and Bowers, 1972). At this time, therefore, the safest course is probably to collect time-series data on attitudes and behavior at multiple measurement points, and then choose the interval that yields the most stable and representative relationships.

A related problem concerning the stability of attitude-behavior relationships is that the size and form of the relationship between these variables can change over time. In the Mirvis and Lawler (1977) study, for example, secondary analyses revealed that monthly time-series relationships between a single item measure of intrinsic satisfaction and teller shortages ranged from -0.67 to -0.06 over a four-month period. Unless this relationship is stable, predicted financial changes will not be accurate. In addition, the behavior costing model assumes a linear attitude-behavior relationship, but the actual relationship may well be curvilinear. Correlational methods are available to deal with curvilinear relations (for example, eta, the correlation ratio), but the point is that both the size and form of attitude-behavior relationships must be monitored over time with periodic corrections in the predicted savings based on the new relationships.

Special care must be taken not to over- or understate potential cost savings. Motivation and job satisfaction are likely to be improved by a combination of factors, such as job enrichment programs, participative management styles, or better employee selection procedures. Since the components of job attitudes (satisfaction, job involvement, intrinsic motivation, and so on) are rarely independent, to estimate separately the cost savings associated with each would overstate the resulting benefits. This suggests that monthly behavior measures should be related to the *set* of relevant attitude measures. This would probably result in more accurate estimates of the attitude-behavior relationships and the eventual financial benefits.

Financial benefits might also be overstated if there is substantial covariation among the rates or costs of absenteeism, turnover, and performance. It would seem appropriate, then, to remove statistically the effects of absenteeism and turnover from performance in estimating behavioral change and financial benefits.

Finally, it is important to stress that the costs of absenteeism, turnover, tardiness, and mistakes in job performance vary widely from one organization to another. Hence, comparisons across organizations may be less useful than intra-organizational comparisons of outcomes relative to baseline data.

A FINAL WORD

The time has clearly arrived for behavioral scientists to begin to speak the language of business. The methods described in this chapter provide a useful start in that direction, but we hasten to add that the nonfinancial impact of changes in employee attitudes and motivation (for example, individual growth and well-being, organizational adaptability, and good-will) cannot, and perhaps should not, be assigned an economic value. Management decisions made solely to optimize financial gains will miss completely the effects of organizational development or attitude change programs on nonfinancial results.

Nonetheless, while there are a number of problems associated with relating attitudes to costs (see Exhibit 5), and refinements may be needed in the methods described here, the potential of cost-benefit comparisons of attitude-behavior relationships is enormous. The potential payoffs in improved personnel and financial planning provide

EXHIBIT 5
Assumptions, Advantages, and Disadvantages of Attitude-Cost Models

Model	Assumptions	Advantages	Disadvantages
Human asset valuation	Salary = value to organization; therefore attitudinal improvement enhances value to the organization	a. Simple framework for measuring human assets b. Attitude Index may serve as a standard metric	a. Effects of improved attitudes on job behavior are unknown b. No validation of predicted savings
Unit cost	Changes in unit costs can be predicted from anticipated changes in attitudes. Therefore cost change = economic impact of attitudes	a. Reduces errors associated with equating to zero changes in the value of human organization from Time 1 to Time 2. b. Offers statistical method for relating attitudinal measures to financial results	a. Inclusion of fixed costs + inflationary trends in cost per unit yields irrelevant variance b. Ignores intervening processes between changes in attitudes and changes in unit cost c. Assumes constant attitude-behavior relationship over time d. Analysis is at work-group level, not individual level
Behavior costing	Attitudinal measures are indicators of subsequent employee behaviors — participation-membership and job performance	a. Relates attitudes to future costs b. Yields the financial measure most closely related to employee attitudes c. Analysis is at individual, not work-group, level	a. Difficult to validate cost savings since analyses are based on correlational data b. "Best" time lag for determining attitude-behavior relationships is unknown c. Instability in attitude-behavior relationships yields inaccurate financial changes

ample justification for expending the necessary effort and resources to develop further methods for estimating the financial impact of employee attitudes.

REFERENCES

Ajzen, I., and Fishbein, M. "Attitude-Behavior Relations: A Theoretical Analysis and Review of Empirical Research." *Psychological Bulletin*, 1977, 84:888–918.

Ajzen, I., and Fishbein, M. *Understanding Attitudes and Predicting Social Behavior*. Englewood Cliffs, N. J.: Prentice-Hall, 1980.

Katona, G. *Psychological Economics*. New York: Elsevier, 1975.

Lawler, E. E. *Motivation in Work Organizations*. Monterey, Cal.: Brooks/Cole, 1973.

Lawler, E. E., and Rhode, J. G. *Information and Control in Organizations*. Pacific Palisades, Cal.: Goodyear, 1976.

Likert, R. "Human Resource Accounting: Building and Assessing Productive Organizations." *Personnel*, 1973, 50:8–24.

Likert, R., and Bowers, D. G. "Improving the Accuracy of P/L Reports by Estimating the Change in Dollar Value of the Human Organization." *Michigan Business Review*, 1973, 25:15–24.

Macy, B. A., and Mirvis, P. H. "A Methodology for Assessment of Quality of Work Life and Organizational Effectiveness in Behavioral-Economic Terms." *Administrative Science Quarterly*, 1976, 21:212–226.

March, J. O., and Simon, H. A. *Organizations*. New York: Wiley, 1958.

Marrow, A. J., Bowers, D. G., and Seashore, S. E. *Management by Participation*. New York: Harper & Row, 1967.

Mirvis, P. H., and Lawler, E. E., III. "Measuring the Financial Impact of Employee Attitudes." *Journal of Applied Psychology*, 1977, 62:1–8.

Mirvis, P. H., and Macy, B. A. "Accounting for the Costs and Benefits of Human Resource Development Programs: An Interdisciplinary Approach." *Accounting, Organizations, and Society*, 1976, 1:179–193.

Mobley, W. H., Griffith, R. W., Hand, H. H., and Meglino, B. M. "Review and Conceptual Analysis of the Employee Turnover Process." *Psychological Bulletin*, 1979, 86:493–522.

Myers, M. S., and Flowers, V. S. "A Framework for Measuring Human Assets." *California Management Review*, 1974, 16 (4):5–16.

Porter, L. W., and Steers, R. M. "Organization, Work, and Personal Factors in Employee Turnover and Absenteeism." *Psychological Bulletin*, 1973, 80:151–176.

Rothenberg, J. "Cost-Benefit Analysis: A Methodological Exposition." In M. Guttentag and E. Struening, ed., *Handbook of Evaluation Research* (Vol. 2). Beverly Hills, Cal.: Sage Publishing Co., 1975.

Smith, P. C., Kendall, L. M., and Hulin, C. C. *The Measurement of Satisfaction in Work and Retirement*. Chicago: Rand-McNally, 1969.

Survey Research Center. *Michigan Organizational Assessment Package*. Ann Arbor, Mich.: Institute for Social Research, 1975.

Taylor, J., and Bowers, D. *Survey of Organizations*. Ann Arbor, Mich.: Institute for Social Research, 1972.

Vroom, V. H. *Work and Motivation*. New York: Wiley, 1964.

Quantifying the Human Resources Function

Jac Fitz-Enz

Few human resources managers — even the most energetic — take the time to analyze the return on the corporation's personnel dollar. We feel we aren't valued in our own organizations, that we can't get the resources we need. We complain that management won't buy our proposals and wonder why our advice is so often ignored until the crisis stage. But the human resources manager seldom stands back to look at the total business and ask: Why am I at the bottom looking up? The answer is painfully apparent. We don't act like business managers — like entrepreneurs whose business happens to be people.

We are all familiar with that most obvious preoccupation of business managers — the bottom line. Management must constantly demonstrate that its efforts make sense quantitatively — in objective, cold, hard-cash terms. Of course, such matters as the quality of worklife, employee morale, social responsibility, and business ethics are also concerns of every company today, and they are attended to — right after the profit plan. Profits aren't measured in terms of goodness, righteousness, or other esthetic indexes. They are expressed in hard dollars. Therefore, if the human resources department wants to join the profit team along with marketing, manufacturing, and the rest of the high-status departments, it will have to start looking for and pointing out its contribution to profits.

WHY DON'T WE MEASURE OUR ACTIVITIES QUANTITATIVELY?

There are at least four reasons that quantitative measures haven't been applied in most human resources departments.

1. *Personnel people don't know how to measure their activity.* Many people in our field have had no experience at all with measurement methodology. If we look at the content of publicly offered personnel workshops, we won't find a section on quantitative techniques. A number of master's degree programs in the behavioral sciences don't require courses on statistics and those that do include statistics courses don't apply them to the personnel function, because academics haven't figured out a way to do it. Those who grew up in the personnel field probably weren't required or trained to measure their results. Given any or all of these quantitative gaps, it is no wonder that personnel professionals don't know how to measure themselves.

2. *Top management has bought the myth that personnel cannot be quantitatively evaluated.* How can we expect top management to be different? Since most personnel departments don't measure results, how can management know that it can be done? It's just part of the cycle: no measurement — no evaluation — no appreciation — no rewards.

3. *Some personnel managers don't want to be measured.* Content to be second-class employees — so long as few demands are made on them — they can be a pathetic group of demeaned and demotivated people. The vice-president of human resources at one firm, for example, was little more than a lackey to senior management. His primary annual objective? To avoid rocking the boat.

Although this type of manager is a dying breed, we still meet many who truly don't want to have their departments assessed by quantitative measures — and, almost without exception, their position in the organization is strictly second-class.

4. *A few brave souls would like to apply some measures to their function, but they haven't been able to do so. Here's a message for those brave souls:* First, it can be done; second, it doesn't mean a lot of extra work; third, there is a valid business reason for doing it; and finally, there is something in it for you. One human resources department that initially balked at the idea of applying a yardstick to its work has achieved such good results that staff members now voluntarily initiate improvements. The scope of this department's measurement system has expanded, as has its recognition in the company.

WHY EVEN TRY TO MEASURE THE FUNCTION?

It is true that personnel departments have existed unmeasured for many years and that some human resources managers have, of late, gained considerable stature in the organization. By and large, however, the function's improved position has come about for negative reasons. With the onslaught of government intervention through EEO, ERISA, OSHA, and other recent legislation, businesses have been forced to hire or advance human resources managers and give them some clout, if only to keep the firm out of Uncle Sam's doghouse.

Serendipitously, this turn of events has brought many bright, creative people into the field. These people have begun to show organizations that it pays to support the human resources department. But for all their efforts, most personnel groups still lack the organizational position and stature they seek. The reasons? Until they start using objective, quantitative indexes in managing the personnel function, human resources managers will never fully realize a status equal to that of managers in other key departments.

There are three criteria for judging the relative value of a department's position within an organization. The first — survival — is negatively based, having to do with avoidance. Positively oriented measures are advancement and power.

Survival

When an organization encounters serious difficulties, it usually reacts by slowing down or cutting back certain functions. Traditionally, the first groups affected are staff departments. Public relations, advertising, planning, and personnel often experience a reduction in budget and staff. The reasons are obvious and usually logical. No one knows the benefits of cost-center departments. We know that if we lay off workers on the assembly line, we will ship less product. But what will happen if we drop the public relations department? What if we stop training? In these cases there will probably be few observable negative short-term effects. Even if there are, we probably won't be able to prove it, since we have no objective measures of the value of staff functions.

Speculate with me for a moment on what would happen if we did have a quantitative technique for measuring a staff function's net worth. Let's assume that management has been shown that over the past couple of years the firm's recruiters have been able to find qualified applicants with minimal use of headhunters and that the cost per hire has been one-fifth that of using agencies. Furthermore, let's say management is aware that these hires stick with the organization an average of 60 percent longer than agency candidates do. Given that the hiring of direct labor and line managers is a continuing need, would the company then choose to decimate its recruiting staff as part of a belt-tightening program? Probably not. The problem is, how do you collect and communicate that type of information to top management? Surprisingly, most of the data on the contribution a trained recruiter makes to the cost-per-hire and retention factor of new employees are already available, if unused.

A sample cost-per-hire analysis is illustrated in Figure 1, which provides a report on a monthly, yearly, and year-to-year basis. All the data shown can be easily collected with either a manually maintained hire log or an automated applicant control system. The year-to-year comparison demonstrates that the average cost per hire in 1979 is running about 7.5 percent lower than it did in 1978. Additional data can be furnished to show the number of recruiters and number of clerical assistants per applicant processed and per hire achieved, retention rate of new hires, and many other effectiveness measures.

Clearly, the numbers are there to prove that laying off recruiters costs more and increases the turnover rate. Few reasonable executives shown such facts and figures would cut off the corporate nose to spite its face. That would be a bad business decision. Therefore, the first reason for objective assessment is simply survival.

Advancement

Every organization operates on a reward system that consists principally of pay and promotions. Theoretically, at least, most people advance on the basis of their ability to obtain positive results. Sales, manufacturing, engineering, and finance all demonstrate the return on their investment. Accordingly, the executive floor is populated by those who have demonstrated that the results of their efforts can be measured down to that favored indicator of corporate health — the bottom line. Now is the time for the human resources department to find ways to show that it can contribute to overall profits.

Although the cost-per-hire figures illustrated in Figure 1 are fairly obvious measures, others are not so apparent. Supervisory and managerial training, for example, represent a function we've been told cannot be measured. But we can poke holes through that notion by setting up a simple pre/postsurvey experiment that will demonstrate the reverse. The fact is, supervisors who invest time in specifically geared training programs improve attitudes and productivity in their units, while untrained supervisors do not.

Such measurable benefits illustrate that the human resources department can be evaluated by means of the same criteria that are applied to other corporate functions. When we begin to operate in this mode, we will obtain a better share of the corporation's rewards.

Power

Professionalism is an attribute we all admire. We like to watch a real pro at work, and we work in a society that promotes professionalism as a desirable goal. People who choose careers in medicine, law, accountancy, and engineering enjoy status, respect and, usually, high incomes. We look to these experts for advice. Their words carry considerable weight in our daily lives, both at home and at work. When dealing with important matters, or in times of crisis, we turn to professionals for guidance, support, and special services. As a result, professionals acquire a good deal of persuasive power in our society.

Some people regard personnel work as a profession. The way it is today, though, I'm not certain I could support that contention. The prerequisites of a profession are a body of scientifically developed knowledge, a formal educational program, and a pub-

FIGURE 1
Staffing Department Activity Report

April: Cost of Hires by Source

	Agency			Ads			Employee Referrals			Non-profit Other		Total Number Hired	Total Cost	Cost per Hire
	No.	Total Cost	Cost/ Hire	No.	Total Cost	Cost/ Hire	No.	Total Cost	Cost/ Hire	No.	Cost			
Exempt	6	$47,500	$7,916	8	$24,375	$3,047	5	$1,500	$300	1	$00	20	$73,375	$3,669
Nonexempt	1	624	624	24	10,078	420	24	2,400	100	9	00	58	13,102	226
Totals	7	$48,124	$6,875	32	$34,453	$1,077	29	$3,900	$134	10	$00	78	$86,477	$1,109

Year to Date: Cost of Hires by Source

	Agency			Ads			Employee Referrals			Non-profit Other		Total Number Hired	Total Cost	Cost per Hire	Year to Year	
	No.	Total Cost	Cost/ Hire	No.	Total Cost	Cost/ Hire	No.	Total Cost	Cost/ Hire	No.	Cost					
Exempt	21	$83,512	$3,977	28	$43,282	$1,546	16	$ 4,800	$300	3	$00	68	$131,594	$1,935	1978	$712
Nonexempt	8	2,843	355	91	26,270	289	69	6,900	100	17	00	185	36,013	195	1979	$662
Totals	29	$86,355	$2,978	119	$69,552	$ 584	85	$11,700	$138	20	$00	253	$167,607	$ 662		

lished code of ethics. The human resources function is incomplete in these areas. No easily accessed, scientifically validated, universally accepted body of knowledge appears to have been assembled. Far too few undergraduate and graduate personnel programs exist, and those that do are not consistent in content and design. The only acknowledged code of ethics seems to be to see that neither the employee nor the organization gets shafted — not quite the equivalent of the Hippocratic oath.

Even if the trappings of classic professionalism can't be draped about our shoulders, we can still perform in a professional manner. Most of our colleagues in human resources today try to do a good job for themselves, their organizations, and the employees. Unfortunately, we have a difficult time proving that our function is directly linked to profits. The most encouraging note is that some personnel people already recognize that measurement is the key that can unlock the door to professional status. Although measurement alone won't satisfy the requirements of formal professional recognition, it certainly will elevate the function in management's eyes and confer upon it an aura of professionalism. To the extent that we can relate to top management on its terms — quantified results — we will be viewed as pros in the operational sense and will acquire the power to match our sense of conviction.

HOW TO MEASURE HUMAN RESOURCES MANAGEMENT BY RESULTS

In public workshops on methodology, I often encounter three reactions from participants: "This is a measure of activity, not productivity." "This doesn't relate to the bottom line for the organization." "There must be a few basic measurements that can be applied in all organizations at all times with equal validity." There are two ways to address these reactions.

Any single measurement is only a snapshot of a moment in time. When we measure the number of insurance claims processed, cost per hire, the number of problems solved through counseling, or cost per man-hour of training in a given time period, we are measuring activity. But if we continue to measure those results over time, we begin to develop an indicator of relative productivity, efficiency, or effectiveness. Some measures, such as cost per hire, are direct indexes of productivity. Others are indirect or partial measures that, when integrated into a whole, yield less quantifiable, but nonetheless valuable, assessments of effectiveness. The point is to generate a meaningful set of measures that can be tracked over time. The result will be trend data that tell us objectively how well we are carrying out our responsibilities.

Whenever possible, include costs as the dependent variable in the measure. Cost is the one factor that everyone understands. Admittedly, it is difficult to apply costs to some tasks — but not, as we have allowed ourselves to believe, impossible. We can, for example — since people perform personnel services — associate costs with both the person and the activity. Costs for our department are costs for the organization. Obviously, if we accomplish better results with the same number of people, we have achieved greater efficiency and productivity. Furthermore, high productivity in areas that count is equated with effectiveness. I've been able to develop more than 60 ratios of personnel activities that either directly or indirectly compute costs/benefits over time. Using a consistent assumption of costs, we can account even for tasks such as counseling in ways that demonstrate savings to the organization.

Of course, there is no magic set of measures that can be applied with equal value to every human resources department. Even such basic computations as cost per hire, for example, are not useful to every organization. Take the captive labor markets or slow-growth companies; in both instances, hire costs would be considered irrelevant. Each organization has its own structure, objectives, and problems that combine to make it unique. And since most personnel managers know and understand their organization's idiosyncrasies, they are in a perfect position to select the appropriate measures.

A Total System

The initial reaction of most human resources managers is that they are already familiar with the basic measure of their work. But is their understanding broad enough to include a total system — one that works across the board? Management itself can be measured only when all functions are put to the test. This doesn't of course imply that we have to implement a full-blown program on Day 1. But certainly the ultimate objective should be to have a uniform system in place for the personnel function as a whole. The design should phase in several aspects of each personnel subfunction, including employment, compensation, employee relations, and training. Experience with the methodology will permit the incorporation of increasing numbers and levels of tasks. And as each new task is added to the measurement system, a synergetic effect takes place. Hitherto unseen relationships between tasks become visible. The staff begins to appreciate how its work is interconnected. In time, the system approach to total department measurement generates a very powerful effect indeed.

Formulas for Subfunction Measurement

Probably the best way to put the system in place is to begin by listing all the variables we would like to measure within a given subfunction. (See Figure 2.) Employment is one function that offers opportunities for many measures. A few of the most important variables in most firms are time; cost; recruitment source; interviews; offers made, accepted, or rejected; job level; EEO classification; performance level; and termination rate. These can then be worked into formulas that can be applied at the corporate, divisional, and departmental levels. The same is true for the compensation, employee relations, and training functions.

Although we cannot hope to undertake a full explanation of all possible formulas and their various uses here, it is useful to examine a partial list of factors for which formulas have been constructed. Brief comments will be made on their value and applicability.

A key point is that any activity in a given function can be viewed from a number of perspectives. For example, any of several formulas can be used to compute hiring costs. Here is one:

$$C = [(ST)^I + (MT)^I + Y]/H$$

C = Cost per hire

I = Number of interviews (120)

ST = Standard cost of recruiter and clerical time per interview ($28.21)

MT = Standard cost of management time per interview ($22.41)

Y = Supplemental costs (advertising, fees, relocation, and so forth: $6,345.00)

H = Number hired (14)

C = ($28.21 × 120 + $22.41 × 120 + $6,345.00)/14

C = $12,419.40/14

C = $887.10

There are dozens of such formulas, many of which start out as simple ratios that evolve into more elegant and powerful measures as time and experience deem appro-

FIGURE 2
Dependent Measures

Variable	Comments
Hiring costs	Can be computed on a gross basis by adding in all costs. Can also be computed in terms of partial measures when you just want to examine applicant sources, time spent interviewing, relocation costs, and so on. Can also calculate new employee orientation costs.
Recruiter productivity	Can be analyzed by the time spent interviewing as compared with time spent on administrative tasks, by hiring rate, average length of interview, rejection rate, retention rate, and so on. Each partial measure provides a different view of a recruiter's effectiveness and productivity.
Staff productivity	Several ways to measure the number of recruiters and clerical assistants required to handle a given volume of applicants: average number of hires per recruiter, per assistant, per month by job types. When tracked over time it is clear that requisition mix has an impact on number of recruiters needed, as well as optimum load per recruiter.
Cost of record keeping	Simple measures of average time required to process a new hire, transfer, promotion, and so forth, multiplied by salary and benefit costs of the processing clerk. Can also be used to project staffing needs for a given workload.
Benefit costs	Can calculate as average cost per employee or as percent of salary. Can also analyze participation in optional plans (such as employee stock purchase, thrift plan) by job level, job group, or department/division.
Salary administration	Objective: to monitor compliance with company's salary and performance review systems. Can compare salary increase or performance ratings across departments and levels. Obviously, external market comparisons of salaries can be made.
Group insurance costs	Simple measures of processing claims by mixing staff costs, number of claims, number of claims processors, volume of claims over time, and turnaround time per claim are ways to get at the efficiency of the benefits unit.
Lost time	Absenteeism can be calculated as a direct cost and as it affects labor utilization. To be meaningful, turnover volume and costs should include such factors as job level, department, length of service, performance level, and reason for leaving.
Counseling	Monitoring the number, type, and time of counseling sessions by level or department provides an early warning system for organizational problems. An effectiveness measure that tells how many sessions resulted in a positive solution can also be developed.
Training	Improvement in knowledge and skills can be proved by making pre/postsurvey tests around each training module. Retention can be tested three to six months later. Utilization, change, and cost impact can be demonstrated through surveys. Cost of training per man-hour of instruction can be calculated and compared between courses and vis à vis outside programs.

priate. Some situations don't even require simple formulas. In such instances, the raw data of frequency or time can be used without manipulation.

Figure 3 shows the number of several types of counseling sessions held and the time spent on each. By plotting these data on a multilayered bar and showing three months at a time, we have developed a trend chart. This type of visualization serves as an early warning system. In this particular example, we see a marked and consistent pattern of increase in problems with employees. Conversely, there is a continuing decrease in policy and procedure sessions. (Note in the figure that session size is in proportion to time, not frequency.)

The first trend tells us that something negative is happening and needs to be investigated. As you study the chart, several other correlations become apparent: The number of exit interviews, career counseling sessions, and personal problems is also increasing. This would support the problems-with-employees trend. Another factor to be aware of is the proportion of time versus frequency of sessions. Our example shows that the ratio is going up in problems with employees and down in policy and procedure discussions. We have found the time/frequency proportion to be a good indicator of complexity or severity of problems.

The second trend shown in Figure 3, policies and procedures, might be attributable to a training program on that topic that took place during May and June. The chart serves as an indirect measure of the effectiveness of the training effort. The data can also be cut by department/division to pinpoint where the problems lie.

Whether you use formulas, charts, or tables, the idea is to start with a system in mind and then build measures that will fulfill the system's objectives. Introduce as few or as many as time and skill allow. As the system grows and trends begin to emerge, the strength and value of these indicators multiply geometrically.

Reporting the Results to Management

Having the best measurement system in the world can be very satisfying to you and your staff. But until you let management know what you are doing, you have reaped only part of the reward for your efforts. We all know that communication in organizations is a critical process that can either build cohesion or create confusion, depending on how well it works. Communicating the results of the measurement system to top management in the form of periodic reports is crucial. A cardinal principle of communication is to understand the personalities of people who will read the report. Only then can you select the best way of communicating the results so that they will be read, understood, and appreciated.

A number of charting techniques are available for this purpose. Trend lines, bar charts, pie charts, tables, and so forth are excellent choices for eye appeal and ready comprehension. Since most top executives are busy people — generally numbers people — and, until recently, people who aren't overly interested in what goes on in personnel, a reporting format that makes for brevity is paramount. It can help the reader speed through a report quickly and pick out only what he or she wants to know. It can also be constructed in a manner that will emphasize major points. To paraphrase Marshall McLuhan, the medium influences the "message." In short, a message can be either enhanced, obscured, or destroyed by the means chosen to communicate it.

THE BOTTOM LINE

To improve any unsatisfactory situation, something has to change. If we are interested in improving our position in the organization, we will have to find and use more accurate, appropriate, and acceptable tools of persuasion. Nothing is more acceptable —

FIGURE 3
Counseling Sessions, May–July

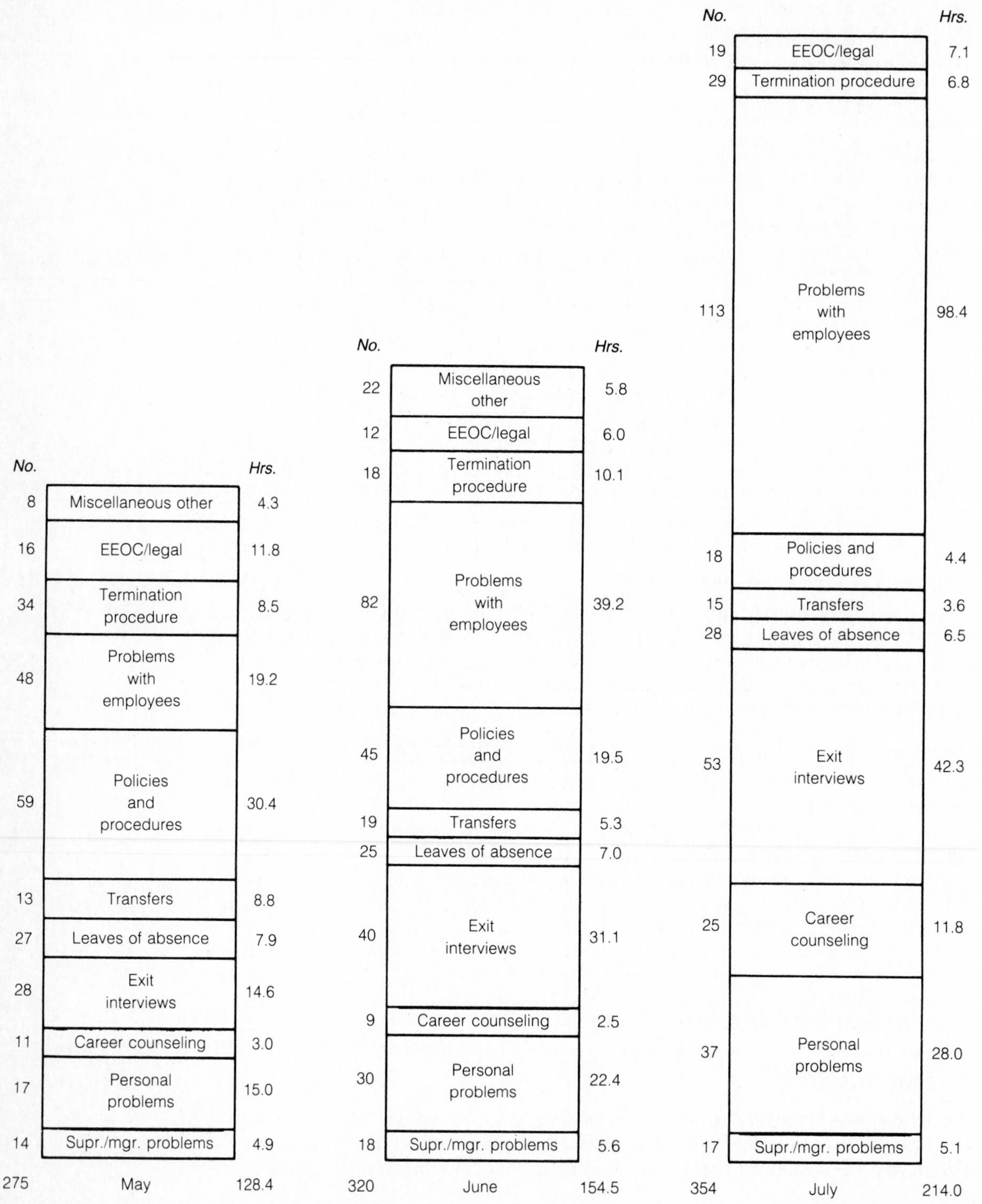

No.		Hrs.
19	EEOC/legal	7.1
29	Termination procedure	6.8
113	Problems with employees	98.4
18	Policies and procedures	4.4
15	Transfers	3.6
28	Leaves of absence	6.5
53	Exit interviews	42.3
25	Career counseling	11.8
37	Personal problems	28.0
17	Supr./mgr. problems	5.1
354	July	214.0

No.		Hrs.
22	Miscellaneous other	5.8
12	EEOC/legal	6.0
18	Termination procedure	10.1
82	Problems with employees	39.2
45	Policies and procedures	19.5
19	Transfers	5.3
25	Leaves of absence	7.0
40	Exit interviews	31.1
9	Career counseling	2.5
30	Personal problems	22.4
18	Supr./mgr. problems	5.6
320	June	154.5

No.		Hrs.
8	Miscellaneous other	4.3
16	EEOC/legal	11.8
34	Termination procedure	8.5
48	Problems with employees	19.2
59	Policies and procedures	30.4
13	Transfers	8.8
27	Leaves of absence	7.9
28	Exit interviews	14.6
11	Career counseling	3.0
17	Personal problems	15.0
14	Supr./mgr. problems	4.9
275	May	128.4

indeed, intriguing — to top management than contributions to productivity and profitability. Since profits are objective indexes, we need objective methods to tell our story.

With much of the data required for an objective measurement system already at our fingertips in the form of voluminous hire data kept at the behest of government regulators, invoices for ads and agencies that cross our desks with regularity, salary and benefit costs detailed by most of us, and absence and turnover files, we need only a format to give the information meaning.

An objective report of recruiting results, record processing, counseling, or training provides top management with a clear picture of the contributions you and your staff are making to the organization. Probably for the first time, higher management will be able to understand, in their own language, the intrinsic value of the human resources function to the organization. Personnel work is not altruism; neither is it benevolence or humanitarianism. It is a necessary and fundamental aspect of any sound enterprise. When the realization finally spreads throughout an organization, work-life in that organization will be better for all of its employees.

E.

LABOR RELATIONS

Lifeboat Labor Relations: Collective Bargaining in Heavy Seas
Arnold Weber

A sweeping change is taking place in labor relations strategies and tactics in the United States. This development has been occurring with such precipitous speed that no expert could have predicted it as recently as three years ago.

In fact, the leading issue in labor relations that titilated attorneys and arbitrators three years ago was the neutrality clause.

Three years later, however, we are talking about a different set of adversities and legal issues that reflect a completely contrary labor-management environment. If I have any text to my sermonette, it is that the current interest in the use of the bankruptcy procedure to abrogate union contracts is best understood within the context of pervasive and profound changes in the labor relations environment. Beyond the important legal considerations, the issue itself is overshadowed by broader issues of structure and strategy within the labor relations area.

It is important first to specify the dominant characteristics of the American industrial relations system, in order to provide a framework for the changes that have been working themselves out during the past few years. Once we look at these ascriptions, we can then identify what, in fact, has happened and is likely to happen in the years ahead. With this perspective, we can perhaps better understand the implications of the bankruptcy issue.

Let us look at the American labor relations system as it existed in the mid-1970s and toward the end of the decade. On the one hand, we can say there was a certain element of self-congratulation, if not smugness, in viewing the American industrial relations system. It had certain problems. Stereotypes such as the hyperaggressive shop steward, the union leader pursuing self-defeating wage policies, and the willful employer had some basis in fact. But by and large, the system had worked and it reflected the character of the American environment.

From *Labor Relations in Transition*, Washington University, March 1984. Reprinted by permission of the author.

In the United States, regardless of deficiencies in labor relations practices, there still was a comforting quality of stability. It was a framework within which, at the end of all the posturing, you could "make a deal."

BASIC ELEMENTS OF U.S. INDUSTRIAL RELATIONS

Three basic characteristics of the labor-management system were taken as given at the end of the 1970s. First, union membership and strength had been maintained in the dominant sectors of the economy, and that strength was accepted as a given. Unions in the United States have had a unique and anomalous role: statistically, they have always been a minority. But in terms of their impact in the labor market, through their emulative impact on the non-union sector, unions have always had a majority effect. Union membership at its peak (and nobody knew it was peaking in 1958) was around 28 or 29 percent of the labor force. Nonetheless, unions clearly have been viewed as a constant in the heartland of the American economy.

Heartland Strength of Unions

Union strength traditionally has been in manufacturing, in the "blue collar alley" curving from Pittsburgh to Cleveland, up into Michigan, and across to Chicago. Construction, the extractive industries such as mining, and particularly the transportation and printing industries defined the deep genealogical roots of the trade union movement.

Adjusting Wages by Formula

The second basic principle governing the labor relations system at the end of the 1970s was the widespread acceptance of a formula approach to compensation. Wage increases were linked to macroeconomics factors rather than to firm- or industry-specific factors. When this development took place, it was proclaimed — and with some justification at that time — as the triumph of statesmanship and long-term perspectives over short-term avarice.

The basic element of this approach was something called the "annual improvement factor," or AIF. In its explicit and robust form, the Annual Improvement Factor was developed in the General Motors-United Auto Workers contract of 1948. Basically, labor and management said, "We are going to change the ouija board, which works on differential pressure, into a slide rule (we would say a computer now) in determining how we divide up the pie." The governing factor was what happened to national trend productivity, which was fixed at that time at 3 percent. The primary consequence was to break the linkage between wages and the firm or industry measures and, instead, tie wages to some macroeconomic variable.

The next step in this formula approach to wage adjustments was to protect the real gain in earnings associated with the Annual Improvement Factor by adding on a cost-of-living adjustment clause, or COLA clause. The explicit theory behind COLA adjustments was that the appropriate approach to collective bargaining and wage determination is to establish a real increase based on the AIF or on productivity, and then protect the value against changes caused by inflation through a COLA clause.

The third element of the formula approach to wage increases was coincidental with the emergence of fringe benefits as a major element of compensation. This took place in the 1950s and 1960s. Every employee has since been exposed to the erosive economic impact of "benefit creep." This phenomenon arises from the fact that employers prefer to negotiate benefit levels rather than costs, because if they became involved with costs, the unions would push for the last nickel or dime.

Consolidated Bargaining

The final element of the pre-existing system was the development and entrenchment of highly consolidated bargaining structures. These structures are of two basic types. The first is a straightforward, garden-variety, multi-employer bargaining arrangement.

In its more subtle and extended form, bargaining structures were consolidated through "pattern-setting" — which developed in rubber, autos, retail food, and a whole range of other industries. This pattern following developed its own protocols which, in some ways, were predictable.

In my judgement, these three elements — the predominance and acceptance of union organization in the heartland of the economy, the development of a formula approach to wages, and the establishment of consolidated, well-defined bargaining structures — were the pillars of the American labor relations system. They stood for a thirty-eight-year period. Lost time from strikes in a bad year was on the order of .18 of 1 percent, which was probably less than the lost time associated with golf.

THE CHANGING LABOR-RELATIONS ENVIRONMENT

The system worked, and we thought it was an expression of maturity. At the same time, it almost had a Toynbee-esque quality. But changes were taking place in the environment which would undermine existing practices and set the stage for the tactics and developments that we identify today — of which resort to bankruptcy is an element.

International Competition

One of these major changes is the emergence of unrelenting international competition. Many industries did not understand this development; they imputed the apparent success of companies and industries to their own managerial genius when, in fact, that success was attributable to their position in national economic development — the fact that many companies operated in protected markets. This was certainly the case in airlines, steel, rubber, autos, and a whole range of industries within which protective practices took root.

Deregulation

Secondly, and most dramatic, has been the impact of deregulation, particularly on transportation. Ten or fifteen years ago, Jimmy Hoffa of the Teamsters was a folk hero in labor relations. Hoffa was a larger-than-life figure who stood astride the Central States Master Freight Agreement like the Colossus at Rhodes. We can recall the legendary stories of Hoffa negotiating global contracts and also serving as the court of last resort in the resolution of grievances. And if Teamster business agents strayed from the existing contract, methods were found to try to bring them back in line.

But look at what is happening now in the deregulation of industries. The best Master Freight could do was agree to a wage freeze which has subsequently been widely eroded through the fragmentation of what appeared to be a monolithic bargaining structure.

Effects of the Recession

A third factor is the extended, deep recession which began in 1979. In this recession we have seen a discontinuity in the trend growth rate of the American economy. Many of the principles inherent in past labor-management relations arose during the era of what I call the "Great American Schmoo Machine" — the Schmoo being the mythic character in the Al Capp comic strip, every part of which was convertible to a delectable pork chop, that would split by binary fission as a gesture of love. That is the situation we thought we had for thirty years. Real GNP was increasing by roughly 4 percent a year, productivity was going up 3 percent, and everybody fell into the trap of linear extrapolation: the expansion was going to go on forever. We finally reached a discontinuity in the 1970s.

The Sun Belt Shift

The next factor of change was the failure of unions to follow geographical and industrial shifts in the labor force. What happened was that the trade union movement, like almost every other institution, acquired a certain "organizational arteriosclerosis." That is, it is much easier to have an office on Sixteenth Street in Washington, and go across the street to the White House, than it is to get out and hustle in small towns in Tennessee and pass out handbills at 5 o'clock in the morning or go around to people's houses and try to organize them. In other words, there was a loss of initiative within organized labor.

Professionalization of Personnel Administration

Another factor which altered the labor environment was the maturation of the personnel administration movement. I think this aspect plays a very important part in understanding the unions' difficulties, because workers now perceive that there are reasonable, non-tyrannical alternatives to joining a union.

Influence of the PATCO Strike

The last important element of change is the following: in order to crystalize any event, there has to be the "Sarajevo phenomenon." That is, World War I was not caused by the assassination of a hapless archduke; it was an incident which merely captured a whole set of historical events.

In American labor relations, in my judgment, the Sarajevo phenomenon was the Professional Air Traffic Controllers' strike. When the PATCO strike took place, many of us dismissed it as exotica. In a way, it *was* exotica. But the very fact that it happened was extraordinary. The fact that the President of the United States — the chief personnel administrator, if you will — took on this group and broke the strike gave it tremendous significance. This was the largest strike broken by any employer since the steel workers' strike in 1919.

In a consequential way, the PATCO strike created the environment that permitted Continental to file for bankruptcy. What is more significant are the recent events (in late 1983) at Greyhound. Imagine calling the union representative in and saying, "You take a 9½ percent wage cut, and if you do not take it in a week we are going to replace you." Furthermore, Greyhound is a company that has been unionized for decades. Such a challenge to an established union would have been unthinkable a few years ago. The Continental bankruptcy issue, the Greyhound shutdown, and a range of other episodes are efforts to redefine the current limits of acceptable behavior. This redefinition process is a legal, managerial, tactical and, if you will, moral issue.

IMPACTS ON U.S. LABOR RELATIONS

Shrinking Unionism

The question is, how have these changes affected the three basic elements of the labor relations system that I outlined earlier? Unions will not disappear or decline to insignificance, but they are clearly defending a shrinking perimeter. Their membership has fallen from a peak of 28 percent of the labor force to 20 percent as of two years ago, and membership to about 18 percent today. They have failed to keep pace with the growth of the labor force in areas such as health services and microelectronics. In addition, unions are now losing membership in sections of former strength through the development of what I characterize as the "neo-open shop movement."

Breakdown of Formula Bargaining

Secondly, the formula approach to bargaining is clearly losing ground. There has been a sharp deflation in union wage gains beyond any reasonable expectations, a deflation which has been associated with moving away from the formula approach. Look at the data. In 1981, wage gains in all major bargaining agreements averaged 9.6 percent. Four years ago, a self-respecting union leader would not dare come forward and say the union had a three-year agreement for anything less than 30 percent. But in the first nine months of 1983, wage gains averaged 1.7 percent. If interest rates had dropped from their peak as much as first-year wage increases have declined, they would be down to about 4 percent.

The next step in the evolution of labor bargaining is the one where the bankruptcy issue comes in. Labor and management have altered the rules of the game with respect to the rate of wage increases, but in many industries that is not perceived as an adequate adaptation. The next step, in management's view, is rationalizing the wage structure.

For example, it is one thing for a firm in the meat-packing industry to declare a zero percent wage increase. But if that wage freeze leaves the firm with employees earning $12 an hour while a competitor such as the old Iowa Beef Company (now MBX) or a non-union city packer is paying only $6 or $7 an hour to its workers, then it is the competitor's wage rate that defines the adjustment which management will seek.

The use of bankruptcy law has taken place in these types of circumstances. The major issue in these cases has not been reducing the rate of increase in wage, but rationalizing the wage structure and labor costs in light of a new economic environment. That is the context in which Continental Airlines and Wilson Foods have attempted to make use of the bankruptcy law.

Fragmentation of Bargaining Structures

The third major change is the fragmentation of large bargaining structures. Indeed, in my judgment, this is probably the most important development in shifting from macro considerations to micro factors in wage determination. For instance, can Uniroyal, when talking to the rubber workers, make its own case or must it always deal within the shadow of Goodyear and Firestone?

Are these trends likely to change? John Dunlop, who is a respected authority in this area and a man of great judgment, basically views all this as a perturbation. Historical parallels can be made with changes in the hosiery industry outside Philadelphia in 1934 and other past episodes; that is one way you can look at current trends. Dan Mitchell at UCLA also takes this view. I do not think what is happening now is a perturbation. I believe the changes are durable and are likely to continue over the next five or ten years.

Several things are changing the current environment. The first of these is government policy. We certainly do not see consequential labor policies coming from President Reagan. As a matter of fact, the curious thing is that the Reagan Administration is the first administration of any party in 50 years not to have an explicit labor policy. Its labor policies are derived from other economic policies. What is happening in the airline and trucking industries comes from the Carter-Reagan policy toward deregulation. What happened in construction and autos, in a real sense, was a consequence of tight money, which dried up demand and put excruciating pressure on the bargainers. Even the most myopic manager has to realize that "the times, they are a-changing."

Even if there is a change in political parties in the White House and Congress in 1984, I do not think we will see a major change. Any President is unlikely to be enthusiastic about increasing a broad array of tariffs, or placing more limitations on employer discretion in plant shutdowns, or altering the array of economic forces that are producing these changes in labor-management relations.

Secondly, are we likely to get any relief from the labor market? In my judgment, the answer is no. Given current unemployment rates and the breakdown of immigration controls — which maintain sort of a permanent elasticity in the labor supply — we will not see a change that would result in a labor shortage and thus tip the labor-management balance of power.

And third, will some Mosaic leader emerge from the unions, as we saw in the 1930s? Is there lurking in some textile mill a prospective John or June Lewis, ready to lead labor out of the wilderness? I see no evidence that this will happen.

What we are more likely to see is the power of the American labor movement diminished at the bargaining table. Unions will then switch toward increased political action in closer accord with the European model. And indeed, in my opinion that is the significance of the bold step taken by Lane Kirkland of the AFL-CIO in having formal labor representation in the high councils of the Democratic Party as well as the early endorsement of political candidates.

Setting aside collective bargaining agreements via bankruptcy poses an interesting and challenging policy issue that will, in one way or another, be worked out. But its true significance can be seen as a tactic within a new and boldly changing strategic labor relations environment. In a tactical sense, I do not know whether filing for bankruptcy is better or worse than threatening to hire replacements or shutting down plants peremptorily. But, in fact, these methods are part of a new array of tactics in a game in which the parties are divesting themselves of previous virtue and trying to re-define the character of new, more difficult, and probably less generous relationships.

The 1982 Union Wage Concessions: A Turning Point for Collective Bargaining?

Daniel J. B. Mitchell

In the past, the perspective taken on labor relations has been decidedly short-run. Prognosticators have concerned themselves with upcoming negotiations and their likely outcomes for the next year or so. However, the rash of concession bargaining in the union sector, which began in 1979, reached a crescendo in 1982. In a number of industries, wages were frozen or cut, existing contracts were interrupted before expiration, and work rules were relaxed. These unusual developments redirected the discussion among academics and practitioners away from the standard short-term focus and toward the longer-range outlook. Specifically, by the end of 1982, debate had crystallized into a spectrum of views. There were those who believed that the large number of wage concessions represented normal behavior of bargainers faced with a deep recession. At the other extreme were those who believed that a fundamental turning point had been reached in industrial relations and that collective bargaining in the 1980s would not return to the practices of the 1960s and 1970s.

What is the correct viewpoint? Has a fundamental turning point been reached? Obviously much depends on what is regarded as "fundamental." It is difficult to imagine that the concessions of 1982 will leave no trace behind; the real question is whether the changes that do occur will be far-reaching. Despite the perils of forecasting, it will be argued below that there is a potential for change inherent in the wage concessions. Increased use of gain sharing in some concessions could be a fundamental change, if it endures and becomes widespread. But the fundamentals of collective bargaining have not as yet shown clear signs of change.

For purposes of this article, an economic perspective is taken. American collective bargaining in the past has been an adversarial system of determining wages and other employment conditions which finds its expression in long-duration contracts. Under these contracts, adjustments in wages have been responsive to the rate of price inflation, often through the use of cost-of-living adjustment clauses (COLAs), but have not been especially sensitive to other economic conditions.[1] Unless this method of determining wage adjustments is altered, the changes caused by the 1982 wage concessions cannot be viewed as fundamental.

AN EMPIRICAL OVERVIEW OF CONCESSION BARGAINING

While it is easy to identify 1982 as a major year of concession bargaining, obtaining a count on the number of concessions which occurred is not easy. Since collective bargaining is a give-and-take process, and since some bargains in any year are inevitably less favorable to the union side than others, it is difficult to define the concept of concession rigorously. As a working definition, however, contracts in which basic wages were frozen or cut are taken to be concessions for purposes of this article. While there are some conceptual problems with this definition, it appears to capture the settlements which would be likely to be regarded as concessions using other definitions.[2]

The Bureau of National Affairs (BNA) maintains a contract file of collective-bargaining settlements covering fifty or more workers. From these files, it is possible to isolate those settlements which involved basic wage freezes or cuts during 1982.

About 12 percent of the 1982 agreements reported by BNA froze or cut wages. Table 1 provides a summary of the industry and union composition of these concession contracts.

Only 12 percent of the subsample of concession contracts involved actual reductions in wages of existing workers, although a number of other contracts provided for wage cuts at the entry level for new hires. Wage freezes were the most common form of concession. The ten industries shown on Table 1 accounted for over four-fifths of the total number of concessions in 1982, with the construction industry accounting for nearly one-fourth of the total.[3] Many of the concession settlements involved relatively small numbers of workers confined to local areas, especially those in construction. Thus, much of the concession bargaining that occurred in 1982 did not make headlines.

Of the settlements that did receive substantial publicity, those in intercity trucking and motor vehicle manufacturing were most prominent. These settlements alone accounted for over nine-hundred-thousand workers, if U.S. Bureau of Labor Statistics (BLS) estimates are taken literally.[4] The Teamsters and the Autoworkers unions figure prominently in the number of concessions negotiated. Over one-fifth of the concessions reported on Table 1 were negotiated by these two unions. In some cases, the concessions made by the Teamsters and Autoworkers outside their basic industries were closely connected with the larger concession settlements; in other cases, the unions simply had the misfortune to represent workers in distressed industries outside their main jurisdictions.

Table 2 provides information on two key, interrelated contract characteristics: the presence of COLA clauses and the duration of the agreement. The proportion of concession contracts with active COLA clauses (shown in column (1)) varies substantially from industry to industry. However, the variation mirrors the propensity to use COLAs in each industry prior to the concession period. That is, in industries such as construction, where COLAs are rare in all contracts, they were also rare in the concession contracts. In industries such as motor vehicles and trucking, where COLA clauses have been standard practice, they were typically found in the concession contracts. In total, 40 percent of the concession contracts had some form of "active" COLA clause — clauses that could provide some payout during the life of the agreement.

Column (2) of Table 2 indicates that while COLA clauses were frequently found in concession contracts, the concession arrangements often involved restricting the COLA's operation. In some cases, COLA money was "diverted" to pay for fringe benefits. Delays in COLA payments, partial freezes of COLA monies, and other types of unusual limitations occurred in 54 percent of the concession contracts which had COLA clauses. There were also instances of more conventional COLA limits such as caps, reduced frequency of payment, and so on.[5]

Apart from the 40 percent of concession contracts which retained some type of COLA, another 17 percent froze or suspended their COLAs but did not completely delete reference to COLA from the contract. Column (3) shows the frequency of such provisions by industry. If agreements with active COLAs are combined with those with frozen COLAs, about two-thirds of the concession contracts retained some trace of the COLA principle. As shown in column (4) of Table 2, only 11 percent of the contracts were reported as dropping completely a preexisting COLA clause.

COLA clauses are rare in one-year agreements; they are generally associated with multiyear contracts. Column (5) shows that the average contract duration for the concession contracts was just under two-and-a-half years. Thus, just as the COLA principle was generally retained in concession bargaining, so was the standard practice of negotiating long-duration agreements.

In many respects, the unionized labor market became bifurcated in 1982. Al-

TABLE 1

Industry and Union Pattern of Wage Freeze and Cut Contracts, 1982

Industry	Union					
	Team-sters	Auto-workers	Food and Commer-cial Workers	Transit Union	Rubber Workers	Carpen-ters
Construction	X					X
Metals	X	X				
Public transit[a]				X		
Motor vehicles[b]		X				
Retail foodstores	X		X			
Rubber					X	
Machinery		X				
Meatpacking			X			
Airlines	X					
Trucking	X					
All others	X	X				
Percent of total wage freeze of cut contracts	13%	9%	9%	8%	6%	5%

Note: an X indicates one or more wage freeze or cut contracts were negotiated by unions indicated in designated industry.
[a]Including intercity bus lines.
[b]Including motor vehicle parts.

though 12 percent of the union contracts negotiated involved wage freezes and cuts, the other 88 percent did not. Table 3 permits a comparison of characteristics of all contracts negotiated in 1982 with nonconcession contracts — those which provided for basic wage increases. The all-contract, first-year median wage increase in 1982 was 7 percent, down from 9.6 percent in 1981, a drop of 2.6 percentage points. If the analysis is confined to contracts providing wage increases, the drop was from 9.9 to 7.9 percent, or 2 percentage points. Put another way, including concessions in the sample raises the amount of union-sector, first-year wage deceleration in 1982 by only .6 percentage points.

During the same period, the rate of consumer price inflation measured by the conventional consumer price index, the CPI-U, fell from 8.9 percent to 3.9 percent, a full 5 percentage points. Even if the less volatile CPI-U-X1 index is used — which avoids problems created by the housing component of the conventional consumer price index — the inflation rate dropped from 8.5 percent to 5.0 percent, a 3-percentage-point drop. No matter what the measure, the degree of wage deceleration in 1982 was not startling, although it was more than forecasters had predicted.[6] Indeed, the 1982 contracts provided for a real wage increase in the face of a severe recession, even if the concession contracts are included in the sample.

Union

Machin- ists	Electrical Workers (IBEW)	Steel- workers	Plumbers	All Others	Percent of Total Wage Freeze or Cut Contracts	Wage Cuts as a Proportion of Wage Freezes or Cuts[c]
	X		X	X	24%	18%
X		X		X	9	21
				X	9	0
				X	8	0
					8	8
				X	7	0
X				X	6	11
					6	11
				X	4	29
X					3	0
X		X		X	18	14
5%	5%	4%	4%	32%	100%	12%

[c]Excludes wage cuts affecting only new hires. Wage cut may not have affected all workers under contract.
Source: Daily Labor Report, various issues.

Thus, most of the 1982 contracts did not provide for substantial deviations from past notions of appropriate wage increases. But a minority of negotiators took the drastic step of imposing wage freezes or cuts when faced with especially distressed economic conditions.[7] Table 3 shows also that the frequency of inclusion of escalators in contracts fell in 1982 relative to 1981. But this was not because of the concession contracts (which were more prone to include escalators than the nonconcession contracts). A more likely explanation is that the drop in price inflation and inflation expectations caused interest in escalators to decrease. Similarly, contract duration in 1982 fell somewhat relative to 1981, from thirty-two months on average to twenty-nine months. But both concession and nonconcession contracts exhibited the same twenty-nine month mean duration. General uncertainty about future economic conditions, rather than concessions, appeared to account for the modest duration decline.

THE TURNING POINT DEBATE

As noted at the outset, the 1982 concessions set off considerable debate concerning their long-term significance for collective bargaining. While some observers have argued that fundamental changes in collective bargaining have occurred as the result of

TABLE 2
COLA and Duration Pattern of Wage Freeze and Cut Contracts, 1982

Industry	Proportion of Wage Freeze and Cut Contracts with COLA in Effect[c]	Proportion of COLA Contracts with COLA Diversion, Delays, or Limitation[d]	Proportion of Wage Freeze and Cut Contracts with Totally Frozen or Suspended COLA[e]	Proportion of Wage Freeze and Cut Contracts Which Dropped Existing COLA[f]	Mean Duration of Wage Freeze and Cut Contracts[g] (Months)
Construction	8%	0%	0%	0%	24
Metals	43	67	7	0	33
Public transit[a]	50	43	36	0	28
Motor vehicles[b]	92	91	0	0	27
Retail food-stores	33	25	0	50	34
Rubber	73	13	9	0	35
Machinery	44	75	11	29	34
Meatpacking	44	100	33	0	39
Airlines	29	0	0	0	21
Trucking	100	100	0	0	36
All other	34	40	0	23	29
All industries	40%	54%	17%	11%	29

[a]Including intercity bus lines.
[b]Including motor vehicle parts.
[c]Does not include contracts reported in last two columns.
[d]Does not include COLA caps.
[e]Includes only COLA clauses frozen over entire life of contract.
[f]Contracts eliminating COLA as proportion of sum of contracts with COLA, with frozen or suspended COLA, and dropping COLA.
[g]Simple average of contract duration.

Source: Daily Labor Report, various issues.

TABLE 3
Union Contracts Characteristics, 1981–1982

Characteristic	All Contracts, 1981	All Contracts, 1982	Contracts Excluding Wage Freezes and Cuts, 1982
Median first-year wage increase	9.6%[a]	7.0%	7.9%[b]
Proportion of contracts with COLA in effect	24%	17%	14%
Mean contract duration (months)	32	29	29
Proportion of contracts containing wage freezes or cuts	3%	12%	0%
Note: percent change in consumer price index			
CPI-U	8.9%	3.9%	—
CPI-U-XI	8.5%	5.0%	—

[a]If this figure were adjusted to exclude wage cuts and freezes in 1981, it would have been 9.9 percent.
[b]The median of the previous column has been treated as a means to make adjustment.

Source: Daily Labor Report, various issues.

the concessions, the view advanced in this article is more skeptical and conservative. Before presenting further elaboration on this personal perspective, however, the opinions of other commentators are considered below.

Freedman: A Breakdown of Pattern Bargaining

Audrey Freedman of the Conference Board, a business research organization in New York City, has been a major proponent of the idea that the fundamentals of labor-management relations were changed by the recession and that there will be no going back to business as usual. In articles in the *Harvard Business Review* (with coauthor William Fulmer) and in *Challenge*, she focuses heavily on "pattern bargaining" (where one lead settlement has a strong influence on the pattern of other later settlements).[8] Freedman notes the erosion of pattern bargaining in a number of industries and concludes that it is dead.

Whether Freedman is correct will depend largely on whether the patterns that existed in bargaining up until, say, 1979, are viewed as fundamental characteristics of collective bargaining. There is no doubt that those pre-1979 patterns eroded due to the concessions. The Big Three automakers (Ford, GM, and Chrysler) became the Big Two, with Chrysler going its own way in 1979, due to its perilous economic situation. Various deals were struck in the rubber industry at the plant and company level which violated the principle of industrywide wage settlements. Similar examples can be cited in other industries characterized by multiemployer or coordinated bargaining. Employers and unions directly involved in such negotiations undoubtedly felt that such deviations from traditional patterns were highly significant for them — and for them they undoubtedly were. But in historical perspective, pattern bargaining has long been an ephemeral and fuzzy concept whose relationship to the basic characteristics of wage determination is, at best, uncertain.[9]

At the end of World War II, the degree of pattern bargaining was much higher than it was in the late 1970s, before the 1979–82 round of concession negotiations began. The old Congress of Industrial Organizations played a major role in coordinating bargaining demands of its constituent industrial unions. And there was continued government intervention, even after wartime wage controls were lifted, which tended to spread wage patterns. But even at that time, bargainers improvised pattern variations to deal with the problems of particular employers who could not afford to match the lead settlements.[10]

The erosion of patterns continued in the 1950s and 1960s. For example, the close connection between rubber settlements and auto settlements began to break apart in the mid-1960s. The special treatment given by the Autoworkers to American Motors Corporation in the 1960s and 1970s, which allowed AMC to pay less than the Big Three, foreshadowed the Chrysler concessions of 1979–81. Moreover, pattern bargaining — even when it was undisturbed — had different meanings in different industries. In some industries it meant uniform wage and benefit levels; in others it meant seemingly uniform wages but with benefit variations; and in still others it meant uniform wage increases imposed on wage levels which varied by plant, firm, or region.

Pattern bargaining can be compared to the surface of the water in a lake behind a dam. The water remains smooth and uniform over the lake's surface so long as there is enough water to cover everything. But if the level of the water in the dam is lowered, eventually the rough points along the bottom begin to poke through and uniformity is no longer possible. Similarly, when there is enough demand in the economy to keep all of an industry's major employers healthy, uniformity in wage settlements is possible. However, as the level of demand decreases, the most marginal firms begin to suffer and plant closings, layoffs, and bankruptcies threaten. Uniformity becomes less and less possible or desirable as demand declines and the economy sinks into deep recession.

But not every recession produces the volume of concessions that occurred in 1982. If a recession looks like a temporary aberration, it is possible for bargainers to ride it out without changing old habits. And this was what happened during the postwar period in many cases. Even the major recession of the mid-1970s was short enough to be ridden out without much disturbance to normal collective bargaining.[11] But the period of slackness which began in 1979 lasted so long that certain existing wage patterns were forced to break down.

It is likely some pattern relationships will be restored after the economy has had a chance to recover, although they may well have different boundaries and be defined in different ways from their predecessors. But such alterations should not be regarded as fundamental changes. Patterns have always shifted; the slump which began in 1979 simply exacerbated the tendency. Hence, Freedman's view is misleading. It is true that pattern bargaining was disrupted by the concessions. But, a particular set of patterns is not a fundamental element of collective bargaining. Therefore, a change in those patterns, unsettling though it may be to the participants, does not mean that collective bargaining has entered a "brave new world" unlike anything that has previously existed.

Kassalow: New Centers of Innovation

Everett Kassalow, in a paper presented to the Industrial Relations Research Association, indicated that the concessions of 1982 caused a shift in the likely base of innovation in collective bargaining and a change in union policy making — not exclusively in the bargaining arena but in the area of policy formation within the union movement.[12] On his first point, Kassalow argued that innovations such as escalator clauses and supplemental unemployment benefits became widespread once they were adopted in the auto and steel sectors. These innovations were often not invented in autos and steel, but their adoption in those industries was tantamount to the Good Housekeeping Seal of Approval for other industries.[13] According to Kassalow, the combination of recession and foreign competition has so eroded the auto and steel base that innovations will have to come from somewhere else in the future. He indicated that the telephone industry and the Communications Workers would have been a good choice to inherit the innovators' mantle — since telephone calls cannot be imported — were it not for the restructuring of the Bell System. Kassalow is unsure what sector will emerge as the new innovator.

There is a problem with the Kassalow position. Even in recession, the auto industry managed to innovate in making a modern concession. Auto industry wages were among the first to be frozen, beginning with Chrysler. But, as part of the quid pro quo for a wage concession, auto industry management conceded various income and employment guarantees to their workers.[14] These arrangements were imitated elsewhere, just as were other auto innovations in more prosperous times. Kassalow may have counted out autos as an innovator too soon. Regarding steel, it is not clear that it ever had the wide-reaching innovating role that Kassalow ascribes to it; steel innovations were generally confined to the metals sector.

Kassalow's second point deals with the balance of power within the union movement. He believes that the central body, the national AFL-CIO, will play a larger role in formation of major union policy than has been the case in the past — that it will be a center of policy innovation. A key question is whether the national AFL-CIO's role will be in the area of bargaining relationships with employers — providing more guidance to member unions than has traditionally occurred at the time of negotiations — or in the political setting.

There have already been moves by the AFL-CIO to involve itself more heavily in national politics, particularly Democratic Party politics. The AFL-CIO might well press for what used to be called national economic planning but which now could be repackaged as "reindustrialization" or doing things the "Japanese" way. Such a program might well include a union role in the planning apparatus. However, the significance of such a development for wage determination is unclear.

Dunlop: No Change in the Fundamentals

In sharp contrast to the opinion that important changes are occurring in labor relations is the view expressed by former Secretary of Labor John T. Dunlop that the wave of concession bargaining was a normal response to an abnormal economic situation.[15] Dunlop points to long historical experience with wage cuts going back to the Great Depression and before. He argues that the fundamentals of union objectives and collective bargaining were not altered by these earlier episodes, and he sees no reason for a different outcome in the 1980s.

Dunlop also points to the bifurcation of the labor market that became apparent in early 1982. Unions — except when faced with employers in dire economic circumstances — did not abandon the fundamental goal of improvements in wages and conditions. Those unions which could make improvements did not hesitate to do so, while others made a tactical (temporary) retreat.

The Dunlop view has been criticized as being too long-run and too historical in orientation. In particular, Kassalow has criticized Dunlop for including pre-World War II experience in his assessment.[16] Such early experience, Kassalow argued, is of little relevance to modern collective bargaining. And it is true that when analysis is confined to the postwar period, although there have been previous episodes of concession bargaining, the number of workers involved and the proportion of contracts included was higher in 1982 than had occurred in those earlier postwar episodes. There was at least a quantitative difference in what occurred.

AN ALTERNATIVE VIEW: POTENTIAL FOR FUNDAMENTAL CHANGE

Certain elements of the 1982 concessions undoubtedly will endure, while others will fade. There were interesting experiments with a variety of innovations in 1982, which go under such headings as quality of work life, quality circles, and worker participation in management. Many of these ideas are not new. Experiments along these lines go back to the 1920s and earlier.[17] Throughout their history, proponents of these experiments — whatever their labels — have tended to promise a great deal. Yet while there have been waves of experimentation, widespread and enduring adoption of such plans has not occurred. During the early 1960s, a period which saw very moderate wage settlements similar to what occurred in 1982, a number of innovations which seemed very significant at the time appeared on the horizon. In steel, there was the Kaiser Long-Range Sharing Agreement and the Human Relations Committee in the basic steel settlement. In meatpacking, there was the Armour Automation agreement. All of these arrangements eroded as the economy expanded and normal collective bargaining resumed.[18]

There is an obvious tension between traditional labor-management relations in the context of collective bargaining and other forms of worker participation. In a situation of employer economic emergency, the so-called adversary relationship between union and management is temporarily suppressed by the evident need for cooperation to avert mass job loss.[19] Thus, the climate for cooperative experiments improves. But the key question is whether such experiments — if promoted at the height of an emergency — can endure once the emergency subsides. Those plans which were adopted in haste may well fade away in the future, unless the general climate of cooperation between union and management is sustained by perceived gains to both sides. But undoubtedly there will be some instances in which the quality-of-work-life experiments succeed in establishing a sufficient base of support to be continued.

Tangible Changes in Income Security

The income and job security guarantees offered senior workers in the auto industry and others fall into the category of tangible benefits which are likely to endure. Senior workers are more likely to be older workers with family responsibilities and high costs of mobility. Income and job protections, therefore, appeal to senior workers whose voice is especially important in determining union policy. Moreover, the guarantees represent a continuation of earlier efforts to achieve income security, such as the supplemental unemployment benefit (SUB) plans. SUB plans, which provide payments to laid-off workers, were popularized during the recession of the mid-1950s when job security was threatened by the economic readjustments following the Korean War. The new programs resulting from the auto wage concession negotiations in 1982 can be viewed as "super-SUBs." Because they extend an earlier concept, they are not as radical an innovation as they may seem at first glance.

There have been concerns in the management community about the potential costs of the new plans, just as there were at the time the older SUB programs became popular.[20] There may, however, turn out to be management benefits in the new plans which go beyond the wage concessions that were received in exchange. A work force which has income security is less likely to feel threatened by new technology, plant relocations, and similar disruptions. Management flexibility in these areas, which can be important in meeting international competitive pressures, changes in consumer tastes, and alterations in the regulatory framework, may be enhanced by the new programs.

Gain Sharing: Potential for Fundamental Change

Since the new income security arrangements represent an evolution from earlier benefit programs, they should not be classified as fundamental changes in collective bargaining. What would more properly be regarded as a fundamental change would be contractual devices which alter significantly the responsiveness of wages to the economic conditions of the employer, industry, or economy. Multiyear contracts, which became the standard type of agreement by the 1960s, tend to be insensitive to the pressures of the business cycle since they expire infrequently.[21] To the extent that wages under these contracts reflect economic circumstances, it is through the use of a cost-of-living escalator clause which responds only to price developments. Adaptation to recession is typically by layoffs of junior workers rather than wage adjustment, except in dire instances when only wage cuts or freezes can avert large-scale job losses.

Many economists believe that the U.S. economy would function more efficiently, and that fighting inflation would be easier and less painful, if there were greater wage flexibility and sensitivity to economic conditions than labor contracts have typically provided.[22] Barry Bosworth, former director of the Council on Wage and Price Stability, has called for a law banning multiyear contracts and COLA clauses for this reason.[23] But such an action would be a drastic remedy which the parties to collective bargaining would strongly resist. Multiyear contracts, while they may not reduce the number of strikes, at least make the exposure to strike risk more predictable and less frequent. As already noted, there was no indication that the parties themselves, even those who conducted concession negotiations in 1982, wished to abandon multiyear contracts.

A more acceptable change than the abandonment of long-term contracts — and one which would be a fundamental reform — would be the wide-spread incorporation of gain-sharing plans into union agreements. Gain-sharing plans, of which profit-sharing is the most common example, link an element of pay to an index of the economic circumstances of the employer. The index may be profitability, sales, production, or productivity. While such plans reduce compensation during bad times, they also guarantee bonuses in good times. In a gain-sharing economy, some of the adjustments to recession that are now primarily handled by layoffs would instead be made through reduced gain-sharing payments.[24] Observers of the Japanese economy have argued that the gain-sharing bonus system in use in that country has helped maintain job security during recessions.[25] The same principle could be applied in the U.S., and it would have the same beneficial effect.

Unfortunately, gain sharing represents only a potential for fundamental change at present. In a number of the wage concession negotiations, modest elements of gain sharing were introduced into the compensation package for the first time. But if these elements remain, and if they eventually become a much larger proportion of total compensation than they currently represent, fundamental change — far more important than shifts in pattern bargaining or who wears the mantle of innovator — will have occurred. The problem is that even the modest experiments in gain sharing made in 1982 may not endure.

In the 1983 Chrysler settlement, for example, profit sharing was eliminated — just at a point when it appeared that Chrysler might again become profitable — in exchange for the normal guaranteed wage improvement factor and escalator clause. Thus, gain sharing may have been viewed by some concession negotiators as a temporary face-saver to be eliminated at the first propitious moment rather than a valuable innovation.

There is potential for fundamental change in collective bargaining via gain sharing but the parties need external stimulus to move in that desirable direction. Gain sharing could bring such social benefits as a more responsive wage structure and a less inflation-prone economy — benefits which are not fully "captured" by individual parties to a collective-bargaining negotiation. Appropriate federal tax incentives to encourage gain sharing are needed to reflect these economywide benefits. Other tax incentives in the past have encouraged the use of pension and welfare plans so there is good reason to expect that tax incentives could promote gain sharing, too.

If gain sharing had been widespread prior to the current period of economic slackness, many of the painful contract interruptions, wage freezes, and cuts could have been avoided. Gain sharing would have automatically effected a "concession" without the need for renegotiation. And it could have done something for workers that is otherwise difficult to do in concession situations. It could have guaranteed automatic recoupment of employee concessions when the economy improves. Despite these advantages, gain sharing remains a potential change in the fundamentals of collective bargaining. As yet, there has been little government interest in promoting its adoption.[26]

CONCLUSIONS AND POSTSCRIPT

The 1982 union wage concessions were dramatic events which naturally stimulated diverse opinions concerning their significance. Clearly, there will be future ramifications of these concessions affecting many aspects of collective bargaining. But from the economic standpoint, the key aspect of collective bargaining is its role in wage determination. In the area of wage determination, the concession impact is uncertain.

The 1983 Basic Steel Settlement

In early March 1983, the major steel producers and the United Steelworkers reached a settlement incorporating a temporary wage cut of about 9–10 percent in take-home pay and a set of severe restrictions on the operation of the COLA clause. Other benefits, such as holidays, were also reduced. But SUB benefits were expanded, and some language was added indicating that the labor-cost savings would be used for plant modernization.

The steel agreement included key features which had developed in the 1982 contract concessions. It preserved the multiyear contract by adopting a forty-one-month duration and the COLA principle. Interests of senior workers in job and income security were clearly expressed in its SUB provisions and early retirement options. But the contract broke no substantial new ground in the areas of worker participation in management (existing arrangements and efforts were continued) or gain sharing (no profit-sharing plan or similar program was included).

In the steel case, the negotiations process seemed more painful to the union than the actual concessions. An attempt to reach a concession settlement failed during the summer of 1982. A second attempt in November was negotiated by the top leadership of the union but rejected by its local union presidents. In that version, the wage concession would have been greater but gain sharing would have been introduced through a complicated linkage of company earnings and the COLA formula. The successful third attempt was not made until the union revised its voting procedures, reducing the electorate of local union presidents to those most likely to approve. Thus, the basic steel negotiations illustrated the ingrained resistance to wage adjustments based on external economic circumstances. Moreover, without gain sharing and with the COLA clause severely limited, wage schedules were set in advance for a forty-one-month period without any contingency for changes in those circumstances, either positive or adverse.

REFERENCES

1. Daniel J. B. Mitchell, "Should the Consumer Price Index Determine Wages?" *California Management Review*, vol. 25 (Fall 1982), pp. 5–21.

2. For a survey using a different set of definitions, see Daniel J. B. Mitchell, "Recent Union Contract Concessions," *Brookings Papers on Economic Activity* (1: 1982), pp. 165–201.

3. Construction contracts accounted for 18 percent of the agreements included in the BNA survey. Hence, they are overrepresented among the concession subset.

4. The BLS estimates for contract coverage may not have fully reflected the decline of the unionized work force in trucking and autos due to layoffs.

5. It was not always possible to tell if the more conventional COLA limitations reported had existed in prior agreements.

6. Daniel J. B. Mitchell, "Is Union Wage Determination at a Turning Point?" *Proceedings* of the Industrial Relations Research Association, December 1982, (forthcoming).

7. Peter Cappelli, "Concession Bargaining and the National Economy," *Proceedings* of the Industrial Relations Research Association, December 1982, (forthcoming).

8. Audrey Freedman and William E. Fulmer, "Last Rites for Pattern Bargaining," *Harvard Business Review*, vol. 60 (March/April 1982), pp. 30–48; Audrey Freedman, "A Fundamental Change in Wage Bargaining," *Challenge*, vol. 25 (July/August 1982), pp. 14–17.

9. There are important methodological difficulties in trying to identify patterns and spillovers in wage determination. See Daniel J. B. Mitchell, "How to Find Wage Spillovers (Where None Exist)," *Industrial Relations*, vol. 21 (Fall 1982), pp. 392–397.

10. George Seltzer, "Pattern Bargaining and the United Steelworkers," *Journal of Political Economy*, vol. 59 (August 1951), pp. 319–331; Mitchell O. Locks, "The Influence of Pattern-Bargaining on Manufacturing Wages in the Cleveland, Ohio, Labor Market," *Review of Economics and Statistics*, vol. 37 (February 1955), pp. 70–76.

11. Mitchell, "Recent Union Wage Concessions," pp. 176–185.

12. Everett M. Kassalow, "Concession Bargaining, Something Old, But Also Something Quite New," *Proceedings* of the Industrial Relations Research Association, December 1982 (forthcoming).

13. Sanford M. Jacoby and Daniel J. B. Mitchell, in "Development of Contractual Features of the Union-Management Relationship," *Labor Law Journal*, vol. 33 (August 1982), pp. 512–518, discuss the development of various innovations in union contracts.

14. Harry C. Katz, in "Assessing the New Auto Labor Agreements," *Sloan Management Review*, vol. 23 (Summer 1982), pp. 57–63, discusses the 1982 auto settlements.

15. "Remarks of Former Labor Secretary John T. Dunlop on 1982 Wage Developments Before Conference of Business Economists," *Daily Labor Report* (23 February, 1982), pp. D1–D2; John T. Dunlop, "Working Toward Consensus," *Challenge*, vol. 25 (July/August 1982), pp. 26–34 (interview).

16. Kassalow, op. cit.

17. Sanford M. Jacoby, "Union-Management Cooperation: An Historical Perspective," in Eric G. Flamholtz (ed.), *Human Resource Productivity in the 1980s* (Los Angeles: UCLA Institute of Industrial Relations, 1982), pp. 173–215.

18. Mitchell, "Recent Union Wage Concessions," pp. 174–175.

19. Calls for departing from the adversarial model became more and more frequent as the economic slump which began in 1979 deepened. See Ben Fischer, "Taking Combat out of Labor Relations," *Business Week* (21 September 1981), p. 17.

20. A poll of management executives indicated substantial resistance to job and income security guarantees. See "A Management Split over Labor Relations," *Business Week* (14 June 1982), p. 19.

21. On the development of the multiyear contract, see Sanford M. Jacoby and Daniel J. B. Mitchell, "Does Implicit Contracting Explain Explicit Contracting?" in *Proceedings* of the Industrial Relations Research Association, December 1982 (forthcoming).

22. Daniel J. B. Mitchell and Larry J. Kimbell, "Labor Market Contracts and Inflation" in Martin Neil Baily (ed.), *Workers, Jobs, and Inflation* (Washington: Brookings Institution, 1982), pp. 199–238.

23. Barry Bosworth, "Policy Choices for Controlling Inflation," *Alternatives for the 1980s*, A publication of the Center for National Policy, (1:1981), pp. 16–22.

24. Daniel J. B. Mitchell, "Gain-Sharing: An Anti-Inflation Reform," *Challenge*, vol. 25 (July/August 1982), pp. 18–25.

25. Masanori Hashimoto, "Bonus Payments, On-the-Job Training, and Lifetime Employment in Japan," *Journal of Political Economy*, vol. 85 (October 1979), pp. 1086–1104; Robert J. Gordon, "Why U.S. Wage and Employment Behavior Differs from that in Britain and Japan," *Economic Journal*, vol. 92 (March 1982), pp. 13–44.

26. The poll cited in footnote 20 indicates that there is much greater receptivity on the management side to gain sharing than to job/income security guarantees.

F.

PERSONNEL RESEARCH

Personnel Research
William H. Holley and Kenneth M. Jennings

Personnel research is becoming more relevant and more prevalent, essentially because of externally imposed demands related to equal employment opportunity and internally imposed demands related to accountability for personnel activities and to increasing the productivity of human resources. Personnel researchers are involved in these challenging areas, which have given impetus for renewed interest in research by both personnel professionals and academicians.[1] However, personnel research also faces problems. One researcher describes the situation as follows:

> Personnel research pervades all of the functional areas of personnel administration. In many respects, the future of the personnel administration field rests upon our ability to refine and develop techniques, practices, and strategic approaches to the ongoing problems in personnel. Research has traditionally produced innovations in areas such as job analysis, staffing, and performance measurements, job satisfaction and employment morale and personnel forecasting and planning. More recently, research has provided answers to organizational problems in the areas of equal employment opportunity and equal pay administration.
>
> Why then does there remain the doubt and skepticism about the practicality of [personnel] research among practitioners and administrators? For years we have observed that there is a large gap between the subject matter and findings of personnel research efforts and the practical problems in the field. Concern over the sometimes "esoteric" nature of personnel research creates frustration on the parts of those who are involved in producing research as well as those who are involved in solving personnel problems. More importantly, however, much potential understanding and useful information is lost because of misunderstanding over the means and ends of personnel research.[2]

Personnel research can be categorized according to six major types — experimental research, case studies, surveys, analysis of employee data, legal and quasi-legal research, and secondary research.

Experimental Research

The most creative type and the one most likely to advance the personnel function is experimental research.[3] Experimental research usually involves a new program or a new direction for an existing program, such as a wage incentive program to increase productivity. The research design calls for an experimental group (a group to work under the new wage incentive program, for example) and a control, or comparison, group (a group that will *not* work under the new program); also skilled researchers must be employed if any sophisticated analysis is required.

Before the new program is introduced on a broad scale, it should be carefully analyzed and assessed. Because many organizations are reluctant to experiment when the risks of failure are high, researchers — especially academicians — often rely on laboratory studies, which can be carefully controlled. Many such experimental studies are conducted on campuses; a typical example might involve a comparison of negative and positive feedback concerning a performance appraisal interview. While the natural concern about the results of laboratory studies involves their transferability to the real world, each experiment advances our knowledge about personnel activities. Ideally, the results should be published so that others can share in the researchers' findings.

Case Studies

The intensive case study revolves around an organization or a specific personnel activity. Personnel researchers may rely on sources of information, such as company policies and records, or interviews with organizational personnel. . . . Many . . . case studies have been written by personnel professionals about their experiences in specific programs, such as job enrichment programs, drug-abuse programs, union-management quality of working life programs, and the like. All help others become more knowledgeable and thus help advance the personnel function.

Surveys

Surveys may be conducted within or outside the organization. Surveys within the organization usually include attitude or organizational climate surveys, which assess employees' opinions, attitudes, and beliefs about their jobs, organization, pay, supervision, and other job-related considerations. Some organizations conduct these surveys routinely so they can continually monitor personnel-related concerns. Analysis of the survey data enables the organization to identify such things as early signals of employee dissatisfaction, possible problems with particular supervisors, and employees' reactions to new programs.

External surveys are frequently conducted by organizations to determine what other organizations are doing with regard to a particular personnel activity. . . . A commonly conducted external survey is the wage survey, which is used to determine the labor market wage rate. On a broader scale, national surveys are conducted by government agencies, trade associations, groups such as the Conference Board, and reporting services such as the Bureau of National Affairs, Commerce Clearing House, and Prentice-Hall. Although these national surveys cannot be readily applied to an individual organization, the survey results give an indication of what other organizations are doing, provide the current status of particular personnel activities on a national scale, and give trends and projections for these activities.

Analysis of Employee Data

Analysis of employee records and data takes advantage of records and data that are currently available within the organization or that can be secured. Exhibit 1 shows various types of employee data that can be obtained. If the personnel data are kept in a computerized form called a *personnel information system* — skilled researchers can analyze enormous volumes of data highly useful to the organization. Typical studies include the relationships between turnover and personnel characteristics such as age, sex, race, education, and so on. Further, measurements of performance can be correlated with test scores, interviewers' assessments and biographical data. Performance, absenteeism, turnover, and other employee data can be translated into employment costs per unit output. Examples of more uses of personnel data appear in Exhibit 2. Such analyses can contribute significantly to the effectiveness of personnel activities by enabling personnel managers to assess the costs of human resources and by making the personnel department more accountable for many of its activities.[4]

The ready availability of personnel records and banks of data stored in computerized personnel information systems has led to a rise in employees' concern about the privacy of their records. Employees are raising the question of possible misuse of these data by unauthorized personnel. Casual handling of private records by personnel departments has heightened the possibility of governmental intervention in personnel activities. In fact, twenty-four states already have legislation to protect employees' privacy; six more states have had legislation introduced; and the federal government has enacted a law guaranteeing privacy of personnel data.[5]

Legal and Quasi-Legal Research

Legal and quasi-legal research may not be considered personnel research in its purest form, even though it is extremely important to the personnel function. This type of research involves analysis of employment discrimination and labor arbitration cases, which may take a sizable amount of time in some large organizations. In analyzing employment discrimination cases, personnel researchers may seek legal cases in which they can identify principles useful to the company's positions in an EEO suit. For example, suppose that a minority employee denied promotion files a discrimination charge and that performance appraisal was used as the basis for the promotion decision. A review and analysis of similar cases would assist the company in formulating the position it would take before the EEOC or, later, the court. While this work may be assigned to corporate attorneys, familiarity with the legal research process will add significantly to the value of the personnel researcher.

Similarly, in preparing for an arbitration hearing (called a quasi-legal procedure), researchers will find it valuable to conduct case analysis to identify principles and apply these principles to the company's positions in the forthcoming arbitration hearing. Such cases are available in their original form from the Bureau of National Affairs, Commerce Clearing House, Prentice-Hall, and the American Arbitration Association. Personnel researchers frequently take advantage of these sources.

Secondary Research

In using the last type of personnel research, secondary research, the researcher synthesizes information from publications on a particular topic for a specific purpose. Although this research is not classified as creative or innovative, it often requires cre-

Personal Data

Name
Pay number or social security number
Sex
Date of birth
Physical description of employee (height, weight, color of eyes, etc.)
Names, sex, and birth dates of dependents
Marital status
Employee association participation
United Fund/Community Chest participation
Minority group classification

Recruiting Data

Date of recruiting contact
Responsible recruiter or interviewer
Source of candidate referral (newspaper ad, employment agency, etc.)

Benefit Plan Data

Medical and/or life insurance plan participation
Pension plan participation
Savings plan participation (U.S. bonds, etc.)
Pay for time not worked (vacation, illness, lost-time accidents, personal time off, death in family, jury duty, military reserve duty, etc.)
Tuition refund plan participation
Etc.

Separation from Payroll Data

Date of removal from payroll
Reason for leaving
Forwarding address
Name and address of new employer
Amount of pay increase obtained with new employer
Eligibility for rehire

Safety/Accident Data

Noise level (in decibels) in work area
Exposure to noxious fumes or chemicals on job
Record of injury (date of accident, date reported, nature of injury, cause of injury, record of medical attention given, name of attending physician)
Classification of injury (disabling or nondisabling, days of work lost, lost time charged)
Physical limitations resulting from injury
Workmen's compensation claim data

Open Jobs or Positions Data

Job request control number
Job title
Position or job code
Educational requirements
Experience requirements
Permissible salary range
Date by which the position must be filled

Work Environment Data

Average educational level of co-workers
Average salary of co-workers
Number of job openings in component
Date of referral of candidate or application to interested management
Names of supervisors or managers referred to
Date of interview(s)
Date of offer of employment
Date added to payroll
Reasons for selection/rejection of candidate
Test scores and interviewer ratings
Number of jobs open for which candidate was potentially qualified
Number of other applicants for same open job or jobs.

Work Experience Data

Names and locations of previous employers
Prior employment chronology
Military service
Job skills possessed
Percent employees terminating employment (for some standard period)
Accident frequency and severity rates for position or component
Relative frequency of job changes in component
Manager's or supervisor's age
Manager's or supervisor's years supervisory experience
Selection or inheritance of employee by present manager
Relative frequency of manager's or supervisor's disciplinary actions
Manager's or supervisor's tendency toward strict or lenient rating of employees
Amount of overtime worked in component
Percent of employees dissatisfied with work, pay, supervisor, etc. in component

Position/Job History Data

Job or position ID number
Job or position code
Date job or position was established
Permanent/temporary classification of job
Identity of past incumbents in the job
Dates of change in job incumbents
Dates of vacancies in positions
Type of change involved for each person leaving the position (newly hired, lateral transfer, promotion from another position)
If a promotion, identity of position promoted from
Location of job in organization structure
Manager or supervisor to whom position reports

(continued)

610

PART VII
P/HRM IN THE
CONTEMPORARY
ENVIRONMENT

EXHIBIT 1 (cont.)

Labor Market Data

Analysis of local manpower availability
Unemployment levels by skill, occupation, age, sex, etc.
Predicted future manpower needs
Identification of scarce and surplus manpower pools
Wage and salary, shift differentials, etc.
Product line experience
Managerial or supervisory experience
Foreign languages spoken, written, read
Publications authored
Special skills or hobbies of potential value to the business
Patents held
Elective governmental positions
Security clearances held

Educational Data

College degree, high school diploma, level of educational attainment
Field of degree
Date of degree
Schools attended
Special employer sponsored courses completed
Professional licenses held

Compensation/Work Assignment Data

Exempt/nonexempt or hourly/salaried classification
Current salary or pay rate
Date of current salary level
Date and amount of next forecast salary/pay increase
Previous pay rates and dates effective
Previous dollar and percent increase and dates of increase
Organizational reporting level
Position title
Supervisor/individual contributor status
Job code
Hours worked
Premium time hours worked

Performance Evaluation Promotability Data

Personal interests
Work preferences
Geographical preferences (for multiplant operations)
Level of aspiration
Rank value of contribution in current work group
Special nominations and awards
Appraisal reports

Date of last appraisal
Growth potential as rated by manager
Previous promotions considered for, and dates of consideration
Dates of demotion
Reason for demotion
Date of last internal transfer
Dates considered for apprenticeship or other special training
Reasons for elimination from consideration for apprenticeship or other special training
Dates of, type, and reason for disciplinary action

Length of Service/Layoff Data

Date hired by employer (actual or adjusted for lost service)
Seniority date (if different from date of hire)
Date of layoff
Last pay rate
Recall status

Employee Attitude/Morale Data

Productivity/quality measures
Absenteeism record
Tardiness record
Suggestions submitted (usually to a formal suggestion plan)
Grievances
Anonymous inquiries/complaints
Perceived fairness of management practices regarding employees
Perceived fairness and soundness of management philosophy
Attitudes about credibility/honesty of management
Attitudes toward work, pay, supervisor, etc.

Union Membership Data

Union membership/representation status
Controlling union contract
Union officer status
Dues checkoff status

Location/Contact Data

Home address
City and state
Zip code
Home phone
Present component and work assignment
Geographic location of work assignment
Office phone
Emergency notification

Reprinted by permission from "PAIR Records and Information Systems" by Glenn A. Bassett in *ASPA Handbook of Personnel and Industrial Relations*, Dale Yoder and Herbert G. Heneman, Jr., eds., pp. 2-66–2-68. Copyright 1979 by The Bureau of National Affairs, Inc., Washington, D.C.

EXHIBIT 2
Uses of Personnel Data

611

F. PERSONNEL RESEARCH

Employee age distributions and retirement analyses
Equal employment opportunity reports and analyses
Budgeting for recruiting
Prediction of success in finding specific work skills at desired salaries
Identification of good and poor selection practices
Description of the candidate pool attracted by the employer
Description of the time span required to fill an open position
Identification of effective and ineffective recruitment sources
Identification of employees for promotion, reassignment, or special assignment
Justification of salaried or job titles
Analyses of the availability of existing job skills for changes in product mix or work
Planning for availability of critical manpower types
Planning college recruitment
Comparison of individual salary growth rates
Creation of salary curves
Control of salary budgets
Tracking and control of pay increases
Tracking of pay increase policies and practices
Analyses of employee losses by component, educational level, quality of performance, etc.
Systematic control of bumping and recall situations
Monitoring appraisal practices
Analysis of absenteeism and tardiness patterns
Tracking of changes in attitudes for comparison with observed changes in the business
Monitoring relations with the union
Sending out special notices and letters
Drawing samples for representative surveys of employees
Identifying geographic distribution of employees for purposes of distributing United Fund gifts,
    encouraging car-pools, etc.
Analyzing the return on investment from benefits expenditures
Analysis of the competitiveness of pay rates from losses to other employers
Identification of patterns of safety hazards
Provision of OSHA reports and analyses
Control of hiring requests to assure consonance with manning authorizations
Identification of environmental factors which most affect attitudes, turnover, productivity, etc.
Analysis of career movement patterns, including identification of fast-track or dead-end jobs, etc.
Prediction of potential skill shortages and training needs.

Reprinted by permission from "PAIR Records and Information Systems" by Glenn A. Bassett in *ASPA Handbook of Personnel and Industrial Relations,* Dale Yoder and Herbert G. Heneman, Jr., eds., pp. 2-71–2-72. Copyright © 1979 by The Bureau of National Affairs, Inc., Washington, D.C.

ative and innovative analysis and interpretation. For example, an organization may be considering the introduction of a management-by-objectives program, a flexitime program, or a retirement preparation plan. Top management may want an analysis of the program's effect on the personnel function, its advantages and disadvantages, the experiences of other organizations, and so on. The personnel professional can research the professional literature, such as the journals in Exhibit 3, to make the analysis and prepare recommendations.

As to the future of personnel research, one view is offered by Herbert H. Meyer, who was General Electric's personnel research manager for two decades.

The success of American industry has been attributed to the fact that technical and organizational problems have been approached in a very *systematic* manner. Innovative practices emanating from the scientific management movement

EXHIBIT 3
Journals Covering Topics Relating to the Personnel Function

Employee Relations Law Journal

Industrial Relations

Industrial and Labor Relations Review

Journal of Applied Psychology

Labor Law Journal

Personnel

Personnel Administrator

Personnel Journal

Personnel Psychology

Public Personnel Management

Training and Development Journal

were adopted and developed to their fullest potential by American business leaders in the first half of this century. There is no reason to expect that in the second half of the century American business leaders will not also apply this systematic approach to the complex area of human relations.[7]

Because the role of personnel research is so important and has so much potential for contributing to organizational effectiveness, it seems inevitable that this role will expand. With rapid technological advances affecting attitudes and behavior of employees, creative approaches to work-related concerns must be sought and examined. Younger employees are less receptive to authoritarian leadership, and researchers must therefore continue to study supervisory behavior and leadership styles. Shifts from a blue-collar workforce to a predominantly white-collar workforce with more education and a stronger need for self-actualization will require imaginative approaches to management of personnel. The value of personnel research and personnel researchers is yet unrealized. However, large companies are organizing specific research units, and small companies are participating in joint research efforts. The latter part of this century will show significant progress in this personnel activity.[8]

NOTES

1. Richard W. Beatty, "Research Needs of PAIR Professions in the Near Future," *Personnel Administrator* 23 (September 1978), pp. 15–16.

2. Reprinted from "Personnel Research for Problem-Solving," by Fred Crandall, pp. 15–16 of the September 1978 issue of *Personnel Administrator*, copyright 1978, the American Society of Personnel Administration, 30 Park Drive, Berea, OH 44017, $26 per year.

3. Herbert H. Meyer, "PAIR Research," in *Planning and Auditing PAIR*, ed. Dale Yoder and H. G. Heneman, Jr. (Washington, D.C.: Bureau of National Affairs, 1976), p. 2–120.

4. *Ibid.*, pp. 2-118–2-120.

5. "Privacy Rights Protections under State Statutes," in *Fair Employment Practices Digest* (Washington, D.C.: Bureau of National Affairs, February 12, 1981), p. 4.

6. Meyer, "PAIR Research," pp. 2-127–2-128.

7. Reprinted by permission from Herbert H. Meyer, "PAIR Research," in *Planning and Auditing PAIR*, edited by Dale Yoder and H. G. Heneman, Jr., p. 2-128, copyright 1976 by The Bureau of National Affairs, Inc., Washington, D.C.

8. "ASPA-BNA Survey No. 41, Personnel Activities, Budgets, and Staffs: 1980–1981," in *Bulletin to Management* (Washington, D.C.: Bureau of National Affairs, 1981), p. 1–4. Based on survey of 507 employers with employment of 1,051,532. One-half were manufacturers; 28 percent were nonmanufacturing businesses; and 21 percent were nonbusiness organizations. Fifteen percent had fewer than 250 employees; 19 percent, between 250 and 499; 23 percent, between 500 and 999; 24 percent, between 1,000 to 2,499; and 19 percent, 2,500 or more.

G.

LABOR UNIONS

Interview with Ronnie J. Straw

Ronnie Straw is presently director of the Development and Research Department for the Communications Workers of America, a position he has held for sixteen years. In this role, he researches and implements projects of national scope in the areas of economics, finance, telecommunications policy, and social reform. He is a member of the American Economic Association and has been a staff economist for the National Telephone Cooperative Association and the National Rural Electric Cooperative Association. Mr. Straw holds a master's degree in economics and public administration from Syracuse University.

1. *Could you please begin by describing the objectives of Communications Workers of America (CWA), the nature of the membership, and benefits you provide to your members?*

Generally the objectives of CWA are to assure that the workers we represent receive proper compensation for the work performed, adequate protection against workplace health and safety hazards, and an appropriate voice in structuring the work and choosing the type of equipment that is used to perform the tasks. The membership that we represent includes 550,000 telephone company workers and 48,000 public employees at the state level.

We provide our membership with the entire range of benefits permitted by law, and have engaged in a wide range of employee participation efforts such as Quality of Worklife programs, Technology Change Committees, and Occupational Job Evaluation programs.

2. *Much has been written regarding unions' response to job enrichment — the use of internal rewards such as autonomy and discretion. Most seem to say union leadership is still economically oriented. Where does the CWA stand on this issue? Are noneconomic gains (such as better, more challenging positions) objectives of interactions with management?*

Since 1980, CWA has had a Quality of Worklife program established by contract with AT&T. The union has participated in developing the program, constructing the training, and supporting the effort from the president's office to the local union. Additionally, we established a Technology Change Committee with the companies to receive early notice of technological changes and to develop worker input into these decisions. We also developed a job evaluation plan with AT&T. As you can see, CWA has engaged in a wide range of programs which could be described as "noneconomic." Our role in all these programs is to help create an environment where the workers can make real contributions to the structure of the work and the efficiency of the company, without becoming victims of the changing nature of work.

3. *What is the role of unions with regard to affirmative action plans? In your opinion, have unions themselves adopted equal employment opportunity (EEO) guidelines effectively?*

CWA has supported affirmative action plans with the companies that it organizes. This support is demonstrated by active support on legislative initiatives, classes on racism and sexism in a local leadership school, and strong support of minority rights in contract administration.

Employees at CWA reflect the make-up of our membership, which is very similar to national demographics. Labor unions were among the earliest and strongest supporters of civil rights, and I feel their employment practices reflect that position.

4. *Traditionally, labor unions have been most successful organizing workers in the industrial sector of the economy. Now, many of these industries (e.g., steel, automobiles) are declining in terms of the number of workers employed, and union organizing efforts seem to be moving toward white-collar, service, and clerical workers. What different approaches and tactics will union leaders need to adopt to be successful in organizing these types of employees?*

The labor unions exist because the membership feels that collective action is a more successful way of securing their rights at work. The approach and tactics used in organizing are to identify the needs of the workers, and then to structure and communicate a program to address those needs.

5. *Are there employee groups that labor will pursue in the 1990s that we are unaware of now? What will the typical union of 1995 look like and how will it differ from present unions?*

Labor has always offered their services to all those eligible under the law. As the economy changes and as the Taylorization of white-collar work continues, you can expect to find increased activity in a wide range of office environments.

If present trends continue there will be fewer and larger unions by 1995. The structure of unions will be very similar to current unions, but a single union will have a larger variety of workers represented.

6. *How has the climate of industrial relations changed over the last twenty years? Have you seen a change in the way personnel managers approach collective bargaining?*

In the last twenty years the legitimacy of organized labor has been severely challenged. When a national labor policy was enacted in 1935 it was to establish a controlled battle of the economic will of the parties. With the 1947 and 1959 amendments (to the National Labor Relations Act), labor's role was diminished as the corporations grew in power and influence. Through the economic boom of the sixties and early seventies, the climate remained relatively constant but since the mid-seventies organized labor has been a whipping boy for all the economic ills that plague this country. The UAW, and not poor corporate planning, is thought to be the reason for the invasion of foreign autos. USW wages, and not the failure of steel companies to reinvest in modern equipment, is blamed for the invasion of foreign steel. The strike by PATCO employees, and not outdated equipment, are thought to be the reason for air traffic difficulties.

The public sentiment generated by corporate America and supported by a conservative administration has severely altered the industrial relations climate.

7. What trends do you perceive in recent National Labor Relations Board (NLRB) decisions? Have they been moving in a pro- or anti-union direction?

The most alarming trend at the NLRB is the inactivity. While the anti-union posture of the Reagan Board is well known and applauded in corporate circles, the most damaging activities have been their unwillingness to do the work. "Justice delayed is justice denied." The actions of the Board in the last five years continue to undermine the rights of workers, which may eventually lead to a new militancy in labor.

8. What has led to the increased incidence of union decertification elections and the growing inability of unions to successfully retain their representation rights?

The refusal of employers to bargain in good faith and the lack of effective enforcement procedures under the National Labor Relations Act, as amended, are the prime factors in the increased incidence of decertification elections. When an employer wishes to rid itself of a bargaining agent for its employees, it need only to call one of the practicing union busters. The formula for such activities is well known: refuse to bargain; the union will file an Unfair Labor Practice (ULP) Charge with the NLRB; the NLRB will take two years to adjudicate the ULP; and if it rules for the union, it will order the company to bargain and the company will repeat the process. At some point the employees will realize that the union is not providing any service and will vote the union out. There are other scenarios but they all include outside counsel, and use of NLRB or judicial backlogs as a tool against the bargaining agent. Because the company always has more money and because the union is so limited in its legal responses, any company can get rid of a union if they are willing to spend the money.

9. Why have unions become involved in the "comparable worth" controversy?

Unions have traditionally attempted to legislate or litigate the prohibition of economic exploitation whether they represented the target groups or not. Almost no organized workers are paid the minimum wage and yet without the efforts of organized labor there would be no minimum wage protection. Our mission is to represent workers; abolishing wage discrimination based on sex is in keeping with that philosophy.

10. Do you believe that unions will become more or less influential in national politics in the future? Will unions become a force in the Republican party?

If union numbers continue to decline, certainly their influence will also decline. The current Republican ideology is inconsistent with the goals of labor unions. Unless they change, there is no role for labor unions in their ranks.

11. Why is union membership declining? Will it continue? Why or why not?

Union membership is declining because: (a) industries that are organized continue to reduce their work force; (b) busting unions and opposing unionism is supported by the president; (c) companies are willing to pay union wages to avoid unions; and (d) the scope of mandatory subjects of bargaining limits the types of worker involvement the union can negotiate. Things will get worse before they get better.

12. *Are there job opportunities for recent college graduates in the labor field? If so, what kinds of jobs are available?*

Appropriately, most of the staff positions in unions are filled from the ranks of the represented workers. However, there are a limited number of jobs for college graduates in the research, legislative, and accounting functions of labor unions.

13. *In what ways have unions assisted personnel managers in carrying out their responsibilities? Could national unions and/or local labor leaders do more in this regard?*

It is the union's responsibility to represent workers, not to assist personnel managers with their jobs. Certainly national unions and/or local labor leaders could do more in this regard, but why would they?

PART VII: FOR DISCUSSION AND REVIEW

A.

Terborg

- How are role demands for women managers different from their male counterparts?
- Explain why societal sex role stereotypes and the lack of nontraditional role models might inhibit the career aspirations of women.
- Why are women in organizations sometimes biased against other women?

Kohl and Greenlaw

- What are the facts of the Gilbert case, and why is it such a critical case?

Faley

- Trace the evolution of the Courts' standards for establishing a claim of sexual harassment under Title VII of the 1964 Civil Rights Act.
- How might employers prevent sexual harassment from occurring in their workplace?

Harrick and Sultan

- What are possible organizational responses to the challenge of an increasingly older workforce?
- What role do human resource departments have in assisting the organization to respond to demographic changes?

B.

Hoffman and Hobson

- How might an organization increase employee participation in a fitness program?
- Summarize the research relating physical fitness to performance and to stress.

- ▢ What issues must be addressed if an organization wishes to implement an employee assistance program?
- ▢ How can these programs' effectiveness be assessed?

Time

- ▢ What is "stress"?
- ▢ What role should organizations play in stress management for their employees?
- ▢ What are an individual's responsibilities in stress management?

C.

Ledvinka

- ▢ What would you recommend to employers with respect to the collection and use of employee information?

Joiner

- ▢ What is the "employment-at-will doctrine"?
- ▢ What terminations at will are prohibited by law?
- ▢ How can problems in this area be avoided?

D.

Cascio

- ▢ What are the weaknesses associated with the Human Asset Valuation and the Unit Cost models presented?
- ▢ What are the underlying assumptions of the Behavior Costing Model?
- ▢ What problems are inherent in costing behaviors?

Fitz-Enz

- ▢ Give four reasons why quantitative measures of effectiveness have not been applied in most human resource departments.
- ▢ Why must human resource managers be concerned with "the medium" as well as "the message"?

E.

Weber

- ▢ Why was the PATCO strike a significant event in collective bargaining history?
- ▢ Discuss the impact that changes in the environment are having and will have on the American labor/management system.

Mitchell

- ▢ What is the author's position regarding wage concessions? Do you agree or disagree? Why?

▫ Do you foresee further wage concessions in the years ahead? If so, what should unions' response be?

F.

Holley and Jennings

▫ What is a personnel information system?

▫ Briefly describe each type of personnel research discussed.

▫ What uses does personnel research have for the line manager and what role would he or she have in the research process?